The Covenant

A Reincarnational Memoir

By Annie Weber

Based on a True Story

Contained within these covers are nine love stories-- spanning 1100 years and stretching from the canyons and mesas of prehistoric North America to the snowy peaks of the Himalayas, from the Serengeti plains of Africa to the inner confines of a sultan's harem, from the Adirondack lakes of the British colonies to the law courts of Victorian London, and finally to the hospital halls of Ohio.

What weaves these tales together is something stronger than death and lasting longer than time as we know it. Beyond the sweeping romance and soul-baring emotional intrigue, Weber delivers nine well-researched historical studies of what it was like to live in those widely varying cultures during vastly different times...and what can happen when you continue to open your heart to love.

This work is a memoir. As such, the episodes related in this book are the product of the author's memory and point-of-view, and, therefore, may at times be one-sided. Although, as much care as possible has been taken to recount the dialogue and events contained herein with accuracy, for reasons of privacy, protection, and respect, the names of most persons herein, living and dead, as well as lesser known locales, have been changed. In order to accommodate those changes in locale, it was occasionally necessary to alter a few, unimportant, details of the narrative to maintain the overall veracity of the larger story.

THE COVENANT

A Reincarnational Memoir

Based on a True Story

By

Annie Weber

Dear Susan – my cousin across the sea!
I hope you enjoy reading this –
especially the Dorset and London
bits – but the entire story, too.

Penney DePas

iv

Dedicated to my Soul Mate

Without whom there would be no story.

And to my mother, who taught me how to write.

ACKNOWLEDGEMENTS

I offer my sincere and humble gratitude—

First, to God for the revelation and subsequent miracles that awoke me to my mission. Second, to my friend Sarah who was my sole witness and kept me sane. Next, to my friend Steve who supported me in my grief in this lifetime and made up for the karma from the previous lifetime when he could not. Next to my coach and "committed listener" Leslie who would not allow me to give up and helped me hold together through the sickness, the silence, and the separation. To coaches Micki and Linda who encouraged me to express myself in many forms of creativity—writing, painting, and dance. To the transformative training that gave me the courage and "unstoppability" to fulfill my mission. To my editor, Sherry, who kept my voice while tightening up my written words. And to the many listeners who have been touched, moved, and/or inspired by all or parts of this story. Finally, to those who have been willing to share with me their own similar, very personal, experiences—often for the first time.

PROLOGUE

Canton, Ohio - September 26, 2002

The rain is relentless the entire drive. Turning off the I-77 exit to Canton, I make a right at the stoplight toward the center of town. The approach to downtown on Tuscarawas Street leads me through a non-descript string of burger joints, gas stations, and strip malls. Seeing a sign to the Visitor Center, I bear left and then make a right; more gas stations, a few low-slung factory buildings, and the torrential, gray rain. I realize I am nearing the center of town as the buildings become taller—an office building, a bank, a branch of Stark State College, and a couple of brick churches.

On my left, I pass a stately, stone church with a square tower, Savior United Methodist Church. "A lot like the one he attended in Cleveland Heights," I remark to myself.

Ahead on the left is the Big Football—the town's symbol. A large, brown, oval sculpture imprinted with "NFL" stands in a small, central plaza, reminding me that Canton was famous for its Pro Football Hall of Fame but has now fallen on harder times since the automobile and tire industries moved offshore. A little east of town, beyond the Big Football, the railroad tracks stretch north-south, much like my own hometown was split in two by the railroad that runs between New York and Philadelphia. Here, the storefronts also remind me of home.

Turning right on Market Avenue and heading south, I wonder where in town his father—a doctor—would have resided and raised his two boys in the 1950s. My next left is onto Third Street, S.E.

"Definitely not on this street," I remark to myself, driving into the section of town where the old tire and auto part factories are located. A map would help. I am usually better prepared to explore new territory, spending hours poring over maps, getting my bearings. Although I did make a copy of a Stark County map before I left, it now seems woefully inadequate for my mission...or was this more appropriately my "destiny"?

Retracing my route, I head back to the center of town on Tuscarawas Street and then turn north on Market Avenue.

After passing some more storefronts—many of them empty or sadly devoid of intriguing merchandise—I enter a residential area. An historic marker, a brown sign with white letters, announces a section of older homes known as the Historic Ridgewood District. "Now we're getting somewhere," I assure myself. Rapidly I scan the staid and stately houses on both sides of the street, each with white columns or brick porticos, but all too quickly I pass through the historic district and am driving past a stretch of unremarkable ranch homes. I turn my car around and look again. I am disappointed; I believed I would instinctively know the house. I catch sight

1

of an imposing brick building up on the hill to my left. "Too official for a residence," I decide.

Approaching the center of town once again, I notice a sign for the Ohio Vietnam Veterans' Memorial Park. "He might have had high school friends in the war, just like my older brother did," I think as I turn left into what appears to be a park entrance. In contrast to the orderly buildings of the residential district, I now find myself in a verdant, over-grown area. To my right in the distance I spy a scoreboard and a football field. "Probably for the high school," I conclude then wonder if he enjoyed watching the games as a teenager. It is the first time since arriving that I felt he actually spent time here.

Returning to the main road, I wind through a neighborhood of newer homes whose outlines are more distinctive than the boxier styles of Market Avenue and probably built in the 1960s. As his father's medical practice grew did he move his family to a newly built home? Somehow I doubt it. His was a family that respected its historic roots.

I head west on 12th Street toward Westlawn Cemetery and the Visitor Center at McKinley Memorial to get a more detailed map and find a restroom. The Stark County Historical Society is located inside the McKinley Monument, a domed brick, stone, and concrete structure that houses the remains of the 25th U.S. President. Atop a hill, the building dominates Memorial Park with 108 steps descending to street level. I turn into the parking lot.

The rain has eased some, but I still need an umbrella. It feels good to get out of the car and stretch my legs finally. I have been driving for well over two hours and will drive for another hour to reach Cleveland.

This visit to Canton was a last-minute side trip, a decision to break up the drive, and a curiosity pilgrimage. At one point, I thought I might share the drive, but when I knew I would be making the journey solo, the idea to come here started to percolate in my mind. I am not sure what I expected to find. And I still have plenty of questions.

A portly, grey-haired woman opens the door and welcomes me to the Visitor Center. I smile politely at her. Near the window on the west side of the office, a mustachioed younger man is keying something into a computer behind a big desk.

"Where are the restrooms?"

"The entrance is outside around to the right." She hands me a key with a football on its chain. "Cute," I remark to myself, as I enter the ladies' room.

Returning to the main room of the Visitor Center, I hand the key back to the woman who asks expectantly, "Are you here to visit the Memorial?" as she hands me some maps and guidebooks to the area.

"Actually, I am more interested in the historic buildings closer to downtown." Glancing around the room, I notice two easels with poster boards displaying newspaper articles and photos of rehabilitated buildings.

2

"May I?" I ask, pointing to the poster boards. The woman nods and turns back to her desk.

I alternately read and skim yellowing articles looking for any clues to help me with my mission to uncover more about his youth as he grew up here. There is an article about two doctors who purchased and restored an old building to use as an office, but neither doctor was his father. In addition, I read an article about the restoration of the home of the Canton Women's Club—that official-looking building I saw on the hill in the historic district. An image of his mother starts to form in my mind as someone who might have been involved with the Club.

Nothing else offers additional clues. I thank the woman and younger man for their help, wish them a nice day, and head back to my car. Scanning the maps and guidebooks I was given, I see most of them are dedicated to the automobile industry. Nothing else draws my interest. Besides, it is eleven o'clock, and I want to be in Cleveland by noon.

I turn left out of the parking lot onto Washington Boulevard toward 12th Street again. As I turn onto 12th, I notice a rather dated, silver diner on the opposite corner. I wonder if he and his fellow Canton High School students used to hang out there in the mid-sixties.

Back on I-77, heading north to Cleveland as the pouring rain resumes, my mind returns once again—for perhaps the hundred-thousandth time—to what transpired between the two of us in the last 16 years.

But let me begin before the beginning...

I KNEW I LOVED YOU

I knew I loved you before I met you
I think I dreamed you into life
I knew I loved you before I met you
I have been waiting all my life

Maybe it's intuition
but some things you just don't question
Like in your eyes, I see my future in an instant
And there it goes,
I think I found my best friend
I know that it might sound
more than a little crazy
but I believe...

I knew I loved you before I met you
I think I dreamed you into life
I knew I loved you before I met you
I have been waiting all my life

There's just no rhyme or reason
Only the sense of completion
And in your eyes, I see
the missing pieces I'm searching for
I think I've found my way home
I know that it might sound
more than a little crazy
but I believe...

I knew I loved you before I met you
I think I dreamed you into life
I knew I loved you before I met you
I have been waiting all my life

A thousand angels dance around you
I am complete now that I've found you

Cleveland, Ohio, 1974

Nervously, the young man stands behind the last pew of the Gothic Revival Amasa Stone Chapel on the edge of Case Western Reserve University campus. Although the Chapel is almost full, a few seats are still available. The dimly lit sanctuary is aglow in candlelight and multi-colored reflections of stained glass. Most of the congregants happily anticipate the ceremony that is about to begin; but in marked contrast to the gaiety of the others, the young man's mood is dark.

His thick, dark hair falls across the left side of his forehead above dark eyebrows and glacial blue eyes. Normally, he would be considered exceedingly handsome with a fine wit and a disarmingly engaging smile. But today his mouth is set in a hard line, his square jaw clenched tight, both hands gripping the curved back of the wooden pew in front of him. At 26 years of age, he is a little over five feet eight inches tall and weighs 165 pounds.

The organ music swells and drifts to the rear of the chapel. Reluctantly, the young man turns to his right, trembling slightly, while the congregation rises and faces the entrance where the sun flows–through double wooden doors, making its way partly down the aisle.

Backlit by the sun, the bride's translucent veil and chiffon white gown glow with angelic brilliance as she glides forward on her father's tuxedoed arm to the familiar strains of Mendelssohn's "Wedding March."

As the bride passes, everyone except the young man steps back into the shadow of the column and watches her steady procession toward the altar and her waiting husband-to-be. Finally, convinced that the wedding of his beloved Suzanne is inevitable, the young man momentarily looks down at the stone floor to collect himself. As Suzanne and her father continue forward down the aisle, the young man suddenly propels himself out of the chapel entrance to leap into the driver's seat of his 1972 Mustang convertible parked out front. He turns the key in the ignition, and the engine fires with a roar. Swiftly backing out of his parking space, the tires squeal as he shifts into first and guns the motor to speed away from the chapel and Cleveland.

"Never," he vows to himself, "will I ever be so out-of-control in love with a woman again."

Speeding west on Interstate 80 across northern Ohio, the young man does not stop driving until he reaches Sandusky where he exits to the Cedar Point Amusement Park. After spending the next several hours on the roller coasters and other thrill rides, he takes a long walk on the beach. Finally, his anger dissipated and his heart steeled, he drives back to the University of Akron Law School, the cool night air blowing through his hair.

5

Ohio, 1985-86

SITUATION

I may be old-fashioned, but I adhere to a strict policy: I don't go after other women's men. Otherwise, this story might have had a different ending. I say "might" because it could have ended in a lot of different ways; I only know how it did end.

Not all women share this value with me. In fact, I distinctly remember another woman going after Auguste, my husband, shortly after we were married; I felt as if my fingernails instantly grew several inches so I could scratch her eyes out. But I did not.

I have another policy: I always keep my promises. At least the big ones. For example, before we got engaged, Auguste asked two things of me: One, any children we would have we would raise in Judaism, and two, if either of us were unfaithful, our marriage would be over—no questions asked. I agreed. What did I know? I was young and in love.

When I was in college, I came across a quotation I liked a lot: "The tragedy of physical love is the perpetual virginity of the soul." Maybe it was sour grapes on my part—still a virgin surrounded by the free love generation—but there seemed to be more than a grain of truth in the idea that sex without love, passion, and commitment, is, essentially, an empty gesture.

However, let me begin my saga in a place that makes sense.

In 1980 when I finished my master's degree in the arts at Trevor State University in Trevor, Missouri, we were in the throes of a presidential election that ended with Republicans in office and very few job prospects. A concentrated job search resulted in two half-time, jobs—both funded with state arts council grants. One of the jobs was managing a performing arts association where I stayed for a little over four years; the other was a fundraising position that I left after only a year and had to work a series of part-time positions before securing another half-time, management position.

Meanwhile, Auguste was unable to find paying work for himself. He had held a bookkeeper job with the University but, during my third year of graduate school, he decided to go back to college for a second bachelor's degree and could only find volunteer positions. In 1985 unemployment reached over 15 percent in Missouri when I applied for and was hired as the executive director of the Arts Council of Newark, Ohio, a position I found very attractive for a number of reasons: Housed in an historic building, it had a small staff already in place, there was a sales gallery on site, it combined the visual and performing arts, and it was full-time, paying more than I was making with my two half-time jobs. Finally, although Newark was a small, rural city, it was only an hour's drive east from the state capitol, Columbus.

The head of the Arts Council's search committee was its past board president, Frederick "Rick" Northfield. A gregarious and kind attorney, Rick was short and heavy-set with round, rimless, spectacles and thinning hair.

"If you ever need anything," he said, proffering his business card after the Arts Council board had agreed to hire me, "please don't hesitate to call on me."

After weathering a winter storm that delayed our move from Missouri to Ohio for three days, Auguste and I arrived in Newark to another delay; the construction on our new apartment was not yet finished. After staying a couple of nights at a nearby motel, we were finally able to move into the apartment and settle into our new life.

Soon, however, things did not seem to feel right. The search committee had not included one key member—the incoming board president. This woman, who represented the Arts Council's largest funding source and, whom most people agreed could be unpleasant, privately had resented the board's decision to hire me. Two weeks prior to her ascendancy to the office of president, she convinced the board to terminate my employment contract after only 10 weeks. Shocked by this unexpected news, I phoned Rick Northfield.

"I think you'd better come see me," he suggested after I explained the situation. When I arrived 15 minutes later, Rick showed me into his office and offered me a seat. I faced him across a wide, wooden desk covered with papers.

"I'm very sorry things did not work out for you here. However, I am not a labor lawyer," he explained sympathetically. "I specialize in health insurance law." Up until that moment I did not realize there were different legal specialties. "This is a small town and in order to find an attorney who would be willing to represent you, you'd have to find one from another city." He paused to let me think about that for a moment. "My recommendation is that you take the Arts Council's offer of a cash settlement and find employment elsewhere."

"By accepting the cash settlement, I would have to agree to resign, otherwise the board said they would fire me," I said, weighing my options out loud.

"If it would make it easier on you, bring your resignation letter to my office tomorrow, and I'll arrange to have the Arts Council's treasurer bring the check so that we can swap them here on neutral ground."

"Thank you." I appreciated his sensitivity to my potential awkwardness in facing the board members.

When I arrived at Rick's office the next day with my letter, the Arts Council's treasurer—also an attorney—had already dropped off my check. "You might be better off considering a position in one of the larger Ohio cities," Rick advised as he handed me the severance check. "People in Newark can still be a bit provincial at times." We shook hands, and I left Rick's office.

Auguste and I spent what seemed like an interminably long, hot summer job hunting. Meeting one morning with my predecessor at the Arts Council of Newark, she suggested I interview with David Fisher, CEO of a professional association management firm in Columbus, the Association Emphasis Management Group (AEMG). When he saw my resume during our interview, Fisher was noticeably impressed.

"We don't normally get applicants who have previous association management experience, much less someone who has previously worked with more than one association simultaneously. If something opens up here, I will give you a call."

Since receiving my master's degree, I thought that I had worked for "arts service organizations," but Fisher used another term for them— *associations*. No wonder my resume finally made sense when I compiled it for our interview.

A month later, Fisher was elected the chairman of the board of an international organization. He arrived in his office on Monday from that group's annual convention to find resignations from two of his executive directors on his desk. Typical of an entrepreneur who has many leadership responsibilities, Fisher did not take long to make a decision and asked me to return for a second interview that Monday afternoon. The interview only lasted thirty minutes.

"Can you start work tomorrow? If so, be here at 8:45 a.m. If not, call me."

After three months of idleness in small and cliquish Newark, just the thought of having a place to go and something to do was a relief to me, so I accepted the position with AEMG.

Among the ranks of the six client organizations David Fisher assigned to me were the Arts Councils Organization of Ohio (ACOO) and the Ohio Association of Health Insurance Attorneys (OAHIA). Ironically, my former employer, the Arts Council of Newark was a member of ACOO and Rick Northfield was a member of OAHIA. I was glad for this opportunity to prove my worth in the arts council community after my unfortunate and unexpected job dismissal from the Arts Council of Newark.

Soon I was in the midst of planning conferences, attending board meetings, writing newsletters, and keeping up with the memberships and finances of my six account associations. The last governing board meeting on my schedule—and the one at which I would personally meet the members for the first time—was the Ohio Association of Health Insurance Attorneys. OAHIA's Vice President, Liam McFarland, was to host the Executive Committee meeting in the 17th floor conference room of the Athenaeum Health Plan's headquarters building in Mansfield on November 13th. In giving me driving directions, Liam instructed me to "exit onto Route 13 North and aim for the tallest building downtown." As soon as I came off the exit ramp, I could see Athenaeum's pyramid roof protrude above the trees in the distance like a lighthouse beacon, and I headed straight for it.

Entering the wood paneled conference room I noticed I was the only female in attendance at the meeting. I took a seat at one end of the polished oval mahogany table and prepared to take minutes. My introduction seemed a superfluous, but requisite, courtesy. The attorneys arranged themselves around the table: Immediate Past President T. Eric Mitchell, Jr., to my left; President Charles ("Chuck") Lincoln, Jr., at the head of the table to preside; Vice President Liam McFarland next to Chuck; Treasurer J. Harrison ("Harry") Whitfield to Liam's left; and Private Practice Section Representative Warren Sullivan who sat across from me. Secretary Keir Mervais was the only one absent.

Chuck Lincoln called the meeting to order by tapping an inscribed wooden gavel on the table. Being the first Executive Committee meeting of the OAHIA administrative year, the agenda covered routine matters: approval of previous minutes, the financial report, next year's budget, and committee appointments. Although primarily intent on capturing the motions for the minutes, I did look up periodically. Glancing around the table, I was struck by how attractive these gentlemen were; by and large, much more attractive than average. Eric, although starting to go bald, was ruggedly good looking. Both Chuck and Harry were distinguished, albeit, silver-haired. Warren was downright stunning, although prematurely gray. "I must have died and gone to heaven to be surrounded by such handsomeness," I thought.

However, when the officers began to consider some proposed legislation regarding a fine point of hospital law, I found it difficult to follow the discussion.

"Excuse me," I interrupted, hesitant to reveal my ignorance, "but I am trying to take meeting minutes here, and I don't understand what you are talking about."

In one movement, six male heads turned toward me quizzically, almost as if they had forgotten I was in the room. "Uh-oh," the reprimanding little voice in my head warned, remembering my recent dismissal in Newark, "I'm in trouble now!"

"No one from your management company has ever asked us about our work," Eric observed, breaking the tension. The men launched into a detailed description of hospital law, health law, and the particular item under consideration. Most of it was too complex for me to fully understand, but I think I made a positive impression on them. When the meeting adjourned, I packed up my items and returned to Columbus, relieved I had successfully completed the meeting.

Before desktop computers, fax machines, and Federal Express began to speed up the business world, I was lucky to have at my desk an electric memory typewriter that self-corrected and had interchangeable fonts. When the minutes were drafted, we mailed them out for review. We wrote our newsletters by typing one column at a time, top-to-bottom, and gluing the columns to a sheet of poster board using melted wax. Every Friday, or for our smaller clients, every other Friday, we called the presidents of our association clients to discuss the status of their organizations. For OAHIA, this usually included a request for the regular *President's Message* column for the quarterly newsletter. In the few days of training I had received from my immediate predecessor on OAHIA, she had warned me that extracting that piece of writing would be a challenge.

OAHIA President Chuck Lincoln intimidated me. He was a tall, imposing man, with a no-nonsense military bearing. Highly intelligent, he graduated from Ohio's best law school at Case Western Reserve University. His manner was businesslike and a bit gruff—or so it seemed to me, still smarting from my termination from the Newark arts council. When I finally received his *President's Message* for the fall newsletter, it was long-winded and wordy, but he appreciated my edits.

The newsletter also included an article announcing my appointment as Executive Director with a professional and attractive photograph of me taken a few years earlier by a fashion photographer when I had held a short-term public relations position with a cosmetics firm.

Ten months after arriving in Ohio, Auguste was still without a job. His resentment over my having paid employment and a place to go every day while he was stuck in inhospitable Newark resulted in daily marital arguments. In Newark, the Arts Council board members still crossed the street or went down a different grocery store aisle to avoid us. Many mornings I commuted along Route 16 to Columbus in tears, only pulling myself together for the AEMG work day when I reached the outskirts of the capital city.

The December holidays were rather lonely in Newark without family or much money to spend. However, in January Auguste and I made arrangements to meet my parents for a weekend at my uncle's large apartment in McKees Rocks, PA. We would visit the Pittsburgh Art Museum's special exhibition of British antiques, a subject on which I had conducted a semester's independent study as an undergraduate.

"Jobs here in accounting are more plentiful than in Columbus," Auguste observed while reading the Sunday newspaper classifieds before we headed for the Art Museum. "What do you think about my trying to find a job in Pittsburgh?" I was not sure if he would be more successful than he had been previously, but I did not want to stand in his way. At least he seemed more hopeful than in recent months. My uncle was willing to let Auguste stay with him for a while, so we agreed that Auguste would return to Pittsburgh in March to seek a suitable position there while I stayed in our Newark apartment and commuted to work in Columbus at AEMG.

With the unpredictable winter weather in Ohio, it was an unusual stroke of luck that the governing boards of ACOO and OAHIA both chose to hold their February 1986 meetings in downtown Cleveland on consecutive days. The ACOO board had been considering if they wanted to continue their management agreement with AEMG or hire their own executive staff directly. This was the principle agenda item when the ACOO board met on February 11 at Playhouse Square.

The ACOO board members had generally been pleased with the quality of my work. Several of them were even inclined to continue to retain me and the AEMG firm. Usually when a board meets to discuss their management staff, contract, or fee, any staff present will recuse themselves from the meeting so that the board may discuss their business in executive session. Instead, the ACOO board members held their discussions openly before me. The debate lasted for five, long, uncomfortable hours.

In the end, the decision to leave our management company pivoted on one statement made by the ACOO treasurer. "There are other fish in the sea," the treasurer asserted, countering most of the board members' obvious desire to retain me as their executive director. By vote, the board authorized the ACOO president to attempt to negotiate a release of my services from the AEMG management contract so that I could continue as ACOO's chief staff officer when the association left AEMG. The board members then hastily concluded the rest of their business, and we adjourned for dinner at a nearby restaurant.

I was tired, my stomach ached, and my head hurt. I excused myself to go to the ladies' room where I fell against the wall and broke down into tears. Not only was my husband moving to Pittsburgh in a few weeks, but the association for which I had taken the AEMG job was also leaving our management company. My boss would not be pleased. I doubted he would agree to waive the contract clause that prevented staff members from going to work with clients who left AEMG. Eventually, I composed myself enough to join the others for dinner and feigned conviviality.

After spending a restless night at the Hampton Inn, I walked the few blocks to the Cleveland Plaza Building for the OAHIA board meeting, pulling my files and suitcase on a wheeled cart behind me.

A tall, boxy, glass structure, the Cleveland Plaza Building housed the legal offices of several OAHIA health insurance member companies. The OAHIA Executive Committee was meeting in the conference room of Cleveland Medical Health Insurance Corporation's suite where Secretary Keir Mervais had his offices. His receptionist ushered me into a pale blue conference room, tastefully decorated with a large, oval table surrounded by deeply upholstered gray chairs. From this 25th floor perch, the view through floor-to-ceiling glass windows of downtown Cleveland, the waterfront, and Lake Erie beyond was stunning.

Since his Athenaeum Health Plan suite was just down the hallway, Vice President Liam McFarland had already arrived. A slender man, Liam was of average height with brown hair, a bushy moustache, and round spectacles. He was the wiry type, overly worried about life in general and, therefore, he was diligent and precise. Liam was engaged in light conversation with Keir when I entered the conference room but turned to greet me.

"This is our new executive director, Annie Weber, Keir." Since the latter had missed my first Executive Committee meeting the previous

11

November in Mansfield, this was the first time we met. Keir and I shook hands.

"How are you, Annie?" Liam turned back to inquire.

Being a person who has difficulty hiding my emotions, and still unsettled from the previous day's ACOO board meeting, I was probably more frank than normal.

"Truthfully, I am a little shaken up. I met yesterday with one of my other client associations, and although the board members approve of my work, they voted to leave our management company." I briefly described the previous day's turn of events as well as the possibility of Auguste working in Pittsburgh.

A few minutes later, the remainder of the officers joined us, and Chuck Lincoln began the meeting. Harry Whitfield's financial report showed the association in dire financial straits. OAHIA would run out of money by late summer unless drastic measures were taken.

"The projected deficit is a result of four factors" Keir explained. I had read in the previous year's minutes that Keir, as treasurer, had repeatedly warned the other officers at each meeting that the association might soon run out of money. "First, when OAHIA conducted its lobbying efforts a few years back, not every health insurance company member paid their share of the lobbyist's invoice. Second, when we sent Jim Frazier to Hawaii to attend the national conference as OAHIA's president, the travel expenditures exceeded the budget. Third, our association's annual sponsorship of the cocktail party during the Ohio Bar Association's Health Law Section convention has also drained our funds. Finally, if our annual convention does not make a profit in any year, the association does not experience a year-end surplus." The room was quiet for a moment as this recap of the financial facts sank in. I was struck by this man's grasp of the situation as well as his clear cut presentation.

"We could invoice for next year's dues in May," another officer suggested.

"I'm sorry," I interjected, "but *my* associations do not bill for next year's dues in mid-year to pay for *this* year's expenses. That's akin to robbing your future." My impassioned certitude surprised even me, but the leaders agreed to consider other options.

One-by-one, each issue was addressed with a new policy. In the future, no lobbying effort would be conducted without collecting the lobbyist's fees in advance from the member companies; the Executive Committee would set a budget cap each year for the OAHIA president's travel to the national convention; individual insurers would be responsible for funding the Health Law Section cocktail party by OAHIA collecting the same amount of money from each company in advance; and, the annual convention budget would be set to earn a profit each year.

In addition, Chuck Lincoln appointed a task force consisting of Harry Whitfield, Keir Mervais, and me, as executive director. Our assignment was to develop a full financial proposal for the remainder of the current fiscal year to be presented in one month at an emergency Executive Committee meeting on March 11th. We then adjourned for lunch in the glass atrium food court on the second floor.

A couple of weeks later, Harry, Keir, and I met in Harry's conference room at SummitCare in Mansfield, midway between my home in Newark and Keir's in Cleveland. Once we were all seated at the conference table, Keir described a comprehensive plan he had already devised: restructuring the association's membership dues, a one-time special assessment to replenish the operational coffers, and a cover letter promising the member companies that the Executive Committee was taking the necessary steps to return OAHIA to prosperity, essentially listing the policies approved at the previous month's meeting.

Watching Keir describe his well-thought out strategy, I was again impressed by his intelligent and holistic comprehension of the association's predicament. I sensed that righting OAHIA's financial ship was important to him. As the previous year's treasurer, or perhaps because of his legal training, he took his fiduciary responsibilities seriously and put his reputation as an attorney on the line in promising the members that their association would not fall on hard times again. Even though Harry was older and Keir was closer to my age, Harry and I both deferred to the wisdom of Keir's persuasive plan.

At the March 11th meeting at Athenaeum's Mansfield office, the OAHIA officers adopted by unanimous vote our task force's proposals, which essentially were Keir's. In addition, they adopted additional membership recruitment procedures, including the development of a membership application brochure for the Health Law Section of the Bar.

Immediately following the meeting, Warren Sullivan and I adjourned to a nearby coffee shop and drafted the contents of the brochure. Warren, who also lived in Columbus, suggested we car pool to future meetings to share the mileage expense. On our quarterly drives to Cleveland, Mansfield, and Akron over the next couple of years, Warren educated me in the basics of health insurance law in Ohio.

By the next OAHIA Executive Committee meeting on May 15th in Columbus, the association had received a majority of the special operating funds the Association had assessed its members. As AEMG's CEO, David Fisher offered to buy lunch for the OAHIA officers at his downtown club in conjunction with their meeting.

Occupying the entire 28th floor of one of Columbus's office buildings, the club's deep green pile carpeting and wood paneling gave the enclave a darkly elegant and hushed atmosphere. OAHIA had been able to reserve one of the private conference rooms for 10:00 a.m. Three new items of business were introduced: development of a health insurance rating bureau, implementation of a uniform health insurance form, and a bylaws change establishing the composition of the Nominating Committee. Subsequently, we adjourned for lunch in the club's dining room, a vast chamber brightly lit on three sides by floor-to-ceiling windows that provided a tri-vista view of Columbus to the north, east, and south.

Keir and I arrived at opposite sides of the extensive club buffet table at the same time. He waited politely for me to scoop salad onto my plate first. "Congratulations on your promotion to vice president of Cleveland Medical," I said in an attempt to make conversation. I had recently received the announcement to publish in the newsletter.

Keir shrugged his shoulders slightly inside his navy blazer as though to deflect the compliment, but a sly smile crossed his lips. "Thank you. It provides the company with an opportunity to give me more work." He chuckled slightly. "David Fisher must be getting ready to raise our management fee," he playfully tossed over to me as he helped himself to salad. I looked at him to ascertain his motives in making this observation. Was he testing my reaction to his theory, trying to divert attention from himself, or merely making conversation?

Although not as classically handsome as Warren, Keir was disarmingly handsome in his own way. His face was square, topped with a luxurious swathe of thick, wavy, dark hair—the kind you want to run your fingers through—that dipped down over his left brow. About 5'8" or 5'9", he was shorter than the other members of the Executive Committee, however, he had broad shoulders and a developed chest that give him a solid yet well-proportioned appearance for his 165 to 170 pounds. When he smiled, his dimples were like parentheses around his perfect teeth. His friendly, easy-going manner and charm were a winning combination. And, with my husband now living away in Pittsburgh, I was particularly vulnerable to male charms. "Why, this man is flirting with me!" I thought. A little disconcerted, I pondered the best way to respond to Keir's imputation of my boss's motives. Meanwhile, my internal voice warned me, "He is very good-looking, so he probably normally relates to women by flirting."

"I'm sure David Fisher just wants to thank OAHIA for its continued business," I responded out loud. As we continued down the buffet line, I changed to a more neutral topic. "I'm glad the special assessment and other revenue measures seem to be working for OAHIA."

"You and Harry have done a great job collecting the money and following up with everyone." Keir seemed to want to deflect any credit for his role.

"We were just implementing your plan," I pointed out. We reached the end of the buffet line and walked over to the table where the other officers were already seated. The conversation turned to shop talk about health insurance law and sports—topics of male interest. Unable to contribute much to this conversation, I had a little time to mull over what had just happened.

Growing up I did not have any male admirers. The only two dates I had in high school were with my pediatrician's son who came out of the closet as a homosexual as soon as he got to college. I had a few blind dates in college and a crush during the junior year I spent abroad in Paris. But

14

Auguste was the first man I ever dated seriously. I met him the summer before my senior year, and we were married exactly one year after our first date.

My self-image was one of being FAT and UGH-LEE. Although I have never tipped the scales at 150 pounds, the woman I saw in the mirror weighed at least 300 pounds, and was over-endowed with a large bosom—a genetic inheritance from my grandmother—and for which I was teased mercilessly in the girls' locker room in junior high school. Occasionally, especially during intimate moments, Auguste pointed out that I was putting on weight which I internalized as additional criticism.

I also don't remember anyone ever telling me that I was pretty. I hung around with the smart girls who wore glasses and carried home armloads of books. Although I was not the smartest graduate, my close friends were valedictorian and salutatorian, and I graduated among the top 25 students in grade point average. As an A-minus student, I never seemed to be quite good enough, smart enough, skinny enough, and definitely not pretty enough.

With stick-straight brown hair, dull brown eyes, and a plain face, I could pass for average on a good day. But, most days I was surprised that our mirror did not crack when I peered into it. Auguste did not like me to spend money on cosmetics, so I only put on my clown face—as he called makeup—when I had a client meeting.

For the time being, Auguste was living in Pittsburgh. He had found work and was now leasing his own studio apartment. We took turns visiting each other on alternate weekends, touring the cultural sites or natural areas surrounding Pittsburgh and Columbus. It was like dating again and, as they say, "absence makes the heart grow fonder." With him working again, his own self-esteem had improved as had our financial situation. We could both lighten up after the months of unemployment and the setback we suffered when the Arts Council dismissed me.

Although I continued my daily commute from Newark to Columbus, I now spent very little time in Newark, occasionally staying overnight in Columbus with arts friends. My husband was less critical and seemed to appreciate me more during our weekend trysts. I must be exuding a new air of confidence, I told myself, and thus dismissed Keir's manner as simply his way of relating to me as a member of the opposite sex. Once lunch was over, the OAHIA officers all headed back to their respective cities.

The 1986 OAHIA annual convention was scheduled from July 31 to August 2 at Beaver Ridge Inn Resort in Cambridge, Ohio. A small, quaint inn, the Beaver Ridge was a white clapboard building with green shutters sitting on a mountain ridge in the Salt Fork State Park area. Its front veranda had a row of old-fashioned white rockers lined up overlooking the golf course that extended into the hills in the distance. Since the inn nestled into the mountains, the facility had no air conditioning, relying on the evening breezes for cooling.

15

To economize, I was the only paid staff member traveling to Cambridge to work at the convention. During the Thursday afternoon OAHIA Executive Committee meeting from 3:00 to 5:00, I left a small sign on the registration desk informing the convention attendees what time I would return to the desk to distribute registration packets and name badges.

I joined Chuck Lincoln, Liam McFarland, Keir Mervais, Eric Mitchell, and Harry Whitfield in the Beaver Ridge board room just off the Inn's lobby for the Executive Committee meeting. Harry informed us that the Association's finances had improved with the influx of assessment monies. At Keir's suggestion, the officers agreed to change the order of officer succession in the future. A new secretary would be nominated and elected annually as the first officer position, and would move up the officer chairs each successive year. Treasurer would be a second-year position on the governing board, rather than the first, allowing the newest officer a year to become more familiar with the association's business before taking on its financial responsibilities. To accommodate the change this year, Harry agreed to serve a second term as treasurer. The officers nominated Henry Spaulding as the new secretary. Eric Mitchell would rotate off the Executive Committee after Saturday's annual meeting and election. The discussion then focused on current and future conventions.

"What should I do about any cancellations and no shows?" I inquired, noting a problem that had surfaced with the convention registrations. Keir made a motion to give me the authority to develop a policy and establish fees for late registrations and cancellations for the 1987 convention, the one he would chair. He then requested suggestions for topics and speaker ideas from his colleagues for next year.

After approving three new company memberships, agreeing to future meeting dates, and discussing a letter from a former president, the committee went into executive session to consider the management fee increase for the following year proposed by AEMG. (Reflecting back on Keir's comment at the last meeting's luncheon, I thought, "Keir *had* been right about David Fisher's reasons for picking up the check.") Before I left the room, I asked Keir, as secretary, to be responsible for taking minutes of any actions during my absence from the meeting and noting the adjournment time. I returned to the registration desk to greet convention arrivals and await the outcome of the management fee discussion.

With my discharge from the Arts Council the previous year and the ACOO board voting to leave AEMG six months earlier, I was anxious about the OAHIA executive session. Rick Northfield was a member of OAHIA and may have told the officers what had happened to me in Newark. "If OAHIA chooses to leave AEMG, my job might be in jeopardy," I reasoned.

However, as more guests began to register, I quickly became absorbed in meeting the delegates, matching their faces and names, so that the hour soon arrived for the Welcome Reception to begin in the lobby. The convention attendees mixed and mingled during the cocktail reception—colleagues, friends, and spouses greeting each other and sharing news since they last encountered each other. I stood off to the side from the crowd. As a new staff member, I was not quite on the same social rank as the members.

Noticing that I was standing apart, Keir approached me. His wife had not accompanied him to the convention, so he was more solitary than most of his colleagues. I detected a mischievous twinkle in his eyes.

"Did anyone tell you what happened during the executive session?" he asked.

"No. I expect that, as president, Chuck will tell me," I responded respectfully. Keir considered this protocol for a moment. The playful light went out of his eyes, but he appeared to defer silently to my assessment of the situation. "Is your wife not attending the convention?"

"No. She works for a large corporate law firm and could not get away." He trailed off as though this was not a subject he wished to pursue further. At that moment, Warren Sullivan, who had missed the Executive Committee meeting earlier, came toward us. Warren and Keir shook hands.

"Nice to see you! Let me introduce you to my wife, Remy. Remy, this is Annie Weber, OAHIA's executive director, and Keir Mervais, who sits on the Executive Committee." We all exchanged greetings and handshakes.

Although Remy was a lovely and willowy brunette, I was surprised that she was not as strikingly beautiful as Warren was handsome. After exchanging a few pleasantries about the Sullivan's drive from Columbus, the architecture of the Inn, and the general state of business, Keir offered to introduce the Sullivans to his boss, Alexander McDowell, on the other side of the room, leaving me to seek out others for conversation. I walked over to Liam and Fran McFarland who were taking photographs of the event.

"May I use some of those photos for the next newsletter?" I asked Liam.

"Sure," he replied. "Once they are printed, I'll send you the best ones. We are using black-and-white film which will be perfect for printing in the newsletter." Liam took a quick shot of a group of people nearby. "I suppose I'll need to identify who is in the pictures for you."

"That would be very helpful."

"Have you met my wife, Fran, yet?" Fran and I shook hands.

"Did anyone tell you what we decided in our meeting about the management fee?"

"I thought Chuck would tell me since he is president."

Just then, Liam, as convention chair, spotted one of the next day's speakers enter the lobby—Insurance Director Donald Carson—and excused himself to greet the state government official.

"Liam is a bit nervous about the convention program," Fran explained. "He's always very conscientious about his projects."

"And I am sure he wants to make a good impression on his colleagues," I observed. We saw Liam turn toward us and signal to Fran to join him in order to meet Director Carson. I headed toward the registration desk to retrieve Carson's convention packet and name badge to hand to him.

That task accomplished, I joined Chuck and his wife, Patricia, who were speaking with the national association's Executive Vice President, Brian Willis, and his wife.

As the hour-long Welcome Reception came to an end, the health insurance company lawyers and private practice attorneys made their way to the Inn's restaurants or out to the veranda. I was tired from the last few weeks of convention preparations and gratefully slipped off to my room at the rear of the Inn for the night.

One of the speakers that had Liam worried was L. Brent Tillet, Jr., an attorney from the Cleveland law firm of Garber, Gay, Jones & Siegel. Tillet's wife was expecting their first child sometime around the dates of our convention, but their son was born prematurely a few days before the convention. Brent had arrived at Beaver Creek but was obviously concerned about leaving his newborn and wife. I later learned that, while I slumbered peacefully upstairs in my room, some of the OAHIA officers gathered on the veranda to enjoy the cool evening air. There, Brent and Keir struck up a conversation. Although childless himself, Keir reassured the new father that everything would be fine.

A few rocking chairs away, Liam and Donald Carson were discussing an important insurance underwriting issue. In essence, all the competing health insurance underwriters were providing liability coverage for a key hospital procedure that the Director did not believe should be covered. Liam had innocently inquired about the coverage and whether, in the Director's opinion, it was a procedure for which the companies could charge a fee under Ohio insurance law.

"I don't even think that procedure is legal in Ohio," Carson admitted in astonishment, "but I will have my legal staff check it out as soon as I get back to Columbus."

Without realizing it, Liam's question and the Director's response would effectively cripple the industry's ability to operate unless a suitable compromise could be worked out. Keir, who had been the Cuyahoga County campaign manager for Carson's election two years earlier, sensed that tensions were mounting at the other end of the veranda and went over to join the conversation. The issue was temporarily sidelined when Keir convinced Carson to meet in a couple of weeks with some key OAHIA members in Columbus to work out a compromise before a full-blown crisis emerged.

Having reached a temporary truce, tensions abated and the delegates on the veranda eventually went to bed. The next morning, the education sessions proceeded without a hitch. All the speakers had arrived, easing some of Liam's worries. After the morning's presentations, a group of delegates went off to play in tournaments on the golf course and at a nearby tennis court, while about a dozen of us followed Harry on a hike through the state park.

Friday evening, after the sports enthusiasts had all showered and dressed, we gathered in the ballroom for another round of cocktails followed by a dinner banquet and presentation of the tournament prizes. The cocktail chatter focused on commentary on the morning's educational topics or the afternoon's activities. Chuck still had not apprised me of the outcome of the management fee discussion. Spying Liam McFarland momentarily free of a conversational companion, I walked over to speak with him.

"Chuck still has not told me what happened in the executive session, so I'll take you up on your offer from last night."

"The Executive Committee voted to accept the proposed fee," Liam explained, "with a counter offer that the fee would remain at the same level for two years with the caveat that you continue to stay as our executive director as long as you continue to be employed at AEMG."

I was relieved that the Executive Committee had accepted the fee increase and wished to continue our management agreement and was flattered that they thought highly enough of me and my services to insist on my continued work with them. I realized that two years would cover both Liam's and Keir's successive presidencies and wondered if they had concocted this plan together. It might also explain Keir's mischievous look the previous evening when he first approached me about the Executive Committee's decision. However, I was simultaneously a little annoyed that no one had bothered to consult with me as to whether I wished to remain tied to their account as executive director.

"Thank you for telling me, Liam. I know David Fisher will want to know what happened when I get back to the office on Monday. I will also need to get that portion of the meeting minutes from Keir before I leave."

The next morning, during the mid-morning coffee break, I asked Keir for the minutes he had taken during Thursday's executive session. From his inside coat pocket he wordlessly handed to me a small note-sized piece of paper where he had neatly printed two motions—one approving the two-year management fee as a counter offer, and the second one with the request that I remain OAHIA's executive director for the duration of my employment at AEMG.

Immediately following the end of the educational sessions late in the morning, Chuck began the annual business meeting. Harry's treasurer's report indicated that the association had regained a positive cash flow and the convention was expected to net a surplus. Keir publicly thanked Harry and me for putting the association's finances back in order.

The membership accepted by acclamation the Nominating Committee's slate of officers for the coming year. As incoming vice president, Keir announced that he expected the 1987 convention to be held in May at the Bayshore Inn in the village of Reno Beach, a popular coastal town near Toledo. As ideas for the convention were suggested, it was clear that the members preferred to hold the convention in July or August rather than in May. The business meeting continued with approval of some bylaws changes.

"Now I want to introduce to you someone who is intelligent, energetic, very diligent, and an outspoken leader for our organization," Chuck announced to the gathered members. I looked up from my minute-

19

taking, curious to discover who this fine creature was. "Annie Weber took over as our executive director last year and has impressed our board members with her ability to manage our association." I was so surprised by this unexpected praise that it took me a moment to gather my thoughts to rise to the podium.

"Thank you, Chuck," I was able to respond and then presented my annual report on the statistics of the association.

Once I sat down, Liam presented Chuck with a plaque of appreciation for the latter's service as president and concluded the business meeting.

That afternoon 20 of us took to canoes for a trip on the Salt Fork Lake organized by Harry Whitfield. Since the summer had been quite dry, the water level was relatively low. In a number of spots, we had to get out of our canoes to dislodge our vessels which became wedged on the rocks.

By the time we arrived back at the Inn, my camera's viewfinder was half full of brown river water, and my sneakers squished as I walked. Aware that we were both supposed to be hosting the Saturday evening farewell cocktail party only 15 minutes later, Chuck and I ran into opposite ends of the Inn, looking too much like drowned rats to go through the lobby. Miraculously, we both were able to shower and dress in time to greet everyone at 7:00 p.m. Not everyone had stayed for the canoe trip and closing reception. Keir, for example, left Saturday afternoon, presumably to return to Cleveland and his wife.

About a dozen or more members gathered on the veranda for cocktails before dinner on the final evening of the convention. Liam was congratulated on his election as OAHIA president, and Chuck was thanked for his service during the preceding year. Once the cocktail reception ended, I drove back to Newark.

Keir again offered to host the next OAHIA quarterly Executive Committee meeting on November 12th at his office. However, upon his return to Columbus, Insurance Director Carson had investigated the situation Liam had raised on the porch at the Beaver Ridge Inn and had issued a "cease-and-desist" letter to the health insurers on September 19th. This action caused an immediate insurance crisis in Ohio. National insurers required the procedure—which was condoned in other states—but was now considered illegal in Ohio. Exercising his presidential prerogative to call a special meeting, Liam McFarland rescheduled the Executive Committee meeting to October 21st. An *ad hoc* group representing the hospital association, insurance agents' society, the Health Law Section of the Ohio Bar Association, OAHIA, the medical association, and several other interested parties, was convened to discuss and present alternatives to Director Carson as well as to determine the legality of his action. Director Carson met with the *ad hoc* committee members on October 8th and, two days later, issued a subsequent letter temporarily allowing until December 1 coverage from any procedures that had already been performed.

Once the OAHIA Executive Committee gathered again, the officers discussed the situation for a considerable length of time. Although I did not completely understand the medical-legal ramifications of these discussions, I was aware that the individual livelihoods of the OAHIA members and the viability of the entire health insurance industry in the state were at stake. The officers agreed to present a modified proposal to Director Carson that would allow insurance coverage under very strict guidelines and only certain circumstances, having prior approval of a hospital's legal department and head of surgery. Chuck and Keir amended the motion further to require agreement on the wording of the policy coverage and a rate mechanism for charging for the coverage.

Having addressed the crisis, at least temporarily, the Executive Committee meeting continued with Harry's treasurer's report.

"I anticipate the Association will have a year-end surplus of $2,000 to $3,000 due to the convention profit of $1,000 and collecting more special assessment income than we expected, with Henry Spaulding's company paying two years' dues in arrears." Everyone murmured congratulations for the improved financial condition of OAHIA.

"Rather than applying the $1,000 convention profit to help underwrite next year's convention budget, I suggest we keep it in the general operating fund," proposed Keir. As next year's convention chair, Keir would be responsible for having his convention break even entirely on its registration revenues without the $1,000 cushion. "I also suggest that Harry and Annie prepare a proposed budget for 1987, determine the annual dues based on the budget, and send around a mail ballot for Executive Committee approval."

"Any new member dues we receive after the convention should be deferred until the following year, since most of the benefit for the year, including the convention, will have already passed," Liam added. The rest of the officers concurred with these two recommendations.

Keir presented a proposed agenda of speakers and topics for the 1987 convention in Reno Beach.

"Since the membership wants to change the convention dates from May to July or August," I observed, "we will need to renegotiate the proposed contract provisions with the Bayshore Inn. The deadline for signing the contract is Monday, November 4. It is more difficult for me to plan a meeting at a location that I have never seen before. It might be worthwhile for me to pay a site visit to the Bayshore before a contract is signed. The hotel will provide me with a free night's stay, but I need approval from the Executive Committee for reimbursement of my mileage and meals." The officers felt this was a reasonable request and authorized the expense and adjourned the special meeting.

Liam, Chuck, and Keir met with Director Carson on October 30th, after which Carson revised his order to accept OAHIA's proposed new rating system for implementation on December 1. However, other affected organizations protested, and the discussions continued throughout

November when Director Carson suspended his previous orders and the December 1 deadline to allow for new legislation to be enacted in the General Assembly the following August.

After living and working for 10 months in Pittsburgh, August returned to Newark. We agreed that we could live together less expensively on one salary in Ohio than we could with two salaries if I moved to Pittsburgh. Being relative social outcasts in Newark, we opted to move into Columbus proper, saving me the 90-minute daily commute. Now that I had a track record of employment for over a year at AEMG, we were approved to sublet a condominium townhouse off Cleveland Avenue in Columbus, beginning the following February.

While making arrangements for my site visit to the Bayshore Inn on November 2nd, I learned about a brand new property, the Sandpiper Suites just a few miles up the road in Maumee Bay, so I accepted an offer from the Sandpiper's sales manager to visit that resort during the same weekend. Auguste accompanied me up to Reno Beach. After checking in, the Bayshore Inn sales manager led me on a tour of the meeting facilities, proud that they had just undergone a complete renovation.

A rectangular, three-story building, the cement Bayshore Inn was about 30 years old, built in the modern style. The lobby faced the lake with a series of floor-to-ceiling windows, but seemed rather dark. I rationalized that, because it was November and the angle of the sun was different, it might appear brighter during the summer. The lobby was furnished in groupings of wicker chairs upholstered in a tacky flower print on a darkly stained, wooden floor. The wall coverings in the ballroom where we would hold the banquet were a bright metallic blue, lit by faux, French renaissance chandeliers and wall sconces. Worst of all, the educational sessions would be held in a musty-smelling, elongated, and windowless room located in the basement, with a low ceiling and a badly painted mural at one end where the head table would be placed. I tried not to let my disappointment show when the sales manager pressed me about signing the contract.

"We have until Monday morning to sign the contract," I reminded him. "We will have a decision by then."

When I returned to our room, where Auguste had been waiting, I used the bathroom. The toilet basin had rusty circles, and the wallpaper was peeling. The furniture looked like Victorian wicker that had sat outside on a porch for too long.

Auguste and I rode the metal elevator down to the dining room for dinner. A spacious room next to the lobby, it also had a lake view. Granted, it was off season, but during our entire dinner, there were only two other people dining there. Our seafood dinner was dull and uninspired, and the table service excruciatingly slow. Auguste and I could not wait to check out on Sunday morning to move over to the Sandpiper Suites.

A completely different environment greeted us at the new resort. Instead of the Bayshore's low ceilings and dark wood, the Sandpiper's lobby had a two-story glass atrium facing Lake Erie with an enclosed pool, allowing sunlight to flood the entrance. The smell was one of fresh air and sand mixed with the pool's chlorine where we could see a family with children frolicking in the heated blue water.

Each overnight accommodation was a one-bedroom suite, individually owned with the resort managing the rental. A hallway door opened on the land side to the outside balcony entrance. To the left was a bedroom with two queen-sized beds covered in fresh, pastel-colored linens. Brand new fixtures graced the bathroom. At the end of the hallway, a large room contained a dining table for four, a chandelier, a pastel upholstered sofa, a large television, and a kitchenette on the opposite side of the bathroom wall. Beyond the alcove with the dining table, the front wall consisted of floor-to-ceiling windows with sliding doors that opened onto another balcony with a clear view of the beach and Lake Erie.

After a swim in the pool, Auguste and I took a late afternoon walk on the beach that extended toward the adjacent wildlife refuge for mallards, cranes, and other water fowl. Our dinner at the resort restaurant was a tasty treat, and we rested well in the soft coziness of our room.

On Monday morning, I met the Sandpiper's sales manager for breakfast and a tour of the meeting space. The main ballroom was above ground, light and airy, and could be divided into three parts. Our cocktail receptions could be held *al fresco* around the spacious outdoor pool or in a section of the ballroom. There was also a small room next to the lake view restaurant for our Private Practice Section breakfast. The meeting space seemed ideally suited for the OAHIA's convention. I excused myself from the sales manager to return to my room to make a phone call. Luckily, Keir was in his office.

"I am at the new Sandpiper Suites resort in Maumee Bay after visiting the Bayshore Inn yesterday," I began, not sure how he would react to my suggestion. "As you know, we are supposed to sign the Bayshore contract today, but frankly, I am very concerned about the quality of that property for your convention next year." I detailed the problems I had encountered. "In contrast, I believe the Sandpiper Suites would be ideal for the convention." I described the resort.

"I agree," Keir responded without hesitation. "How soon can you get a contract from the Sandpiper Suites?"

"The sales manager promised me one within a few days."

"Let's add switching convention locations to the mail ballot with the proposed budget and dues for 1987 to get Executive Committee approval. Thanks for checking out the two resorts. It sounds like the Bayshore would be a big mistake for our group."

"I can send out the mail ballot tomorrow or Wednesday after I return to Columbus," I assured him as the relief of his trust in my judgment washed over me. After hanging up the phone, I called the Sandpiper sales manager and asked her to prepare the contract, then called the Bayshore Inn's sales manager and told him we were releasing the space. Auguste and I checked out of the Sandpiper and drove home.

The Executive Committee approved the items on the mail ballot unanimously. Subsequently, I mailed the 1987 OAHIA dues renewals that resulted in a 98 percent renewal rate. The Association had a small financial reserve in the bank, the Department of Insurance crisis was being worked out, and plans were in process for the 1987 convention to be held at the new, high-rise, full-service condominium, Sandpaper Suites resort complex on Maumee Bay. Auguste and I began packing to move from Newark to Columbus.

Hisat Sinom (Anasazi) & Patayan (Cohonina)

circa 900 A.D./C.E.

We were out of breath. We had been running since before dawn. The sun was beating down on us like fire even though it had not yet reached its midday zenith. Nanko was bent over, his strong, beautifully shaped hands resting on his knees. I scanned the horizon of the rocky, cactus- and yucca-strewn mesa, searching for other signs of life.

Early this morning, Nanko had stealthily approached my parents' hut, nestled partway into the ground near the edge of our village. He tossed a few pebbles toward the opening in the clay-covered, woven-twig roof. I had been waiting in silence for our signal to escape.

I loved and respected my parents dearly, but they were dead set against my relationship with Nanko. I had unsuccessfully pleaded and reasoned with them. Now Nanko and I were running away together.

Nanko had arrived in our village some months ago. He did not talk much about his ancestors, his tribe, or from where he came, but he recounted wonderful tales of his travels and spoke of the many wonders outside our canyon walls—rivers that flowed a blue-green color, intricate caves, and exotic animals.

He was not afraid of work and pitched in to help with the agricultural tasks, guarding our fields against raiders or digging ditches for water. No one seemed to refuse his willingness to help or his winning smile. His easy-going manner and good-natured personality made him welcome.

Although somewhat shorter in stature than the men in our tribe, his muscular shoulders and broad chest gave power to his slighter build. There was no arguing that he was particularly handsome, but his good looks seemed second nature to his ability to make the person to whom he spoke feel important and the center of his attention. It was not long before most of the women, and even some of the men, were enchanted by Nanko. I was not immune to his charms either.

I was surprised when Nanko began to pay special attention to me flashing his engaging smile at me when I passed or seeking me out to speak to me when I was standing by myself at the evening campfire. His melodious voice settled around me like a warm blanket. At first I thought he was just making the rounds among the different girls, and I kept warning myself that he would soon move on to his next interest. But those few, simple, encounters alone with him seemed to shimmer with a magical quality I had never felt before.

25

Nanko's eyes hinted at deeper mysteries and hidden pain that simultaneously excited and frightened me. I felt strongly and uncontrollably drawn to him, even while my mind warned me that once I relinquished my guard and allowed myself to be swept up in the current of his personal river, there would be no turning back.

One evening, we hung back from the others in the twilight of the evening as everyone returned from tending the fields. Nanko and I ended up in a side canyon watching a small eddy pool. He slipped his left arm around my waist and gently pulled me toward him. Our closeness was dizzying to me. As our faces moved together, I stopped resisting and melted into his kiss.

In an instant, he raised my cotton sheath tunic and, without a second thought, I surrendered to him against the rock wall. Waves of pleasure pulsated throughout me. I could not get enough of him, at times biting, scratching, and devouring like a mountain lioness, at other times, soft, warm, and moist like a doe. We panted and sweated until our ardor finally cooled with the evening air. We walked back to the village in silence, hand-in-hand.

When we reached the edge of the cluster of pit houses comprising the village, Nanko squeezed my hand, then let go to head off towards his hut. I stopped to watch his figure silhouetted against the canyon rocks by the light of the agave fire from the center of our kiva then headed to my own pueblo.

My family must have been in the kiva with the other villagers, so I did not have to explain my delayed return. I snuggled down under the skin blankets atop my straw pallet and drifted off to sleep while still thinking of the warm feel of Nanko's body and the sweetness of his lips.

The next morning, while grinding corn for our supper, I was still basking in the warm memories of the previous evening's encounter when my father suddenly returned from his chores.

"Nanko just asked my permission to marry you," he scowled down at me. "Under no circumstances are you to ever associate with him."

"Why not?"

Just then my mother appeared at my side. "What's happened?" My father repeated to my mother what he had told me.

"But, why not?" I insisted. I knew my defiance was serious disobedience.

"He's a stranger."

"But that doesn't make him a bad person! Nanko works hard and has made many friends here. I think he hopes to stay."

"I have spoken." My father turned on his heels to return to his chores. I ran after him.

"But what did you say to him?" My father stopped and turned towards me, his fists clenched.

"My decision is final. I will not be questioned by my daughter. If you pursue this further, I will marry you off immediately to Muav."

Muav was the village idiot. Muav drooled. He could not speak coherently. He could not bathe or feed himself. I shuddered at the thought. I would rather die than marry Muav. The tears rolled down my cheeks. I started to sob and ran back to the house, past my mother who looked on in silence.

As the day wore on, I resolved that I could no longer live with my father's ruling or stay under his roof. I gathered some yucca-fiber baskets and, going into our food storage area where red-and-white pots decorated with black geometric shapes and swirls stood, I filled the baskets with dried berries and meat and filled a leather pouch with water that I tied under my skirt.

At dinner, I appeared subdued and obedient.

After supper, I accompanied my family toward the kiva fire in the center of our village, but hung back in the shadows, scanning the crowd for Nanko, afraid he might have left the village in disappointment or shame. Then I saw him. He was also hanging back in the shadows. Our eyes met. I smiled shyly. He moved his hand in a circular gesture suggesting that we should meet behind the grain storage pueblos. By moving his right forefinger to his lips and raising his left hand he signaled that I was to wait until he was out of sight, lest someone discern our clandestine meeting.

When I arrived behind the pueblo, Nanko grabbed my shoulders and kissed me swiftly.

"Do you know I asked your father if I could marry you?"

I nodded, telling him in a hushed and quickened voice the scene earlier with my father. Nanko looked down at the ground, then back up, questioning me with his eyes.

"I have prepared water and food, should you want me to leave with you tonight." My determination surprised me.

Nanko seemed to weigh the matter quickly in his mind.

"I will come to your house when all are asleep. We will make our escape then." Nanko brushed my cheek with his lips while squeezing my hands, then left abruptly.

I walked slowly back to my home. Tonight my intermittent slumber under the blanket skins was so different from that of the previous night. I was about to sneak away under cover of night, to head off into the unknown wilderness with a man I scarcely knew.

As Nanko straightened up out in the desert, I asked, "Do you know where we are going?" In the light of day, our escape plan seemed less sure than before. At first, we had hiked along a stream bed on a primitive trail, crisscrossing it several times to hide our tracks. Then we ascended to an upper trail leading out of the canyon to the mesa rim above.

"Your village lies on the southern edge of the canyon," he reassured me. "I know of some settlements on the eastern edge and beyond. I came from that area. I guess it is time to go back." Then he took my hand, using his other to designate a direction in the distance.

"We will head towards those cliffs so that we will have some shelter tonight," he said, pointing northeastward. "But we should probably have a bite to eat and some water first."

Later, upon nearing the cliffs he indicated earlier, Nanko set a trap for a jack rabbit and built a fire of mesquite branches over which to roast our dinner. After we watched the glow of the sunset fade from red to orange to purple, we both fell asleep exhausted in each other's arms sheltered by a rock overhanging from a cliff.

As the fire burned out, the early morning cold enveloped us, and bats flitted across the sky. A swell of homesickness and fear overtook me, and I began to cry. Nanko tried to comfort me, but his own confidence was waning as he began to fathom the full extent of the journey and his responsibility for me. He knew the risks and the dangers, but he had traveled alone on his previous trek. There were now two mouths to nourish and, I was bound to tire more easily. I would slow him down and make it more difficult for us to evade dangers.

I watched these concerns flicker across Nanko's face. I was touched by his tender regard for me while aware of his wish to protect me from his worries. We sat, our bodies touching, while we silently pondered our own thoughts. My head dropped onto his shoulder. He put his arm around me, and we soon fell asleep again.

When we awoke, we ate the last of our small food supply and had a small gulp of water each. Nanko was so deep in thought while we ate, I dared not speak.

We stood up to begin the day's journey. But first, Nanko pulled a pouch from under his tunic that had hung, hidden, around his neck. Then he looked straight at me for the first time since we awoke. His eyes burned with a faraway intensity I had not seen before.

"My parents were killed in a raid on our village by another tribe. I found them both dead and badly beaten when I returned from a scouting expedition." He stopped, and then continued more tenderly. "For as long as I can remember, my parents were deeply in love with each other." He opened his pouch and pulled out two silver bracelets. The wider one was inlaid with striated bands of alternating turquoise, black onyx, red coral, and mother-of-pearl. The other was a more feminine band that narrowed on the sides. It contained stripes of similar stones but also triangles of onyx and alabaster in the center of its inlay pattern.

Nanko hesitated for a moment, reasserting control over his emotions.

28

"These bracelets represent my parents' pledge to each other. When I found them, their left arms, the ones with the bracelets, were outstretched towards each other."

Again, Nanko hesitated.

"I don't kno..." he started again, "I don't know where, or how, our journey will turn out, but I do know that you are the one...the one whom I want to wear my mother's bracelet."

He took my left hand and encircled my wrist with the silver band, clasping it so that the two prong ends bent toward my skin. He then placed his father's bracelet on his own wrist as my tears overflowed and coursed down my cheeks. His hands cupped my face as he kissed me. My tears rolled over his thumbs clasping my chin. Nanko smiled, turned, and took my hand in his. We began to walk. In my heart, I knew that, in the simple act of giving me the bracelet, Nanko had revealed his deepest pain to me. He had also made to me a sacred pledge of eternal devotion.

All day, we ran and skipped, swung our arms together, laughed and hugged. Nanko pointed out birds, animals, and plants to me.

During the third night in the wilderness, I was suddenly awakened by a hand covering my mouth, my arms pinned behind me. As I was lifted to my feet, my eyes shot open. Two young men from my village had hold of Nanko who was struggling to get free but was overpowered. Two other men held me from behind.

"Your father sent us to drag you back," snarled one in my left ear, "but he doesn't want that one to come back." I looked at Nanko, who struggled in vain. His captors spun him around and pushed him toward some rocks. It was then that I saw his wrists were bound.

"We are going to leave this one for the vultures," the largest man spat out.

"No," I screamed through the hand covering my mouth. I tried to pull away. I bit the fingers covering my mouth. That hand withdrew in time for me to scream, "Nanko!" before the hand slapped my face. I winced. I tried kicking, but lost my balance and was yanked back to my feet.

By this time, Nanko's captors had tied him to a thorny cactus and stripped him of his clothing. He would die slowly and horribly. If he did not succumb to thirst and starvation, his skin would burn and blister in the sun. Then, if the insects didn't infect his raw skin, the birds of prey would be attracted to his body—his beautiful body.

I struggled harder, until a swift blow rendered me unconscious.

When I woke, I realized I had been carried quite a way from our night's encampment. I tried to look back for a final glance at Nanko, but we had already traveled too far. The sun was almost overhead.

29

We did not stop until nightfall. The men took turns watching over me to ensure I did not escape. I began to contemplate my fate—marriage with Muav. I couldn't imagine what harsher punishment would be awaiting me. And even if by some miracle I could escape, I knew I would not be able to find the cactus again where Nanko was tied. Even if he could escape, would he even try to come for me?

I could think of no way we could be together again. In sharp contrast to just the day before, my heart now was heavy and I was without hope.

The second day of travel brought us closer to our village and the terrain took on more familiar aspects. I remembered that we would pass near the rim of the canyon high above a river. As we drew closer to home, the men seemed to become more confident and less vigilant of me.

The afternoon was waning when we veered close to the canyon edge. A couple of the men began to argue, and the other two attempted to intervene. Seeing my captors thus distracted, I broke into a run straight toward the canyon rim. The men shouted for me to stop, but I ran faster, jumping into mid-air as I went over the edge.

For a few moments I felt the freedom of a bird soaring high over the canyon floor. Then my body began its descent and crashed into the rocks below.

Ohio, 1987-1988

FLIRTATION

My work assignments at Association Emphasis Management Group altered and shifted periodically as staff members and client associations changed. When I started there in August 1985, I was executive director of four organizations and newsletter coordinator for two others. Three of those organizations left AEMG during my first year, but I was given conference management responsibilities on one of my national accounts plus a large statewide group. Except for the "special services" clause, included when the OAHIA management was renewed, I might have been taken off that client; however, my boss, David Fisher, was smart enough not to tinker with that group of attorneys. OAHIA had been his first client when he opened the firm ten years earlier, and David bought his house from an OAHIA officer. During the negotiations, they had discussed David's new business and the recently formed association's need for staffing. If OAHIA was now pleased with my services as executive director, then that was one less management concern for David.

One of AEMG's senior executive directors, however, was having difficulty with a national insurance regulator's society. David decided to assign me to that client group as assistant executive director for a six-month trial period to see if my personality and management style would be better suited than that of my senior colleague. If it worked out, the promotion would be ideal for me to graduate to the national scene.

With a more secure employment situation for me, Auguste and I moved into a Columbus townhouse in February 1987. By May, with his Pittsburgh work experience on his resume, Auguste was hired by the Huntington Bank in their mortgage accounting division. With two incomes, I now hoped our previous tensions were behind us.

The OAHIA Executive Committee met again on the 17th floor of the Athenaeum Health Care Plan headquarters in Mansfield on February 13th. Although the Association had a secretary, the Executive Committee usually dispensed with the reading of the minutes I had taken and approved them as distributed. Treasurer Harry Whitfield reported that, after a $10,000 net surplus for 1986, of which $5,600 was used to pay off OAHIA's 1985 shortfall, the Association now had a cash reserve of $4,400. Keir quickly expressed the Executive Committee's appreciation to Harry and me for this positive financial news, diminishing his own critical role in the turnaround.

I again noted that Keir preferred to work behind the scenes while giving others the credit and limelight. I also sensed that, although Liam (OAHIA's President) appeared to be in the forefront of the insurance rating controversy, it was likely Keir's charm and easy-going manner—as well as his relationship with Insurance Director Carson—that had greased the skids during the tough months of negotiation surrounding the controversy. I

31

admired how Keir seemed to know instinctively when to break the tension with a joke or clever remark, as well as the way he could clearly see multiple sides of an issue and bring a holistic resolution that satisfied all parties in a difficult problem.

To implement one of the financial policies from the previous year, the Executive Committee members agreed that each health insurance company would pay $300 towards sponsorship of the Health Law Section's annual convention, and OAHIA would purchase a black sign with changeable plastic letters to display each year with the names of each of the company sponsors. In addition, Liam suggested OAHIA purchase its own satin banner with the OAHIA logo for display behind the podium at its conventions.

During the meeting, we viewed videos of the Delroy Resort and the Deerwood Lake Lodge as the proposed 1988 convention sites. Keir also presented the speakers and suggested topics for the 1987 convention program, and registration fees were established.

Since past president Chuck Lincoln was absent, there was no report on the proposed establishment of a rating bureau, a separate organization that would develop a specific rating structure for health insurance premiums to the Department of Insurance.

"Don't you all adhere to the rates *already filed* with the Insurance Department?" new Secretary Henry Spaulding of Safety Assurance Health Plan asked naively.

A pregnant silence enveloped the conference room. Keir, who was seated a couple of empty seats from me, shifted uncomfortably in his chair. Eyes darted about the room. Instinctively, I knew this was a legal question, and these men were all licensed attorneys. I rather noisily banged my pen down on my note pad and stuck my right hand inside my purse, muttering under my breath, "This broken nail is driving me crazy!" I pulled out an emery board and started filing my nail, feigning oblivion to what had transpired in reaction to Henry's pointed question.

"Let's take a break," Liam suggested, signaling a recess. I was very glad I was the only female and could go alone into the ladies' room. I do not know what occurred in the men's room, but I suspect Henry received a reality check because, when he returned to the meeting, he suggested the Executive Committee consider purchasing directors' and officers' liability insurance.

The officers' conversation then turned to specific issues in health insurance law and practices in other states. Liam presented a copy of proposed legislation to permit as legal the practice that had precipitated the insurance crisis the previous fall. The meeting ended with the tentative selection of Deerwood Lake Lodge for the 1988 convention and Liam's appointment of a Long-Range Planning Committee, consisting of immediate past president Chuck Lincoln, president Liam McFarland, and vice president Keir Mervais.

During the spring, the health insurance industry experienced upheaval when Cleveland Medical purchased Safety Assurance Health Plan, Attorneys Assurance Health Plan aggressively expanded and hired key employees from SummitCare, and, several new branch offices opened in suburban locations around the state. I was starting to the get the feeling that, no matter how genteel and polite these attorneys were around the conference room table, out in the marketplace they were fiercely competitive with each other.

The May 6th OAHIA Executive Committee meeting was again hosted by David Fisher at his club in downtown Columbus. After the approval of minutes and the treasurer's report, Keir confirmed his lineup of national and statewide convention speakers, including Insurance Director Carson—again, and Health Law Section Chair Patch Damien. Attendance at the Sandpiper Suites was expected to be considerable, so I was urged to block ten additional suites. Henry Spalding, whose offices were located near the Sandpiper in Toledo, had identified potential locations for golf and tennis tournaments, and names of potential tournament chairmen were suggested to Keir. I presented the results of my research on the cost for a OAHIA banner in green and gold satin.

Henry and Chuck reported on some cooperative efforts among organizations interested in health law and controlled premium schemes, while Liam informed the Executive Committee members of the status of the new legislation that had been developed.

"Despite our increased cooperation with the Insurance Department, Director Carson is still planning to conduct company audits of premiums and statements," Keir warned his colleagues.

Privately, I wondered if these audits had been precipitated by the practices to which Henry's question at the previous meeting had alluded, but I now knew enough about the subtleties of this group of men not to voice my question out loud. The Nominating Committee was appointed to consider the candidates put forward for the position of secretary. The three officers on Long-Range Planning agreed to meet on Wednesday, July 8th, at Liam's office in Cleveland. The meeting adjourned so that we could enjoy the club's buffet luncheon.

Two months later I dutifully drove up to Cleveland to meet with the Long-Range Planning Committee. Upon arriving at the Cleveland Plaza Building, I rode the elevator up to Liam's office in suite 2560. When I entered, Liam was on the phone with his Athenaeum Health Care main office, but he covered the mouthpiece to speak to me.

"Chuck Lincoln called to say he couldn't get out of a commitment in Akron, but we should go ahead without him. Why don't you go to Keir's office to get him? I'll be finished by the time you two get back."

Keir's office was just down the hall, so it took only a few moments to enter the Cleveland Medical offices. I approached the high, wooden receptionist's desk.

"I am here to get Keir Mervais for a meeting."

The receptionist rang his extension. A few moments later he emerged from his office, dressed in a light blue, button-down shirt, a tie, and navy slacks.

"Liam was on the phone so he sent me to bring you to his office for the Long-Range Planning meeting. Chuck Lincoln cannot get out of an appointment in Akron, so it will only be the three of us," I explained.

"I can't meet with you today," Keir said unexpectedly. I hesitated, not sure what to do. After all, I had driven nearly three hours from Columbus for this meeting. Sensing my puzzlement, Keir headed toward the suite's exit door.

"Come with me," he directed. I turned and followed him. He held the mahogany door open for me to exit first.

I noticed that the hallway was dimly lit but with an understated, sophisticated look; the walls were a burgundy color and the carpet was gray with burgundy and ivory speckles. As the suite door closed behind us, I sensed Keir had stopped and I turned back towards him.

"I just learned…my mother has cancer…" Keir fell backwards against the wall and broke down into tears.

For a moment I was not sure what to do. I had only know Keir a year—essentially five Executive Committee meetings—and here he was, crying before me. Quickly, my mind reasoned, "As the branch manager, he cannot break down in front of his staff, his family is not around, and he cannot appear like this in front of Liam. I am it—the only person neutral enough with whom he can be vulnerable right now. As a crier myself, I know he needs to cry and what a catharsis that can be."

"I'm sorry," I murmured out loud. I stood quietly and respectfully at a distance until Keir could pull himself together again. I sensed a level of trust that Keir had in me and the depth of his love for his mother. My intuition told me this was a private moment, not to be disclosed to his colleagues.

After a few moments, Keir stood back up from the wall and pulled out a handkerchief.

"I'll tell Liam you cannot participate in the Long-Range Planning meeting today," I offered.

"Thank you." Keir re-entered the door of his suite, while I made my way back to Liam's office. He had just finished his phone call and was gathering up a pen and pad for the meeting.

"Keir just learned his mother has cancer and won't be joining us."

"Oh, dear. Well, while you are here, let's brainstorm how we should proceed." We agreed to hold a full Executive Committee planning retreat in Columbus after the annual convention which was scheduled for August. I recommended conducting a membership survey to gather additional information. An hour later, I was back on I-77 driving southward to Columbus.

One of the several reasons I had accepted the association executive position at AEMG was that I had been impressed with David Fisher's assistant, Evonda Spectin. A stately and dignified older woman, Evonda exuded a deep warmth and concern for her fellow human beings. Although her education consisted only of a high-school diploma from a one-room schoolhouse in Minnesota, Evonda had a keen intelligence about people and thoroughness about her work. Often her grammar, spelling, and writing skills exceeded those of younger, college graduates whose work she corrected. She had a strong moral compass that was refined with a graceful personality and tempered by the school of hard knocks. A divorced mother of three children the same ages as my siblings and I, she had originally been hired by David Fisher, whom she had known from church, as his secretary and confidante in the fledgling association management business. If David was the "patriarch" of AEMG, Evonda was its respected "matriarch," dispensing guidance and direction with grace and good humor to those employees who were savvy enough to be open to it.

In the association management company, changes in staffing happened quickly. The person initially assigned to me as my second on several groups, including OAHIA, was soon assigned to other clients, so Evonda was assigned to assist me with OAHIA and another association of electrical contractors. In those pre-computer days, membership information and finances were tracked manually—on index cards, ledger sheets, and the previous year's hard-copy membership directory. With the complicated, multi-level dues structure that Harry Whitfield, Keir Mervais, and I had developed for OAHIA, I needed Evonda's keen attention to detail to help me keep track of their membership information, especially since my own office duties were increasing.

Shortly after my return from the truncated OAHIA Long-Range Planning meeting with Liam in Cleveland, I flew to Orlando for the 500-person annual conference of a national society of state regulators, NIRS. Assuming their fifty board members and twelve Executive Committee members liked me well enough, the plan was that I would replace the current executive director. By the end of the five-day conference, I had been approved for that promotion—a position that would command at least fifty percent of my time and attention.

Returning from Orlando, I turned my attention to the OAHIA annual convention, August 6-8, at the Sandpiper Suites in Maumee Bay for which Keir was convention chair. Since the change in hotel location had been my suggestion, I was a little anxious that the officers be impressed. Auguste had received permission to take two days off from his new banking job and accompanied me on the trip. Pre-registration attendance was at an all-time high with 115 delegates. Since one of the complaints from the previous year's convention at Beaver Ridge had been that I was the only staff member on-site and, therefore, the registration desk had been self-service, I asked Evonda to attend this convention with me, serving as registrar to hand out convention packets and greet people while I was participating in the meetings.

Evonda and I set up our registration desk in the sun-filled atrium lobby of the Sandpiper, across from the resort's check-in desk, so that our attendees would have the convenience of registering with the hotel and then with us in the same location. We could smell the chlorine from the indoor pool behind us and feel the breeze from the lake through the open doors. The members of the OAHIA Executive Committee began to arrive first, in time for their 3:00 p.m. meeting in Liam McFarland's presidential suite, before the convention officially began with a poolside Welcome Reception at 6:00 p.m.

Gathering my Executive Committee files and a notepad for taking minutes, I left Evonda in charge of our registration desk and headed for the glass elevator to proceed to Liam's sixth floor suite. As the elevator arrived and the doors opened, Keir and a curly-haired brunette came to the elevator. I entered first, followed by the couple.

"Annie, this is my wife, Abigail Anderson. Abigail, Annie is our executive director. She picked this resort." I noted that Abigail had retained her maiden name as my mind assessed that she was not as pretty as I would have expected for Keir's wife, rather more cute and ingenuous, but she appeared extremely intelligent. I liked her immediately.

"I like how open and airy the hotel feels," Keir continued. Through the glass walls of the elevator, we could see the sun sparkling on the lake waves as they approached the shoreline. I could tell Keir was feeling the nervous excitement of the convention that he had spent months planning.

The elevator stopped on the fifth floor to allow Abigail to go to their room, while Keir and I continued to the Executive Committee meeting on the floor above. Liam's wife, Fran, was leaving to go out to the lakefront beach as we entered. The McFarlands had brought in beer, soda, potato chips, and pretzels for snacks, so the officers settled in for a more relaxed meeting, sitting on the sofa and in easy chairs. The curtains were pulled open to provide a spectacular view of Lake Erie through the floor to ceiling windows. The western afternoon sun caused glittering, diamond-like, reflections across the water's surface.

Once everyone had arrived, Liam called the meeting to order. After dispensing with the reading of the minutes, accepting Harry's positive treasurer's report, and hearing an upbeat overview of the convention from Keir, Chuck Lincoln nominated Herbert Howell of Attorneys Assurance Health Plan—Lincoln's company—to be the incoming secretary. Since Chuck, Keir, Liam, and I had not been able to hold the Long-Range Planning meeting back in July, the Executive Committee members agreed to hold a planning retreat at the AEMG offices in Columbus on September 23rd to be facilitated by David Fisher.

Several attorney memberships were approved at the meeting. Harry Whitfield and I reviewed some details of the 1988 convention logistics at Deerwood Lodge, while Henry Spaulding suggested several locations for the 1989 convention site: Lakeside Inn in Lakeside, Castaway Bay Resort at Cedar Point, or the popular South Beach Resort in Marblehead.

President McFarland reported that the health insurance legislation had passed; this essentially allowed, under very specific circumstances, the procedure that had precipitated the previous year's crisis with Insurance Director Carson. However, Chuck Lincoln warned that controlled premiums would be the next big concern for the industry. The officers agreed to postpone addressing this issue and future conventions until its September 23rd planning retreat. The meeting adjourned to allow everyone to relax and freshen up before the poolside reception. I went downstairs to see how Evonda was doing with registration in the lobby.

The convention delegates began to arrive in greater numbers for resort check-in before the reception.

"I think I made a mistake," Evonda admitted to me between handing out packets. "I put the name badge for Keir's wife, Abigail Anderson, in with the packet for Anthony Andersen, thinking they were spouses as their last names were so similar."

"We'll give Abigail her name badge at the cocktail reception and apologize for the mix-up in last names," I reassured Evonda.

The setting sun was still glinting off Lake Erie as the convention delegates assembled on the concrete pool deck for libations and socializing. A fresh breeze blew in from the lake as gulls squawked overhead. I circulated among the crowd to greet the members and guests. Across the pool patio, I spotted Rick Northfield, the attorney who had helped to extricate me from the situation at the Arts Council of Newark, and his wife, Patti.

"How are things in Newark?" I asked.

"The fundraising is going well for the theater renovation," Rick replied, avoiding the direct subject of the Arts Council's activities and new executive director, my replacement.

"I'm glad they are going to renovate the historic theater." We were avoiding the topic of how my forced departure had been handled. Rick shifted from one foot to the other.

"Looks like we are going to have a superb weekend for the lake," Rick said. "Keir Mervais has put together an interesting program of speakers."

"The weather forecast is excellent," I replied, relieved to move to a more neutral topic. "Now, if you'll excuse me, I've just seen one of our speakers join us, so I'll need to greet him." I smiled my goodbye then walked determinedly in the direction of a man in a suit who was standing hesitantly at the gate to the pool. From his speaker photograph I recognized the senior counsel for the parent company of Buckeye Health Insurance. He had flown in from Los Angeles for his presentation the next morning.

"Hello, Mr. Morgenstern. Welcome to Maumee Bay! I'm Annie Weber, the Ohio Association of Health Insurance Attorney's executive director. Did you have a pleasant trip in?"

"Yes, I did. Thank you," he replied, still scanning the crowd. A middle-aged man with a receding hairline, Mr. Morganstern looked like a fish out of water in his California polyester leisure suit amongst the Hawaiian- and golf-shirted OAHIA members. I surmised that the most accommodating course of action was to find the Buckeye Health Insurance delegates and quickly glanced around the pool for Eric Mitchell who was conversing with Mike Johnson, the state president for Buckeye, and Jon Patrick, a fellow agency manager.

"I see Mike Johnson, Eric Mitchell, and Jon Patrick on the other side of the pool," I pointed to the cluster of men and their wives. "Would you care to join them or get a drink first?"

"Both," Morgenstern said, relieved and relaxing a bit. I led him toward the bar, waited patiently while he ordered, and then led him toward the knot of his colleagues, before discretely moving away.

Not too far away, Keir was standing with Liam, their spouses Abigail and Fran, and Insurance Director Carson whom I recognized from last year's convention at the Beaver Ridge Inn.

"I've made our dinner reservations at the Harborview Restaurant for 8:00 pm.," I overheard Keir tell Director Carson. About 15 miles due west of the Sandpiper Suites, the Harborview was one of the better known steak-and-seafood restaurants in the area. Located at the bend in Otter Creek Road, across the Maumee River from Toledo where the river opens to Maumee Bay and Lake Erie beyond, I knew the restaurant offered a sunset view of the Toledo harbor traffic, as well as of several nearby waterfowl and wildlife refuges including Mallard Club, Cedar Point, and West Sister Island wildlife refuges, Grassy Point Island in the middle of the Bay, and, further away, Luna Pier in Michigan. Keir would be sparing no expense to entertain the Insurance Director.

In the OAHIA's photo archives from two years prior to my employment at AEMG, I recalled seeing a photo of candidate Carson with Keir who was proudly displaying Carson's election button on his sports coat.

As I approached the cluster, Keir's boss, Alex McDowell, the state president for Cleveland Medical Insurance Corporation, arrived with his wife, Phoebe, and the head of Cleveland Medical's parent company, Kenneth Taft, who was also attending the convention to represent and speak on behalf of the board of the American Association of Health Insurance Attorneys. Sensing that I might be intruding on their business discussions, I changed course and went to greet Warren and Remy Sullivan who were talking with Emmanuel Stevens, an attorney speaker from Columbus, and the Health Law Section Council chairman, Patch Damien. They, too, were discussing dinner options, selecting from the seafood houses along the lake front to the east of the Sandpiper.

I excused myself and returned to the lobby to find Evonda still standing at the registration desk.

"I don't think many more people will come tonight. Why don't we pack the badges and packets away so that you can go have a drink and some hors d'oeuvres yourself?" Even though Evonda was old enough to be my mother and had children my age, in my role as executive director, I was her supervisor which created a strange dance of roles between us. Often I would seek her advice and guidance as the older, wiser, more tenured staff member and confidante of our boss. But the management decisions were mine to make.

"What do you want to do about dinner?" she asked as we packed the convention materials into boxes to store away for the night. I remembered my husband was upstairs in our suite. Not one for socializing at the cocktail receptions, he was likely watching television.

"I'll phone Auguste and see if he wants to join us for dinner. I am okay with just eating here in the hotel restaurant."

"I'm not that hungry myself," Evonda admitted. "Something light to eat here would suit me just fine."

By the time we rejoined the reception crowd poolside, small parties of delegates were gathering to leave for their respective dinner outings. Glancing at my wristwatch, it showed 6:55 p.m.

"Last call, last call," I announced going from group to group amongst the remaining clusters of attendees. "The bar is about to close." A few men stepped toward the bar while others graciously took their spouses' elbows, touched their backs, or patted a colleague's shoulder to usher them toward the pool exit gate. Within fifteen minutes, everyone had disbursed, and the hotel banquet staff began to dismantle the food and beverage set ups. Evonda and I re-entered the hotel lobby so that I could phone Auguste from a house phone.

"I've already ordered from room service," Auguste told me.

"Okay. Then Evonda and I will eat in the restaurant, after which I'll come up to the room."

Following dinner and a shower, I was drying my hair, when our room phone rang. Shutting off the dryer, I entered our bedroom and reached for the phone on the nightstand.

"Hello?" I was not sure whether to expect bad news or some emergency.

"Annie, it's Keir. I am calling to invite you to join Director Carson, Liam, and me for breakfast at 7:30. Can you make it?" I immediately recognized this as a special admission to the "boy's clique" and quickly rifled through my morning duties in my mind. I would just have to arise earlier.

"That would be great!"

"We'll meet at the restaurant in the morning then." I noticed the soft, melodic cadence of Keir's voice.

"I'll see you then. Good night."

"Thank you and good night." I was honored that Keir thought it was important that I be included in their breakfast powwow. I felt a warm glow inside as I walked into the parlor where Auguste was watching television.

"Auguste, I have to eat breakfast with some of the officers and a speaker tomorrow."

"Okay. I'll probably sleep in late tomorrow anyway." He did not take his eyes from the television set. I returned to the bathroom, finished drying my hair, set the alarm for 6:30 a.m., and crawled into bed, both nervous and excited about the next day's activities.

It was still dark when the alarm sounded. Turning off the alarm button, I tried to ease out of bed with the least disturbance to Auguste. Although we were on my business trip, I felt like my every movement inconvenienced him. He saw the weekend as his vacation time and my working detracted from his expectation and desire to relax. In an era of post-women's liberation, it would be politically incorrect for him to voice his displeasure, but I had long ago learned to read his resentment towards my earning more money than he did while taking advantage of my employment perks. As stealthily as I could, I gathered my undergarments and suit from the drawers and closet and tiptoed into the bathroom to dress, turning the light on only after gently closing the door behind me.

While donning my standard issue black skirt and suit jacket along with a blue-and-white striped blouse, I realized I had forgotten to bring my jewelry into the bathroom. Assessing myself in the mirror, it was obvious from the gap between my second and third buttons that a safety pin would be necessary to keep my blouse modestly closed.

Inherited from my paternal grandmother, the amplitude of my breasts was a source of constant embarrassment to me. As a young teen, the other girls would make derogatory comments in the locker room, and once, a male driver who stopped to ask me directions observed, "Nice tits," before driving away, leaving me in tears. I learned to hunch my shoulders forward to attempt to minimize the protrusion of my offensive mammary glands into the world's space in front of me. Adding insult to injury, I never had a flat stomach; instead, soft rolls of flesh were stacked in my midriff, like used tires at the auto mechanic's shop.

With all the superfluous flesh up front, it was unfair that my behind was comparatively flat and useless in its own way. I considered my best feature to be my shapely legs. But fashion lengths had fallen from the mini-skirts of the early 1970s to the below-knee, straight skirt of my nondescript black suit.

"At least the stripes are vertical," I consoled myself as I attempted to safety pin my blouse opening.

Combing my straight, fine, mouse-brown hair, I considered whether or not to take 20 more minutes to use a curling iron and chance being late for breakfast. To save money when Auguste and I were both unemployed, we had begun a ritual of cutting each other's hair. Essentially, my locks resembled those of a Dutch boy—straight cut bangs in the front, a center part, and a straight bowl cut around the sides and back.

Eschewing the idea of curling my hair, I spent five minutes applying makeup. I applied blush to my cheeks, lipstick, eye shadow, and felt I had enhanced my, at best, plain visage: an oval face, flat cheek bones, bushy-brown eyebrows inherited from my father which overhung darker brown eyes, and pale pink lips. "I am definitely *no* threat to the 'trophy wives' of this group!" I observed to myself. I dug into my toiletry bag for a small vial of sample perfume in a last attempt to enhance my femininity. I would have to grab my earrings, necklace, purse, and convention notebook in a few muffled movements as I donned my black flats and headed on my way out the door.

In my rushed attempt not to disturb Auguste, I dropped my purse on the linoleum floor, my metal lipstick tubes clattering as they rolled away from me.

"Damn!" I whispered with annoyance under my breath, grabbing wildly for the scattered purse contents.

"Goodbye!" I heard Auguste's displeased voice emanate from his pillow.

"I'll be back for lunch," I promised as consolation then headed for the exit door of our suite. I felt the familiar knot in my stomach and the ache of stifled tears begin to form in my throat. Struggling to pull my emotions together, I strode along the hallway toward the glass elevator.

"Not even the privacy of an enclosed elevator!" my psyche lamented as I pushed the lowest button for the lobby. As the doors slid apart on the first floor, I remembered to, "Put on a happy face!" Walking over to the registration tables facing the elevator, I pulled the convention boxes out from under the table and placed one atop a banquet chair, glad at least to have something to do. It was 7:15 a.m. I would set up registration for Evonda who would be down about the time I was expected in the dining room for breakfast.

I arranged the remaining name badges and convention packets neatly in alphabetical order, facing outward and upside down to the staff side of the table, then walked around to inspect my work from the other side.

Rick Northfield sauntered toward me from the restaurant, coffee cup in his left hand and newspaper in his right. I turned to face him.

"Good morning, Rick!" I said cheerily. "Did you find someplace nice to eat last night?"

"Yes, Patti and I joined Patch Damien, Emmanuel Stevens, and the Sullivans for dinner at a little Italian bistro in town. As usual, I ate too much!" Rick indicated the curve of his stomach with the edge of his newspaper, then turned to head back up to his room before the education sessions were scheduled to begin at 9:00 a.m. "I'll see you later," he called out as the elevator doors slid toward each other. I watched him ride up for a floor or two before pulling some brochures out of a box and walked around the front of the registration table to display them.

"You're up early." I heard Evonda's voice behind me as she came out of the elevator. She must have caught it returning from dropping Rick off on his floor. "You didn't need to put all the registration things out for me, but thank you." Evonda was authentically and endearingly polite.

"It's alright. I have to meet Liam McFarland, Keir Mervais, and the Insurance Director for breakfast at 7:30, and I was a little early."

"I was going to see about getting something quick to eat myself."

"Go ahead, Evonda. The registration desk is not scheduled to open until 8:00. I'll walk over to the restaurant with you."

We passed the hotel registration desk and a small gift shop on our left and the condominium sales office on our right. The meeting rooms were next on the left while across from them were the restrooms. Once past those, the double glass doors to the hotel restaurant were open, and the smell of strong coffee and frying bacon assailed us as we entered.

"Breakfast for two?" the hostess politely assumed.

"No, one," Evonda replied at the same time as I said, "No, I'm meeting some others." I turned back to look expectantly down the hallway while Evonda followed the hostess to a seat by the windows.

Because the hallway back to the elevators curved a little, I heard the men before I saw them: Liam's higher-pitched, grainy voice and Director Carson's sonorous bass. Both men were dressed in dark business suits. Keir, however, sported a well-tailored navy sport jacket with a brightly-colored Hawaiian shirt tucked neatly into khaki trousers. He appeared almost too relaxed and affable to be the convention chairman on the first morning of the program. I had to admire his aplomb. Upon seeing me, Keir's face broke into a broad grin of perfectly aligned white teeth, likely the result of orthodontia work when he was a teenager—dental work my own parents could not afford for me.

"Insurance Director Carson, may I present our Executive Director, Annie Weber. She's been doing a great job for us at OAHIA."

Liam and Director Carson interrupted their conversation to acknowledge my presence and allow me, as the only woman, to follow the hostess first to our table. "Keir must have reserved the table," I thought, since we were obviously expected.

After a few moments examining our menus and placing our orders, Director Carson pointed to a star-shaped pin on his lapel, similar to a deputy's badge.

"I'm a descendant of the founders of Carson City, Nevada, the state capital," he told us proudly, obviously a story he told often. "My great grandfather was the city's first sheriff when outlaws with six-guns held gun fights in the city streets. I come from a long line of tough, no-nonsense, law preservers."

The conversation turned to health insurance law, and although I listened politely and feigned interest, there was not much I could add to the conversation. Carson was not particularly good-looking. His middle-aged face was rectangular, ending in a jowl-like jaw. His dark glasses framed almost beady eyes that darted quickly, constantly assessing the situation. I gathered that what he may have lacked in intelligence he made up in political savvy and connections. He would be your best friend as long as you did not cross him.

As Carson spoke about the Insurance Department, I slowly realized that my appointment last month by AEMG as the new NIRS executive director might be a conflict of interest with OAHIA—not a direct one, as the NIRS membership consisted mainly of deputy directors of insurance from each of the fifty states, but perhaps in any dealings I might have with the Insurance Director. The management company policy was generally not to disclose the names of client associations to other clients, but I suspected there was a higher level of probity needed here. I would have to look for an opportunity to speak to Director Carson alone for a moment.

"Most of your audience this morning will be private practicing health law attorneys and in-house legal counsel with the key health insurance entities in the state," Keir advised Carson. "We're most interested in hearing about expected legislative initiatives that might affect us and your handling of any disciplinary cases related to violations of the new premium rating rules."

"I was planning to cover those two topics as well as give an overview of the interstate collaboration being fostered by the National Association of Insurance Commissioners."

Nodding his satisfaction with the Director's speech outline, Keir signaled our waitress for the check. I glanced at my watch: 8:35 a.m. We were due for Liam and Keir to open the convention at 9:00 with a welcome.

"I should check the audio-visual and room setup; please excuse me." I rose and backed my chair away as each man rose partly from his seat. Keir stood to pull my chair out further with his left hand while holding his napkin with his right.

"Thank you for joining us," he said gently.

"Thank you for inviting me." I smiled and then quickly headed across the hall to inspect the table lectern microphone setting, the continental breakfast and coffee stand, and count the number of chairs set in the meeting room. Assured that the room was properly set, I dashed out to check on Evonda and grabbed the box containing copies of speaker handouts, before re-entering the meeting room where delegates were beginning to claim their seats.

"Just like in church," I thought. "The back rows fill first." Already a dozen men had seated themselves in the last row with coffee cups, pastries, and the morning's paper. Several others were scattered around or standing in line at the breakfast buffet.

Heading back outside into the hallway in the direction of the ladies room, I encountered Director Carson exiting the men's room.

"Director Carson, I thought you should know that I was appointed the new executive director of NIRS last month."

"Congratulations!" he offered in return. "They are a good group of folks."

43

"Thank you." Pointing toward the meeting room, I continued, "I believe Liam and Keir want you to sit at the head table with them and with Emmanuel Stevens, another speaker." Carson nodded and headed toward the meeting room while I ducked into the ladies room to freshen up, hoping to be back out before Liam convened the session at 9:00. Upon my return, I slid sideways into my seat at the rear of the room just as Liam stood behind the centered table lectern to greet the assembly. After joking about Keir's choice of casual clothing, Liam turned the microphone over to his colleague for speaker introductions.

"Tonight's banquet menu is a Hawaiian luau," Keir explained good-naturedly. "I just thought I would dress the part!" He continued only slightly more seriously. "After last year's nearly disastrous premium crisis when Liam single-handedly almost brought health insurance sales to a halt, I was very surprised that Insurance Director Carson agreed to even lay eyes on us again, but he graciously accepted our invitation to address our industry today. Please welcome the Director." The delegates greeted the Director with polite applause.

The Insurance Director was not the only one to do an about-face, I thought as I watched Keir's unselfconscious welcome. Was this the same man who had been in tears in my presence only a month earlier? During the previous several weeks of phone calls exchanged between us regarding convention planning, I had been sufficiently sensitive to his privacy not to bring up his mother's condition in conversation.

Keir puzzled me. He was definitely masculine with a square face, lantern-shaped jaw, and dark eyebrows. But there was a softness to him— his luxurious, dark hair so tempting to run one's fingers through; his long, dark eyelashes shading almond-shaped eyes that crinkled at the corners; and two slightly lopsided dimples surrounding the all-too-perfect teeth when he smiled. He could pal around and be one of the guys, but he also set himself apart by his quicksilver intellect. His humor and compassion made him inclusive but the cut of his clothing and gracious bearing signaled someone who had been surrounded by affluence and good breeding for so long, it was simply part of the fabric of his being. He was quick to compliment others but unwilling to allow the spotlight to shine on his own achievements for very long.

Director Carson finished his remarks, which were met again with polite applause. Keir rose to make an announcement and introduce the next speaker.

"During the morning break, the golf and tennis tournament chairmen would like to meet with the respective participants to arrange car-pooling, pairings, and other logistics. Tennis in the left corner," Keir pointed to the back corner farthest from the door, "and golf in the right front, over here." He pointed over his shoulder.

Emmanuel Stevens' speech on corporate law issues impacting health insurance was too technical for my limited legal knowledge, so I took the opportunity to check the quantities of coffee in the urns and to slip outside to see how Evonda was faring at the registration desk. She was writing personal correspondence since there was no other work for her to do. There were only a few badges left to pick up: two attorney speakers (one from Cleveland and the other from Columbus) plus the regional counsel for Cleveland Medical's parent company located in St. Louis. The latter was flying in today and was expected later in the afternoon. All three were speakers scheduled for the next day. I gave Evonda permission to break down the registration desk.

Remembering that Kenneth Taft, Keir's top boss and CEO of Cleveland Medical, was speaking after the break, followed by Mr. Morgenstern, I hurried back into the session to provide moral support, if nothing else. How was it possible for Keir to appear so nonchalant? In his place, I would have been a nervous wreck. I imagined that the moot court sessions in law school must provide good training in staying calm under pressure, but all I had to do was observe Liam's anxious behavior, and my theory was immediately disproved.

The presentations during the second half of the morning were not that much more intelligible to me than the first half, but I tried my best to take notes and pay attention. I admit I was relieved when it was over, and the golf and tennis players left for their tournaments.

I headed upstairs to change my clothes and eat lunch with Auguste. We planned to spend the afternoon sunning at the lakefront pool. He was in a little better mood than when I had left him. Since my travel expenses were reimbursable from OAHIA, he instructed me to buy myself a lunch that we would both split to save on his expenses. I changed into a one-piece bathing suit, covered by a tee-shirt and shorts, and donned a pair of sandals. I stuffed a beach bag with towels, sunscreen, and a novel.

Auguste and I found a secluded area on the pool deck to relax and eat the lunch I bought at a poolside cafe. I was torn between insisting he attend tonight's luau as my spouse and to save on food costs, and discouraging his attendance in case his domineering attitude toward me would embarrass me in front of my association clients. Besides, Auguste did not enjoy socializing as much as I did.

"You don't have to join us tonight for dinner," I offered tentatively. "Most of the talk will be about health insurance law. I could barely follow the speeches myself this morning." Not getting much reaction, I continued. "Do you want to order something from the restaurant? There's a microwave in the suite. Or maybe we could find a Chinese restaurant in town and you could get some take-out?"

Auguste stared out at the lake, squinting. I tried to judge his reaction from the set of his jaw and the narrowing of his eyes.

"That's alright. I'll get something from the hotel restaurant. Perhaps they have some fish and French fries I can eat." I could hear the veiled accusation of "you are not taking care of me" in his voice.

I looked down at the pattern in the lounge chair between my feet and began to rub the soles against the plastic weaving for a minute or two.

Then I pulled my knees up to my chest and rested my chin on them, turning my face away from Auguste and back toward the hotel. "Keir and Abigail had not signed up for golf or tennis; perhaps they might come out to the pool, too," I thought to myself. "I would like to see Keir in a bathing suit, but I would not want him to see me in mine." I pulled my legs up even closer to my body and closed my eyes. If Keir and Abigail came to the pool that afternoon, I never saw them.

Evonda and I met downstairs about thirty minutes before the banquet was scheduled to check the food stations and put up a sign at the door. We sat down together on a bench in the foyer facing the entrance to the hotel restaurant and bar. A ruckus erupted in the bar as competitors Mike Johnson (Eric Mitchell's boss), who was the state director of Buckeye Health, and Gordon Frazier, the state director of SummitCare, began arguing loudly in the doorway. Mike pushed the taller Gordon in the chest. Evonda and I froze, not knowing what to do or whether to intervene, as we watched Gordon clench his fists and a furious glare rise in his eyes. But he hesitated, thought better of it, and walked out of the bar and down the hallway.

"I've known Gordon Frazier for *years*," Evonda exclaimed to me. "He and his wife, Susan, were friends with my ex-husband and me. Gordon has always been an extremely courteous gentleman." I nodded in assent from my own experience of Gordon. "Mike must have really provoked him." Relieved that the crisis had passed, at least temporarily, we stood to greet Liam and Fran McFarland as they came down the hallway.

About half the delegates appeared wearing Hawaiian shirts or colorful dresses at the luau buffet banquet. I wore a black dress with simple leaves outlined in white with a few mauve flowers. I had an imitation mauve orchid pinned to my left shoulder and a string of white beads. Some others, like Patch Damien and Gordon Frazier, wore loud plaid shirts or sports jackets. Coincidentally, Keir and Mike Johnson both sported the same Hawaiian shirt, so they posed for a photo together. Keir's broad smile showed he was obviously enjoying himself. He was likely relieved that his most prominent speakers, Director Carson, Kenneth Taft—the head of his own company—and Phillip Morganstern, had already presented their talks. The mood around the room was light and fun, so Evonda and I silently agreed not to mention the earlier altercation, especially since Mike and Gordon seemed to be staying away from each other. A positive and enthusiastic hum engulfed the room as people conversed over cocktails and during dinner about the golf and tennis matches or other activities they had enjoyed that afternoon.

As the banquet attendees began to return to their rooms or adjourned to the hotel lounge for a night cap after dinner, Evonda and I went to the lobby to take the elevator. Spotting Abigail Anderson, Evonda went over to apologize to her for the name badge mix up, while I spoke with Keir.

"Everyone seemed to enjoy the luau."

"Yes, it was a great time! Thank you for suggesting that menu and all your help with the convention planning."

I noticed Keir's eyes were a light, sea green color, similar to the pale green just before the height of an ocean wave rolls over into thunderous foam. As we continued our casual conversation about the convention, I experienced a magnetic sensation, like an ocean undertow, of being pulled into Keir's eyes. "This shouldn't be happening...!" my panicking mind warned me. "Where's Abigail?" I tore my eyes from the depths of Keir's to look over my left shoulder where Abigail was standing about ten feet behind us, her back towards us and still speaking with Evonda.

Moderately reassured that Abigail was not aware of what I thought had just transpired between me and her husband, I turned back to Keir. The same "eye drowning" experience occurred again. I did not know whether Keir was having the same sensation, but the voice in my head immediately cautioned me, "Where's Auguste? Oh, he is safely upstairs in our suite." Before I could relax, my conscience warned me further, "Any moment now, Abigail's wifely radar is going to sound an alarm, 'Beep, beep, beep— husband in danger!'" I further rationalized, "Okay, the convention is going well. Keir is grateful to me for my role in making it a success. We've both had some drinks. We are probably both a little drunk. That's all this is." Out loud, I excused myself to Keir.

"I've got to get up early tomorrow morning to check on the private practicing attorney section breakfast, so I am going to call it a night." Evonda and I entered the elevator to return to our respective rooms. I had the feeling of having just averted grave danger.

The next morning, a record twenty-two attorneys attended the private practicing attorney breakfast in the Lakefront Room and elected a new representative to the OAHIA Executive Committee, replacing Warren Sullivan who had been very helpful to me in teaching me the fundamentals of health insurance law and with some private legal matters. Following the breakfast, the educational sessions recommenced with Patch Damien providing an update from the Health Law Section first, followed by a Cleveland area attorney and by the regional counsel for Cleveland Medical.

During the annual business meeting, Harry Whitfield was able to report a $10,000 net surplus for 1986, offsetting the $5,000 loss for 1985, leaving OAHIA with a $5,000 cash reserve, a remarkable turnaround for the Association. The OAHIA members elected Keir as their next president, Harry as vice president, Henry Spaulding as treasurer, and Herbert Howell as the secretary. Harry announced the following year's convention would be held at Deerwood Lake Lodge. Keir presented Liam with a plaque of appreciation for his presidential term and adjourned the meeting.

During my biweekly phone calls with Keir as OAHIA's president, we discussed association business. However, seduced by Keir's easy-going manner, we sometimes found ourselves sharing snippets of our personal lives. On a call shortly after the convention, I casually asked him, "Where did you meet your wife?"

"She's the daughter of long-time friends of the family." Somehow, in the matter-of-fact way Keir related that piece of information, it struck me

47

like he had just described an arranged marriage. But why would someone as bright, good-looking, and charismatic as Keir need an "arranged" marriage?

"I met Auguste when we both worked at a European banking house in New York City after I returned from my junior year in Paris." Turning to association business, we discussed the logistics of the upcoming strategic planning session to be held at AEMG's office.

Since OAHIA's strategic planning session from July was postponed until September 23rd to include all the Executive Committee members, we had some extra weeks available to us. Liam and I created a membership survey. Respondents complained that one of the key issues plaguing the industry was the way hospitals were being "forced to direct their reimbursement business to certain health insurers to the exclusion of others."

On September first, as I was collating the surveys in preparation for the strategic planning meeting later in the month, news broke that two OAHIA members, Attorneys Assurance Health Plan and Athenaeum Health Plan, had sued another member, Paramount Blue—the state's only domestic and its largest, health insurance company—in state court over the issue of "directed business". This lawsuit would be the subtext of the Association's business agenda over the next couple of years, occasionally surfacing obliquely during an Executive Committee meeting but, because of restrictions regarding discussing ongoing legal actions, unable to be discussed openly. Having only recently survived the previous health insurance crisis with the Department of Insurance, the industry was now facing another disruption. Keir would need all of his deft tact and leadership skills to steer the Association through this split.

I had asked AEMG's CEO, David Fisher, to facilitate the strategic planning session so that I could participate. Under David's guidance, the Executive Committee members examined OAHIA's strengths (an active, interested, talented membership with respect for one another), weaknesses (public misunderstanding, weak lobbying, directed business, and outside pressures), and potential programs that could improve the Association's less effective aspects by utilizing its more productive ones. Together the members drafted and adopted a mission statement and five main goals. OAHIA's primary focus would shift to governmental advocacy by establishing a Legislative Committee, developing a reserve fund for hiring a lobbyist, and maintaining regular communication with the state insurance department. To respond more rapidly to crises, I would create a communication phone tree among key members and use the new technologies of conference calls and facsimile machines. The Executive Committee would establish committees to develop generic, industry-wide, health insurance forms and to create educational programs for constituent groups. The president would appoint a member of the Executive Committee to serve as newsletter editor and solicit industry-specific articles, including case studies. These committees would involve other OAHIA members beyond the current officers to distribute the workload and provide a vehicle to identify future leaders. We postponed identifying specific timelines and responsibilities for achieving the goals until the next Executive Committee meeting on November 12.

As a result of Keir's close relationship with Director Carson, Keir was asked by the deputy insurance director to pull together a committee of OAHIA volunteers to develop a new state health insurance agent's licensing examination for the Insurance Department to administer. Keir consulted with Gordon Frasier, his newly appointed General Counsel on the Executive Committee. After making a few phone calls to their colleagues, Gordon and Keir were able to find seven other OAHIA members willing to come to Columbus at their own expense for two days in mid-October to help draft the new examination questions.

Meanwhile, with the surplus funds in the OAHIA treasury, the Executive Committee voted to fund its president's travel to the national convention. In early October, Keir and Abigail flew to Seattle for the AAHIA convention.

In place of our biweekly call, Keir suggested that he and I meet for lunch before going to the Department of Insurance offices on Thursday, October 15th. A few minutes past noon, Keir picked me up at the AEMG offices on the 10th floor of the Grandview Building and for our lunch, we selected a new sandwich shop on the first floor. After ordering our respective sandwiches, we found a linoleum-topped, high table with two stools. As gracefully as possible, I hoisted myself onto the elevated seat, wondering why I had selected to order a messy, chicken salad croissant that would assuredly drip in an embarrassing manner. I tried to refrain from being self-conscious while eating and made small talk with Keir about the weather, association business, and the involvement of OAHIA in the exam-writing process.

Although our conversations could be light-hearted and Keir sometimes teased me, he also wanted me to understand the politics and dynamics of the health insurance industry.

"Insurance Director Carson made it clear to us at the convention that his Department will be assuming more regulatory authority over our industry. The Department is planning to review several aspects of our business in the coming months. Participating in the exam-writing process is a way to strengthen our mutual lines of communication. I am hoping to develop regular avenues of liaison with the various divisions of the Department."

Once we finished eating and disposed of our refuse, Keir held the glass door for me to walk out onto the sidewalk. The day was one of those pristine Indian summer days when the sky is a pure, rich, cloudless, cerulean blue and everything seems to appear crisper and brighter. The autumn leaves hung red, gold, orange, and yellow, and the day's gentle warmth made you feel glad to be alive.

"The day is so beautiful, let's walk to the Department of Insurance," Keir suggested. "It will be difficult to find a parking spot close to the building anyway."

We turned west along Goodale Boulevard and headed toward the Scioto River and Riverside Drive. Walking next to Keir, our steps easily fell into rhythm together, although I had to force myself to walk a little faster than normal in my black high heels in order to keep up with him. I noticed he took the gentleman's outside position on the sidewalk; even when we turned a corner he shifted sides behind me. "Something Auguste never did," I noted silently. As we neared the State Office complex on Stella Court, I acknowledged to myself how much I simply enjoyed being in Keir's company. I wished we could have continued walking along together, but we had reached the Dexter Insurance Building, and Keir opened the door for me again. (I was beginning to like these chivalrous gestures.)

The hallway seemed dark and narrow after the splendid sun outside. Keir, familiar with the building, headed straight for the elevators where he waited while I entered, then followed me inside and pressed number 4. The doors closed, and the car shuddered slightly before ascending. I reminded myself that, "Keir is a very nice gentleman, and I should not allow myself to be too easily spoiled by his polite ways."

Getting out on the fourth floor, Keir indicated a conference room to the right. We entered. Insurance Department staff members introduced themselves to the OAHIA contingent, several other members having already arrived ahead of us. Once seated, the deputy director explained the protocol for the question-writing, the confidentiality, and the resources available— text books, volumes of state statutes, and copies of the previous exam. I was to be one of the question recorders.

The OAHIA volunteers spent the first hour developing an outline of subject areas and assigning each to groups of two. During the next three hours, each of the small groups poured over the old exam questions for their section and developed tentative, new questions. Sometimes the statute volumes or another small group were consulted. We finished our work just around five o'clock.

Since most of the OAHIA volunteers resided in Columbus, and Keir was the only one from out of town, Gordon Frasier offered to accompany Keir to a nearby bar for a few beers and dinner before he retired to his hotel room. Knowing they would likely talk shop, I politely declined to join them and walked back to my parked car at the municipal lot two blocks from my office. The walk gave me the opportunity to slough off my lingering impressions of Keir before heading back home to dinner and the evening with Auguste.

The exam-writing team reconvened the following day and finished its work around 3:00 p.m. The deputy director and Keir thanked everyone and shook hands. Since all the OAHIA volunteers had been given parking passes to the Dexter Building garage, we all descended together in the elevator and parted company.

In addition to everything else going on in the health insurance industry, Keir had moved his offices down to suite 1730 in the Cleveland Plaza Building which is where he hosted the November 12th OAHIA Executive Committee meeting. So that we could review the strategic plan ideas, I had brought along AEMG's collapsible easel and OAHIA's newsprint pad with notes from the September 23rd meeting. The day was sunny and relatively warm for November—weather that belied the dreary winter days to come. I parked my car in the deck that was connected to the Cleveland Plaza Building by a second-story walkway and, so as not to need a second trip to my car, I did my best to carry the awkwardly large easel and pad together with my briefcase and pocketbook.

The reception area for Keir's new office suite was carpeted with an oriental rug. The light green wallpaper reflected one of the hues in the carpet, while the waiting room sofa and arm chairs picked up its burgundy and light blue. I approached the mahogany receptionist desk, and the fashionably dressed young woman with frosted hair seated behind it looked up quizzically. A small, oblong, bronze plaque standing on the desk in front of her read, "Katherine Shipley."

"I am here for the Health Insurance Attorneys Association Executive Committee meeting," I announced.

"Just a moment please," Katherine replied as she picked up the telephone receiver and dialed. "A woman is here for the Health Insurance Attorneys' meeting," she announced into the receiver then appeared to listen for a moment before hanging up. "Keir will be right out," she told me. I walked over to a grouping of chairs around a coffee table.

As promised, a minute or two later, Keir came down the hall dressed in a navy blazer, white button-down shirt, burgundy tie, and grey slacks. He flashed a welcoming smile, and held out his hand in greeting which I shook. "How are you? Did you have a good drive up?" I nodded my head affirmatively. "The conference room is back here," he indicated with a hand gesture the hallway from which he had come, then stepped back so that I could pass him. As I headed down the hall, I could hear men's voices coming from a room about fifty feet further down the hallway. When I entered, Liam and Harry stopped speaking to greet me just as the intercom announced to Keir that more of the officers had arrived. "Thanks, Kathy," he replied to the intercom, and excused himself to head back out to the reception area, returning a few minutes later with Gordon Frazier, Herbert Howell, and Henry Spaulding.

"Private Practice Section Representative Douglas Roberts was unable to come," I announced, "so I think everyone else is here." I set up the easel in a corner of the conference room and screwed the newsprint pad onto its top rail as the officers took their seats around the conference table. When I had seated myself ready with my legal pad and pen to take minutes, Keir called the meeting to order.

Due to a recent change in company affiliation by General Counsel Gordon Frazier, the Executive Committee now had three OAHIA Executive

Committee members—Gordon, Harry, and Herb—all working for the same company, Attorneys Assurance Health Plan.

"I can resign as General Counsel," Gordon offered. However, the consensus of the officers was to decline his resignation and to table any further action to redistribute officer designations evenly among company members until the following year's Nominating Committee report. The minutes of the previous Executive Committee meeting were approved as distributed, so we now turned our attention to Henry's Treasurer's Report.

After proposing to reimburse the Health Law Section Representative—Douglas—for mileage expenses and declining to purchase directors and officers liability insurance in the wake of some recently enacted legislation that afforded greater protection to nonprofit organizations and volunteers, Keir changed the order of the agenda to have the Executive Committee take action on some items that had surfaced during the strategic planning session, most notably, establishing a Legislative Committee that would serve as an *ad hoc* committee until the next annual meeting when a bylaws amendment would be proposed to make it a Standing Committee. Next the officers approved, with a few minor changes, the telephone hotline I had developed. The establishment of three more committees—Forms, Education, and Editorial—was tabled until the next meeting so we could recess for a thirty-minute lunch break in the building's atrium food court.

Upon reconvening, Harry requested and was given several speaker and topic ideas for the 1988 convention at Deerwood Lake Lodge. The officers considered various locations for the 1989 and 1990 conventions, including Sandusky, Marietta, and Cincinnati.

I presented three new attorney members who were accepted for membership and proposed moving the directory publication date from post-convention (autumn) back to springtime after the dues renewal cycle was complete to have more accurate information. In turn, other officers gave their reports. Subsequently, Keir described the two-day exam development process with the Ohio Department of Insurance.

"Director Carson would also like OAHIA to sponsor the publication of an educational brochure aimed at consumers that explains health insurance and distribute it through our company agents." The officers were aware that Carson was up for re-election soon and that this was an attempt to gain positive leverage with voters. The Executive Committee members encouraged Keir and Gordon to continue discussions with the Insurance Department regarding directed business and the creation of a rating bureau. Keir adjourned the meeting at 3:00 p.m., and the officers quickly left to head back to their respective offices or cars.

"May I help you carry some things to your car," Keir offered as he folded up the easel. In my experience, none of my association board members had ever offered to assist me with packing up. Keir was again displaying his chivalrous tendencies. I remembered my struggle earlier in the day.

"Why, yes! With the easel and newsprint pad, I have more than I normally carry."

Keir took the easel, which was now packed in its carrying case, by the handle and the newsprint pad by the opening in the top, while I picked up my briefcase and purse. As we passed through the office reception area, he turned and said, "Kathy, I'm helping Annie take these items to her car." I reached the suite door first, so I opened it, allowing us both to pass into the building hallway.

"I think the meeting went rather well, don't you?' Keir said as we waited for the elevator. I was not sure whether he was just making conversation or whether he was really seeking my opinion of his first meeting as OAHIA president. I opted to bolster his esteem.

"The other Executive Committee members supported your ideas about creating new committees and developing a brochure for the Insurance Department." Keir appeared to relax a little bit. The elevator doors opened, and we entered. He continued as we descended.

"It is in OAHIA's best interests to maintain close ties with the Insurance Department and to rebuild our legislative advocacy efforts—even to the point of funding a war chest, if possible."

We made our way across the elevated walkway into the parking deck. "My car is on the far side," I pointed toward the cement wall opposite that rose half way and was open above to the outside where the afternoon sun was beginning to wane.

"We appreciate what you did to get the Association back on financial track," Keir continued with his train of thought.

"You were the one who championed the special assessment and restructuring of the dues." I did not think that much credit should be accorded me when all I did was follow the instructions the officers had given me.

Arriving at my car, I opened the trunk of my light blue, 1986 Nissan Sentra. Keir placed the easel and pad inside. My expectation was that he would now return to his office, having completed his gentlemanly duty. Instead he stayed to talk with me for about twenty more minutes.

I was not conscious of the words we spoke but to a sensation similar to being in high school and having the cutest guy in school walk you home and carry your books—or at least I imagined how that would feel since it had never actually happened to me. "It's just flirtatious banter," I told myself, "nothing of any consequence." Finally, aware that time was fleeting with a two-and-a-half hour drive still ahead of me, and hopeful of arriving home before it got dark, we said our goodbyes.

As I drove home, I went over in my mind the other moments when Keir and I had been...well, what? *When something uncommon had occurred.* I remembered the meeting we had at Harry's office when Keir already had the solution to the financial crisis. I remembered when he trusted me enough to cry over his mother's cancer diagnosis in my presence. I remembered "drowning" in his eyes at the Sandpiper Suites, walking to the

Department of Insurance after lunch, and now, the conversation in the garage. "Keir is just being nice to me," my mind justified. "Besides, he's married to a bright, attractive woman, who is nicely shaped, so what could he possibly see in *me*?" I shook off the incident as best as I could. "Maybe my intelligence, similar height and hair color, and *naiveté* remind him of his wife." Like the afterglow of a heady wine, the lingering impression of Keir's agreeable personality stayed with me all the way home.

A couple of weeks later, near the end of November, I noticed Keir had not yet sent me his "President's Message" for the fall newsletter. Granted, a lot of activity had transpired since his election, but I had the responsibility to publish the newsletter on schedule. I was already accustomed to delays after Chuck Lincoln's and Liam McFarland's terms. Since it was time for our biweekly conversation, I called Keir to remind him about his newsletter column as well as to review Association business since the Executive Committee meeting. He was not at his desk, so I left a message.

I was in the AEMG workroom making copies when Keir returned my call. The workroom contained the large copier, the postage machine, supply shelves, and the desk of the young man who handled our copy and supply orders. Seating myself on the outside corner of the desk, I took the call on a wall-mounted phone with a 25-foot cord, and explained to Keir why I had called.

"I have upgraded nagging for the 'President's Message' to a fine art," I teased, swinging my crossed left leg. "In fact, Liam had to write an ex-President's column for the summer newsletter because his last article was so late it came in after your election." Keir chuckled and promised to get the article to me the next week.

I do not know whether it was Keir's disarming manner and sense of humor, my assumption that we were close in age, or the few moments of intimate familiarity we had occasionally shared, but our calls did not have the usual professional distance that I had had with his predecessors or even had with other association clients' officers. That is not to say that I have not developed close, personal relationships with other association presidents, but I could not put my finger on why this relationship felt different. I chalked it up to being the one who convinced the OAHIA Executive Committee to take the actions necessary to stop the financial bleeding about which Keir had warned during his year as treasurer before I came on board, as well as convincing Keir to switch resorts from the rundown Bayshore Inn to the Sandpiper Suites, essentially saving his convention. I settled on the explanation that he was grateful to me.

When I received Keir's "President's Message," it was worth waiting for. He wrote of his trip to Seattle with Abigail for the national convention, the agent's exam preparation with the Department of Insurance, the strategic planning retreat, and the 100 percent dues renewal rate. He also thanked Liam for his service as the immediate past president.

Auguste had been working for about a year in Huntington Bank's mortgage services department in Columbus. With both of us middle-aged and my biological clock ticking, we made a couple of attempts to get pregnant. While visiting my parents over the Christmas holiday, I lost an embryo one morning before I had even been aware that I was pregnant.

"I didn't think you and Auguste wanted children," my mother replied when I told her that morning, feeling a little stunned and saddened about this spontaneous abortion.

"I never wanted to be barefoot and pregnant, living in a trailer. Now that Auguste has a full-time job, I can afford to take some maternity leave. We have already started house-hunting."

Our one-year lease in the Cleveland Avenue condominium was due to expire at the end of February 1988, so we visited a few realtors to determine if we had the ability to buy a house for ourselves. During the previous summer, we had worked with a realtor who had made a mistake on our bid for a house in Gahanna, a southern suburb of Columbus. We were not exactly thrilled with the area, so when our deal imploded, we stopped looking and moved into the condominium where we were now residing. When we began to look again, I decided to use three realtors in order to hedge our bets. I did not want to have a child in a townhouse that I did not own and that lacked a fenced yard.

Every Saturday after the first of the year, I would go out with one of the realtors and look at anywhere from four to fourteen properties for sale, continuously comparing the one I was looking at with the one I liked best. If I found a house that had potential, I would have Auguste go with me to look at it again. One realtor showed us several substandard homes for sale, but the other two realtors had a better sense of what we were seeking.

"How are these homes appealing to you?" the third realtor asked me late one Saturday afternoon in January.

"On a scale of one to ten," I said, "you are showing us sevens and eights."

"What would it take for you to buy one?"

"If you showed us a nine."

Around nine o'clock the next morning, the realtor called us.

"I've found you a nine! When can I show it to you?" We agreed to meet her at her office at 11 o'clock.

The one-and-a- half story Williamsburg house, located in a quiet cul-de-sac only two miles from our current residence, was similar to my childhood home. Sitting on a hill amidst a tree-shaded yard, the house had a sizeable living room with fireplace, master bedroom downstairs, a bathroom and walk-in closet, an open kitchen-dining area, a covered front porch, a rear deck, two smaller bedrooms with bath upstairs, and two walk-in attics. Only four years old, the home was in excellent condition. It was, indeed, our "nine." By that evening, fighting the angst normal to first-time home buyers, Auguste and I put in a bid on the house. We called my parents in New Jersey with the exciting news.

"We hope you don't need to borrow any money from us, because your younger brother just bought a house, too, and we lent him $5,000 for the down payment!" my father told me. I reassured him that Auguste and I were not planning to ask for a loan. Once our bid was accepted and the various home loan application papers were signed, our closing was scheduled for the end of March with a move-in date of April 6th and 7th.

For OAHIA's February 10th Executive Committee meeting, we returned to Athenaeum Health Plan's headquarters building in Mansfield. Liam's new boss, Chuck Parker, attended the meeting as a guest. As OAHIA President, Keir presided at the meeting. The Association had had its first financial audit since its 1985 financial crisis, and Treasurer Henry Spaulding was able to report a surplus just under $4,000. As vice president and 1988 conference chair, Harry Whitfield received quite a few speaker suggestions for the upcoming convention at Deerwood Lake Lodge. Henry presented 1989 convention proposals from Sandcastle Resort, Island Point Resort, and Lakeside Inn. The latter's room rate was too high, so the officers instructed Evonda and me to conduct a site visit to the first two before a final decision would be made.

The four committees that had been recommended during the strategic planning process were established: Legislative, Forms, Editorial, and Education along with respective committee chairs and member appointments. Keir also appointed two *ad hoc* task forces to address some pressing issues that needed representation from various member companies. Keir chose himself as Legislative Committee Chair, and Chuck Parker proposed a piece of legislation for the Committee to consider as its first order of business. Liam would head the Forms Committee, Harry would chair the Education Committee, and I was appointed as the acting chair of the Editorial Committee, along with two members who were to help me identify pertinent newsletter content. The Executive Committee voted to recommend past General Counsel and Athenaeum Health Plan founder, Fred Peterson, as an Honorary Member. Peterson was a kindly and affable man of the old school who, after retiring as Athenaeum CEO, had entered private legal practice.

The Executive Committee spent some time discussing a visit by Keir and Gordon with Insurance Director Carson, the Deputy Director, and the department's legal counsel regarding continued incidences of directed business and rumors of filed rate violations, although the Department's audits of health insurers had found no such violations. The on-going state lawsuit among the three health insurers in the state also muddied the issues since the Attorney General's office could not provide any guidance as to whether certain acts were illegal or not. Unable to move forward with these concerns, the Executive Committee members approved a sponsorship for the Health Law Section annual convention and changed its next meeting location and date from Columbus on May 12th to the Sandpiper Suites on May 6th. Keir agreed to raise the issue of OAHIA obtaining blanket approval from the Insurance Department for nationally-promulgated policy forms rather than having each health insurance company file essentially the same forms with the Department, thereby eliminating duplication of effort and cost.

On February 23rd, since the state action had not made any progress, Athenaeum and Attorneys Assurance filed a federal lawsuit against Paramount Blue, alleging violation of laws concerning directed business. OAHIA members quietly took sides, and any official discussion of the cases was silenced. In mid-July, Paramount Blue Health Plan counter-sued Athenaeum and Attorneys Assurance in federal court, making the issue even more complicated.

A few weeks later, Evonda and I drove up to Sandusky for our site visits to Sandcastle Resort and Island Point Resort. Although both were nice resorts, we agreed that the older Sandcastle Resort was too large and impersonal while the newly-built Island Point Resort with condominium housing and smaller, lakefront, meeting rooms would be more appealing to the OAHIA crowd.

Auguste and I moved into our new house in early April as planned. The neighbors warned me not to drink the water, because almost every young couple who had moved into the neighborhood became pregnant a short time later. Together, we silently thought, "That *is* our plan."

A rainy, gray Friday greeted the OAHIA Executive Committee meeting in the Lakeview Room of the Sandpiper Suites on May 6th. Henry Spaulding thanked the Executive Committee members for traveling to Maumee Bay on such a dreary day to accommodate his schedule. Evonda had prepared a thorough report from our March site visits to the two Sandusky resorts. Upon staff recommendation, the officers selected Island Point as their choice for the 1989 convention.

Liam had convened the Forms Committee that was redrafting some key health directives forms to be used by health law attorneys with their clients. Harry's Education Committee had crafted the wording for the Insurance Director's brochure and proposed developing a speaker's bureau and a series of educational seminars for paralegals and legal secretaries to be presented around the state by OAHIA members. Harry had also made substantial progress with his 1988 convention program at Deerwood Lake Lodge and proposed a Saturday afternoon river tubing trip on the Deer River south of the dam that created Deer Lake. He would also arrange for a hiking trip on Friday afternoon for those convention delegates who did not wish to play golf or tennis.

Keir reported that the main malpractice liability insurance carrier for the health law attorneys had met with a group of OAHIA members to ascertain the extent of expected future claims. Although the meeting did not provide the information the malpractice carrier had hoped, OAHIA sent the message that the Association members shared this concern and that they were open to an on-going dialogue. Before adjourning the meeting, Keir also appointed OAHIA members to write articles on a rotating basis for the Health Law Section newsletter.

The previous year, when I went to the trophy shop to order a presidential plaque of appreciation for Liam, I noticed a sample plaque hanging on the wall with a beautiful, light blue, metal plate and a silver gavel. I had not been pleased with the black and gold brass plaque given to Chuck Lincoln, so I asked the trophy shop to make Liam's using the light blue and silver. Returning to the trophy shop in late July 1988 to order Keir's presidential plaque, I intended to order a silver and light green plaque to match his eye color, but was very disappointed to learn that the silver gavels had been discontinued. The light green and brass did not have the same color effect, and I was highly dissatisfied with the look of the final product but with only days to spare until the convention, I had no alternative.

Having settled into our new house, Auguste and I made another attempt at parenthood. As he was 43 and I was 37, we suspected it might take six months or more for me to get pregnant, assuming there were no fertility problems. In addition, I was not home much. My AEMG clients' convention schedule had me traveling some place almost every month: Georgia's Calloway Gardens in mid-May; Copley Place in Boston in mid-June; and Burlington, Vermont, in mid-July.

One day, Auguste and I argued about how much traveling I was doing for work.

"I thought by this time in my life I would have a house and kids!" he shouted at me.

"We're living in the first and working on the second!" I shouted back. We definitely did not know on August 11th that I was already pregnant when Auguste and I left for the OAHIA convention at Deerwood Lake Lodge.

A scenic, hilltop resort with a rustic stone lodge as its centerpiece, Deerwood's central lodge was surrounded by villas and townhouses. The main lobby was constructed of massive pillars, made from the local rocks holding up wooden beams, and a slate floor. The floor plan of the lobby consisted of a central, open staircase rising in three sections, dividing the lobby into the front registration area and rear entrance leading to the restaurants and conference center plus two wings of specialty boutiques and condominium sales office. On the opening day of the convention, Evonda sat at the OAHIA registration desk, situated in the front lobby across from the hotel registration desk so that the OAHIA delegates would be able to obtain their registration materials upon check-in.

Due to the rustic nature of the lodge, there was no elevator. However, the Lodge rooms on the second floor were one-bedroom loft suites, each with a small parlor, kitchenette, and dining area downstairs with an open staircase leading to the balconied loft bedroom and bath upstairs. Auguste and I had a blue-themed loft suite to the left of the main lobby staircase. On the opposite side of the stairwell was Keir's and Abigail's red-themed suite where the OAHIA Executive Committee was scheduled to meet.

Abigail left the suite as the officers arrived for the meeting. Keir had set out beer, soft drinks, and salted snacks for this more informal meeting. The issue of having too many officers from the same member company had been resolved when Herbert Howell had switched companies to take over Gordon Frazier's former job at SummitCare, so the Nominations Committee simply nominated a new secretary, Jonathan Patrick of Buckeye Health Care. The Executive Committee reviewed the convention plans and provided updates on several industry issues.

At the close of the meeting, the Executive Committee went into executive session to discuss a proposed three-year management contract with AEMG that contained a graduated fee increase: $10,000 for 1989, $10,500 for 1990, and $11,000 for 1991. Although the officers agreed that a fee increase was warranted, they voted to counter-propose $9,000 for 1989, $10,000 for 1990, and $11,000 for 1991, under the condition that I would remain the executive director of OAHIA as long as I continued to work at AEMG. Harry Whitfield, as the incoming president, was given the authority to negotiate and sign the three-year contract and to type in the addition of the special services clause about me. When the contract was signed, David Fisher made it a perpetual contract, requiring that only the fee be negotiated annually, requiring that the Association's Executive Committee meetings be held at AEMG headquarters (to save on staff travel costs), and agreeing to a management fee of $9,500 for 1989, $10,500 for 1990, and $11,000 for 1991.

While the officers were effectively deciding my future in perpetuity as the OAHIA Executive Director, I went outside to check on the preparations for the Welcome Reception to follow that evening. Deerwood Deck— a brick patio and site of the cocktail reception—was located behind the lodge, affording a sweeping view of the Appalachian foothills and Atkins Lake. The resort staff had placed tables, sheathed in white tablecloths, at strategic locations around the patio with the *hors d'oeuvres* displayed buffet-style, and the bartender was ready to serve drinks.

As the OAHIA members arrived and obtained their beverages, they gathered in clusters and conversed; they wore a mix of sports jackets, golf shirts, plaid shirts, dresses, skirts and tops, and suits. Sporting a summer tan, Keir wore a Hawaiian-style shirt and khakis while Abigail dressed in a chiffon, watercolor print, ensemble. Liam photographed them standing together in a close-up, Keir holding a napkin-wrapped beer bottle in his right hand with his left hand casually thrust into his pants pocket and smiling enigmatically, while Abigail leaned backward in an intimate and familiar fashion toward her husband's left shoulder.

Knowing how easily alcohol affected my system, I chose to wait until the reception was half over before ordering a whiskey sour. Auguste joined us for the reception in order to have something to eat and drink, but he soon grew bored and left to return to our suite. When the reception ended, everyone broke into company groups to eat in the resort dining room. In order to save money, Auguste had prepared sandwiches for us in our suite. He was watching television when I got back to the room. As I drifted off to sleep that night, I remembered Keir and Abigail were in their almost identical suite on the opposite side of the stairwell.

Keir wore another Hawaiian print shirt for the opening educational session on Friday morning. After welcoming everyone, he turned the program over to Harry Whitfield to emcee. After the morning's session, a group of 14 conventioneers went to play in the tennis tournament and a group of 16 golfers headed for the mountain-view course for that tournament. Harry had organized a hike through the foothills behind the lodge. Auguste decided to join us, but Evonda chose to read by the pool.

Classified as a moderate hike, the trail termed "The Plummet" was, in fact, an hour-and-a-half trek down into the Deer River gorge along a rock-strewn trail alternatively speckled by sunlight and leaf shadow. On an August afternoon, even along a shadowy trail, the summer heat and humidity found us. At times, we needed both hands to grapple our way up the rocky path ascending from the river. All of a sudden, one of our hikers, a heavy-set woman, slipped and wrenched her knee. We stopped to ascertain the nature of her injury. I was afraid we might have to carry her back or send for medical assistance. I felt the hot sweat trickle down the side of my face, but I was afraid to wipe it away with my dirty hands that hung limply at my sides. The injured woman stood up and agreed that she could continue on the walk under her own power if we would proceed more slowly.

Just then, looking ahead on our trail, I saw Keir and Abigail walking toward us on the path from the direction in which we were headed. In contrast to us—hot and sweaty hikers—the picture-perfect couple appeared cool and elegant, as if on a mere stroll. In that moment, I hated them and was even more conscious of my disheveled condition. I attempted to hide myself behind the other hikers ahead of me as everyone greeted the Mervaises.

"At least we cannot be too far from the trailhead if Abigail and Keir are just starting their walk," I consoled myself. About 15 minutes later, we exited the woods onto the asphalt path leading back to the lodge where I opted for a shower and a short nap before the evening's banquet while Auguste changed into his swim trunks and headed for a dunk in the pool.

Although Auguste did not enjoy mingling with the convention delegates, he joined us for the cocktail party and dinner. After everyone was assured a seat at dinner, Evonda, Auguste, and I seated ourselves at a half-empty table. I was glad to be able to stay more in the shadows and leave the limelight to the officers and tournament chairs to present the prizes.

Following Saturday morning's continuing education program, Harry had organized a tubing flotilla down the Deer River. Thirty-two of us grabbed box lunches and cold drinks before driving twenty minutes to the site of Deer River Runners. I realized during the drive that I had not taken time to say anything to Keir after the annual meeting when he had passed the presidential gavel to Harry upon the latter's election, and Harry had presented Keir with the green and bronze plaque of appreciation for his year serving as OAHIA President. Abigail and Keir had not signed up for the tubing trip, so I was not sure I would see them to say goodbye.

But I was also relieved that Keir would not see me in my bathing suit. I thought, "Abigail is such a cute, petite woman in comparison to my pitiably plump shape that no bathing suit can hide." I was able to enjoy the leisurely tube float with no more than my usual self-consciousness. I could simply phone Keir from the safe distance of my office in Columbus the following week after the convention was over.

Since Liam had written his ex-President's column for last summer's newsletter so late, we had combined it with the fall issue, thus Keir needed to write only three presidential columns rather than four. When I received Liam's black-and-white photographs from the convention for the newsletter, the ones of Keir and Abigail made my heart skip a beat. "Why did Keir have to be SO GORGEOUS???" my mind involuntarily asked.

I dialed the number to Keir's office. His receptionist put me through to his phone.

"Hello, Keir. I am sorry I did not get the opportunity to say goodbye when we were at Deerwood since we had to hurry up and leave for the tubing expedition."

"Thank you for all the assistance you provided me during my presidency and for how the convention ran so smoothly. Liam just sent me the convention photos."

"I just received the ones for the newsletter from him."

"Liam took a wonderful picture of me and Abigail."

I agreed, thinking of the sets of photos I had received from Liam: two full-length photos of Keir and Abigail, a group shot of the tennis players, several crowd shots of the reception, and Harry presenting Keir with the latter's presidential plaque.

"Yes, it's great Liam is a good photographer. I'll be using several of the shots in the newsletter."

"Thanks for calling. I've got to take another call." We bade each other goodbye. Hanging up, I thought about how much I would miss my biweekly phone calls with Keir.

Harry Whitfield convened the mid-November OAHIA Executive Committee meeting in the AEMG conference room in Columbus with vice president Henry Spaulding, treasurer Herbert Howell, secretary Jonathan Patrick, Attorney Representative Jeffrey Charles, and General Counsel Gordon Frazier. Now immediate past president, Keir Mervais was absent. The Deerwood Lake convention had lost $1,215 in revenues, and although the comments about the educational sessions were positive, there had been some negative feedback about the choice of accommodations and remoteness of location.

After I presented the proposed budget for 1989 Harry observed, "We should hold the fall Executive Committee meeting in October to approve the budget *before* the dues invoices are mailed in case we need to increase the dues charged." Henry proposed that the budget be approved with the caveat that it be reviewed again at the February meeting when we had a better idea about the status of dues collections. The officers then reviewed a series of legal forms for health insurance that had emerged from Liam McFarland's Forms Committee. As OAHIA president, Harry appointed Henry as the new Forms Committee chairman, retaining Liam and several others as committee members. In Keir's absence, Harry presented the Legislative Committee report, initiating discussion as to the amount and type of legislative monitoring and involvement necessary for the Association which had limited financial and people resources.

Henry Spaulding already had several topics and speakers lined up for the 1989 convention planned for Island Point Resort. Herb Howell suggested several Cincinnati hotels for the 1990 convention location, including the Hyatt Regency, Omni Netherland Plaza, Terrace Hilton, Westin, and Manor Grove Inn. Henry suggested that one of his branch manager colleagues located in Cincinnati could visit the hotels and provide his feedback for selection. (I worried that a health insurance attorney might not be looking for the same features that a professional meeting planner, like Evonda or I, would consider during a site visit, but I did not voice my concern out loud.) With no other business to discuss, Harry adjourned the meeting.

Auguste had been working at the Huntington Bank's main office on Cleveland Avenue and 17th, about five minutes' drive from our house, when the Bank's management announced it would build a Grandview Heights location, effectively located directly across the street from the building housing AEMG's office. As the 21-story structure rose, it blocked David Fisher's 10th floor corner office view of the city skyline and points northeast. David took steps to relocate AEMG's office to a more suburban location with adjacent free parking rather than the current arrangement that required us to pay monthly rental fees for parking in the municipal deck. As the 1988 holiday season approached, I entered my fifth month of pregnancy, and my body was beginning to show signs of the impending arrival of our first child.

In the Shadow of "Ol Doinyo Lengai" – Maasai, Africa

c. 1400 C.E.

I waited with the other girls and women of our tribe at the edge of the *kraal* to greet our victorious warriors as they returned from a glorious lion kill. Standing on a fence railing, I was anxious to see Natani Ole Naudo, one of the most attractive and my favorite, to learn if he was one of the first to spear the lion. The two victors would get to dance with the girls of their choice at tonight's festival. My companions giggled, argued, and pushed each other in a teasing manner, claiming their warrior to be the best. I stood to the side, not willing to be distracted by their playfulness, intent on watching the horizon.

Under my bare feet, I felt the relentless heat rising from the parched, red earth beneath the stubbly grasslands that stretched as far as I could see in each direction, interrupted only occasionally by an acacia or baobab tree or a grouping of rocks, a *kopje*. Peering into the hazy distance, the foothills had a wavy, shimmering, appearance. When an occasional breeze blew a path through it, the gold and green straw would gently sway. Far away, I could just see a herd of zebra, wildebeest, antelope, and gazelle, the size of black dots, crossing the seemingly endless plains, the *Serengeti*.

Our *kraal*, or *engang*, was enclosed by a circular fence built from poles tied together using thorn bushes and the prickly branches from umbrella trees. Close to the fence were our dome-like homes, *inkajijik*, made of branches and grass, cow hides, and sealed with cow dung. Cattle grazed in the center of the enclosed settlement. Older women scurried about the *manyatta*, a secluded area of 49 houses reserved for the most privileged warriors, their mothers, and their uncircumcised adolescent girlfriends.

We had spent the afternoon adorning our bodies with large circles of our best, multi-colored beaded necklaces, long loop earrings, and our prettiest red leather skirts. Having not yet reached puberty, my breasts were not fully formed and my pubic area was still smooth and hairless. I was betrothed in infancy to Loomali Ole Pesai. When my body would start to show signs of maturity, my head would be shaved, and I would be circumcised in preparation for my marriage.

I climbed to a higher rung of the fence to get a better view of the handsome heroes returning. I shaded my eyes with my hand and squinted into the horizon. Natani was not very tall, so I hoped he would be visible in the front.

I strained my eyes in the hazy and dusty direction of the brown savannah and the sparse acacia trees that dotted the distance between our village and Ol Doinyo Lengai, "The Mountain of God." We were near the end of the dry season, *alamei*, May to October, so the *moranees*, the warriors, had to hunt and herd further afield in the highlands than earlier in the season. This time they were gone for nearly a week, but a runner preceded the main party to alert us to the returning victors.

Dust rising in their wake, I heard their chants before I saw them. Since the land is so flat and far-reaching, the spears of our men were first visible over the curved horizon of the earth as their distant voices filled the air.

The throng of waiting women, girls, and elders jostled for positions at the gate for the best view. Their own shouts of excitement drowned out those of the chanting warriors. In the distance, I soon saw the plaited hair atop the young men's heads. Then their strong shoulders appeared, draped at one shoulder with solid or checkered red togas, followed by their graceful hips and long legs.

My heart pounded in my chest as I distinguished the shape and gait of Natani near the front of the crowd. I sensed his presence as much as I saw him. Although compact in body shape, he walked with grace, his head held high. As the group moved closer, his proud face became clearer. Seeing me, his mouth broke into a gleaming smile. For a moment, time stood still, the rest of the world passed away, and there was only Natani and me.

Before I realized it, the warriors had passed through the *kraal* gate and were surrounded by the waiting crowd, all clamoring to know who killed the lion and earned the right to dance with the prettiest girls. In the momentary confusion, I lost sight of Natani, only to find a few moments later that he had found me, casually slipping his arm around my waist. He pulled me toward him and whispered in my ear.

"Tikako, will you dance with me tonight?" Turning my face around toward him, I nodded while my gaze sunk into his dark eyes.

"I wouldn't want to dance with anyone else."

Squeezing me swiftly then releasing his hold, Natani left to seek his hut and don his ceremonial ostrich plume headdress and thigh bells. I returned to my own hut to prepare my share of the milk for the evening's festivities.

The entire village was buzzing with the ceremonial preparations. As shades of rose, magenta, peach, turquoise, and soft green painted the sky from the setting sun, and the first stars dotted the night's firmament, mothers, elders, and children gathered in the center of the *engang*.

The elders blew their kudo horns, announcing the warriors' arrival. I could scarcely contain my excitement, and I scanned the pack of entering warriors for Natani. The men were magnificently dressed in lion manes, eagle feathers, and ostrich plume headdresses. I hoped Natani would be in the front again, but I did not see him.

The men's shields were decorated in elaborate patterns, and they carried their spears upright as they paraded into the circle of people. Reaching the center of the *engang*, the warriors formed two opposing lines and tilted their spears toward a facing warrior, forming an arch. Standing on my toes, I saw their sun-glazed bodies were adorned with ochre paint and beaded ornaments—earrings, necklaces, ankle bracelets, and armbands. As they started to chant a song, Natani and the other heroic warrior, Kakombe, arrived to enter the far end of the arch of spears. Pride swelled in my chest.

Soon Natani and Kakombe reached the end of the arch. When Natani walked over to me to take my hand for the first dance, my surroundings, the other people gathered for the ceremony, and even the sounds and singing, all melted away.

I do not know how long we danced or how many dances we were together. I was only aware of his presence, breathing together, and his grip on me preventing me from floating off into the air above.

"May I have a drink?" Natani asked, sweat easing down his cheeks.

"Oh, I forgot the milk!" Tearing myself from his arms, I rushed back to my hut for the precious liquid. When I returned to the ceremonial circle, another girl, Loiyan, had captured Natani's attention. I would have poured the milk out onto the ground if he had not seen me just at that moment and smiled in my direction. He took a few steps toward me and broke whatever spell Loiyan had attempted to cast on him.

Now I was under his spell instead. As he took the container of milk from my hand, our eyes met and locked before he raised the milk to his lips. A drop of white liquid slipped from the corner of his mouth. Wiping it from his chin with my forefinger, I licked it. Dropping the container to the ground, Natani enveloped me and brought my body in close to his glistening chest. When he released me, I noticed we had attracted some attention.

Natani slipped his fingers between mine and indicated without words that I was to follow him to his hut. Once outside, he stabbed the blunt end of his spear into the ground and drew aside the cow hide door covering so I could enter.

After the bright light of the camp bonfire, my eyes took a moment to readjust to the darkness inside his hut. A small fire smoldered in the center of the rectangular room and gave it a smoky smell. The inside was not unusual—sparsely decorated with a bed of skins to one side, some rawhide containers, and dung pots with body paints.

65

I felt Natani slip inside the entrance behind me, also hesitating to adjust his vision. Placing his strong hands on my shoulders, he turned me to face him and gently brought his face down to where our lips could meet. His kiss was soft and warm. His hands slid down both sides of my back, circled around my waist, and then rested on my almost breasts.

Previously, I had not had a favorite among the warriors so everything Natani did was new to me. He was a slow, tender lover, making sure I was comfortable. We spent the night exploring each other's bodies, experiencing wonderful sensations and discovering how we complemented each other. When the dawning light found us wrapped in each other's arms and rapt in each other's eyes, it was much too soon.

Remembering his duties, Natani rose and gathered himself together to join the other warriors to eat and tend the herd before heading out on another hunt. I returned to help my mother gather firewood, fetch water from the river, and milk the cows and goats.

The day seemed to drag on forever. Every few minutes I would scan the horizon searching for him even while knowing the men would not be back for hours. It was even more likely some of them would not return for several days.

Word had gotten around the *kraal* that Natani and I had been together last night, and several times the other girls or younger boys teased me about it. Mostly, I ignored their taunts, preferring to replay in my mind our special moments together.

As evening came upon us, a small band of warriors returned to camp, but my *asanja,* my special one—as I had begun to think of Natani—was not among them. I thought about him out there on the savannah at night and wondered if he was missing me the way I ached for him.

I was staring up at the stars, thinking that at least we were sharing the same heavens above us, when Tajewo, a younger warrior came over to me. I was aware that he had desires toward me but had always been too timid to act on them. Tonight he must have drunk some honey beer because he swaggered with a little too much self-assurance.

"So the lion killer has left his fresh prey for the rest of us, has he?" Tajewo smirked exultantly. Since I had been "broken in" the night before, he expected me to bed down with him as my *oljipet* or second lover, "the skewer." I turned to walk away. "What's the matter—too good for the likes of me?" he called out.

Before I could run away, Tajewo grabbed me from behind, covered my mouth with his hand to muffle my protests, and carried me to his hut. I squirmed and fought his grip, but he was too powerful.

Tajewo and I went through the same basic physical acts as Natani and I had the night before, but Tajewo's force and violence was so opposite of the pleasure I had found with Natani.

"Stop, please stop!" I cried, first as screams, then as a whimper, but Tajewo kept ramming his body into mine. With my arms pinned behind me, I thought his hammering body would never stop, the action causing a painful, ripping sensation between my legs. Why had Natani left this morning, leaving me unprotected?

Tajewo arched and shuddered finally. His anger and passion spent, he withdrew and left his hut. I rolled over onto my side, pulling my legs to my chest in a useless attempt to soothe my raw insides. I felt dirty and ashamed. I knew Tajewo would brag about his conquest, and there would soon be others vying for the spot of my crossover, or third, lover, *olkeloki*. Through my tears, I prayed for Natani's return.

I knew I would need to declare my love for Natani formally to my parents and obtain their blessing. I expected that when Natani returned, we would have a special feast day with much drinking of milk and singing. "When they see how happy we are together, perhaps my parents will end my engagement to Loomali and allow me to marry Natani," I thought.

At night, I tried my best to stay out of sight of Tajewo and the other warriors in the compound, doing my best to hide among groups of elder women or stay in the shadows. Tajewo appeared satisfied, however, and he pursued other girls. As a younger warrior in training, he used the absence of the more virile men to his advantage. I was thankful he did not come after me again.

It was several nights before the main band of warriors, Natani among them, returned to the *engang*. I had fashioned a special upper armband and necklace for him. I was excited about an evening of dancing, playing games, and making love with him. I especially wanted him to know he was my *asanja* and invite him to a feast with my parents.

But Natani did not join with us in the merrymaking. As the evening wore on, I sought him in his hut where he was stretched out on his bed of skins, staring at the ceiling. When I entered the doorway, he jumped up and ushered me out.

"You should not be here with me," he warned me in a whisper.

"Why not?"

He looked down at his feet. "Because you are betrothed to Loomali," he said quietly.

"But my parents could stop that when they know you are my *asanji!*" I regretted spoiling the tender surprise I had prepared and practiced for days.

67

"No, Loomali has more cows for your dowry than I do." His shoulders slumped forward, and he looked forlorn.

"I will ask them tonight."

Without saying a word, Natani kissed the top of my bare head and ducked back into his hut.

For a few stunned moments, I stood there with tears rolling unimpeded down my cheeks and chest to the ground. Then I turned and dashed home to my hut only to realize my parents were still in the grand circle with the rest of the villagers. I was not sure whether to seek them out or wait until their return home. I paced inside our hut, practicing what I would say.

As a child, I could not imagine my parents denying my request, but Natani appeared so certain that our situation was irreversible that doubt clouded my thinking. I tried to word convincing arguments in my mind, but the ideas seemed to tumble around and become twisted like brambles. I even lay down hoping that my thoughts would slow down and allow me to think more clearly.

I must have fallen asleep, because some time later my parents returned and shook me awake.

"Loomali has accused us of breaking your marriage contract!" my father said, folding his arms across his chest. "You've been seen with Natani."

"That's not true!"

"You have not been with Natani?" My father eyed me suspiciously.

"Plenty of girls spend time with warriors they do not marry."

"The marriage agreement with Loomali does not allow that."

"But I don't want to marry Loomali. I want to marry Natani!" After all my planned speeches and convincing arguments, I was being defiant and defensive rather than persuasive.

"Loomali has many more cows for your dowry than Natani," my father said.

"I don't care about cows, and I don't like Loomali!" I screamed. "I want to marry Natani!" I could feel the ground I was losing slipping from under my feet. My father and mother exchanged glances.

"Perhaps this discussion will go better in the morning when we have had some sleep," my mother suggested. My father and I shot each other a look, knowing neither one was likely to relent by morning. My father headed to his bed in the corner. My mother lay down next to him. I stood there for another few moments with clenched hands, my heart still pounding. There was no one to storm at any longer. I returned to my bed and lay down, my thoughts racing and jumbled again until nearly dawn when I slipped into a fitful slumber.

As the household began to stir with the sunrise, I felt even more sullen. Our father's word was law, and marriage contracts could only be annulled in certain circumstances. One of those was if a warrior was selected to be the *Alaunoni*, a great honor for bravery. The village elders selected for him a marriageable girl from a reputable family. She and the *Alaunoni* must wed despite any previous agreements of engagement.

But the chances of Natani being selected as the *Alaunoni* and me being selected as his designated mate were unlikely. Natani, if appointed the *Alaunoni,* could be paired with another girl, or I could be the one forced to marry another *Alaunoni*.

I needed to speak with Natani before the warriors set out this morning. I set about my chores, quickly fetching the water and firewood for the family. When I was done, I ran over to where the warriors were beginning to gather.

As I came closer to the cluster of warriors, I saw that Loomali and Natani were arguing loudly. The other warriors encircled them, in some cases, appearing to take sides and shouting.

As I neared the outside of the group ring, several warriors fell silent and parted to allow me entrance to the circle. The sun glinted off Loomali's unsheathed sword. I looked at Natani and saw he was weaponless. Natani noticed me, taking his eyes off of Loomali.

"Go away. Get away from me," he hissed at me.

I watched Loomali thrust his sword into Natani's chest. Stunned, Natani stood for a moment before crumpling onto the ground. Loomali withdrew his sword then backed away as the rest of the men parted in surprise and shock behind him. I dove forward to gather the bleeding Natani in my arms.

I clung to my lover's limp, blood-covered body, trying to catch my breath between sobs. For the longest time, none of the remaining warriors made a move but stood around helplessly, watching me mourn Natani's lifeless form.

Eventually, arms encircled my shoulders and pulled me up. Other arms lifted Natani's body and carried it outside the *engang* for a considerable distance beyond the fence. In the shade of an acacia tree, the men lay his body down, facing east.

The horror of leaving Natani's body to be devoured by vultures or hyenas gave me the strength to struggle free and sprint towards Natani's resting place. Perhaps I could keep the predators at bay.

For a long time, as the morning sun mounted the sky, I knelt on the ground with Natani's head in my lap. I did not feel the burning heat of the sun as it crested at midday, nor did I notice the warriors wordlessly move out into the fields to tend the cattle.

For a while, I swatted ineffectually at the insects that attempted to settle on my deceased lover's corpse. Then, I began to sing and sway to a soft melody, like a lullaby.

As the sun began to slide toward the horizon, my mother came out to me, placed her hands on my shoulders to stop my body motion and capture my attention.

"Let Natani go home to the spirits now, Tikako," she said softly. "You can do no more here. Come back home now." She gently lifted me to my feet, and putting her arm around my shoulders, she directed me back to our *manyatta*. Several times I turned my head to gaze at the outstretched person of Natani.

All night long I lay on my pallet, tears coursing from my eyes, imagining the vultures tearing at his body. I did not want the morning sun to rise because I was afraid to see what the night had wrought. At moments, I could almost feel his presence next to me in the hut, but the sensation would vanish before I could hold on to it, returning me to my sadness.

My head ached. My skull felt about to burst, the pressure was so strong. The throbbing expanded from behind my eyes, upwards over my head, and down my spine. I felt a rigidity set into my backbone and my legs tighten. My body began to shake uncontrollably. I felt simultaneously hot and cold, sweat sprouting from every pore. My tremors increased. Then, suddenly, like a snap of a twig, every sensation stopped. I was dead.

EDUCATION

In January, and seven months' pregnant, I made a site visit to San Antonio, Texas for the NIRS conference planned in July 1989. Shavonne, the co-worker who was slated to plan the convention during my maternity leave, accompanied me.

One of the tourist features of San Antonio's downtown is the river-level walkway that adds a second level of shops and open-air cafes to the city along with scenic tourist boats plying the waters. In the mild winter weather, a plague of black birds nested in the Riverwalk trees, affecting tourism. Each afternoon, the police shot blank bullets into the air to scare off the birds.

After checking into my hotel room, I lay down trying to rest my bulging body, but the sudden *crack-crack* of the guns made me jump. The baby inside me must have hated the noise, too, because while I was supine on my back, she decided to change position in my womb by 180 degrees and head down towards the birth canal. I lay stock still, concerned whether I should go to the emergency room, but thankfully, after that dramatic movement, she settled down, and we both drifted off to sleep until dinner time.

As Shavonne and I made our way down the Riverwalk to our restaurant, a river rat suddenly crossed our path heading toward the river. Shavonne nearly jumped into my arms with alarm, which I found amusing since I was the pregnant one, but she regained her composure. The next day, while visiting the Alamo, an exceedingly small, dark, dank building with a mud floor, Shavonne felt faint. We exited the claustrophobic monument so she could catch her breath away from the Texas humidity inside. Since neither of these two incidents appeared to bother me, my concern about a premature visit to the hospital subsided.

However, when I went for my next doctor's visit, my blood pressure from my middle-aged pregnancy had risen.

"You will need to stop working," my obstetrician advised.

"Then you won't get paid," I said, implying my reliance on employer-paid health insurance.

"How about cutting back to half-time?"

"I'll see if I can work that out with my employer."

"You'll need to rest for an hour before you go into work and every two hours thereafter. Listen to relaxation tapes while you rest."

Once I obtained permission from David Fisher to cut back to twenty hours per week, I fell into a pattern of sending Auguste off to work, then lying down to listen to the tapes for an hour, arriving at work at 10:00 a.m., resting during my lunch hour on a too-short leather loveseat in the ladies' room—again listening to tapes on my Walkman, working two more hours, then heading home to rest again before making dinner.

At AEMG, we made arrangements for support staff on each of my client associations to cover for me during my maternity leave from mid-April to mid-June. I would be absent from three board meetings and two conventions. Evonda would take care of two of my smaller groups, including OAHIA. My two national clients would require a team of staff members to cover in my absence.

As a woman's body gets ready to give birth, her hormones do strange things; certain emotions and memories stand out while others pass by completely unnoticed. The only thing I remember from the February 16th OAHIA Executive Committee meeting was during Keir's Legislative Committee report. I was taking minutes, seated to Keir's left. He was dressed in typical conservative, attorney work attire—navy sports jacket, grey slacks, white long-sleeved shirt, and red tie with a small print—however, I noticed one curious abnormality: instead of a gold watch, peering out from underneath the left sleeve of Keir's white shirt was a silver, Native American-style bracelet with inlaid stripes of red, black, turquoise, and mother-of-pearl stones. I was intrigued; why would an attorney, otherwise attired in standard business dress, be wearing such anachronistic jewelry?

By early April, I could scarcely waddle down the street from the municipal parking garage to our office building. So that there was sufficient space for my expanding stomach behind the steering wheel, I had pushed the driver's seat back so far only my toes touched the pedals. I switched to a back-tilting desk chair and extended my arms as far forward as possible to type. The baby was pushing and stretching her legs against my fundus—the top of my uterus—with her head pushing downward into the birth canal. I felt as if my pelvic joints were ripping apart. My blood pressure reached 140 over 90—the lower limits of the danger zone. My expected due date and the commencement of my maternity leave were still a week away.

Reluctantly, I decided to use a precious week of vacation to start my leave earlier. On my last Friday, contrary to doctor's orders, I worked eight straight hours to get caught up. On Monday morning, with my feet stretched out on a hassock and using the ironing board as a desk, I completed a meeting budget for one of my clients then stopped by to put it inside Evonda's home mailbox on my drive to the obstetrician's office.

"Your blood pressure is too high. I am going to bring your case up at our management meeting on Wednesday to determine whether or not to perform a C-Section," my doctor informed me. "Meanwhile, I am ordering you on complete bed rest." I relaxed; there was nothing else to do but wait. Auguste could make our supper. The pelvic stretching pains began again that night. I felt like a swollen seal and could not find a comfortable position in which to sit or lie down.

Around three o'clock in the morning, my water broke—just a trickle, but, when we called, the doctor on duty ordered us to drive to the hospital. Auguste was still half asleep, while I was suddenly totally awake and barking orders to him.

"Get your pants on. Don't forget my suitcase. Take your keys." I waddled out to Auguste's car and eased myself into the passenger's seat, tilting the seatback so that I could recline.

Once I was admitted to the hospital I learned that by losing some amniotic fluid, the pressure was relieved in my uterus and the baby settled down. With little change during the rest of the morning, Auguste and I played cards and read, both of us needing naps but too excited to sleep. Since the baby would need to be born within 24 hours of my water breaking, by late morning, I was given an intravenous drip with Pitocin to stimulate contractions. An hour later, because the contractions were so severe I required an epidural injection into my back to numb the pain. After a couple of hours enduring the side effects of chills and tremors from the two drugs, I finally reached the sufficient threshold of dilation and was wheeled into the delivery room. Mireille was born at exactly five o'clock in the afternoon, the moment my doctor was scheduled to go off duty from an 18-hour work shift. Luckily, we had no emergency complications. The nurses slapped her butt, and Mireille let out a cry. They placed her on my, now shrunken, stomach while Auguste and I stared at this strange, new creature.

Mireille only weighed five pounds and eleven ounces, but she was fully formed with magnificent large, dark-blue eyes. I had decided to nurse her. After I was settled into a private hospital room, she was wheeled to my bedside in a Plexiglas bassinette to spend the night. Lying on her stomach, she lifted her head (something most newborns are unable to do) and gazed over at me with those large, dark eyes as though to ask, "Who are *you*?" I looked back at her with the same inquiry. We bonded instantly.

Half of all newborns contract jaundice, and Mireille was one of them. We extended my stay in the maternity ward two additional days, and then moved over to the pediatric ward for one night before finally being released after a total of five days in the hospital. The night Auguste and I arrived at the hospital there had been some snow flurries. When we left, pink, red, white, and purple azaleas were in bloom everywhere. I had not been outside in five days; the sun and freedom felt wonderful. The OAHIA Executive Committee sent me a baby pink azalea bush as a gift. Auguste planted it in our backyard.

During my eight-week maternity leave, I tried to figure out how to stay home with Mireille permanently, but Auguste and I were too dependent on my salary for me to be a stay-at-home mother. At the time, there were very few books or magazine articles for women who wanted to work full-time and continue nursing, and I only found one that addressed what to do in the case of a traveling mother who breastfed.

In the end, we put Mireille into a franchised day-care center—almost cold turkey—using breast milk I had expressed the previous day, frozen, then thawed. I went back to work and to a monthly convention-travel schedule. The airplane tickets for the San Antonio NIRS conference in mid-

July had been purchased before Mireille was born. Now I realized that being away for five days would wreak havoc with our nursing schedule. After considering several options, including hiring a babysitter to go to the conference with me, I used a doctor's excuse to shorten my trip to two days away—enough time to participate in the first board meeting and kick off the conference with the keynote speaker.

Upon my return when I walked back through our door, Mireille nearly leapt out of Auguste's arms into mine. In my absence, she had drunk infant formula from bottles and was extremely relieved that her mother had returned with the real thing.

During the summer my parents retired from New Jersey to live in Columbus, only two miles from our new house and their new grandbaby.

"I can help take care of Mireille when you go to work," my mother offered cheerfully.

"We've already put her in fulltime daycare." Noticing my mother's crestfallen expression, I added, "But you can help us when she is sick or the daycare is closed, as well as over weekends when I travel. I don't expect you to be tied down as Mireille's permanent babysitter. You have just retired and have earned your freedom from parenting."

My parents and Auguste decided to accompany me to Island Point Resort for the 1989 OAHIA annual convention in early August. My father wanted to play golf, Auguste wanted to enjoy some time at the lake, and my mother could mind Mireille when I was in meetings. Since the sleeping accommodations were townhouse villas, our units were next door to each other and equipped with kitchenettes.

As I spent most of my time that year caring for Mireille's infant needs or keeping up with work, my recollection of 1989 is vague at best. During the past year or two, like a game of musical chairs, General Counsel Gordon Frazier had switched employment from SummitCare to Attorneys Assurance, causing agency branch managers from SummitCare to follow him to Attorneys Assurance, with the one exception that Harry Whitfield's transfer was thwarted when Chuck Lincoln, already at Attorneys Assurance in Akron did not want another office in nearby Mansfield. Herb Howell, now displaced from his position by Gordon, moved from Attorneys Assurance to take Gordon's former job at SummitCare. Meanwhile, Harry turned to his relationship with Keir to seek employment with Cleveland Medical as their Mansfield office branch manager.

When Gordon worked out a deal to return to SummitCare again, Herb was once again displaced, but this time his (and Gordon's) former position with Attorneys Assurance was already filled by someone else. When the dust finally settled, Herb was left without employment in the health care legal field, putting his membership on OAHIA's Executive Committee at risk.

We held the summer 1989 OAHIA Executive Committee meeting in Henry Spaulding's villa parlor at Island Point Resort. Despite Herb's unemployed status, Keir's Nominating Committee report included Herb on

74

the Executive Committee slate as vice president for the upcoming administrative year.

"Gordon's two-year term as General Counsel is also ending, but since he has been a valuable asset on the Legislative Committee both with the General Assembly and the Insurance Department, I move that we appoint Gordon to another year as General Counsel," Keir said. Jonathan Patrick quickly seconded the motion.

The strained tension in the room between Herb and Gordon was palpable. The officers considered their options in silence.

"Any discussion?" Harry asked, glancing around the room. "All those in favor?" The motioned passed with Herb's lone abstention. It felt to me as if each officer had gotten out of his chair, one at a time, to walk over and slap Herb on the face. All the officers had done was to reappoint Gordon, but the air in the room was saturated with a playground feeling of kids picking teams for a game and one child being deliberately left out. Herb sat in stoic silence, accepting defeat like a gentleman without allowing his dignity and honor to falter. I felt badly for him but knew it was not my place to protest. For me, this OAHIA Executive Committee action would ever remain in my mind as one of its lowest points. I was glad when the meeting adjourned.

Auguste brought Mireille to the poolside reception to show her off, but I found it difficult to pay attention to my five-month-old and to my executive director duties at the same time. Luckily, Evonda was still helping me with the registration and social events so I could excuse myself early from the reception and take Mireille and Auguste back to our villa.

"I want to go fishing. When do I have to watch Mireille tomorrow?" Auguste asked when we got back to the room.

"I have to work during the morning, but should be back at the room for lunch and the afternoon. Maybe my mother would be willing to watch Mireille?" Auguste shrugged his shoulders and turned on the television set while I bathed Mireille and put her to bed.

All weekend I was annoyed at Auguste for not being more helpful in taking care of Mireille. After all, we would not be here at the resort if not for my job. He seemed to resent having to watch her because it interfered with the freedom to be on vacation. I was also feeling uncomfortably bloated and fat from the fullness of lactating. I spent the morning coffee breaks in the restroom expressing milk and all my spare afternoon time in the villa with Mireille. Even though I knew Keir's wife had not accompanied him to the convention this time, I was too embarrassed by my shape and Auguste's behavior even to approach him during the social or educational events to acknowledge that he would be rotating off the Executive Committee with this meeting. Was it possible that he sensed my annoyance and embarrassment and politely avoided me so as not to cause me further discomfort? I was very thankful when the convention concluded, and we could all, mercifully, go home.

Although still out of work, Herb Howell worked diligently on the 1990 convention program for the Hamilton Hilton in Cincinnati. In addition to his General Counsel duties, Gordon Frazier took over as OAHIA's Legislative Committee chair from Keir who was no longer on the Executive Committee.

Following the OAHIA convention, I traveled to an Arizona resort in September, a California resort in October, and to Orlando, Florida, in November. Although I had never before been bothered by hay fever or allergies, throughout the autumn I experienced all the symptoms of runny nose, itchy eyes, and post-nasal drip. Over-the-counter remedies did little to eliminate the effects, and by October I experienced a deep, barking cough that worried Evonda.

"You should see a doctor," she admonished.

"It's just post-nasal drip from allergies," I insisted, but when I awoke one November morning with a fever of 102, I called my mother to ask the name of her doctor.

"You have walking pneumonia," the doctor said. "People die of pneumonia. You should be in bed." Easy for him to say—Thanksgiving was coming, along with my mother-in-law. I needed to cook and clean. My mother offered to clean my house for the holiday, but I knew that the accumulating dust and a season of dead leaves had gotten the better of me.

"When we move into our new office in December," I told Auguste, "I will no longer need to pay $50 per month for parking. May I use that money to hire a maid to clean our house?"

"I don't want a stranger touching my things!"

"We can keep one room closed off that the maid won't touch. I just can't keep the house clean enough to prevent Mireille and me from getting sick!" Auguste relented finally.

Between Thanksgiving and Christmas, Mireille learned to pull herself up to stand and started to walk. By February 1990, she was climbing stairs. She delighted in helping her mother with the laundry by pushing the full laundry basket from the bedroom hamper, through the hallway, across the living room and dining room rug, and through the kitchen to the laundry room, then back again. After a few hours of energetic activity, she would abruptly climb onto the sofa or a bed with her blankie and immediately drop off to sleep.

My days seemed to run together in a never-ending blur of getting Mireille, Auguste, and myself up, dressed, fed, and ready for daycare and work; responding to the demands of my various association clients; picking Mireille up at daycare; and returning home to feed, undress, bathe, and get everyone into bed to start the next day. Often I would bring paperwork home at night for proofreading or drafting while Auguste watched television. I was responsible for the inside of the house while Auguste took care of the outside yard and the repair chores for the house or cars. Sometimes he would cook meals or bathe Mireille, but often I was the one reading her bedtime story or rocking her to sleep (and often dozing off myself in the rocker). She was frequently bothered by ear infections, and underwent an ear-tube insertion operation under anesthesia for her first birthday.

OAHIA was going through its own growing pains. Herb Howell finally found a position with the Administrative Office of the Courts and resigned as OAHIA vice president in February. Jonathan Patrick moved up from treasurer to vice president, and Chuck Parker moved into the Treasurer's slot, while the Executive Committee voted to add Marcia Tuttle to its officer ranks, the first woman in a dozen years. On a career fast-track, Marcia came highly recommended by the CEO of The Health Plan of Ohio, but she was not herself an attorney.

The health insurance industry was also undergoing changes. Hospitals and physician groups were forming their own health insurance companies and directing business to them. Non-affiliated hospitals and doctors were forcing the other health insurance carriers into a bidding war despite the system of filed premium rates with the Insurance Department. Meanwhile, the U.S. Department of Health and Human Services was filing disbarment suits against a few health lawyers, while the Insurance Department was demanding to raise the financial reserve amounts held by the insurance companies to pay the escalating level of claims. Not only were the health insurance claims mounting, the malpractice lawsuits against doctors, hospitals, and their health care attorneys were increasing, too. The climate was getting vicious. The lawsuit (and countersuit) of <u>Athenaeum Health Plan and Attorneys Assurance Health Plan v. Paramount Blue of Ohio</u> along with the suit by the Attorney General against Paramount Blue, were combined into a single case and appealed up to the U.S. Supreme Court.

In order to stay competitive with each other, the health insurance member companies of OAHIA were expanding by adding branch offices in different Ohio cities and by hiring marketing representatives. In 1983 Keir had hired Katherine Shipley as the receptionist in his Cleveland office, but by 1989 she was the sales manager for the entire state, doubling the sales of the three existing branches and adding more staff. Other companies were exhibiting similar growth, accompanied by employees also switching company allegiances.

In my five years as the Association's Executive Director, OAHIA had managed to overcome a six-thousand dollar deficit and accumulate a cash reserve of $20,000—an amount over fifty percent of its annual revenues. By now, all of the officers who had originally endorsed me under the special services clause had ended their terms on the Executive Committee and rotated off, so when the OAHIA-AEMG three-year management fee arrangement was due to expire in October 1990, the OAHIA Executive Committee chose to seek competing bids from other management firms.

The program content that Herb Howell had planned for the 1990 convention at the Hamilton Hilton proved to be very timely, but the hotel itself was not up to the quality standards that OAHIA had come to expect. (I had not paid a site visit to this hotel before the contract was signed.) This was the first convention that Keir did not attend since I had joined OAHIA. I assumed that the five-and-a-half-hour drive from Cleveland to Cincinnati was a deterrent, although his colleagues Liam McFarland and Eric Mitchell made the trek down from Cleveland.

In her position as secretary and confidante to David Fisher, Evonda was privy to the inner workings at AEMG. She confided in me that Alexander McDonald, chief executive officer of Cleveland Medical Health Insurance Corporation and Keir's boss, had been involved in an extramarital affair with former AEMG staff member Linda Peters, who had worked on OAHIA when McDonald was the president in 1980. As a result of this dalliance—an ethical conflict of interest for an AEMG employee—David Fisher had fired Linda. I agreed with the decision for the reasons of moral and ethical impropriety as well as conflict of interest.

Not being an attorney or having studied health law, I did not always understand the problems and dilemmas facing the OAHIA members. However, I sensed that members were bowing to outside, competitive, marketing pressures in ways that made some of them feel uncomfortable. The OAHIA officers, and many of the members, were essentially honorable men who wanted to do the right thing and took seriously their sworn oaths to uphold the laws. But the real world was murkier and greyer that the hallowed halls of law school. Laws and practices varied from state to state and many parent companies were domiciled elsewhere. Every few years, a contingent of OAHIA officers visited Insurance Director Carson to see if he could provide some regulatory or legislative pressure to force conformity within the state. His intervention came in the form of a series of market conduct audits that revealed some rate violations.

Now OAHIA president, Henry Spaulding used his quarterly newsletter column to draw attention to the internal industry problems:

"We have a lawsuit by the Attorney General's Office pending against one of our members. We have a lawsuit by two other members against the same member, a countersuit against those two, and at least two other members suing each other over an incident arising out of attorney fraud, something over which neither one of them had any control."

I suggested to Henry that he might become the Pied Piper of the industry.

"Actually, I feel more like Don Quixote, tilting at windmills!"

We surveyed the membership, and the respondents agreed on the very same issues. Spaulding—who had initially questioned rate violations—again warned in the newsletter, *"We need to consider the possibility that we are increasing premiums in the short-term at the expense of profits in the long-term for those companies who pay our salaries. To the extent that we reduce the profit of our underwriters by taking risks that add to their claims experience, by bringing pressure to bear for them to reduce their rates to meet our competitors, or by violating the Ohio Department of Insurance-approved rates, we are putting our long-term security at risk."*

Unfortunately, the Executive Committee could not come up with a mutually agreeable solution to the dilemma.

Fatehpur Sikri (India)

1581-1595 C.E.

The Sultan had called for me. It had been at least a year since he had summoned me from our palace, the harem where I had lived with Akbar's other Rajput wives since my marriage to him in 1581. After I was impregnated, he had had little to do with me or our son. The less attention I attracted, the happier I was, absorbed in daily harem activities and young motherhood. But I knew what the summons required of me, even though I was puzzled by this sudden interest.

Of the four *Haresara* buildings housing women in the city of Fatehpur Sikri, ours was the most elegant because Mariam uz-Zamani--the Amber Princess--was Akbar's favorite and mother of Jahangir, Akbar's first-born son. The high walls of red sandstone afforded us much seclusion, as did the imposing gateway guarding the enclave. In the middle was our splendid courtyard garden, edged by two-storied pavilions that were connected by four colonnades enclosing our beautiful sanctuary.The walls and columns were ornamented with bells, niches holding various Hindu deities, and chain designs. The graceful architecture reflected both the delicate Persian influence and the ornamental decor of the Gujarati style.

The Emperor had 300 wives and 5,000 women and children in his harem. I was one of Akbar's minor wives. I had come from Jathpur in the province of Rajputana, the daughter of Rao Mal Deo and his concubine, Tipu Paswan. Mariam uz-Zamani, also known as Rajkumari Hira Kunwari, was the first of Akbar's Rajput wives, acquired when Akbar had created alliances with our chiefs by placing them in positions of power within his government and involving them in his empire rather than trying to defeat them militarily.

By courting favor with the fierce Rajput warriors, repealing *jizya*—a Muslim tax on members of other religious sects—and marrying our princesses, the Sultan had cleverly solidified his rule.

We Rajputs, a powerful Hindu land-owning military clan, were proud of our lineage. Our men were fierce in battle and punctilious when it came to etiquette and chivalry. Any occupation not involved with the bearing of arms or governing was considered beneath our men, but there was also a level of equality of rank; a Rajput yeoman had the same aristocratic rank and privilege as a landowner. With Akbar's religious tolerance and permission, Rajput chiefs pervaded the Mughal Empire in the roles of officers, soldiers, and governmental administrators.

My *bayadere* helped me dress for my audience with the Emperor. After rinsing my breasts with rose water and applying sandalwood paste to my ankles and wrists, she rubbed my dark tresses with scented oils. She helped me step into a *ghagra* underskirt of gold and silver-threaded brocade silk. Next, she swirled over my head a short-sleeved silk shirt, *choli*, with decorative jewels and gold stitching, barely hiding my breasts and leaving my stomach bare. Then, with a deftness born of much practice, she wrapped my hips in a transparent yellow *sari*, folding the cloth in nine pleats over her fingers and tucking it into place in the waist of the *ghagra*. She lifted the other end of the *sari*, heavy with gold embroidery, across my chest and over my shoulder.

I sat on a small stool. After dabbing the corners of my eyes with black kohl and placing a single dot of red *kumkum* between my eyebrows, the *bayadere* opened my box containing fine gold jewelry. She selected a pair of earrings that dangled to my shoulders, a dozen bracelets, and a necklace inlaid with numerous precious and semi-precious stones. Finally, she adorned my hair with gold ornaments, adding a pearl headdress with teardrop that lay on my forehead above the *kumkum*. Standing again, with my hand placed on her shoulder to balance myself, I slipped my feet into *mojari*, silk shoes embroidered with gold and ending with turned up toes.

I was now ready to be escorted to Ankh Micholi, the building housing the Sultan's private quarters and the throne room where Akbar would receive me. Because of *purdah*—the seclusion of women from public view—and to avoid the possibility of being seen, I would be led by a specially selected guard through a maze of corridors and hallways from our female sanctuary to Akbar's Hall of Private Audience, Diwan-i-khas. I raised the loose end of my *sari*, draping it over my head and holding it in front of the lower half of my face in preparation for my walk to meet the Sultan.

As a slave girl opened the ornate door to my chamber, and I stepped over the threshold into the foyer, I was startled to find a Rajput warrior bowing to me. His long *jama* tunic was wrapped to the left with a *patka* sash, indicating that he was Hindu. I had expected one of the palace eunuchs to be my escort.

As his turbaned head came back upright, I saw the flashing and enigmatic dark eyes of a strikingly handsome countryman. Our eyes met for a brief but telling instant before modesty and self-consciousness lowered mine. That momentary exchange had ignited me so quickly that I found my heart racing with both impassioned surprise and unexpected delight.

As the soldier turned to lead me to my destination I realized that—although we had never met before—my heart had known him in an instant. Following him through the corridors, my mind began to note the details of his dress, his manner, his carriage, and I began to speculate on what might lie beneath his clothing and within his heart and intellect. I was floating instead of walking. I completely forgot I was going to meet my husband for his conjugal prerogative.

81

From behind, staring at his *puggree* headdress, I noticed my escort's long, silky dark hair caressed his strong, dark neck. My eyes memorized the curve where his neck met his broad shoulders clothed in the *sherwanis* brocaded jacket that encased the subtle muscles of his back and was cinched with the *patka*. When I was not contemplating this man's physique, I wondered why the Emperor ordered my presence and how it had come to pass that a Hindu guard, still in possession of his full male faculties, would be assigned to escort me to my encounter with Akbar.

I noticed how nicely the guard's pajama trousers tapered to his bare ankles. On his slippered feet, he wore *majaris*. From behind, the tip of his *khurkuris* knife was visible, denoting his role as a soldier.

Usually the soldiers stood guard outside our *zenana* while armed females or eunuchs were assigned to protect the Emperor's women—mothers, aunts, sisters, wives, and concubines, as well as our children, attendants, servants, and slaves. We women spent most of our time indoors at the royal residence, venturing outside only in the company of a male relative and with our heads and faces covered by a veil, an *odhni* scarf draped around our shoulders and hair.

I shifted my own scarf around my face and shoulders, causing my bracelets to make a clanking sound. The guard looked around and smiled at me. I felt a deep sense of security in his presence and returned his smile before lowering my eyes to the ground before me. Had I not been so engrossed in studying the gorgeous male figure before me, I might have been more nervous and wary of the unfolding events.

The Sultan's wives and concubines did not participate in public audiences or *durbars* where the courtiers gathered to debate issues of philosophy, theology, history, and diplomacy. Akbar was considered a great patron of literature and the arts, so I understood that his public audiences were very lively. He proved to be a good judge of character, surrounding himself with talented administrators, counselors, and effective military strategists. Revered by many to be a wise and benevolent ruler, Akbar successfully won allegiance from those of many different faiths. He had been politically astute enough to enlist the Rajput leadership in order to consolidate Moghul power. After a long period of fighting and unrest, it was comforting to know the Empire was at last relatively peaceful.

When he tired of holding court with his nobles, Akbar would sometimes retire to one of his harem cities like Fatehpur Sikri where he sought the pleasure of his wives and mistresses.

As we approached the anti-chamber to Diwan-i-khas, I could already hear the faint strains of drums, tambourines, and horns. I was loathe to separate from the company of my handsome protector who, upon reaching our destination, stopped and stepped aside, bowing again as the door to the inner chamber was opened for my entrance.

In the center of the throne room was a pillar with a few dozen scroll-shaped brackets that supported a circular platform topped by the Sultan's throne where he sat upon a Gaddi cushion. As I approached, the Badshah Akbar waved his hand to signal a halt to the music and festivities. Out of respect I bowed low to the floor with my eyes and head pointed downward, averting my gaze away from the Emperor.

"*Namaste*, Johdi Bibi," Akbar greeted me in my native tongue. "*Aapkaiseh hein?*" ("How are you?") I was surprised he still knew my name. "How is my son?"

"Your son and I are well, with thanks to your munificence, Dhanyavaad," I replied, keeping my visage downcast.

"You have come to dance for me."

As a dancer, I had been endowed with an ample chest and favored with flexible limbs. A slave handed me a pair of *sagat*—finger cymbals—and I stepped out of my slippers. Akbar signaled the musicians to begin again. I was glad the piece was slow so that I had time to limber up my choreographic movements.

With my *sagat* setting the rhythm, I languidly moved my chest in a circle to the left, then my hips in a circle to the right. After some side undulations and a few hip drops, I began a movement to a *beledi* rhythm. My ankle and wrist bracelets added tinkling sounds to the main music as it began to increase its tempo. All eyes were on me as I made my barefooted way around the Persian carpet before the Sultan's throne. As long as I kept dancing, I could delay what was expected next.

Although the Sultan was not cruel, he was strong and his power absolute. He was not to be denied—whether it was his ambition to conquer and annex lands or to possess the women of his former opponents. He had an avid and wide-ranging intellect, but became bored easily, so the mandate of his court was to find new and exciting ways to entertain and amuse him.

I tried to invent some new dance movements and use my *sari* veil in a sultry manner. However, after only two dances, Akbar signaled the musicians to stop and descended from his pillar. He held out his hand to me, and I followed him to his inner sanctum.

For all the lavish décor and splendor of the rest of his palace complex, Akbar's private chamber was relatively modest. The white satin, cushioned bed was surrounded by white silk drapery. Two small, gold-and-jewel-encrusted tables were nearby, topped with ewers which I assumed were filled with beverages, and a small *hooka*, but otherwise, it was Spartan. I had only been here once before—to consummate our marriage and conceive our son. I was nervous.

The Emperor began pulling at the edge of my *sari* until it was completely dislodged and fell down around our feet. Next he pulled down my *ghagra* skirt and removed my *choli*. I stood before him completely unclothed. As his broad hands explored my body, I slowly removed his sash, tunic, and jewelry. His moustache tickled as his kissing became more ardent and his lovemaking more urgent. Trying to distract my mind from what was physically happening, I began to fantasize in my mind about my escort earlier in the day. What if it were his arms that held me and his kisses caressing my body? The prospect quickly excited me and must have provided an increased level of passion in my response to Akbar, because I was soon feeling waves of pulsating relief coursing through my groin.

As the ardor of the moment began to wear off, I sensed Akbar's full weight on me. He lifted himself both out of and off of me to roll over onto his back.

"Did you like the gift I sent to you?" he asked.

"The *gift*...?" I echoed back.

"Yes," he replied. "The soldier from Jathpur. He was recommended to me by your father. I thought you might enjoy seeing one of your countrymen again."

"I was very surprised." I looked away, trying not to reveal the depth of my interest in the handsome soldier.

The Sultan studied me for a moment, almost said something, and then changed his mind. Instead, he pointed to a small ewer on the table.

"Massage some of that oil into my back and shoulders." The Sultan turned his back towards me, sitting cross-legged. I fetched the container and poured the liquid into the palm of my hand. When I was finished rubbing the oil into his bare skin, I stood back. "You may go now," he said without turning around.

I bowed, gathered up my clothing, swiftly slipped my skirt and shirt back on, and reassembled my *sari* about me. Akbar had lain down with his eyes closed. I picked up my jewels. Leaving by the door where we had entered, I located my slippers at the edge of the carpet where I had begun to dance. As I looked up to determine how I should exit the Diwan-i-khas hall, a harem eunuch seemed to appear out of thin air to lead the way back to my own building. I quickly covered my head and face for the return trip and followed my escort out towards the courtyard.

As we passed through the anti-chamber, I noticed a group of soldiers standing to one side. Before I could avert my eyes, I caught sight of my Rajput escort from earlier. Our gazes locked momentarily, my heart skipped a beat, and I smiled involuntarily before I looked down at the feet of the eunuch walking ahead of me. I could feel the soldier watching me as I walked away down the hallway.

I do not remember the rest of the walk back to my chambers. My mind was swirling with the all-too-brief moments and memories of my two encounters with the Rajput warrior.

I had never felt this way before. I had had very little exposure to men at large. Even in my father's house, I had been fairly well sheltered; the only opportunity to meet and talk with members of the opposite sex was limited to the *melas*, festival days conducted at the Royal Bazaar where merchandise was sold to the courtiers and nobles. And even then, we were escorted by our servants and interaction was minimal. Still, my reaction to this soldier from Jathpur had left me both dazed and excited. I could not stop thinking of him.

Once back at Mariam uz-Zamani's quarters, my four-year-old son ran to me, and we went to the courtyard garden so that he could play with some of the other children. I stirred the cool pool water absent-mindedly with my hand when my friend Aram came to speak to me.

"You look like you are in another world," she said. Startled back to the present, I looked up.

"The Emperor called for me this morning." She nodded in understanding.

"How did it go?" It had been a long time since Akbar had called for her.

"He wanted me to dance for him in the hall, but after only two dances, we went to his private chambers. It was not too bad. He let me go after I applied oil to his back." I completely left out any mention of the soldier. I still wanted to sort out that memory alone. We watched our boys play for a little while, and then supper was announced. We gathered our sons and proceeded to the dining hall.

After the usual dinner festivities of talking, music, and dancing, I retired to my chamber to ready my son for bed. Even though we had servants and nursemaids, the quiet time just before he fell asleep allowed us our special moments together. He asked me where I had gone earlier in the day.

"Your father, the Great Sultan, wanted my attention for a while to discuss our son's well-being and education." I kissed him goodnight then retired to my bedroom.

I removed my clothing, replacing them with a thin silk night chemise. I lay the oil lamp on my bedside table and pulled the bed curtain aside to climb in. I was completely startled to find the Jathpur soldier reclined on my bed, obviously waiting for me.

"How...how did you get in here?" I asked in a forced whisper. Men—other than the harem eunuchs—were forbidden inside the women's quarters. The penalty was severe.

"It was surprisingly easy," he grinned. He held out his arms to me. Despite every warning in my head, I knew it was exactly what I wanted to do.

Embracing him, drowning in him, coming together as one, was completely natural. My hands caressed his smooth shoulders and chest then slid down to his waist and over his tight buttocks to pull him closer into me. The smell of his skin, moist and glistening with effort, was heady. We indulged in one another, the passion mounting, reaching crescendo, then warm, loving, and entwined. In between, we dozed, dizzy and exhausted, before waking again, once more consumed with the desire to meld and merge, until the early morning light reminded us of the mortal danger we were courting.

After several last kisses, my soldier stole out of my room to find his way out into the undercover safety of the early morning darkness. I lay in bed in the afterglow, partly filled with the bliss of the night's lovemaking and partly filled with the terror of our scandalous behavior.

I do not know how I got through the next day. It was almost as if I were two people. One—a shadow of myself—went through my daily routine of bathing, dressing, eating, and being with my son. The other—an observer outside me—was terrified and on edge lest someone discern that something illicit had happened the previous night.

I retired to my bedroom that evening with great relief. No sooner had I blown out my oil lamp and lay down when my bed curtains parted to admit my soldier. He quickly silenced my surprised gasp with his mouth on mine.

"I couldn't stay away." He raised my chemise over my head and started caressing my body with an intensity heightened by the previous night's intimate familiarity. In succumbing to each other, the rest of the world—and our worries—faded, leaving only the ecstasy of being together, feeding off of each other's heightened desire until every ounce was spent. He again left me as dawn was breaking.

I was numbed with the fatigue of almost two nights of physical exertion and little sleep, aggravated by a heightened sense of alertness. My audience with Akbar seemed like it had occurred two thousand years earlier, not just two days, and I dared not even wonder if my soldier would have the audacity to attempt to appear for a third night. And what if he did not? Would I ever remember how to fall sleep again without his arms encircling me?

As I went to bed that night, every nerve in my body seemed to be on fire. I cautiously pulled the bed curtains aside and climbed onto my bed. I lay there, tense in heightened anticipation, twitching with every sound. Time passed excruciatingly slowly, but my soldier did not appear. At some point I must have fallen asleep, because I awoke with a start as the sunlight came into my bedroom. I was still alone. Turning sideways to bury myself in the pillows, I cupped my face in my hands and cried as a wave of longing, mixed with relief and regret, washed over me.

Finally, my tears stopped. I remembered it was time to wake my son and join the others for our morning meal of sweet potatoes, mangoes, and pomegranates, accompanied by hot *chai* tea. As we entered, most of the harem women were seated on mattresses at the *bajots*, low tables where the servants set plated foods on silver *thalis* trays. Aram waved at us from where she had saved us space to sit.

Once seated, she asked me, excitedly and in a hushed voice, "Did you hear what happened?" I shook my head in the negative and looked at her quizzically, only slightly aware of a creeping feeling of cold dread seeping through my veins.

"They caught a male intruder inside our palace last night!" she exclaimed conspiratorially. "The Emperor had him beheaded at dawn." She waited a moment for my reaction.

I could feel the bile start to swirl in my stomach and begin to rise. The room began to shrink and my eyesight narrowed from darkness at the edges.

"Are you okay?" Aram asked, slightly alarmed.

"I do not feel well," I said weakly. "Would you please watch my son? I need to return to my room to lie down." I rose without waiting for her answer and stumbled almost blindly back to my quarters where I proceeded to heave and vomit until I thought my stomach had turned inside out and there was nothing left.

That is why my soldier had not appeared last night! He had been attempting to visit me a third time and his luck—or caution—had run out.

When I stopped vomiting, I began to hyperventilate. I blamed myself for not discouraging him sooner. I worried that he had been tortured—or even maimed—before the decapitation. I could not—would not—imagine his handsome head severed from his magnificent body—the body and face that had given me so much pleasure only one night earlier! What would they do with his body? Would they cremate it and sprinkle his ashes in the river as with a normal funeral or would they desecrate it?

I got up and wandered to the window overlooking the Yamuna River in a foolish attempt, or even wish, to see whether his funeral pyre could be seen.

My breathing had scarcely begun to slow down when my mind was consumed with agitation that I, too, might be tortured or beheaded as a result of my infidelity—or my son hurt in some manner. My mind began to race with schemes of escape and suicide. This time the room did close in on me, and I fainted into a heap on the floor.

I returned to consciousness after smelling something nasty and acrid then hearing voices around me. Aram must have sent some servants to my aid because there were several in attendance, applying rose water, giving me drink, and fanning me. For a moment,

I forgot where I was or what had happened, leaving me slightly disoriented as I was helped to stand. But then the cruel memory swept over me, and I swooned again. I was carried to my bed where the servants applied cold compresses and further fanning.

I was about to send everyone away so that I could be left to die when my son ran in.

"Mother, are you ill?" he asked with curiosity tinged with trepidation. As I turned towards him, my maternal arms opened automatically for his embrace. With this permission and reassurance, he ran straight towards me, flinging himself into my arms while I lay on my bed.

Seeing that my maternal instincts had roused me somewhat, the attendants backed away slightly to allow for our moment of parent-child intimacy. Just then, another servant entered carrying some weak sugared tea that I was encouraged to sip. Moments later, the crowd around my bed parted and bowed as the Amber Princess glided to my bedside. She immediately placed a warm, compassionate hand on my forehead. My son sat up on his knees and bowed.

"Are you feeling a little better now?" she inquired. My eyes searched her kind face for any sign that she was aware of my complicity, but I saw only reassurance and genuine concern. I nodded slightly in the affirmative. She then ordered the servants away, and taking my son's hand, she told me to "rest now" and turned to leave.

"Thank you, Your Graciousness," I murmured, closing my eyes and turning my body away from the entrance to conceal the tears that were beginning again to slide down my cheeks with increasing speed.

I must have finally drifted into sleep because I dreamt of my lover. We were flying together on a carpet through the stars. Suddenly, I fell off the carpet and the fall startled me awake. For a few seconds, I basked in the afterglow of feeling his presence again, but then the reality of his loss overtook my senses again, and I was racked with sobs. As my tears began to slow, I dozed off into a dreamless sleep.

The next days seemed to blur together. I could scarcely stomach much food, and I was often beset by crying spells. I do not know whether anyone guessed why I was so devastated or whether they thought I was just dramatically ill, but no one inquired as to the source of my uneasiness. They simply acted patiently with me and, gratefully, watched over my son.

As the weeks went by, I found myself drawn to a secluded courtyard with a view of the river where I would go to be alone with my memories. Little by little, the weight of my grief lifted, almost imperceptibly at first, and often circling around again after a short period of subsiding, but eventually there were more hours, then days, when I did not cry as I had before. And life went on.

The Sultan never called for me again. Somehow I surmised that it was his way of publicly ostracizing me while privately conceding to his own complicity in the affair, but it was a blessing not to have to face him again. In a somewhat convoluted manner, I suppose it allowed us both some measure of private forgiveness for each other. He allowed me the space for my personal feelings and devotion that, to the outside world would have been treasonous, but privately was a love match that Akbar had arranged. At the very core, he had a soft spot in his heart, either for me or for true love.

After the marriage of Akbar's favorite son, Salim, to his cousin, Man Bai, in 1585, the Sultan left for Lahore to conquer Kashmir. The court abandoned Fatehpur Sikri, and the entourage traveled as a caravan behind him. Since there were also concerns about water shortage, our departure was hastened. It was both distressing and a relief to leave the scene of my greatest passion and worst heartache, but in the end, it was probably for the best.

Ten years later, when our son turned 16, he left the confines of the harem to join the world of the courtiers and participate in the administration of the realm. That summer, my motherhood duties ended; I succumbed to a case of malaria and, mercifully, died quickly.

Ohio, 1991-1992

SUSPENSION

OAHIA President Jonathan Patrick arrived early for the February Executive Committee meeting; a balding and be-speckled man, he appeared to get along with everyone. In the Association's early days, before I joined AEMG, Jonathan had served on the Executive Committee as the Private Practice Attorneys' Representative.

"May I speak with you privately for a few minutes?" Jonathan asked. His rather wiry voice seemed to be a higher octave than usual.

"Sure. Come back to my office," I replied, turning to head down the hallway. For some reason, David Fisher always gave me the office furthest from his. Whether he had total confidence in my ability to work autonomously, or he wanted to keep me out of his sight as much as possible, I never knew.

"As you know," Jonathan said, seeming to weigh his words, "the OAHIA Executive Committee has been looking into other management options, and well...You're the *best!*" Jonathan grinned. A flood of relief washed over me. I was not sure whether he meant that AEMG was the best management firm or I was the best executive director for OAHIA, but it did not matter, the result was the same. "When we go into executive session today, Marcia Tuttle and I will recommend continuing our agreement with AEMG." Thus reassured of OAHIA's continued esteem, Jonathan and I headed toward the conference room to begin the Executive Committee meeting.

Meanwhile, David Fisher started to find ways to avoid talking to me. I suspected it was due either to OAHIA's decision to reconfirm its management agreement, naming me in its special services clause, or because I spent an entire day "bonding" with the president of David's premier association while we were grounded in the Cleveland airport en route to a site visit. Whatever the reason, our communication was reduced to memos left in each other's mailboxes. Our relationship deteriorated further through the spring when he contracted an abdominal infection and was laid up for eight weeks. David returned to work in mid-June, just in time for the Seattle convention I had planned for his premier association.

The following month I was back in Portland, Oregon for the NIRS educational conference. Instead of my usual five-conventions-in-five-months schedule from May to September, this year I planned five conferences in only two-and-a-half months with three of them back-to-back.

Evonda, who had always kept me informed about behind-the-scenes activities at AEMG, was now reaching retirement age and surprised us by announcing her engagement to her son's widowed father-in-law. Without any retirement package at AEMG, Evonda's retirement plan was to marry well.

Losing Evonda, I now befriended Susie Tillett, our new office manager. A CPA, Susie managed the AEMG office during David's illness. Susie was well-liked by the AEMG staff and sometimes ran interference between staff members and David. On the Sunday following my return from Portland, Susie phoned me at home.

"Annie, I called to warn you," Susie began, "I went into the office today to pick up some documents, and I found a copy of a strange, four-page, hand-written memo from David addressed to you in my mailbox. I'll read it to you."

In the letter, David accused me of being drunk and insulting members at the Seattle convention among other incidents of conduct outside my normal behavior.

"That's very strange," I said. "I didn't drink at the Seattle convention because David wanted Cabernet Sauvignon and Chardonnay wines, and I don't like them, so I consciously chose not to drink at the dinner. David *has* been acting erratic lately..."

"I knew it did not sound like something you would do. But in any case, David wants us to meet with him at 10:00 a.m. in his office tomorrow. I just did not want you to arrive tomorrow morning and find this in your box without some time to think about your response."

"I really appreciate your looking out for me."

I knew Susie had taken a chance with her own job security to forewarn me about the memo, but in the five years that I had worked for David his behavior had never been as unpredictable as recently. Maybe I did not always agree with him, but at least I could follow his reasoning. I felt badly for Susie who had to administer David's decision within her CPA ethical guidelines, when she did not know herself whether he was going to be rational or not.

Reading David's letter the next morning at the office, it made even less sense. I was glad Susie had given me a day's notice so that I could act more calmly. In our meeting, I defended myself.

"I was not drunk at dinner because I did not have any wine. I don't like Cabernet or Chardonnay, so I only had iced tea." I started to wonder if David was becoming jealous of my growing relationship with the board members of his premier association. I was the group's convention coordinator, but they had made it clear that they did not want a female executive director, so David had no reason to feel threatened. But that was what my intuition was telling me was happening. David was acting paranoid, and his response to our meeting was to place me on probation.

Meanwhile, OAHIA continued with its own inner strife. In his presidential newsletter column, Jonathan Patrick admitted that, *"directed business and violations of approved rates are the biggest problems facing the health insurance law industry in Ohio. The problems existed before I became a part of the industry, and I don't have a solution."*

Rather than approach the issues head on as Henry Spaulding had attempted to do, Jonathan Patrick took a more indirect and benign approach.

"I do believe we can take steps to help with these problems through education," he told the members. Under his auspices and those of Marcia Tuttle, OAHIA developed a series of educational workshops held in Cleveland, Columbus, and Mansfield, followed by Cincinnati, Toledo, and Marietta. Both the workshops and the annual convention, which returned to the Sandpiper Suites during the summer of 1991, included an hour-long ethics session.

Being back at the Sandpiper brought back the memory of that moment in the lobby with Keir when I started to "drown" in his eyes. He did not attend the convention again, but I overhead someone say that he and Abigail were expecting a baby—their first. I don't know why, but I wondered if seeing me with Mireille at Island Point Resort had somehow motivated his interest in starting his own family. Yet, following that thought was another—why would my actions and life be of any consequence to him? Maybe after his mother died of cancer, he realized that the timing was right, or before Abigail's biological clock ran out of time, or their careers had been sufficiently developed to slow down, or—like Auguste and I did—they bought a house. I tried to push these thoughts to the back of my mind to concentrate on the work at hand, but that singular first impression lingered.

In mid-September Auguste, Mireille, and I went with my parents for a weekend at Cedar Point, meeting my older brother and his girlfriend from California to enjoy the amusement park. The next month I had a convention in Disney World.

While on a trip to Montreal in October, David Fisher telephoned our new office manager, Kathy, who had been hired to replace Susie Tillett, whom David had fired suddenly only two weeks after he put me on probation.

"Kathy, we need to schedule a six-month follow-up review with Annie about her probation when I return." Kathy, unaware that I was even on probation, came into my office. New to the office culture, Kathy had befriended me over the intervening months to help her acclimate to the office.

"I didn't know you were on probation!" she exclaimed, barging into my office. "Mr. Fisher just called me to say he wants us to schedule a follow-up review." I related to her the strange circumstances surrounding my earning the Scarlet Letter 'P', as I sarcastically called my probation.

"The whole thing is totally bogus," I told her. "I didn't do what he accused me of. He's just been acting so erratic lately."

At my performance evaluation review the next week, David Fisher took me off probation and gave me a raise. However, to keep out of each other's way, David agreed to remove me from the role of convention coordinator for his premier association. Our communication returned to normal. (Ironically, a year later, David fired Kathy.) Meanwhile, my scope of work was expanding to executive director roles solely with more national associations and fewer state associations.

OAHIA was still plagued by directed business concerns and violations of approved premium rates. The new Executive Committee, with Charles Parker as President, G. Fulton Burke as General Counsel, and Gregory Grisham as Secretary, visited Insurance Director Carson again who warned them that it was incumbent upon the industry to adhere to the filed premium rates. They also approached the issues on the state legislative front. The U.S. Supreme Court ruled that the use of a state-controlled rating bureau by a health insurer was in keeping with the Constitution. Meanwhile, an Ohio Representative in the U.S. House backed away from a proposed statutory amendment that would allow banks to sell health insurance on a national level—a potentially threatening action that would remove health insurance regulation from state insurance departments and open it up to the banking sector.

In early December, I took Mireille, now a year-and-a-half old, and Auguste on a site visit to the historic Lexington Lodge and Conference Center in Kentucky. I thought we would all enjoy the time away while visiting the historic area. On the Friday evening that we arrived, the temperature was slightly above freezing and there was a bone-chilling rain. Auguste and Mireille were both temperamental at dinner—Auguste angry that Mireille was unsettled and picky about eating, and Mireille becoming more defiant when he scolded her. I was embarrassed and relieved when we finally could pay the bill and leave the quaint restaurant.

Since we opted to walk back to our hotel, I carried Mireille and an umbrella to protect her a little from the chilling rain. Auguste insisted she wear her knit cap which she kept pulling off. She was wiggling in my arms to avoid her father who continued to shove the cap down tighter on her head. As we approached the corner, I did not notice that the brick sidewalk did not have a curb-cut, and I tripped over the curb. In an attempt to protect my baby from hitting the bricks as I lost my balance, I purposely sank straight down onto my knees and then sprawled forward, Mireille clutched to my chest, and the umbrella flying out of my hand. The pain from my knees hitting the brick surface shot up through my body like a fireworks explosion, but I was able to keep Mireille from directly hitting the ground. We both began to cry, Mireille from the shock of our sudden fall and me from the searing pain in my left knee that took the first and strongest hit.

"Take Mireille from me so that I can get up! I'm hurt," I seethed at Auguste through clenched teeth. He reached down and took the crying bundle from my arms then fetched the umbrella that had rolled away. Relieved of my child, I used my arms to push myself back up to a standing position. I tried taking a few limping steps. "I'm not sure I can walk..."

"If you hadn't been struggling with your hat," Auguste scolded Mireille, "this would not have happened! Now, let Mom put your hat on!" Auguste indicated the cap that Mireille still gripped in her hands. Silently I took it from her and slid it over her short hair. More subdued now, she did not struggle.

I took a few more steps, a little less painful than the first. In furious silence we slowly walked back to the hotel.

"I'm giving Mireille a bath and putting her to bed," I announced tersely as I took her from Auguste's arms and removed her outer garments. Gathering up her pajamas, we headed into the bathroom. At home, I had a Styrofoam knee pad to kneel on when I bathed Mireille, but here I had only the hotel bath towels that I could fold up to protect my damaged knee. In addition, the bathtub was deep, so it was even more uncomfortable for me to bathe my daughter, but I did it anyway. After she was dressed, I sat on the toilet seat and examined my knee. It was already starting to swell and look bruised.

Once I had placed Mireille in our king-sized bed, I took the plastic bag from the ice bucket and thrust it in Auguste's direction. "Get me some ice!"

He had already lain down on the sofa in the parlor and was using the remote to scan through the cable channels. Begrudgingly, he left the suite to search down the hallway for the ice machine. Meanwhile, I found a television channel in the bedroom broadcasting the cartoon *Roger Rabbit* for Mireille to watch with me. After Auguste returned with the ice and went back to the parlor to watch his adult show, I slammed the bedroom door and locked it. Auguste would be sleeping on the sofa tonight, something I had never previously forced him to do.

After a night's sleep and with the level of our vexation and animosity reduced, Auguste and I were curtly civil enough to eat breakfast in the hotel dining room together as a family and sketch out the morning's tour plan. The rain had stopped, but it was still a damp and chilly day. The throbbing in my knee had stopped and the swelling was reduced, but secretly I was worried that I might have fractured some part of my left knee cap. I did not wish to ruin our visit to Lexington by not being able to tour around the historic area, so I took a couple of aspirin and toughed out the morning. Mireille seemed subdued as well and, luckily, distracted by the sights and activities on the tour. By lunchtime, our little family had re-established an uneasy peace, and by the next day, I was able to use my left leg with the manual transmission's clutch in our car to drive back home. Upon visiting my physician on Monday, he reassured me that I had only bruised my knee but not broken anything.

With a toddler, the holiday season was full of fun events for Mireille. For Hanukkah, Auguste and I agreed to give her one gift on each of the eight nights, provided she behaved. If she did not behave, she could play "Dreidel" with me; this is a game that uses a four-sided wooden top that the player spins to win Hanukkah *gelt*—chocolate "coins" wrapped in gold paper. Any gifts she was not allowed to open we would save for Christmas Day with my parents.

We lit the Menorah candles together after dinner and then offered her the evening's gift. Mireille was also awed by our Christmas tree, her eyes as large as saucers and her hands clasped together in delight at the lights and decorations. Her daycare also had many planned holiday activities, but I was relieved she was not interested in having her photograph taken with the shopping mall Santa.

As winter melted into spring 1992, I received word that Keir and Abigail Mervais were the proud parents of a new son, Sean. I sent Keir a congratulations card. He called to thank me, his voice bursting with pride.

"We have something new in common–I'm a middle-aged parent, too!" I knew little Sean would benefit from the attention, opportunities, and educational direction available from his more financially stable and emotionally mature parents than he would have if he had been born to younger parents.

Meanwhile, I was in the throes of studying for a national certification, using every one of Mireille's naptimes to read the twenty-some books on the reading list, often succumbing myself to the lure of sweet sleep. Within ten days of our eight-and-a-half-hour written exam, I was running my first of five conventions that summer: two in the Sandusky area, one split between two hotels in Montreal, one at the enormous Opryland Hotel in Nashville, and one in Dayton. Having passed the certification exam, I also flew to Atlanta for the installation ceremony during the national convention.

In early September, I had a dentist appointment to place caps on two teeth. In order to do the work, the dentist held my mouth open for a very long time. As someone who now suffered from allergies, I often ground my teeth at night while sleeping. When annoyed, upset or stressed, I also tended to grit my teeth—especially when suppressing the desire to say what was really on my mind. At some point after that dental appointment, I started to notice a pain in my right jaw but I could not find the source—was it under my bottom teeth, coming from the jaw joint, or from the top teeth? Attempting to relieve the pain, I tried everything I could think of: shifting my lips and bottom teeth to the right, warm compresses, cold compresses, various over-the-counter pain killers, and a variety of other treatments for the constant discomfort. I finally visited an orthodontist who made a hard, plastic mold of my mouth for $250 and told me to sleep with the device for what was now diagnosed as TMJ (Temporomandibular joint disorder), a chronic inflammation of the joint that connects the jaw mandible to the skull. The device was even more uncomfortable, so I sought other medical advice—including neuromuscular therapy, acupuncture, and use of a $50 soft, generic plastic, mold for my teeth for night sleeping. Nothing seemed to help or give me relief. I learned to live with the constant, nagging pain by ignoring it as much as possible.

OAHIA's plate was as full as mine. Asked to submit an *amicus curiae* (Friend of the Court) brief in the case of <u>Attorneys Assurance and Athenaeum Health Plan v. Paramount Blue</u>, the OAHIA President, Charles Parker (who was also president of Athenaeum), recused himself, letting Vice President Marcia Tuttle preside during that portion of the February Executive Committee meeting. However, the remaining officers maintained their long-standing policy of not taking a position in a dispute among members. The Association was still conducting its regional educational workshops, maneuvering through various legislative activities, developing generic forms, supporting the Health Law Section's convention and planning OAHIA's own, and sparring with the Ohio Department of Insurance.

Smart and capable as Marcia Tuttle was, she was not an attorney herself, which gave her a distinct disadvantage as she advanced through the office ranks toward the OAHIA presidency. Her term was going to have to be shored up with dependable legal counsel from the other officers and her own boss, Fulton Burke, the man quasi-responsible for OAHIA being managed by AEMG.

To complicate matters, the OAHIA Nominating Committee selected Lawrence Hammersmith as the incoming Secretary, a brilliant yet sometimes sarcastic lawyer with Attorneys Assurance, whom Marcia had confessed to me that she disliked. Leading up to the 1992 convention and Marcia's election as President, Marcia and I discussed whom she might appoint as OAHIA's General Counsel. The pool of candidates consisted of former OAHIA presidents whose companies were not currently represented on the Executive Committee. My heart beat a little faster when Marcia agreed with my suggestion that she appoint Keir Mervais to that position.

"Keir is about our age," Marcia speculated, acknowledging her approval and observing that he might be less intimidating a personality than the senior statesmen of the industry who had previously served in the General Counsel capacity. "I'll call Keir and ask if he would be willing to serve." I crossed my fingers.

Although my suggestion of Keir as General Counsel was based upon tradition and balanced company representation, I was secretly thrilled when I learned he had accepted Marcia's appointment. To avoid being disappointed, I repeatedly reminded myself that "the little flirtation" I had imagined occurring between us previously was in the past and over. "He is just a nice man being kind to me, a pitiful, fat, 'ugh-lee' woman in a less-than-satisfactory marriage. As a new father, Keir has additional responsibilities as well as the desire to build his career. Besides, we've not seen each other for three years."

Having moved out of the Grandview Heights-Goodale Street area of Columbus in December 1989, AEMG had traded its skyscraper offices for a suburban location in Upper Arlington with free parking and an A-rated suite of offices, complete with baby grand piano in the center of the marble-floored, a two-story atrium lobby, and central bronze elevators set in mahogany paneling.

For her first meeting as OAHIA President, Marcia Tuttle took her seat at the head of the conference room table in the AEMG offices. Our second-floor conference room had one wall of floor-to-ceiling windows overlooking the landscaped and curving front drive and the four-lane street beyond. I sat on Marcia's left, facing the windows, prepared with my legal pad and my file of meeting documents.

One-by-one the remainder of the officers arrived and took their seats around the table: Treasurer Gregory Grisham, Vice President Patricia Rosewood, Secretary Larry Hammersmith, Past President Chuck Parker, and Health Law Section Representative Deborah Paul Sayres. The seat to Marcia's right and the one to my left were still vacant.

Traveling the farthest and from Ohio's largest population center, Keir arrived a few minutes late for the ten o'clock start. All my self-admonitions dissolved as he entered the conference room door at the far end of the room, and my heart did a somersault in my chest.

"It's *not* over," the little voice in my head declared as I quickly turned my head and lowered my eyes to my legal pad to take minutes. "He will likely sit on the other side of the table at Marcia's right hand," the voice rationalized.

Keir swiftly scanned the available vacant seats, then, making the least disruption as possible, walked over to sit down in the empty chair next to me. "Maybe he does not know any of the other officers that well and just feels more comfortable next to someone he knows," the rationalizing voice continued. (At the time, I was totally unaware that Keir and Larry had been law school classmates and both had been private practicing attorneys along with Greg Grisham in Akron before all three had gone to work for the legal departments in different health insurance companies.)

Throughout the meeting, I struggled to keep from being distracted by Keir's presence next to me. In contrast to when I first joined OAHIA, the Association now had over $25,000 in reserves and had used some of those funds to pay its new lobbyist, Kevin Bodwell. The officers spent a good portion of the meeting discussing the 1993 proposed budget, dues, committee appointments, regional seminars, the newsletter, legislative activities, new forms development and the convention program. It was close to three o'clock when we adjourned.

"Would you like to see photos of my son, Sean?" Keir asked, pulling out his wallet.

"Of course!" I leaned on the left arm of my chair to get a closer look at the adorable, blue-eyed baby. In turn, I pulled out a day-care photograph of three-year old Mireille. After exchanging the appropriate oohs and aahs, we returned the pictures to our respective wallets. The remainder of the OAHIA officers had already left the conference room to return to their homes or offices.

"Before you leave, I'd like you to meet OAHIA's new staff assistant, Sylvia. Evonda left AEMG when she remarried," I explained as Keir gathered his papers into his briefcase. "Sylvia was hired by David Fisher to run a travel agency subsidiary of AEMG, earning commissions by booking travel for association client board members, convention speakers, and staff, as well as from hotel bookings. For a while, Evonda had assisted Sylvia with the agency part-time while still helping me on OAHIA and another client. When Evonda left, a full-time travel agent was hired, and Sylvia took on Evonda's duties as my part-time assistant while still managing the travel agency."

Although Sylvia had attended the 1992 annual convention at the Cedar Palace Hotel with me where she had already met the other OAHIA Executive Committee members, Keir had not been there. Together, we walked into the adjacent office serving as the travel agency.

"Sylvia, excuse me, but I wanted to introduce you to Keir Mervais, OAHIA's General Counsel and a former President." Sylvia and Keir shook hands and exchanged pleasantries for a moment. Then I turned to address Keir.

"We usually don't encourage our association members to cut through the travel agency to exit from the conference room to the outside hallway and elevators, but since you are already here, the most direct route out is through this door." I pointed to the travel agency entrance. One could clearly see the second floor atrium balcony through the agency's office windows overlooking the atrium. I led Keir out through the door and to the elevator bank where I pushed the button.

"I hope you have a safe trip back to Cleveland."

"Thank you," replied Keir as he stepped to the back of the elevator and smiled at me. As the brass doors slid closed, I turned and walked back to the conference room to clean up. Suddenly, I was aware of the pain in my jaw again.

Druk Thul—Land of the Thunder Dragon (Bhutan)

c. 1650 C.E.

I watched the tiny speck of a man grow steadily larger as he climbed the mountain path towards our village. We were isolated in our highland valley, nestled among the terraced fields in the shadow of the mountains, so strangers were a rare cause for celebration. I wanted to run to tell my parents of his approach, but for some reason, his mere appearance forced me to stand my ground, and I could not move.

He became larger and closer until he was near enough to be heard.

"Where are your parents, girl?" he asked, a little out of breath in the thin Himalayan air.

He was dressed in the traditional Bhutanese garb of a *gho* – a large-sleeved, knee-length tunic that was tied around his waist with a *kera* belt and close-fitting trousers with felt boots. Over his left shoulder was a *kabne*, or sash. His bald head had begun to sprout a day or two's growth, and his face was beginning to show the creases of middle age and the effects of squinting in the bright sun.

The stranger did not seem threatening or unkind, but he seemed to be traveling on some official business. Without saying a word, I turned and led him toward our family's hut.

Our home was a humble structure of three floors constructed of whitewashed mud walls standing on stilts. The outside walls were decorated with animals and spiritual folk symbols in fading paint. Large rocks held down the wooden roof shingles. Inside, the hay-covered ground floor stabled our mountain goats, chickens, and sheep. From there, a ladder rose to a heavy wooden door that opened onto the second floor where our family ate and slept around the central charcoal fire pit. Narrow slits in the walls were shuttered to keep out the cold and rain or let in the bright Himalayan light. On the third floor, wooden barrels, leather boxes tied with ropes, and gourds filled the crawl space under the eaves.

My mother was weaving on her loom when the stranger and I entered. She immediately rose in a flurry, bowed low out of respect to the man, and offered him *seudja*, a tea flavored with salt and yak butter, and *churpi*, snack cubes of yak cheese. After settling him in front of the fire, my mother stepped outside to whistle for my father who was in the rice fields, then returned to serve our guest.

From the shadows, I studied the stranger, trying to guess the nature of his visit. He seemed in no hurry while he sipped his beverage and contemplated the fire. Of medium height, he was squarely built, with dark, almond-shaped eyes deeply set above high cheekbones.

"*Lyonpo*, we are honored by your presence," said my father to the government official, as soon as he had crossed the threshold, bowing in his turn.

As customary, our guest handed a white scarf to my father who refused it. The giving of a white scarf meant an important event, so now my curiosity grew.

I watched my father talk with our visitor. At first they made polite comments about the man's trip on foot, the weather, and the crops. Another gift was offered which my father firmly refused. The conversation now turned to life in the capital, government, and religion. While the men spoke, my mother prepared our dinner of *bjashamaru*—a chicken stew flavored with garlic butter, and *daal-baat*, rice and lentils flavored with curry, chilies, and pickles. The meal was served with warm barley beer, *bangchang*, which my father offered in an unusual mood of generosity.

"*Zhé, zhé*—drink up, drink up," he kept saying.

The men talked well into the night. At some point, between the drone of the low voices, the warmth of the fire, and the numbing sensation of the *bangchang*, I feel asleep.

At dawn, our household began to stir as my mother prepared the *zheng-chang*, our morning elixir, to warm and wake us in the bracing cold of the early morning.

Our guest arose and was greeted by my parents. This time, I realized the topic of conversation was me.

"Jamtsho, Jamtsho." My mother roused me. "You are going away with the Lyonpo," she told me. "You will need to pack your things and take some food for the journey."

I shook the fog of sleep from my head. I thought it was strange that I would be selected to escort this man, since he appeared to have arrived on his own without guidance.

"Hurry," my mother ordered as she placed a bowl of boiled bulgur before me with the *zheng-chang*. As I ate, she placed *momos*, steamed cheese dumplings, and *shabalays*, fried mincemeat turnovers, in a yak-skin sack.

When the Lyonpo and I had eaten, he took the white scarf out of his *gho* and again presented it to my father who accepted it this time with grace and a deep bow.

"We will leave now," the Lyonpo announced. My mother gave me the yak sack of food and my father handed me a rucksack with a blanket and change of clothes. Without another word, my parents hugged me, and the visitor walked back over the threshold as easily as he had come. He began walking in the direction from which he had arrived.

100

I followed him out the door and was almost blinded by the early sunlight raining down from a stunning blue sky and ricocheting off the immaculate whiteness of the snow-covered Himalayan peaks that surrounded our alpine valley village. My head throbbed from too much *bangchang* and the sharp intensity of the light and altitude. I turned around just in time to see my parents disappear behind the closing door to our home. Then I ran to catch up with the man who was already descending the rock-strewn mountain path.

When I caught up to him at his side, he turned to me and asked, "Your name is Jamtsho, is it not?" I nodded in assent.

"Do you know where we are going?" I panicked and stared dumbly up at him. Had I missed some important directional instruction from my parents? "We are going to Paro." At least he had knowledge of our ultimate destination.

The Lyonpo strode along the path with determination. As I trotted along beside him, trying to keep pace in my bare feet, he explained the purpose of our travels together.

"We are going to the capital city where you will be indentured to the governor's administrative household and have the opportunity to gain more education and be more useful than you would be staying in your village. You will learn from the monks so that you will have a better life and not be a drain on your parents' limited resources."

My pace slowed. Although first excited about this new adventure, I now realized my carefree life in the village as I had known it was over forever. As a nine-year-old girl, I was expendable to my family. A lump rose in my throat in the knowledge that my parents had sent me away, and I might never see them again. I stopped walking. Hot tears rolled down my cheeks. I would now be expected to obey and work for people I had never met in a place I had never known.

Up ahead, the Lyonpo stopped and turned around. "Come along now, Jamtsho. We have far to go."

Reluctantly, I walked toward him. Turning back in the direction of Paro, we fell into step again.

As we descended from our alpine village down the stony path bordered by red and purple primroses emerging from the melting snow, I became interested in the new vegetation around me. Bright, sunlit fields of golden buttercups and lilies dancing with butterflies alternated with cool, dark forests of shiny oaks and maples, slippery rocks, and fallen tree limbs. Some trees had bright red flowers and others large, white, magnolia blossoms. Inside the forests were rhododendrons of pink, purple, and white blooms. The ground was covered with small, round, fallen fruits. Alongside the now, almost imperceptible moss-covered path, were fan-shaped, feathery ferns in full bloom or still in fiddle heads.

101

Above me I heard the squawking of a crow with black, velvet-like feathers and a gray band around its neck. The crow darted and glided through the trees as though he was taunting us to play.

Around midday, we reached a clearing with some rocks. Here my guide stopped to sit and indicated we should eat. In the near distance, I could hear the rush and gurgle of a mountain stream coursing its way over boulders and felt the dampness rising from the forest floor.

We rested our legs and ate our turnovers in silence. I had so many questions in my mind: How much longer would we need to walk? What would it be like when I got there? What would I be doing? Where would I sleep? Who would become my friend? But, the demeanor of my traveling companion seemed to forbid me from expressing my innermost thoughts out loud.

After taking a few moments to urinate, we continued our trek downward.

Suddenly, the moist, dark forest that had felt like a quiet enclosure opened to a dizzying gorge that dropped down to a roar of water below. In front of us a long rope-and-plank bridge precariously spanned the gash between the mountains. I must have gasped with surprise because the Lyonpo grasped my hand firmly and pulled me onto the bridge behind him.

As we threaded our way across the swaying lifeline of a bridge, I was torn among closing my eyes, staring determinedly ahead, and the natural draw to look downwards at the dazzling yet crushing scene below. Above us, the stark blue of the sky seemed to create a curving sensation of a dome. The claustrophobic effect was enhanced further by the sharply-pointed snow-covered peaks just visible in the distance above the never-ending greenery of the trees.

Eventually we walked out of the gorge, leaving the turquoise and white surge of the river behind us, and plunged back into the dark, cool forest. After a couple more hours of walking, we emerged into the full sunlight again. The light seemed to scorch my skin and the humid air made it more difficult to breathe. Here, the fields of flowers were a riot of colors that seemed to shimmer in the afternoon heat. Butterflies and birds in all sorts of color combinations—gold and red, black and turquoise, green and maroon, bright blue and yellow—flitted and darted among the bushes with star-like leaves. A little further away, umbrella trees held blossoms that looked like flames. Gray langur monkeys swung through a grove of banana trees heavy with stalks of green and yellow fruit and played a game of hide-and-seek.

Occasionally my escort would point out an animal, bird, or plant to tell me what it was, but mostly we marched along in silence. He appeared to be in a graceful, meditative state while my head was on a swivel trying to take in and experience all the wonders around me, while eagerly anticipating what might be around the next bend in the path.

On our journey, we walked uphill and downhill along twisted, gnarled paths that had been deeply rutted by packs of mules or yaks or along narrow ridges subject to landslides. We also passed through hamlets of two or three homes and villages of several houses and a central marketplace. Everywhere we traveled, we felt the unrelenting and towering presence of the snow-capped, conical mountains that pierced the overarching, extraordinarily blue sky.

As the sunset splashed peach, fuscia, gold, and light green colors across the sky, we came to a house shaded by a citrus tree hung with large, round fruit. The family welcomed the Lyonpo as my parents had. After several offers of gifts, the head of the household took what was offered in exchange for a supper of *emadatse* and *sip*, a combination of melted cheese and hot, green chilies served on flattened rice cakes and washed down with cider. Within moments of placing my head down on the straw pallet and covering myself with my blanket, I was fast asleep.

The next morning, the Lyonpo shook me awake. After a brief breakfast of eggs cooked in butter and some tea, we were again on our journey. This time, as we traveled along a clay track, we followed the river. As the sky reversed its sunset color scheme to one of dawn—magenta to pink to peach to yellow, green, and blue—we started to ascend again.

As we reached each plateau and the day became hotter, we found that the top of each climb only revealed another incline to mount. At about mid-morning we suddenly veered to the river's edge where my traveling companion knelt down and splashed himself with water and took a long drink, and instructed me to do the same. As I drank and splashed, the chill of the water relieved my burnt skin and parched throat. He filled a yak stomach pouch with water.

We fell into a rhythm of walking together. It was about all I could do to keep up with his adult strides, so the absence of conversation did not bother me. There were too many sights, sounds, and sensations for me to absorb without trying to talk as well. The overstimulation kept me trudging alongside the government minister instead of collapsing from exhaustion.

Just when I thought I was going to faint from heat and fatigue, we again ascended into a mossy, emerald sanctuary of fir trees and dense, gnarled oaks. We passed waterfalls tumbling into frothy white whirlpools. The forest was alive with the sounds of cicada, chirping birds, and the scurrying of small animals. Near nightfall we found a clearing with an outcropping of rocks under which we took some cover. The Lyonpo built a small fire. We ate our dumplings in silence, and again I quickly fell asleep.

Sometime during the middle of the night, the skies opened up and a torrential wall of rain descended in a waterfall over our small, rocky roof that only provided modest protection. I snuggled closer to the Lyonpo's back and fell asleep again to the pouring sound.

When I awoke, our world seemed shrouded with a foggy white mist making the world appear surreal. The man grabbed me roughly and pulled off my now-drenched *kira*. With a stick tipped with a red ember, the Lyonpo burned the leeches off my body and did the same to himself. He withdrew the change of clothes from my *jhola* rucksack and handed them to me while he, too, replaced his soggy *gho* and trousers with other ones only slightly less damp. He handed me a piece of citrus fruit from our previous night's hosts, and we began to walk again.

As the day wore on, the mist slowly lifted. We could see further in front of us, and I marveled that my companion seemed to know the way through the woods. Abruptly the forest opened up, and below, as far as the eye could see to the mountain's edge, was a lush green vista sloping into a deep valley dotted by miniature buildings.

"Before we arrive in the Wong Valley and then onto our destination of Paro," my escort said, "we will stop for lunch at the Punakha Dzong monastery."

We continued our trek down the curving, clay road through fields of sun-bleached grass and undulating terraces of crops, past large white or yellow houses trimmed with dark wooden beams and decorated with stenciled symbols and images. The path forked, and we continued upward toward the monastery. All along our journey, we had seen white strips of prayer flags along the route and the occasional *chorten*, small reminders of the Buddha. However, this time we began to see multi-colored prayer flags--blue, green, red, yellow, and white--announcing our approach to the holy site.

After a couple of hours of walking, we arrived at a carved wooden, cantilever bridge covered with a shingle roof that stretched over an icy blue river, the Puma Tsangchu. Sitting on an embankment above the bridge was the imposing monastery with its high, white-washed, stone walls gradually tapering inward at the top. The building was crowned with a crimson band of roof supports where the walls were also pierced with narrow windows beneath an overhanging, shingled roof.

We passed through the stone gates of the *dzong* (fortress), past massive wooden doors painted with deities. The trapezoidal shape of each wall provided an even more imposing impression of strength and impenetrability. Once inside, we entered a stone courtyard. At the opposite end, a huge watchtower arose skyward. Painted and decorated wooden galleries and balconies supported by pillars hung from the second floor. To one side of the courtyard, a group of crimson-garbed monks sat cross-legged in three rows.

One of the monks rose and came to greet us, bowing to the Lyonpo and indicating that we should follow him. We entered a long room with row upon row of wooden benches and tables. At one end of one table there were two bowls set across from each other. The Lyonpo sat on one side before a bowl and pointed to the other side for me to sit. The monk disappeared through a door while I looked around the dining hall with wonder.

The ceiling rose twenty-five feet above our heads, supported by massive wooden beams. The whitewashed walls were frescoed with both benevolent and evil-looking figures, animals, clouds, and other natural objects and designs.

Soon the monk returned with a large, steaming bowl of noodles, pork, and spinach, which he ladled into each of our bowls. We ate while I continued to gaze at my surroundings.

After eating, the monk and my companion spoke for a while. Warmed with a full belly and lulled by the murmur of the men's voices, I stretched out on the bench and fell fast asleep. The next thing I knew, the Lyonpo was shaking me awake, and we exited the dining hall, back to the courtyard and through the dzong gates. Crossing the cantilever bridge and returning to the winding path, we passed through more villages of yellow-tinted houses of stone and wood. We traversed rice paddies occasionally shaded by large, fragrant, eucalyptus trees. We crossed small footbridges spanning rivers. And, as the sun began to set, we were welcomed into a small family farm where we spent the night.

Our journey began again as usual the next morning, but this time the clay road seemed to flatten, and we saw more travelers heading in our direction or going the opposite way. As the sunlight rose over the crests of the surrounding mountain peaks, the golden mist dissipated and the wispy trails of haze melted away.

By mid-morning, as we wound our way through the increasing throng, the footpath widened for a while. We crossed over another bridge and then our route converged into narrow, crooked streets made of stones. Here, the street was filled with primitive stalls displaying boots of chewed yak leather, corn husk flour, bins of charcoal, wool sweaters and caps, and hand-loomed rugs. Merchants hawked their wares. A man was seated dipping pan leaves into a green paste while a woman arranged sweet potatoes and corn in bushel baskets. At another stall, green and red chilies hung to dry, and at another, rice beer and other warm drinks were offered for sale. Animals and children ran in the streets.

I stayed close to the Lyonpo, afraid of losing sight of my protector and guide—the only person I knew, fascinated with the completely unfamiliar scene and hubbub around me.

105

We passed through a courtyard where water streamed out of pipe holes. People were washing themselves and their clothes or fetching water for cooking or drinking. Three-storied buildings with intricately carved balconies lined the crooked streets and rose overhead.

As we wound our way upward, we walked through another market area where the shops encircled a huge prayer wheel holding metal cylinders inscribed with mantras—prayers to be chanted as the wheels are spun clockwise. Religious men, holding prayer beads, cards, or dice, told fortunes to the faithful. We stopped for a few moments to observe a group of men and women chanting and slowly moving in a circle, alternately raising and lowering their arms. Horns, cymbals, and bells accompanied their prayers. The rhythm of their song changed unpredictably with the melody soaring and then dropping abruptly in a melancholy manner.

Continuing on, we turned a corner, finding a huge stone staircase before us. My eyes rose following its ascent and were met with the stark whiteness of the Paro Dzong thrusting skyward. All alongside the narrow walls of the staircase were poles holding prayer flags snapping in the wind. We began to mount the stairs.

The white walls seemed to pulsate in the sun, and the heat and height pressed down on me, making me dizzy. When we reached the top of our climb two guards dressed in navy *ghos* similar to that of the Lyonpo, pulled open the heavy wooden gates and allowed us to enter.

We crossed an open courtyard of cobbled stones and entered a dark, cool hallway to the left. Wooden balconies lined the corridor above where we could see young monks looking down on us. Halfway down the hall, we stopped in front of a door with a wooden sign carved with gold letters. The Lyonpo knocked. A monk opened the door and ushered us inside where we sat on a bench along the wall. We were offered tea and sweet wafers.

Some moments later, the door to an inner chamber opened. My companion rose, pulled me to my feet, and we entered the room.

Rising from his seat behind a stark wooden desk, another man in a black *gho* with a red sash across his chest rose and bowed slightly to the Lyonpo who returned the bow more deeply.

"Welcome," the other man said. "I hope your journey went well?"

"Yes, we were blessed." The Lyonpo turned to me. "This is the *Dzongda,* the secular district administrator of the dzong fortress and right-hand to the *Penlop,* the provincial governor of the Valley. You may address him as *Dasho* or 'sir'." Facing the Dzongda again, he said, "And this is Jamtsho."

For the first time, I looked at our host who had turned his focus to me. His strong, square face was kind, yet handsome. The

Dzongda appeared to be younger than my escort, but his intense eyes were intelligent and warm. I suddenly felt safer than I ever had before. I noticed his expressive hands, his high cheekbones, and pleasantly shaped mouth. I was so intent in studying him, I paid no attention to my surroundings, and seemed to absorb his question to me through my skin rather than actually hear it.

"Have you enjoyed your trek?" the Dzongda asked gently. "Are you ready to stay here and assist me with my duties?"

I nodded my head. His lips parted in a brilliant smile. My knees almost buckled beneath me. I knew I would do whatever he asked of me.

The Lyonpo turned to me, bowed in farewell, and was escorted out the door by the monk, who returned a moment later. The Dzongda sat down behind his desk and pulled out some papers. Removing his attention from me had the effect of the sun being eclipsed. The monk took me by the shoulder and turned me toward the door. Without raising his head from his work, the Dzongda said, "We will begin your lessons tomorrow." His voice had the effect of warm liquid pouring through my veins.

"Yes, Dasho," I whispered and exited with the monk. He led me down two long corridors to a small, stark cell with a high, narrow window, a straw pallet for a bed, a woven blanket, and a small metal brazier with glowing coal embers. A clean woven *kira* and a yellow robe lay atop the blanket. On a small table a bowl with water and another bowl with steamed dumplings rested. The monk left, closing the wooden door behind him. I heard the metal latch secured. I devoured the dumplings stuffed with minced meat and cheese and garnished with chili sauce. My stomach filled, I changed into the saffron robe and slid beneath the blanket into a deep slumber. One journey had ended, and another was about to begin.

I awoke the next morning to the sound of the metal bolt sliding open. The monk handed me a brass bowl of pinkish-brown, cooked rice mixed with egg and a cup of *seudja* tea. He stood, waiting while I ate and washed my hands and face, and then led me back to the Dzongda's office where the deputy governor was already bent over his desk in deep thought. The monk indicated I should sit on the bench facing the deputy governor's desk and then left the room.

After a short wait, the Dzongda looked up and smiled at me.

"Good morning! Did you sleep well?" he asked. I jumped up from my seat to bow and then stood, nodding my head.

"Yes." I could not say more. I was too happy to have the direct attention of such an important adult.

The Dzongda came out from behind his desk and reached out his hand for mine. When his hand encircled mine, a small charge like lightening resulted from our touch. We left his office, and I began to skip as we headed down the hallway together. For a few moments, he allowed me my childish and whimsical action but then, after stifling a small grin, he placed his other hand gently on my shoulder to settle me down into a walk as we saw another minister coming towards us from the far end of the corridor.

I was pleased to have this new friend so different from the stoic Lyonpo. I felt a warm familiarity with the Dzongda as if we had known each other our whole lives.

Turning a corner, we mounted a flight of thick, steep, planked stairs, walked down a shorter hallway, and turned into a small chapel, elaborately decorated with frescoes, carved pillars, butter lamps, and an altar adored with brass objects. Above the altar was a large, nude sculpture seated cross-legged and surrounded by a jewel-encrusted halo. On the altar were offering bowls of water, fruit, and rice.

"His Holiness, the Buddha." Dasho pointed to the statue dominating the altar. Seating himself cross-legged on a small pillow on the floor facing the altar, the Dzongda indicated that I should sit down next to him on another pillow to his left. Next, he pressed the palms of his hands together, his fingers pointing upwards. He closed his eyes and bowed his head slightly. I copied his movements. I knew I wanted to please him. We stayed in that pose for a long time. Occasionally, I opened my right eye to check that he was still in that same position next to me.

Finally, I heard him stir and stand. I stood and followed him outside of the chapel. We turned the opposite way down the hallway from where we came. As we passed various official-looking adults in dark robes, the *Dzongda* nodded and greeted them with equanimity. I was so busy looking around me that I did not realize for a moment that my escort had stopped at a door.

We entered a cool, dark chamber with cushions on the floor and decorated walls. Again, the Dzongda pointed at one cushion for me to sit as he seated himself on another. Looking at me for a moment to evaluate me and to collect his thoughts, I sensed that what was about to transpire would be important, and I waited with anticipation.

"Do you know why you were brought here?" he began. I shook my head. He looked down at the floor as though organizing his thoughts.

"Do you know where we are?" Again, I shook my head.

"You were brought from your mountain village and parental home to the regional capital of Paro, to this dzong, a fortress that serves as the seat of the provincial government and a monastery. As the Dzongda, I am responsible for administration of this province, the fort, and all non-religious activities of the monastery. From time to time, we select a few young people from the villages to study and work here. Most of the time they are young boys who enter our midst, but we learned about you from someone who was concerned that your parents might soon be unable to support you. The idea of training a young girl fascinated me, so I sent the Lyonpo to fetch you."

As he paused, his eyes studied me to see how much of this I understood. I smiled. He appeared satisfied and continued.

"While you are here—under my protection, tutelage, and supervision—you will be both learning and working. You will be asked to do tasks of which you are capable and you will be trained to perform administrative tasks and, also receive religious instruction." He hesitated, his forehead creasing a little. "If at any time, you feel endangered in any manner or worried about anyone's behavior here toward you, including mine, please tell me immediately. You will not be punished."

I nodded even though I did not comprehend entirely what he meant.

"I have been treated nicely," I said in a hushed voice. His face relaxed into a smile.

"I am glad to hear that. Hopefully, it will continue that way, but do not hesitate to tell me." He gathered himself up off the cushion, and I followed suit. "Tomorrow we will begin your lessons. But for now, we will go into the garden for a walking meditation."

After another walk through the maze of corridors of the dzong, we entered a magical place: a square stone enclosure, roofed only by the cerulean blue of the sky. This garden could only be entered from inside the dzong. A covered, wooden colonnade ran around the perimeter, while two perpendicular pathways crossed in the middle of the central open space, dividing it into quarters. Each quarter section was filled with jewel-like flowers in shades of lavender, grape, yellow, crimson, and white hanging from outstretched branches. The Dzongda noticed my awestruck countenance and moved his hand in a vague arc.

"Orchids."

Placing both arms behind his back, the Dasho began his circumambulation around the edge of the garden. I followed him, respectful of his purposeful silence while enchanted by the varieties of uniquely shaped flowers decorating the sacred space. I stopped to admire a particular cluster of orchids when I was surprised to hear his gentle voice from behind me.

"Just as these blossoms grow from a small seed, sprout blooms, and die, so do we people. Everything has a cycle; nothing stays the same. A few days ago, you were a village girl in the mountains. Today you are in a monastic garden inside Paro's dzong. What makes us happy in one moment—the beauty of a bloom—can make us sad when it shrivels and dies. It is the nature of life that things change, but as humans we try to hold onto them too long, and this is what causes us pain. By letting go of what we love, we can more fully embrace it during the moments we are with it. It is a contradiction, a paradox, that by letting go, we can more fully have it. This is your first lesson. Now we must go as there is much work to do inside." He turned and walked toward the entrance, slipping back into the dark hallway. I scurried to catch up.

We spent the rest of the day working on the civic affairs of the dzong. I took messages to people and brought the Dzongda water and small portions of food. I rolled up scrolls and stacked them, and I stood quietly in the corner while he consulted with various officials.

I noticed the Dzongda never became upset or angry but remained serenely calm with all his interactions. He was sympathetic and understanding of the issues people brought before him, and they always left more happy or delighted than when they entered.

At the end of the day, the Dzongda once again focused his full attention on me. It felt like morning sunlight breaking over the mountain tops.

"Do you remember how to return to your room from here?" he asked. I had a moment of panic as I realized that I had forgotten but did not wish to displease my master. I shook my head once.

"Then someone will have to take you there. Pay particular attention to the route you take so that you can come back here tomorrow morning on your own. Your supper will be waiting for you in your room. Goodnight."

He went outside to the anti-chamber to instruct one of the monks to accompany me back to my room, then left. I felt as if the sun had gone behind a dark cloud. I followed the monk, noting our turns and the hallway décor that could serve as my guideposts.

Once alone again in my starkly furnished cell, I ate my simple supper then fell asleep.

As dawn light entered the high, small window, illuminating my room, and I heard people stirring in the outside corridor, I woke from my deep and dreamless sleep. I remembered where I was, and especially that I would again go to the office of the Dzongda to be with him.

There was a slight tap on my room door, and a servant entered wordlessly with my early meal on a tray, then left.

After eating my breakfast and dressing, I emerged into the hallway to retrace my steps back to the Dzongda whom I found already at his desk working. I entered quietly but he looked up at me, and his smile brightened the room. His eyes were uncommonly clear with a slight note of amusement.

"Did you sleep well?" he asked. I eagerly nodded. He then stood up, and we went to the same chapel where we had gone the day before and resumed our prayerful positions. However, today we did not leave after the prayer session. Instead, the Dzongda pointed to the altar statue.

"The Enlightened One," he pronounced, "who brought us the Four Noble Truths. As people, we experience much suffering: childbirth, hunger, cold, and painful wounds. We suffer because we wish to hold onto the temporary pleasures in life—food, people, animals, a beautiful day, a flower. The true nature of things is that they do not last. It is our ignorance and illusion that anything is fixed in time and space. It is out of our ignorance and our denial that we believe what we see and feel is permanent, that we all seek to grasp and hold onto to that with which we form attachments. This is Samsara.

"There are, however, eight principles to help us let go of our attachments and eventually put an end to our suffering. I will teach you each of these as we go along, but, in essence, not hurting others, and being kind, gentle, compassionate, patient, and peaceful are at the heart of them. Any unkindness or kindness that we do creates ripples far out into the world and then back to us in another form."

I listened, absorbed in both his words and his demeanor, trying to pattern myself after his goodness, but the lesson was soon ended. We left the classroom and ventured back into the meditation garden, eventually retracing our steps to begin the daily administrative duties.

Each day fell into a similar pattern of lessons, meditative walks, and work. I came to cherish those lessons and our time alone in the garden. After a while, the Dzongda would question me, testing whether the learning was taking effect. Sometimes he would praise me for my learning or how I did a particular task. I hungered for those moments akin to rays of golden light from the heavens.

"Tomorrow we will take a journey," the Dzongda announced one day at the end of our lesson. "We will travel to a temple near the Phobjikha Dzong in the Tongsa region. We have official business there. I think it would be good for you to visit another temple. It will require a long walk similar to the one you took with the Lyonpo, but not as far. We will end our duties earlier today so that we can rest for our journey."

I was both excited at the prospect of being alone with the Dzongda for an elongated period of time, but also anxious that the purpose of the trip might be to send me to live at the other dzong. I dared not mention my fear to the Dzongda in order not to appear ungrateful. However, I watched him even more closely than usual for signs that would indicate that I was about to be transferred. I could not find any, but I spent a restless night.

We went again to the chapel that morning, but instead of a lesson, the Dzongda explained that he placed offerings on the altar

111

for a successful journey. We then gathered food and bedrolls for our trip that we fastened to our backs. We descended the long, stone steps to the marketplace and wound our way through the streets toward the river, crossing the wooden bridge where I first entered the city.

We turned and walked on a dirt track along the ice-blue river as it splashed over large, smooth rocks. Our path was lined with large, shady trees. In the distance, I again saw curving terraces planted with rice, corn, and other crops. Smaller footpaths curved toward wooden houses on stilts—some white with dark wooden trim, others made of yellow stucco and stone. Beyond the terraces arose steep hills covered in thick forests of maple, cypress, and fir. Farther away, the mountains rose and rose again—black, jagged peaks with shimmering, snow-capped summits. Dotting the hills were long poles with white prayer flags floating in the wind.

Just the sight of the mountains, reminding me suddenly of home, quickened my heartbeat. I was soon skipping alongside the Dzongda who trekked onward with a steady gait. This time, however, he did not still my girlish display.

About mid-morning we entered a bamboo forest and a while later ascended into a higher forest where large oaks and towering cypress shielded us from the noonday sun. The cool, humid forest floor was covered with chestnut-like fruit and ferns. We stopped to eat beside a waterfall. The Dzongda again took up my lessons.

"The self is not permanent. There are no individuals, and we are not separate entities from anything else. It is just an illusion that you are there and I am here. Who we are is a matter of experiences, circumstances, faculties, and conditions that, at the moment of death, break down and all that remains is the *karma* of that life which helps determine the condition of the next. That is why karma is so important.

"The Buddha gave us these simple rules for living: never act thoughtlessly or carelessly; be sympathetic and helpful to all living things; do no harm, do not steal, and do not kill; be generous and kind to others; take only what you need—no more; and, do not lie or say unkind things about others. Following these rules will help you increase the good *karma* in the universe."

As we began walking again, I thought about what the Dzongda had said. It was not so much what he had said, but that there seemed to be a certain urgency or expediency behind what he was telling me—as if this journey was a concentrated lesson and that we no longer had the leisure of our special time in the chapel or garden. I again began to worry that I was being transferred to the next location, and the Dzongda was trying to teach me everything I needed to know before we arrived.

On the third day of our trip, we awoke to a thick mist clinging to our surroundings. The path was rocky, slippery, and muddy, and the air was cool, dank, and dark. As we slowly wound our way, the thick sunshine began to dissolve the fog and, suddenly the woodland opened onto a bright, golden meadow, dancing with butterflies.

The somewhat gloomy mood of the morning gave way to one of delight. I looked over at the Dzongda to see him smiling brilliantly. It was genuinely good to see him smile again that way. I so loved his company that I never wanted the moment to end. I thought my heart would burst with happiness.

A short while later, partially secluded in a grove of trees, we saw a small temple, its gold-and-red decoration glinting in the sunlight. Large, golden prayer wheels lined the path to the temple.

"Each cylinder holds a mile of prayers that are sent out to the heavens with each rotation of the wheel while the devotees recite mantras and prayers, adding to their karmic merit and invoking higher powers." The Dzongda stopped and showed me the proper manner to use the prayer wheel.

Once our devotion was complete, the Dzongda lead me onto the portico of the small temple, between two ornately decorated red columns, supporting a slanting roof. The entrance was a carved, wooden door, painted in gold-and-black. The Dzongda grasped the vertical cylindrical door handle and pulled the door outward to the left, allowing me to enter the dark room. The coolness was refreshing after the hot sun outside.

In the center of the floor were two black satin cushions. By habit, I sat down on one; however, my master remained standing. I glanced around and saw the usual altar adornments and requisite statue of Buddha. A door to the left of the altar opened, and a small man in a dark robe entered silently and sat on the cushion opposite me. The Dzongda withdrew behind me. Experiencing a momentary rise of panic, I wondered if my care had just been shifted to this strange little man who, with his eyes closed, was rapidly reciting prayers. After moments that resembled an eternity to me spent fighting the urge to run after the Dzongda, the caretaker monk focused his attention on me. He placed his right arm into the wide left sleeve of his robe and withdrew a glass-like tube encased in gold metal tendrils. Inside the cylinder was a rolled parchment.

The monk handed the scroll to me, and I sensed that I was not to worry. I was not even aware of him saying the words or telling me why he was giving me this scroll; he imparted this knowledge directly into my mind.

The monk then rose from his cushion, motioning me to do the same. He pointed towards the door with an outstretched hand, and I turned to go, looking back over my shoulder once to be sure I had not misunderstood. But the monk had disappeared behind the altar again. I pushed open the heavy door and walked out into the bright sunshine.

The Dzongda was waiting outside for me. Relieved he was still there, I ran to him and slung my arms around his waist. He hugged my shoulders in return with one arm and patted the back of my head with his other hand, appearing almost as relieved as I was.

"Now we will go back home," he said. "Do you want me to carry that for you?" I had forgotten I was still holding the scroll. I looked down at the object in my hand and then handed it to him with a smile, grateful not to have to carry the delicate object.

"Thank you, Dasho."

He tucked it inside where his *gho* was tied. Then he took my hand in his, and we began retracing our route back to Paro.

I remembered what he told me about everything being connected, and through our hands, our arms, our shoulders, and the rest of our bodies, I felt the connection, that indescribable peaceful oneness, that perfect love which I thought he had meant. For a long time, we did not talk; we were content.

The return trip seemed to pass more quickly than the original journey. As we neared a rest stop, we noticed some travelers ahead—a woman and her son. The woman appeared to be in some distress and signaled us urgently. We hurried until we were much closer. The boy had dropped to the ground, doubled over and writhing in pain.

"Stay where you are," the Dzongda said, as he hurried to the boy's side, and dropped to his knees. The woman also bent over the boy. For a few moments more the boy trembled then he shuddered and stopped moving. I heard the woman gasp and saw her begin to rock with sobs. The Dzongda held out his arms to her, and she collapsed against him. I began to cry, the tears rolling down my cheeks, both in the realization that the boy must be dead, but also at the stance of my master's shoulders which revealed to me his feelings of helplessness and sorrow more than words.

Eventually, the mother's grief subsided, and she pulled herself from the Dzongda. They both stood up, apart from each other.

"Crying will make it more difficult for your son's spirit to leave," the Dzongda said. "He will remain attached to your love here on earth. You must accept his death, so that he can move onto his next lifetime more quickly." The woman nodded.

The Dzongda and the mother carried the boy's body off the path.

"Help us gather stones, dry sticks, and burnable brush," my master called to me.

Slowly, we collected enough rocks and dry matter to create a small circle around the boy's body. When we added enough sticks, leaves, and brush, my master rubbed two of the sticks together and lit a fire. All three of us stood holding hands around the circle as the boy's body burned and melted into ash. The mother then hugged us both, and we parted company to head our separate ways.

As dusk began to fall, the Dzongda and I stopped next to a river to eat our supper.

"Have you noticed that the river is everywhere?" he asked me. "It is in the mountains as snow—its source. It is also at the end—in the ocean and at its mouth. It is in the waterfall, the forest, the valley, and alongside the arid lands. It flows only in the present, although it has a past and a future. It has no sense of time. It is in thinking of our past or worrying about our future that we have sorrow, fear, and self-torment.

"We can learn much from the river. It can roar, it can gurgle, it can drip, and it can rush, but it continues on, experiencing all seasons with equanimity. So we must face our lives with the steadfastness and malleable flexibility of the river. Do you understand?" He looked me squarely in the face. His kind eyes searched mine, as though he was reading into my soul. His gaze was both magnetic and unsettling. I began to feel a little dizzy as if I was floating on the river of his eyes.

I did not understand anything. Not the boy's death, not the scroll the priest gave me, not the river, and certainly not the uncanny way my master seemed to see through to my core. In that moment, nothing else seemed to exist but his eyes.

"Do you understand?" he repeated. I nodded my head, if only to please my master and to shake the mesmerizing sensation of the last moments from my psyche. I do not think he believed me, but he seemed satisfied.

"We will sleep here tonight and resume our journey in the morning." The Dzongda made camp.

"Sir?" I asked. He turned to me. "Why did that boy die?" I was shaking a little.

"Encephalitis," the Dzongda stated with finality. Even the name of the disease sounded scary to me. My master must have noticed my fear because he continued. "I told you to stay back because it can be given to others. The boy was very ill. I could not do anything for him, only comfort his mother."

"Will *we* die of en-, en-, encephalitis?" I blurted out.

"We will die whenever it is our time to die." He reassured me with a smile. "But hopefully it will be a peaceful release and not a tormented one."

As I lay down, I thought about the events of the day but soon fell asleep. During the night, a heavy thunderstorm awoke us. We ran for cover under a rocky outcropping but our clothing was drenched. I was shivering, so the Dzongda wrapped his *gho* around me leaving him with little protection from the elements. When the rain stopped the next morning, we continued on our journey.

The day's heat seemed to rise rapidly as we descended again toward Paro. The Dzongda looked deep in thought, so I said little to disturb him. He appeared a bit flushed from our exertion. Since he wanted to be back at the dzong before sundown, we pressed on. A few times I noticed he held his hand to his brow and winced.

We were both glad to see the wooden bridge across the Paro River once again and began running—not dignified for the administrative head of the dzong but indicative of our relief at being close to home.

Happy to be in familiar surroundings once again, I do not recall falling fast asleep back in my room.

When I awoke from my sound sleep, I noticed the gold-entwined canister containing the scroll had been placed on its end at the foot of my bed. What was written on the scroll was indecipherable to me, the letters were unfamiliar, and the parchment rolled in such a manner as to hide most of the writing. I decided to take it to the Dzongda that morning and ask its meaning.

I ate my customary breakfast and hurried down the hallways to see my master again. We had been separated for the first night in nearly a week, and I missed him as if a key piece of me had been severed for no reason.

When I arrived at the Dzongda's office, there was an unusual hush. The other monks spoke in whispers to each other. When I approached the Dzongda's office door, which was strangely closed, the monk from the first day grabbed me by the shoulder and stopped me.

"The Dzongda is tired from his journey," he informed me. "You have been assigned to help the deputy Dzongda today." I was led down another corridor into another office that was a bustle of activity. I was given only one mundane task that I quickly finished.

I was saddened not to see my beloved master, to be separated from him for a full day. I missed our lesson in the chapel and our walk in the garden. But I wanted him to rest from our trip, so I dutifully did what I was told, hoping to earn his pleasure when I saw him next.

Returning to my room that night, I picked up the scroll, turning the cylinder around in my hands and examining its intricate design as well as the letters I could see on the parchment. I remembered the priest and how I understood that I was not to worry.

My thoughts turned to the boy and his mother, how the Dzongda had warned me to keep distant, but he had bent near the boy and comforted the mother. I remembered how he had given me his own robe during the rain. Were these the things I was not to worry about?

I shook my head to change my thoughts, concentrating on my memory of the butterfly field and how content my master was when we knew we were coming back together. I remembered his smile as I drifted off to sleep.

The next morning, I barely ate my breakfast before dashing off to the Dzongda's office, but once again the monk stopped me at my master's closed door.

"The Dzongda is not feeling well today," he said. "Go to the marketplace to buy some mushrooms, sweet potatoes, bamboo shoots, cheese, and chilies." The monk handed me a sack and a few coins.

I had not often been to the marketplace. I was pleased to have been given an interesting errand and took my time gazing at the different wares in the various stalls before selecting my purchases.

As I turned the corner to mount the long dzong steps to the entrance, I saw a crowd starting to form at the top of the steps. Civic officials and monks alike were lining the stairway amidst prayer flags floating in the breeze.

A small knot formed in the pit of my stomach. The blood at my temples started to throb. I mounted the steep steps as fast as I was able, weighted down by the items I had bought in the market. As I reached the middle of the crowd, the large double doors to the dzong opened, and a hush fell over the crowd. I stepped to one side as the group of people parted to allow for a processional.

Several maroon-robed monks came first, hands folded and heads bowed. Behind them, carried by three monks on either side was a type of stretcher with poles extending out at the bottom, middle, and top. On the stretcher, enshrouded in bright, white scarves, was a man's body. A murmur went through the crowd as they pressed forward for a closer look, blocking my view.

I pressed my smaller frame through the crowd to the edge just as the bier passed in front of me. At the top end of the shrouded figure, I saw the ashen visage of my beautiful master, his eyes closed and his lips sealed shut.

"NO!" I heard myself scream as I lunged forward to embrace him and stop the downward movement of the procession. But arms grabbed me from behind and held onto me tightly. I stood on my tiptoes to catch one last glimpse as the crowd closed in behind the procession and moved down the steps toward the river.

The image of the boy's mother falling into the Dzongda's arms came to me along with anger toward her for exposing my master to that disease. "Now, who will comfort *me*?" I thought in angry desperation.

117

My legs felt as though the bones inside them had dissolved. My head felt dizzy and dislocated. My breathing was suffocating, coming in short, staccato bursts. To steady myself, I managed to move to one side of the crowd and sat down on the steps. Then the tears came. I crossed my arms on my knees and sobbed to wring every ounce of pain from my heart. I did not care that my market purchases had been scattered, rolled down the steps, and crushed. There was no one left to please.

When my crying subsided enough to lift my head, I saw the funeral procession had reached the river, and the flames from the Dzongda's pyre were visible over the heads of the mourners. An acrid, smoky smell filled the air. I could barely imagine that my master's hand that I had held just three days ago was now merely wisps of smoke. The tears started to fall again. I sat all alone on the cold, hard steps.

As the flames subsided, and the crowd began to disperse, a group of men and women gathered in the prayer ring in front of the dzong. Slowly, the group moved in circular fashion, their voices and arms rising and falling in a melancholy, lulling manner. The rhythm of their chant was unpredictable like the changing landscape, ascending and plunging in an irregular pattern. Their voices and movements came together in a simple, yet beautiful dirge.

No longer in possession of the items from my shopping task and no longer needed by the Dzongda, I stood up stiffly and, undetected, made my way back to my room.

Once inside, I spied the scroll at the foot of my pallet. I picked it up and threw it against the wall, shattering the glass and denting the gold casing. I picked up the parchment for a moment and once again attempted to decipher the writing.

"Who will explain this to me now?" my heart cried out. I ripped it up into many pieces and threw them as well. I tossed myself down on my straw bed and cried myself to sleep thinking, "If crying keeps the deceased spirit tethered to the earth, then I shall cry forever!"

Dawn was just breaking as I awoke. There was a moment before I recalled that my beloved master was no more. The only memento I had of him was the scroll and parchment, so I picked up the torn pieces and placed them inside the belt of my kira. My stomach rumbled, reminding me that I had not eaten much in nearly two days.

Then I remembered what the Dzongda had said about the river and its similarity to the flow of our lives. I imagined that his cremated mortal remains were either still on the pyre near the river or were tossed into the river to float downstream towards the ocean. I knew I must go to the river.

In the hubbub of the early morning marketplace setup and the awakening activities of the dzong, I easily slipped outside and made my way unnoticed toward the river's edge. A smoky smell of cremation still lingered in the cool, morning mist.

The funeral pyre had been swept clean, so I clamored over the rocks at the river's edge to view its downstream flow. The wooden bridge blocked my view. I climbed across the rocky edge under the bridge, trying to balance on the slimy, moss-coated boulders that anchored the bridge end. My foot slipped. I fell into the icy, black water that snatched my breath away. As I tried to grab onto the rocks, I was caught in the current. I flipped over and was pulled down by a rapid. My head smashed on an underwater rock, and I became one with the river.

Ohio, 1993-1994

REALIZATION

Appointed as OAHIA General Counsel by Marcia Tuttle, Keir Mervais was responsible for chairing the Legislative Committee and fielding any specific legal matters that arose for the Association. Rather than a full frontal assault, Keir preferred to work behind-the-scenes. Although the Association was in the throes of drafting, negotiating, and lobbying for its first major legislative effort, Fulton Burke and Larry Hammersmith appeared to be the members who were most heavily involved with OAHIA's lobbyist, Kevin Bodwell, rather than Keir, while Jim Frazier sat on the General Assembly's legislative drafting committee.

When two hospital attorneys were accused of malfeasance, Keir undertook an informal investigation but concluded that he could not find a violation of law in either case. In contrast to his more lively and interactive involvement during the Executive Committee discussions several years earlier when he was an officer, Keir now was more stand-offish, almost as if he did not belong to the governing group. I did not understand if this was because as a new father he had shifted his priorities from career to family; his own career was rising less dramatically than Abigail's; he deemed the General Counsel role to be more cautious and advisory; he had a concern with how he might appear to his colleagues on the Executive Committee if he were more forthright; he did not wish to eclipse Marcia Tuttle's leadership; he was possibly putting his leadership efforts into other organizations; or there existed some other, to me, unfathomable, reason. I was simply vaguely aware that Keir's animation and zeal were tempered to the point of almost being withdrawn, and I did not feel it was my place to question him about it.

Marcia was relying on Keir to provide the legal and government relations expertise that she lacked as well as to act as the Executive Committee's intermediary with, and even emissary to, Insurance Director Carson, lobbyist Kevin Bodwell, the statute writing committee, and the Health Care Attorneys malpractice claims task force. If Keir participated in these activities at some level, I was unaware of it. If he did not, his slack was picked up by the other officers.

Even though I did not think my work life could get busier, 1993 proved hectic and fraught with changes. The previous August David Fisher had assigned me to a national alternative health care society that was in financial trouble. I succeeded in turning it around in one year from a $7,000 loss to a $23,000 surplus on a $150,000 budget. My largest national society, NIRS, launched a half-million dollar lawsuit and experienced a two-thirds staff turnover in six months. I was travelling an average of four days every six weeks, and in June I was gone three weeks in a row.

In August, Sylvia and I headed to the Lexington Lodge and Conference Center in Lexington, Kentucky, for the OAHIA convention. We had barely pulled up to the front entrance when a panicked Marcia Tuttle came running up to my car.

"Annie, someone is in my suite and won't checkout! We need that suite for the Executive Committee meeting in a couple of hours and for the children's program. Can you do something?"

"Let me talk to my hotel contacts once I get inside," I calmly tried to reassure Marcia while stepping out of my car. I was sure there would be a reasonable explanation or other accommodations provided, once I could get all the facts straight. Sylvia stayed with my car while I entered the cool, dimly lit lobby and proceeded to the front desk to check in and ascertain the situation around the availability of the OAHIA President's Suite.

"The woman occupying the suite originally reserved for Ms. Tuttle became ill last night," the front desk manager explained to me. "The Kentucky lodging law mandates that the occupant may stay in the room as long as she pays. However, we have a similar suite down the hall for Ms. Tuttle." I thanked the woman and returned to my car with a bellman and luggage cart to help Sylvia unpack the car, get the convention boxes and supplies to our registration area, and inform Marcia that she had another suite reserved for her use.

An hour later, having eaten a quick lunch, Sylvia and I met with the hotel staff for our pre-convention meeting and to set up registration for the afternoon. Once that was done, I walked over to Marcia's suite for the Executive Committee meeting. I was the first one to arrive.

"Pat Rosewood and Larry Hammersmith already checked in at our registration desk," I told Marcia, "but Keir Mervais is not registered to attend the convention. I suspect the distance from Cleveland is a deterrent."

"Keir hasn't been as helpful to me as General Counsel as I had hoped," Marcia said. "With everything that's been going on with the premium rate problems with the Insurance Commissioner, malpractice task force, and legislatively, I could have used more support and guidance." Since I was the one who had suggested Keir to her for the position, I detected a subtle accusation from Marcia. I remained silent. Just then, the other officers began to arrive for the meeting.

Lexington was a fun venue for the convention. We had tours and children's activities along with the traditional golf and tennis tournaments and legal educational sessions, so the weekend passed quickly. On Saturday morning, Marcia Tuttle passed the presidential gavel to Pat Rosewood, and Sylvia and I were soon on our way back home to Columbus.

My association client mix continued to change, adding more national and international organizations. My travel for work took me to Montreal, Orlando, and San Diego. Meanwhile, Mireille, a cute five-year-old, full of imagination, conversation, and curiosity, entered kindergarten. I had promised Auguste before we got engaged that we would raise our child in the traditions of Judaism, so we joined a Reformed Synagogue, Temple

121

Beth Torah, located on High Street, north of the State University campus. Mireille entered Sunday School there, and we attended Friday evening services regularly.

We were also in the process of convincing Auguste's mother to move to Columbus from Brooklyn, New York, since most of her friends and relatives in New York had either died or were too ill and housebound to visit. We worried about the possibility of my mother-in-law's own declining health and mental state as well as the impact of potential crime on her quality of life in New York. Auguste and I felt she should live near her son and granddaughter so she could enjoy what family she had left.

When Pat Rosewood became the OAHIA President, she asked immediate Past President Chuck Parker to serve as her General Counsel to maintain consistency with the legislative and regulatory efforts that had taken place during Marcia's term. She wanted his leadership through some bylaws changes and related articles of amendment as well as to continue to shepherd its key legislative bill through the State Assembly that was in the re-drafting stage. At the October Executive Committee meeting, I was instructed to invoice for dues and a special assessment for government relations immediately and hold fast on the December 31st deadline with the added incentive that the OAHIA membership directory would only include those companies whose dues and special assessment payments were received by year-end.

As I was opening the OAHIA envelopes with dues renewals one day, my heart skipped a beat as I saw the distinctive Corinthian columns of the logo of Keir's company, Cleveland Medical, on the envelope containing his dues renewal. A few weeks later, while Sylvia and I were proofreading the OAHIA directory pages together, my heart skipped a beat again as my eyes saw Keir's name listed. I silently wondered whether he would attend the 1994 convention in Cincinnati at the historic Manor Grove Inn. He had been absent for the last four conventions, and now that he had held all the positions on the OAHIA Executive Committee, there were no other official OAHIA occasions at which I could expect to see him again.

I quickly admonished myself that we were each married with children, and that I should not misinterpret his kindnesses toward me as any more than his polite upbringing—not to mention the professional conflict of interest. In addition, there was the negative precedent of his boss's affair with my predecessor, and, why would he be interested in fat, ugly me? I put the whole train of thought behind me—at least until the next time I saw his name, or the logo of his company, or even the word, 'Cleveland'.

During my year-end performance review session with David Fisher, I lamented that I had joined AEMG in 1985 to manage ACOO, an arts association that subsequently left the firm the following year, and I wanted to manage another one.

"Go find one," was David's response. Meanwhile, he placed me on another national client in a different field. At least this time, it was not in alternative medicine.

In January 1994, while in Los Angeles to attend a citywide convention of associations affiliated with a national umbrella group, the president of one of them—a North American arts society—announced that they were interviewing for an executive director. I almost leapt across the conference table with my AEMG business card. Unfortunately, the board members were already in the final stages of their selection process. Nevertheless, by May, they had not been able to reach an agreeable negotiation with anyone for the position, so they considered association management firms, narrowing their selection to AEMG and a firm based in Washington, DC. AEMG won the client, because I had previous management experience in the arts and another key aspect of their field. I added yet another client to my list of growing accounts: five national associations and OAHIA, my only statewide client.

My largest client, NIRS, was going through the legal discovery process as the plaintiff in its intellectual property lawsuit. During the 1993 year-end holiday week, I personally packed fifteen storage cartons with documents, shipped them to our attorneys and, in 1994, would participate in two grueling depositions—one in Columbus and a follow-up in Denver.

OAHIA President Pat Rosewood, a relatively young and attractive blond attorney with Trust Medical—now headed by Gordon Frazier—went out on maternity leave for her second child in late January. Managing an association with the president *in absentia* is difficult, although the rest of the officers pitched in and Pat was willing to be contacted at home. Vice President Greg Grisham presided at the February Executive Committee meeting in Pat's place, and I ghost wrote Pat's *President's Column* for the newsletter's spring issue.

The previous fall, Pat had recruited and appointed a pretty extensive group of committees and had encouraged conducting a membership survey in anticipation of revising OAHIA's strategic plan. General Counsel Chuck Parker and Attorney Representative Deborah Sayres were revising the OAHIA bylaws. Three former Capital University Law School buddies, who had all ended up in the health insurance legal field together—J. Mark Thomas, Mike Talbot, and Kevin Raines—were recruited by Pat for the Education Committee to re-think the OAHIA seminar program since OAHIA company members were now offering similar, competing seminars for free.

Personally, I was experiencing some health issues. The dust allergies I developed after Mireille was born had developed into walking pneumonia in 1989; following a course of antibiotics to treat the pneumonia, I developed *candida*–an alimentary canal yeast infection that systemically pervades the body causing, among other things, fatigue, back and neck aches, and discomfort in the sexual organs. Trouble breathing at night and work stress caused me to grind my teeth, further compounding my TMJ jaw pain as well as that of my back and neck. One day, while standing in line at the drug store for yet another prescription, I saw a book about yeast infections. Following the dietary guidelines and adding lactobacillus acidophilus to my regime for several months resulted in most of my symptoms subsiding as well as a loss of 30 pounds, although the TMJ pain remained ever present.

Being in constant pain did not help my relationship with Auguste. Although he was working, he never made a salary equivalent to mine. We often argued about money. He was also afraid that my *candida* infection could be transmitted to him. We focused most of our attention on Mireille, probably not the best for our child. Auguste informed me, "If you are going to travel for work all the time, I cannot take care of two kids while you're away," effectively squashing further consideration of a sibling for Mireille.

Mireille was a bright, articulate, and observant child. When she was only two, she complained to me of the unfairness of apologizing, "Daddy never says he's sorry!" I began to pay attention and found Mireille's observation accurate. It occurred to me that Auguste was more considerate of the plants in our garden where he spent most of his spare daylight hours than he was for the women in his family.

Legislatively, OAHIA was still in the midst of drafting an end-of-life state statute while yet another Congressional initiative was pushing to switch health insurance regulatory authority from individual states to the federal level under a 'health insurance czar'.

By the May 10th Executive Committee meeting, OAHIA President Pat Rosewood returned from maternity leave. After the sixth draft the proposed end-of-life healthcare legislation was readied by the drafting committee that included OAHIA former president James Frazier. The Association hired Patch Damien as its lobbyist and used the special assessment of $1500 from each health insurance company member collected the previous December to underwrite Damien's retainer. But opposition to the proposed legislation was already mounting from the Estate and Family Law Sections of the Ohio Bar Association as well as from the hospice, medical, and funerary fields. Once introduced into both houses of the General Assembly, the bill was referred to the Judiciary Committee. Due to the bill's complexity and multiple areas of opposition, Damien predicted that it would not reach the floor of the Assembly until 1995.

Vice President Greg Grisham planned the 1994 OAHIA convention at the Manor Grove Inn in Cincinnati, now a favorite location. His program included several returning speakers: Professor Shuman from Capital University Law School presenting his annual case law update; OAHIA's own Chuck Lincoln, representing the national society, AAHIA; and Larry Burris, a law partner in the same firm as Deborah Sayres. One of the more interesting speakers was expected to be divorce attorney Allen Sommers who was going to talk about the impact of health issues on domestic relations. In addition to the Health Law Section update, a representative of Buckeye Health Care's national office and an attorney specializing in long-term care insurance were scheduled to speak.

Before Friday morning's educational session was to begin in the O'Henry Room of the Manor Grove Inn, I was surveying the remains of the breakfast buffet at the rear of the room with my back to the entrance. The room was arranged in rows of parallel, narrow, draped tables, with banquet chairs facing forward, and a head table for four at the front where Greg Grisham and Pat Rosewood were seated along with the first two speakers of the morning, Professor Shuman and Larry Burris.

Unexpectedly, I felt an arm slip familiarly around my waist and a kiss on my right check.

"You look *great!*" Keir declared. This level of physical intimacy with any of my professional association members had never occurred. I was surprised but not offended since his behavior did not seem to be disrespectful. I sensed he was simply glad to see me after several years and was acknowledging my recent weight loss.

"Thank you."

"I did not attend last year's convention in Lexington because Abigail had a miscarriage, and I did not feel right in leaving her at the time." Keir said in a hushed voice. I nodded my understanding, accepting this confidential admission of a private family matter as another instance of his trust in my discretion. I was honored that he felt he owed me any explanation, suspecting he was one of those people who kept most of his personal trials and tribulations extremely private.

President Pat Rosewood stepped to the microphone and asked the convention delegates to take their seats.

"I guess I arrived too late to sit in the back row," Keir said. I watched him squeeze himself behind the chairs of his colleagues already seated in the second to last row. As he made his way to the seat at the far end near the wall, I noticed his eyes were light blue in color, coordinating with his navy golf shirt.

"But I thought his eyes were *green*," I reflected, as I recalled those moments in the Sandpiper Suites lobby when I had been drawn so magnetically into them.

The rest of the morning's agenda went along as usual and, during the afternoon, participating members enjoyed the golf and tennis tournaments. Sylvia and I toured the Cincinnati Museum of Art. Since Keir did not play golf or tennis, I wondered how he would spend the afternoon.

That evening while prizes were distributed by the tournament chairmen at the banquet, I photographed the event. I also snapped a picture of the delegates at their banquet tables enjoying the humorous remarks. In contrast to the forward-looking and smiling faces of his table companions who were obviously engaged in and enjoying the remarks from the podium, Keir's face was downcast and introspective. I recalled he had not spoken to me during the cocktail party preceding dinner.

At eight o'clock the next morning, I was in the unoccupied O'Henry Room seated in the back row, setting up the new office laptop in preparation for taking minutes during the annual business meeting scheduled at the end of the morning's educational sessions. (With the introduction of laptop computers, I no longer used a pad and pen, thereby speeding up the process of producing the typed minutes.) Once that was done, I planned to check the podium microphone and place the speaker gifts near the lectern for Greg Grisham to distribute at the end of each talk.

With my slimmer figure, I was wearing a new, blue-and-green floral, one-piece skort outfit cinched at the waist with a wide belt of the same material. Around my neck I wore an emerald-and-diamond chip necklace—a gift from Auguste. The V-neck of my outfit revealed just a hint of cleavage.

"Good morning!" Keir had entered the room through the door behind me, arriving plenty early to get a choice seat at the back of the room. "You look GREAT!" he noted again as he rounded the end of the table where I sat and entered the center aisle next to me. "How's Mireille?"

"She's five now and has taken up playing miniature billiards at daycare. Did you ever see the movie, *Cinderella Liberty?*" Keir nodded affirmatively, his eyes twinkling—I guessed he was recalling the moment in the film when actress Marsha Mason, dressed in a very short, burgundy dress, leans over a pool hall table far enough to distract the male customers with the view of her skirt barely covering her backside while she hustles them at snooker. "I'm afraid my daughter is going to grow up like the character Marsha Mason played in that movie!" I exaggerated slightly in a teasing manner. "How's Sean?"

To continue our conversation, Keir sat down in the seat in front of me, turning to face me over the back of his chair. "We bought him a wooden train set for his birthday that he loves to play with."

As we continued to talk, I noticed his eyes this morning were the same light green as I remembered from the Sandpiper Suites seven years earlier, and that unique "drowning" sensation began again between us. However, this time I could not blame the experience on having had too much to drink or from the excitement of Keir's successful conference. "He must wear contact lenses," my mind registered as our conversation carried on in a light, bantering tone. Another thing was different this time, too; both our spouses were miles away in Columbus and Cleveland, respectively. "Hmmm, let's see where this leads..." my thoughts challenged.

It seemed as if we were having two conversations; one, coming out of our mouths, had no real consequence; the other, subliminal, was more substantial and earnest. I don't remember what we talked about, but twenty minutes later, I was abruptly brought back to the reality of our surroundings: Greg Grisham was introducing the first speaker. I was astonished that, during my twenty-minute conversation with Keir, the meeting room had filled up with convention delegates. I had not yet checked the microphone, nor plugged in my laptop in anticipation of the annual meeting later, nor given Grisham the speaker gifts. Oblivious to anything but Keir seated before me, I had forgotten to do my job while wrapped in the cocoon of Keir's warm, velvety, voice and crystalline eyes.

I was relieved that the microphone Greg was using worked and, as unobtrusively as possible, I darted to the front of the room to hand him the speaker gifts. Returning to my seat, I wondered if Keir had experienced the same sensations as I had.

Allen Sommers, the divorce attorney, was telling an amusing story when I noticed Keir had turned his face over his shoulder toward me. Self-conscious, I stared straight ahead at the speaker as if I was totally absorbed in what he was saying. Keir turned back toward the front of the room and leaned his chair somewhat precariously back on its two rear legs, something I had never noticed anyone else do in a similar educational session.

As the morning wore on, I noticed Keir would occasionally look back over his right shoulder, lean back in his chair again, and even bite the cuticle edge of his fingernail. When he was not gazing in my direction, I studied the back of his neck, his hairline, and his shoulders. I suspected Keir was not paying any better attention to the program than I was.

"I probably shouldn't even give him continuing legal education credits for today," I thought to myself, "except *I* am probably the one responsible for his lack of attention."

During the refreshment break, I took some photographs of speakers and officers for later use in the newsletter, while Keir conversed with some colleagues. We all returned to our seats for the remainder of the presentations and the annual business meeting, the last event of the official convention program, except for the President's Reception that evening.

As the meeting room emptied of delegates, Sylvia and I began to clean up the remaining documents. I noticed that Keir had lingered behind in the room speaking with our lobbyist, Patch Damien (who had been the Health Law Section Council speaker during Keir's convention in 1988). I remembered that Keir had always been interested in politics and legislative activities, so their conversation could very well be explained as the result of a natural interest but instinct told me something else was afoot. Was Keir actually lingering, stalling, on the pretense of conversing with Patch but really in the hopes of talking with me alone again? Did he have a sixth sense about my presence in a room the way I had about his?

During Keir's presidency six years earlier, the Association had purchased a custom-made, green-and-gold, satin banner with the OAHIA logo, gold tassels, and fringe that hung from a horizontal wooden pole. So as not to damage the wall, I customarily let the hotel banquet staff hang up and take down the banner from the wall behind the speaker lectern since it required a ladder and special hardware.

Suddenly, a devilish test of whether Keir's attention was focused more on me or Patch occurred to me. I would imitate Marsha Mason's pool hall pose. I strode purposely across the room, grabbing a banquet chair from the head table along the way. Climbing atop the chair in my skort, I stretched my right arm, hand, and fingers high up to touch the pole of the banner in an effort to remove it from the wall, most likely revealing more of my legs than I would normally consider proper. In a heartbeat, Keir was standing next to my chair.

"May I help you with that?" he offered in his gentlemanly style. Just at that moment my fingers grasped the pole, and I released the banner from its hooks. I looked down at Keir triumphantly thinking to myself, "You are *so busted*!" but managed a gracious smile.

"No, thank you. I have it now." I descended from the chair and began to roll the banner around the pole. Keir returned to his conversation with Patch. I inserted the rolled banner into its packing tube while Sylvia collected the remaining OAHIA items. At the same time she and I headed out of the meeting room, Keir turned to exit the room with Patch. Once out in the hallway, Sylvia and I headed toward the hotel elevators while Keir and Patch continued walking in the opposite direction toward the main lobby.

Sylvia and I planned to change clothes before our rendezvous for lunch and tour of the Taft Museum of Art and its formal garden. As I exited the elevator on my floor and walked down the hallway to my room, I reflected on the morning's events with Keir and exclaimed to myself, "I just hope he is having as hard a time with this as I am!"

I needed another person's opinion of the situation to ascertain whether or not I was imagining things. A half-hour later, as I was driving out of the Manor Grove Inn parking deck with Sylvia in the passenger seat, I risked confiding in her.

"How do you know if a guy is flirting with you?" I began.

Sylvia shrugged her shoulders.

"What do you mean?"

I spent the fifteen minutes of our drive to the Museum recounting the different instances I recollected of Keir's possible flirtations: in the buffet line at David Fisher's club, the special services clause, Keir crying in front of me when his mother had been diagnosed with cancer, the "eye drowning" incident at the Sandpiper Suites lobby, teasing conversations on the phone, the walk to the Insurance Director's office to rewrite the agents' exam, yesterday's arm around my waist and kiss on the cheek, this morning's second "eye drowning" experience, and finally the incident with taking down the banner.

"I really don't remember which one he is," Sylvia said.

"But I have introduced him to you at least *four* times," I protested in frustration. We had arrived at the Taft. I parked the car, and we approached the entrance ticket kiosk.

"I'm sorry," Sylvia concluded. "I really don't know what to advise you."

"Please don't tell anyone else what I told you."

"I won't."

We dropped the issue and enjoyed our afternoon admiring the art, architecture, and gardens of this 1820 Palladian-style mansion containing Old Masters, Chinese and Renaissance porcelains, and intricate watches. When Keir did not attend the President's Reception that evening, I surmised he had driven back to Cleveland that afternoon —to Abigail and Sean.

Despite having dropped the inquiry about Keir's behavior toward me with Sylvia, the topic was not complete in my own mind. Being a ruminator, I went over the various incidences in my mind while driving to work or taking walks. I would consider them from various points of view, trying to dismiss them as examples of Keir "just being nice to me" or "just the way he relates to women." When Auguste would say something particularly unkind to me, the voice inside my head would immediately issue a silent protest: "Keir would *never* have said that to me!"

Nermernuh "Our People" – Comanche

1695-1712 C.E.

Our band was on the move again. The women were quickly pulling down the *tipis*—tents—and folding the skin coverings and blankets. The skins and blankets were laid on top of our *travois*. A simple "trailer," the travois was made of two poles harnessed to the *puc*—horses—and reaching to the ground with hides stretched between the poles. In a matter of moments, we could pack up the village and be on the trail seeking buffalo and other game.

Our band followed the buffalo herds. Following a successful hunt, we women spent our days butchering the massive beasts and scraping the meat from 1500 pound animals, separating it from the skins with sharp bones, then drying the strips of meat using lime from the soil to absorb the grease. We also rubbed the buffalo brains until they were soft. Children would run up to beg for the liver and gallbladder while we saved the intestines for future eating. The work was dirty, greasy, and smelly. I would often be covered from head to toe with blood, marrow, and insects. By each full moon, it was my duty to have dressed seven skins, so I often took the skins with me when I went with the others to tend the horses at night.

By the light of our campfires, we beaded and decorated our braves' shields and other tools of war. We sewed clothing and tipis made from deer, antelope, and buffalo hides, and cooked. To supplement our meat diet, we also gathered berries and roots. Most of the dried meat was saved for the long, cold winters, but a smaller portion was mixed with the berries to create *pemmican* snacks, stored for traveling in parfleche pouches made of hide.

Many squaws were needed to bear strong warriors to hunt and sturdy girls to help with the chores. Usually after a raiding party on another band, more women and children captives were added to our ranks. Often men took three or four wives.

As the granddaughter of our band's medicine chief, Grey Willow, I was betrothed to Red Cloud. Having my marriage arrangements settled, I did not think too much about the other marriageable braves. None of them interested me that much as I passed through puberty and began learning the duties of women and wives.

In the morning, when everything was packed, Red Cloud, astride his *puc*, gave the signal to march forward. Most of the adults walked alongside the packed horses while the children rode on the animals' backs. The elders told us that formerly we used dogs with *travois*, but as our people moved further south from the Black Hills along the north fork of the Platte River, we had gained more horses in trade from the people who live in pueblos and from raids on other bands. With the horses we could travel more swiftly and carry more supplies. We followed the buffalo herds that were heading toward more plentiful grazing lands on the undulating plains. As our band made its way through the dusty grasslands and hills of the savannah, across plateaus and down valleys, the *travois* poles made parallel tracks in the ground.

I liked watching the large, white clouds slide across the deep blue sky and the tickle of the tall grasses against my legs. In the distance, the horizon was completely flat, our world stretching as far as I could see, with purple, yellow, and white flowers dotting the landscape all around me. It was still spring. The merciless hot days of summer, bringing the danger of lightning strikes and wildfires, were still ahead of us, while the bitter cold winter, blinding snows, and biting winds were gone for the time being.

Once we found bison, mounted warriors would pursue the multitudinous herds of black beasts; they stretched far into the horizon in front of us like a black cloud over the prairie. The herds would run until they reached the edge of an escarpment, their sheer momentum pushing them, tumbling over in a swirl of dust, to the bottom of the canyon. Whooping and yelping, the men rode atop their mounts, or sideways, rapidly shooting arrows or long lances into the buffaloes' sides. Once a buffalo was mortally wounded, the beasts on either side would stop in their tracks, making them an even easier target.

Our band, *Kotsoteka* or "Buffalo Eaters," was heading more directly southward to avoid other existing bands, like the Nokoni or the Quahadis. Each time we moved, we sought out a large grove of trees and bushes that would indicate a nearby river where we would have access to water and shade to make camp again. After several days of walking, we found a fork in the river where a beaver dam had caused a crystal clear lake to form, and there we set up our camp.

Each family had its own *tipi*. The women tied four peeled cedar poles together at one end with hide strips then splayed the legs to form a pyramid shape. Between twelve and thirty smaller poles were set around the main frame. A covering of tanned and sewn buffalo hides was raised to sheath the cone-shaped wooden frame and fastened in place with foot-long, wooden skewers and rocks placed at the bottom to hold the hide in place. At the top of each *tipi,* the corner flaps were turned out to adjust the air flow, while inside a cloth was hung from about shoulder height to the floor to keep moisture out.

After the 25 *tipis* were set up, each wife set about the task of building a fire inside her family's *tipi to* prepare the evening's meal. Other girls were sent to gather twigs and branches for firewood while I went to fetch water.

The evening was pristine, the air so clear you could see for miles, and felt pleasantly warm. I was dirty from the trail, and the lake water looked very refreshing. A waterfall spilled over some rocks. I wandered off a ways from our camp and approached the water's edge near a small grove of cottonwood trees. I could smell the distant smoke of mesquite as the *tipi* fires were set. Birds called to each other as the sun began its descent for the night, the sky turning colors of blue, green, and yellow.

Getting too near the edge, I lost my moccasin foothold on the wet rocks and splashed headlong into the lake. The water felt delightfully cool, so I paddled around in it for a short while.

Since it was getting hard to maneuver in my wet deer-cloth dress, I took it off and threw it open to dry on some nearby bushes. Soothed by the freedom and sensation of swimming without the encumbrance of clothes, I closed my eyes and leaned back to float in the water's buoyancy.

After a little while, a horse's snort abruptly disturbed the silence and my serenity. My eyes flew open as my legs dropped deeper into the water. Standing on the bank was a *dupsi kumma*, a brown horse with a black mane and tail. Astride the horse, sitting tall, erect, and unwavering, was the most beautiful man I had ever seen. His smooth skin was more reddish-brown than that of our darker skinned Comanche braves. He had broad shoulders and a well-formed chest. He sat atop his mount with the dignity of a chief.

The brave's long, black tresses cascaded from a central part running from his intelligent-looking brow to the crown of his head, atop which rested a horned buffalo headdress with the *cuntz,* or buffalo hide, covering his back, a useful form of disguise for a scout on the flat plains. His leggings had triangular flaps at each hip, a design not used by our people.

His face was square more than oval with high cheekbones and a strong jaw. His lips were parted in a slight smile showing a gleam of teeth. But it was his gaze that held me the most. He seemed to regard me with a combination of respect and amusement. His look was one of caressing a treasure that one had unexpectedly found.

Neither of us moved, but the space between us felt compressed, bringing us closer until I was only truly conscious of his dark eyes—warm, slightly mocking, but gentle.

Almost imperceptibly, he nudged his horse forward to enter the water. Without taking his eyes from me, he drew a hide blanket from behind him which he handed down to me without a word, then turned his horse around and walked it out of the lake. Once he reached ten feet beyond the shore, he turned his horse slightly so that he could look back at me. Momentarily, he nodded his head in farewell, turned back, and galloped away from our camp in a cloud of dust.

After he was out of sight, I took the blanket he gave me and wrapped it around my naked body as I walked onto the shore. My dress was nearly dry. Using the blanket as a covering in the chill air and, in a greater sense of modesty brought on by my encounter, I slipped back into my dress. Not sure what to do with the stranger's wet blanket, I left it drying by the trees rather than bring it back to camp where it might draw attention. I was not sure at all whether the brave would dare to come back to retrieve it.

I suspected that, if any of our warriors had encountered an unprotected woman as I had been, she would have been captured and raped as a matter of course. His bearing, coloration, and markings indicated that he was not a Comanche. We had encountered other tribes on our journeys, but I did not ever recall ones who had such regal bearing.

He was probably on a reconnaissance mission and had come dangerously close to our new camp. Under no circumstances did he want to alert our braves to his presence. But then why did he stop to give me his blanket and potentially give his location away, even chance an ambush by our warriors? And would his own band now come to attack us?

I knew I should warn Red Cloud about this encounter, but as I fetched water in the two hide containers I had brought with me and walked slowly back to camp, my heart told me to keep this meeting a secret.

As I finally lay down to rest that night, the stranger's spirit flooded back to me. Every detail of him seemed to have been carved indelibly into my mind. Sleep did not come easily. I was certain he did not intend to harm me and even counted on me not to give his appearance away. I did not know how I knew that, nor even that his handing me the blanket was a signal to cover myself. Without speaking, our spirits had flown to each other. I did not even know his name.

I did not know if I would ever see him again. At this thought, I began to cry.

As the days in camp passed, I slipped away at every opportunity to go to the lake and the grove of trees, but the blanket was still there. I began to worry that it would blow away or be discovered by someone else. Kneeling down on the ground and using a sharp stone, I dug a hole beneath a bush, and I buried the blanket so that only a small corner with markings protruded.

I knew it was very unlikely that he would return. It was too dangerous to come back for the blanket much less for—what I secretly hoped—me. Yet, I went every day.

A few weeks later, Red Cloud announced that we would again be pulling up camp and following the buffalo migration. How would my brave find me if we decamped? Could I leave a message with the blanket? But how could I communicate where we were going when we probably did not speak the same language, and I did not even know where we were going?

I had never been one to worship the tribal spirits, but I remembered the teachings that the River Goddess was a protector. On our last day in camp, I took a collection of feathers, rocks, and berries to my blanket burial place and performed a ritual service asking the River Goddess to help my brave find me again—wherever we might roam.

As the days, weeks, and months passed—riding, walking, camping, riding, walking, and camping again—I began to doubt that I had ever encountered the stranger at all. Perhaps it had been a vivid vision or a dream? As we moved on, my hopes and prayers left by the lake shore faded, replaced by a slowly growing resentment against Red Cloud and his constant need to keep traveling. Logically, he was doing what was in the best interests of the tribe. But my disappointment found a target in him, and like a small seed that grows into a tree, my anger grew in strength the further we traveled away in time and distance from my encounter. My parents accused me of becoming sullen and disobedient. I withdrew into my own world of thoughts and dreaming of when I would once again behold my brave. These episodes alternated with those when I scolded myself that he had long ago forgotten me.

After traveling south across the shimmering grasslands, we encountered the Naponee River and turned eastward again, stopping where the Naponee, Beaver, and Sappa Rivers converged to form another lake. The women set up our camp site while the men tended to the horses and their war gear, hanging their shields on tripods outside the *tipis* to ward off evil.

As the sun began to set, a bonfire was built in the center of the camp and our people gathered around to dance, eat, and converse. There was a general sense of excitement as our scouts had discovered a buffalo herd nearby and plans for a hunt were discussed among the elders and warriors, including my father, Black Hawk; my grandfather, Grey Willow; and Red Cloud.

Although several of my female friends were gathered in a small group, talking and laughing, I chose to sit apart, using the light of the full moon and fire to sew beads and feathers to a deerskin shirt for my father. Eventually, the fire burned down, the men's powwow ceased, and the drumming stopped as everyone but our lookouts wandered back to their family *tipis* to sleep.

Deep into the night, the camp was awakened by the pounding of horses' hooves and war cries of an attack. I heard someone shout, "*Tashĭn!*" referring to Kiowa Apaches, a fierce tribe with a reputation for horse-stealing and kidnapping. I hesitated, not knowing whether I would be safer inside our *tipi* or running for shelter away from camp. Something made me choose to go outside—if only to see what was going on.

Outside our *tipi*, the camp was in chaos with women, children, and old men screaming and running everywhere. My father and the other men had mounted their horses in pursuit of the invaders who were also on horseback, and there were several skirmishes in progress about the camp. I glanced about, looking for my mother who had left our *tipi* before I did. I spotted her knocked on the ground in the midst of rushing horses and headed toward her.

I do not know whether I sensed him first or felt his arms around my waist first as I was lifted from the ground and thrown face forward across the base of the horse's neck. It happened so quickly and swiftly. The air was knocked out of me as I landed and was only able to watch the ground rushing past. My eyes, nose, and mouth were filling with dust, but the din of the camp raid began to fade, and I realized that I was being taken away. I struggled to raise my head and back to get a better look at my surroundings and captor, but his hand was pressed against my back with too strong a grip, securing me to my position on his speeding horse.

We rode this way for several hours until dawn was about to break. I gathered from the way the light was coming up that we had been heading west so as to have a longer period of darkness. Although our initial flight from camp seemed to be driven more by excitement than a sense of clear direction, I sensed that my captor was confident of the direction in which he was heading.

We were alone; no other horses or braves were with us. I knew from fireside tales of raids by our band's warriors that they would often separate and ride alone so as to make it more difficult for those seeking revenge to follow them.

Whether from the constant pounding of the horses' hooves, my view of the ground slipping past, the initial shock of being captured, the realization of my hopeless situation, or having my head below my heart for too long, I grew light-headed and faint. My captor may have felt my limpness or he may have just needed to stop himself, but we halted near a rock outcropping where we could have some shelter from the sun and be out of the sight of any potential pursuers.

The warrior slid off his horse then pulled me down to where my feet touched the ground, but not as roughly as I had expected from a kidnapper. I knew that I was completely at this man's mercy, but I was not afraid. My knees buckled a little as I turned to face my fate, but my captor's strong arm supported me and lingered with his hand solidly against the small of my back.

I lifted my head to look at the brave's face. My heart jumped as I stared into the familiar countenance of the scout who had given me his blanket. He grinned.

I could not have resisted his kiss even if I had wanted to. I knew every moment of my life had led up to this instant.

But as quickly as he had embraced me, he drew back, immediately alert again to the danger of my village in pursuit. He jumped back on his horse, stretching both arms down to lift me, astride in front of him this time, as he kicked his legs against the rear haunches of his horse to start us in rapid motion again.

We glided through time and space together as one unit—horse, scout, and me. This brave was more comfortable riding his mount than walking on the earth. But I realized my added weight was likely slowing us down, and his horse would tire more quickly than if I was not part of his flight. I wondered how far and for how many days we would need to ride before he would deem that we were a safe distance from my encampment and my tribe's warriors tracking us.

When the sun was at its zenith, we stopped at a stream to let the horse rest and drink. The scout pulled *pemmican* from his pouch and handed me some. I nodded my head in appreciation and watched the expression on his face as he looked around with concern and calculation.

Lightly, I touched his bare wrist and then motioned to myself.

"Tuaahtaqui,"I said. It was the Comanche word for "cricket" and my name.

He appeared to understand, pointing to himself and replying,

"Duu Sarrie." I repeated his name softly.

While I chewed my *pemmican*, I continued to study him. As he moved about his horse, I caught glimpses of the red color on the inside triangular pleat of his leggings. On the sleeves of his war shirt were various red and yellow marks, indicating the numbers of horses he had stolen, villages raided, and enemies killed. The toes of his moccasins were pointed and covered with diagonal beading. His war shield was covered with bear symbols, a sign of strength, while his club displayed a scalp and coup feathers hanging from its handle. Obviously, this warrior was not afraid of combat or dangerous situations.

After we ate, we again mounted his horse and continued riding. I wanted to know if he had come to my camp deliberately to abduct me or, if upon seeing me during the raid, he had impulsively grabbed me as an added prize.

Duu Sarrie wrapped his left arm around my waist, and he pulled me closer to him. I could feel the solid strength of his chest against my back as I nestled into him and the resultant stirring of his loins against my buttocks. If this was going to be a long ride, we might as well enjoy it.

I felt his warm breath on the left side of my cheek. I reached backwards to caress the side of his face which he turned to kiss the inside palm of my hand. Slowly, I withdrew my arm and placed it on top of his arm about my waist as his kiss to my neck sent shivers down my spine. He squeezed his legs together to encourage the horse beneath us to move faster.

We came to a river and rode through it for a while to hide our tracks. We exited the river on the north side, rode for a while, entered the river again, doubled back, and then exited the river on the south side. By nightfall, we found ourselves in a foothill region where we stopped to make camp and rest. I sensed that Duu Sarrie would have pressed on through the night if I had not been with him. If warriors from my tribe were following us, we would lose precious advantage by stopping, but perhaps our evasive maneuvers through the river had thrown them off our track.

We did not light a fire but ate our *pemmican* ration in the quickly fading light. As we finished, licking our fingers, Duu Sarrie took my left hand in his, withdrawing a knife from the sheath at his waist. With a swift movement, he slit his left thumb, then hesitating, he looked at me. I lifted my thumb and nodded assent. He cut my thumb and pressed the two wounds together, co-mingling our blood in the symbol of a marriage.

To stay warm that night, we used our body warmth by nestling together under his blanket as the rapidly cooling plains winds blew over us.

I was startled awake by someone dragging me across the dirt and away from Duu Sarrie's warm body, while I heard a loud yell and the ominous thud of a rock hitting bone and flesh. My eyes flew open, and I strained to see what was happening.

Several braves from my village were gathered around, standing over Duu Sarrie, taking turns to club him around his head and body. I could see spurts of blood flying through the air. I struggled to pull away to stop them and screamed when I could not budge.

They dragged me away as I kicked and twisted. The warriors finally tied me down with strips of hide onto a *travois* so that I could not move. They piled a buffalo blanket on top of me.

As they stepped back, I could see the mutilated and scalped corpse of my scout as they carried him to a nearby ditch. I could see from his fallen arm that they had cut off his fingers as well to use the bones later as necklace ornaments.

My grandfather bent down toward me lying on the *travois*. He leaned his face in to assess my condition and asked, "Are you all right?" I knew he wanted to know if I had been raped or otherwise violated by Duu Sarrie as that would diminish my worth as a virtuous bride for Red Cloud. I spat in his face. Angry and surprised, he pulled back.

At the foot of the *travois*, arms akimbo stood Red Cloud, smug in his victory over Duu Sarrie. Hatred filled my heart. I wanted to die right then on that *travois*. My tears stung the backs of my eyelids but refused to fall.

The trip back to camp was tortuous. The *travois* bounced over endless rocks and crevices, jarring my bound body. The dust from the horses caked my face, and lined the inside of my nose and throat, already sore and swollen from swallowed tears. Red Cloud would not stop to rest.

The revenge raiding party returned to our village in triumph. The warriors whooped and yelled while the village drummers hammered a welcome. I was delivered to my parents' *tipi* where I rejected their open arms and sullenly lay inside during the evening's celebrations.

Shortly before dawn, I awoke and left our *tipi*, taking my father's knife and some fireplace soot to the edge of the camp. There I roughly cut my hair, blackened my face with ashes, ripped my dress, slashed my calves, and cut my fingertips—the traditional mourning for a husband.

Staggering back to camp, weak from blood loss and the shock of grief, I heard a menacing rattling sound. There in my path, coiled just a few inches from my feet was a prairie rattlesnake. Trying to remain still, my body was wavering while my calves and finger tips bled. The snake shot out its forked tongue, sinking two holes into my left leg. I started feeling a numbing sensation in various parts of my body as I stumbled back to camp.

When I crumpled to the ground, I heard someone call for my grandfather to cast out the evil spirits and heal the venomous wounds. I closed my eyes. My chest felt tight. My body started to perspire and shake violently. My throat began to swell, and I vomited. I slipped into blissful oblivion.

REVELATION

Mireille caught chicken pox over the 1994-95 Christmas-New Year's holiday. Luckily, I had already planned the time off from work as vacation. Together, we built a dollhouse for all of her Disney Princess/Barbie dolls. I also taught her to read and roller skate. While she was napping one day, I read a newspaper article that interviewed a local woman who called herself a *life coach*, an emerging field. Not only was I attracted to the concept of assisting people to overcome their roadblocks and achieve success by working with a personal cheerleader, but the lifestyle could enable me to have a more flexible work schedule to spend more time with Mireille.

"I suggest you enroll in Coach University," the life coach recommended when I called her to find out more information. Researching online, I learned that Coach University conducted its entire 36-module curriculum through telecourses, including a free, introductory conference call/seminar. After participating in the introductory call, I did not feel ready to embark on a three-year course of study with a $3,000 price tag; my life was already full. I was directing four North American associations and OAHIA; our family had joined the reformed synagogue; I was traveling nearly every month; and, Mireille was now involved with gymnastics and soccer. My accelerated work environment included three types of email, voicemail, faxes, overnight packages, and two-foot high piles of snail mail each week. At the same time, OAHIA was in the midst of mounting an intensive legislative campaign and conducting educational workshops in the major Ohio cities of Cleveland, Columbus, Cincinnati, Toledo, Mansfield, and Dayton.

I enjoyed working with Greg Grisham, OAHIA's new president. For the first time in ten years, OAHIA had a president who sent me his newsletter column on time, if not before the deadline. Like Keir, Greg was a handsome and charismatic leader, and a respectful gentleman. But as the economics of the health insurance industry were tightening, there were efforts underway in the nation's capital to regulate the industry at a federal, rather than state, level. Inexpensive service lines were being introduced to consumers that appeared suspiciously like health insurance but bypassed the normal channels of regulation while undercutting OAHIA members' revenues.

In contrast to Greg Grisham's easy charm, Vice President Larry Hammersmith struck me as an uptight, although brilliant, attorney. Ironically, Larry had switched companies and was now working in the same company as Marcia Tuttle. Fortunately, she had been able to change her opinion about him to a more favorable one than she held when she was OAHIA president.

The rest of the OAHIA Executive Committee members were relatively laid-back as well. Chuck Parker remained for a sixth year as General Counsel. Pat Rosewood was finishing out her term as Immediate Past President, L. Brent Tillet, Jr., the attorney who was the speaker at my first convention with a prematurely born son, was the Health Law Section Representative for a second year. In addition to President Grisham and Vice President and Convention Chair Hammersmith, two Capital University Law School friends, J. Mark Thomas and Michael Talbot, were Treasurer and Secretary, respectively. The Chair of the Sponsorship Committee, Kevin Raines, and his wife were expecting their first child as was my co-worker, Sylvia.

For the 1995 convention, OAHIA returned to the elegant Cedar Palace Hotel in Sandusky. The polished and ornate Cedar Palace, with chandeliers and Chinese pottery adorning its public spaces, was in keeping with Larry's personality as the Manor Grove Inn's rustic casualness had matched that of Greg's.

Keir registered to attend this convention with Abigail and their four-year-old son, Sean, whom I was eager to meet finally. Knowing that Keir and his family planned to attend, I had purchased a new dress to wear to the Welcome Reception: a beige, ankle-length, Regency style with an Empire waist and small buttons down the entire front. Sprinkled across the entire fabric was a field of burgundy flowers. The front was modestly cut in a low curve, and the sleeves were a flattering short cape style. Without any appropriate jewelry, I tied a narrow band of burgundy ribbon at my throat. I wore beige sandals with a wedge heel.

Sylvia and I anticipated a record convention attendance. The lights in the ballroom for the Welcome Reception were dimmed as the OAHIA delegates arrived for their cocktails and *hors d'oeuvres*. At the rear of the ballroom Sylvia and I stood next to our registration desk while clusters of members conversed. Although never good at estimating crowd sizes, I guessed we had about 75 or 80 of our 125 expected attendees in the room. The late summer sun was streaming through the large windows in the foyer and through the double entrance doors to the ballroom.

The moment I glimpsed Keir enter the door at the far end of the room, my heart did a flip-flop in my chest. I saw him just long enough to glimpse he was wearing a navy blazer, yellow golf shirt, and grey pants before my self-preservation instinct urged me to regain my self-composure by turning and attempting to hide behind Sylvia's tall, rounded, pregnant form. I expected Abigail and Sean to follow Keir's entrance, so I feigned being busy with the remaining name badges laid out on the table behind her, searching for the Mervaises' badges.

I turned back to face Keir, ready to shake his hand in greeting. However, instead of facing me, Keir had turned 180-degrees around, slipped his left arm around my waist, and kissed me on my right cheek.

"You are the *most beautiful woman* in the room," I heard him say.

Caught completely off guard, the first thought that flashed through my mind was to suggest he visit an eye doctor to check his contact lens prescription, but that would have been ungracious of me. It was the nicest thing anyone had ever said to me—but wait, was he making fun of me? No, he seemed sincere. I next thought, "You wouldn't say that if *Abigail* was here... but, wait, where IS Abigail?" I worried he could feel my love handles, but remembered that I had donned a figure-slimming body suit under my dress.

My right arm felt awkward hanging, squeezed down between us, so I slipped it under his jacket and lightly rested my hand around his waist. I could feel the taffeta lining of his nubby sports jacket on my arm as well as his leather belt. I hoped the gesture was unseen by anyone else but tacitly understood by Keir alone. My mind was still racing to figure out what to say in response to his compliment. The seconds ticked away but felt like hours. Finally, I encapsulated all my thoughts and emotions into one, slightly admonishing, exclamation.

"Oh, Keir!"

At that moment, I felt him stiffen slightly and drop his arm from my waist as he became aware of Sylvia standing beside us, likely staring at him in disbelief. He thrust his right hand out toward Sylvia who returned his handshake.

"Hello, I'm Keir Mervais." Sylvia handed him his convention packet with its three name badges. He handed Abigail's and Sean's badges back to Sylvia, explaining, "They aren't coming." Taking his own badge and packet, he walked away through the crowd of delegates toward the bar.

"*Ho*, boy!" Sylvia let out her surprise. "Has *he* got the *HOTS* for *you!*"

"Are you absolutely *sure*?" I watched Keir's receding back. I was even more flabbergasted at Sylvia's assessment than Keir's behavior and comment. "Maybe he's a womanizer?"

"No, honey, that was just for *you*."

As the evening wore on, the little voice in my head tried to make sense of this new development. "Was there really something to Keir's attentions to me after all and not just the desperate, romantic imaginings of a lonely woman? And why didn't Abigail come? Did they have an argument? Maybe he was angry with her, got worked up over it during the drive over from Cleveland, and decided to get even by playing a naughty, 'Peck's bad boy' and planting his attentions on me, a person he knew would not expect him to follow through."

Sylvia and I socialized with the other OAHIA members at the reception, but after his unabashed greeting, Keir and I did not go near each other again. As the reception ended, I saw him talking with some clients and colleagues as they exited the ballroom for dinner. Sylvia and I found a nearby restaurant for our own supper.

Friday morning's educational sessions were held in the same ballroom, but now the room was set with banquet chairs and classroom tables facing the dais. For the first time in my nine-year experience as OAHIA's executive director, rather than a straight lecture, one of the speakers had requested an overhead projector. I went to the back of the room to dim the lights.

The last row of seats was completely filled. Standing, I leaned against the back wall next to the light panel. In the darkened room, I noticed Keir had managed to sit in one of the back row seats. From my vantage point I could study him undetected: the softness of his dark hair, the curve of his hairline, the broad shape of his shoulders and back. I noticed he was wearing a peach-colored golf shirt and khaki trousers. I felt the urge to go behind him and slowly trace a line up his spine with my thumb nail, but I imagined he would have leapt out of his chair and disturbed the session and colleagues around him. I suppressed the desire by placing both my hands behind my back and leaning on them against the wall for the duration of the talk.

I surmised that Keir might have regretted his sudden forwardness toward me the previous evening, so I did not approach him during the refreshment break or after the session was over. By this time, I had fully convinced myself that he had been angry that Abigail decided not to attend the convention again, and he had retaliated by flirting with me the prior evening. After a night's sleep, his vexation now spent, I concluded he would want to put his presumptive act behind us both.

That Friday afternoon Sylvia and I planned to visit two historic homes in downtown Sandusky, the 1834 Greek Revival Follett House and the 1844 Eleutheros Cooke House. But first, we found a quaint, upscale, storefront bistro for lunch a couple of blocks from the hotel. Seated at a table for two next to the wall toward the back of the restaurant, I faced the front window. Midway through eating our lunch, I spotted Keir outside the café reading the menu in the window, contemplating whether to enter.

"What if he comes inside?" I asked myself in a slight panic. I knew Sylvia could not see him. "Should I invite him to sit with us? We'd have to pull up a chair, and it's a very small table. Besides, we are almost finished with our lunch." I was still considering how to react when I saw Keir turn and move on down the street.

With deference to Sylvia's mid-term pregnancy, we took our time on the house and garden tours and allowed sufficient time to return to the hotel to shower and dress for the evening's reception and banquet. I was pleased with my soft, chiffon, cocktail dress covered in pastel flowers with an open boat-neck and large ruffled collar.

The ballroom was dimly lit for cocktails. Round banquet tables and a podium were situated at the far end and two bars were set up close to the entrance doors. Only two couples had arrived so far. I went over to the banquet tables to select a seat near the podium to provide a good vantage point from which to photograph the golf and tennis tournament winners. To reserve my seat, I placed my meeting planner's binder on the chair.

Bent over the chair, my heart did a familiar somersault in my chest. I turned around to face the door and confirmed my heart's intuition that Keir had indeed entered the room.

"Now I even know where he is without even seeing him first!" my internal voice chided me. I advanced forward to greet him and exchange the customary pleasantries. Since I had seen him outside the café, I knew he had not participated in the golf or tennis tournaments.

"How did you spend your afternoon?" I asked.

"I went over to Lakeside. Abigail and I are planning to buy a vacation home there, so I was looking at some real estate." In a more confiding tone, he said, "Something came up at her office, so Abigail and Sean did not attend the convention." Then a little brighter, he continued, "What did you do?"

Before I could respond, Keir's boss, Alex McDowell, and his wife, Phoebe, entered the room. Without a word, Keir left my side in pursuit of Alex and Phoebe. I was perturbed that he had not even excused himself before I answered his question.

I had little time to stew about Keir's behavior. OAHIA Secretary Mike Talbot, his wife, Ruby, and Treasurer Mark Thomas's wife, Marianne, entered the reception and walked over to me.

"Mark injured his leg at the tennis tournament," Mike said. "He spent the afternoon at the emergency room and is resting in his room, so just Marianne is attending dinner."

"Mark is okay," Marianne reassured me, "but he'll be in a wheelchair for a while. I think he is pretty embarrassed, though."

Since the tournament was an OAHIA-sanctioned activity, I worried about the Association's liability, but the Thomases used Mark's insurance to cover the medical costs of his-injury.

As the cocktail party was winding down about an hour later, and the convention delegates were finding their banquet seats, Sylvia and I stood aside to be sure everyone else had a seat before we seated ourselves.

"Annie will know," I overheard Keir's voice say to someone at his table. He walked towards me. He reached out and, to get my attention, grabbed my left shoulder. He caught a handful of the shoulder pad in my dress. Still miffed that he had walked away from me in the middle of our earlier conversation, I turned icily toward him. "Our table wants to order some wine. What are we having for dinner?" Keir's natural tone indicated he was completely unaware of my annoyance with him. I pulled the paper menu out of my purse and coolly recited the entrée.

"Would you like to join our table for dinner?" Keir offered. Some of my irritation with him melted.

"Thank you, but Sylvia and I have to be sure everyone has a seat before we ourselves can sit down." Keir shrugged his shoulders slightly then returned to his table. When everyone else was seated, I noticed Keir's table was fully occupied. Sylvia and I found empty, single seats at two other tables.

I photographed the winning teams of golf and tennis players. When the tennis tournament prizes were presented, Mark Thomas was awarded a consolation prize which Marianne accepted in his absence.

As the last diners straggled out after dinner, I spotted Keir among them, but he was again surrounded by colleagues from his company and not easily approachable. Sylvia and I walked together down the Oriental-carpeted foyer toward our rooms on the other side of the second-floor mezzanine which overlooked the marble-floored lobby downstairs. Passing the balustrade, we noticed a cluster of convention delegates had congregated to go to the bar.

While showering, I fantasized about various scenarios. I noticed the marble bathtub and shower that was large enough for two. I studied how my new burgundy night gown with spaghetti straps and black lace fell across my body. I wondered if Keir would dare to telephone my room—or if I should dare to call his? What might have happened if I had printed my room number on a scrap of paper and slipped it to him during dinner?

"He is probably at the bar having a night cap with his co-workers or clients, or even back in his room calling Abigail," I scolded myself as I slipped into bed.

The next day, prior to the mid-morning refreshment break, I was standing alone, checking on the refreshment supplies in the foyer next to the meeting room when Keir approached me.

"I've been looking *all* over for you!" he said.

My mind responded, "I've been right here," but I did not reply out loud, waiting instead for him to continue.

"It's been a *great* convention!"

"Sylvia did most of the planning for it," I admitted. Was there another motive behind this compliment? Had he been looking for a pretext to seek me out to talk to me?

"But, I know who is *really* behind her planning." He smiled.

Just then, several convention delegates came out into the foyer to obtain beverages and snacks. Keir grabbed a soft drink and walked away.

After the last half of Saturday's educational sessions and the annual business meeting were finished, I headed out of the ballroom to our registration desk in the foyer where Sylvia was seated, deeply engrossed in conversation with Greg Grisham who was sitting next to her. I slipped behind them to join their conversation, standing between them with one hand on the back of each of their chairs.

Suddenly feeling self-conscious, I looked up across the foyer. Keir was standing beneath a royal portrait hanging on the opposite wall, staring intensely at me as though memorizing how I looked. In modesty from the heat of his gaze, I glanced down. I quickly looked up again to verify what had just happened, but Keir had completely vanished. I hastily scanned down the foyer toward my right, then across to another hallway, but there was no sign of Keir. "He must have *run* toward the lobby to have disappeared so rapidly," I told myself.

Once Sylvia and I were alone and packing up the remains of the convention supplies in our staff office behind the registration desk, I told her what had transpired between Keir and me that morning.

"All I know is what I saw and heard on Thursday at the reception," she stated.

Keir did not attend that evening's cocktail reception for outgoing President Grisham and incoming President Larry Hammersmith. I concluded Keir had driven directly back to Cleveland and Abigail after his hasty departure from the hotel foyer.

On our long drive back to Columbus from Sandusky through rural north central Ohio on Sunday morning, I played my cassette album of "Tapestry" by Carole King. Sylvia and I sang along with "(You make me feel like) A Natural Woman", "You've Got a Friend", and "I Feel the Earth Move". The lyrics for each song now held a special meaning for me.

When I arrived home, my mother phoned to invite our family for a Sunday afternoon swim in their apartment complex's outdoor pool. While I was collecting my swim paraphernalia, I wondered out loud within Auguste's ear shot.

"Should I change here and wear my bathing suit over to the pool or should I wait and change at my folks' apartment?"

"Who cares?" Auguste said with disdain. "*No one* is looking at *you!*"

Stifling the blow to my ego, my mental voice protested silently once again, "Keir would never say anything that unkind to me!"

Overnight I resolved to phone Keir on Monday to find out what was going on—was I imagining things or was there really some level of romantic exchange happening? As the rationale for my call, I decided to offer Keir a refund of the registration fees he had paid for Abigail and Sean, suspending my strict cancellation policy of "no refunds for no-shows" I had adopted the year he was convention chair.

AEMG was expanding. As a result, David Fisher had decided to move me and my entire support staff to non-adjacent space on the other side of the building. While Sylvia and I had been at the OAHIA convention, our offices were packed and moved to the annexed office space. Arriving at the office on Monday morning, the first problem we encountered was that Sylvia's office furniture did not fit into her new office space, and she would have to be moved back to the main office space, splitting up my staff.

Next, my phone line was not working right. I could make outgoing calls but not receive incoming calls which were directed to my voicemail box instead. When I called Keir that morning, he was temporarily away from his office, so I left a message with the woman who answered his phone. He returned my call, but with my phone not ringing properly at my desk, he left a message. I called back again, but he was out again. This continued three more times throughout the work day.

By mid-afternoon, Sylvia and I were both sitting on her office floor in tears; her pregnancy hormones were raging, she was overtired from the weekend, and her office was too small, and I was frustrated and nervous with unsuccessfully attempting to reach Keir and ascertain the situation.

While I was putting away some OAHIA files later that afternoon, I happened upon a manila envelope that contained two copies of the black-and-white photographs Liam McFarland had taken of Keir and Abigail at Deerwood Lodge seven years earlier. I thought I had mailed Keir a set of those photographs, but then I remembered we had discussed on the phone after the convention what a great photo Liam had taken of them, so I figured Keir already possessed copies of the pictures. Thinking to myself, "I might want these someday," I took one set and left the other set in the OAHIA photo morgue. I placed the manila envelope in a secret zippered pocket inside my briefcase.

As I was getting ready to leave that evening at 5:15 p.m., I tried one last time to reach Keir. This time he answered the phone himself, his soft, melodic cadence wafting through the line to me.

"Since we had such a good turnout at the convention, I've decided to refund the registration fees for Abigail and Sean," I began.

"Thank you." I tried to ascertain Keir's mood, but it was not obvious to me, so I attempted a different approach.

"In the past, you have always behaved like a gentleman to me..." I was thinking particularly of his uncharacteristic rudeness when he left me in pursuit of Alex McDowell on Friday evening. "What's going on?" I wasn't sure if he would realize I meant his walking away on Friday or his arm around my waist on Thursday.

"What do you mean?" Keir's response was guarded.

"You seemed in an awful hurry to go after Alex and Phoebe," I said, choosing the lesser offence to address.

"Alex McDowell is retiring soon. He wasn't even supposed to be at the convention. I needed to be sure he didn't mess things up."

I got the sense that Keir was in line for Alex's job as state manager for Cleveland Medical. Keir could not afford any mishaps at this point. He might have even been a little worried that I was about to accuse him of sexual harassment. My intuition told me he was backpedaling, so I did not press him for a more exact explanation. I suspected that he had arrived back home on Saturday, made up with Abigail about missing the convention, and now regretted his rash behavior toward me at the convention.

We wished each other a good night and hung up. The next day I prepared a refund payment requisition for Abigail's and Sean's registration fees.

About a month later, when Alex McDowell actually retired, Cleveland Medical did not name a state manager. Instead, the health insurance company was to be managed by a quaternion—a tetrad—of four branch managers: Keir in Cleveland, Harry Whitfield in Mansfield, Allen Farmer in Columbus, and Alex McDowell's former office manager in Akron. I felt sorry for Keir; he had seniority and had worked hard to build up the Cleveland market. In my mind, he was the crown prince in line for succession but now had his right to the throne thwarted. With no one single person in charge, I was privately skeptical about how this management structure could function for very long.

When the OAHIA Executive Committee met in October, the officers put a two-year moratorium on continuing the regional seminars and voted to focus more on the upcoming legislative battle. Each health insurance company member would again be assessed an additional membership fee for 1996 to cover the costs of lobbyist Patch Damien's retainer fee. Mark Thomas's Education Committee changed its attention from planning the regional seminars to developing a speakers' bureau.

The officers asked me to conduct another site visit to Deerwood Lake Lodge in November. The resort had expanded and renovated its facilities, and I was to ascertain Deerwood's continued suitability for the 1996 OAHIA convention the following August.

Sylvia quit AEMG to be a stay-at-home mom after giving birth to her baby boy, Kevin. In her place, Gabriella Synchik was assigned as my deputy staff on OAHIA. Young, smart, and capable with computers, Gabriella was an efficient worker, although she tended to be a bit moody and somewhat of a loner. However, I was too busy handling my several national accounts to spend much time concerned with her demeanor. She was getting the job done, and that was what mattered to me.

The winter of 1996 saw its share of severe weather and setbacks. My largest national association client, NIRS, was still in the midst of its trademark lawsuit. Due to a bad snowstorm in January and a conflicting convention for another, smaller, national client in San Antonio, I was not able to attend the jury trial—only 90 miles away in Austin—which ended, disappointingly, in an inconclusive victory for the other party. While at the San Antonio convention, unbeknownst to me, the Board members of that association client voted to leave our management firm. I wondered if the outcome might have been different for NIRS if I had attended the trial instead of working at the convention for the ungrateful client.

On Saturday morning, February 3rd, our family awoke to a loud crash as one of the large trees in our front yard, top heavy with ice, fell, bounced off our chimney, and crashed onto our front porch roof. Luckily, it did not fall directly through our bedroom or living room ceilings but was caught on the porch overhang. Five other homes in our neighborhood had trees land on their roofs that night. Auguste busied himself locating a tree trimmer to lift and remove the leaning conifer and then a contractor to repair the damage to the gutter and porch roof. Meanwhile, I packed up the departing client's documents and possessions and helped NIRS sort through the process of obtaining a post-trial settlement agreement and negotiate the legal bills. We were happy to see spring arrive.

In mid-April, Evonda and her new husband, Lloyd, were in Columbus for a visit, so she and I met for lunch at a nearby restaurant to catch up.

"You'll never guess who Lloyd and I met at the Hideaway Country Inn when we were coming through Bucyrus at Easter!" Evonda was right; I had no idea. "Keir and Abigail Mervais were there with their son, Sean. We noticed Lloyd's grandson playing with another little boy, and when we saw his parents, I recognized Keir. I'd forgotten what a nice man he is."

I related to Evonda the flirtatious manner in which Keir had interacted with me at the Cedar Palace Hotel the previous summer and Sylvia's observation about his attraction to me. Evonda appeared bewildered.

"I thought Keir and Abigail made the perfect couple."

"When Keir arrived home after the convention, I think he made up with Abigail because he seemed to back down when I called him that Monday morning," I tried to reassure her, describing our phone call. I had never told her about the "eye-drowning" instances with Keir in the Sandpiper Suites lobby or at the Manor Grove Inn, nor had I ever mentioned to her about the moments in the Cleveland parking deck, on our walk to the Insurance Director's office, or our other brief conversations and encounters.

To avoid any further concern to Evonda, I switched the subject of our conversation. Our lunchtime visit ended soon, and I returned to my office.

Mireille had begun to complain of headaches and was having difficulty with reading comprehension in first grade. After consulting with a specialty optometrist, we learned that Mireille would need twice weekly vision therapy in Gahanna, a thirty-minute drive from our home. With school ending in mid-June, a family vacation the following week, planning for a mid-July convention in Pittsburgh, an early August board meeting for my art association client in San Antonio, and OAHIA's convention at the Deerwood Lake Lodge in mid-August, my summer was extremely hectic.

Auguste chose to stay home from the OAHIA convention, this time to take care of our newly adopted cat, so Gabriella, Mireille, my mother, and I packed ourselves into my compact Saturn sedan along with our suitcases and the OAHIA convention materials for the drive to Deerwood Lake Lodge. Keir had registered to attend, but I had not spoken to him since our phone call the previous year.

Subconsciously, I had always left it to Keir to take the lead in our relationship, so I was not sure what to expect from him this time. When he did not appear at the Welcome Reception on the outdoor patio, I was not sure whether to be disappointed or relieved. I rationalized to myself that he had chosen to work the entire day in Cleveland then drive south to the Lodge after work that evening. Hoping he would remember that the final approach to the Lodge was hilly and a bit treacherous in the dark, I prayed silently for his safe arrival.

As the seats for Friday morning's educational session began to fill up, I saw Keir arrive at the door closest to the front of the room. I noticed immediately that he was more subdued than I had ever seen him before.

"Hello, Keir." I pointed at the rear of the room. "Our registration desk is in the hallway outside the door." I walked with him outside into the foyer. "Keir, this is my new assistant, Gabriella, who will give you your name badge and registration packet." I returned to the meeting room.

While Keir was serving himself from the continental breakfast buffet, Mireille burst into the meeting room from the front door, excitedly waving a stuffed animal perched on her raised right hand.

"Mommy! Mommy! Look what Grandma bought me!"

Outside of the front door, I could see my mother stop in hesitation. I quickly met Mireille midway down the center aisle. So as not to disturb the gathering attorneys and the educational session about to begin, I took Mireille's free hand and walked with her to the rear of the room and out into the registration hallway.

"Let me see what you have, Mireille," I feigned excitement in my voice to cover up my slight annoyance and embarrassment at being disturbed while working. Mireille showed me the red fox puppet my mother had bought for her.

"I'm going to call him 'Foxy'," she announced proudly.

"That sounds like a good name," I said as we continued to walk past the registration desk, out the glass doors, and around the building to where my mother was waiting.

"I'm sorry, Annie," she offered. "Mireille wanted her mother to see her new toy, and she ran into the room before I could stop her." I nodded my understanding of my daughter's childish impulsiveness. I bent down to address Mireille.

"Mireille, Mommy has to go back inside and work now. You need to stay with Grandma this morning. I'll come get you at lunch time, and then we can all go to the swimming pool together." My mother took Mireille by the hand and led her away toward the children's playground while I returned to the meeting room where the educational session had already begun.

Sitting in the back of the room while the case law update was presented, I had a moment to glance around the room. Keir was seated on an end seat midway down the aisle next to Brent Tillet. I remembered that Keir and Brent had become friends at Beaver Ridge Inn during my first OAHIA convention when Brent, one of the speakers, was concerned about his prematurely-born first son, and Keir had offered kind words of assurance to him even before becoming a father himself. Brent and his wife now had three children who were all attending the convention.

Instead of Keir's usual, neatly trimmed hair, I noticed that his soft, dark hair was overhanging the collar of his golf shirt. Since I regularly cut Auguste's hair, similarly thick and soft like Keir's, I daydreamed about taking the pair of scissors from OAHIA's supply box and offering to cut Keir's hair. "Excuse me," I would say to the person sitting behind him whose view I would be blocking. "Don't mind me. I'm just giving Keir a little trim." I smiled to myself over the audacity of my little fantasy.

149

When the morning's session was over and after our lunch together, Mireille, Gabriella, my mother, and I went first to the outdoor pool. I hoped nine-year-old Mireille would not notice Gabriella's pierced bellybutton jewelry and leopard-skin bikini, so I kept Mireille occupied playing in the pool while Gabriella lay out to tan. About an hour later, the sky clouded over, and we all moved inside to the spacious indoor pool lit with skylights. Mireille found some other children with whom to play, and I sat on the edge of the pool to watch.

Recalling that Keir did not play golf or tennis, I wondered if he might come to the pool. The last time OAHIA had been at this resort, Keir and Abigail had walked on The Plummet Trail, so perhaps he was hiking in the woods. Or maybe he retired to his room to work or watch a ballgame. I wanted him to come to the pool, but I was self-conscious of how I looked in my one-piece bathing suit. The bikini-clad Gabriella did nothing to enhance my self-esteem in that arena.

"It's time to return to our rooms to get ready for this evening's activities," I announced at four o'clock. I had planned a reception and banquet for the adults and Kids' Night Out for the children —chicken fingers, hot dogs, games, and videos. I wore the same beige dress with burgundy flowers I had worn the previous year when Keir had told me I was beautiful, only this time I wore a black jacket over it in case I was chilly in the air-conditioned ballroom.

The cocktail reception was held in a long, L-shaped foyer outside the banquet room with the bar in the far corner. A few sofas and chairs lined the walls. After dropping Mireille at the Kids' Night Out program, my mother, who was tired from having chased after my energetic child all day and who knew very few people in the group with whom to make cocktail conversation, sat on one of the sofas.

As the foyer was filling up with OAHIA delegates gathering in small conversational clusters, I saw Keir enter from the far end of the room. He was dressed in a navy sport coat and khaki slacks with a yellow button-down shirt, open at the collar, setting off his summer tan. Similar to the previous year, my heart somersaulted in my chest, only this time I did not have a pregnant Sylvia to hide behind. I quickly turned around to find someone with whom I could converse while I recomposed myself.

About ten minutes later, I noticed that Keir was momentarily standing alone. I thought of something I could tell him, so I moved in his direction.

"Hello, Keir. How are you doing this evening?"

"Fine and you?" We faced each other.

"Kathy Shipley called me a few weeks ago about how we could work out her membership status affiliated with your office while she worked from her home in Mentor-on-the-Lake. I think we came up with a workable solution."

Katherine Shipley was Cleveland Medical's marketing representative assigned to Keir's branch office. OAHIA's directory listing and membership policy allowed for additional staff members to be listed in the directory as members if they were operating out of the main or branch office address. Kathy's desire to be listed at her home address created a deviation from the normal policy.

"Thanks for helping Kathy." Although sounding genuine in his appreciation, Keir appeared a bit distracted and uncomfortable. To put him more at ease, I changed the subject to our neutral protocol of family inquiry.

"How are Abigail and Sean?"

"As usual, Abigail is busy with work. As a corporate attorney, she has difficulty getting away for a weekend." I thought I detected a slight note of resentment mixed with gratification that his wife was both intelligent and in demand. "Sean will be entering kindergarten this fall." Keir's demeanor shifted to one of pure fatherly pride. "I can't believe he has grown up so fast!"

"Mireille has had some vision difficulties lately, but we've been seeing an optometrist who specializes in vision therapy this summer. We are hoping to see a marked improvement in her reading ability this year."

So as not to appear that we were spending too much time together, Keir and I separated to mingle with others. Twenty minutes later, I turned around to find Keir and Chuck Parker speaking with each other. Chuck was the current President of SummitCare which had recently purchased Athenaeum Health Plan which in turn, had merged with Ohio Community Insurance. Liam McFarland had left the Cleveland office of Athenaeum to work in private practice, leaving a vacancy in that branch.

"How are things going at Cleveland Medical?" Chuck asked Keir, referring to the four-person management structure that had been in place since Alex McDowell had retired the year before.

"I'm just the marketing guy now," Keir replied, his tone tinged slightly with sarcasm and a little bitterness. I noticed Keir shift slightly before continuing. "How do you like working with SummitCare now?"

While Chuck launched into his response, it dawned on me that Keir was subtly feeling Chuck out for job prospects—possibly Liam's former position—and he was doing it unconcerned that I was privy to their conversation. Once again, I was surprised at his unspoken trust in my discretion.

As Keir and Chuck continued to converse, I was suddenly aware of a remarkable sensation; I felt an electrical energy charge between Keir and me at the level of our groin areas (the area I now know is called the second chakra). I dared not look down for fear I would actually see a lightning bolt pass between us. Privately, I wondered if either Keir or Chuck sensed the same energy that I was experiencing. I was aware, however, that Chuck did not seem to be picking up on Keir's subtle job searching hints.

"Excuse me, but I should check on the banquet arrangements inside the ballroom," I said and slipped away down the hallway. Since the servers were ready, the banquet tables set, and it was nearly eight o'clock, I returned to the foyer to announce "last call for alcohol" and encourage the convention delegates to move from the reception area into the banquet ballroom for dinner.

Once everyone was seated, Gabriella and her boyfriend, who had driven from Columbus in the afternoon, my mother and I, and a private practicing attorney, Harry Smith, with his wife sat together to eat our dinner at the remaining unoccupied table.

As the evening wore on, the golf and tennis prizes were presented, dessert and coffee were served, and the banquet finished. I was just about to arise from the table to go fetch Mireille when Keir appeared at our table.

"Mom, this is one of OAHIA's past presidents, Keir Mervais. Keir, this is my mother, Frances Weber."

"Nice to meet you," she said to Keir. Sensing that I might need to converse with Keir, my mother rose from her seat. "I'll go get Mireille," she offered.

"That would be great. Thanks, Mom." I wondered if her mother's intuition could sense the chemistry between Keir and me. He turned the banquet chair next to me out from the table so that he could sit down in it. I turned my chair out to face his and sat as well, our knees almost touching. I found myself leaning forward, my arms crossed with my forearms resting on my lap. I wondered how much cleavage my dress might be showing but dared not look. Keir leaned forward as well.

"I've been meaning to tell you," he began, "that Abigail and I ran into Evonda at the Hideaway Country Inn last spring. Sean played with her husband's grandson." Although I already knew this from my lunch with Evonda, I thought Keir might be using it as a pretext to speak with me, so I nodded but remained silent.

While the wait staff cleared away the banquet dishes and the remaining convention delegates filed out of the ballroom, Keir and I spent a few minutes immersed in conversational intimacy until my mother returned to our table with Mireille. Keir had not seen my child since she was a baby. I put my arm around her waist.

"Keir, this is Mireille. Mireille, this is Mr. Mervais." Keir fell back into his chair. I was surprised that he did not mention how pretty Mireille was with her shiny, long, brown hair; dark, almond eyes; high cheek bones; and bow mouth. I sensed that Keir was in a bit of a quandary about what to do or say next. I also noticed my daughter was very tired since it was already ten o'clock and past her bedtime.

"I should take Mireille up to bed now." Keir and I both stood up. "Good night." I headed upstairs with Mireille and my mother to our room, hastily putting our tired selves to bed. Mireille was already asleep in the king bed she and I were sharing when, after my shower, I slipped under the covers beside her.

But sleep for me that night was elusive. I went over and over in my mind the moments with Keir that day, and the other fleeting moments we had spent together in the past ten years. Although Auguste had not accompanied me on this trip, I wondered if Keir had not realized— until

152

Mireille and my mother came back to the table—that my mother and daughter had.

Was it possible, in coming over to speak to me, Keir had perhaps hoped to "get lucky" that evening and his plans had been thwarted by the presence of my two female relations? Had he even thought that far? Should I have asked him if he wanted to go to the bar for a night cap, while instructing my mother to take Mireille up to bed and not to wait up for me?

Then I wondered what the next day would bring. By morning I had resolved that, should Keir stay after the annual meeting to visit with me and we had a few moments alone, I would caress his cheek lightly, tell him I was sorry that his job was going badly, and give him a gossamer kiss on the lips.

I rose from bed the next morning with mixed feelings—tired from a sleepless night while excited about what might occur that morning. I checked on the Attorney's breakfast and the general session setup. Soon, the convention delegates arrived for their continental breakfast and to find seats for the educational sessions. The last rows filled up first.

Keir arrived just before the session was about to begin, so he and Brent Tillet sat together off the left side aisle in the middle. I thought they looked like Mutt and Jeff—Brent tall and Keir of moderate height.

The morning wore on with a few legal talks about health care, most of which went over my head. During the annual meeting, I rose to the podium to give my usual Executive Director's statistics about the OAHIA administrative year. Already tired and a little nervous, I looked out over the audience and felt Keir's eyes looking at me. Not wanting to reveal my heightened emotional state, my gaze bypassed him and rested on Brent before looking back at my notes on the podium before me.

As the delegates exited the meeting room at noon, I noticed Keir stayed behind to speak with Sara Sue Miller, one of Cleveland Medical's agents. Since Gabriella's boyfriend had arrived the day before, I gave her permission to leave rather than to stay behind to help me clean up. I began to collect the leftover copies of handouts and agendas.

The room had emptied. I was alone and on my knees packing a box with handouts, name badges, and registration leftovers when Keir appeared in the rear doorway, his hands thrust into his pockets.

My joyful elation that he had come back to tell me goodbye privately was immediately quelled by a vague sense of ill-boding. Keir looked—there is no other word for it—forlorn. I immediately sensed that he had come to tell me that he was planning to quit Cleveland Medical and did not know if he would ever see me again. But he could not—would not—say for certain out loud what his body language conveyed. I broke the tense silence.

"Are you leaving now?"

"My father has Parkinson's. I thought I would stop by the nursing home in Richfield on my drive home." I remembered his mother had died of cancer about eight years earlier, sadly, before her grandson was born. I knew it must be heartbreaking for Keir to be losing a second parent.

"I'm sorry," I said, not knowing what other comfort to offer. Still on my knees, I was physically too far away to execute my plan of a sympathetic caress to his cheek and gentle kiss. Keir shrugged his shoulders, turned, and walked away.

I now realized that I had too many items to carry back to my room in one trip. I could have asked Keir to help me carry them to my car and have prolonged our time together a few minutes more. Sinking back on my heels, I cried—at Keir's sadness, at the realization of what might have been a final goodbye, and at my tender moment being thwarted by the physical and emotional distance between us.

Drying my tears, I divided the convention items into two manageable piles to carry to my room. I took the two most valuable items first—the laptop computer and OAHIA banner—leaving the box of handouts to be retrieved on my return trip some minutes later. Rising to my feet, I tucked the banner tube under my arm, picked the laptop up by the case handle, walked to the door, crossed the outside patio, and entered the hotel lobby.

A wheelchair ramp was set up in the lobby to supplement the first flight of stairs. Being burdened by the weight of the bundles I was carrying, I opted to walk up the ramp. As I approached the ramp's corner passing near the stone front desk, I noticed Keir and Sara Sue Miller conversing again in an alcove at one corner of the front desk.

I thought I would slip past without capturing their attention, but Keir must have sensed or seen me, because he turned his gaze in my direction and nodded to me. I nodded back, sensing in that moment that he must have been stalling in the lobby, hoping for one last chance to see me before he left. I rounded the ramp's corner and mounted the stairs to my room, my footsteps and heart uplifted by this last encounter. I wondered if Keir could tell from my face that I had been crying.

After depositing my load in our room, I descended the staircase a few minutes later to retrieve the remainder of the convention supplies in the meeting room. Keir was no longer in the lobby.

"This will *not* be the last time we will ever see each other again!" I swore to myself.

After returning a second time to our suite, Mireille, my mother, and I went to the restaurant for lunch and then spent the afternoon in a paddleboat on Deerwood Lake. Being with my mother and daughter did not allow me much time to ponder the events with Keir. I thought it wisest not to reveal my flirtatious indiscretion to my mother.

Gabriella had driven back home with her boyfriend. I drove my car home to Columbus on Sunday with my mother and Mireille napping in the rear seat. I played the Carole King "Tapestry" cassette and mulled over the weekend's events.

I knew Keir and I were drawn to each other in some way, although I could not fathom why someone so handsome, rich, funny, and smart would be interested in me. Perhaps I reminded him of Abigail in some manner,

154

such as her ingenuousness or intelligence. Or perhaps it was his trust in me and emotional bonding during those moments when he stood in the hallway with me upon learning of his mother's cancer diagnosis. It had to be more than simply my being a good executive director, saving the Association from financial catastrophe, and helping Keir through the OAHIA leadership offices. I also wondered what kind of job he would land next and when I would get to see him again.

In early September, Auguste and I celebrated our 23rd wedding anniversary at a quiet dinner for two at a local restaurant. We kept the conversation light about movies, art, and other things we both enjoyed and not just about Mireille. My parents, who were babysitting that evening, planned to dine at the same restaurant three nights later for their 49th anniversary. However, before they could go out that evening, a freak and terrifying night of violent thunderstorms and tornadoes intervened. In addition to flooding, uprooted trees toppled onto the roofs of houses, cars, and sheds, including our own home, and an extraordinary number of tree limbs and downed power lines covered the streets and yards with attendant widespread power and phone outages. Mireille and I slept badly on a pile of pillows on the floor of my walk-in closet, while Auguste stood vigil from the living room sofa, flashlight in hand, all of us jumping each time a tree slammed into our roof and shook the house.

We awoke to what looked like a war zone in our quiet neighborhood. We had seven trees down in our yard, crisscrossed like a game of pickup sticks. Three trees had hit our house—one of our own and a double-tree from the neighbor, barely missing our bedroom by a foot and the neighbor's car by an inch. Others were not so lucky; one house was split in two, while two more had bedrooms smashed as the frightened children were being pulled to safety. As one newspaper editor described it, "...sleep- and caffeine-deprived residents of Columbus wandered their neighborhood streets in a daze..." as we all surveyed the damage.

For several days without electricity, we cooked thawing meat and boiled water for coffee on the outdoor gas grill, scouted frequently for bagged ice, and listened to the news in the evening on a battery-powered radio by candlelight.

Auguste wielded his new chain saw while I filled a wheelbarrow and began building piles of tree debris at the curb. Our pile eventually stretched thirty feet wide and four feet high. All the neighbors had similar curbside piles in front of their homes, the piles winding their way in either direction along our street as far as the eye could see, interrupted only by space for driveway entrances and the mailbox deliveries when the streets were sufficiently clear to resume vehicular traffic.

Tree services from other states and insurance claims adjusters descended on us. Within a week, the trees were removed from our roof, and a blue tarp covered the holes. From the sky, it must have looked like the entire city had installed roof-top pools as blue tarps were everywhere, and everyone began the long process of rebuilding.

As I returned to work and a sense of normalcy a week later, I learned that Chuck Parker had been ousted as President of SummitCare. "There goes Keir's prospect of getting Liam's old job there," I thought ruefully.

By the time our roof was repaired in December, we had sixteen more damaged trees cut down, including one large tree which had been perilously close to Mireille's room. Auguste began creating a new, more open landscape design for our yard.

Lake Horican-Colony of New York, Americas

1732-1757 C.E.

My husband died in 1754. Since then, I had managed our homestead for nearly two-and-a-half years by myself. I had no other family.

At first, it was very hard, missing him both as a companion and as the farmhand and heavy lifter. I was lonely, and it was hard, physical labor. Eventually, by the second year, it became easier, and I had enough to eat and keep myself warm. Weather permitting, in the spring, summer, and fall, I could visit neighboring settlements to exchange food, cloth, and news. Occasionally, neighbors would stop by with deer meat, squirrel, tools, or other necessary items to make my life more comfortable.

But winter was the most difficult. In mid-November the snow started to fall and did not seem to stop for weeks. When it did, the sky was a cloudy grey with a weak sun making only an occasional appearance. The wind howled between the cracks in the logs of my cabin. My husband would have patched the cracks before winter set in. Besides, his body had been so warm in bed. Now I stuffed rags in the cracks and had only our dog for comfort at night.

I lived on the west side of the lower end of a crystal clear lake which, only last August, General William Johnson had renamed 'Lake George' after our sovereign, George II, but the natives called 'Horican' and the French called 'St. Sacrament'. Tensions were mounting between our British settlements and the French who had planted themselves some ten leagues north in St. Frederick for the purpose of constructing Fort Carillon at the point where Lake Champlain met the north end of our lake. Three British strongholds existed in the area: Fort Edward, below Wing's Falls to the south, Fort Ann to the east, and nearby Fort Nicolson, at the southern tip of the lake where it met the Hudson River. General Phineas Lyman had arrived in early 1755 to supplement Fort Nicolson with a log-and-earthen four-bastioned fort on a rise just west of General Johnson's camp. The proximity of this fort gave me and my neighbors a greater sense of security.

However, on September 8, 1755, the British troops had three serious skirmishes with the French. In the morning, soldiers led by Colonel Ephraim Williams and some Mohawk natives ambushed and repelled a French force that had descended the east side of Lake Horican towards Fort Edward, but both Colonel Williams and the Mohawk chief were killed. The French then redirected their march towards our weakly defended Fort Nicolson. Hearing the musket fire from the morning battle, the troops at the fort's construction site

157

overturned boats and wagons and felled trees to protect themselves. General Johnson attacked the French troops which retreated south only to run into a surprise detachment from Fort Edward who routed the French and imprisoned their leader.

To reinforce British defenses, Major William Eyre finished the Lake George fort in November, naming it Fort William Henry. The fort was designed to garrison 300 to 400 regulars with an additional force of 1,500 provincial soldiers and attachments encamped in the southeast. With this more secure fortification and larger troop force from Albany, most of the year 1756 passed relatively free from any serious military engagements.

Nevertheless, in the fall of 1756, I learned from neighbors that our military scout, Robert Rogers, and his Rangers had continued their raids and brought word of additional French buildup to our north at Forts Carillon, St. Frederick, and Crown Point, amassing 3,000 troops and 30 cannon.

When Lake George froze in late December, our mounting concern of an attack by the French descending on sleighs was confirmed when Major Roberts pitched a feverish fight in a ravine near Carillon. Rogers barely escaped himself and lost twenty-six men but was successful in cutting the French force by a thousand men. Now, retaliation by the French was considered inevitable.

In early March 1757, one of my neighbors warned me that our sentries had spied a few bands of Indians and Frenchmen a couple of leagues north. It had been eighteen months since our area had seen any action; we had almost forgotten there was a war. Another reason I missed my husband was that he was a good shot with a hunting rifle. I had also nearly forgotten what it was like to eat venison, pheasant, and rabbit. Instead, I contented myself mostly with the chickens and geese in our barn. There was no need to hunt and shoot them with precise aim. But if Indians and French soldiers invaded our territory, they would want my fowl, and I would have to defend my food supply.

After several clear days, the weather gave way to another snowstorm on Monday, March 20th. It snowed hard and long with big, clumping flakes.

"What was that?" I awoke with a start early the next morning. The fire had died down to embers, and it was still dark outside.

There it was again! I sat up in bed, clutching the quilt to my chest. It sounded like the low moan of a wounded animal. I grabbed my husband's long hunting rifle from its mounting over the fireplace mantle. Too late to worry about the last time it was cleaned or the amount of ammunition powder it may or may not contain. How I wished my husband was here now!

I wrapped the quilt around my nightgown. I unlatched the front door, my hands shaking with cold and fright, and opened it just enough to peer out, ready to close it in an instant.

The smell of burning wood hung in the air. The moon was shining, casting shadows and glitter on the snow. A thin, fresh layer of snow covered the ground, so the intermittent dark spots running toward the house did not make any sense. The spots glistened wet in the moonlight. They appeared to lead to the corner of the cabin. I thrust my head out a little farther. That is when I saw the dark form on the ground. At first I could not make out the shape. Then I heard another moan. I slammed the door shut. I had to think.

I slowly reformed the image in my mind. The way the form lay stretched out, it did not seem like an animal, but more like a human. I opened the door again slightly to take another look. The moaning became steadier.

I pulled the quilt tautly around me and tightened my grip around the rifle. Quietly, I crept outside and alongside the house to the figure face down in the snow, my dog following.

The form appeared to be a dark-haired man in only a dirty white blouse, trousers, and leggings. A pool of blood had formed under his head. The dog sniffed the body. Dawn was starting to break, so as the light began to spread across the eastern sky, I made out what appeared to be a gunshot wound or a sharp blow to his forehead.

I ripped at the hem of my nightgown to form several bandage strips. Using the snow, I cleaned his head wound as best as I could and enable the blood to congeal to be able to judge the situation better. But what if he was dangerous and regained consciousness?

Leaning my rifle next to the cabin door, I laid the quilt flat on the snow next to the man's body and rolled him over onto it. Seeing his face calmed my fears and spurred me into action. Besides, it was freezing; I had taken off my quilt and shortened my nightgown for bandages. I pulled the four corners of the quilt together and, with all my strength, fueled by a mix of determination and fear, I tugged and pulled the quilt holding the man's body toward the open door of my cabin and, with a final yank, over the threshold. I retrieved the rifle and placed it next to the fireplace.

I stoked the fire embers, added a couple of logs, set a kettle of water on the hearth, pulled a shawl over my shoulders, and lit two candles. Holding one of the candles in my hand, I surveyed the wounded man lying on my floor before me.

He was a white man with dark hair and a complexion darkened by the sun. Despite a day or two's growth of beard, he appeared strikingly handsome. His face had a boyish quality to it.

Taking a damp rag to his broad forehead, I blotted the dried blood around the wound. Carefully I lifted the bandage above his left eye to see if I could tell whether the wound was from a bullet, bayonet, or a blow to the head. From the round appearance of the wound, surrounded by black powder, it looked like he had been shot, but I could not detect whether the shell was still lodged inside his skull. I cleaned the wound as best as I could and re-wrapped his head with fresh bandages. I covered his body with blankets and raised his feet to prevent shock.

The kettle began to boil, so I made myself a pot of coffee and sat down to think. I could not leave this man lying in the middle of my floor. There was only one bed, and I would somehow have to lift him on to it. Would it be possible to fetch the surgeon-barber from the fort? Should I ask a neighbor for help? Should I at least try to move him onto a pallet of straw and blankets so he would be more comfortable? What if he regained consciousness? What if others came to fetch him? I started to worry about my own safety and my dwindling winter food stores. I poured myself another cup of coffee.

There was a low moan. My heart leapt; I leaned forward. The man stirred slightly and then he ceased movement again. I sat back in my chair.

A louder moan. This time his hand instinctively went to his forehead. I went to his side. His eye lashes fluttered a few times then his eyes opened to reveal two sky-blue irises with the clarity of mountain pools. He stared up at the ceiling for a moment before his gaze landed on me. His smile seemed to fill the room like the sun suddenly breaking over a mountaintop at dawn. Our eyes locked for a long instant. He winced suddenly, closing his eyes again. I dropped into my chair. He said something I could not quite make out.

"Qu'est-ce que m'est arrivé?" His eyes were still closed.

I was not sure what he was asking, but I offered, "You've been shot in the head, I think, but I'm not sure how bad it is."

"Je ne comprends pas." I began to realize that we had another problem, one I had not anticipated. He was an enemy French soldier, separated from his fighting unit. I took another sip of my coffee, now lukewarm. He sniffed and opened his eyes again.

"Café?" He pointed at my cup.

"Would you like some?" I reached for another cup from the shelf—my husband's cup—and picked up the coffee pot to pour more hot liquid into both mugs.

I tasted his coffee to be sure it was not too hot. I knelt on the floor behind his head and gently elevated it onto my lap while holding the cup to his lips so he could drink.

"Merci," he whispered.

As I lay his head back down, he groaned in pain then seemed to doze.

I busied myself making some porridge—a breakfast I thought he could eat. Hearing the Frenchman's regular breathing, I took the opportunity to dress swiftly while he slept.

While I spooned the porridge into two bowls, he stirred again.

"Would you like something to eat?"

His eyes opened again. I walked toward him and indicated the bowl and spoon.

"*Oui*," he muttered, appearing to agree.

Placing the bowl and spoon temporarily on the floor within easy reach and again kneeling behind him, I carefully lifted his head onto my lap and began feeding him small spoonsful of the cereal.

Waiting between mouthfuls, I looked around the cabin and considered how to make him more comfortable.

First, I would make a blanket and straw pallet on the floor in one corner of the cabin, moving the table and chairs closer to my bed for more floor space. I would then try to move him onto the pallet. Perhaps after resting and eating, he might even have some strength to move himself.

Once he was comfortable, I resolved to strike out in the snow to my nearest neighbors a half league east, to see if they would fetch someone from the fort, another league further southeast. Although the Frenchman no longer felt like a danger to me, I worried that the seriousness of his wound could be fatal.

Using a combination of gestures and words, I tried to explain that I was going to the barn to get some straw. He closed his eyes and slipped into deep, rhythmic breathing again.

As I closed the cabin door behind me, I wondered if, in seeking assistance from the fort, I might be endangering the soldier by disclosing his existence. Would he be imprisoned there?

With each step I sunk into the nearly calf-high snow. Getting to the barn was difficult. Even wearing snow shoes, would I be able to reach my neighbor's house and return before nightfall? Besides, it was nice once again to have the company of a man under my roof.

In the barn, I filled three sacks with straw. I would have to sew the open ends closed when I got back inside. I also fetched the results of the chickens' laying—six eggs—and milked the cow. It took me three trips to move the bags of straw, eggs, and milk into the cabin.

He was still resting, so after storing the eggs and milk, I took needle and thread to sew up the open ends of the straw sacks. With some difficulty, I moved the table then laid the sacks on the floor adjacent to each other, evening out the straw. On top, I placed one blanket and one of the two pillows from my bed.

I heard a scratching sound at the cabin door and realized that I had forgotten about the dog. He entered panting, his breath warm from the cold outdoors. He quickly went over to investigate the

Frenchman who, feeling and hearing this intruder so near, awoke and put his arm out, partly in greeting and partly in self-defense. Once satisfied with sniffing this new addition to the household, my dog went to the hearth and lay down in his usual spot.

It occurred to me that I was making a somewhat permanent place for this man, this stranger, and we had not been properly introduced. I walked around to within his view again, and was again struck by the clarity of his blue eyes. I smiled, and he smiled back.

"My name is Elizabeth Pruett." I pointed to myself. "Elizabeth Pruett."

"*Lizbet*," he murmured.

His voice had a warm cadence. I liked how his French accent colored the pronunciation of my name.

"What's your name?"

He closed his eyes again and, for a moment, I thought he might not answer.

"*Je m'appelle Jacques Phillipe*." He opened his eyes again. Their brilliance almost knocked me off my feet. "*Jacques Phillipe*."

"Well, Jack Phillip." I pointed toward the pallet in the corner, "Do you think we could move you over to a more comfortable location?"

His eyes followed my gaze, and he nodded almost imperceptibly. I again gathered the corners of the quilt near his head and began to pull and turn him toward the corner. After another effort, I was able to drag the quilt alongside the pallet. I stood up and noticed a dark red spot was beginning to appear in the center of his bandage.

I moved across the width of the pallet so that my back was against the cabin wall. Grabbing one corner of the quilt by his head and the other near his right foot, I tugged the quilt and his body on top of the pallet. His groan seemed a mixture of pain and relief to be laying on the straw rather than the wooden floor.

I heated some water and ripped up more bandages from one of my husband's night shirts. Returning to Jack's side, I knelt to unwrap the bandages on his head and clean the wound. At first he reached out and grabbed my wrist, but then he released my hand, wincing as I pulled off the last strips closest to the wound.

To clean Jack's wound, I would have to trim his hair on the left side. His dark hair was thick, curving down over his left eye. I gently smoothed the curve across his forehead. The left side was matted with dry blood. I crossed the cabin to retrieve a pair of scissors with which I used to cut my husband's hair then returned to the Frenchman. He looked at the scissors then closed his eyes with silent assent.

Gently, I trimmed away the hair near the wound. I figured the bullet must have entered his left temple lobe, missing his eye, and

162

then exited the left top of his head where there was also some dried blood. I cleaned around the two wounds, examining them for signs of infection. I considered whether I should attempt to stitch the forehead wound with needle and thread and treat it with the remains of a jug of whisky I had kept for emergencies rather than to go for help.

I let him rest after I finished. Next, I prepared some soup with dried chicken pieces and root vegetables I had stored. While the mixture was simmering in a pot on the hearth, I went outside to gauge the weather. Grey clouds were moving rapidly, rolling to fill the sky. Another storm was building. I turned back inside to finish the soup and to check the contents of the whisky jug. It was half full—more than I expected.

"*Lizbet?*" I was startled to hear my name. "*Lizbet?*"

I went over to see what he needed. He made a drinking gesture with his hand to his mouth.

"Coffee?" I asked.

"*Non. L'eau.*"

I must have looked perplexed because I could tell he was thinking how to explain what he wanted. His egg-shell blue eyes darted around the room until he spotted the water bucket near the door.

"*L'eau.*" He pointed to the bucket.

"Water?" I scooped up some water, using the dipper cup, and indicated the cup.

"*Oui,*" he nodded and smiled. I brought the water to him, and as I had done before, I lifted his head carefully so he could drink.

"*Merci,*" he murmured.

As I began to stand, Jack grabbed my empty hand, bringing it to his lips for a kiss. The look in his eyes made my knees suddenly feel weak. I glanced away to break the intensity of his gaze and rose to my feet, returning the water cup to its place above the bucket. I went to stir the soup, hoping that the simple, routine act would still the unexpected pounding in my chest. As my heart returned to normal, silence descended in the cabin again. I dared not turn to see if Jack had fallen asleep—at least not until I got my emotions completely under control.

I took a sip of the broth steaming in the pot. It was not yet strong enough. Soon I would have to decide whether to attempt stitching his wound or seek a surgeon. I peered outside the door. Snow had begun falling again, and the wind was blowing. It was not looking promising for a trip for assistance.

"*Lizbet?*"

I was again startled out of my thoughts. The way he spoke my name this time made me realize that his request would not be as simple as a drink of water. Suddenly, it dawned on me what our next

163

challenge would be after his consumption of coffee and water. One look at his expression confirmed it.

During periods of bad weather and cold nights, my husband and I had preferred to use a tin bed pan urinal but this required someone with the ability to sit up. I would have to devise something for a bedridden man to ease himself—and quickly. I remembered I had a tin watering pitcher I used for the vegetable garden in the warm months that might serve. I removed the pieces of wood kindling sitting in it and placed them in the corner near the hearth. I took the watering can over to Jack.

I suspected he was more relieved that I understood his need than amused at my solution. I handed him the can, walked back to the soup pot, and kept my back turned until I heard the stream of liquid stop entering the tin can followed by the thud of the can as he placed it on the floor.

Without a word, I picked up the watering can and went outside a little distance from the cabin and emptied it. I then re-entered the cabin.

"*Merci*," Jacques murmured.

"The soup should be ready soon."

Once the piping hot broth with pieces of chicken and vegetables was cool enough to eat, I went to spoon feed my patient again. He ate slowly but with the relish of someone who had not eaten a home-cooked meal for some time. I wondered if Jack had a family, perhaps even a wife, who was worried about him.

After I had fed Jack his soup, I served myself a bowl and carried it over to sit near him for company.

"*Tu est une ange*," he said, probably knowing I would not understand what he meant.

I could feel him watching me as I ate. I sensed his gaze appraising me—perhaps he was wondering if I was married, and if so, when my husband would come home? More likely, he was wondering whether I planned to turn him over to the colonial military authorities.

After being watched for a bit, I looked up, again smiling as our eyes locked. For a few moments, I completely forgot everything as I was drawn further into the depth of his irises. I forced myself to look away. My glance found the needle and thread on the table. I heard the wind gusting outside and resolved that I would have to sew up his scalp myself, relying only on my sewing skills and the half-full whisky jug.

I stood up with resolve and walked to the table, picking up my mending implements. I reached above the fireplace mantle for the jug, standing still for a moment to gather my courage. Then I turned to face him.

So different from our emotional bonding of a few moments before, this time I saw the fear behind his eyes.

"*Je comprend*," Jack said, nodding slightly, and closed his eyes.

When he opened his eyes again, they seemed to mirror my own resolve. I poured some whisky in his cup and lifted it to his lips. While I let the liquid numb his senses, I put some on a cloth to clean the wound.

"This may burn."

"*Oomph!*" The fingers on his left hand dug into my knee. I gave him some more whisky then threaded my needle.

"I could use some whisky myself," I thought, but then admonished myself that I needed my nerves and hands as steady as possible for the task at hand.

I lit two more candles and placed them near Jack's forehead. I heard the wind howling outside. I gave Jack another sip of the golden brown liquid.

"Are you ready?" I asked him. He nodded and closed his eyes tightly. His hand gripped my thigh as I pushed the needle up through a piece of broken skin on his temple and down through another, pulling them together. As I pushed the needle through again, I felt the grip on my leg deepen, but he made no sound. A few more movements with the needle and I sealed the point of bullet entry in his temple. I cut the end of the thread. His grip on my leg had eased. I placed my free hand over his briefly then picked up the cup to offer him more whisky which he gulped.

I then moved to position myself above his head. This would be harder as there was not as much play in the skin atop his skull. I held his hand again. After a squeeze to signal that I was about to begin again, I let go to use that hand to guide my sewing. Jack grabbed a hold of my lower leg. I took a deep breath then plunged the needle into his skin again, and again several more times in rapid succession. Among the dark spikes of his trimmed black hair, you could scarcely see the stitches.

"*Finis?*" The one-word question was barely audible. I leaned forward and kissed his forehead. Pouring more whisky on the cloth, I gentle patted the sewn area at his temple and atop his head. He winced.

"*Tu est mechante! Une ange comme diable!*"

I let him vent his pain. Again I wrapped his head in bandages.

"I'm finished now." I let him rest. This time I took a sip of the whisky then peered outside the door. The sky had turned a leaden grey, and the snow was falling heavily. I lay down on my bed and fell into a deep slumber.

When I awoke, I was hungry. For a moment, I had completely forgotten about the morning, but then my eyes spied the cups and sewing supplies where I had left them on the table. I arose and went over to check on Jack. Since he was still sleeping, I stirred the fire embers and began making supper.

Either the sound or the smell of eggs and bacon frying awoke him because Jack called out again from the corner.

"*Lizbet?*"

He tried to raise himself on his left elbow, but the exertion was too much, and he fell back down onto the pallet blankets, his right hand instinctively moving to the bandaged wounds on his head to stem the pain.

"More?" I held up the whisky jug.

"*Non, d'abord...*" He pointed at the urinal tin.

When I was sure he had finished his necessary, I again disposed of the tin's contents.

"*Maintenant, je veux du whisky en plus,*" Jack requested, pointing at the jug. I poured him a few swallows in the cup, reserving the rest of the golden liquid for later needs. As I lifted the cup to his lips, his left hand covered mine, partially in guidance and partially in gratitude. I felt a warm sensation travel up my arm from my hand.

"Would you like something to eat?" I asked. "Some eggs and bacon?" Not waiting for an answer, I returned to the fireplace to serve two plates of food.

After we had both eaten, his eyes turned to me, silently asking me the same question that had been going around and around in my head. Can he simply stay here with me, insulated and isolated from the rest of the world, while he healed and got his strength back? Or must I disclose his existence to others? The longer our eyes held each other, the deeper we seemed to be drawn to the other. The darkness of the cabin enveloped us in a cocoon.

Then, like a candle snuffed out, his eyes closed and he fell asleep. I drew the blankets up closer around his neck.

"Good night, Jack." I whispered then stood up and went to clean up the dishes. I fell asleep later to the steady and reassuring rhythm of his breathing.

When I awoke the next morning, Jack was still sleeping. The snow drifts outside my cabin door were nearly up to the windows, and I could only open it because the wind had blown a small trench in front of it. Stepping through the snow up to my thighs, I forced my way with difficulty to the barn where I went about my routine morning chores: milking the cow, collecting the hens' eggs, selecting pieces of wood for the fire, and raking the straw in the barn.

"*LIZBET!*" Jack's voice pierced the morning calm. I ran out of the barn only to see two native savages on snowshoes leaving the

166

cabin, dragging Jack backwards behind them by pulling at both his arms.

"NO!" I ran after them, not certain whether to run inside for the rifle or to continue to pursue them. I trudged through deep snow, but my long skirt and falling shawl made it difficult for me to progress forward fast enough. The three men were getting further away from me. The Indians seemed to have an agility borne of practice escaping winter skirmishes. They were clothed skimpily in loin cloths and fur—and now I realized they had my rifle, too. Jack called out my name again, more plaintively this time.

Lifting my skirt and legs higher, I attempted to run faster. I tripped and fell face forward in the snow. As I looked up, I saw a dark red spot forming on the bandage above Jack's left eye. The three men disappeared from sight over the ridge.

I picked myself out of the snow and drove my legs forward as fast as I could to the top of the ridge. But when I got there, the men had vanished into the forest. I leaned against a nearby tree and broke down in sobs.

Part of me wanted to lie down in the snow and die right there. But my survival instinct was too strong. I slowly retraced my steps back to the cabin in the path I had made earlier, seeking warmth and protection. Had Jack only been with me one day? How could I have fallen for him so fast? I had been married to my husband for five years, and yet I had not felt this heart-broken when he died. Had I fallen in love with Jack? We spoke different languages—how could I have told him how I felt? I tried to think what to do next.

I entered my cabin, chilled to the bone. Inside I could see where the men had struggled and dragged Jack from his slumber. The rifle was missing from its perch over the fireplace, and the table was tipped over. I slowly began to straighten up, knowing in my heart that going for help would be a futile waste of time. He was, after all, the enemy.

I also suspected deep in my heart that he could not long survive his head wound with the rough handling he had received.

Several weeks later, a neighbor stopped to tell me the news of the French retreat and the extent of the damage to Fort William Henry's outbuildings and sloops. He told me some French were found scalped, frostbitten, or missing appendages. While my neighbors celebrated the rout, I quietly alternated between the certainty that Jack could not have survived the return to Fort Carillon and the distant hope that miraculously he had. We existed on opposite sides of the conflagration. The safest course of action for me was to forget.

Thanks to "Lizbet's" handiwork and some Indian herbal remedies, Jacques survived the arduous journey back to Fort

Carillon. By summer, his wounds had healed, leaving only scars. His superiors were planning another mission southward against Fort William Henry (or "Guillaume Henri," as the French called it). Jacques owed his life to Lizbet and worried that another ambush on the British would likely endanger her as well. With an ill-formed, heroic notion of finding her again and protecting her, Jacques joined the intimidating French force marching and floating south in early August. They landed two leagues north of Fort William Henry on the west side of the lake with 35 cannon and five mortar. From this point, the French stealthily moved their artillery and stores to within sight of their military objective.

From some scouts for Fort William Henry passing near my cabin on July 31st, I learned that the French commander, General Louis-Joseph Marquis de Montcalm, had arrived at Carillon a few weeks earlier and had amassed some 8,000 troops, including nearly 2,000 native warriors. Over the summer, native Ottawa, Huron, and Mohawk savages had been attacking on frontier settlements up and down the lake.

I was advised by the scouts to seek shelter at Fort William Henry, now under the command of Colonel George Munro. Munro had replaced General Daniel Webb who had withdrawn to Fort Edward further southeast. I gathered a change of clothing and some food stores wrapped in a blanket and set out on foot with my dog for the journey to the Fort.

Fortified Fort William Henry now held a garrison of 500, consisting of the 35th Regiment, with another 1,700 colonial militia and foot soldiers camped outside the fort's wooden walls. The encampment was a bustle of activity with carts of food and ammunition, tents and campfires, and horses and people getting ready for the French approach. Below the hill and west of the fortress walls lay the vegetable garden. On the other side of the fort was the morass—a swampy area produced by the delta of the Hudson River. Further southeast was Johnson's former encampment and the older Fort Nicolson. The only path for retreat was the road to Fort Edward.

As a woman alone, my dog and I were admitted to the interior of the fortress. Frontier people and soldiers were everywhere, huddled in small groups on the ground, near the walls, or napping on the dirt floor. I found a protected corner for ourselves and spread out my blanket to sit and wait.

We heard the first cannon fire around five o'clock on the morning of August 3rd. People screamed.

"To the ramparts," a soldier shouted while troops ran in several directions.

"Fire!" I heard yelled above me. Our cannon fire responded loudly, filling the air with smoke. A protracted artillery bombardment followed. I covered my ears as I squatted down in a corner. My dog ran to hide under a wagon.

"The French entrenchment is six or seven hundred feet northwest of the fort with two batteries at either end," I overheard a soldier report to his officer. I had been very lucky to get to the fort just ahead of the enemy's approach.

The sky was lit with cannon fire and shot as both sides volleyed at each other for hours. People scurried everywhere—the red-coated regulars mixed with our colonial militia in civilian garb. If the French had 8,000 soldiers and our Fort could only house 500 with fewer than 2,000 outside, I knew we were badly out-numbered.

The bombardments continued throughout the day. The explosions were constant, the sound becoming louder and the sky smokier.

"The French have begun an approach trench," a redcoat told his colleague. "If they dig thirty yards a day, within three days their 30-inch mortars will only be 200 yards from our fortress walls!"

By morning, rumors circulated around the fort that Colonel Munro's daughters, Cora and Alice, had miraculously arrived under cover of darkness that night from Albany, having made it through a skirmish with the enemy accompanied by some Mohicans, a white scout, and Major Duncan Heywood of the 60th Regiment who reported the rest of his attachment had been slaughtered en route from Fort Edward. Learning from Major Heywood that General Webb was not aware that further reinforcements were desperately needed at William Henry, Colonel Munro dispatched another courier to Fort Edward, twelve miles away, describing the siege and need for assistance. At best, reinforcements would need three days to arrive, if the courier got through the French lines at all.

From the ramparts, soldiers reported small skirmishes between the natives and our provincial militiamen on the outskirts of the fort. Colonel Munro ordered two lines of our red-garbed soldiers to fire upon the grey-and-navy coated French front lines as they plunged forward out of the trenches. The fighting was so brutal and savage I was secretly glad my Frenchman was no longer among them.

The summer countryside looked so different to Jacques than during the winter that he was afraid he might not be able to locate Lizbet's cabin again. The forward units of natives and scouts had plundered a number of British settlements for food and ammunition then burned them to the ground. Hoping to find her first, Jacques volunteered to serve in the first wave of grenadiers to be sent against the armed fort and lines of firing British redcoats.

The sky was thick with smoke as both enemies faced and fired on each other at short range. Jacques was hit in the chest with a cannon ball, thrown backward by the force of the impact, and died from loss of blood only 300 yards from the fort's walls.

Inside the Fort, I could find no relief from the smoke, noise, and fear from the bombardments that continued day and night for several, interminable days as the French inched closer, aiming their 30-inch mortars to penetrate our fortress walls and explode in the courtyard.

When Webb's reinforcements still had not arrived by the fourth day, a weary Colonel Munro sent a flag of truce to General Montcalm. The fighting ceased as they met on the field of battle to discuss the terms of a British surrender. Montcalm's forces had indeed intercepted the dispatches between Munro and Webb. However, in a gesture of civility, the French commander offered our soldiers their freedom if they agreed to return to England without any further fighting. Munro agreed to accept Montcalm's terms for surrender.

On the morning of August 10th, Colonel Munro, on foot himself, led the remaining soldiers and camp followers on a solemn march southward on the dirt road toward Fort Edward. At midday, we had barely arrived at the point of General Johnson's former camp when out of the woods from both sides came hundreds of bare-skinned natives, wearing black war paint and screaming. Horrified, we did not know which way to turn. Standing back-to-back, our soldiers attempted to defend our line. Swinging rifles and hatchets, the natives had no mercy. Confusion, blood, and smoke reined.

I started to run for the woods when a soldier in front of me was shot down with an arrow. As I turned around to find cover, I was struck from behind on my neck by the butt end of a rifle, knocking me to my knees. I looked up pleadingly as a savage swung the rifle again, smashing the right side of my face. Senseless, I fell forward to the ground.

FORLORN

Even as the storm from the previous September had disrupted and buffeted our lives, other events created less dramatic, but more long-term upheavals. I began to investigate a possible, new career of life coaching. Now reduced to 30-hours-per-week to give more attention to Mireille, reorganizing my job schedule at AEMG also enabled me to take some exploratory courses and attend some introductory networking meetings. More and more, I realized I was dissatisfied with my job, unhappy in my marriage, and unfulfilled in my life.

Over Mothers' Day weekend in May, I participated in a three-day transformational, personal development course in Akron—ostensibly to learn coaching skills; however, I also uncovered that I had a deep-seated verdict of myself as "not good enough" that had compelled me to overachieve and had colored my view of my career, my marriage, and my life.

Still pondering these insights on Monday morning as I drove home from Akron, I stopped off in Mansfield for an OAHIA Education Committee conference call meeting at Mark Thomas's office at Buckeye Health Care. Mark was then vice president of OAHIA and chairing the Association's Education Committee that had switched its focus from regional seminars to creating a speakers' bureau. Mark's large, imposing presence was softened by his teddy bear–quality of deep caring and gentleness. Frequently apologetic for things he had not done—real or imagined—Mark struck me as comfortably familiar, but I could not figure out why.

Since I arrived for the conference call a few minutes early (being rigorously on time was one of the virtues instilled in us by the personal development course), Mark and I had a few minutes to chat, so I told him about my weekend. No longer trying to prove myself good enough—at least for the moment; I was serene and centered, a quality that Mark noticed as something he did not often achieve in his own life. I invited him to join me for the next evening's closing session back in Akron. Mark had a previous engagement but seemed interested in learning more.

At the top of the hour, we dialed into the conference bridge line to join with Kevin Raines and Frank Spheres, two younger members of OAHIA whom Mark had selected for his committee. The national association, AAHIA, had developed a slide show and script for state affiliates to use in public relations campaigns. Mark, Kevin, and Frank discussed the development of an OAHIA speaker's bureau to disseminate the slide show and script. The Education Committee would identify the organizations and locations to present the talks and which OAHIA members we could select to make the presentations.

Once the conference call was finished, I continued on my return drive to Columbus. Still peaceful from my transformative experiences over the weekend, I had to keep reminding myself, "Remember to exit in Columbus." I was in such a state of tranquility that I could have driven myself straight to the state line and into the Ohio River.

Auguste, on the other hand, was quite anxious to return Mireille's child care to me as soon as I walked in the door and was not happy to learn I was returning to Akron for Tuesday evening's closing session. My condition of serenity did not last long at home.

In addition to the duties of planning NIRS's 650-person national convention in New Orleans in July and OAHIA's 80-person convention in August in Louisville, I was also the chief planner for my parents' 50th wedding anniversary gathering, also in Louisville, a few weeks later. Luckily, my personal development course also included a ten-week seminar that helped reinforce the concepts of the course. In June, after an argument-fraught vacation at Cedar Point with Auguste and Mireille, I began my Full of Life seminar. Ironically, the homework for the seminar was to throw parties and events on the principle that a large aspect of aliveness is a function of one's participation in social activities. I started to see the meetings and conferences I was planning as parties rather than work and obligations.

Realizing I had been missing a social life in my marriage to Auguste, I also held two smaller social gatherings for my female friends—a tea party and a jewelry demonstration party. Whenever we had hosted non-family guests for dinner or an event, after everyone had left, Auguste frequently accused me of offending our guests by something I had said. I was always surprised and saddened to learn that I had hurt someone's feelings. Over time, we ceased to invite people to our home. Planning gatherings enabled me to do something I enjoyed once again.

From the Full of Life seminar, I experienced an increase in confidence and vitality. In preparation for my parents' 50th anniversary party, I went to a beauty salon for my first professional haircut in ten years. (Auguste and I had economized by cutting each other's hair.) I also went shopping for an appropriate dress for the occasion and came home with three.

"We can't afford your extravagant spending!" Auguste shouted.

"I can use these clothes for work and convention attire, too," I pleaded. Auguste slammed the door as he went outside.

Privately, I hoped that Keir would attend the Louisville OAHIA convention this year to see me with my new hairdo and wardrobe, which included a long red dress that was particularly flattering to me. But I knew that Louisville was a long drive from Cleveland, and I doubted he was particular friends with Mark Thomas who was the convention chair, or Mike Talbot, the OAHIA President that year. I was disappointed but not surprised when Keir did not register.

Mark Thomas planned the educational sessions around a changing national health insurance industry. Former OAHIA President and current AAHIA Board member Chuck Lincoln described the climate in the national magazine after having been an AAHIA member for nearly 20 years:

"...I previously have not seen the industry change as rapidly and profoundly as in the past three or four years. Consider the effects of modern technology; the consolidation of the underwriter community through mergers and acquisitions; the changed AAHIA stance concerning the involvement of financial institutions in health insurance; changing national and state regulations; alternative products entering our business and potentially replacing it; the concern over the role of the independent agent; and, the resulting question of what type of education should be offered to our members on national, state, and local levels."

The sands were starting to shift again, portending another industry crisis on the horizon. The OAHIA members elected Mark Thomas as president, Kenneth Farmington from Paramount Blue of Ohio as vice president, Kevin Raines as treasurer, and (instead of original nominee Sara Sue Miller) Gordon Geddes of the Health Plan of Ohio as secretary. The members had partially reconciled themselves to the outcome of the antitrust lawsuit among Paramount Blue, Attorneys Assurance, and Athenaeum Health, which had favored the former, and had voted Farmington onto the OAHIA governing council because Paramount was too large an insurer to ignore. As a fellow attorney, Farmington understood the other issues key to the industry's agenda. Mark Thomas's fellow law school classmate and friend, Mike Talbot, continued on the Executive Committee as immediate past president. Thomas asked Mark Brown of The Health Plan of Ohio to serve as OAHIA's general counsel.

The consolidation of the industry through acquisitions and mergers was reflected in a dramatic decline in OAHIA's membership of health insurance companies, dropping from a high of twenty-two companies to fifteen companies. In addition, the health lawyer membership dropped from 105 to seventy-two. The OAHIA Executive Committee formed a task force to review its membership structure and again consider potential bylaws changes.

The OAHIA officers invited the chief executive staff member from the Ohio Bar Association and its Health Law Section Director to attend the October OAHIA Executive Committee meeting. The officers planned to discuss sponsorship, exhibition parameters, and the budget for the OAHIA company members to participate in the Health Law Section annual convention on an equal footing, as well as corollary opportunities for OAHIA to promote attorney membership to the Section and to serve on the Section's governing council.

In the relatively rare moments I had alone, mostly driving to or from work, I would think about those brief, singular interactions I had encountered with Keir; I turned them over in my mind, trying to remember the order in which they had happened, why they had happened, and what he might have been thinking. Something did not fit and did not make sense to me; an important piece was missing—something I could not understand, and for the life of me, I could *not* figure out.

However, somewhere, in the deeply primitive recesses of my heart and mind, I knew that, if anything should ever happen to Auguste—perhaps, a heart attack from one of his angry outbursts—I would want to marry Keir. (I did not think about what might happen to Abigail to make it possible.)

During the summer, David Fisher, AEMG's founder and CEO, put the association management firm up for sale so that he could pursue other interests. He placed a friend of his—a nice but less charismatic leader—at the helm to oversee the company through the sale. I was not immediately concerned for my own livelihood because the firm's key collateral was its clients and the employees' relationships with those clients; I was an essential component in that. In fact, my knowledge about the company and willingness to share it with the new CEO helped ensure my job security.

About every three years, the health industry legal field played musical chairs and a series of job switches would take place. In the continuing atmosphere of mergers and acquisitions, 1998 proved to be one of those years. Attorneys Assurance purchased Buckeye Health Care, the Health Plan of Ohio bought Safety Assurance Health Plan, and Trust Medical acquired Cleveland Medical.

Having lost his position as State President at SummitCare the previous fall, Chuck Parker was hired as General Counsel at Trust Medical, Kevin Raines left Attorneys Assurance to work for The Health Plan of Ohio and, a young non-attorney from Pennsylvania, Kenneth Sven, was appointed the new State President of Attorneys Assurance in Cleveland; a year later, he was tapped as the new State President of Cleveland Medical at Keir's office. I imagined what a slap-in-the-face it must have seemed to Keir who, wanting that position so badly himself, and having the tenure, the maturity, the network of contacts, the understanding of Ohio operations, and the law degree, would now have to report to Sven. (To replace Sven, Attorneys Assurance also hired an out-of-state non-attorney for its State President.) The OAHIA Nominating Committee lamented the lack of lawyers now available to serve on the Executive Committee.

When Kenneth Sven and his wife registered to attend the 1998 OAHIA convention at the Sheraton Swiss Inn in Mentor, I suspected it was unlikely Keir would attend as well. As the registration deadline approached, I plucked up the courage to phone Keir's office one afternoon to inquire hopefully if he planned to be there.

"I would rather go to our vacation house in Lakeside," he admitted. Since Lakeside was a more posh resort than Mentor, I wondered if Keir was justifying his absence as much from snobbery as from realizing that Cleveland Medical and Sven would likely not approve his travel expenses. I wondered also if another component of Keir's decision may have been still smoldering resentment of Kenneth Farmington of Paramount Blue, residue from the old lawsuit.

"I am sorry. We'll miss you." I had no arguments in my repertoire which might convince him to attend the convention where he potentially might have to face embarrassing career questions. I tacitly comprehended he would much more enjoy his private weekend getaway at his new lake house with his family.

During the OAHIA convention banquet dinner I found myself seated next to Kenneth Sven. A charming and good-looking man, Sven was hard not to like. Nevertheless I felt like I was sleeping with the enemy. Loyalty was important to Keir, and I felt guilty and disloyal for even conversing with Sven. However, I rationalized that getting to know Sven would give me the opportunity to learn whom Keir was up against. Besides, it was my job to know the State Presidents of the OAHIA member companies.

"Mommy, I don't feel good," Mireille had said just before the dinner banquet.

"Go ahead; I'll stay with Mireille in the room and order room service." Auguste was more content watching cable television than networking with the OAHIA members.

By Saturday noon, Mireille's temperature had reached 103 degrees, so we left Mentor a day earlier than expected to drive home. Her virus caused her to miss the first week of fourth grade, and I caught the illness two weeks later, causing us to postpone until October our 25th anniversary celebration trip to Marietta's historic Washington Lodge, our first stay at a bed-and-breakfast.

The Washington Lodge was within walking distance of several historic museums, including The Castle, the Campus Maritus Museum, and the Ohio River Museum, as well as several vintage and picturesque restaurants. Mireille accompanied us on the trip, sleeping on a cot in our room which was outfitted with a four-poster bed. After a whole day of museum visits and adult activities, Mireille was itching to act like a youngster.

"Mommy, can I go swing?" Mireille pointed to a playground inside the wrought iron fence of a Marietta churchyard.

"No, you cannot," August scolded. "That's trespassing!"

I opened the gate to allow Mireille entry to the playground while Auguste proceeded to walk onward to the Washington Lodge alone. I would give him an hour to blow off steam while I worked through being angry. Even on our special anniversary weekend, we could not avoid a spat.

By the time Mireille and I returned to our room, Auguste was ready for happy hour, so we left Mireille in our room watching television while we joined the other Lodge guests for an hour of adult refreshments and snacks in the drawing room. Then we retrieved Mireille and headed out to a riverside restaurant for dinner.

My personal development training now gave me the ability to "pull apart an upset" in minutes rather than stay miffed and not speak for days. However, the frequency of arguments had me in pull-apart mode almost constantly. Every conversation with my husband seemed to be about how I was not a good enough mother or wife, my failures in housekeeping and cooking, and my inadequacies as a friend or neighbor. Instinctively, I would clam up but the little voice in my head would protest, "Keir would never say that to me," or "Keir would never treat me that way." The mantra became the salve for the psychological wounds multiplied by Auguste's criticisms.

I continued to participate in the series of related personal development courses, completing the Level II Course in May 1998, as well as several seminars. In addition to caring for Mireille during my business travels, Auguste was now responsible for her on Monday evenings while I attended the transformation seminars. Although he did attend a couple of orientations to the preliminary course I had taken, he was adamantly against participating himself. Instead, two of my AEMG co-workers took Level I as did OAHIA's President, Mark Thomas, who also went on to take the Level II Course and attend some of the same seminars that I did, providing us with a much closer personal relationship than we might otherwise have had.

Fynchingham, Dorset, Regency England

1792-1842 C.E.

I had never been so happy in all my eighteen years! My silk slippers barely touched the ground as I skipped towards the grey stone bridge over the River Teasley. The warm sun illuminated my golden curls, cascading and bouncing from the knotted ribbon centered at my crown. My straw bonnet had already fallen backwards, only tethered to my neck by the pink silk ribbon tied in a large bow. As I scurried down the dirt path, past the laurel hedges, my right hand clutched and lifted a handful of the flower-strewn muslin of my narrow, high-waisted, morning dress, revealing a bit of the ruffle-edged slip beneath.

The large, grey stones of the bridge formed two curved walls on either side of the dusty, gravel path, partly shaded by low-hanging branches of ancient oak and sycamore trees native to our part of England. The clouds of green leaves provided a welcoming embrace of cool shadows, pierced with sparkling sunlight that danced across the river below as I skimmed across the bridge.

He was waiting on the other side, standing by the open door of his family's carriage, a four-wheel, enclosed barouche. I could just see the two inside bench seats facing each other, the entrance steps lowered in anticipation.

He was by far the most handsome man I had ever encountered, and the sight of him caused my heart to leap within my chest and gave wings to my feet.

Of average height but perfectly proportioned, Christopher, Lord Crevven of Fynchingham, was elegantly dressed in the prevailing London fashion of 1810. His black leather top boots encased the calves of his slim-fitting, black trousers. His black riding coat had a high collar that caressed the back of his neck and medium-wide lapels that extended down his solid chest. Encircling his neck and flowing down his chest was a gleaming white, silk stock and lace cravat over which his luxurious dark hair spilled slightly at the nape of his neck. Crowning this image was his black silk top hat that he took off as he saw me coming toward him.

Lord Crevven's wide, full lips broke into a huge dimpled smile, baring perfect, even, white teeth. A lock of soft hair curled slightly above his left eye. His lantern-square jaw was clean-shaven. His cheeks were softly encased in smooth skin that also dimpled at the sides, and his medium-length nose was perfectly modeled to his face. However, under the slight black bushiness of his eyebrows and the curve of his dark lashes dwelt his best features: two light blue, crystal-clear eyes, the color of the winter sky. When I looked into those eyes, I always had a slight dizzying sensation as if my feet no longer knew where the ground was.

As I neared the carriage, the horses snorted and stamped their feet from impatience which mirrored my own. Without thinking of the propriety and lack of breeding of my actions, I leapt off the ground into Lord Crevven's arms, which he reactively threw around my waist to catch my hurtling form. We kissed hard and unreservedly for a moment before we came to our senses and surroundings. He lowered me to the ground and looked beyond me to the struggling, overweight form of my governess, Miss Tilling, who, out of breath, was running to catch up with me. She was to be our chaperone on our visit to Crevvenwood, Lord Crevven's home, where we were to announce our engagement to his parents, the Earl and Countess of Fynchingham.

As I turned in the circle of Christopher's—Lord Crevven's—arms from our embrace, I could see the mix of anger, embarrassment, and dismay at my behavior in Miss Tilling's face and body. In her role as chaperone, her job was to prevent such unbridled public—or even private—displays of unguarded affection as she had just witnessed between me and my intended. All three of us knew it was a serious breach of morals and etiquette; however, there was no way to erase it.

Silently, Christopher and I stepped apart as Miss Tilling drew near, and he dipped his head in acquiescence of respect and apology, holding his hand out to help her into the carriage doorway. He then turned to assist me in, careful not to let her see his sly, but mischievous, wink to me just before I turned to put my dainty foot onto the entrance step. Once I was seated next to Miss Tilling on the upholstered bench, Christopher pulled himself onto the bench opposite, stifling with difficulty his smile of pleasure at both my exuberant greeting and our chaperone's discomfort.

"I am sure you will find the rest of the journey less taxing, Miss Tilling," Lord Crevven observed in a steady voice.

"Hmmph. Thank you, Lord Crevven. I certainly hope so." Miss Tilling rustled in her seat and then looked sideways at me. I smiled back and turned my attention to our host.

My father, the Reverend Edward Beechcroft, was the rector of Fynchingham in Dorset with a subordinate living at Melmont. My mother had died along with my younger sibling in childbirth when I was three years old, effectively leaving me the only child of the widowed rector. My father had adored his wife, feelings he then bestowed on me, and did not succumb to the kind attentions of the many spinsters and widows who earnestly sought to replace my mother in his affections. Instead, my father hired Miss Tilling to help educate and raise me, and to manage our household.

The Rectory, Briarcliff, where we resided was a simple rectangular structure with stucco walls and beamed ceilings. It was set back from the lane with a low hedge and wooden gate enclosing a typical English flower garden of roses, asters, tulips, daffodils, and pansies.

Stepping through our front door, to the left was our modest but welcoming parlor and to the right my father's study where he conducted his church business. His Chippendale secretary desk was overflowing with half-finished sermons, books, receipts, and other papers, while the library table was piled high with bibles, hymnals, texts, and other books in Latin, Greek, English, Italian, and French— some open and others with book marks protruding from between the pages. In addition to his high-backed desk chair, there were two visitor chairs, their upholstered seats also covered with papers and books which would have to be removed for any guests. The walls were relatively bare except for three paintings of religious scenes and a sweet, early pencil-and-wash likeness of my mother. My father spent many hours sequestered in his study, devoting his time to erudition, first as a way to ease his personal grief and later, as the years passed, simply as a habit to keep his mind sharp.

As a result of my father's preoccupations and my governess' light disciplinary hand, I had more leeway to roam and explore than I might have been permitted under the watchful eye of a mother. Miss Tilling woke me early, and, after a cup of hot cocoa, we would spend two hours in my academic schooling of writing, geography, and French. Then, I would accompany her to the kitchen to oversee the scullery staff as they prepared our breakfast, consisting of porridge, tea, coffee, rolls, and eggs or dried fish, at which point my father joined us in the dining room, located behind the parlor.

After breakfast, Miss Tilling would supervise my needlework or gardening duties. In addition to our flower garden, we had an herb garden near the kitchen and a small vegetable garden in the back. Our cook and scullery maid were responsible for the daily marketing, drying, and storing of the fruits, vegetables, and herbs; cooking and serving our meals; and cleaning the kitchen, dishes, and utensils. We also had a housemaid who kept the remainder of our house, oversaw the fireplaces, and laundered our clothing and linens with the assistance of the scullery maid. Since Miss Tilling's duties included those of our housekeeper as well as being my governess, I often found my afternoons free to amuse myself after a light luncheon of cold meats, bread, and fresh or dried fruit, depending on the season.

Sometimes I would play the piano forte in our parlor or retreat to my upstairs bedroom where I would read or stare out the window to watch the comings and goings of the villagers. From my window seat, I could just glimpse part of the village market square.

But, as a curious, independent, and spirited young girl, I would frequently venture out of the house for the afternoon, sometimes heading into the churchyard or down by the riverbank. Although our village was populated sufficiently with children, there were no girls and few boys of the same age and suitable gentry class to socialize with me, with the exception of William Taylor, the innkeeper's son. As the son of an independent tradesman, William was considered of a higher social rank than the children of the tenant farmers who leased their lands from the Earl of Fynchingham.

After finishing his own chores around the tavern and inn stables, William would sometimes meet me in the churchyard to join me for a couple of hours of play and freedom from adult supervision.

Around most people, William generally appeared shy and withdrawn, preferring to study events and conversations than to join the activity. He used the material he gathered through his observations to invent wonderfully imaginative scenes and games in which we would engage together for hours: knights and ladies in distress, Napoleonic battles, Henry VIII and Elizabeth I, and Shakespearean-like dramas.

Skinny and wiry, William would quickly scramble up an ancient oak tree with me in pursuit. We would sit up high and regard the village and the Teasley Valley spread out before us, as the breeze gently lifted his straight blond hair that sometimes hung teasingly in his eyes.

"Who should we pretend to be today?" William's blue eyes twinkled with merriment once we reached the high branches. "Did you hear about the mix up with the shoes the cobbler made for the baker?" Even if I had heard the story before, William's recounting would double me up with laughter.

In the summers, we would spend many idyllic afternoons exploring the surrounding woods, skipping stones on the river, catching white-clawed crayfish, climbing trees and rocks, or running after each other as we imagined ourselves in different times, places, and roles.

In other seasons, we might sneak into the church where I would read out loud or we played hide-and-seek. Alternately, we would go to his stables so that I could pet the horses or play with his dog. Sometimes, William would break into a song, and if I knew the words, I would sing along with him.

Eventually, as we grew older, my friendship with William reached a point when it became strained. He spent more time working for his father at the stables and in the inn, while I was expected to help my father with his vicarage-duty social calls. Society already forbade two young, single people of the opposite gender—but with affection for each other—to spend unchaperoned time together. Coupled with the disparity of our social classes, by the time we reached fourteen years, we only saw each other on Sundays at church services, nodding a silent greeting to each other and quickly turning away lest our former affection give rise to a suspicion of anything more.

As Lord Crevven's carriage bounced along the country road toward Crevvenwood, we exchanged flirtatious and grinning glances at each other across the expanse of the dark leather interior as the dappled sun played across us in alternating light and shadow. Miss Tilling sat in a stony silence, staring out the window at the passing countryside. Her role as my governess was about to end, and although she could be very proud of the match I was about to enter, her own future was far less secure. My impropriety at greeting Christopher and my blatant disregard for her last moments of supervision had not pleased her.

The rutted dirt and rock-strewn road gave way to a more even, gravel path as we entered Crevvenwood's double-towered gate. Lord Crevven had placed himself on the carriage bench so that I would be facing forward with a full view of the elegant Palladian mansion's façade during our approach up the tree-lined drive.

Although I had been here previously—on the night of the dance to welcome Lord Crevven home from his grand European tour—the daytime effect of the great house was stunning. The façade consisted of an Ionic-columned portico facing eastward, with colonnaded pediment and staircase to either side of the entrance in the center. Two wings and rectangular pavilions balanced either side, while two-storied pilasters rose on either side of tall, pedimented windows to support a balustraded cornice.

I could hardly believe that this estate would become my home should Lord Crevven's parents, the Earl and Countess, formally approve of our match. My earlier giddiness gave way to anxious anticipation at the presentation that was about to take place. My concern was only heightened by the array of servants lining the drive to greet the arrival of our carriage.

A footman opened the carriage door and unfolded the steps so we could disembark. Lord Crevven alighted nimbly from long habit then turned to take my hand to help me descend as well as to steady me on my feet. Standing before the entrance to the manor house I was instantly flooded with memories of the night one month earlier when I had met Lord Crevven.

Although the Earl and Countess of Fynchingham had occupied Crevvenwood during the country season, their son spent most of his youth at boarding schools and University, visiting his parents only in London before being sent abroad to finish his education during a lull in Napoleon's activities on the Continent.

When news reached the inhabitants of Fynchingham village that the only son and heir to Crevvenwood would be visiting for the first time, the tone of speculation and excitement reached an almost feverish pitch. When invitations went out for an elegant ball to be held in honor of Lord Crevven's homecoming, townsfolk could not have been more ecstatic than if the King had been expected. The latest fashions were ordered—ball gowns and men's fancy dress. Inquiries went out to rent extra horses, carriages, and equipages for the evening, and many social visits were spent sewing and discussing the upcoming festivities.

Finally, the night of the ball arrived. The procession of carriages through Fynchingham village, past our house, and up the lane to Crevvenwood gave the impression of a parade. Our own carriage made its way slowly up the drive to the great house. Several local boys had been hired to help the drivers with their liveries during the evening's festivities, and I glimpsed William among them, assisting the occupants of the open phaeton in front of us. Part of me wanted him to notice my arrival and admire me in my new ball gown, while another part of me knew that it would wound his pride, since I would spend the evening inside, mingling as a near-equal with the gentry, while he would be outside stabling their horses. As my father, Miss Tilling, and I descended from our rented carriage, I hurried quickly across the gravel drive and up the steps, hoping William was too busy to notice me.

The entrance hall was ablaze with several standing candleholders and crowded with newly arrived guests excitedly waiting to be presented to our hosts. The anticipation of the assemblage in the entrance hall increased to mild impatience once the strains of the musical ensemble emanated from the grand hall beyond as the first country dance got underway. I began to tap my foot in time with the music to disguise my impatience to move from the formal greeting line into the activity of the other room.

Eventually, our threesome was next in line to greet the Earl and Countess. The Earl of Fynchingham was tall and stately, distinguished in his looks and manner. His greying hair was cropped closely to his head rising above his starched stock and cravat. His elegant pale gold silk waistcoat showed off his lace front shirt and contrasted with his black silk riding coat with tails.

The Countess was decidedly shorter and rounder with ringlets framing her face. Her Empire-waisted ball gown was embroidered with pearls, her neck and ears swathed in diamonds, and she held a lace shawl over her shoulders against the evening chill.

Both had the manner of dutiful and slightly bored landowners opening their home to the less-than-equal local entourage. I drew myself up to evoke as much elegance and gentility as I could muster in my subordinate position of vicar's daughter as we moved up the greeting line, at which moment the guest of honor, Lord Crevven, joined his parents in the receiving line. My cool reserve vanished as my eyes absorbed him, and a schoolgirl blush enveloped me.

"Reverend Edward Beechcroft and his daughter, Emily Beechcroft," the footman announced.

"Lord Fynchingham, Lady Fynchingham, Lord Crevven." I smiled and curtseyed as I greeted them, but I only recall the warm grasp of their son's hand in mine as I dropped lower but kept my gaze riveted on his eyes, my smile broader and more revealing than modesty should allow. Did I see a responding twinkle in his eyes? Was there an increased amount of pressure in his grasp of my hand, and did he hold it a moment longer than usual?

As I turned to enter the grand hall with my father and Miss Tilling, I felt an eerie sense of dislocation and floating.

The Hepplewhite-style furniture in the room had been pushed to either side to allow for the orchestra at one end and the dancing in the center. Already several couples had formed a line and were going through the steps. My father espied a baronet of some acquaintance and his wife settled midway down the right side of the room and strode as purposefully as possible into the crowded room to where they were seated, warmly greeting parishioners and other people he knew as we passed.

The gentleman arose as we approached. After introductions to Sir Philip Crestwell and Lady Olivia, I was seated on the divan with the baronet's wife while my father and Sir Philip went for refreshments.

"A lovely night for a ball," Lady Olivia observed politely, as she smoothed the lap of her ball gown, a field of petite pink flowers against pale green gauze overlaying a petticoat. Her neck was garnished with a simple strand of pink pearls with matching earbobs. Her face and manner revealed a sweet disposition with only a mild intelligence.

"It is indeed. How far have you come?" I responded, trying to bring my focus to the woman at my side after my first encounter with the Earl's handsome heir.

"We came from Hawkworth Heath. It took us about two hours to drive the twenty miles."

"How do you know my father then?"

"Hawkworth Heath is in the parish of Melmont," Lady Olivia replied. Melmont was my father's other, smaller living where he would occasionally visit to oversee the caretaker curate. "Have you been there with your father?"

"Not since I was younger. After my mother's passing when I was a little girl, I have been responsible with Miss Tilling for the affairs of the household." Upon hearing her name, Miss Tilling, who had been standing to the right side of the divan quietly observing the scene of the great hall, turned toward us and curtseyed to Lady Olivia.

The men returned with our glasses of punch just in time to hear the musical tempo change, announcing the official opening of the dance. The Countess of Fynchingham was escorted to the center of the floor by the Duke of Newchester and the orchestra began a minuet.

As my conversation with Lady Olivia was thus momentarily interrupted, I quickly scanned the room until my glance alighted on Lord Crevven standing next to his father at the doorway watching his mother being led around the room by her dance partner. He must have felt my stare because he glanced in my direction as I quickly looked away, but probably not soon enough to escape his detection. An inescapable warm flush rose up my neck to my cheeks. To restore my demeanor, I looked around the remaining half of the room in the opposite direction.

Someone was speaking to me. I looked up at Sir Philip Crestwell's proffered hand and deep bow as I came out of my embarrassed daze and heard the end of his question, "...with me?" I realized the minuet had ended and couples were lining up for a country dance.

"I would be honored, Sir Philip." I rose and curtseyed, both out of the need to be in motion to shake off the confused state caused by Lord Crevven's attention and simple courtesy to the baronet. I took hold of his outstretched hand to be led to the dance floor. We took our places facing each other in the middle of the line.

The Earl and his wife, at the head of the line as the top couple, began their way to advance to the center, twirled together, and retreated in the first figure. Next in line was Lord Crevven who advanced the center to circle with a female cousin. As he turned in front of me, he caught my eye for an eternal second and then retreated to his place. Each couple thus completed their set, Sir Philip and I advancing and retreating like the others, until the dance was complete. As customary, Sir Philip promenaded me around the room until we returned to our party of my father, Lady Olivia, and Miss Tilling.

My father danced the next set with Lady Olivia, while Sir Philip and I chatted about the dance, the house, and the weather. Sir Philip then danced with his wife, while I sat with my father for a while before he rose to cross the room and greet the family of the Earl's brother, the Viscount Glendowne, including Lord Crevven's cousin, the Honorable Sophie Glendowne. I was watching this encounter from my perch on the divan when I sensed the approach of a dark-dressed figure from the other direction, my heart skipping a beat.

"Emily Beechcroft, if I recall correctly," he said, more a statement than a question, and bowed slightly as I turned my eyes upward toward his impeccable countenance. Lord Crevven's engaging smile showered me like sunlight breaking through storm clouds.

"Yes," I answered, rising out of respect for his position and from being drawn into the source of his energy. Suddenly remembering my manners, I curtseyed.

"Would you honor me with this next dance?" Lord Crevven's eyes displayed a distinctive glint, reflecting the candlelight or an inner glow. From the moment he took my hand to lead me to the dance floor I completely lost awareness of anything other than his presence in the room. When we were touching, I felt complete happiness; when we separated, I felt as if a limb had been severed. And when he was obliged to dance with other partners, it seemed like I was enveloped in the dark of a sunless room.

As the dancing ended, the supper interlude was announced.

"May I escort you to refreshment?" The Fynchingham heir was next to me again.

"I would be delighted," I heard my voice say. I placed my hand and arm on his as we walked together toward the dining hall.

Once I was seated, as customary, Lord Crevven stood behind me sipping from his wine glass, while I attempted to swallow bites of the elaborate dishes of negus soup, meats, and sweets lain before us. Already light-headed from the exercise of dancing and the proximity of our host's son, I knew any further imbibing would merely make matters worse. I limited my beverage intake to lemonade and managed a few polite nibbles, which were all that my excited stomach would allow.

After my repast, Lord Crevven again took my arm to return me to the dance floor and my father's side.

"Will you be staying at Crevvenwood for a while?" I asked, hoping to mask my personal self-interest and apprehension over his answer with casual disinterest. My escort slowed his gait and turned his visage toward me. I felt my breath and heartbeat stop, poised for his answer as though my life depended upon it.

"It depends," he began thoughtfully, "on whether I can find sufficient activity here to hold my interest." Did his eyes hold the same question for me that my heart was holding for him? Modesty, upbringing, societal mores, and simply the fear of being too presumptuous silenced the question I wanted to ask. Instead, I posed the opposite one.

"And, if not?" It seemed to break the tension that had mounted from the unspoken inquiry between us.

"I suppose I would return to London to handle our family obligations there." He turned back to our walk. I thought his voice held a hint of sad resignation.

"Then, I hope we can supply you with many activities to pique your interest while you stay here," I wanted to revive his gaiety.

"I most sincerely hope so." Lord Crevven leaned over my hand to take leave of me and greeted my father.

"Reverend Beechcroft, I have enjoyed dancing with your daughter and look forward to hearing your next sermon."

"You are too kind, Lord Crevven," my father responded with a bow.

Bowing in return to both of us, the Fynchingham heir quitted us and headed back in the direction of the supper room.

"It seems you made a favorable impression on his Lordship...?" My father was interrupted as Viscount Glendowne approached us.

"Reverend Beechcroft, may I dance with your delightful daughter?" I was grateful for the interruption because I had no definitive answer to my father's—or my own—question.

As the evening wore on, I noticed I was either physically aware of where Lord Crevven was positioned in the dance hall, envious of every interaction he had with others, or seeking in near panic to find him when he slipped from my sight. Although I knew I could not monopolize his attentions for the remainder of the evening, I experienced myself as being slightly petulant and dissatisfied with my other dance and conversation partners. In one way, I never wanted the evening to end—even if I was no longer the nearest planet to be lit by the sun of my solar system—and, yet, I also could not wait for the evening to be over so that I could be alone and replay in my mind my precious moments with Lord Crevven.

Eventually, the evening did end and the tired guests filed out of the entrance hall after expressing appreciation to our hosts. As our party approached the Earl's family, I frantically searched for something brilliant and memorable to say, but instead my father startled me by extending an invitation to a dinner party at the vicarage. Embarrassed because our home was far too modest in comparison to the Fynchingham estate, I hoped our hosts would graciously decline but Lord Crevven squeezed my hand warmly and turned to gaze at me.

"I cannot respond for my parents, but I would enjoy that very much."

If he had not been grasping my hand at that moment, I am afraid my weak knees would not have held me, but I managed to answer with a responding compression to his hand.

"We will be delighted to have you to dinner."

I do not remember my feet touching the ground for our exit but my mind swirled with potential plans for a dinner and quickly rejected most of my ideas. Miss Tilling must have been equally occupied with her thoughts because she silently stared out the window of our coach as we returned home while my father chatted contentedly about the evening's events.

I finally broached the subject that was occupying Miss Tilling's and my thoughts.

"Father, were you serious about having the Earl and Lady Fynchingham over for dinner?"

"Why, I thought you made a good impression on their son," he retorted.

"That's not the point," I protested. "The vicarage is not suitable for guests of their status! Plus we would have to invite the Viscount and Viscountess Glendowne and their daughter, Sophie. Our house just isn't big enough." But as I said it, I realized that it was not the humbleness of our house that was my strongest objection, but the competitive presence of Sophie Glendowne, vying equally with me for her cousin's amorous attentions. I was afraid I was not a superior match on my merits alone.

I slipped into a brooding silence, wanting to bask in my memories of those delightful moments with Lord Crevven, not wishing to cloud or upset them with thoughts about tenuous future encounters. Earlier, I hadn't wanted the evening to end, and now I could not wait to go to bed.

When our carriage arrived at the vicarage, my father and Miss Tilling stepped out before me, but I was the first to enter the front door. After a quick kiss to my father's cheek and a good night to them both, I virtually sailed upstairs to my room. After a few mental re-enactments of the evening, I fell into a deep, blissful sleep.

The next morning, when I descended for breakfast, I found my father and Miss Tilling discussing how to rearrange the furniture for the dinner party he was planning for the Fynchinghams and the Glendownes.

"You don't even know if they will accept the invitation!" I stamped my foot.

"We should know soon." My father smiled with pride. "I sent the invitations out this morning."

A feeling of despair descended over me, punctuated slightly with the hopeful glimmer of anticipation at seeing the object of my romantic speculations again. I dared not hope for a further positive encounter, while every ounce of my being yearned for exactly for that. My mind barricaded hope behind a wall to protect it from disappointment, while my imagination stoked the very fires of anticipation.

I was miserable in my self-imposed limbo between heaven and hell. There was nothing to do but fret and await the outcome of my father's impatient invitations. I escaped to walk in the woods where William and I used to frequent, wishing to recapture those more carefree days.

"Where have you been, Miss?" Miss Tilling and cook were not happy with my absence. "Without your assistance, dinner is delayed. Now hurry and set out the dishes and silver."

We had just finished eating when we heard the garden gate bell sound announcing we had a visitor. Miss Tilling answered the door and returned to the dining room.

"Reverend, Sir, Lord Crevven has come to see you."

"Thank you, Miss Tilling. Are you coming, Emily?" My father rose and led the way into the parlor.

Having walked in the woods earlier, I was not at all prepared to receive such a distinguished guest, and yet there was no retreat to change my mud-edged dress and walking boots.

Despite my memories from the night before, I was physically struck once more by Lord Crevven's charm, gentlemanly bearing, and splendid good looks. I blushed uncontrollably while trying not to betray my infatuation. Something akin to the power of lightening passed between us as he took my hand in his to greet me. I was afraid to meet his eyes with mine, lest I melt into a puddle at his feet.

My father invited our guest into the parlor. As Lord Crevven let go of my hand to enter the room, I was able to regain a bit of my composure, as behind me, Miss Tilling cleared her throat and, in a loud whisper, said, "Emily, come help us prepare some refreshment for our visitor!"

I followed Miss Tilling to the rear of the house to assist with the preparations for tea, but my thoughts were in the parlor, straining to catch the gist of the conversation. Although I could not catch their words, I could hear the soft hum of the male voices—my father's a slightly higher pitch than the sonorous lilt of Lord Crevven's tone. Hearing it reminded me of the pleasure of walking on soft moss in the woods.

"Emily! Watch what you are doing!" admonished Miss Tilling, bringing my daydreaming mind back to the kitchen. I quickly mopped up the spilt tea water and put the cups, teapot, and plates on the tea tray. Lifting the tray, I followed Miss Tilling, who was carrying the cake, into the parlor. Both my father and our guest rose as we placed the tea items on the table.

"Would you like some tea and cake, Lord Crevven?" I offered, managing to address our special guest with an even voice.

"Lord Crevven has come to tell us the Fynchinghams have honored us by accepting our dinner invitation for Tuesday next," my father interjected excitedly. I turned a quizzical look towards our guest.

"With pleasure," Lord Crevven added, parting his lips in a radiant smile bestowed in my direction.

"We've also invited the Glendownes," my father inserted.

"It all sounds splendid," our guest pronounced. "And, I would like a cup of tea." The cup rattled softly in the saucer as I handed it to him, while I attempted to appear as calm as he was despite my receiving confirmation of the dinner party.

As though not wanting to give me any further discomfort on the subject, Lord Crevven turned back to my father.

"What topic will your sermon address this Sunday, Reverend?"

As my father and Lord Crevven began to discourse on the subject of his forthcoming sermon and the affairs of the village in general, I was able to study our visitor's visage and bearing in more detail: the line of his jaw, the curve of his cheek, the dimples that creased his face when he smiled, and the curl of his eyelashes.

In addition to his looks, he had a stately, self-confident bearing, gentle and sensitive to those around him, yet with a deep-seated strength that would serve him with an adversary. I tried to soak in every aspect about him—his mannerisms, his dress, and his very being. All too soon, however, Lord Crevven announced his departure, goodbyes were exchanged, and the light when out of the house when he left.

In anticipation of the dinner party my days were spent in planning, cleaning, baking, and all sorts of preparations for the upcoming event. When I was not helping Miss Tilling and cook, I would spend my time sewing my dress for the evening, a pale blue muslin frock with cap sleeves and a white dotted Swiss under-chemise. The high-waist was tied with a white silk ribbon to match the one for my hair. Silver slippers plus a simple pearl necklace and ear bobs would complete my outfit. Since I would be unable to compete with Sophie Glendowne's wealth and dazzle, I opted for austere simplicity.

Our guests arrived, as custom, shortly after 7:00 Tuesday evening. After an exchange of greetings and polite conversation in the parlor, we adjourned to the dining room. My father escorted the Countess of Fynchingham, seating her to the right of his head table seat. Her husband, the Earl, followed with the Viscountess Glendowne who was seated to the Earl's right at the other end of the table from my father. The Viscount took my arm and sat me to the Earl's left and himself in the center to my left, while Lord Crevven and his cousin entered last, Sophie seated to my father's left while her escort placed himself in the last remaining seat in the middle.

Thus sandwiched between his cousin Sophie and his aunt, Viscountess Glendowne, Lord Crevven would, disappointingly, not be available to me as a conversational companion for the length of the dinner. Rather, I was locked between the Earl and his younger brother who discussed hunting, politics, and estate affairs. As the dinner wore on, I slipped into silent observation.

In contrast, Lord Crevven appeared maddeningly at ease, equally at home conversing with his cousin or his aunt, while in my own home, I was clearly out of my element between two pillars of the peerage—his father and his uncle. Once or twice in passing, he glanced my way but was immediately drawn back into conversation by one or the other lady beside him. It was almost a relief when the gentlemen withdrew to the parlor for their port, but then I was aware of being excluded from the female gossip about people I did not know, as the Countess, Viscountess, and Sophie chatted primarily amongst themselves. I was fighting back tears of frustration when the men returned.

"Do you play whist?" Lord Crevven inquired of me upon re-entering the dining room.

"A little," I brightened, basking in his sudden attention.

Lord Crevven advanced to behind my chair, pulling it from behind me as I rose.

"Would anyone else like to join us in a game?" Lord Crevven looked around the rest of the room while he offered me his arm. All present being in assent, we retired to the parlor and set up two tables of four.

"Will you be my partner for the game?" Lord Crevven asked me once the tables were arranged.

"I would be delighted."

The Countess and Viscount joined our table while the Earl, Viscountess, and the Honorable Sophie Glendowne joined my father.

Despite my limited experience with the card game, Lord Crevven and I won most of the hands. He would look across the table at me almost to divine which trick to play, and then he would play the perfect card sequence. I could tell he liked the intellectual challenge of it—remembering which cards had been played and deducing who had the remaining cards in their hands from the ones they played—all the while delightfully recounting news of London or stories from his travels, as though his attention was not on the cards. I was both charmed and entertained.

All too soon, however, the game was over, and our guests rose to depart, each gentleman, in turn, bowing slightly over my hand as my father did the same to the other ladies.

Two days later, my father was called to Melmont while I was helping our house staff rearrange the furniture in the parlour and dining room to its customary set-up. Because we had opened the windows to the warm air of a fine day, I heard a horse approach our gate followed by the bell announcing a visitor. Since Miss Tilling was back in the kitchen, I opened the door to find Lord Crevven in his riding dress. As delighted as I was by this unexpected surprise, our house was in too much disarray to receive him properly.

I curtsied. "My father has gone down to Melmont," I began regretfully. "I don't expect him back until nightfall." Even if our home had been perfectly presentable and Miss Tilling able to sit in the parlour with us, as a single young woman, it would not have been entirely appropriate for me to entertain a single young man.

"I see." Our handsome visitor appeared to size up the indelicate situation. "Would you please tell him I will return tomorrow?" He bowed slightly and turned to remount his horse. I stood watching him ride away.

The following day, Lord Crevven returned as promised, and my father was home to greet him. The rooms had been put back to rights, and I was dressed in a light pink frock with darker pink flowers. After a pleasant half-hour of talk, my father suggested we take a walk through the church grounds. I donned a periwinkle blue spencer jacket against the slight chill, and Miss Tilling joined our party.

My father pointed out gravestones of noteworthy former residents, the cornerstone dating back to 1765, and the small contemplative garden to the rear, before heading to the front to enter the sanctuary with Miss Tilling behind him. However, Lord Crevven hung back momentarily, and I stayed with him, partly as an act of being a gracious hostess and partly out of curiosity.

"Miss Beechcroft..." He hesitated as though not sure what to say next. I waited out of respect and nervous anticipation.

"Miss Beechcroft, my parents are expecting me to marry soon." He stopped again and rubbed his hands together, visibly searching for his next sentence. He looked at the ground. "If I do not select someone of my own choosing soon, I believe they will match me with my cousin, Sophie Glendowne. Although Sophie has certain charms, I..." He looked up at me.

I was aware that our unchaperoned absence would very soon be noticed. Lord Crevven's unasked, unanswered question hung in the air between us, but without him actually asking my feelings toward him out loud, any direct response from me would have been presumptuously out of place. Instead, I laced my arm through his and began walking to the front of the church, hoping my gesture, at once both respectful and intimate, would answer his doubts. He reached over with his loose hand and patted mine resting on his arm, smiled tenderly, and relaxed as we rounded the front of the church. I am not sure my feet touched the ground as we walked.

When we entered the sanctuary, Miss Tilling gave me a disapproving look that I ignored, but my father began his tour of the inside with enthusiasm. Lord Crevven appeared to listen politely, occasionally asking questions, while I was lost in my recollection of the exchange between us moments earlier.

When my father had completed his tour, Miss Tilling and I exited through the stone portico and headed down the walk toward the opening in the stone wall surrounding the churchyard. She and I stopped at the aperture and turned to see my father appear surprised at something Lord Crevven must have said to him, then he clasped Crevven's right hand with both of his own and shook it vigorously. Then they both descended the stone steps from the portico to the gravel path and headed in our direction. Both men were smiling—my father broadly and the Fynchingham heir less conspicuously but essentially pleased.

I was on tenterhooks to learn what had just transpired between my father and Lord Crevven but knew I would have to wait until my father and I were alone together later. Lord Crevven took his leave at our garden gate, mounted his horse, and rode back in the direction of his parents' manor house.

However, I was not to have the audience alone with my father. As we neared the house, cook intercepted our party of three.

"Reverend Sir, Farmer Owing has been crushed by a mule and might not live through the night." Farmer Owing was one of the village yeomen and father to ten children. My father left immediately to tend to the dying farmer and his family, leaving me and Miss Tilling perplexed by the earlier events.

I was awakened the next morning by the *nine tailors*—nine tolls of the "passing bell" for Farmer Owing followed by a peal for each year of his life. My father was sequestered in his study most of the day, preparing for the funeral that would be attended by the male members of the village. Once the death knell had tolled, I knew the deceased had been interred.

My father would expect a repast after the funeral. When I heard the garden gate bell ring, I went to the front door to greet him, but instead I was astonished to see Lord Crevven, dressed in mourning, standing in the entrance instead. He must have come straight from the gravesite since his boots had fresh mud on them. His manner was serious, not unusual considering the sad duty that he had just attended.

"My father has not yet returned," I started, at the same time Lord Crevven was saying, "I suspect your father has likely been too occupied to speak with you..." We both hesitated. I could not invite him into our house without my father present, yet I sensed Lord Crevven had something important to say.

Appearing to come to a decision, Lord Crevven offered me his arm and asked, "Would you walk with me a bit in your garden?"

Although it was small, the flower garden extended from the front around to the side of the house and ended in the kitchen garden to the rear. If Lord Crevven was about to ask me what I hoped with all my heart, it would little matter that we were unchaperoned in my own garden for a few moments. I took his crooked elbow in assent.

When we turned the corner of the house to enter the side garden and were less conspicuous to passersby, Lord Crevven released my arm but continued to hold my hand in his.

"I had hoped your father would have spoken with you first, but as his duties and circumstances have prevented it, I hope you will not object to my impatience in speaking with you first." I nodded slightly, encouraging him to proceed. For someone who had been so self-assured in our previous encounters, Lord Crevven appeared agitated and unsure of himself while, in contrast, I felt glacially calm. With my free left hand, I lightly but reassuringly placed it atop his hand holding mine. His eyes looked penetratingly into mine. I felt slightly unbalanced by his sudden intensity. With a deep in-breath, he gathered his courage and exhaled his question in a rush of words.

"Miss Beechcroft...Emily, my dear, your father has permitted me to propose marriage to you, should you be willing...?"

"Oh, yes!" A wave of joy and relief washed over me. "Oh, yes, I am willing!" My body swayed slightly toward him.

After a blink of incredulity swept across his face, Lord Crevven gathered me in his arms and bestowed a kiss on the top of my head.

"Ahem!" My father cleared his throat behind me. "I gather that Emily has assented to your proposal, Sir?"

Releasing me from his grasp, Lord Crevven beamed and nodded affirmatively.

"This requires a toast," my father suggested and turned to cross the threshold of our house, while arm-in-arm we followed him inside.

Once Miss Tilling was called and joined us, the port was poured and a congratulatory toast was made and drank. We all agreed that Lord Crevven should return to Crevvenwood at once to announce the news to his parents, after which arrangements would be made for my presentation to the Earl and Countess as their son's fiancée.

And now I stood before the façade of Crevvenwood on the cusp of becoming Lady Emily Crevven. It felt unreal like a dream, everything had happened so quickly, and yet I also felt solid and sure when I was with (dare I call him now?) Christopher. I repeated his Christian name over gently in my head.

The interview with the Earl and Countess of Fynchingham was reserved but not difficult. They may have placed some hope on a match between Christopher and the Honorable Sophie Glendowne, but they would acquiesce to their son's choice of a wife.

Wedding plans were discussed. My father would marry us by license at the village church within a month's time. A wedding breakfast would follow on the grounds of Crevvenwood, after which Christopher and I would depart by sailing vessel from Weymouth for Falmouth where we would spend a month visiting with the Countess's sister and her family. Our wedding night would be spent at Stacie's Hotel on the Esplanade in the port city so that we could sail on the next day's tide. A dressmaker from Salisbury would design my dress in grey silk with a matching cape to double as protection during the windy two days in the Channel. All the details seemed to have been so well outlined that I suspected that the plans had been in place for some time, merely awaiting Christopher's choice of a mate.

With so many items to execute in a short month's time, Miss Tilling and I were soon returned to my home by Christopher and his carriage. On the return trip, my former governess was too full of excitement, schemes, and projects to stay angered at my earlier behavior. Now formally engaged to be married, Christopher and I shared the same leather bench on the return trip, and he held both my hands in his, too overcome for words, while I softly hummed.

Once back at the Rectory, we told my father of the wedding plans.

"Where will you settle after your honeymoon in Falmouth, Lord Crevven?" my father inquired, aware that his daughter would no longer be able to provide the comfort of her company to him as frequently.

"We will divide our time between Crevvenwood and London for the season, I suspect," reassured Christopher.

Hugging my father swiftly, I generously added, "I will visit you often, and you will be welcome to come dine with us."

Since everyone seemed satisfied with the projected events, Christopher took his leave with a promise to return within the week.

The month disappeared quickly in a flurry of activity, and our wedding day dawned sunny and full of promise.

I wanted to linger in bed and savor the last time I would be an unmarried girl at the Rectory. But I also wanted the excitement of the day and my new life with Christopher to begin. Questions and wonder about our life together swirled in my head like the butterflies in my stomach. I wished my mother were here. Since she had died and my father had not remarried, I did not have a role model for wifely conduct. I could not imagine myself seeking the Countess's counsel on such matters. I would have to rely on Christopher's affection, understanding, instruction, and forbearance.

I dressed in my grey silk wedding gown with the determination of someone who is not fully aware of that which she has undertaken. When I was ready to have my hair dressed, I called for Miss Tilling's aid.

My former governess displayed a mixture of unsettled excitement and pride that did nothing to calm my own jitters. This was not the moment to approach her with my own fears, especially since she had no direct knowledge of matrimony herself. Instead, I thanked her for her devoted years of service to me and my father and gave her a hug which brought tears to both of our eyes. Then we descended the stairs and exited the house.

At the gate, I turned to look back at my childhood home for the last time as a youth, then lifting the front of my skirt, hurried along to the church.

The Fynchingham estate carriage with the family coat-of-arms on the doors had already arrived along with those of the Glendownes, the Crestwells, and several other distinguished families. An open barouche also stood directly in front of the gate. I surmised that this was the vehicle that would transport Christopher and me from the church to Crevvenwood for the wedding breakfast.

In addition to the assembled nobility, throngs of villagers had gathered and overflowed the church to witness the marriage of the only heir to Crevvenwood and the Fynchingham estate to the only daughter of the village rector. This was the event of a generation, if not a lifetime, for many of them, and they would not miss it for anything.

The crowd parted to let me pass into the church grounds and ascend the steps to the portico. At most weddings, a father, brother, or uncle would accompany the bride down the aisle, but my father was officiating, and I had no other male relatives to perform that honor. I was to walk the church length on my own. I chastised myself for not realizing sooner that I would want someone to lean on at that moment, but I could not think of anyone I would have wanted, other than William, who would not be appropriate.

I realized that I had not seen William in the crowd and wondered if he would come at all. But before that thought could linger, a village boy serving as an acolyte told me that all was ready for the service to begin.

I had a moment of panic as I stepped to the head of the center aisle, but my gaze fell on Christopher waiting for me near the altar and then on my father standing in readiness. Christopher broke into a smile like the sun breaking through the clouds after a downpour and erased my fears. I flushed and returned his elated expression with relief and joy. My father, too, was smiling in benevolent fashion, pleased and proud that his daughter had grown up to enter into a match that raised and secured both our stations in life.

With the two men I most loved in the world standing at the front of the sanctuary, I was drawn down the aisle as if on a cloud.

I do not remember much of what was said. I just remember standing before Christopher totally entranced by his eyes. Nothing else existed or mattered around us.

And then it was over. We both signed the parish register and, my father hugged me and shook Christopher's hand. Linking arms, Christopher and I strode together out of the church between the cheering groups of villagers on either side of the path and toward the waiting barouche.

The footman helped first me, then Christopher into the carriage. As I turned to wave to the throng of well-wishers, I glimpsed a downcast William standing in the middle of the churchyard. He must have arrived too late to be seated inside the stone church. He was dressed uncomfortably in a loose-fitting suit, his Sunday best, and slowly turned a broad-brimmed straw hat between his hands. I detected a mixture of reluctant happiness for me tinged with sad regret at the event putting a final end to our friendship. It was the one blemish on an otherwise perfect day.

I soon forgot William's demeanor once I was caught up in the festive spirit of the celebratory breakfast, greeting the Fynchinghams as my new in-laws and the rest of the guests at Crevvenwood. All too soon, it was time to depart for Weymouth. Our trunks were loaded on the back of a closed carriage while Christopher and I bade farewell to our respective parents. We climbed onto the carriage bench and were carried off down the drive amidst the throwing of old shoes. I nestled into the shelter of Christopher's arm as I realized that, except for the coachman and footman aloft on the front of the carriage, we were alone together in the confines of the leather interior for the next several hours of a jolting ride to the port and the mysteries of our wedding night.

"Are you nervous?"

"A bit," I looked up at Christopher's face for reassurance. He kissed me to transfer some of his confidence to me. From here forward, everything would be new to me, whereas he had been to sea and knew his mother's family. He was comfortable in the upper class world of London and country houses. I was entering his world a complete ingénue with only him to guide me.

"You will be fine." But I was not sure to which aspect of our future life together he referred. I hoped he was right. To distract me from the concerns beginning to crowd my thoughts, I watched the passing scene through the window—the familiar scenes of my home, village, and surrounding countryside slowly retreating as the landscape became less and less familiar.

Christopher placed his right arm around my shoulder, while I nestled into his form. He took my right hand in his left. We sat for a while in contented silence. Then I turned to face him.

"Tell me about Europe."

For the next hour, he entertained me with descriptions of the European capitals, court intrigues, and exotic countrysides. Although first the French Revolution and then Napoleon's dominance on the Continent had made travel there difficult, during a lull in the wars of the French Emperor's increasing land grab, Christopher was one of few young Englishmen who had successfully been able to visit Europe.

In Dorchester, we stopped for a short rest and refreshments at a wayside tavern before we returned to the carriage to continue on our journey to Weymouth.

With a full stomach, I dozed for a while. I awakened to the call of seabirds and smell of salty air.

"Did you enjoy your nap?" Christopher planted a kiss on top of my head.

I sat up, lifting my weight from his arm and side, stretched, then turned to smile bashfully at him. I was struck again by his handsomeness, then remembered suddenly we were now married.

"Yes. Do we have much further to travel?"

Pulling out his gold pocket watch, he replied, "Likely another half-hour."

I leaned out of the carriage window. The height of the sun told me it was mid-afternoon.

"I think you'll like Weymouth," Christopher suggested. "Tonight we will stay at Stacie's Hotel and Assembly Rooms overlooking the bay and beach, but first we will walk along the Esplanade this afternoon after this long ride. Our ship will leave from the Custom House Quay in the harbour area. King George III swam at Weymouth in 1789, and since then it has taken on more fame as a seaside resort in addition to its traditional role as a port."

"How long will it take us to get to your aunt's home?"

"We will likely be at sea for two days to reach Falmouth, depending on the weather and sailing winds, then a half-day by carriage."

I returned to watching the passing vista. I remarked the differences in vegetation and cottage architecture as we neared the coast. Approaching the outskirts of Weymouth, I noticed the buildings were closer together—some made of stucco, others of stone.

When we crested a hill, I saw the bridge over the Wey River, and further in the distance, the sparkling waters of the Weymouth Bay and, farther out still, the Channel was visible, taking my breath away. Descending across the river bridge into the city on St. Thomas Street, we passed several rows of townhouses in the process of construction, lining each side of the cobblestoned streets. Chandlers and costermongers, packmen and pie men, sailors and sweeps, and all sorts of workers all went about their business mingling among more high-class folks, various street children, apprentices, clerks, and cooks shopping for food.

On the left, Christopher pointed out the Royal shrubbery and then the Royal Palace. Each building was three stories high and three bays wide. One of the bays on the ground floor served as an entrance door. Some windows had arched heads while others were encased with columns or topped with elliptical fanlights. Many of the first floors were rusticated stone. Some of the second stories had wrought iron balconies or verandahs with trellis supports. They made a charming spectacle of sentries.

The coach proceeded up the waterfront, past five stately, newly fashioned, pastel-colored, bow-windowed town houses. We halted in front of Stacie's Hotel, a more austere but dignified three-story stone structure. Different from the other buildings, the hotel also had two semi-circular bowed corners of three windows wide. The center pavilion was flat, although also three bays wide and three stories high, and was topped by a triangular pediment. The lower central bay had an arched doorway set in rusticated stone. More townhouses extended as down the street as far as I could see.

Christopher helped me alight from our carriage while the footmen brought down our trunks and took them inside. I waited inside the elegant candlelit lobby, surveying my surroundings while Christopher registered us with the desk clerk. Then we were led upstairs to our sleeping suite on the top floor of one of the curved bays. In Adamesque-style, the light blue walls were crowned by a white stucco ceiling in low relief.

Our four-poster bed faced the window with a spectacular view of the sea. In one corner was a screen hiding the dressing area, water basin, and commode. The adjacent parlour had a mantled fireplace that backed up to the one inside the sleeping room. The warmth from the lit fire emanated outward.

The furniture was thoroughly modern, exhibiting the heavier, rounded, Egyptian influences of the Continent beginning to replace the more lightly playful rococo elements of the Hepplewhite and Sheraton furniture of the previous decade. I noticed motifs of lotus leaves and reclining lions, the use of inlaid ebony and satinwood on mahogany veneers, and curved cross frames ending in lions' paws. Chairs, reclining sofas, and a settee were all covered in light blue satin patterned with gold designs. I was so thoroughly enchanted with my fairy tale surroundings that I did not realize for several moments that Christopher was silently watching me as I inspected this new environment. When I finally turned my attention back to him, he simply inquired,

198

"Would you like some refreshment before we take a stroll outdoors or after we return?"

"Afterwards, please!" I did not wish to miss a moment to see the wonders of this new place.

Together we descended the hotel staircase and walked out again into the hubbub of the street, crossed it, and mounted the parapet alongside the white sands, passing the royal enclave once again, although this time on foot. I was not sure which was more delightful to my senses—the elegant Georgian architecture of the King's seaside palace or the magnificent nature of the Channel and the expansive curve of the sandy beach.

As we strolled down the Esplanade, Christopher pointed out the York Terraces, Harvey's Assembly Rooms, and the Royal Theatre. Behind Charlotte Row were the Oxford Hotel and Ferry Inn, and as the Esplanade curved toward the open Channel, the Clarence Buildings gave way to the Alexandra Hotel and Gardens framed in the background by the Devonshire and Pulteny Buildings beyond.

By this time, the excitement of the day's events was taking its toll on me, so we retraced our steps to our hotel. We found the dining room where we ordered a light supper before ascending to our room.

Christopher seemed to enjoy his role as my guide and instructor. He tried not to overwhelm me while imparting information in his understated manner. I appreciated that he had so much more to teach me but he was in no particular rush, allowing me to absorb it all at my own pace.

Back in our suite, he discreetly permitted me to take off my gown behind the screen and wash off the dirt of travel and our walk while he read in the parlour. I donned a simple white, lace-trimmed, chemise-style nightgown and climbed under the covers of the bed.

The feel of the cool sheets on my legs was soothing as I sunk into the softness of the down pillow and closed my eyes.

I dozed off quickly but awakened as Christopher blew out the bedside candle. I felt both his body weight on the other side of the bed and cool air as he lifted the covers to slide in next to me. His arms pulled me toward him, surrounding me and nestling the curve of my backside against his warm, masculine form. Our arms were interlaced around my waist, and I could feel his warm, sure, rhythmic breath in my left ear.

"I love you," he stated simply.

"Mmmm, I love you, too," I replied sleepily.

After a few moments of this blissful hug, Christopher concurrently moved his hands up to cuddle my breasts and licked my ear. My eyes flew open as an unexpected surge coursed through the female recesses between my legs, creating a warm, moist feeling there.

"Ohhhh," I moaned involuntarily.

In a few swift movements, Christopher rolled me over toward him, slipped his arms under my shoulders, pressed his mouth to mine, and lay upon me. His tongue was inside my mouth, exploring, until it found mine, and they danced together.

I was not sure quite how to react, although the sensations he was evoking were pleasurable. I slid my arms around his back, realizing for the first time that Christopher was completely undressed, and I was totally at his mercy in my ignorance.

Christopher pulled his body to one side and slid his left hand up under my nightgown towards my right breast, alternately cuddling and massaging it. Exploring a little further, his forefinger and thumb found my nipple. I inhaled a quick breath and felt more warm feelings between my legs. In response, I arched my back. Christopher took the opportunity to pull my nightgown off entirely to have full access to my breasts and nipples, taking one in his mouth to suckle. My brain felt comprised of fireworks. My breath quickened sharply.

The room was lit only by the moonlight and its reflection off the Bay outside. As my eyes became accustomed to the darkness, I could see my husband's dark form above me.

Christopher guided my hand to a hard, skin-covered object between his legs surrounded by coarse, curly hair covering two pouches. His manly hand still covering mine, we stroked the object together until it was completely hard and erect. All the while, Christopher was kissing my face, neck, and shoulders.

"Keep stroking me," he encouraged as he removed his hand from mine, and raising himself on one elbow, it sought out the hair-covered area between my legs. Gently prying them apart, Christopher's fingers found that moist place and began to cause wonderful sensations throughout me. Suddenly, he thrust his finger inside me. I tensed my body, but he used his other hand to reassure me with a stroke on my shoulder.

There was a soft, sucking sound as he withdrew his wet finger from within me. Gently removing my hand from his rod-like protrusion, Christopher whispered, "You're ready."

Separating my legs into a V-shape, Christopher knelt between them, and then thrust his rod inside me where his finger had been.

"Aeeiih!" I protested as a searing, white-hot pain ripped me apart.

"It only hurts the first time," Christopher tried to soothe me as his hips began to move closer and farther from me, thrusting the rod deeply then withdrawing it part way. Sometimes he kissed me, sometimes my breasts.

I reached up and touched his chest, lacing my fingers through the soft hair and, finding his nipples, I kneaded them in tentative reciprocity. Flashing his brilliant smile, Christopher murmured, "I like that."

Thus emboldened, I applied similar strokes and touches to my husband's body as he had done to me, becoming more of a partner in the night's erotic exchange.

In response, Christopher's rhythmic pushing and retracting quickened and took on a greater urgency. Soon we were both intently concentrating solely on the colliding of our pelvises.

Suddenly, almost without warning, a wave broke over me, sending a series of pulsations through my female recesses. Within moments, Christopher tensed, thrust one last time, and released his fluid inside me.

Still inside me, but much softer, my husband's body weight relaxed on top of me. I slowly glided my fingers down the length of his bare back and gently caressed his bare buttocks. We were both spent and perspiring. I noticed we had a special, musky smell of our combined body fluids and odors.

After several still moments of lying on top of me, I felt the full weight of Christopher's body bearing down on me. Slowly, he pulled himself off and apart from me, rolling over onto his back. Involuntarily, I began to cry at this act of separation, so Christopher gathered me in his arms to his chest, and so enwrapped we fell into our night-long slumber.

By the time I awakened, the sun was fully up, and Christopher was dressed. Through the open doorway to the parlour, I could see he was already eating the breakfast that had been delivered to our room. I scanned the bedroom to determine where my nightgown had been so cavalierly thrown the night before. Christopher must have anticipated my return to modesty, because it was carefully hung on one of the posters of the bed. Holding the covers close to my chest to hide my nakedness, I retrieved my garment and slipped it back on while still hidden by the covers. Then, furtively, I disappeared behind the screen to wash and dress in a reverse of last night's chain of events.

When I appeared at the parlour entrance, Christopher looked up from his reading, closed his book, and greeted me with a seductive gleam in his eyes.

"Good morning, sleepy head." As he poured me a cup of coffee, he observed, "In the future, you will be doing this for me."

We ate our toast and eggs in companionable silence for a few moments. Then with a brashness born of intimate familiarity, I asked somewhat tentatively,

"How did you kno...Where did you learn...what we did last night?"

Christopher chuckled softly—whether at my question or his answer—I know not which.

"There are many French and Italian women who are more than willing to teach a young lord the ways of the *boudoir*." Sensing that I was not sure how to react to his response, he added with a smile, "You will make a very agreeable wife in that regard." To emphasize his satisfaction, Christopher lifted my hand and kissed it. His demeanor then shifted from one of personal intimacy to one of dutiful business.

"Now, if we do not hurry, we will miss our passage." My husband downed the remaining coffee in his cup, pushed his chair back from the table, and stood.

"While you are finishing your packing, I will settle our account then order the carriage round with the footman to assist with our trunks." Then he left me alone in the room to descend to the main lobby.

Unexpectedly, I had almost a physical sense of loss and dread, a heart-rending separation like the night before, or as if a limb had been severed off. I told myself that this was silly; he was only downstairs and would return shortly, but I could not seem to shake the sense of apprehension even when I proceeded to repack my things into my trunk. When I was finished, I wrapped myself in my grey silk cloak and pretended it was Christopher's arms around me. I stood at the window looking down at the Bay, the Esplanade, and the bustle below me. I tried to reassure myself that it was simply my anxiety about my first experience on a sailing ship and the anticipation of meeting Christopher's relations in Cornwall.

Several minutes later, Christopher returned, like the sun after a long, hard rain, accompanied by the footman and a hotel servant for our luggage. Then we all went down to the street to load the carriage for the trip to the docks on Custom House Quay.

After passing the terraced Gloucester Row and the Royal Lodge, our carriage went left along the Promenade, past the York Buildings and Harvey's again, the Library, and Charlotte Row. However, instead of heading straight as we had on our previous evening's walk, we turned to the right at the Royal Theatre and entered East Street, passing the Oxford Hotel and Ferry Inn. As we approached the quay, I saw a series of seventeenth century stone cottages whose rear once faced the Channel but whose view was obstructed by Belle Vue Terrace, now overlooking Alexandra Gardens and the sea instead.

The Quay itself was lined with timber-framed seamen's inns and extended several blocks along the mouth of the River Wey. The harbour was chaotic with the bustle of loading and unloading freight and passengers, sailors and seamen, drunk and sober, fishermen and fishmongers, all weaving in and out, shouting and singing. I was both fascinated and a little overwhelmed with the bustle. I was grateful to be under the protective guidance of my husband.

202

The carriage stopped as Christopher alighted and turned to help me out. He pointed out a Tudor house in the next block with a cannonball embedded in its gable end before leading me towards a tall-masted, black sailing schooner, the *Francesca*, which would take us to Falmouth. Something about the ship made me shiver. I wondered to myself how such a small vessel would fare in a squall in the Channel. I had heard stories of ships being lured to wreck on rocky shores for their cargo and tales of smugglers plying the coastal waters.

I could not fathom why I was imagining these frightening events when I was on my honeymoon with a wonderful man. I shook my head to clear it of these fearful fantasies.

As we ascended the *Francesca's* gangplank, the ship's captain appeared on deck to greet us. He was tall and rather thin, almost scrawny, with a couple days' growth of beard. His short-waisted, dark blue, velvet jacket was outdated, faded, and worn. The lace neck stock he wore was limp, with a yellowish tinge, and his waistcoat was stained. A pair of scuffed boots rose to cover his loose-fitting sailor pants. The left side of his face was contracted with a slight palsy causing his left eye to squint and the left side of his smile to be higher than the right.

Arranged all around the captain were sailors of various shapes and sizes, some in the striped shirts of ordinary seaman and others in the waistcoats of midshipmen. All-in-all, my impression of the captain and his crew was one of scruffiness, and I instinctively clutched Christopher's arm more tightly as we alighted onto the deck. I wondered how many of the crew had been impressed into service.

"Captain Josiah Carpenter, at yer service, sir," the captain stepped forward to introduce himself. "Welcome aboard the *Francesca*, a no more seaworthy vessel ye'll find," he boasted unconvincingly.

"Lord and Lady Crevven," Christopher responded, "bound for Falmouth. At what time do you expect we will sail?"

"We still be loading some cargo, and the tide, she's still out, so it'll be early aft'noon a'fore we depart. Meanwhile, ye might make yerself familiar with quarters below deck." There was something a little too ingratiating in his attitude, a false servitude that hid untrustworthiness. He instructed one of the sailors to guide us below.

I was a little wobbly moving across the deck to the bulkhead and down the narrow ladder after my husband. The smell below was foul after the sea air, and the space was cramped. We entered a claustrophobic and compact, wood-paneled room with a cot that was more a padded box than a conventional bed. The paneling consisted of cupboards while the table and chairs were bolted to the floor. The seaman who accompanied us pointed out the toilet facilities that consisted of a wooden platform with a hole open to the water below and a ceramic basin bolted to a shelf where rainwater would be provided for washing. I noticed that the basin did not appear to have held any clean water for a long time.

Shortly, our trunks were brought in to the cabin, making it even more crowded. Thankfully, the seaman left to return above deck, leaving us alone to contemplate our situation. In comparison to the elegant suite at Stacie's Hotel the night before, these accommodations were shockingly wanting.

"How long will it take us to get to Falmouth?" I searched Christopher's face to ascertain whether he was as dismayed as I was by the ship and the journey's prospects.

"We should be there the morning after tomorrow, barring a bad storm," he replied deep in thought, obviously weighing our options in his mind. "With our navy protecting our seas from French encroachment, the best vessels and crew have been required for service elsewhere," Christopher justified, as much to himself as to me.

All the travel arrangements had been made by Christopher's family without my direct knowledge, so I relied on their far greater experience in these matters. As a new bride, it was not my place to question my husband or these arrangements. We would just have to make the best of an uncomfortable situation for a couple of days.

However, the undulation of the tide and putrid smell were having their effect on me.

"May we go back on deck, Christopher?" My husband straightened up from rummaging through his belongings and looked at me with an expression of relief.

"If we will not be sailing for another couple of hours, we should sup at a tavern on the quay," he suggested. "I think you will feel better once you have eaten and our ship gets underway." Christopher closed his trunk and took me by the hand to lead me back up to the main deck. Once above, he briefly consulted with the captain, checked his pocket watch, and then escorted me down the gangplank and into a nearby public house where we passed a good hour in dining.

Thus satiated, we returned again to the schooner deck to await the captain's cast-off orders and the unfurling of the sails as we lifted anchor and slid our way down the Wey and out of the harbour.

I thought it magical as the buildings and terraces of Weymouth glided past us and shrunk in size as we entered the bay. Christopher and I stood arm-in-arm at the stern rail while we passed the Isle of Portland and rounded its southern tip before turning westward and then northward to hug the coast of Lyme Bay.

Breathing the salty air and sensing the steady movement over the deeper water of the bay did make me feel better, but as the sun began its descent, I became chilled and asked Christopher if he would fetch my silk cloak from our cabin. While he was conducting this errand below, the captain startled me from behind. As I turned to face him, he pressed my back hard against the railing, his leering visage too close to mine and his arms encircling me, pulling me forward to embrace him. I quickly turned my face to avoid his distasteful lips and tried to pull his gripping arms away from me.

At that moment, Christopher, in possession of my cloak, emerged again from the bulkhead and discovered the captain's unwelcome advances toward his new wife. As my husband rushed to my aid, dropping the cloak on deck, he was violently restrained by two sailors who appeared to be enjoying both my struggle and that of my husband. Wrenching Christopher's hands behind his back, the sailors bound him with rope while two other mates picked his feet up. Together, the four men lifted him up and over the railing and threw him overboard.

"NO!" Christopher!" I screamed thrashing and fighting with all my strength against the grip the captain had on me. It was all he could do to hold onto me, until another sailor came along side us. I felt a crushing blow to the base of my neck where it intercepted with my right shoulder, rendering me unconscious.

I woke to the awful smell of tar, brine, and vomit. I was in pitch black darkness. I tried to pull myself onto my knees and elbows, but the rocking sensation and the clammy, wet, slimy-covered surface made it slippery, and I fell forward. Again I tried to pull myself up but soon realized that my hands were bound by a rope that was securely fastened to some permanent object. My neck, elbows, and knees ached; my head throbbed; and my stomach was roiling around.

I did not know where I was or what I was doing there. Above me, I could hear shouting voices, the slap of water, and a crack of lightening. Suddenly, I was thrown forward and again splayed out on the slick surface. The next moment I was thrown to the rear and rolled sideways, my arms almost pulled from my shoulders and my wrists scraped by the grip of the rope. The shouting above was muffled but now became frantic.

There was a loud, cracking sound of splitting wood, followed by a huge wave of seawater over me, slamming me backwards against a curved wall. The water entered my mouth and nose, causing me to choke and sputter. Then that same wave sucked me forward, tumbling and clutching for a hold, but to no avail. My knees, arms, and torso were scraped and scratched as I was cast out upon rocks and boulders of some headland. The seawater receded again, leaving me beached.

As another bolt of lightning descended from the dim, grey light of the storm clouds and lit my surroundings, I looked behind me to see the gaping gash in the schooner's hull as the boat ebb backwards from the rocks toward the Channel waters. Whatever had tethered my rope-bound hands to the interior of the ship was gone.

Ascertaining that no one was pursuing me, I wildly scrambled up the rocky escarpment until I reached the top. I shot a glance over my shoulder one more time to assure myself that no one was following then hurriedly moved away from the edge lest someone see me. I found myself on a cliff walk, blindly half walking and half running away from the terror of the shipwreck below.

In contrast to the solid black of the boat hull interior, now outside with an enshrouding white fog and driving rain, I still could not see very far in front of me.

I do not know how far or long I traveled, but when I came to the end of the cliff walk and the path began to descend, I stopped to catch my breath and untie the remaining rope from my wrists. It must have been morning because the fog became increasingly lighter. As I stood at the cliff precipice, the fog lifted enough to reveal below me a picturesque fishing village snuggly nestled in a semi-circular harbour.

Glancing down at my feet, I became conscious for the first time that I was barefoot. My grey silk gown was heavy and wet from rain and salt brine as well as ripped in several places from crawling on the rocks. My hands, knees, and feet were bloody from cuts and scrapes. Wet drops slipped from my hair to my face then dropped onto my shoulders and chest. I was shivering. I started down the path towards the fishing village.

The air brightened as the early morning mist continued to dissipate and I clamored down the pebble-strewn incline. Several village fishermen were on the beach readying their boats and nets in preparation for seeking the day's catch, and they turned to eye me with suspicion. I approached the nearest one.

"Excuse me, sir, but where am I?"

The fisherman screwed his face a bit as he squinted into the direction of the sun rising in the east and looked me over to assess how he should answer, then said simply,

"Why, yor in Gorr'n 'aven, Miss."

I thanked him and continued to cross the wet sand toward the seafront buildings and battery wall. I mounted an ancient stone staircase to the quay lined with small stone cottages and a few meager shops. I had never heard of the coastal village of Gorran Haven, but I was now very hungry. I entered a small public tavern that smelled of cooking food. A small bell made a tinkling sound as I pushed the entrance door open. While standing at the counter awaiting the tavern's serving attendance, I saw my reflection in the bottom of a huge, metallic lobster pot hanging on the wall behind the bar.

I looked a sight. My blonde curls were elongated and hanging in disheveled disorder around my face and down my seaweed- and algae-decorated dress, so it was not surprising that the woman who emerged to assist me eyed me as strangely as the fisherman.

"May I 'elp you, Miss?" she asked hesitantly.

"I'm hungry," was my reply.

"Eggs, kippers, an' coffee are two quid," she offered guardedly. I suspected she had artificially inflated the price for a stranger, who, although bedraggled, wore the garments of the upper class.

"Oh," I responded, crestfallen, as I realized I had no money on me. "I came from the boat..." I pointed my hand in the direction from whence I had arrived.

"Which 'boat'?" Then, with an enterprising comprehension, she asked, "'as there been a wreck?" I nodded affirmatively. She came out from behind the counter and crossed the floor to peer out the door. "There was a fierce storm last night. Could 'ave wrecked up at Pen-a-maen Point..." She trailed off in thought and then turned back to me. "Any other survivors?" I shook my head from side to side and then stopped as I wondered if I was correct in my assumption. She looked out the door again as though assessing the situation, then turned back to me.

"What's yer name, dearie?"

I started to respond, but then realized I could not remember. I raised my left hand to the bump on my brow and winced as I touched it. She must have noticed, because she softened.

"Don' ye worry, now. Let me git yer a bite, and then I will send ye up to the priest. 'e'll be knowin' what to do with ye." She went back into the kitchen and brought forth a plate of eggs, toast, and piping hot coffee.

The warm food was very welcome, and I ate ravenously. Satisfied that I was momentarily occupied, the woman left the pub— likely to tell other villagers of the night's shipwreck up at the Point and to seek any likely salvage booty.

As I was finishing the last drops in my coffee mug, the woman returned to the pub.

"T'ere was a wreck up 'ar the Point last night. Some o' the fish'men found floatin' debris and stores from 'er. We'll be see'n what floats up the beach this way in the next day or so. Now, we'll see if the curate kin find ye a place to stay ere ye recollect yer name and ere ye be from." She motioned for me to follow her outside. She turned right and walked past two houses to a cobbled street heading up and further inland through the village. She directed me up the street in the direction of the square church bell tower visible on the horizon above.

"Thank you for your kindness to me." I shook her hand and then turned toward the hill before me.

Carefully making my way up the cobbles in my bare feet while lifting the skirt of my still damp clothing, I tried to remember what had happened before the shipwreck, before I had woken up in the dark bowel of the ship, but I could not remember anything.

As I rounded a bend toward the summit of the street, the sight of the stone church with a square portico was familiar and reassuring. I entered the churchyard through a rusted gate in the low stone wall. The priest was bent over tending a grave, but turned his head as he heard the creaking gate and then rose to greet me.

"Good day to ye, Miss. May I 'elp ye?" he began.

"The kind woman at the pub below sent me to you to help me find some lodgings. I was in a shipwreck last night at..." I tried to recall the location the woman had mentioned. "..at the Point. ...'Penamen Point'," I think she called it.

"I see." The curate looked me up and down. "What's yer name?"

"I appear to have forgotten that and everything that occurred before the boat collided with the rocky coast line. I think I must have hit my head," I again touched the tender spot on my forehead. "But something about this church feels very familiar to me."

"Well, p'haps getting ye out of yer sea-soaked garments and 'aving a few days' rest will restore yer mem'ry. The Widow Smythe 'as an extra room. I believe she'd be willing to have ye stay for a while." With that, the priest led me out of the churchyard and down a street heading away from the one I had mounted to find the church.

Very soon we came to a cottage with stucco walls and a small, enclosed flower garden in the front. The curate rang the small garden bell, and a kindly woman with grey hair, covered by a white lace cap, opened the door. The curate explained about my unfortunate circumstances—the shipwreck and my apparent memory loss. He then asked if she would be willing to give me lodgings for a time until my identity could be discovered, hopefully, in a few days, once I recovered my strength with rest, care, and nourishment.

The Widow Smythe welcomed me into her home, found me dry clothing, and provided me with a tub of hot water in which to bathe.

Sitting in the steam of the warm water, I began to relax a little from the recent traumatic events. Closing my eyes, I envisioned a stone church and yard—but not the one here in Gorran Haven. Familiar faces floated through my mind, but I could not name them. They were just loving, warm entities that made me feel safe and secure.

After my bath, I dressed in a nightgown left out by the kindly widow and stretched out on the bed, falling fast asleep. I dreamt of familiar people and places, including a very handsome, loving man, but I awoke with a start as my wonderful dream turned into a nightmare filled with the dread of an impending disaster.

I could smell the enticing results of my hostess cooking in the kitchen and realized that I was again famished. Quickly donning the simple gown she had left me, I ventured into the kitchen to assist with dinner preparations.

"Did ye sleep well?"

"Yes, I did. Thank you. Can you please tell me about this village and the life here?"

I learned that Gorran Haven was on the south Cornwall coast between Mevagissey and Falmouth. The mention of the latter city seemed to revive a fleeting memory, but it quickly evaporated.

While we were supping, we heard voices outside, and the garden bell announced visitors. Two fishermen had come with a donkey cart bearing two leather trunks, both embossed with gold lettering: Ld C. Crevven and Ldy E. Crevven, Crevvenwood, Fynchingham, Dorset, England.

"These 'ere trunks floated t'ward the beach at 'igh tide. Are they yer'em?" One of the men directed at me. Not sure, I hesitated.

"Yes, yes, of course. Bring 'em in," the Widow Smythe instructed. She turned to me. "Weren't it kind o' these gent'men to take the trouble to bring 'em 'ere?" She reached into her apron pocket and gave them each sixpence for their efforts.

The fishermen carried the trunks into the widow's parlour.

"Per'aps ye can 'elp us open 'em as the Lady 'as lost 'er keys."

Using a metal tool and a large rock from the garden, the men broke open both locks, then tipped their caps and left.

All the while I had been staring at the trunks. If they did belong to me, my name and home were emblazoned on the front. If the contents of the female trunk were not badly soaked or damaged, my clothing would be inside and available to wear. But something about opening the chests to reveal their contents caused me trepidation. In contrast, the widow did not hesitate except for my permission, which I gave reluctantly, with the instructions to open the Lady's trunk first.

It was a testament to the trunk's fine construction that the items packed inside were scarcely damp and still relatively neatly packed.

"My trousseau!" escaped involuntarily from me as we pulled out fashionable gowns, spencers, pelisses, slippers, and various undergarments and a box of jewels. We also discovered a bible. Inscribed on the cover page in a learned hand was: "To my darling Emily from her proud father, Rev. Edward Beechcroft, Briarcreek Manor, Fynchingham, July 15, 1804."

One of the faces from my dream came rushing back to me along with the church memory that had been floating through my mind.

"It's from Papa," I croaked out and sat down to cry. The elusive mystery of my name and where I came from had been solved, although how I got here was still locked inside my stubborn memory, and perhaps, in the other trunk.

"We'll write yer father straight away and tell 'im where yer are, safe and sound," the widow declared reasonably. As she moved to get a pen and writing paper, I rose and slowly approached the man's trunk.

Lifting the lid ever so slowly as if it were Pandora's Box, the scent from his clothes and the sight of his finely tailored riding coat and silk shirt struck me like a dagger to the heart.

"Oh, Christopher!" I moaned as I sank to the floor racked with sobs. The widow rushed back to my side, then took me in her arms and rocked me, sympathizing, one widow to another.

Between sobs, I tried to explain what had happened.

"They...threw...my...husband...overboard...The...captain... he held me...I was...in the hold...of the ship...The water...rushed in...I floated out...onto the rocks...I walked here..."

"Ye poor dear! 'ow 'orrible! What an ordeal. Too sad. We'll send for yer papa on the 'morrow's post," the widow reassured me.

Closing Christopher's trunk, she lifted me from my heaped posture on the floor and half carried, half led me back to my bedroom. I lay on my side completely dressed but crying more softly than before. The widow covered me with a blanket then quietly left me alone to explore the depths of my grief that the temporary amnesia had hitherto kept at bay.

True to her word, the widow sent for my father who, coming overland post chaise by private coach lent by the Fynchinghams, took four days to arrive in Gorran Haven. While I awaited his arrival, I kept imagining and hoping against hope for Christopher to arise miraculously from the sea, even while knowing he had been tossed overboard too far to the east. At night, I slept fitfully, often crying myself to sleep.

When he finally arrived, my father was tired from the journey but extremely relieved to see me again. His joy at my personal safety was much tempered by his sorrow at our mutual loss of Christopher.

"The Earl and Countess are beside themselves at the premature and criminal loss of their son and only heir. They were too overwrought to fetch you themselves, but generously loaned me their carriage and driver. We shall return to Fynchingham on the morrow."

After staying overnight to rest, my father and I thanked the widow for her hospitality and care and gave her several guineas. The widow had provided me with a simple black dress from among her own mourning garb. It was outdated and slightly large, but I cared little about my appearance. After a hug goodbye, we mounted the carriage for the long, sad trip home with the two trunks—all that was left of my honeymoon voyage. Father held my hand and patted it occasionally while I stared out the window, oblivious to the passing scenery as tears flowed down my cheeks. In one week I had gone from the bliss of marriage to Christopher to the torment of his premature and murderous loss.

"Emily, I loved your mother very much. It was very hard when both she and the babe died. Sometimes the only thing that kept me going was the knowledge that you were dependent on my care." My father stopped when he realized that I did not even have a child as a reason to live. Yet, now I understood fully for the first time why he had never remarried.

The trip felt interminable—through Plymouth, then Exeter, and along the Dorset Coast. When we reached Dorchester, north of Weymouth, we retraced the journey that I had shared with Christopher the afternoon of our wedding day only a week earlier.

Word must have reached the village of our impending arrival for, as we reached the outskirts of Fynchingham, the inhabitants were lined up on both sides of the road, some wearing black armbands or other somber costume, the men with their hats off. I was very touched by this natural demonstration of their support and admiration for Christopher, for his family, for my father, for me.

We stopped at Briarcliff Manor first. Miss Tilling fell upon me in a hug.

"We are so happy to see you home safe, my dear, but I am heartbroken for you. It must have been horrible for you." Once she released me from her embrace, she presented father with a letter from the Earl that had been received during his absence. While reading it, I noticed his expression quickly turn from shock to crestfallen to angry to resigned.

"What is it, Papa?"

"The Earl and Countess have considered the circumstances of their son's death and the extremely short duration of your marriage," he paraphrased. "They will not mar your reputation by withdrawing your rights to use the family name." He stopped and cleared his throat. "However, they do not feel that you should in any way be entitled to any of their son's allowance. They have returned to London for the foreseeable future to mourn their inconsolable misfortune. Any meeting with you would only wound them further." He folded the letter back and quietly ripped it into small pieces.

Christopher's awful death was not torture enough, but that his family should scorn me too, was more than I could bear. I collapsed disconsolate into Miss Tilling's arms. My former governess half carried, half walked me up to my former bedroom and sat with me while I lay in misery until exhaustion overtook me and, mercifully, passed into a deep, dreamless slumber.

Waking late the next morning, I noticed my trunk had been placed in my room. I descended the stairs to join my father for breakfast.

"I have sent the driver and carriage with Christopher's trunk onto Crevvenwood." I nodded in silence, not sure whether I wanted to retain some of my husband's things as a memento or if I was better off without the reminder. Father and I began to eat in silence, but I sensed my father had something difficult he wished to discuss.

"Emily, dear, I think it is only fair to you to allow you to stay at the Rectory for your year of mourning. At the end of that time period, however, I think it best that you should find a suitable position as a governess unless another suitable marital match has been found."

In my present emotional state, I had not thought that far into the future. I had assumed I could stay with my father interminably, but I now supposed his living in Fynchingham might come to an end, and he wanted to be sure I would be situated independently and maybe even have more opportunity to find an eligible husband. Since I was the widow of the eldest son of an earl, my social standing now put me in the ranks of the upper classes, so I would no longer be marriageable to anyone else here in Fynchingham.

Everyone here knew the dreadful account of my late husband's tragic demise at the hands of the unscrupulous crew of the *Francesca*, and they all eyed me with pitying inapproachability. Growing up I had had few friends of equal age and rank; now I was even more isolated. From a distorted viewpoint, some people even blamed me for Christopher's fate.

Dealing with my own sorrow, I would have naturally been reclusive, but now I became almost a social outcast, visible only on the grounds of the Rectory or in the churchyard. Having lost my titled husband, the villagers began to refer to me directly as "Lady Emily," instead of "Lady Christopher Crevven," "Dowager Lady Crevven," or even "Emily, Lady Crevven," as proper respect should have afforded me, and behind my back simply as "Widow Emily," an even more unenviable title.

One afternoon while sitting morose and alone on a bench under a broad tree among the grave markers in the church cemetery, William came over, wearing a heavy linen smock frock—the sign of a country workman—his hat in his hands. He stood a respectful distance away, nervously twisting the hat brim between his hands in a circular fashion.

"Er, Lady Emily," he hesitated, coughed, and looked down at his hands. With a deep intake of breath, he pronounced every word. "I am profoundly sorry." He looked down again, then turned and left the churchyard. I started to cry again for I knew he was not just sorry for my bereavement, but for my changed situation in life and for the closure of our friendship, the gulf of the distance between our social stations now uncrossable, and, for one additional thing I did not know until three weeks later, when the marriage banns for William and Mary Farthing were read in church.

The solitary weeks and months passed. Occasionally, while I was quietly engrossed in some routine, menial task, or even once while sitting at silent prayer during church service, I could feel Christopher's presence palpably near me; a slight hand touch on my shoulder, a whisper of "Emily, dearest" in my ear, or a whisk of gossamer wings against my cheek. I tried to grasp and hold onto the fleeting sensation of his presence, but it was gone almost as soon as I was aware of it.

At times I would see someone who reminded me of Christopher. There were days when I almost believed he had washed up on a distant shore, forgetting for a time—as I had—who he was, but one day he would come back to me. Other days I deeply despaired and wished my life were at an end. Why was I the only one spared in the shipwreck? Was my wretched continued existence punishment for marrying above my social rank? Were my few days of joy and pleasure in Christopher's company to be counterbalanced with years of aching misery?

As our first wedding anniversary approached, I hardened myself in an attempt to protect myself from the bittersweet memories and in anticipation of the time when I would have to seek a life elsewhere. For several days I was anxious and restless, uncommonly annoyed with my father, Miss Tilling, and the servants. When I was indoors, I wanted to be outside; when I was outdoors, I wanted to return to the isolation of my room.

The anniversary day dawned, tauntingly and ironically, cheerful and sunny. I could hear the birds chirping without a care. I pulled the covers over my head and stayed in bed much longer than usual, but Miss Tilling eventually knocked on my door to rouse me, her voice just a little more tender and understanding than normal.

Neither my father nor Miss Tilling mentioned the remarkability of the date, but went about their ordinary business except for making few demands on me, for which I was grateful.

However, with the post came an advertisement from the Countess Fynchingham for a governess position in Salisbury. There was no accompanying letter or greeting—the message was clear. It was both a gesture of reconciliation and one of further distancing me from the Crevven-Fynchingham family with finality. It only served to darken my mood and symbolize the approaching end to my hitherto protected life at Briarcliff Manor. To me, it resembled an eviction notice.

My father let the subject rest for a fortnight, then brought it up one night at supper.

"Emily, you might write to the Salisbury merchant to inquire about the open governess position before it is filled by someone else."

A response to my correspondence was received almost by return post that a governess was still sought for the three children of a middle-aged widower and that it would please the man for me to come to Salisbury to interview in a few days' time.

Accompanied by Miss Tilling (for my father was called away to Melmont on urgent church business), I made the half-day journey to the cathedral city for my audience with Harry Frederick, owner of a tannery, shoe-making, and glove-making establishment, and father to three children. For propriety sake, Mr. Frederick had arranged for us to meet at the White Hart on St. John Street. The hotel had a classic Georgian façade whose columns towered above a life-sized stag.

We found Mr. Frederick seated on a bench in the restaurant, having already ordered our meals for us. He wasted no time asking me about my own education and qualities suitable to help rear his children. When he appeared satisfied by my responses, he explained that his beloved wife, Lucy, had succumbed to consumption some six months earlier. Because he was necessarily involved with business, their children had been left in the hands of servants who were also too busy to mind them. As a result, the two boys and their younger sister had become spoiled and wild. It was necessary that they should be disciplined with the structure of regular lessons and order.

Looking back on my own childhood, I was not sure I was the best choice to guide the Frederick children, but the matter was settled that I should return to Salisbury in a fortnight to assume my new duties as the Fredericks' governess. Miss Tilling and I returned to Fynchingham that afternoon with few words exchanged between us. Both of us were acutely aware of the impending end of our life together, the high aspirations of my governess that her charge would marry well both fulfilled then quickly dashed to such an extent that I had now sunk to equal her status. I felt as guilty in disappointing her as she was in her sense of failing me.

The two weeks until my final departure from Briarcliff Manor passed all too quickly. I was soon saying a tearful farewell to my father, Miss Tilling, and the servants.

The return trip to Salisbury was uneventful. After several weeks of struggle to assert my authority and direction, the Frederick children and I reached a peaceful understanding. Essentially, they wanted rules and a consistent mother figure—one that I endeavored to provide.

In turn, I was in need of distraction and some place to devote my loving energies and intelligence. Although sometimes gruff and

214

often businesslike, Mr. Frederick was not an unkind or unfair master. He allowed me Sunday off every week when I would often walk around the Cathedral Close after services. It was in this quiet sanctuary that my thoughts would turn back to my memories of Christopher, our courtship, and our wedding night. In the longer days of summer, I would venture past the High Street shops to the Market Place before returning to the Frederick house for the evening and writing my weekly letter to my father before the candle tallow burned out. Twice a year I was even permitted to visit my father.

One-by-one the Frederick boys grew up and went on to being tutored, then entering public school and university, while the daughter found a suitable marital match.

That same year, my father died.

No longer bound to Fynchingham, I ventured further from my roots to become the governess of a wealthy family in Bath, that of Lord and Lady Titus Jones. The lively elegance, fastidious architecture, and open park spaces suited my disposition after the staid solemnity of Salisbury. Although I did not partake directly in the social activities around me, I was, at the least, on the periphery, recalling my own halcyon days at Crevvenwood. I took pride in the social successes of my charges and comforted them when things did not go well. Those children grew up, married, and left home, but Lord and Lady Jones graciously allowed me to stay on, as if I was their children's aging aunt.

Eventually, I developed tuberculosis of the lungs. Perhaps it had lain dormant from my years exposed to tannery dust in the Frederick household or from some other manner. I was tended gently by the household staff and visited occasionally by the apothecary offering me a dram of this or that to lessen the cough or provide me with more energy.

When they were visiting their parents, the Jones children would come upstairs to visit me. The disease was in its later stages one afternoon when Sir Anthony Jones, the youngest son of my employer, came to see me.

I had been lying quietly under the voluminous covers with a lace mob cap on my now silver-white curls, drifting now and again into sleep. I woke to find Sir Anthony sitting in a chair near the foot of my bed, his shiny dark hair catching a glint of light from the window and looking very handsome in his green velvet riding coat and grey trousers.

"Christopher! You've come for me at last!" I greeted him. "I've been waiting so long." I sat up with my arms outstretched towards Sir Anthony who realized I was not completely in charge of my wits. As I made the extra effort toward him, I began coughing violently, with the telltale disgorging of blood from my lungs onto the bedclothes in front of me. Finally, the coughing stopped, and I sank back onto the pillows.

I came out of a dark tunnel into a glorious light in which Christopher was awaiting me. Alongside him were my father, my mother, and many others I recognized. I felt complete, unconditional love as Christopher enveloped me in his arms.

KARMA

Having taken personal development training courses Level I and Level II, plus a few seminars, Mark Thomas caught up with me to participate in Level III from January to April 1999. The Level III course builds on what is learned in Levels I and II. In Level I the focus is on one's own humanity and the methods and beliefs we adopt that limit our natural, expansive, conscious beingness. Level II focuses on inventing and expanding one's potential to impact the world in a positive, powerful way; it provides the tools to enable an individual participant in Level III to become a positive force in his or her selected community (e.g., church, work, neighborhood, family, etc.) in such a way that s/he is now known and listened to in this new way of potentiality, while the selected community itself transforms.

Potentiality is a concept and a way of being that does not currently appear to exist in space and time but for which a person may create a steadfast position that the intention of it will show up in one's presence. When your potentiality is functioning, the universe moves in synchronization with what you think and say, sometimes described as being "in the flow" or "in the zone." (I have heard it portrayed as, "When you say 'table', a table falls out of your mouth into existence.")

Throughout the Level III course if I was caught in a traffic jam, all I had to do was to think of the potentiality of "velocity" to "push" the cars forward in front of me with my mind, and the traffic in my lane would clear out of my way. At work, my potentiality was in full gear—I would think about a report or information I needed, and immediately, a staff member would appear at my door with the report, or I would receive a phone call at the moment with the information I was seeking.

My Level III project was to encourage the potential of "creative self-expression" in my community of friends and family by organizing a trip to the Reinberger Galleries of the Cleveland Institute of Art in University Circle. I followed the course guidelines to initiate conversations to motivate, excite, and enlist others into the project. Although other people seemed to be inspired and encouraged me about the idea, most of my friends opted to focus on their own version of individually *self*-expressed creativity. In the end, only my mother and Mireille accompanied me on the day trip to University Circle.

From the moment that March morning when we exited in my car into Cleveland Heights and walked around University Circle, many of my early memories of OAHIA Executive Committee meetings, of Keir, and of the Arts Councils Organization of Ohio came flooding back. This was the first time I had been to Cleveland without seeing Keir there; however, I felt that his spirit permeated the very air.

After a few hours of viewing art at the Reinberger Galleries (and not touching), Mireille was getting antsy, so we proceeded over to the Children's Museum to allow her to let out her own, youthful, self-expression before the three-hour car ride home.

As soon as the Level III course was over on April 1st, Auguste, Mireille, and I flew to San Francisco to visit my older brother and his life partner. While there one day, we decided to visit Alcatraz, but when we arrived at the ticket booth, the queue was very long. My brother, who became exceedingly perturbed that we would miss the boat, was pacing in a nervous fashion.

"We have plenty of time," I calmly told him, using my Level III velocity-potential training. The line started to move more quickly. By the time we arrived in front of the ticket booth, we changed our minds and agreed to take the boat to Sausalito instead of Alcatraz. We purchased our tickets and moved into the boarding line just as it began to move forward so we did not have any needless waiting on the dock.

After an enjoyable, but breezy, afternoon visit to Sausalito, we realized we had only twenty minutes to walk the mile back to the boat. As adults, we could have walked very quickly and arrived in sufficient time, but nine-year-old Mireille with her shorter legs was tired of walking already and could not be pressed to keep up with the rest of us.

"We can make it back to the boat in time," I confidently reassured everyone, "but I suggest we take turns carrying Mireille on our shoulders so we can keep up our gait." We arrived back at the boat dock to be the last ones to board before it left its moorings to return to San Francisco.

I invited a couple I had met in my personal development courses, Marilyn and Allen McDuff, to dinner one evening. We had a great time laughing and talking. After the dinner was over and our guests had left, Auguste and I cleaned up.

"You really insulted Marilyn and Allen with what you said," Auguste said.

"What do you mean?" I was totally surprised by this revelation. "I thought the evening went well."

"You could tell by the look on their faces." Auguste turned his face to the wall in a manner that let me know the discussion was over. I was crestfallen. My personal development studies had taught me that when you hurt someone, you can tidy it up with them. I resolved to call Marilyn the next morning.

"Marilyn, I want to apologize for offending you and Allen last night."

"What are you talking about?"

"Auguste said I had offended you and Allen last night by something I said."

"We were not offended. I can't imagine what Auguste meant."

After I hung up with Marilyn, I realized that Auguste had lied to me, or at least made the story up. "Why would he do that? Why would he want to ruin a perfectly good evening?" I began to speculate about what other things he had told me in the past that might have been purposely untrue or unkind. Another wedge of distrust slid into the mortar of our marriage.

While I was in the Level III course, I had invented the potentiality of *community and integrity* for OAHIA. For me, *community* meant members of the organization working together in fellowship rather than in discord while *integrity* meant intact, complete, and *bona fide* with oneself, as well as operating inside moral and ethical guidelines.

When I had received Cleveland Medical's 1999 OAHIA membership dues renewal from Kenneth Sven, Keir was no longer listed as an employee. Over the years, whenever I happened to glimpse Keir's name in the OAHIA membership directory, saw the Cleveland Medical's logo, or even noticed the word Cleveland, my heart had skipped a beat. Now I would have to remove him from the OAHIA directory without knowing his whereabouts.

In mid-April, while attempting to reach OAHIA Treasurer Gordon Geddes at the Cleveland office of The Health Plan of Ohio to discuss a financial matter, I was told by the receptionist that he no longer worked there. To ascertain Gordon's whereabouts, I called Fulton Burke, the State President of The Health Plan of Ohio at his Columbus office. Fulton had served as OAHIA General Counsel a few years earlier and was a long-time and well-respected member of the health insurance industry. Although this could be a delicate business matter, I trusted that Fulton would exhibit professionalism.

"Fulton, I just heard that Gordon Geddes has left The Health Plan. As you know, Gordon is the OAHIA Treasurer, and I need to speak with him about the Association's finances. Do you happen to know how I can reach him?"

"Although Gordon is violating the non-compete clause in his employment agreement with us, I am willing give you his home address and phone number." I noticed Fulton's voice was tight with suppressed anger.

"Thank you for being helpful and gracious." I wrote down Gordon's contact information.

I then called OAHIA President Mark Thomas to alert him about Gordon's change in company affiliation.

"Mark, remember I created the potentiality of 'community and integrity' for OAHIA? Well, I have a sense of displaced integrity regarding the OAHIA community: I don't know where Keir Mervais is."

"I heard he went into the new agency with Gordon."

After concluding my call with Mark, I dialed the phone number Fulton had given me.

"Gordon, I initially called you to discuss OAHIA's investment strategy concerning some certificates of deposit due to mature, but I learned you were no longer employed at The Health Plan. In order for you to remain OAHIA Treasurer, you'll have to join OAHIA with your new agency and any additional branches or staff members you want listed." I refrained from mentioning Keir by name in case what Mark had told me was confidential.

"Send me an agency membership application," Gordon replied, "and I'll return it as soon as we have all our agency contact information set up."

Now I wondered if Keir, too, was violating a non-compete clause with Cleveland Medical. When I received Gordon's application for his Summit-United Health Care agency a couple of weeks later, the application listed Keir and Linwood Ashton, who had previously been working for Trust Medical. The OAHIA directory was going to have a lot of changes in it this year, but I was happy I did not have to remove Keir from its listings. I remembered how forlorn Keir had looked the last time I saw him at Deerwood Lake Lodge and my sense he was planning to leave Cleveland Medical. At least he had been able to remain in the health insurance legal field.

The creation of this start up agency was not the only news about to shake up the health insurance industry. In early May, responding to a message I had left for him the previous day, OAHIA vice president and 1999 convention chair Kevin Raines returned my call. He was now working in Henry Spaulding's office in Toledo.

Kevin's dry wit endeared him to people instantly. In his late thirties, Kevin had come up with some pretty ironclad excuses for not attending OAHIA Executive Committee meetings: for one meeting, his wife was due to give birth any day, and for another, he changed companies and was required to fly out to California for training at the parent company. The Executive Committee had even formulated the "Kevin Raines Rule" about excessive meeting absences.

"I've got something that I'd like to get off my mind," Kevin began.

"What's that?" I braced myself for a funny punch line.

"I was out playing tennis a month ago and was in the process of serving the ball when I blacked out, and the next thing I knew I woke up in the Toledo Hospital. Seems I've got a spot on my brain they are calling brain cancer. Since I am undergoing radiation treatments, I can't travel to Columbus for the Executive Committee meeting next week. However, I still expect to plan and attend the convention at the Manor Grove Inn in August."

What a punch line; more like a punch in the stomach! I had never known anyone with brain cancer, but I suspected it was not very curable. With breast cancer, colon cancer, testicular cancer, or even lung cancer, parts of one's body can be surgically removed along with the offending cells. I thought about Kevin's wife and three children. I recalled back some fifteen years before when the treasurer of one of my Missouri associations had died of a heart attack two days before our board meeting, and how I had slumped against the wall in my office in shock and cried.

When I hung up the phone with Kevin after wishing him well, I walked over to my office door and closed it quietly, then returned to my chair and started to cry.

220

In mid-May, I had a day off and volunteered at Mireille's elementary school at a book fair held in the school library. We had a surprise visit from the Ohio Governor at the book fair while I was there, although I did not have the opportunity to meet him in person.

A couple of weeks later, right after Memorial Day and my 48th birthday, I awoke and noticed my joints felt unusually stiff. When I looked at my hands, they were so swollen that the normal lines and skin indentations were as smooth as the surface of an inflated balloon. I had to ask Auguste to fasten my bra for me and putting on pantyhose was definitely not an option that morning.

I telephoned the doctor's office but was told it would be several days before I could secure an appointment. I experienced difficulty getting into the driver's seat of my car, and using the clutch and stick shift felt as uncoordinated as when I first learned to drive a manual transmission.

A few evenings earlier, I had received a call from a local seminar leader from my personal development courses, Don Jensen, inviting me to participate in a five-week evening Coaches Academy in Dublin, Ohio, to train the coaches for the next Level III course. I had been very excited about being part of this program, but now, the day the Academy was slated to begin, I struggled to drive to work. I seriously wondered if I would be physically capable of driving myself to Dublin and back home that evening.

Once I arrived at my office, I spent a couple of hours training a fellow employee, Leslie, how to prepare meeting specifications on the computer for the national NIRS conference we would be running six weeks later in Las Vegas. As I rose from my chair to take a break, I could scarcely move. I told Leslie what I was experiencing.

"You need to call the doctor right away," Leslie insisted.

"I did this morning, and they told me it would be several days before they could see me."

"Then you need to call them back and explain it is an emergency. Don't get off the phone until the doctor agrees to see you *today*."

The strategy worked, and I got an appointment for mid-afternoon. My doctor ran a battery of tests. To curb the swelling and ease the accompanying pain, he prescribed 100 milligrams of Prednisone, a powerful corticosteroid drug that works as an immunosuppressant. After picking up my prescription, I immediately popped the recommended dosage into my mouth at the pharmacy water cooler and drove home to make dinner before heading over to Dublin, about 20 miles away.

I arrived ahead of the rest of the participants at the Quaker Meeting House where the Coaches Academy was to take place. Only Don Jensen, a cardiologist, and Smitty Smythe, the other course leader, were already there.

"How are you?" Don greeted me.

"Well, I'm not so sure…" I explained what had transpired with my health. "But I am committed to being in this program, no matter what!"

"Prednisone is a powerful drug," Don observed in his understated, yet caring, physician tone, "and explains why you were able to drive yourself here in spite of your symptoms. Let me or Smitty know if you need anything tonight during the session."

I was able to last the entire three-hour session but had bouts of discomfort and frequently changed sitting positions on the love seat, sometimes with my legs up, crossing and uncrossing them, sitting forward and back, and changing my arm positions. I made it through the evening and the drive home but found my sleep was short-lived. I awoke at four o'clock in the morning, completely wired. With the rest of the house asleep, I played with our new kitten that was very happy with the nocturnal company I provided.

My doctor had instructed me to take 100 milligrams of Prednisone for two days, reduce the dosage to 60 milligrams for two days, reduce it again to 30 milligrams for two days, and then go off the medicine. After following the instructions precisely, I was back in his office a week later with the same symptoms as before with the added side-effects of sleeplessness and anxiety. One of my co-workers, Adelaide, who suffered from severe arthritis, was dismayed at my dosage.

"I go from 5 milligrams to 4.5 milligrams when going off Prednisone. Going from 100 milligrams to 60, then 30, is far too abrupt!"

"Would you be willing to be my health coach for this disease, whatever it is?"

"You need to schedule lots of rest periods," Adelaide warned. "The medicine makes you manic, wanting to take on the world."

At my next appointment, my doctor examined the results of my blood tests.

"You tested slightly positive for Lupus," he pointed out. I knew David Fisher's youngest child had Lupus—it was incurable and undesirable. "I want you to go to a rheumatologist and get your blood retested, because it is not yet definite what you have. Meanwhile, I am going to put you back on 100 milligrams of Prednisone, but I want you to reduce the dosage more slowly—on your own schedule." I swore to myself that I would be completely off the Prednisone by the NIRS convention in Las Vegas, five weeks away.

Ten days later, I entered the rheumatology lab and was subjected to the removal of 15 vials of blood for sampling. A few days later, the rheumatologist's nurse called me at my office.

"You have human parvo," she announced and hung up. I do not know if I was more relieved about not having Lupus or baffled by this unknown disease.

"Human parvo?" a co-worker exclaimed. "I thought parvo was a *dog's* disease!" She promptly researched the term on the internet, while I was still sitting stunned that the nurse had not given me more information. I decided to call the rheumatologist's office back.

"Human parvo is also known as 'Fifth Disease' or the 'B-19 Virus,'" the nurse explained. "It's usually something children catch, like mumps or measles. I really don't know much more about it."

My co-worker returned with several web site printouts for me to read. The disease was "discovered" in 1799 in England and is related to German measles. Children tend to contract it in the spring and not suffer much from it other than pink cheeks, but adult women who contract it suffer more severely. Remembering back over my activities for the two-week incubation period, I remembered the school book fair. I now had a diagnosis and a likely source, so I could address the disease directly. What I needed was the most knowledgeable epidemiologist in the country about this virus. After calling a few association contacts, I located Dr. William Sheets who was attending a medical conference in Boston.

"The bad news is that B-19 virus is incurable," Dr. Sheets related to me over the phone, "but the good news is that it will eventually go away after about five months. You will continue to have symptomatic attacks, but each one will be milder than the last. Your symptoms should disappear by Thanksgiving. I would encourage you to reduce your reliance on Prednisone as much as possible, using a less potent arthritis medicine, for example." I was very relieved that this was not a lifelong, debilitating, or life-threatening virus.

Throughout the month of June, while still trying to obtain a diagnosis, I had continued with the Coaches Academy sessions. We were each assigned a fellow participant to coach and one to coach us while Don and Smitty served as head coaches. Hillary, who had been one of the coaches in my Level III course and was the housemate of the man who had been my coach for that course, was assigned as my coach for the Coaches Academy; Hillary and I had our first telephone coaching appointment on Sunday afternoon.

"What do you want to get out of the Coaches Academy?" Hillary asked.

"For years I've wanted to own a fine craft gallery. And, although I have declared that I want to be a coach, I have not yet registered for the 36-month Coach University training program that costs $2,800." I thought that was a pretty tall order to accomplish in five weeks.

"What might be in the way of your achieving those things?" Hillary probed, practicing the skills we had learned about listening to another's commitments and holding a steadfast and non-judgmental position of unconditional support for those commitments.

"First, I'm afraid to use up our family's savings to pay for a gallery or Coach University's tuition. Auguste would not approve of it. Second, I don't know how to exhibit the sales items in the gallery or how to obtain the artists' works. In addition, I don't know what items would be more likely to sell."

"I hear all your concerns about money and not knowing how, but maybe there are ways around both those issues." I agreed to be open to investigating other options during the coming week.

The following Wednesday, after I dropped Mireille off at her YMCA day camp, I passed a strip mall shopping center and saw "Gallery"

223

spelled out in white letters on the green roof. I immediately pulled into the parking lot and parked in front of the storefront. Getting out, I looked into the window to see beautiful specimens of glass, pottery, and wooden items with paintings hanging on the interior walls. I noted the store name and hours on a piece of paper from my purse. I promised myself that I would leave work sufficiently early to visit the gallery later that afternoon before picking Mireille up from day camp at six o'clock.

At 5:30 I pulled up in front of the gallery again, got out of my car, and headed through the glass doors with a slight uneasiness. A light tinkling of bells signaled my entrance, and a gentle woman in her late thirties with crimped hair and soft blue eyes approached me from behind the counter.

"Hello, welcome to our Collector's Gallery. Please look around and let me know if I can answer any questions for you." I immediately warmed to her.

"Are you the owner?" I ventured.

"I'm one of five partners. We're all potters, but some of us also paint and make jewelry, too."

I thanked her and began to look around, my eyes caressing each *objet d'art*. "PARTNERS?!?!?! What a concept!" My mind began to churn. I had always envisioned that I would have to be the sole owner of a gallery, or maybe have one partner; but here was a collective group of partners sharing in the costs and the work.

Later that evening I could barely contain my excitement when I called one of my former co-workers, Marilyn Fields, who had taken the Level I Course from my recommendation while working at AEMG and then, after a dramatic breakthrough in the Relationship seminar, had quit to become a potter herself.

"Marilyn, do you know anything about the Collector's Gallery?" I was almost out of breath.

"Sure. I've placed some of my work there."

"Do you know any of the partners?"

"Yes, I know them all. They are a neat group of people."

"If I wanted to talk to them about possibly investing or partnering with them, with whom should I speak?"

"I would talk to Anthony Bocci. Let me get you his phone number."

The next evening, being consciously present to the personal development lessons I had learned, sensing excitement mixed with trepidation, and exuding the potentiality of "partnership and investment," I phoned Anthony Bocci.

"Mr. Bocci, Marilyn Fields suggested I call you about the Collector's Gallery. Would you be interested in having another partner or investor?"

"Well, we recently lost a couple of partners and are looking for another one or two," Bocci replied in a deep, thoughtful voice. "Let me speak with the others."

224

A week later, Auguste and I were invited to meet with the gallery partners to discuss our possible investment. At a $2,500 investment per partner, Auguste declined for himself, but we all agreed that I would initially purchase a 1/100th share and work on Saturdays from 10:00 to 6:00 for a six-month trial period, after which we would all evaluate whether or not I would become a full partner. I consulted with an attorney to draft up the partnership agreement that became effective on December 1st.

Although the Coaches Academy course lasted only five weeks, Hillary continued to coach me. I also registered for the Coach University program, beginning November 1st. Both my outcomes of the Coaches Academy were, in fact, realized within five months of our first coaching call.

While my B-19 virus was being treated during the summer of 1999 and I was on Prednisone, OAHIA was facing a federal legislative challenge that had been brewing for several years. A Congressional bill was calling for greater federal regulatory oversight of the health insurance industry, especially impacting the way health laws were regulated in Ohio. Never one to be interested in government relations, advocacy, and lobbying, I had always left those matters up to others.

The American Association of Health Insurance Attorneys (AAHIA) was particularly active in this fight and enlisted its state affiliates to rally for grassroots support. I telephoned OAHIA's president, Kenneth Farmington, to determine what we should do as an association to spread the call to action. Kenneth was less than enthusiastic.

"I don't plan to get very involved in this fight," Kenneth admitted, "But if you think we should alert the membership, you can go right ahead."

"I have forty-five minutes before I have to leave for the day. I'll spend that time calling the state presidents and agency heads to see how everyone reacts." I began working through the membership directory listed alphabetically by company name, mostly leaving messages, but occasionally speaking with a company head. Most of them agreed to contact their Congressional representatives.

When I called Summit-United Health Care to speak with Gordon Geddes, Phyllis Buckley answered. I explained why I was calling.

"Gordon is not in the office now," Phyllis replied. "Would you like to speak with Keir Mervais or Linwood Ashton instead?"

It took less than an instant for me to make that choice; I scarcely knew Linwood, but it had been a year since I had spoken to Keir and three years since I had last seen him. In addition, I recalled that Keir had established OAHIA's Legislative Committee and been involved with Director Carson's election campaign. He would likely be interested in a grassroots legislative effort.

"Let me speak with Keir, please."

"This is Keir Mervais." His familiar voice seemed to lack its usual verve, but I was too glad to hear it again finally and too impetuous from the Prednisone and my mission to take much notice.

"Keir, I am calling to urge OAHIA members to contact their Congressmen to oppose the legislation now in the House that would increase federal regulatory authority in the industry." I noticed I was speaking faster than normal, partly due to the medicine and partly due to my nervousness in speaking with Keir again.

"I doubt that would do any good. The two things you don't want to watch being made are sausage and legislation."

Even in my rather euphoric, unstoppable, and drugged condition, I was taken back. This was not the cheerful, hail-fellow-well-met, charming, and flirtatious man I had known previously. Keir sounded discouraged and sarcastic. As I hung up, I stared at my phone and said out loud to it, "That man is *not* a happy camper! I doubt he will be staying much longer with *that* job."

I made a few more calls, but my heart was no longer in the task. I began to think that maybe I should tell Keir about the Level I Course and how it might give him a new perspective. However, with the Las Vegas conference in a couple of weeks and the OAHIA convention at the Manor Grove Inn a few weeks after that, I had little time to dwell on Keir being out of sorts until later that evening.

As I lay on my bed resting after supper and listening to classical music, I was aware that the constant TMJ pain in my jaw was even more intense with the viral joint pain from the B-19 virus. As Tchaikovsky's *Sleeping Beauty* waltz played, I remembered my favorite Disney movie of the same name and the scene where Aurora dances in the woods with Prince Phillip. My mind wandered to what it might be like to waltz with Keir. For a brief moment, the pain in my jaw subsided.

Astounded by the sudden, although only momentary, cessation of the chronic pain that had been ever-present for the last seven years, I tried the daydream of dancing with Keir again. The pain suspended and then ebbed back. I tried the slow dancing vision again, and again the TMJ subsided. After a few more attempts, I knew I was on to something...but what?

By the time I headed to Las Vegas on July 23rd for the NIRS conference, I had weaned myself off the Prednisone and used another arthritis medicine for a few weeks instead.

On August 10th, my parents and Mireille accompanied me to Cincinnati for the OAHIA convention at the Manor Grove Inn. Since our family had celebrated my parents' fortieth wedding anniversary at the historic resort in 1987, they looked forward to a return trip—my father to play golf and my mother to care for Mireille while I was working and to enjoy the cultural and artistic attractions of the city when I was not.

Again, Keir did not register for this convention. I was disappointed but rationalized that since Summit-United Care was a new agency and Gordon Geddes, the OAHIA treasurer, was expected to attend, they had likely decided it was not economical to spend the money to send two of the agency partners to the convention.

Most of the attention at the convention was focused on Kevin Raines, the OAHIA vice president and convention chair who showed up bald from his brain cancer treatments and looking dapper in a seersucker suit topped with a bowtie. Kevin led the introductions for the education sessions valiantly and with good humor, but I knew he spent all his free time resting in his room to preserve his energy for his appearances in public, especially for the closing of the annual business meeting when Kenneth Farmington passed the gavel upon the Kevin's election as OAHIA's next President.

Due to his continuing treatments, Kevin announced he was unable to attend the AAHIA fall annual convention at The BroAdmoor in Colorado Springs as OAHIA's representative. The Executive Committee members agreed to send me in Kevin's place in October. I had never attended the AAHIA convention before due to budget restrictions, but with OAHIA's own Chuck Lincoln finishing out his term as AAHIA's president, I thought it would be an especially auspicious occasion.

I arrived at The BroAdmoor late in the evening to check into my room. All the regular rooms were filled, so I was upgraded to a Junior Suite in the middle of the Main Inn. My suite had a spectacular view overlooking the man-made Cheyenne Lake and Pike's Peak rising from the Rocky Mountains in the distance beyond. To exercise, I resolved to walk around the lake a couple times each day of the convention, even though the air at 2.5 miles above sea level made it difficult to breathe.

On the second evening Chuck and his wife, Patricia, invited me up to their Presidential Suite for a glass of wine. The suite atop the Main Inn stretched the full extent of the Inn's top floor. I counted five fireplaces and balconies on both sides overlooking both downtown Colorado Springs and the Rocky Mountains.

"This suite is bigger than my house!" I remarked to Chuck when he finished giving me a tour.

"It's bigger than *our* house, too." I knew Chuck was far more affluent than Auguste and I, so I suspected he must have been really impressed by his accommodations.

"I'm sorry Kevin couldn't attend the convention, but I think it is great that I got my chance to attend when a member from Ohio was the AAHIA President." I smiled at Chuck.

"You know, Annie, I hired Kevin Raines into our industry. He had a lot of potential. I hate that this has happened to him." I nodded in agreement. We joined Patricia in the parlor and finished our wine. Chuck led me to the suite door.

"Thank you for the refreshments. See you tomorrow!" I exited and returned to my room.

With the two-hour time difference, the next morning I took a few moments before my walk to call back to Columbus to check my office voicemail. Kevin Raines had called and left me a message.

"The doctors have found two more spots on my brain. I am going to have to undergo radiation and chemotherapy treatments together. Unfortunately, I have to resign as OAHIA president." Kevin would not even have the opportunity to preside at his first OAHIA Executive Committee meeting scheduled for two weeks later.

Although shocked and devastated for Kevin, I knew I should contact Chuck Lincoln, and Kevin's boss, Fulton Burke, who was also at the convention.

"Kevin called me, too," Fulton acknowledged when I reached him in his room. "He still seemed upbeat, but this is not good news."

By now, the initial numbness was starting to wear off. I called Mark Thomas back in Mansfield. Hearing Mark's reassuring voice broke the flood gates, and I began to cry.

"I've known Kevin since he was just a youngster in church camp and I was his counselor," Mark explained. "We lost touch with each other over the years, but then we were sworn into the Ohio Bar on the same day. Later, when he came into the industry, we struck up our friendship again, and I put him on the OAHIA Education Committee, as you know. He has brought a great deal of levity as well as business integrity to our industry. I'm so sorry for Kevin and his family to have to go through this."

After I hung up from my call with Mark, I realized that OAHIA did not have a clear plan or bylaws provision for dealing with presidential absence or incapacitation. I knew I was going to have to think about the options before I called past president Kenneth Farmington and vice president Gordon Geddes. A slow walk around Cheyenne Lake would give me the opportunity for contemplation.

The day was beautiful, crisp, and sunny. Pike's Peak and the Rockies were covered in snow from a storm the previous afternoon, but at the lower altitude of The BroAdmoor, the aspen trees still retained most of their golden leaves which fluttered slightly in the chill morning air. As the air was cold enough to see my breath and chill my extremities, I put on my gloves and hat.

At the northwestern end of the lake a small, man-made island was anchored with a footbridge extending to it from the western shore of the lake. On all my walks previous days, the gate across the footbridge to the island had been locked and barred, but this morning the gate was open, beckoning me.

I slipped undetected over the bridge and onto the circumambulatory island path, secluded amongst the aspens and firs that seemed to cloister the island from the rest of The BroAdmoor complex. As I walked, it occurred to me to dedicate the island mentally to Kevin. Walking back across the footbridge to the western shore, I entered the West Building and walked into its gift shop. I found a golden aspen leaf ornament that I purchased to send to Kevin. Even though he had not been able to come to The BroAdmoor himself, I wanted him to have something of the experience. When I got back to Columbus, I mailed the ornament with a short note thanking Kevin for the opportunity to attend the AAHIA convention in his place. Kevin phoned me after receiving it.

"Thank you for the beautiful golden aspen leaf. I'm going to put it on our Christmas tree."

"You're welcome. How are your treatments going?"

"When I first get the chemo, I feel worse than death with the side effects. By the second week, I feel like warmed-over death. The third week is a little better, and the fourth week I almost feel human again. Then, *wham*, I get more chemo, and it starts over again." Kevin was trying to make light of the situation.

"I certainly hope that we will speak again, Kevin, but in case we don't, I want you to know how much I have enjoyed knowing and working with you."

"I've enjoyed it, too."

"I want you to know, if..., if..., if the worst should occur, and I certainly hope it does not, I promise that OAHIA will remember you with a named award."

"Thank you. That would be very nice."

On the following Thursday, the newly elected OAHIA Executive Committee, except for Kevin Raines, sat around AEMG's conference room table in a leadership crisis without a president and without a plan. If we pulled Kenneth Farmington back to president from past president status, then we would not have a past president. If we bumped Gordon Geddes up to president from vice president—and he did not feel ready to take the reins yet—we would have to re-order the succession, something that we had to do ten years earlier when Herbert Howell had left the industry. The most favored idea was to bring back an earlier former president to serve out Kevin's vacant term, but whom? All the officers at the table turned to me.

"Who do *you* think would be the best choice?" Kenneth asked.

Since I had actually given some thought a few days earlier to who might be a potential candidate to recycle, I responded without hesitation.

"Greg Grisham," I announced. "Greg has just rotated off the Executive Committee, so there will be very little gap in his familiarity with the current issues facing OAHIA. I believe he will be sensitive to the situation and willing to serve as an acting president in Kevin's place. Besides, he's the *only* president who ever got his President's column to me on time or even early!"

The officers looked at each other, nodding in agreement. I was honored that the OAHIA officers had asked my opinion and concurred with my suggestion.

"We wouldn't expect Greg to write all the newsletter columns," Kenneth suggested. "I can write the fall one, Annie can write the winter one, and Gordon can write the spring one. Annie, would you please call Greg and set up a conference call at 2:00 p.m. tomorrow so that Gordon and I can ask him to serve out Kevin's vacancy?"

The next morning I called Greg at 9:00 a.m. to verify if he could make a two o'clock call.

"What's this about?" Greg was naturally curious.

"Kevin Raines has resigned as OAHIA president since they found two more spots on his brain, and he'll be undergoing chemotherapy and radiation simultaneously." I let that news sink in for a moment. I figured the simplest thing was to be straight with Greg. "We now have a vacancy for the Association president. The Executive Committee met yesterday and agreed that we should have Kenneth and Gordon ask you to serve as acting president."

"I'm honored that you've asked me and am willing to serve again." Greg responded without hesitation.

"Kenneth and Gordon need to ask you officially, but I am pleased you'll accept. You were one of my favorite presidents. We'll be splitting up the writing of the president's column for the newsletter. Quite frankly, since you had just rotated off the Executive Committee, it made the most sense to ask you."

Both my working at the Collector's Gallery and my participation in the Coach University courses started in earnest in December. I worked from 10:00 in the morning until 6:00 at night on Saturdays at the Gallery. At first, Auguste appeared supportive, but he would routinely start an argument with me every Saturday morning before I left for the gallery. I was working over thirty hours a week at AEMG, eight hours a week at the gallery, attending a professional development seminar session almost every Monday evening, taking a couple of Coach University teleclasses in the evenings, helping Mireille with her homework, taking her to Hebrew School and Sunday School, and trying to keep up with the household chores. We also attended Friday evening services at the synagogue.

Auguste was working 25 hours a week as a bookkeeper for a local consulting firm. I thought, perhaps if Auguste had some hobbies besides working in the yard and watching television, he might be less envious and happier. Over the course of several months, I encouraged him to explore interests of his own: *t'ai chi*, bonsai plants, and making pottery. However, instead of an increased atmosphere of joy and harmony, the level of competition and tension seemed to escalate. Both our conversational sharing and marital intimacy continued to decrease.

Auguste would criticize Mireille's behavior then demand that I discipline her even though I did not agree with him that her behavior was as severe as the punishment he wanted to mete out. After work one Monday evening, I returned home and found Mireille crying in her room with her door locked.

"What's wrong?" I asked her.

"Daddy...tried..." she forced out between sobs. "Daddy...tried...to...strangle...me." I rubbed her back to attempt to calm her.

"I'll talk to him," I promised.

230

Auguste was in the other room working at his desk.

"Mireille says you tried to strangle her," I tried to stay calm and give him some benefit of the doubt. "What happened?

"I didn't strangle her. I just shook her a little by the shoulders," he said with practiced calm. I suspected he was trying to make the situation less grave than it likely was.

"You tried to strangle me once when we lived in Newark," I said tersely, my mounting ire just barely under control. Between my teeth, brooking no further argument and leaving no room for doubt as to my seriousness, I warned him, "If you *ever* do that again to her, I will call the police on you." I turned and left the room, closing the door emphatically behind me.

Normally, I would have attended my Monday evening seminar, but this evening I called the seminar leader.

"I won't be able to attend the seminar tonight. An emergency has arisen." I did not feel I could leave Mireille alone in the house with her father that night, and it took several weeks before I felt able to trust him alone with her again. When I went to work at the gallery on the Saturdays during the height of the Christmas sales, I took Mireille with me or made sure she went to a friend's house or her grandparents' home for the day.

Those of us with computers were in the grips of the predicted millennium-year-end anticipated apocalypse known as "Y2K" when all computer programs and systems were expected to melt down at midnight on December 31, 1999. Computer software designed in the twentieth century was not expected to be compliant with the millennial date change. AEMG's data processing staff was pressed to migrate to newer software that accommodated the millennial year-end.

Amidst the Y2K uncertainty and the holiday festivities, Congress quietly passed the federal health insurance legislation that OAHIA had been fighting. However, a last-minute amendment removed the most inhibiting aspects of the new law, allowing many of the state-chartered health insurers to continue to operate. This provided an aspect of relief to the OAHIA members who were about to be struck by a blow of a different sort.

On the Tuesday morning following Christmas 1999, I had an eleven o'clock routine appointment with my gynecologist. Having taken the day off, I was dressed in a comfortable sweat suit to make disrobing easier in the doctor's office. At 10:30 a.m., I received a phone call from Gabriela Cynchik in my office.

"Deborah Sayres and Alicia Tomlinson called. They said they were on their way to Toledo for Kevin Raines' funeral and thought you should know that Kevin died on Friday, December 23rd. The funeral begins at eleven o'clock this morning." Both Deborah and Alicia were on the OAHIA Executive Committee and worked in Mansfield. I calculated that they must have been on the road for an hour already and were less than thirty minutes from Toledo.

231

After I sent Kevin the golden aspen leaf from The BroAdmoor, I also sent him a few emails through a Caringbridge web site some friends of his had set up to receive progress updates on Kevin's treatments and to send him encouragement. I had not received any responses to my emails. I knew his death, just before Christmas, would be especially tragic for his wife and three pre-school children. Their holiday would always be tinged with that sad reminder.

However, with only a half-hour notice of the funeral in Toledo—at least a two-and-a-half-hour drive away—and about to leave for doctor's appointment, there was no way I could attend Kevin's funeral, especially since I did not know where in Toledo it was scheduled to be held. After the initial shock of the news, sadness sank in upon my return from my doctor's appointment. Kevin's death hit me hard. Then the memory of Keir slumping against the hallway wall outside his office just after learning of his mother's cancer diagnosis also flickered through my mind.

Over the next couple of weeks Deborah Sayres sent me copies of the Toledo newspaper obituary, eulogy, and touching funeral service that Kevin had prepared in the last months of his life. In turn, I wrote a short obituary for the OAHIA Winter 2000 newsletter about Kevin, largely based on the newspaper version. This was the newsletter issue in which I had been assigned to write the president's column after Kevin's resignation, so it was an even more poignant task. The Association had lost a favorite son.

In writing the obituary, I realized I had not known much about Kevin's personal life. Just shy of forty years of age, Kevin's children were aged two, four, and five. His wife, Becky, was a stay-at-home mom. Since Kevin had expressed concern during his last few months that he had been unable during his abbreviated life span to make financial provisions for college educations for his three youngsters, a group of his civic and attorney friends established an education trust fund for his children. We requested donations in the newsletter.

When I received Summit-United's membership renewal form from Gordon Geddes in January 2000, Keir Mervais was no longer listed as employed with the agency. I remembered how unhappy he seemed on the phone the previous summer, so I was not completely surprised. However, once again, I did not know where he was working.

Meanwhile, other changes were afoot. Harry Whitfield left Cleveland Medical in Mansfield and went into private practice with a local law firm, and Alicia Tomlinson was hired by Kenneth Sven to replace Harry. I privately wondered whether Harry's departure was in any way related to his friend Keir's departure from Cleveland Medical the previous year before Keir had joined Summit-United. I hoped I might learn more about Keir's whereabouts during the February OAHIA Executive Committee meeting.

The start of the February meeting was delayed by an hour as two officers driving from Mansfield were delayed in traffic driving to Columbus. OAHIA's new acting president, Greg Grisham, was caught in the same traffic jam only further behind. He turned around and returned to his Akron office to preside over the meeting via conference call.

No one at the meeting, and especially not Gordon Geddes, mentioned Keir's employment, and I thought it best not to bring up the topic. Instead, I mentioned the promise I had made to Kevin about some type of award to honor his memory and honor young professionals in the field. Before the meeting was adjourned, Greg assigned the task of developing the award guidelines to the Nominating Committee.

With her attention to detail and proficient writing skills, Alicia Tomlinson was selected as OAHIA's newsletter editor. One morning in March she sent me a facsimile of an advertisement from the weekly publication, *Ohio Attorney*, announcing that Keir Mervais had opened a new health insurance agency, Health Cuyahoga.

I was livid with Keir. "I thought we were closer than that," I thought. "He *knows* it is my job as OAHIA executive director to keep track of the member companies in the state. Surely, after all this time, for Keir not to tell me he had changed jobs again...!" I took the copy of Alicia's fax and marched into Gabriela's office, thrusting the document into her hands.

"Invoice him for new agency dues!" I directed her. I did not even wish to send him a note of congratulations or even enclose a cover letter. I remained angry and righteous even after the membership dues check was received in our office.

The economy was doing well, unemployment was very low, and AEMG employees began to leave our employment for better opportunities. My largest association client, NIRS, was particularly hard hit, losing half of its assigned staff in less than six months.

Our interim CEO, who had been retained by AEMG's new owners after David Fisher left in 1998 to take a more prestigious position, had also quit in April 2000. AEMG's new parent company, another association, conducted a nationwide search for a new CEO, hiring Jack Spencer who began work on July 21, 2000, by attending a statewide conference of one of AEMG's less satisfied clients.

The board of NIRS had also been conducting its own search to hire a different management firm, in spite of my thirteen years of devoted service. Since the NIRS annual convention was scheduled to begin on July 24th in San Diego, I met with Jack Spencer for one hour during the afternoon of his first day on the job to give him a crash course in the eighteen-year history of NIRS and AEMG. I urged him to fly out to San Diego that very weekend to make the AEMG management presentation in person.

An affable and gentle giant of a man whose amiable personality belied his perceptive intellect, Jack and I bonded immediately—perhaps because he had been an art gallery owner himself twice before or because he respected my thorough informational briefing about, and understanding of, the NIRS issues. He agreed to fly out to San Diego for the Sunday, July 24th NIRS board meeting in a last-ditch effort to save them as one of AEMG's largest clients.

By the time Jack attended the board meeting, he had studied all the materials I had given him and memorized my resume. However, his association background was in the medical field, whereas AEMG's two previous leaders had come from a financial background—an area important to NIRS. The competing management firm bids were expected to be presented in a board executive session (no staff in attendance) on Wednesday, July 27th. During the intervening days, our staff members managed the NIRS convention, registering members, checking on meeting logistics, and essentially conducting business as usual.

On Wednesday afternoon we four AEMG staff members planned to relax poolside while the NIRS board met in executive session for a few hours interviewing the other management firms. Before retiring to my room to change into my bathing suit after the conclusion of the morning sessions, I went into our staff office to check my voicemail messages back in Columbus. It was the last day for the early registration discount for the OAHIA convention scheduled in Cleveland in a couple of weeks, so I expected I might have some phone messages about that.

There was one. Phyllis Buckley of Health Cuyahoga—Keir's new agency—had called about whether she could receive an extension of time on the early bird discount since she had just received a registration form in the mail, delayed because it had been mailed to the agency's previous address. I recalled Phyllis had previously worked with Gordon Geddes, Linwood Ashton, and Keir at Summit-United Health Care.

"Phyllis, I am actually out in San Diego and won't be back to the office until Friday morning. Can you get me your early bird registration and payment by then?"

"It's contingent upon the approval of the person in charge of our agency, and he won't be back until tomorrow." I suspected Phyllis might be referring to Keir.

"Who's that?" I feigned some innocence.

"Keir Mervais." Phyllis hesitated a moment. "Are you aware that he has been ill?" I wondered if he had a summer cold or the flu.

"No."

"He was diagnosed in the early spring with brain cancer."

I felt like I had been hit in the stomach with a steel girder. Every vestige of ire I had been holding against him since March vanished in a heartbeat. I started sobbing out loud on the phone as my mind raced. "Brain cancer! Kevin Raines died of brain cancer. I know how this goes—first you get some spots on the brain, they hit you with chemo and radiation, and then you DIE. This could not be happening again…and to Keir, of all people!"

"I'm so sorry to have upset you," Phyllis offered kindly.

"You…don't…understand," I blurted out between sobs. "I've…known… Keir…for 15 years…" It did not explain much, but the depth to which I was experiencing shock and grief probably spoke volumes. I composed myself a bit. "Do you have the Mervais's address so that I might send Keir a card?" I wrote down the home address that Phyllis recited to me.

Suddenly recalling the initial purpose of the call, I added, "Of course, I will waive your late registration fee once you have approval to attend the convention,"

Still stunned, I picked up my belongings and went out into the bright California sun to head back to my room. I felt dislocated and dazed as I ascended the elevator to my room. "You should not be alone at this time," the voice inside my head warned me. I wanted to call Sylvia, my confidante and only witness to my relationship with Keir, but I remembered it was her day off. My next choice was to phone Mark Thomas, the only OAHIA member to have taken the personal development courses with me. He would understand why I was distraught over Keir's news so soon after Kevin Raines's death. Luckily, Mark's office had an easy phone number to remember. I checked my watch and added three hours—it would be 4:30 in the afternoon back east.

"Mark, please be there," my mind pleaded. And he was.

"Mark, it's Annie. I am out in San Diego at a convention and just heard...Did you know Keir Mervais has *brain cancer*?"

"Uh, I think I remember Greg Grisham mentioning something like that..." I was not sure whether Mark's hesitation was coming from uncertainty or a wish to deny this bad news.

"You were *supposed* to let me know if you heard *any* news about anyone in the industry!" I started to cry again.

"I wish I was there to give you a hug," Mark was contrite.

"I just want to beat up the pillows on my bed!"

"You do that if it makes you feel better."

After I hung up with Mark, I changed into some shorts and a tee shirt and went back down the elevator to the pool deck where my three co-workers were waiting for me to join them. I briefly explained what had happened.

"Instead of swimming and sunning myself, I think I'll write the Mervais family a note." I went to the gift shop and found a card with a photo of a Pacific sunset on the outside. I located a seat and table in the shade on a veranda not far from the room where the NIRS board meeting was being held and began to write.

"Dear Keir,

I have just learned from Phyllis Buckley of your illness. My thoughts and prayers are with you and your family at this time. I am currently in San Diego at a convention—hence the Pacific Ocean-themed card."

The entire note was four paragraphs in length. I was a bit surprised that the composition came out of my pen so easily. I hesitated over how to sign the card but decided on, *"Fondly, Annie."*

As I finished writing the card and addressing the envelope, NIRS president Derick Smith came out to tell me the board had finished its executive session and the officers would reconvene after a 15-minute break.

"I just learned that one of the former presidents of another client association has brain cancer," I explained to Derick, suspecting that I might look like I had been crying.

"A good friend of mine just died of that last week." Derick appeared to me to be rather emotionless.

I followed Derick back inside to the meeting room and set up my laptop computer to take minutes. The Executive Committee session was relatively short, and although the issue was not addressed directly, by the time the meeting was adjourned, it was pretty clear to me that my largest client would be leaving AEMG by year end while a very dear man was now living under a death sentence.

On the way to the airport the next morning for our return flight to Columbus, I mailed my card to Keir. One of the NIRS convention speakers had given me a copy of the popular book, *Who Moved My Cheese?* I read it on the plane. Obviously, Keir's "cheese" had been moved. One of the key questions in the book is "What would you do if you were not afraid?" The answer that came to me immediately was to call Keir after I got home and he had time to receive my note.

While we were in the process of changing airplanes in Dallas-Fort Worth Airport, I telephoned Sylvia at the office with the awful news about Keir.

"I am so sorry," she said. "My mother-in-law died of brain cancer. We'll talk when you get back home."

What would I do if I wasn't afraid? A week after I returned from San Diego, I called Keir's office at Health Cuyahoga. Phyllis Buckley answered, thanked me for my help on the convention registration fee, and put me through to Keir. His voice was as warm and affectionate as I remembered (with the exception of our last call when he was still working with Gordon Geddes), but his speech pattern had slowed.

"I've just finished four months of radiation treatment that has caused me to lose my hair." I silently lamented the loss of that thick, dark mane of hair through which I had always wanted to run my fingers. "I haven't been able to work full-time, only coming into the office when I feel up to it. My doctors estimate that I have two years to live." I quickly did the math—that put him into spring 2002, around Mireille's *bat mitzvah* date.

"You wouldn't have opened the Health Cuyahoga agency if you only expected to live two more years," I chided him encouragingly.

"No," Keir agreed. "I'm the type of person who always sees the glass half full, rather than half empty. I plan to live a long and happy life." I silently added, "With me in it!"

"How are you feeling?"

"The radiation leaves me feeling zapped, and I have some difficulty with numbers..." I could almost sense the twinkle of humor in his eyes as he added, "I'm dangerous with a tip." We talked about Mireille and Sean, the gallery, and my coaching practice.

236

Over the previous fourteen years, I had wondered who had come up with the idea for the special services clause in the OAHIA-AEMG management agreement. In the past, I had asked Liam and Harry, both of whom had only very vague recollections of it. I had always suspected it had been Keir's idea.

"You know, Keir, I am still working with OAHIA after all these years because of that special services clause."

"It was meant to be a *lifetime* contract," Keir teased me. I knew he did not intend it as job slavery, but it was definitely an admission that he both recalled and understood the clause's initial intention and was, therefore, the likely author of it.

"The OAHIA convention is going to be at the InterContinental Hotel at the end of next week. I know Phyllis has registered to attend. Would you like me to visit you while I'm in the Cleveland Heights area?" I had already checked MapQuest for Keir's home address and its proximity to the hotel.

"I would enjoy that, but my brother is taking me, Sean, and my two nephews to our vacation home in Lakeside that weekend."

"Oh, like a male bonding weekend?"

"Something like that." Keir chuckled.

"Perhaps I can visit another time I am in Cleveland then...?" I wondered when that might be. OAHIA was the only statewide group I still managed, and I had not been to Cleveland for business at all in recent years. "May I call you after the convention to let you know how it went?"

"I'd like that."

Our conversation lasted forty-five minutes. The aura of love between us on the call felt so thick you could have cut it with a knife.

Gabriela Cynchik had resigned from AEMG earlier in the summer, and Jennifer Erwin, whose father had been in association management for his career, was assigned by Jack Spencer to assist me with OAHIA. Jennifer was right out of college, having worked as a catering manager at the Hyatt in Columbus. A beautiful brunette, Jennifer was at ease in the association world, eager to do a good job, and more extroverted than Gabriela had been. A member of The Ohio State University swim team, Jennifer took to the job like a fish to water. I was able to delegate to her many of the meeting planning aspects of the OAHIA convention that I had not been able to trust with subordinate staff members since Sylvia had left to have her first child back in 1996.

Being held in Cleveland, the OAHIA convention was the most poorly attended of any I had witnessed. I did not know whether it was avoided by most of the members from Cleveland because it was in their own backyard, because Gordon Geddes—convention chair and former employee with Kevin Raines' company—was not popular, or because there were conflicts with most members' schedules. Certainly, the hotel was of a high caliber and situated in the shopping, cultural, and educational mecca of Cleveland Heights. Gordon Geddes and Phyllis Buckley (who had left

Geddes' agency when Keir had) were the only two Cleveland-area members who attended the convention. Mark Thomas commuted daily from Mansfield as did several other members from Akron and Youngstown. Even acting president Greg Grisham had not brought his wife to the convention this time—and regretted it once he saw the elegant President's Suite he was assigned by the hotel.

In his capacity as acting president, Greg opened the convention on Friday morning with a touching moment of silence for Kevin followed by a prayer for Keir.

After Friday morning's educational sessions were over, I drove over to visit the Reinberger Galleries in University Circle. Just as in March the previous year when I had visited the Reinberger with my mother and Mireille, Keir's spirit felt pervasive. The following afternoon, I returned to the Circle to visit the Cleveland Museum of Art, an imposing classical structure on a hill overlooking Wade Lagoon. After viewing a portion of the art treasures inside the museum, I went outside to sit in the Fine Arts Garden surrounding the lagoon.

Ironically, I thought, "Here I am in Cleveland Heights and Keir is in Lakeside." Just as I had mentally dedicated the island in The BroAdmoor's Cheyenne Lake to Kevin Raines, I dedicated this garden to Keir Mervais. The tears rolled down my cheeks as I surveyed the peaceful setting of the garden.

Exiting Wade Oval onto East Boulevard in my car, I became turned around and ended up heading south on Martin Luther King Junior Drive rather than west on Carnegie Avenue toward the hotel. In an attempt to turn around, I headed west on Cedar Glen Parkway which turned into Cedar Road. The names of the streets sounded familiar from my MapQuest search a couple of weeks earlier, so I knew Keir's house was nearby. However, so as not to get completely lost, I pulled into a Sunoco filling station and turned around to retrace my route back past University Circle and onto Carnegie Avenue in the direction of our hotel.

The only attendees that evening at the Presidents' Reception—an event designed to congratulate the incoming and outgoing OAHIA presidents—were Gordon, his wife, Jennifer, and me. Gordon presented both of us staff with $50 gift certificates, a relatively rare occurrence, as a thank you for our convention assistance. For a half-hour, Gordon and his wife chatted with Jennifer and me, waiting to see if anyone else would show up for the reception, but none did. Apparently, everyone else had left for home already. I felt embarrassed for the apparent lack of support for Gordon's presidency.

"I think it is futile to wait any longer," Gordon acknowledged at 7:30 p.m. "Why don't you ladies leave for your drive back to Columbus?" The only time I had ever previously left an OAHIA convention before the weekend was over was the time Mireille had contracted the flu a few years earlier.

Our featured gallery artist for August was a Dublin potter, Susan Graham, who specialized in shino-glazes, incorporating an iridescent, blue-green-turquoise glaze in some of her pieces. I was very taken with her work and had already splurged by purchasing two turquoise-lined bowls, two burnt sienna-orange bowls, and a teapot. (The subtle modulations from light blue to light green in the two turquoise bowls, and especially the circle designs in the shallower bowl, reminded me of the colors I had seen in Keir's eyes the two times I had "drowned" in them.)

I was tempted to buy a sixth piece--a six-sided, faceted vase standing about seven inches tall with a darker, cranberry-hued, shino glaze, that had a more masculine feel than some of the other pieces. Although I could not justify purchasing more pottery for myself, I felt I could buy a gift for someone else. Just as I had selected the golden aspen leaf for Kevin Raines, I bought this shino vase for Keir, wrapped it carefully to protect it during shipping, enclosed a photograph from one of our gallery openings, and sent it along with a note with my hope that, whenever he was feeling zapped, looking at the vase would give him strength.

Two days after I shipped the vase, around early evening as I was preparing dinner in the kitchen, I felt an adrenaline strike like a sudden kick in my stomach—my intuition told me Keir had just received the vase. The next week I telephoned Keir at his office again.

"Thank you for the vase," he said in his understated manner.

"Did it arrive in one piece?"

"Yes."

I then told Keir a little bit about the artist and the other pottery I had bought, the personal development courses I had taken, and how I had gotten involved with the gallery. I also gave him a brief synopsis of the convention and its disappointing turnout.

"See," he observed, "We have *so much* to talk about!"

"How are *you* doing?"

"I'll be going back to the Cleveland Clinic for an evaluation right after Labor Day. I am hoping that I will be allowed to drive again. Abigail is afraid of the liability if I have an accident."

Remembering his wife was also an attorney, I could understand her concern. I quickly guessed, if Keir had not been driving for the past several months, how this could complicate his family's schedule—driving to and from work, to doctors' appointments and hospitals, to Sean's school and extracurricular activities, not to mention Keir's own feelings of increased dependence and reduction of freedom.

"Abigail and I make a great team."

"Team?!? TEAM?!?!" my mind protested. Again I had the sense that their marriage was more a match of two companions who were intellectual equals rather than a love match. I so wanted him to adore her and be unable to live without her, lest, I be tempted to drive a wedge into that crack in their marital foundation.

"I hope your medical evaluation at the Clinic goes well, and you'll be able to drive again," I said out loud. "Do you mind if I inquire about you from time to time?"

"No, I don't mind." The warmth in his voice assured me that he would look forward to future conversations between us.

After Labor Day, I called Keir's office again. Phyllis Buckley answered.

"They have started Keir on chemotherapy." I heard the sorrow and regret in her voice. I suspected from her tone that Keir's availability as the agency's manager would be greatly diminished by the side-effects of the chemotherapy treatments. I thanked her for letting me know and hung up.

On the home front, I was being coached by two of my fellow Coaches Academy participants, Hillary and Allen McDuff, participating in the Being Remarkable seminar, and standing for a perfect marriage with Auguste based on the potentiality of being "treasured and tender."

My horoscope one day read: "Your life will become much less tense once a domestic problem is resolved." Auguste accused me of not "acting like a wife" and did not speak to me for days. Hillary suggested I write Auguste a letter in the vein of, "When you do this, it makes me feel _____," which I did.

One Friday evening in mid-September I also wrote a letter to Keir. My first draft was ten pages long. I edited it down to a more reasonable five pages. I tried to be upbeat and cheerful about the chemotherapy treatments—how he now had time to catch up on episodes of "Judge Judy" on television and how I imagined the chemotherapy eating away at the cancer like "Pac-Man." But I thought it sounded lame and silly. The moment I slipped it irretrievably down the mailbox chute, I was mortified about what I had written—and even the fact that I had written at all.

A couple of weeks later, I sat in my office paralyzed with fear for fifteen full minutes before dialing Keir's office. A young woman answered. She put me through to his office phone, but only his voice mail answered. I hung up and silently noted the irony of having been so afraid and yet not getting through to him anyway.

On October 1st, ninety days before the end of the management agreement termination date, the NIRS President, Derick Smith, informed AEMG's CEO, Jack Spencer, that they were leaving AEMG's management after eighteen years and directly hiring their own executive director, effective January 1, 2001.

NIRS was AEMG's third-largest client with nine staff members assigned to it. Our firm had already lost some other, smaller clients since Jack had begun working with us. In addition, Jack's predecessor had signed a lease agreement for new office space, large enough to house 65 staff members and an estimated 33 association clients, where we were expected to move at year-end. However, in the aftermath of switching CEOs, we had shrunk to only twenty clients with a surplus of staff members. Jack confided in me that he was faced with making some drastic staffing cuts in order to stem the tide of the rising red ink.

Jack was a pretty sharp judge of character. The list of personnel he chose to layoff included the weaker contributors to the overall viability of the firm. He also had identified a few who could turn their specialty skills into entrepreneurial ventures outside the company while retaining some of our mutual clients for graphic and web design. Jack needed me to stay to oversee the three-month transition move out of NIRS as well as retain me on several other clients.

With this increased stress level, and Mireille wanting to visit the Ohio State Fair with her girlfriend, I took a vacation day on October 15th to accompany them. By mid-afternoon, we were all tired of walking and returned home. While the girls were upstairs playing in Mireille's room, I dialed Keir's home phone number. There was no answer, only Abigail's recording that they were unable to come to the phone. I did not leave a message.

Two weeks later, I wrote Keir another letter. This time the first draft was five pages that I edited down to two-and-a-half. In it I quoted a Hebrew prayer for the ill called *Mi Sheberach* (The One Who Blessed) that I had learned at synagogue. I wrote that I was afraid that he would go without saying goodbye. I also enclosed for him a copy of Oriah Mountain Dreamer's popular prose poem, *The Invitation*. Upon mailing the letter, I immediately wanted to retract it.

Since I was not sure whether Keir was well enough anymore to read my letters to himself or whether Abigail, Sean, or a home health care worker might read them to him, I sanitized them by keeping them as light and friendly as possible. Never one to keep a diary or journal, I found myself writing a private log of my feelings of concern, incompletion, frustration, and quiet desperation. After every letter I sent, my coach Hillary assured me that, "The ball is in his court."

Every night before falling asleep, I would clasp my hands together as though holding Keir's hand and pray for him, imagining his tumor evaporating from his head. Each morning as I first became consciously awake, I would repeat the process.

After supper one November evening, Auguste used a particularly mean tone with me.

"If you don't stop treating me like this, I'll leave," I retorted angrily, meaning I would leave the room or the house for a while.

"Don't let the door hit your ass on the way out!" he replied matter-of-factly. I knew now that Auguste no longer cared for me, and in that instant, I fell out of love with him.

I mailed Keir and Abigail a Christmas card.

Victorian London, England

1852-1891 C.E.

"Cab! Cabbie!" Papa shouted, raising his cane in a white-gloved hand to signal the hansoms in Drury Lane. Together we emerged with the crowd from the Theatre Royal performance of Wagner's *The Flying Dutchman* one July evening in 1870. I hung onto his other arm so as not to lose him in the throng of men in top hats and evening coats, with ladies in opera dress, who were similarly engaged in seeking transportation home or to a late-night dinner party.

My father, Lloyd Graham, Q.C., was a distinguished senior barrister—or bencher—who had been conferred with the honor of Queen's Counsel at Lincoln Inn. He was moderately tall, his broad shoulders filling out his waistcoat with an expanding stomach from a life of eating well. He had an almost full head of salt-and-pepper grey hair and a full beard with a moustache descending from the middle of his nostrils to either side of his lips. He exuded an air of commanding presence and confidence that came with the status, rank, and privilege of a Queen's Counsel.

Presented at Court the previous year, I had been thrust into a whirlwind social calendar of dinner parties, dances, concerts, performances, and exhibitions, escorted by my parents. However, since Mama had taken ill earlier in the day, Papa and I eschewed our family carriage to attend the opera in a two-person cab so as not to be burdened with its livery during the performance. The downside of this decision was the competition for cabs at the end of the evening.

"Why, Mr. Graham, sir! What a pleasant surprise!" In one movement the gentleman had removed his top hat with his left hand while extending his right in greeting. We turned to see a very pleasant-looking man in his late twenties—handsomely attired in a dark green frock coat, beige silk waistcoat, and grey trousers—making his way toward us among the other opera patrons. Smiling broadly, my father enthusiastically clasped and pumped his greeter's hand.

"Ralph Thomas! So nice to see you! What did you think of the Wagner? Oh, forgive my manners; Amanda dear, this is Ralph Thomas who is in chambers at Lincoln Inn. Ralph, may I present my daughter, Miss Amanda Graham."

I curtsied slightly and raised my ivory-gloved hand so that Mr. Thomas could bow over it from a respectable distance.

"I'm honored, Miss Graham. I was about to offer you a lift. My carriage is just over there." He pointed to a brougham waiting some distance down the lane.

"We live in Belgravia. Are you sure it is not too far out of your way?" Papa asked.

"It's a fine evening for a ride. It would be my pleasure to give you a lift and discuss the opera with you." Mr. Thomas signaled for his driver to approach.

My father lent me his hand as I put my booted right foot on the carriage step. Stepping into the carriage, the warm smell of the horsehair leather seats and sawdust permeated my nostrils as I carefully positioned my grey satin skirt on the rear bench. In recent years, the bulky, round crinoline had given way in fashion to panniers, looped skirts, and rear puffs with flounces of lace, ruching, and flowers plus a train. To protect my V-neck, off-the-shoulder bodice from the night chill, I wore a pink cashmere opera cape—a tent-like garment buttoning down the front with pagoda sleeves and triangular collar ending with a tassel in the middle of my back.

After giving directions to the driver, my father mounted the carriage steps and seated himself to my right. Mr. Thomas followed, sitting across from us with his back to the front of the carriage. Once settled, he tapped twice with his cane on the inside of the carriage roof, signaling his driver to proceed. With a jolt, we began to move forward.

Although the carriage interior was dimly lit, when we passed under the street lamps, I was able to study the features of our host while the two men conversed about the opera. Together, they discussed the stormy, dramatic motif of Wagner's condemned Dutch captain seeking a woman who will be faithful until her death and how it was interwoven with the melodious and romantic ballad of the woman.

Having doffed his top hat again, a strand of thick, black hair descended over Mr. Thomas's left temple. His slightly bushy eyebrows roofed two crystal-clear irises of citrine green encircling dark, penetrating pupils, enlarged in the darkness. He had a strong nose descending to a pencil-thin moustache overarching soft, flat lips. Although his facial shape was broad, the overall countenance was extremely open and pleasant—quite handsome, in fact.

The carriage wound its way along the Aldwych Crescent, then in a straight line down The Strand, crossing St. James Park along The Mall. My father and Mr. Thomas now turned their discussion to matters of law. First, they spoke of the merits of prison reform and then of the prospect of moving the law courts from Westminster Hall to the north side of The Strand near Chancery Lane.

"The relocation of the courts would make it far more convenient for the barristers, juries, and judges to conduct legal business than having to crisscross The Strand and Victoria

Embankment to get to Whitehall and Parliament," Mr. Thomas observed.

Under the influence of the steady murmur of their male voices and the rhythmic clip-clop of the horses, I dozed off only to awaken abruptly at our doorstep.

Mr. Thomas stepped down from the carriage after the footman opened the door, followed by Papa who helped me alight. We expressed our gratitude and said our goodnights to Mr. Thomas who again bowed over my hand.

"I hope we did not bore you too much with our courtroom chatter, Miss Graham."

"Thank you, no, Mr. Thomas. I was interested very much in your discussion of the opera, but I leave the legal matters to my father." I turned and ascended our newly white-washed steps to the front door opened by our house man. My father waited until Mr. Thomas's carriage drove off then followed me into our front hallway.

"Even when he was a student," Papa remarked, "Ralph Thomas struck me as someone with rare intelligence and superior ambition." As Mama came down to greet our arrival and inquire about the opera, Papa turned to address her. "We should invite him to a dinner party sometime soon."

My mother, Marie Franklin Graham, was ideally suited as a helpmate and companion to my father. She ruled the household with a gentle and quiet strength. The servants knew not to cross her because she would not stand for disobedience. But she was also gracious and considerate of those who served her well. Mama kept all the household concerns and issues from Papa when he arrived home from chambers or the law courts. She was tender and attentive to his needs, whether providing his slippers, pipe, *The Times*, and some quiet time reading, or listening to his discourse on politics, the economy, or the law. She turned a blind eye when he stayed out too late at his club or other activities in the city and returned inebriated, quieting his loud demeanor and dressing him for bed. She also made sure we were well-fed, well-churched, and represented at Sunday services and charitable occasions.

But my mother was at her finest when entertaining. The suggestion of a dinner party added an excited glint to her otherwise tired eyes that night. I knew she would be up early the next morning assembling the menus for the event. I gave her a swift kiss on the cheek and sailed upstairs to my bedroom and grateful slumber.

I had a dream that night, tossed about on stormy seas with the *Flying Dutchman*. But instead of the lonesome operatic figure, it was an enigmatic Ralph Thomas who played the role to my Senta. As I jumped off the cliff into the sea, I awoke with a start, my heart pounding.

244

Even though it was still dark outside, I could hear the kitchen staff moving around as breakfast preparations began. Then I heard stirring in my parents' room, as my mother dressed and made her way downstairs.

I would have enjoyed lazily lying in bed, but I knew Mama would want to have breakfast cleared away from the dining room so that she could concentrate on her morning room duties. After she prepared the guest list, I would be enlisted into writing out the invitations to the dinner party.

Once the servants were given their duties and the cook her instructions for lunch and dinner, Mama consulted her social book to select the appropriate guests for our dinner soirée in a little more than a fortnight. My role was to observe and listen to how she ran the household while quietly sewing caps and collars or embroidering. Occasionally, my mother would ask a question out loud in my direction, not actually expecting my independent opinion but only my concurrence.

Eventually, she selected seven guests suitable for the party: the young barrister, Ralph Thomas; our vicar and his wife, the Rev. and Mrs. Randall Stevenson; a neighbor and banker, Mr. Theodore Palmer; my mother's dearest friend, the widow Eugenia Kendall; and another barrister from Lincoln Inn chambers and his wife, Mr. and Mrs. Neville Hall.

While I wrote out the invitations in my neatest hand, my mother developed the menus and schedules for ordering the ingredients and cooking the dishes as well as cleaning our public rooms. She then ordered our footman to deliver the invitations while we looked over pattern books for the latest dinner fashions.

The following days entailed visits from a dressmaker for measurements and later, fittings, plus shopping for trim and decoration. In addition to the normal, time-consuming duties of meal preparation, bed airing, laundry, and general daily household duties, we supervised and assisted the servants with cleaning lamps, washing windows, airing curtains, polishing furniture, blackleading grates, making preserves and puddings, baking, and generally getting ourselves and the house ready.

"Amanda, dear, I expect you to practice some of your best piano pieces, as well as read your Bible and the newspaper each day, so you will be a knowledgeable and charming dinner companion and capable of providing light entertainment after our repast," my mother reminded me frequently. My parents had moved my matrimonial prospecting into a high state of readiness. The second London season since my debut was nearing an end and an eligible suitor had not yet come forth. Mama and Papa appeared to be setting their sights on Mr. Ralph Thomas, and if not him, perhaps the banker, Theodore Palmer.

The day of the dinner party was filled with cooking, setting the table, floral arrangements, and training new staff hired for the occasion. I did not have time to become nervous until I retired to get dressed.

We had chosen an evening dress of light blue *peau de soie* with an overskirt and underskirt looped in the front—one longer than the other—both trimmed with burgundy ruffles and lace, a matching bustle and short train, with a pleated and flounced hem. The bodice was curved low and off my shoulders, also trimmed with white ruffles and lace, with the latter serving as my sleeves. With the help of my lady's maid, my hair was pulled back and up in a chignon with soft curls cascading from the top and decorated with a comb and lace. A pearl and crystal necklace with matching pearl ear bobs complemented my dress, and I wore white satin sandals, short white gloves and carried a lace fan to complete my outfit.

I carefully assessed my appearance in the looking glass, pinching my cheeks to add glow and applying a bit of pomade to my lips to add a soft sheen.

Our guests were due to arrive at 7:30, so I slowly and carefully descended to the hall foyer at 7:15 to receive my last instructions from Mama. With the corsets, crinoline pannier, petticoats, and several layers, I was easily wearing thirty pounds or more of clothing. Breathing, much less moving, was somewhat difficult. Even if I had not been anxious, I would likely not be able to eat much of the splendid banquet we had planned.

The Reverend and Mrs. Stephenson arrived at 7:35 with Eugenia Kendall soon after. Theodore Palmer arrived next, followed in quick secession by Mr. Thomas and the Halls so that our entire party was assembled in our drawing room by 7:45. Mama had arranged for the following dinner escort pairings: Papa would escort Mrs. Stevenson, followed by Mr. Hall who would escort Mrs. Kendall, Mr. Palmer with Mrs. Hall, then Ralph Thomas would take me into dinner, while Mama would bring up the rear with the Reverend Stephenson. The escorts were introduced to their dinner partners for light conversation prior to the dinner bell.

"It was so kind of you to offer us your carriage after the opera, Mr. Thomas." I was again struck by the clarity of his eyes.

"Not at all, Miss Graham. It was my pleasure to be in the company of you and your father." Mr. Thomas flashed an engaging smile. "It was certainly more pleasant than heading straight back to my bachelor rooms." Noticing my discomfort to his allusion, Mr. Thomas changed the subject. "It must be enjoyable to promenade around the squares in this quieter part of London. Do you prefer to walk or ride, Miss Graham?"

"I like both, rather. The Flower Garden in Kensington Gardens is a lovely walk, but Hyde Park is so extensive that a carriage is necessary. Is there a place you prefer to exercise, Mr. Thomas?" He knitted his eyebrows together slightly in thought. I noticed his dimples recede slightly. At the sudden memory of my dream, I blushed slightly.

"There is a park at Lincoln Inn Fields and a smaller one, New Square, near where I reside, but the Victoria Embankment is the closest open space of any size before St. James or Regent's Parks. Sometimes I weary of the crowds, however."

The dinner bell rang, and we proceeded down to supper, Mr. Thomas offering me his right arm for the staircase descent. I could feel his body's warmth through his black dinner jacket. I noticed that he looked even more attractive in the candle and gaslight of our home than in the street light of the other evening.

Reaching the dining room, Mr. Thomas pulled out one of the two remaining empty chairs at the table for me then seated himself to my right. I removed my gloves and placed them in my lap.

My mother had selected the more modern *service à la russe,* requiring printed menus, additional footmen to serve the foods, and a table setting with displays of fruits, nuts, and flowers down the center runner. The first remove consisted of beef consommé and artichoke soup. Next we were offered fillet of salmon, leg of lamb, a salad, boiled new potatoes, and stewed sea kale. Following this was roast pigeon and French beans, ending with apple pudding, blancmange, greengage plums, apricots, grapes, and a cherry pie. With each service, a suitable wine was offered, ending with champagne.

While we ate, Mr. Thomas continued polite conversation.

"How did you like *The Flying Dutchman*? I am afraid your father and I did not allow you the opportunity to comment."

"The music was rather tempestuous, I am afraid, but I liked how Wagner repeated refrains to weave the story together. Do you think it is possible to love someone that you barely know so deeply that one would fling oneself from a cliff to save the other's soul?"

Mr. Thomas turned to look at me squarely. I noticed how the candlelight played on his cravat pin, and the corners of his collar bent downward as he swallowed. A slight cast of rose appeared to color his face. I had the sensation of everyone and everything else fading from the room as I raised my eyes to look directly into his while he gave my question serious consideration.

"I would hope one need not throw herself over a cliff to prove her love, but I hope that measure of devotion is possible between two people."

The intensity and sincerity of his expression was so genuine that I averted my eyes briefly to break the spell as a blush rose to my own cheeks, necessitating that I use my fan which he likely took as a coquettish ploy. Once again, he had unsettled me in a pointed way.

Needing to change the topic of conversation, I asked about his family.

"My parents and younger brother live near Derby, but I came to London ten years ago to read for the law. Sometimes I do miss the countryside." He looked away in what appeared to me as a brief moment of nostalgic sentiment. His thoughts then came back to our conversation and he continued.

"Nonetheless, there are many activities to keep one occupied and interested in London. I can easily walk to the British Museum or Sir John Soane's collection. Did you see the exhibition of masters at the Royal Academy's new home this summer?"

Before I could respond, Mama signaled for the ladies to repair to the drawing room with her. I excused myself from Mr. Thomas's company, and he rose to pull out my chair. As I left the room, I could almost feel his eyes following me. The men stayed behind to consume their port and to smoke.

I was not quite sure what to make of Mr. Thomas. Perhaps he was a little jittery, too, aware of his role as a potential suitor for me. I mulled over our interaction in my mind as tea and coffee were served. I knew Mama would inquire of my opinion of him—if not tonight while she was relishing her hostess role, then in the morning. It was also obvious that she was interested in Eugenia Kendall's opinion of Mr. Palmer. Although they had not been dinner partners, they had exchanged some comments during the meal.

"Mr. Palmer appeared to have enjoyed my little supper," Mama began.

"He certainly showed good appetite," added Mrs. Hall.

"He likely does not get many home-cooked meals, especially ones as elegant as your suppers, Marie," complimented Mrs. Stevenson.

"You are very kind, Glenda," returned mother. "Eudora, you have been unusually quiet this evening. Are you feeling ill?"

"Perhaps I had a little too much of the claret. I am afraid my knowledge of banking is very limited, so I did not have much to add to the conversation." The widow redirected her attention to me. "Amanda, you seemed to have held an engaging discussion with Mr. Thomas."

"We talked about the performance of Wagner's *The Flying Dutchman* and his family. He comes from Derby. I believe he spends most of his time in the city. He has rooms there." I tried to maintain a matter-of-fact tone so as not to reveal any emotion that I might have been feeling. I needed some more time to sort out my thoughts.

Thankfully, the men entered the drawing room then. My mother signaled for me to play. I rose and navigated my way around the furniture and seated guests to the piano where I performed a piano quartet by Schumann, Beethoven's *Für Elise*, followed by a

Chopin *étude*. At the conclusion, Mr. Palmer rose to his feet immediately.

"Bravo! Bravo! Well done, Miss Graham!"

Reverend Stephenson added, "Excellent!" As I curtsied and smiled at my small audience, I caught Mr. Thomas's pleased expression, and my heart skipped a beat.

"Your daughter has a refined talent, Mr. Graham," Mr. Thomas observed. "It has been a very fine evening, but I have an oral argument to prepare in the morning and must beg my leave." Bowing to the assembled company, Mr. Thomas thanked Mama and then went downstairs accompanied by Papa. That signaled the end of the evening's festivities, and all our guests soon left.

"Marie, you have outdone yourself tonight. It was a splendid party." My father placed his arm affectionately around my mother's shoulders.

"Indeed, Mama, it was a wonderful evening, but I am tired and would like leave to go to bed now." Kissing each parent on the cheek, I climbed the two flights of stairs to my bedroom. Once undressed by my maid, I stretched under the bedclothes. I fell asleep to the strains of Senta's ballad in my head.

The next day was spent in recovering our house from the dinner party. The following day while Mama and I were out paying our morning visits, we received an invitation to dinner at the Hall's home and a *carte de visite* from Mr. Thomas. I was disappointed that we had not been at home to receive his call. I had imagined various circumstances where we might properly meet again, including the hope—albeit it distant—that he would be included among the guests at the evening planned by Mr. and Mrs. Hall, which he was not.

The end of the London season was nearing and the prospects for a more propitious encounter with Mr. Thomas dimmed. As my family was not part of the fashionable upper class that deserted London for a country estate, the number of social occasions—theater, opera, and balls—would be greatly reduced for the next several months.

On one particularly warm and pleasant Saturday afternoon in early autumn, Papa suggested we take some air in our barouche on a drive through Hyde Park. The fall foliage was resplendent in all its colors, and the trees were remarkably brilliant against the deep cyan sky.

We were not alone on our drive as the sandy tracks of Rotten Row, Serpentine Road, and The Ring were quite congested with carriages, riders on horseback, and strollers, all of which seemed to find acquaintances with whom to stop and chat, adding further to the glut of traffic.

Attempting to overcome my frustration with the overpopulation of equine and human beings who impeded our

249

forward progress and, thus our pleasure of the glorious day, I found the balance suddenly tipped in the favor of the latter as one familiar rider emerged from the throng and, leading his horse, strode purposely toward us.

I do not know whether I saw or sensed him first, but I was grateful that my parasol could momentarily and partially shield the uncontrolled smile and warm flush rising to my face. I only had a moment to restore my composure as he approached.

"What pleasant good fortune, Mr. and Miss Graham, to find you in this crowd!" Ralph Thomas removed his top hat in respectful greeting.

Papa signaled for our driver to stop so that we, in turn, became a traffic impediment to others.

"It is such a fine day that most of London must be out taking the air." My father indicated the crowd with his hand.

"Why, Mr. Thomas," I chided in a mildly flirtatious manner. "I thought you preferred promenading on foot as your exercise."

"As I often do, Miss Graham." He looked straight at me in open fashion without acknowledging my slight petulance. "But the day was so favorable, I gave myself leave to venture farther and for a longer time on horseback. And my reward is the fortuitous pleasure to encounter you both here."

Papa then inquired of Mr. Thomas about a court case in which the latter was involved—a topic that quickly exceeded my knowledge, releasing my mind to re-examine the eligible bachelor at hand, this time in natural light rather than by gas, street, or candle light.

In any light, this man would be very pleasing to the eyes. His proportions appeared classic in the manner of the Greek sculptures secured for The British Museum by Lord Elgin in the earlier part of the century. Although his conversational politeness and style were forthright, there was always a glint of humor in his eyes that shielded others from their quicksilver intelligence. He appeared to absorb and understand everything going on around him while seemingly giving his whole attention to the person with whom he was engaged in conversation. His smile was broad, bright, and disarming, relaying warmth that I am sure served him well in both judicial and social settings.

I was still immersed in my contemplation of the charms of the gentleman before me when he again directed his attention to me.

"I hope I may again have the opportunity to favor my senses with your delightful talent at the piano, Miss Graham." Although his comment could have been interpreted as a flagrant attempt to secure another dinner invitation, Mr. Thomas's gracious delivery was entirely respectful and complimentary. I was momentarily speechless from his obviously favorable attention to me, but fortunately my father took his cue with generous good humor.

"Mrs. Graham plans our social calendar, but I am sure we would be pleased to welcome you again amongst our dinner company soon." With that, Papa tipped his hat and motioned our driver forward, while Mr. Thomas, too, lifted his top hat in a departure salute. I peered over my left shoulder to regard him as we drove away. He did not turn away to resume his ride until our carriage was quite some distance away. My face was tight from having kept a smile on my lips the entire time, but my mind felt giddy and light-headed while my heart was beating uncommonly loudly.

"Do you think Mama would wish to invite Mr. Thomas to dinner again?"

"I think it would be worth making some discrete inquiries into his background first," Papa responded thoughtfully. "Although he has shown much promise as a young barrister in chambers, he is rather private about his personal affairs. It would be wise to know more about his family and social standing." I crossed my fingers under my shawl as we rode on.

Anxious as I was about my father's research regarding Mr. Thomas, I was wise enough not to pester him with inquiries. So, when a week later, Mama announced that she was planning a tea and *soirée musicale* in a fortnight that included Mr. Ralph Thomas on the guest list, I found it difficult to contain my excitement. Several of the other guests also played music or sang, so I would share the responsibility and limelight for entertaining our guests, allowing me time to converse as well as showcase my abilities at the piano again.

We ordered another special dress for the occasion—a balance between a day and an evening dress. The latest fashion featured a light cream, silk underskirt with several rounded overskirts in lilac satin, trimmed with cream-coloured pinked flounces and lace. The bodice was a heart-shaped corsage with double-frilled lace chemisette. In the back, this new frou-frou style dress was pulled into a small bustle with a short train, while the sleeves were gathered at the elbows with more lace and pinked flounces to allow me freedom of movement at the piano. My hair was swept up into a braided chignon, capped with a lace bow, while an orchid adorned my crown. A delicate lavender crystal necklace and earbobs, cream gloves, and cream-coloured silk shoes completed my ensemble. Even I had to admit that the vision in my looking glass was very pleasing.

In addition to assisting Mama with the invitations, menu planning of the refreshments and finger sandwiches, house preparations, and sewing of my dress trimmings, I practiced my two piano pieces feverishly, a Beethoven sonata and a Chopin nocturne. I fell asleep each night imagining Mr. Thomas smiling with deep pleasure at my playing, sometimes standing behind me while I was seated at the piano, and at other times being so enthralled that he rose from his seat to come forward and stand facing me. My music would so move him that he would clasp my hand to his chest and ask me to marry him on the spot.

When I awoke I was racked with doubt about my playing, fearful that I would disappoint Mr. Thomas or, worse, fail to appeal such that he would beg leave at the earliest possible moment, or, perhaps spend the evening more attentive to another lady of greater charm, intellect, and beauty.

I dared not express my desires or concerns to anyone out of my superstition that it would negate my positive wishes or strengthen the chances of a negative outcome.

Anxiety and anticipation caused me to have very little appetite the day of the planned *soirée musicale.* I went through the motions of the day's preparations as if in a trance, necessitating Mama to admonish me sharply on more than one occasion for not paying attention or moving too slowly. Finally, at two o'clock, she sent me upstairs to rest and dress, convinced that I was of no further good use in my agitated state.

Even lying down, my mind whirled with various potential scenarios for interacting with Mr. Thomas, so that after more than an hour of attempted repose, I rang the bell for my lady's maid to help me dress and do my hair. The pleasant vision of my reflection in the looking glass only a few days before, now was suddenly open to my every criticism. It was very nearly five o'clock and our guests were soon expected.

"Amanda, dear, you look lovely this evening," Papa said as I entered the drawing room to await the first group of our guests.

"Yes, daughter, you look very becoming." Mama smiled her approval.

All of the other guests had arrived before Ralph Thomas finally made his appearance. I was already in conversation with two other gentlemen when my heart involuntarily skipped a beat as I beheld him in the doorway. My perturbation at his delayed arrival melted under my gratitude and relief to see him again.

Mr. Thomas had taken as much care as I had in outfitting himself to impress. He was elegantly dressed in a fashionable yet classic black cutaway coat, black trousers, white waistcoat, and white gloves. In that ensemble, he was nothing short of stunning.

He stood for a moment in the doorway, scanning the room until he located my mother whom he approached to acknowledge as the hostess. She, in turn, sent him in the direction of her husband to greet him properly at which point they were joined by a widow who, to my chagrin, proceeded to monopolize his attention.

"Miss Graham?" One of the gentlemen at my side had asked me a question that I did not hear, so intent was I on the whereabouts of Mr. Thomas.

"Oh! I agree with you whole-heartedly!" I feigned, fanning away my embarrassment at being distracted. He looked perplexed by my odd response.

"I was inquiring of you if you wanted me to get you some tea and perhaps a sandwich?"

"Yes, of course. Thank you." I recovered slightly, fanning myself more furiously, my gaze wandering off again in search of the object of my affections. Mr. Thomas was engaged in deep conversation with another barrister. I wondered how he could be so exasperatingly calm!

A few moments later Mama clapped her hands to get everyone's attention and announced the order of the musical entertainment. I was to be last on the program. We all took seats. I noticed that Mr. Thomas sat at the rear of the drawing room on the settee near the widow. I was closer to the center of the room so I would be unable to watch him or his reactions to the music while the others played. This was *not* how I had imagined the evening would go at all! We had not even spoken a word of greeting to each other. And I would not be able to ascertain if he was watching me without purposely turning my head to look, an action that would be obvious to everyone present.

I was so disconcerted over the turn of events that I did not even hear the violinist and harpist perform their solos. Next, the widow rose to sing accompanied on the piano by her daughter. I examined them both closely, trying to decipher whether they were rivals for Mr. Thomas's affections but without being able to watch him in their presence, I could not be sure.

Finally, my turn to play arrived. As I came around the end of the piano to take my seat, I glanced in Mr. Thomas's direction to see whether he was more intent on the widow's return to his side or on me. But he was no longer on the settee. I had a moment of panic until I spied him alongside Papa at the other end of the room. Both men gave me an encouraging smile. I sat down on the piano stool, smoothing my silk-and-satin skirts around me, paused a moment to recompose myself, and then began moving my fingers across the keys.

Some days, my playing can be automatic and rote. My connection with the music is missing, and I feel dissatisfied and unfulfilled with the result. But this night I felt the music at a much deeper level, as though my hands and body were one with the piano. I understood better than ever the description of well-played music as a "transportation of the soul."

Almost before I realized it, I was finished with my performance and stood up to enthusiastic applause. The guests who sat nearest the piano congratulated me. Others came forward lavishing their praise. Then, one-by-one they thanked my parents for the evening and departed—except for Mr. Thomas who lingered until he was the only guest left behind with me and my parents.

"This is the moment," I thought to myself. I fairly tingled with anticipation, yet there was also a deep calm inside me. I nearly floated across the carpet toward the three most important people in my life. It was as if I were two entities, one serenely watching the other being nervous and excited, as the scene evolved in slow motion.

Mr. Thomas turned his dazzling countenance toward me as I approached. A radiant smile slowly broke across his face.

"Your playing was rapturous tonight, Miss Graham! It will be a performance difficult to surpass."

"You are too kind, Mr. Thomas," I responded, lowering my eyes in modesty, basking beneath the warmth of his regard, yet, all the while hoping for further commendation.

"Very inspired, Amanda," Papa added. "A delightful finish to a totally agreeable evening." Turning to my mother, he added, "Another tour-de-force, my dear Mrs. Graham."

"I am indebted to you for including me in your enchanting soirée, Mrs. Graham. However, the lateness of the hour requires that I depart your pleasant company." Mr. Thomas bowed to each of us then repaired to the foyer where the footman held his top hat and cane out for him.

I stood immobilized in the drawing room. Once again I had no reassurance of Mr. Thomas's intentions toward me, although I was certain of his admiration. How and when we might encounter each other again was out of my hands.

After I heard the front door close, I was able to move toward the staircase to ascend to my bedroom. Suddenly, a deep weariness washed over me from the anticipation, the depth of feeling expended in my playing, and the disappointment that Mr. Thomas did not express any future ambitions toward me. Once inside the doorway of my room, the withheld emotion and fatigue broke over me. I collapsed upon my bed in a bath of sobs and tears. Too exhausted to ring for my lady's maid to undress me, I succumbed to sleep still wrapped in lilac-and-cream silk, satin, and lace.

Waking to the sound and the bright sunlight ushered in by drawing back my window drapery, I arose stiffly from my side where I had lain all night, my back bustle making it difficult to move. I was a bit startled to realize that it was Mama rather than a servant who was in my room and had brought me a light breakfast on a tray.

"I thought you might be a little disarranged from yesterday's events, so I instructed the servants not to disturb you this morning," she said matter-of-factly, hiding a depth of sensitivity to my situation; this was unusual for her, or at least, a characteristic that I had never before noticed in her drive to have me adhere to the social conventions of a young lady's upbringing.

Mama sat down on the edge of my bed.

"Men do not have the subtleties of social understanding that women do. We must be patient and guide them to their best selves without being obvious of their shortcomings. Every decision must appear to be their own even though a woman may have planted the seed." I was surprised by her openness and candor. She continued with her unusual delicate understanding.

"You will need to respect that Mr. Thomas may need more time to consider his financial position or he may simply be proceeding with the customary gentleman's caution and delicacy."

Abruptly, Mama stood up, returning to her normal unemotional and objective state.

"Now I will leave you in solitude today to contemplate your position and behavior. I will explain that you are unwell due to your over-exertion from yesterday. However, I fully expect you to recover your sense of duty, gentility, and submissiveness by tomorrow. You will not behave in such an emotional manner again."

Turning on her heel, Mama stepped outside my room, closing the door quietly, leaving me to ponder the sudden transformation of my mother before my eyes. I understood that while she sympathized with my impatience for Mr. Thomas to declare his intentions toward me, it was neither seemly nor in my best interests to press him or even to give the appearance of a lack of good breeding by displaying my discontent. She was giving me a lesson in male-female relations as well as one of proper societal behavior while allowing me a fair amount of time to resolve my competing woman-child emotions. My awe and respect for my mother bloomed alongside a deeper fondness. That evening I was able to rejoin my family for supper in the dining room, chastened and subdued but more mature and wiser.

In addition to managing our household and social affairs, Mama was also active in a variety of charities. During the autumn, charity bazaars were held in the city to help raise money for the distressed widows and orphans of veterans and wounded military men. Some weeks after our *soirée*, Mama and I were wandering among the various stalls at the All Saints' Bazaar when to our surprise we encountered Ralph Thomas.

"Why hello, Mr. Thomas," Mama bowed slightly. "I was not aware of your charitable interests."

The gentleman tipped his top hat to us and bowed in return.

"Mrs. Graham, Miss Graham, always a pleasure to see you both. Yes, there are always those unfortunate persons who need our assistance." Mr. Thomas turned to walk with us. "We see more than our share in the criminal courts, so I do what I can to help prevent more poor souls from taking up a life of crime, for once they start down that path, it is very difficult to set them back on the route of virtue."

"Indeed, Mr. Thomas! I applaud your desire to help at both ends of the path," Mama proclaimed. "Having the time, inclination, and generosity to assist these less fortunate persons is very admirable. Mr. Graham usually leaves such matters in my hands."

"And such capable and generous hands they are, Mrs. Graham."

"You are a kind young man." Mama paused for a heartbeat. "Amanda and I were going to stop for some refreshment in a nearby tea shop before heading back to Belgravia. Would you wish to join us?"

"That would be delightful!" Mr. Thomas smiled first at Mama and then at me. I cast my eyes down quickly under his gaze but could not hide the pleased smile that took over my mouth. I was working hard at maintaining my demure demeanor to please Mama, but it was difficult to hide my overjoyed gratification at the happenstance meeting and the opportunity to prolong Mr. Thomas's company.

Since our male guest had walked to the bazaar from his chambers, we rode together in our carriage along Piccadilly to the tearoom at Fortnum and Mason's emporium. Mama held sway in the conversation with her observations on the bazaar, the less fortunate, the weather, and the traffic until we were suitably settled at a table and had ordered our refreshments.

"Mr. Graham has told us that you are one of the more successful young barristers at Lincoln Inn, Mr. Thomas." I sensed that Mama was beginning her interrogation.

"Thank you, Mrs. Graham. I do what I can to help the wretches who end up in the courts."

"Have you plans to marry and have a family one day, Mr. Thomas?" Embarrassed by my mother's directness, I looked down at the gloved hands folded in my lap. I sensed Mr. Thomas stiffen slightly then dart a swift glance at me. The tone of his reply indicated to me that he knew I did not condone my mother's forthrightness.

"Yes, Mrs. Graham, I hope someday to enjoy the blessing of marriage to a fine young woman and have a family. As I come from the countryside near Derby, I would prefer to reside in a part of London or its outskirts that has more country-like open space and fewer crowds than the city proper." Turning to look at me, he added, "I have already confessed to Miss Graham of my leisure-time escapes to the Embankment, Hyde Park, and Kensington Gardens." He smiled at me as though to confirm our shared understanding. I smiled shyly back, hoping Mama would not later scold me for being too forward.

Mr. Thomas's eyes held mine for a brief moment, and then I looked down quickly at my lap. I sensed—or maybe hoped—he was gently trying to ascertain both Mama's and my willingness to permit me to live further afield than if we married and moved to a home inside London and close to my parents' home. It was obviously an important aspect of his future plans and a potential deterrent to marriage.

"You would not wish to live so far out of town so as not to partake of the social and cultural advantages of London," Mama countered. I was not certain if it was a question or a statement on her part.

"I shall need to live close enough to be able to attend to my duties in chambers and in the courts," Mr. Thomas explained. "It will require me to ride in each day, whereas now I live close enough to walk. But I am willing to trade that inconvenience for the serenity of more countryside and a happy home life."

Mother shifted in her seat as though not quite sure if he had answered her underlying question of easy access to her daughter and grandchildren should I marry Mr. Thomas and move to his idyllic home setting.

As though anticipating her next question, Mr. Thomas continued, reassuringly, "I have set aside a sufficient sum to secure comfortable lodgings in a suitable townhouse and have sufficient earnings to maintain a more than adequate lifestyle." He hesitated, weighing his words carefully. "Marriage is a solemn state. So much of one's happiness relies on the suitability of the man and woman. I do not wish to rush into it carelessly."

"I am sure you will choose well," Mama commented and looked at me, silently indicating her consent and approval of Mr. Thomas's plans.

For a moment we each sat with our own thoughts. I kept wishing to think of something brilliant, witty, or charming to say that would convince Mr. Thomas to propose immediately. Instead, I blurted out,

"I think your plans are wonderful! Any young lady would be delighted to be your wife!"

Mama shot me a disapproving look at my effusiveness, but Mr. Thomas smiled at me as though both relieved and slightly embarrassed from my compliment.

"You are too kind, Miss Graham. Now, I regret having to leave such delightful company, but I must return to Lincoln Inn." He waved over the waiter and paid our bill. Even though we had invited him to tea, his gentlemanly gesture of payment elevated him further in Mama's eyes.

Having passed muster with Mama, Mr. Thomas now had the upper hand in deciding whether and when to offer a marriage proposal. That he had so charmingly and deftly maneuvered around my mother's potential objections elevated him in my eyes. What nagged at me was whether Mr. Thomas was cautious because I did not match his image of and standards for a wife or whether he was concerned that my father might object. I reflected back on the times we had met Mr. Thomas and determined that Papa had always been supportive and encouraging. Mama had also spoken of Papa's esteem for Mr. Thomas. That left it up to me; what would I need to do to sway Mr. Thomas's affections in my favor? I ruminated on the matter during our carriage ride home. I concluded that I would need to learn more about Derby.

With Michaelmas Term in the law courts along with the All Saints/All Souls and Guy Fawkes' Day observances, the opportunities to encounter Mr. Thomas socially again would be rare, if any. I consoled myself that the Christmas and Boxing Day festivities might provide other fortuitous occasions for a meeting.

Not one to put all her eggs into one basket, Mama also included her second cousin, Dr. Henry Russell, in some of our family gatherings. A jovial fellow well-met, "Dr. Henry," as we all called him, had been a long-time bachelor, so it was not very likely that he would suddenly indicate a matrimonial interest in me. However, I think my parents were hoping that Mr. Thomas would learn of this potential competition and be forced to declare his intentions toward me sooner. I was concerned that a contrary result might be produced, and Mr. Thomas would lose any interest in pursuing me.

When our Christmas party invitations were finally issued, I was crestfallen to learn that Mr. Thomas had declined in favor of traveling to Derby for a fortnight holiday, effectively precluding any meeting during the social period before the beginning of Hilary Term. Although I made some attempt at cheerfulness when we entertained our guests, the truth is that I spent the period sullen and ill-tempered, spending my few leisure hours sulking in my bedroom when I was not occupied with household preparations.

At first, Mama chided me for my attitude but when she realized that her attempts at elevating my spirits were unsuccessful, she left me alone when my presence was not absolutely required, hoping time would rectify the situation.

In some cases, time and absence does heal heartbreak, and there are those who seem to recover more quickly than others. However, I was one for whom injurious losses endured.

A week after Epiphany, I felt my melancholic state to be even darker with the passing of the holidays and the black, coldness of winter stretching before me. During breakfast, Papa put his morning paper aside and announced to us,

"I saw Mr. Ralph Thomas at my club last night." With a slight smile and more than a little twinkle in his eyes, he turned to Mama and suggested, "I think it is time to invite him to dinner again!"

Mama and I both looked up at each other in surprise and silently questioned each other. Satisfied with my positive reaction, she merely said, "Of course, Mr. Graham."

I wanted Papa to tell us more about his conversation with Mr. Thomas and what marriage proposal hopes I might have, but my father excused himself from the table and made his final preparations for going into the city for his daily barrister obligations.

Mama and I began our usual dinner party preparations, but instead of inviting others guests, the only invited guest was Mr. Thomas. After the invitation was dispatched and a menu chosen, I had some leisure moments to enter my father's library in search of information on the geography and history of Britain that contained sufficient description of Derby to impress our guest with my knowledge. My search revealed two books, William Howitt's *The Rural Life of England* and *Whitaker's Almanac 1869.* Settling on a chair near the window, I was quickly engrossed in absorbing the details of Derbyshire.

What I learned help me understand Mr. Thomas considerably better. Derby was primarily an industrial and rail center with cotton and silk mills. Many of its leading citizens were relatively enlightened and benevolent toward the needs of their employees, while others were on the cutting edge of science, art, or philosophy—values that appeared to have molded Mr. Thomas's outlook on life. Derby natives Sir Charles Fox and Sons were renowned for the engineering innovations on some of Britain's finest railway bridges, stations, and other railway equipment, including the invention of switches. In 1840, former mayor and industrialist John Strutt had donated parkland—the Arboretum—to the city that was free to the public on Sundays and Wednesdays. Entrepreneur Thomas Evans had built a factory village of three-story cottages for his 500 employees across the river from his mill.

Among Derby's most intellectual native sons were Dr. Samuel Johnson, creator of a *Dictionary*; Dr. Erasmus Darwin, father of Charles who authored *Origin of the Species*; and Joseph Wright, painter of *chiaroscuro* works extolling the virtues of the Enlightenment and scientific discoveries. I could see where Mr. Thomas's respect for innovation, intelligence, and artistic prowess had been developed.

Contrasting with the nineteenth century industrial and scientific aspects of Derby, the rolling farmland of the East Midlands, famous for herds of deer and the gardens of Elvaston Castle, as well as the Arboretum, described a pastoral serenity that would understandably be absent from Mr. Thomas's experience of London.

Armed with this background about his hometown, I felt more confident than I had in weeks about successfully flirting with Mr. Thomas and seeing more deeply into his personality.

My dress was also designed to be more alluring than previously. Of turtledove satin, it was in the new *polonaise* style, with a low bodice off my shoulders that was pointed in front and back. The sleeves were tight and elbow-length ending with a lace ruffle. The underskirt was a Princess shape with a round, gauze tablier overskirt in a light shade and a train with lace ruffles matching the sleeves. The front of the skirt gave a flatter appearance while the rear bustle was more pronounced. Bunches of ivory flowers were clustered on the looped sides of the skirt and trailing down the sleeves.

For my jewelry, I donned ivory pearl teardrop ear bobs and a ribbon necklace with a larger, matching, ivory pearl teardrop. A comb inlaid with pearls and flowers adorned my chignon. To complete my ensemble, I wore ivory satin shoes with ivory lace gloves and matching fan. The satin rustled softly as summer leaves when I moved. I used more rose water than usual, pinching my cheeks vigorously before descending to our drawing room.

I secretly pitied Mr. Thomas. I was not sure when he accepted our dinner invitation if he realized he was the sole guest walking into the lair of three people intent on securing his marriage proposal. Papa seemed to think Mr. Thomas was ready to make an offer, but I was hoping we would not intimidate him into backing away. I would have to be highly flexible and attuned to his sensibilities so as to know when to press forward and when to hold back with my affections. Needless to say, this additional alertness intensified my excitement and nervousness as we awaited Mr. Thomas's arrival. I decided to pass the time funneling my trepidation by playing the piano.

As I heard Mr. Thomas's voice in the foyer, however, my heart somersaulted in my chest. I finished the last few bars of my piece to gain sufficient time to compose myself and greet him sweetly but coolly and assess his temperament.

"Bravo, Miss Graham!" he exclaimed behind me—more closely than I expected. I swiveled around on the piano stool and rose to give him my hand and a slight curtsey. Mr. Thomas's demeanor and dress were resplendent. Even resolutely hardened not to be obviously affected by his appearance, I still was nothing short of dazzled by him. My knees felt a little weak, so I placed my hand on the piano to steady myself.

"I did not expect to be regaled so soon in the evening by such a musical treat!"

Why did my mind go blank in his presence? Where were all the brilliant lines I had so diligently rehearsed in the days leading up to this moment?

"You don't think the piece is too emotional...too passionate, Mr. Thomas?" I managed to blurt out.

"I think you translate the power of the music perfectly, Miss Graham. It is your sensitivity to its emotional nuances that makes your playing so exceptional."

There was a moment of awkwardness between us as I basked in his compliment, and a warm glow rose to my cheeks. Social protocol required that I divert the conversational attention to him.

"Did you pass an enjoyable Christmas holiday visit with your family in Derby?" I asked a little more ardently than the question warranted.

"It was a bittersweet visit. Alas, my parents have spent too many years working in the cotton and silk mills. The dust has affected their lungs. They have developed persistent coughs. I try to encourage them to spend more time in the natural areas but the weather was too cold and damp to spend much time outdoors. However, I did spend some leisure hours walking on my own."

"I understand that the Arboretum and Elvaston Castle Gardens are splendid for a promenade."

Mr. Thomas examined me for a moment, registering that I must have acquired some knowledge of his home shire since last we spoke.

"Yes, if you enjoy manmade spaces, there are serpentine walks and trimmed hedges in fascinating shapes. But I prefer to indulge myself in the God-designed countryside of rolling hills and craggy downs, heather and rocks of the Peak areas and Tissington Trail." He stopped to gauge my reaction.

"If you enjoy the country so much, what drew you to London?" I raised my eyes to meet his in earnest, trying to tap into his deeper character. He looked away as if to dislodge a painful memory. Mr. Thomas gazed across the room so as not to reveal too much of himself.

"My grandfather was accused of a crime he did not commit. He spent two harrowing years in Derby Gaol before he was..." Mr. Thomas hesitated to protect me from a full description of the horrid facts as well as to suppress the rising well of his own emotions.

"...before he was executed. I determined that I would become a barrister to help prevent future such false accusations and punishments. London is where one best studies for the law." He looked down at the floor while I studied his countenance. This was a man of strong moral convictions. His interests in life were not frivolous. Although he appreciated the finer aspects of life—music, art, and the theatre—he had come up from working class roots. It dawned on me that he might be concerned that this honest revelation of his family background might weaken his prospects. To reassure him, I lightly touched the lower arm of his coat sleeve.

"That is very noble of you."

"I am not entirely altruistic." Mr. Thomas seemed to recollect himself. "London wages are significantly higher, so that I have been able to help support my family more than if I had returned to Derbyshire to ply my barrister practice."

"Does your brother work in the textile factories, too?"

"No, he is an ironworker for the Andrew Handyside foundry. Although the wages are somewhat better, the work is more dangerous."

"So, you are the one professional in the family?" I tried to make the question more of a compliment to his ascendancy in class status than the accusation it might seem.

"I demonstrated a talent for academic studies and persuasive argument early in school and was encouraged by an enlightened school master." Then Mr. Thomas smiled as though at a private joke. "Besides, I have never liked manual labor."

All this time, my parents had been discreetly making last minute dinner arrangements while, I suspect, trying to eavesdrop on the tenor and substance of our conversation. Sensing a momentary opportunity to interrupt, Mama rang the dinner bell to get our attention then took Mr. Thomas's arm to be escorted into dinner. Papa and I followed.

Dinner was served à la française with the courses arranged around the table. Papa sat at the head with soup, and Mama was at the foot with fish, while Mr. Thomas and I faced each other across the table over the lobster cutlets and boiled eggs. Our footman passed the dishes of soup served by Papa, while our butler served the wine. With the servants present, we made small talk about the weather and the latest news of the Queen. Mr. Thomas helped Mama carve the fish which was also passed by the servants who then offered us each a cutlet and egg. After the remove of these dishes, roast leg of lamb and boiled turkey were served along with fried broccoli and herbed potatoes.

The conversation turned to the situation on the continent between the French and Prussians and what affect, if any, it might have on domestic British affairs. Once the main course was removed and a new cloth placed on the table, the servants returned with macaroni, cheese, brandy bread pudding, apple fritters, and currant dumplings. Along with these savories and sweets, the discussion switched to the politics of reform. Mr. Thomas was respectful of Papa's opinions but was deftly able to make his point when he disagreed but without offense. By the time Mama and I repaired to the drawing room, I was certain my father and Mr. Thomas fully had enjoyed each other's company.

Not long afterward both gentlemen entered the drawing room for coffee with us. I saw Papa send a meaningful glance toward Mama from behind Mr. Thomas's back as the latter crossed the room to where I was seated on the sofa. Mama rose from her seat to where Papa had stopped. They quietly exited as Mr. Thomas took the cup and saucer I offered him.

"Shall I pour you coffee or tea, Mr. Thomas?"

"Coffee, please," he replied and walked over to the fireplace mantel to weigh his thoughts. I wanted so much to help him but did not know what to say.

"Are you familiar, Miss Graham," he began, turning his head to address me finally, "with the village of Hampstead, to the north of London?"

"Yes, I have heard of it and of the large parkland, known as the Heath, nearby, but I have not had occasion to visit it." I was curious to understand why he began this line of questioning.

"The Heath is indeed as large as Regency or Hyde Park but is not so manicured or developed. The village has begun to grow with newly built terrace houses and several new shops on its main thoroughfare. It is on the route to Derby, so I have had a chance to watch its recent growth as I passed through." Mr. Thomas stopped again as though gathering himself for a leap into the unknown. He was watching me intently for reaction.

"I have of late been considering removing my lodgings from Lincoln Inn chambers and settling in Hampstead. Although it will be a longer ride into the courts each day, I would be closer to Derby and countryside..." He hesitated to gage my response. A slight panic arose within me, and I looked down at my hands.

"Would you still be willing to attend our evenings here?" I inquired anxiously, afraid that he might be announcing that he was exiting my life.

Mr. Thomas crossed over to sit beside me on the sofa.

"My dear Miss Graham...I was hoping...If you would consider...If it is not too far..." He stood up again and went back to the safe distance of the fireplace.

"For a man who pleads criminal cases before the Royal Justices, this should not be so hard!" I heard him chide himself under his breath. He placed his left hand across his brow.

I arose and walked over to him, touching his raised arm gently. He lowered his hand and looked pleadingly into my eyes. I smiled tenderly up at him.

"If you are trying to ask me what I hope with all my heart, the answer is yes," I whispered.

263

His relief was visible, and the resultant smile that broke across his face was dazzling. Quietly he asked, "Miss Amanda Graham, would you honor me by accepting my humble offer of marriage?"

I clasped his hand and brought it to my cheek as tears of joy and gratitude glistened in my eyes.

"...and live with you in Hampstead, if that would make you happy."

Withdrawing his hand from mine, his arms enveloped me. I could hear his heart beating beneath his waistcoat as he kissed me on top of my head. For a moment, nothing else in the world existed beyond us.

I raised my head from his chest and pulled back slightly to face him again.

"We should inform Mama and Papa." Although I loathed dispelling the sweet magic of his embrace, I excused myself, leaving Mr. Thomas—Ralph—for a moment, to find my parents in the dining room. They understood in an instant from the expression on my face what had transpired. Each stood and hugged me then followed me back to the drawing room.

"Mr. Graham, sir, and Mrs. Graham, your daughter, Amanda, has agreed to my proposal of marriage for which I now request your permission."

"We could not be more pleased to welcome you into our family," Papa exclaimed, clasping Ralph's right hand in an exuberant handshake while slapping his shoulder. Mama's handshake was more gentle but as heartfelt. I knew her mind was already busy considering wedding preparations.

"To plan for a wedding properly," she warned, "will require at least six months. When do you expect to marry?"

"Between Easter Term and Trinity Term we will be at the height of the season and, there might be too many competing social events," Papa observed." Perhaps between Trinity Term and Michaelmas Term, after the upper classes retire to the country for grouse season, might be wiser."

Ralph and I looked at each other as though mutually reading each other's thoughts: September seemed like a long way off after finally getting to this point. In fact, we had only known each other a little over six months. But we both bowed to the better judgment of my parents in these matters. The long engagement period would allow us more time to become acquainted with each other in our moments alone. A later wedding date would relieve some pressure to rush through the details of setting up a household and making the other necessary arrangements.

During the ensuing months, our respective solicitors worked out the marriage settlement of a separate estate and jointure for me.

Ralph and I exchanged rings and lockets of our hair—inside a gold necklace for me and in a gold watch chain for him. Time was spent assembling the elements of my trousseau, finding a suitable townhouse in Hampstead and furnishing it, as well as sewing the wedding and bridesmaids' dresses. Princess Louisa's wedding cake that year was over five feet tall, created over the course of three months by the Royal Confectioner, and although not quite as elaborate, our own wedding cake was beautifully crafted. As the date of the impending nuptials came drew nearer, we obtained the marriage license, reserved the church and assembly hall for the wedding breakfast, issued invitations, planned and cooked the wedding breakfast, and made the social rounds as an engaged couple.

Ralph's parents and brother, Royce, came down to London to meet my parents. I knew my fiancé was particularly concerned with the class differences that he himself had successfully bridged. Although his father was a foreman at the mill and Royce had recently been elected Mayor of Derby, there were still a rung or two of the social class ladder between them and my father, as well as the advantages of advanced education that Papa and Ralph had enjoyed. Nevertheless, Ralph's keen intelligence had provided him with a respectable annual income sufficient to provide a comfortable living for both of us plus assistance for his family. Upon further acquaintance, Ralph's father and brother demonstrated remarkable ambition and intellectual curiosity not routinely expected at their societal level and proved stimulating company. Mrs. Thomas also had refined tastes and a developed artistic sensibility that pleased Mama. The encounter proved far more successful and enjoyable than anticipated and removed the last of Ralph's misgivings about our forthcoming union.

On a Saturday in mid-August, Ralph and our family rode out in Papa's new brougham to inspect the terrace house Ralph selected to serve as our home. We wound through the London streets: north on Park Lane alongside Hyde Park, east on Oxford Street past the fashionable shops, north again on Regent Street to Portland Place, around Park Crescent (just below Regency Park) to head east again on Euston Road, north again on Hampstead Road, and then along Camden High Street, before finally passing through increasingly suburbanized countryside. I had not often been in this part of north London and was enthralled with the sights and sounds along the way. Ralph appeared to take delight in my rapture, and occasionally when our eyes met, we both broke into simultaneous smiles of joyful anticipation.

Upon our approach into Hampstead, I noticed the avenue was flanked by rows of brick shops, some with awnings. A Romanesque Revival town hall with a clock tower that rose above

265

several buildings with Dutch dormers gave an almost-European feel to the village center.

We stopped for rest and refreshment at The Bull and Bush public house, a stone and clapboard establishment with two bowed windows advertising "Dinners" and "Teas" on one and "Foreign Wines and Spirits" on the other. The latter window was behind a tree while a wrought iron, arched lamppost welcomed diners to the front entrance. To the left side was another, larger arch announcing its "Entrance to Terrace Gardens, Private Dining Rooms, Coffee Room, Saloon Bar, Billiards, and a Brewery." Ralph had made reservations to have us led to one of the private dining rooms where we partook of a splendid luncheon.

Once fed and rested, we left our carriage at the pub's livery and walked to a side street lined on either side with rows of brick, terraced buildings. In the middle of one of the rows, Ralph led us through a low garden gate in a brick wall that surrounded a small garden and up the front steps. He seemed both excited and a bit on edge. I tried to calm him by placing my gloved hand lightly on his arm as he turned the key in the lock of the front door.

We entered the hallway of the ground floor. The smell of new paint and wood assailed our noses as the outside sunlight angled into the dark foyer. One by one, Ralph showed us the dining and morning rooms, then upstairs to the drawing room. Further upstairs, we viewed the bedrooms and dressing rooms. Without mounting further, Ralph indicated the servants' and children's areas above. As we descended to the main floor again, he described the scullery and kitchen areas in the basement.

The rooms were tastefully, yet simply, decorated in an elegant yet practical style. I surmised that Ralph preferred to rely on the quality of material rather than elaborate decorative effects. Moving from room to room, I tried to imagine myself in each one as mistress of the house. When we reached the master bedroom, I blushed upon seeing the large, four-poster bed. As we made our way back into the drawing room, I hugged Ralph's arm in delight. He patted my gloved hand and looked down at me benevolently.

"Do you like it?"

"Oh, yes!" I beamed back into his loving glance. My parents looked at each other and nodded their approval.

"Ralph, my boy," Papa effused. "I think you have done a fine job locating and furnishing the house. I expect Amanda will be a happy housewife under its roof and my grandchildren will be here soon!" He finished with a wink, while I quickly looked down in embarrassment.

"A very fine abode, Ralph," Mama quickly added. "Have you hired the servants yet?"

"Since the house servants will be under Amanda's supervision, I thought it best to let her select them, although I have already engaged the livery staff and a manservant for myself."

"Very good. I will help Amanda recruit the household staff." Mama was still reluctant to allow me full adulthood status. "There will likely be a larger selection pool in London." She trailed off a moment in thought. "Of course, we will also order the proper household linens to finish Amanda's trousseau."

Having concluded the tour, Mama turned toward the stairs to exit, Papa behind her, with Ralph and me following behind. Ralph locked the front door behind us, and we retraced our path to The Bull and Bush, requisitioned the brougham again, and returned to London.

My last few weeks as an unmarried young lady passed very quickly. On the afternoon before our wedding day, we had an "at home" for friends and acquaintances not invited to the wedding and subsequent breakfast. We had agreed to keep the wedding party small: two cousins of mine to serve as the bridesmaids and Ralph's brother, Royce, to serve as best man. A young male cousin of Ralph's would be the page boy to carry my train.

Although Ralph appeared calm and gracious to our guests, I could sense his level of tension as much as my own. We endured much public ceremony and ritual to get to what we both wanted— the privacy of being together.

The next morning, Ralph sent a bouquet of orange blossoms to me, a tradition begun by the Queen, and two flower bouquets along with two delicate bracelets for my bridesmaids.

To signify our unity, my wedding dress was claret satin with an ivory lace veil while Ralph's morning coat was claret velvet with trousers of pale drab and an ivory quilted satin waistcoat. However, even knowing what he would be wearing, as I stood with Papa at the head of the church aisle, I could not remember seeing Ralph so handsome. As he turned to behold me, his smile beamed like a ray of sunshine, lighting my way as I almost floated toward him.

The short ceremony was dreamlike. The Reverend Stephenson spoke and we repeated his words of devotion, duty, and obedience. Once my veil was lifted, we signed the church register, the license was witnessed, and we progressed to the assembly hall for the wedding breakfast.

The food tables almost groaned with the weight of the meats, pies, fish, fruits, jellies and galantines, epergnes of flowers and nuts, creams and blancmange, and the towering wedding cake. Family members from the Grahams and Thomases gathered, as well as respected barristers from Lincoln Inn and close friends.

Having greeted and received congratulations from everyone and eaten a bite or two of the repast and cake, I traded my veil for a carriage hat. Ralph and I proceeded to take our leave in a Victoria with its top down; the requisite slippers were attached to the rear denoting that I now belonged to my husband. (We had barely left Belgravia before Ralph stopped the carriage to untie the slippers, loathe to attract such attention upon ourselves.) We rode the rest of the distance to Hampstead as though merely out for an afternoon ride.

A spectacular day in early autumn, the sky was a pure, unsullied blue. The slight breeze caressed us as I leaned against Ralph's right side and laid my head on his shoulder, his arm wrapped around mine. Our driver kept up a steady but not disturbing pace for the horses. We were enveloped by the sweetest sense of bliss and perfection on a day that anyone would be tempted to preserve under glass. Ralph and I did not need to speak, we felt so in tune with each other's being, experiencing the delight of the day as a part of our own peace and joy.

I was almost disappointed as we pulled into the village of Hampstead because our intimate, idyllic ride was coming to an end; it seemed a suspension of time between the sheltered life of a daughter and the responsibility of a wife, when I needed only to be present to the fervor of our being in love.

As the carriage pulled up in front of our town home, Ralph jumped out enthusiastically and came around to the curbside to lift me out. Sliding his left arm under my right and around my back, and placing his right arm under my legs, in one movement he swung me around, carried me out of the carriage, and through the garden gate, placing me down on the path to the front steps. He dispatched our driver with a hand signal then led me up the path to the front door that was immediately opened by his man servant. The rest of our recently hired servants dutifully stood along the hallway to greet us.

"Congratulations and good afternoon, Mr. and Mrs. Thomas." The manservant greeted us and bowed as did the rest of the household staff.

"Thank you, Frederick," Ralph replied, handing the manservant his top hat and gloves. "Have our trunks arrived?" Frederick nodded affirmatively.

"Good. Then Mrs. Thomas and I will be ready for our dinner at seven."

Ralph took my arm and we ascended the staircase to our bedroom. Once inside, I removed my hat and placed it on the bureau. Momentarily alone, Ralph enveloped me in his arms while I placed my cheek against his chest. He kissed the top of my head then pulled away enough to regard my face.

"Are you tired? Do you want to change now or have some tea?"

I loved him for his consideration of my needs. Then I remembered my own duty as a wife to defer to him.

"What would you prefer, husband?" I let the word linger on my tongue.

"I have some legal briefs to review in my study," he said thoughtfully. "After I change, I will take my tea there. You should rest here," he pointed to a chaise lounge by the window, "and I will have your lady's maid bring you your tea. The cook already has her instructions for tonight's dinner menu and tomorrow's breakfast, but after that the staff will need your direction."

Ralph pulled the servant's bell and entered his dressing room. I perched on the chaise lounge for a few moments, trying to collect myself from the events of the day and Ralph's swift transformation from attentively affectionate husband to business-like barrister.

My lady's maid, Sophie, soon appeared with a tea tray and to help me change into dinner dress. While I rested, I remembered that Ralph had also experienced a life disruption—moving from his chambers in the city to a terrace house on the outskirts of London, requiring him to navigate a long commute back and forth each day. My job was to create his home as a routine and peaceful sanctuary so that the worries and stresses of the day would disappear when he crossed our threshold. By demonstrating his attentiveness to me, I realized, he had been modeling how he wanted me to behave toward him. I committed myself then to being the dutiful, solicitous wife he deserved.

I must have dozed off because the dinner bell woke me from a dream that dissipated as I hurried to the staircase. Ralph came out of his study and met me at the foot of the staircase. He was wearing a green velvet smoking jacket that heightened the light green of his eyes. I was more formally dressed in a grey satin dress. A smile of pure pleasure lit up his face, and I returned one to him. He took my arm and turned us to go into the candlelit dining room.

And so our wedded life began. After the excitement of the day and the wine at dinner, we retired early to our bedchamber, content simply to lie in each other's arms and exchange a goodnight kiss before we quickly fell into deep sleep.

Just before dawn Ralph stirred and woke me as well. This time, his kisses were more ardent and urgent, rousing deeper feelings within me. His manly hands explored my body, first through my nightgown, then slipping the gown off my shoulders and baring my breasts. I was at once startled, modest, and excited. Ralph did not rush but was confidently persistent. He also guided my hands to explore his flesh while alternately he nuzzled and stroked me. My body responded with sensations I had not previously imagined.

Before long I helped Ralph completely remove my nightgown, and he mounted me. Our naked bodies pressed against each other as he thrust his manhood deeply inside me in the first, painful, virginal insertion while covering my mouth with his own, instinctively muffling my responding outcry. He was a sensitive and respectful lover while asserting his rights as a husband with a practiced skill. Ralph whispered words of encouragement and reassurance that the sexual act would be easier and less painful the more frequently we engaged in it.

Ralph's thrusting movements inside me became faster and more rhythmic while he concentrated his energy and power. I was not sure what to expect, how long this would go on, or whether or not I liked it. A tension between my legs began to build as our pelvises bumped each other. Suddenly Ralph stopped, arched his back, and shuddered. I felt an internal explosion and release, my insides pulsating around him. Panting, he collapsed atop me, and I began to giggle and cry simultaneously. My husband lifted his head and looked at me quizzically. Assured that I was okay, he kissed me firmly then pulled his wet, shrunken manhood from within and rolled over onto his back.

Gradually, I became aware of my tingling nudity as my body cooled. Chilled, I sat up and reached for my nightgown. Ralph's fingertips caressed my back just before the cloth of my gown descended over his bare arm.

Our lovemaking concluded, Ralph arose from our bed and headed toward his dressing room, tugging at the bell pull as he went, thus signaling Frederick to come dress him. I followed suit, ringing for my Sophie. Within thirty minutes, we met downstairs for breakfast.

"Mrs. Thomas," Ralph's addressing me so formally surprised me after the naked intimacy between us earlier. "I expect to return from chambers at 6:00 this evening. Please have dinner served at 6:30."

"Yes, husband," I replied in my dutiful role as his wife.

Ralph then read the morning paper, occasionally commenting on an article or notice of importance. I sipped my coffee and ate my toast in silence, still contemplating what had occurred in the bedroom between us and pondering this sudden change in Ralph's demeanor. I concluded that my husband was acting more formal in front of the servants.

Shortly after finishing the newspaper and the remainder of his breakfast, he kissed me on my forehead then left for his commute into the city. Since I was only familiar with the routine followed by my mother, I adjourned to the morning room to begin the tasks of planning menus and ordering the household.

Due to his schedule of court cases, Ralph had decided to postpone our wedding trip until after Michaelmas Term ended.

Instead, we alternated hosting the social calls of family and friends—visiting as bride and groom—and returning those visits. For a while, I struggled with the newness of managing the household, planning meals, and juggling a social calendar, but eventually we fell into a routine. I was motivated by a deep desire to please Ralph, missing his presence during the daytime and seeking to provide for his every comfort and wishes at night. We kept a more formal demeanor around the servants, so it was only when we were alone in the bedroom that we allowed ourselves any demonstration of affection or intimacy. But as time wore on and our duties seem to require more of our energy and attention, even the easy familiarity of the bedroom waned. I hoped that our wedding trip would revive our romantic moments.

Even though Ralph had selected Hampstead as our home due to its proximity to the natural surroundings of the Heath, he appeared to have little time to take advantage of it. I could see that his daily ride into London in the morning and return at night, in addition to the increasing number and severity of his cases, was taking its toll on his vitality. At the same time, as my activities fell into an easier regularity, my sense of isolation from London society, and especially from my parents, wore on me.

One unseasonably balmy afternoon in late November, I chose to walk into the village of Hampstead, gazing into the shop windows as the Christmas novelties began to make their appearance. I found myself drawn to a narrow shop window with three framed paintings: a country landscape with a farm lass and geese, a tall sailing vessel, and a vase of roses. As I entered a small bell overhead signaled my arrival and a slightly hunched over elderly man in spectacles came from behind the shop counter.

"Good day, m'lady!" he greeted me with a slight twinkle in his eye. "How may I assist you?"

"I noticed the paintings in your window," I began then hesitated because I was not sure what I wanted.

"Are you interested in buying a painting?" he asked, trying to mask a certain excitement.

"No...I want to be able to paint like that!" I surprised even myself.

"Ah, a budding artist!" He clasped his hands together in delight. "Watercolor is a fine medium for a lady. Have you used them before?"

I shook my head. Although some young women receive that training, my mother had favored music, embroidery, and sewing for me.

"Let's see," the old man gazed around his shop. "You will need watercolor paper, pigments, a palette, and proper brushes..." He moved around to different shelves selecting the items. I wondered if he was picking the most dear merchandise since I was obviously naïve about the process. Almost in response to my thoughts, he said,

"You should start with a limited palette of colors so you will practice mixing the pigments. You only need a few, basic, brushes, but the paper—the paper must always be first rate." He placed the items on the counter. I had stood still in the middle of his showroom while he gathered the merchandise. He turned back to me.

"Do you need painting lessons?" Until that question, I had not fully realized that I did not know exactly what to do with the artistic implements he had so carefully collected. I was also aware that I had no concept of how much of my meager allowance I was spending. Noticing my hesitancy, the old man added, "I have a few other female students whom I instruct on Tuesday afternoons. Perhaps you'd like to join them? I sell my students their art supplies at a discount."

"I will need to ask my husband…"

"Of course, of course. If you wish to study with me, just come back on Tuesday at two o'clock. I will hold your supplies here until then. You can bring me three guineas then—one for the supplies and two for the lesson."

I clasped my hands together under my chin both in excitement at my new venture and fear that Ralph would disapprove. But later that evening when I asked him at dinner, he smiled benevolently and gave his unreserved blessing. I could not wait until next Tuesday to experience the new lesson and my new art tools.

My first attempts at the watercolor medium were awkward, but after a little while, my results began to show some promise and, I was pleased enough to brave showing them to Ralph who was supportive and complimentary. My joy spilled over into our lovemaking that night. (My creativity was not confined to sheets of watercolor paper!)

For our wedding trip, we had determined to visit Ralph's family in Derby and the Peak District between Boxing Day and Twelfth Night. Ralph would be able to get away from his Law Court concerns while I would be freed from the daily household tasks. We looked forward to having some time alone wandering in the hillsides and river valleys even in the midst of winter. Nearby were spa towns where we could take the waters and generally benefit from a change in the air.

On the Tuesday two weeks before Christmas, I was particularly pleased with my painting—a still life with vase and fruit—and I was anxious to show it to Ralph. I had also been organizing the items for our wedding trip and wished to consult my husband over dinner about the anticipated weather in the East Midlands. Our dinner was ready for service at 6:30 as usual. The evening had become quite chilled and damp, so the dining room fire had been supplied

272

with a few additional logs. As usual, I kept my ears alert for the sound of Ralph's horse arriving.

As 6:15 arrived I became concerned and looked out the heavily curtained window. My breath formed an icy mist on the pane that made viewing difficult. Around each gas street lamp was a misty halo, and I could see some small icicles beginning to form. The few horses and carriages on the street were moving cautiously. I rationalized that Ralph was delayed because he was riding more carefully.

When 6:30 came, I again peered out. I asked the housemaid to go out to the street to see if she could see her master in the distance, which she could not. I began to pace nervously in the dining room, going to the window more impatiently each time.

At last, at 6:55, I heard horse hooves and ran to the hallway as the maid opened the front door to urgent pounding. Instead of Ralph, a street boy stood holding his cap between his bare hands. Behind him at the curb was a carriage with two gentlemen carrying a hatless and limp Ralph—one man holding his legs and the other grasping the body under his arms. Ralph's head had dried blood across his forehead.

"Ralph!" I ran out into the cold to meet the men as they struggled under the weight of my husband's lifeless form. "No! No! No!" I whimpered, realizing that Ralph was more than injured.

As we all made our way up the front steps and into the hall, cook and Frederick arrived and directed the men upstairs into our bedroom to lay Ralph's body on our bed.

"Fetch a doctor!" I instructed Frederick.

"Beggin' your pardon, Ma'am, but I am 'fraid it is too late for the doctor," one of the men said. I pressed the back of my hand against my mouth to stifle my scream, my other hand grabbing the night table for support as I fought off the urge to faint.

"I'm truly sorry, Ma'am," he finished.

"What happened?" I barely spoke above a whisper.

"There was the usual traffic snarl at Ludgate of omnibuses, 'ansom cabs, wagons, carriages and 'orses, but with the addition of the ice, 'twas more dangerous. We were be'ind 'im when the gentleman's 'orse bolted and threw 'im off. 'E 'it his 'ead on a lamppost and went limp. We were going to take 'im to 'ospital, but...well, Ma'am, there didn't seem to be any point. 'E 'ad 'is address on 'is card. Since 'e was obviously a gentleman, we did not wish to leave 'im on the street. We've come a long way and the traveling 'as been difficult..." He trailed off.

"Yes, of course. Thank you so much for your kindness. You must have some dinner. Cook, you may serve them in the dining room. Please, make yourselves welcome." I felt like I was two people—one operating in a calm, rational manner; the other watching the first one but barely holding onto her sanity.

I turned to look at Ralph's cold body—his corpse—lying on the bed as though napping. As though in a dream, or more accurately, in a nightmare, I pulled off his boots and covered him with a blanket. I poured water from the ewer into the wash basin and carried it to the nightstand. I began to wash the dried blood from his cold brow. My movements felt vaguely, yet strangely, familiar.

But there was something about how his skin moved. I touched his cheek—unusually cold from both the outdoors and...and something else.

As the complete realization that my beloved was lying dead before me, I retched violently into the wash basin. Then I could not catch my breath—sobbing, moaning, and rocking back-and-forth. My entire *raison d'être* destroyed even before we had taken our wedding trip! I lay my head on the blanket covering Ralph's chest and cried and cried.

Sophie, my lady's maid, entered the room quietly, pulling me by my shoulders to sit upright on the bed.

"Frederick 'as gone for the doctor, Mrs. Thomas. 'e'll know what to do." I put my left hand on top of Sophie's hand on my right shoulder to demonstrate the appreciation that I could not speak. Then I turned and melted into her arms, crying inconsolably again.

Cook came up some time later to announce that she had fed the two gentlemen and the boy and had given them £5 for their trouble, after which they had left. Shortly afterward, a doctor arrived with the undertaker. Everything was happening too fast and in slow motion.

"Mrs. Thomas," the doctor explained, "Undertaker Hall and I believe it best to take Mr. Thomas to the drawing room or parlor so that you can rest more peacefully here. I am going to give you a small potion to sleep tonight. We will come back in the morning to make further, ah, arrangements."

As the two men began to move Ralph from our bedroom, I lunged forward, but Sophie restrained me. The doctor had left her with a draught of laudanum to calm me. Sophie helped me to undress then placed me under the covers like a rag doll. I turned toward Ralph's side of the bed where he had recently lain—for the last time, I realized, setting forth a fresh set of tears. I pulled his pillow toward me, crushing it in a bear-hugging squeeze. I heard a faint church bell tolling in the distance. The sedative, gratefully, took its effect quickly.

"There is something I need to remember..." I told myself as I slowly came to consciousness. I rolled over to face Ralph and opened my eyes to gaze on his...empty pillow.

The full realization of his death struck me like an iron forge in my chest. "*That* is what I had needed to remember." My mind went numb. I felt as if the wheels of my mind were stuck in deep, impenetrable mud. My body was made of lead. I needed someone to tell me what to do. I needed my mother.

"Oh, *that* is what I needed to remember. Summon my parents. They will know what to do." Then I also remembered Ralph's family. I would have to summon them as well. A funeral would need to be planned. I covered my open mouth to stifle a scream, and I started crying again as another wave of grief overwhelmed me.

There was a light tap on the door, a brief moment of hesitation, and then the housemaid entered with a tray holding my breakfast tea and some buttered toast.

"So sorry to disturb you, Ma'am, but Cook said to bring this up to you. You need your strength, she says, Ma'am." I pulled myself upright to a sitting position and indicated that the maid should place the tray across my outstretched legs. I leaned forward so she could prop up my pillows as if I was an invalid.

"Thank you," I managed to say. I was not sure how I was going to stomach any of it, my insides felt so queasy. But I was grateful for the servants' concern and their consideration of my delicate state. I had to make an effort, even if all I wanted to do was die myself and lie next to Ralph.

"And where is…where is Mr. Thomas?" I tentatively inquired, then understood that she might think I was in denial. "I mean, where have they laid his…?" I could not continue.

"Oh, in the parlor, Ma'am. Surrounded by candles, all proper like." As though she had been too informal, she straightened up and backed up a step.

"Thank you. You may go now, but please tell Sophie that I will need to dress." I did not want her to stay and watch me eat.

Once the door had closed behind her, I took a few sips of tea and a bite of the toast. I waited to see how those items would land inside me. Not well. I scrambled out of bed and lunged for the wash basin on the dresser across the bedroom, arriving just in time. I had not really eaten since lunch the previous day but whatever was in my stomach came out. My internal organs felt as if I was on the high seas on a stormy night. A few bars of the theme from *The Flying Dutchman* came to me.

When the wave of nausea was spent, I wiped my mouth with the back of my hand, but the vile taste remained. Returning to my bedside, I retrieved the tea cup, then walked cautiously to the wash basin and poured it out. Then I poured water from the ewer into my cup and drank it slowly. I rested my elbow on the dresser top and my forehead in my upturned hand, trying to steady my body and nerves for the day ahead.

A few moments later, another knock on my door caused me to stand upright and take a deep breath. I bade Sophie to enter. She curtsied slightly, her head bowed in deference to my loss. Something about the normalcy of the routine of getting dressed revived me a little, until she pulled out the only dress in my trousseau that was even close to suitable color for mourning—a silk black-and-white striped afternoon dress. I had worn it when Ralph and I had received our post-wedding visitors. Seeing it again, I collapsed in tears onto the floor still in my undergarments.

"Oh, Ma'am! I did not mean to upset you!" exclaimed my maid, frantically looking for a handkerchief. Collecting herself while I attempted to halt my tears, she offered, "You are right, Ma'am. This dress is not suitable." Instead, she found a plaid morning dress of green and brown and held it out to show me. I nodded approval then straightened myself for the dressing process.

"I will have Black Peter Robinson's in Regency Street send their fitters around. The servants as well as I will need mourning garb. I shall send for my parents after dressing. Mother will know what to do."

"Very good, Ma'am," Sophie finished dressing me in silence then left quietly while I took a few more moments to collect my courage and stamina. My stomach still felt unsettled, so I determined to have a receptacle near me in the morning room as I slowly descended the stairs to the second floor. As I came to the landing, I smelled a slight scent of burning candle wax and saw the closed door to the parlor. I hesitated—not sure whether I could face seeing Ralph's body but wanting to see him again. Was he alone in there or was someone sitting with his body? I steadied myself with the staircase handrail.

As if to answer my question, Ralph's manservant came out of the parlor. He may have heard my footsteps on the staircase.

"G'day, Ma'am. Do you want to come inside?" Frederick asked uncertainly. Somehow, knowing Ralph was not alone, helped me decide what to do.

"Thank you, but not just yet. You may continue to sit with Mr. Thomas." I turned and continued walking down another flight to the morning room, slipping behind my desk. I pulled out writing paper, pen, and wax, then realized I had to dig deeper to find the small supply of black-trimmed stationery that mother had insisted I add to my store of desk supplies. Neither of us had ever imagined I would be using the first sheets to write to her. I sat there and stared at the black-edged paper, not knowing what to write. Finally, I put the pen point onto the virgin sheet and wrote the bare essentials:

Dearest Mama and Papa,

There's been an accident. Ralph is dead. Please come soonest.

276

Your loving daughter,
Amanda.

Next I wrote to Ralph's family. This one was even harder. I scarcely knew them. They were expecting us to visit after Christmas. Ralph had been helping them financially. They would be devastated. They would have to stay at this house to attend the funeral. Then an even more heartbreaking thought occurred to me: what if they wanted Ralph's body to be interred in Derby? No, I could not think of that now. First things first. They needed to be told. And, as simply and directly as I had written to my own parents, I put pen to paper.

Dear Mother, Father, and Brother Royce Thomas,

There has been a horse accident. Your precious son Ralph is dead. Please come to Hampstead at your earliest.

Respectfully,

(Mrs.) Amanda Thomas.

I rang the bell for the footman, handed him my two missives, and instructed him to post the one letter to Derby and then drive to my parents' home in Belgravia with the other and await a response. If neither of my parents were at home, he was to proceed to Papa's chambers in Lincoln Inn, notifying both my father and the clerk of Ralph's accident. On his return trip, the footman was to stop in Regency Street at Black Peter Robinson's warehouse to request the fitter. If all worked out, my mother would be here before the Robinson brougham arrived in Hampstead.

I was emotionally spent, but the household still needed to be run. I rang for cook. We planned the day's meals for the staff as quickly as possible.

"Thank you for your thoughtfulness in sending my breakfast to my room. I only wish some chicken broth for my lunch. Until my parents arrive, I will take my meals in my room. "

"Very good, Ma'am." Cook curtsied and turned to exit.

Judging it would be several hours before the footman returned, I retired back upstairs, again hesitating near the closed parlor door but deciding to wait to enter until my parents arrived. I told myself I was too young to be a widow. "Oh, Ralph!" I lamented. I had barely entered through my bedroom door before I collapsed on the bed, weeping myself back to sleep again.

Awakened by the arrival of my luncheon broth, I moved to my reading chair by the window. Cook had added a slice of bread, some cold mutton, and an apple to the tray. I nibbled at the bread, ate a few bites of the apple, and swallowed most of the clear soup while staring out the window and the turbulent winter clouds. They appeared as unsettled as I felt. Suddenly I knew what I had to do.

I had always stored my painting supplies in my dressing room so as not to clutter up the more public rooms of the house. Now I was glad they were nearby for me to retrieve them handily. I pulled out a fresh piece of watercolor paper and, pouring some fresh water into the basin (that had, thankfully, been cleaned by the housemaid while I was downstairs), I began to paint the clouds. Once that picture was ready to dry, I worked on a still life of the ewer and basin. The occupation of studying my subject and planning my approach to the painting provided me with a sense of calm focus. I was channeling my emotions onto the paper. As I stood back to examine my work from a distance, I knew I would need to paint Ralph's portrait—and soon. It would be my medium for preserving him and our love. A wave of relief swept over me.

I was startled by a quick tap on my door. Sophie entered again and curtsied.

"Excuse me, Ma'am, but Mr. and Mrs. Graham have arrived, and the footman 'as returned."

"Thank you. I will be right down." I swiftly cleaned my brushes and put them down. I nearly flew downstairs into Mama's open arms and then Papa's, melting into fresh tears as the warmth of their love, the depth of their concern, and their shared grief overtook me.

"Ralph's footman explained to us about the accident," Papa said. "His loss is great—both to our family and to the legal profession."

"How are you faring, Amanda, dear," Mama stepped back to assess me while holding onto both my arms.

"I have not had the courage to see him lying in the parlor until you have come. I have been painting..." The latter statement did not seem to make sense, and yet it was what was allowing me some semblance of coping. "I also sent Ralph's family a letter asking them to come. And I have sent for Robinson's mourning fitters. The undertaker is supposed to come back today. I did not know what else to do. Ralph's manservant has been sitting with him." Each sentence felt like a lead ball dropping. "Would you...? Do you...? We should relieve Ralph's manservant and go inside," I concluded.

My parents each took one of my hands. As we entered the parlor, the burning smell was tainted with another one, slightly acrid and more pungent. Frederick stood and left the room quietly. He looked as drawn as I felt, and it suddenly dawned on me that he, too, had lost his place and purpose in serving Ralph, relegated now to standing watch. My heart swelled with compassion, and I formed a new bond with him.

Our attention was drawn to the table in the center of the room where the corpse was covered with a white sheet. All three of us stopped; it felt as though time stood still. Papa, being closest to Ralph's head, slowly drew the sheet back off Ralph's face and then winced—I am not sure whether at the wound or the beginning of the blue-grey death pallor. Mama took in a sharp breath and squeezed my hand. I moaned a whimper. What I missed immediately were his green eyes. Someone had put coppers on his eyelids, giving them an eerie, brown, open-eyed look. Papa covered his own eyes with his free hand, squeezing his brow together.

Pulling himself back together, Papa asked, "Do you know when the Thomases will arrive? We should not delay long before the burial." He was hinting at what we all knew standing there—Ralph's body was beginning to decompose.

"I only posted the letter this morning. Even if it arrived in Derby tonight, they may need a day or two to make arrangements to come to London and, a half-day by train..." I trailed off unable to do the simple mathematical calculation in my head.

"Then we should proceed with planning the funeral and interment arrangements so as not to delay too long when they arrive," Papa continued. "If you don't have a strong preference for a church and pastor here in Hampstead, we can use our church and the Reverend Stephenson who married you to perform the service." Papa knitted his eyebrows together as if making a difficult decision, then added gently, "After this is over, you may want to move back home with us, and having Ralph's...Ralph's marker nearby will be a comfort."

My face screwed up in pain as I contemplated the thought I had pushed out of my mind earlier.

"What if they want to take his...him back to Derby? We have not been married that long."

Mama and Papa exchanged glances as though confirming that this might be the family's wishes, and we would be powerless to stop them—unless the Thomases did not have the funds to bury Ralph, and instead, my parents would offer with the caveat that his remains stay in London. I did not want the already sad occasion to turn into a family struggle, however. I prayed the Thomases would arrive soon.

The servants readied a guestroom for my parents to stay the night. We had a quiet dinner together. Mama and Papa retired early to their chamber, but I remembered that Ralph had so admired my piano playing. Ironically, I had not often played during our few months of marriage. I slipped into the parlor, past the table with my husband's body, and settled myself on the piano bench. I silently resolved to paint his portrait tomorrow when natural light was available, but tonight the candlelight, the drawn curtains, and the silence enveloped us in a solemn intimacy. My fingers softly stroked the ivory keys. I hoped he could hear the music in heaven.

The nausea struck with full force again the next morning. I was still voiding into the washbasin when Mama knocked and then entered to tell me the Robinson fitters had arrived and were fitting Papa first since he would be returning to London to inquire about the funeral arrangements, but she was obviously concerned with my state.

"Tears and lethargy are common to a new widow, dear Amanda, even little appetite, but it is not emetic." She paused thoughtfully, and then laid her hand tenderly on my shoulder. "'The Lord giveth, and the Lord taketh away.' The only time I was as sick as you look right now was when I was first carrying you." She let the insight seep into me. When she saw me start to crumple under the realization at the news at which she was hinting, she caught me and half-carried, half-led me to the bed. I fell over sideways onto the covers in a fit of fresh grief.

"I'll send for the doctor," Mama said quietly as she left the room.

I wanted to die, but Ralph had left me with a piece of him growing inside me, so I could not neglect it. And, if this child inside me was the product of our love, then I could do no less then love it, too. This little person we created together would comfort me, would be a daily reminder of my husband. These thoughts provided some consolation, and my tears subsided sufficiently so that I could be dressed and go down calmly for the mourning fittings.

After the doctor had confirmed my mother's astute diagnosis and I was properly admonished about eating and caring for myself, I retrieved my art supplies and entered the parlor, dismissing Ralph's manservant from his doleful watch.

I blew out the candles—the smell of which had somewhat masked the body's deterioration—and the remaining smoke gave the room a slight otherworldly look. I pushed open the heavy draperies to capture the full morning light.

Since Ralph was lying on top of a table, I would have to position myself above him in some fashion to capture his likeness. I moved one of the heavier parlor chairs as well as a small table on which to place my paints and water, then mounted the chair to sit, carefully balanced, on top of the chair back. I slowly pulled back the sheet to reveal my husband's countenance. At first, seeing his beautiful face with the gash across his forehead caused a feeling in me as if a knife had been thrust into my chest and slowly turned. I steeled myself, and then began to sketch the outline of his face on my paper. Once engrossed in the artistic evaluations of line, shape, color, value, and shadow, a feeling of detached tenderness returned. Time seemed to stand still.

I knew the eyes would be the most difficult. I wanted to capture their shifting color, their intelligence and sparkle. Above all, I wanted to demonstrate the love and soul behind them. I knew I wanted to show our child what a wonderful man his father had been.

I drew and painted as best as my meager skills allowed me. At one point, it seemed to me that Ralph was above and behind me, watching, guiding my hand, approving, but the sensation was only momentary. When I tried to hold on to it, it slipped away.

The morning light gradually shifted, darkening the room, and I found there was nothing more I could add to my portrait. Dismounting from the chair, I cleaned up my supplies and returned the chair and small table to their original locations, remembering how Ralph had once supervised their placement. I lingered a moment for one final look, then slowly recovered him with the sheet. I gathered up my supplies, closed the curtains, softly exited the room and, returned to my bedroom where I placed Ralph's portrait on the dresser facing the bed. After a last glance at my picture, I returned downstairs for lunch.

Mama had spent the morning supervising the fittings for the servants, ordering the mirrors covered, and making a list of people to notify of Ralph's funeral—the list was very similar to our wedding invitation list. She had also been thinking about becoming a grandmother.

"Amanda, there is no question now that you will need to move back in with me and your Papa." Mama wanted to supervise my confinement. "You cannot continue to live out here in Hampstead—so far away—as your condition progresses." I knew this would mean releasing all the servants, selling the furniture, and essentially, erasing the reminders of my short life as a married woman. My confinement period would coincide with my bereavement; in fact, I would give birth while still dressed in mourning. I acquiesced; I had no fight left in me.

The afternoon was wearing on when the Thomas family arrived. They had wasted no time by taking the morning train from Derby station. Once hugs and verbal condolences had been exchanged, as well as a somewhat more detailed description of the accident as I knew it, Ralph's family was admitted to the parlor for a viewing. Over lunch, one of the servants had re-lit the candles and added some incense. Mama and I withdrew to allow the family some private time and to order refreshments. Mama would return to London this evening so that the Thomases could use the guestroom.

Papa joined us again for supper to inform us of what funerary arrangements would be available to us.

"For the memorial service, we may select among the historic churches in the city, such as St. Paul's Church in Covent Garden, St. Stephen Walbrook, or St. Nicholas Cole. Since Ralph had been a barrister, the Temple Church is also an option. We may also use our family's church in Wilton Place, Belgravia, where the children were married." This suggestion made me wince. We all agreed that recognizing Ralph's affiliation with the Inns of Court made the most sense, so we selected the Temple Church, which was also able to accommodate our earliest preferred funeral date. My father looked at each of us briefly, weighing his next words.

"Then the question remains, where shall we bury the dear boy? Most of the graveyards in London proper are filled. Since Ralph seemed set on living near the countryside of Hampstead Heath, I suggest we consider Highgate Cemetery. It is nearer to Derby than any of the others." I had to admire Papa's style of argument honed by years in court.

Ralph's family members looked at each other. Clearly, they had not thought this far along. Ralph's father nodded his assent.

"We'll select an elegant marker," my father offered. "The undertaker will be by in the morning to fetch the...to fetch Ralph." Tonight would be the last night he would be in the house, and the Thomases would also need to say goodbye. The blood in my veins ran cold as the concept of my life without Ralph began to sink into my psyche. The next several days would be almost unbearable.

"There is some good news, however," Mama interjected to uplift the company's spirits. "Dear Amanda here is with child. We are to become grandparents!"

I smiled wanly as I realized this news had not produced the desired effect. I suspected the Thomases were instantly calculating how many additional mouths there would be to feed now that their source of additional revenue was gone.

"That's wonderful," Mrs. Thomas responded half-heartedly, making me fully aware that the promise of Ralph's baby was not considered by her to be sufficient compensation for the loss of her own boy. I felt guilty for Ralph's death even though I had not been the actual cause of it.

"Of course, we have told Amanda that she must come back to live with us," Mama explained to ease the tension. "She cannot live here on her own in her condition."

The Thomases relaxed slightly, no longer responsible for my well-being and that of the baby, but they also knew that, once back under my parents' roof, the likelihood of their grandparental visitation rights might well be curtailed, if only due to the geographic distance between Derby and London. Their son's gravesite would be distance enough to travel.

"Once the child is old enough to travel, we can visit you in Derby," I offered weakly. Ralph's parents nodded but not with much enthusiasm, seeing little in me to honor that resolve. The baby had to be born first then survive several winters. By then, I could very easily have forgotten my promise or even re-married. The silence hung thickly in the room.

"Your mother will post the funeral announcement letters tomorrow, and I will prepare a notice for *The Times*," Papa directed to me. "A carriage will arrive for Mr. Thomas and Royce at nine o'clock on Saturday morning."

"But *I* want to attend Ralph's funeral," I protested.

"It's not proper for a lady," Mama countered.

"I don't care; I want to be there."

"Very well," Papa conceded, finding it difficult to deny his only daughter. Then, as though not to exclude anyone, he asked, "Do you other ladies wish to attend, also?" Both Mama and Mrs. Thomas declined—the former because she acknowledged her societal place and the latter likely because she felt more at ease around our servants than at the Inns of Court.

As another awkward silence began to descend, Papa stood up to signal my parents' departure. He appeared more than a little relieved to be leaving the company of the somber Thomas family, although feeling equally guilty about leaving me. Under other circumstances, Ralph's relatives would have been more jovial, but being almost strangers in their own son's house and of a lower social class was making them visibly uncomfortable.

As the front door closed on my parents' departure, I suggested the Thomases might like to sit with Ralph. Without another word, I ascended the two flights of stairs to my bedroom and sanctuary. Two nights had passed since Ralph's untimely death—it seemed like a split second...and an eternity. Another whole day would need to pass before the funeral took place. I determined to rise early the next morning to say goodbye before the undertaker arrived. I fell asleep pretending that Ralph's arms still encircled me, my tears softly sliding down to the pillow like raindrops from a windowsill.

Accustomed as I was to servants, there had been few mornings in my life when I took it upon myself to dress without assistance, and this was one of them. I donned a peignoir robe and a woolen shawl and then tiptoed down to the parlor where I startled the housemaid who was just lighting the morning fire. The room was chilly—a good thing for preserving the body lying in state, but it caused me to wrap my shawl tighter around my shoulders as I crossed the floor to my dead husband's side.

My dead husband.

It amazed me how the reality of it needed to keep sinking in, day-by-day. Would I ever come to accept it?

I knelt down and took Ralph's lifeless hand in my own and placed it against my cheek.

"Ralph, darling, I am going to have our baby." My face screwed up in anguish, and I burst into tears again, heaving a deep sigh between sobs. The wave passed, and then calm took over.

"I don't *want* to say goodbye! There are so many things I wanted us to experience together...I hope I can make you proud of me as a mother. Thank you for leaving a part of you behind." I placed his hand back beneath the sheet and rose to my feet. I touched his chest lightly then turned to leave the room, stopping at the door to look back again.

As I closed the parlor door, I heard the arrival of the undertaker's men. I stepped back into the room to get out of their way as they wrapped Ralph's body in a shroud, placed him in a plain wooden coffin, covered it, and then removed it all to the hearse parked on the street outside. I stood, watching from the parlor window, as the men went about their emotionless, business-like manner of securing the coffin in the carriage, suitably draped in black crepe.

"Goodbye, Ralph," I whispered, fogging the window glass with my breath. I watched the hearse until it was out of sight, then went down to the dining room to await the Thomas family's arrival for breakfast. I was not sure at all how we would pass the day together.

After polite inquiries about one's comfort and how one had slept, Mr. Thomas cleared his throat.

"Amanda, we are simple folk used to country funerals. If we are going to be sitting among Ralph's peers at the Temple Church, Royce and I will need to buy ourselves some city clothing."

"Of course," I replied. "Do you want me to fetch the Robinson fitters to return for you?"

"No, I was thinking more that, if we could borrow your driver and carriage, we could go into London ourselves. That is, if you can spare them?"

"Naturally. I have no need for them myself today. Take what time you need." I was, perhaps, a little too relieved to be rid of my social obligations for the day. "I will give the driver instructions to be at your disposal—even to show you a bit of London, if you would like." The Thomases appeared to perk up at the idea of some sightseeing in addition to the more painful duty of buying mourning garb. Mrs. Thomas wished to accompany her men folk, and it was not long after that I saw them off, and the normal household silence returned. I could almost pretend that Ralph was at work in the city again.

Our household mourning clothing was delivered in the afternoon. As the servants donned their black, the household took back its darkened tone. I took a nap.

When my visitors returned, they were anxious to recount their adventures, so the day and evening of the third day passed more easily than I had initially feared.

The next morning, I awoke with *The Flying Dutchman* libretto playing in my mind. Sophie dressed me in first mourning: a tight-waisted, black velvet, *polonaise* dress with bustle, the cuirasse bodice of which was embossed with black crepe. I had a small, black velvet, Eugenie hat tilted forward on my forehead to allow room for my coiled hair braid falling from my crown. Both my gloves and my high button boots were black suede.

The undertaker's coach was an open, four-seat brougham draped in black velvet with four horses adorned with black ostrich plume headdresses.

Mr. Thomas was dressed in a stylish black frock coat, waistcoat, trousers, and top hat with black weeper. Royce had opted for a bowler; a dark grey, tweed country suit consisting of a matching four-button jacket, vest, and trousers of which only the top button of the jacket was fastened. He wore a black arm band.

We drove into the city in silence together, each with our own thoughts. At the cobblestone courtyard of the Temple Church, Royce exited from the carriage then he turned and extended his hand to allow me to descend from the carriage as well. This first gentlemanly act he had offered me reminded me of Ralph such that unshed tears burned in my eyes. Trying to regain some composure, I looked away and recognized my parents' carriage parked in the courtyard. Papa came over to hug me and solemnly shake the Thomas men's hands.

Six pallbearers--Ralph's manservant, driver, and footman, as well as those of my parents--carried the coffin inside while several male "mutes" walked alongside. We followed the coffin into the church. Papa directed us to sit in the first row. Behind us, the sanctuary filled as barristers, judges, solicitors, and others of Ralph's and my father's acquaintances filed into the remaining pews. I recognized Neville Hall and Reverend Stephenson among the mourners. The clergyman who would conduct the service came over to express his condolences in turn to me, my father, Mr. Thomas, and Royce.

I was amazed that so many people knew my Ralph—people I did not know myself. Several men spoke in eulogy extolling his virtues of hard work, justice, compassion, friendship, and generosity. Silent tears coursed down my cheeks as a mixture of pride, love, and loss mingled in my emotions.

When we came out of the church, I noticed a slight drizzle had begun. My father instructed me to take his closed carriage home to be with my mother in Belgravia while he and the Thomas men continued on to Highgate Cemetery in the undertaker's carriage for the burial. From Highgate, they would return to Hampstead where I was to return later that afternoon with Mama so that she and Papa could return home in his own carriage. I also strongly suspected the men would spend some time in a Highgate public house before arriving back in Hampstead.

As Papa leaned into to hug me goodbye, he said, "On a more pleasant day, we will go together to Highgate to view the vault I selected."

I was relieved to be alone on the familiar ride through the City streets to Belgravia. I leaned back, closing my eyes, recalling that night after the opera when Ralph had lent us his carriage.

In the months that followed, my morning sickness waned, we dismantled the Hampstead household, and I moved back to my parents' home. My second mourning coincided with my second trimester, so my bombazine and crepe clothing were widened around the middle to allow for my expanding womb. I often worried that all this somber demeanor might result in an all-too-serious child, but instead I was delighted to give birth to a son of gleeful personality whose energy sometimes helped me to erase our sadder circumstances from my mind.

Many afternoons I would spend in the nursery watching my son, Randall, sleep in his bassinette draped in white lace, or playing with him when he was awake. Tired of the drab mourning, I would sometimes don an outdated white chemisette blouse and tartan glacé plaid skirt just to provide a change in mood. As Randall slept, I painted or read quietly. Soon, however, he was crawling then walking. Before I quite recognized what had happened, Randall was old enough for boarding school.

As my son grew older and his care became less of a major occupation for me, I looked for other outlets to occupy my time and contribute to society. The Education Reforms of 1870 and 1880 created government supported schools and compulsory education, so I turned my talents to teaching in a lower class elementary school in South London.

Being around young children helped ease the loneliness of my own son's absence. My father paid for his grandson's education at Eton and later at Oxford, so my meager teacher's earnings provided me with a small stipend for discretionary expenditures.

Father had indeed purchased a vault for Ralph's remains in the Circle of Lebanon section of the fashionable necropolis of Highgate Cemetery. The cemetery was perched on a sloping hillside off Swain's Lane. One approached the Circle, built around a massive cedar tree, along Egyptian Avenue, a narrow lane that descended through iron gates and then through an underground Pharaonic arch bordered by sixteen vaults of its own. The Circle was further below ground and housed twenty more vaults. As it was quite a distance from Belgravia, for several years I visited Ralph's gravesite thrice each year—on his birthday and on the anniversaries of his death and our marriage.

As time wore on, however, my visits to Highgate became less frequent. Yet, as the twentieth anniversary of his accident arrived, I acquired an unusually strong urge to pay my respects.

During the week leading up to the anniversary, we experienced an unusual cold snap and a few of my students had complained of chills and illness. One had gone so far as to be nauseous in class and was sent home.

I, too, was feeling a bit tired and achy that day as I set off in the omnibus, then the train to Highgate, and finally walked from the station to Swain's Lane and entered the cemetery gate. At one point, I had to lean against a gate due to lightheadedness, but I persevered onward to the vault. I wanted to tell Ralph about our son's academic achievements at Oxford.

I lit a candle I had brought and knelt for a few moments in prayer on the cold, stone slab floor. A draft came through the gate; the candle sputtered and died out. I pulled my coat and scarf closer around me, the chill deepening into shivers as I made my way back to the station. Gratefully, I slept a little on the train.

Once back in London, I opted for a cab to take me home. I scarcely remembered stumbling into the house and being half-carried upstairs by one of the servants. I spent the night half-delirious with fever, alternately soaking my sheets with perspiration and shaking uncontrollably with shivering. I went in and out of consciousness, the pain in my joints very severe at times. Catarrhal systems also developed, and I was administered quinine, although the paroxysmal coughing kept me awake for several nights.

After a week, my symptoms subsided, although a prolonged lethargy and nervousness followed for a number of weeks, as well as continued bronchial coughing. Regaining my strength took far longer than expected. Nevertheless, I went back to teaching a week after my first attack, returning exhausted each night, often foregoing supper to go to bed.

In late March, a few warm days heralded the onset of spring. The improved weather brightened my spirits for the first time in months, and we looked forward to Randall's homecoming from University for Easter. I took advantage of the pleasantness of the day to stroll along the Thames on the Queen's Walk and cross over Westminster Bridge.

I realized I must have over-calculated my recovering strength as I faltered part way across the bridge and had to lean on the wall before continuing the remainder of my walk, gratefully catching a hansom cab at the Houses of Parliament. By the time I reached home, I was again in the throes of a high fever.

This attack was worse than the previous one. Pain was everywhere—my head, my eyes, my neck, my shoulders, and my limbs. Nausea alternated with voiding. I lost track of time, so I was delightfully surprised one evening when I was awaken by a warm hand holding mine on the bed cover.

"Mother," a familiar voice said. "I'm here."

I opened my heavy-lidded eyes and smiled wanly through parched lips as my gaze fell onto Randall's welcome but concerned face. Behind his left shoulder, I saw a glow. Focusing my eyes with effort, out of the halo of light I could just make out another figure emerging with outstretched arms.

"Ralph!" I whispered and closed my eyes again.

Sixteen thousand people died that year from the influenza epidemic in London alone.

Ohio, 2001

FAITH

Most of AEMG's staff members spent the week between Christmas 2000 and New Year's 2001 packing our offices and files for the move to our new headquarters building in early January. I had already packed up most of the NIR records in preparation for pick-up by commercial freight to transfer to their new management, so my remaining files were less voluminous. Among some old OAHIA convention badges I was cleaning out, I found one with Keir's name on it, likely from the last convention he attended at Deerwood Lake Lodge and the last time I had seen him. "I might want to keep this," I told myself and tucked it away separately.

As a result of my personal development seminars, I had begun walking regularly on my lunch hour for thirty minutes for both fitness and stress reduction. Our new office location was in a new section of the city undergoing construction, so I discovered two options for my daily walks. One sidewalk path curved through an apartment neighborhood and up a hill to a more industrial area and then circled around back to our office building. A second route went past some offices, a Montessori school, and into a townhouse neighborhood, but required doubling back to return to the office. On Tuesdays and Thursdays, when she was working, Sylvia would join me on the walk. The other days, I walked solo.

The walks helped clear my head and improved my productivity after lunch. Often I recalled the sporadic moments and conversations I had had with Keir over the years. I turned them over in my mind, like a lottery tumbler, not fully able to understand how the pieces fit together but not wanting to forget them, either.

One mid-January morning while at the office, I learned that Linwood Ashton, who had been in business together with Keir, Phyllis Buckley, and Gordon Geddes at the Summit-United agency, had purchased Health Cuyahoga from Keir. I remembered that Mark Thomas had mentioned to me a month or so earlier that Lin Ashton had left Summit-United and was job hunting. In the process of Lin's previous conversation with Mark, Lin had mentioned that he and Keir were in the same book club together, the Golden Retrievers.

"Lin told me that Keir's speech has slowed and he wears a bandana on his head to the book club meetings," Mark had related to me.

Even though I assumed that Keir and Lin had used their friendship to enable Lin to have a new job and business while alleviating Keir of the burden of the agency's responsibilities, I interpreted the news of the sale of Keir's agency to Lin as another defeat for Keir, adding to his earlier losses of freedom and independence.

Mulling this over, I went out for my lunchtime walk. A cold, grey winter day, I wore my ankle-length, down coat, a knit hat, lined gloves, a scarf, socks, and sneakers against the chill. I trudged up through the quiet apartment community.

About half-way up the hill, the full realization dawned on me that Keir was now no longer in the health insurance law business and, therefore, no longer a member of OAHIA. I had just been in the process of updating the OAHIA membership directory, removing Kevin Raines from the active members and placing an asterisk (denoting "deceased") next to his name in the list of Past Presidents. Now, I would also have the additional, heartbreaking task of removing Keir from the OAHIA directory as well. I further comprehended, with Keir no longer a member of OAHIA, our professional link and, therefore, any pretense for further communication was now gone.

Warm tears welled up in my eyes and slowly rolled down my cold, winter-parched cheeks. "But Keir is *not* dead...yet!" my mind protested. I would have to devise a rationale and a method to keep his name in the directory and to stay in touch, to be able to inquire from time to time about him as I had promised, and even to visit him if I went to Cleveland.

A germ of an audacious idea popped into my head, and I hurried back to the office to check the OAHIA bylaws and call Mark Thomas. The bylaws allowed for a member who had contributed significantly to the industry to be elected as an "Honorary Member" of OAHIA by either unanimous vote of the Executive Committee or two-thirds of the members at the annual meeting. Presently, OAHIA only had two Honorary Members, both elected during Keir's presidential term. I would need to make a very strong and convincing case, especially since I had heard rumors that Keir and Gordon—now OAHIA's President—had not parted ways on the best of terms from Summit-United; and now, Lin, who had also left Summit-United, had taken over Keir's agency and was one of Gordon's competitors. I would need Gordon's permission to even put the item on the February Executive Committee agenda.

"Who else served on the Executive Committee when Keir was on it and who might support your case?" Mark was helping me strategize. "You'll want to get your votes lined up before the meeting."

I found it difficult to identify Keir's supporters among the current OAHIA officers. Alicia Tomlinson worked for Keir's former employer, Cleveland Medical, but her allegiance was likely with Kenneth Sven who had let Keir go from his post. The two newest officers, Tom Taylor and Philip Feldberg, had not been in the industry long enough to have known Keir. That left past president Greg Grisham and Chuck Lincoln, now serving as general counsel, but who had served with Keir when I first started. (Unbeknownst to me at the time, Greg knew Keir when they both worked in private practice in Akron right after Keir had graduated from law school.) I thought Chuck, as general counsel and a "senior statesman" was my best bet, so he was my next phone call.

"Chuck, I learned this morning that Lin Ashton has bought the Health Cuyahoga agency from Keir Mervais so the latter can more fully concentrate on his health treatments. I was thinking the OAHIA Executive Committee could make Keir an Honorary Member."

"Honorary Membership is given to only a few outstanding leaders who have made a substantial contribution to the industry." Chuck seemed reluctant to the idea. I was going to have to make a strong case with him first.

"Don't you remember how Keir was responsible for turning OAHIA around financially when I first started? OAHIA was almost out of money. Then, when Liam got the Association in trouble with Insurance Director Carson, Keir helped to smooth things over. Plus, Keir started the Legislative Committee."

"You're going to have to get Gordon to agree to put it on the agenda," Chuck advised. I sensed his resistance had abated a little.

"Yes, I will."

Gordon was actually more agreeable to placing Keir's Honorary Member nomination on the agenda than I expected, so I did not pursue lobbying the remaining officers to line up their votes in advance of the February 13th Executive Committee meeting.

Instead, I wrote Keir another letter, letting him know that, even though he was no longer working, we in the Association were still pulling and praying for him. I acknowledged that he could now fully concentrate on his health. The letter was originally three pages, but I edited it back to one-and-a-half pages. (Each letter I wrote appeared to be shorter than the last—I was finding it difficult to know what to write without any sort of response.)

My personal coach, Hillary, and I met for dinner on the evening of January 21st at a health food store café. When I began to vent my worries about Keir, we adjourned to my car. For the next two-and-a-half hours, I talked about Keir and Auguste, crying almost non-stop. Hillary handed me tissues, one after the other, and listened. I nearly emptied the tissue box. From the hidden compartment in my briefcase I dug out the fifteen-year old photograph of Keir and Abigail and showed her. Hillary allowed me the space to express all my emotions. When I was spent, she gave me a hug and got out of my car so that we could return to our respective homes for the night.

I sent an email to Keir's former officer and co-worker Harry Whitfield to ask what he thought about the Honorary Membership idea for Keir. Harry had left Cleveland Medical a couple of years earlier to go into private legal practice but had remained an OAHIA member as a private practicing attorney. Harry wrote back:

"I am planning to visit Keir on February 6th, a week before the Executive Committee meeting, and will ascertain how Keir might respond to the gesture."

After his visit, Harry emailed me again.

"Keir is getting around some—reading, walking, and watching television. He would like to continue to receive the OAHIA newsletter.

However, he would be amused to be made an Honorary Member at this point in his life."

I was not sure why it would be amusing, perhaps more ironic, but I took Harry's email as encouraging even though I was distressed that Keir-- this once handsome, outgoing, lively, intelligent attorney--was now home-bound and restricted in his activities. My heart went out to Keir for what must be his hours of loneliness, incomprehension, and frustration. How does one reconcile oneself to terminal illness? Does one wonder if it is punishment from the Almighty? Is it simply bad luck from the gene pool? After all, Keir's mother had died from cancer. Is it an opportunity to re-evaluate one's life and priorities? How do you keep up hope through the side effects of weakness, nausea, diarrhea, or worse?

Every night before I fell asleep, I continued to pray for Keir. Some nights while taking a shower, I would cry, mixing my salty tears with the fresh water and drying them both before exiting the bathroom lest I should have to explain it all to Auguste. And, every time I heard "I Hope You Dance," sung by LeAnn Womack, I would think of Keir—because he loved the water, because I did not want him to lose faith, and because I wanted him to keep fighting for his life.

The OAHIA Executive Committee meeting on February 13th was a difficult one. OAHIA's lobbyist, Patch Damien, had missed a couple of key issues at the General Assembly and, even though he was an attorney member of OAHIA himself, he had charged the Association for attending its convention to make his report. OAHIA had to hire an additional lobbyist for a matter dealing with the Insurance Department, and together these items had incurred a $15,000 year-end loss. The officers took Patch outside our office building for a conversation about their concerns. They reached an agreement for a much reduced lobbyist retainer for the year while having the member volunteers take a more active role in legislative activities.

After Patch Damien left the meeting, the Executive Committee approved language to establish an award in Kevin Raines' memory that would recognize a new member in the profession who demonstrated Kevin's attributes of humor and service. Then Gordon asked for Alicia's convention report, passing completely over the agenda item to consider Keir's Honorary Membership.

"Gordon," I interrupted. "I think you skipped an agenda item."

"Oh. Okay. Why don't *you* explain it?" I did not expect Gordon to do that, so I had not prepared anything to say.

"I don't know how many of you know that Keir Mervais has sold his agency to Lin Ashton because he is unable to continue working while he is undergoing treatment for his brain cancer," I began. "Because Keir is no longer working in the health insurance legal field, I thought it might be good to consider making him an Honorary Member." The officers were all listening respectfully. I spoke extemporaneously while my mind was frantically trying to recall all Keir's contributions to the industry and select the ones that would be the most convincing.

"When I first started with OAHIA, the Association was in serious financial trouble. Keir came up with a plan to get the Association's finances back on track. When the industry was in trouble with Insurance Director Carson and health insurance sales almost came to a standstill, Keir used his personal influence to create a workable agreement with Carson. He established the OAHIA Legislative Committee, wrote the agent's licensing exam, devised the membership structure under which the Association still operates today and, helped push through several advantageous legislative initiatives. If he had not crafted the special services clause in the management agreement, I would not still be OAHIA's executive director today."

My heart was pounding in my chest. When I placed my fingers on the laptop keyboard to record in the minutes a synopsis of what I had just said, my hands trembled so much, I hid them in my lap. "I'll type that part later," I assured myself. "I can remember what I said."

A palpable moment of silence settled in the room while the officers considered what should happen next. Greg Grisham spoke first.

"I make a motion that we bestow Honorary Membership on Keir Mervais."

I was relieved my speech had persuaded him but regretted he was not authorized to make the motion. "I'm sorry, Greg, but the bylaws require the motion to be made by a Full Member. Only Chuck or Gordon can make the motion."

"Well, *I'm* not going to make the motion," Chuck stonewalled.

I thought Chuck had relented during our call, but then I remembered that Chuck's and Gordon's agencies both represented the same underwriter. As general counsel, Chuck was deferring to Gordon as OAHIA President. I suspected that Gordon's rocky relationship with Keir when they worked together might influence him not to go ahead with the nomination. I held my breath. I was afraid we were deadlocked.

Philip Feldberg broke the silence.

"Gordon Frazier is going to retire on May first..." I recalled that Gordy had been Keir's general counsel when Keir had been OAHIA president and was a highly respected, senior member of the industry. Gordon Geddes now had a way to save face and could do the right thing.

"I move that we nominate both Gordy Frazier and Keir Mervais for Honorary Memberships." Greg seconded the motion immediately and Gordon's motion passed unanimously.

The last time Honorary Membership had been bestowed on anyone was eleven years earlier during Keir's term as OAHIA president. Even though I had arranged for those plaques to be made, I had not had the foresight to keep a copy of the wording. By the time I was aware I would need to craft new wording, Gordon was away on vacation in Mexico; therefore, I awaited his return in a couple weeks to approve the plaque wording. In early March, I took the wording down to the trophy shop. For the plaques, I selected a light green metal color with silver underneath (the colors I had originally wanted for Keir's presidential plaque because they reminded me of his eyes but I was forced to settle for bronze at the time because the trophy company no longer carried silver gavels). A week later, when I went to pick up the plaques, I discovered the trophy company had made a typographical error on Keir's plaque. Re-engraving the plaque required an additional week.

I was increasingly concerned that the sand in Keir's life hourglass was running out. Feeling a bit guilty for the delay in preparing the plaque, I called Keir's home and left a general "thinking of you" voice message. The call was not returned.

I really wanted to present Keir with his plaque in person since both he and Gordon lived in Cleveland, but I realized this would require arranging a surprise meeting with Gordon, Keir, and me. When the plaque was finally ready, I consulted Gordon about the possibility of visiting Keir and giving him the plaque in-person.

"I don't think Keir's death is imminent. Ship it." Gordon instructed.

I wrote a cover letter from Gordon and me explaining the reason for bestowal of the Honorary Membership, reiterating Keir's achievements and contributions. In the first line, I used a French word, a subtle signal to Keir that I had composed the letter, and enclosed the plaque. I felt *certain* Keir would acknowledge this honor with some form of response. Eight months had passed since we had last spoken.

Mireille's *bat mitzvah* was scheduled by the Rabbi for April 13, 2002, a year hence. She began the one-year, weekly, intensive Hebrew School program in preparation. To help her learn her Torah portion, I also took a one-day, Hebrew immersion course, learning the *alef-bet*.

Mireille was now in middle school and having some difficulty keeping up with her subjects. The eye doctor diagnosed her with "dyslexic tendencies," but she refused further vision treatments. Auguste alternated between scolding one or both of us and acting sullen and withdrawn, retreating to his job or the yard during the daylight and occupying the living room sofa and the television in the evenings. The air at home hung with anger and resentment. Whatever room he was in was the room for me to try to avoid. We stuck to our own sides of the queen-sized bed, going to bed and rising at different times.

One afternoon while Mireille and I were at the nearby shopping mall, I stopped by the bookstore to purchase a coaching book. Sitting on the shelf next to the book I was planning to buy and facing fully outward was *The Verbally Abusive Relationship: How to recognize and how to respond* by Patricia Evans. I bought both books. Within four days, I had read Evans' book completely, hiding the cover from Auguste and highlighting parts in yellow and pink; underlying in red, blue, and black; and adding asterisks at key passages.

Evans explained that the verbal abuser and his (her) victim live in two different realities. The victim believes in mutuality—a mutually supportive and nurturing relationship based in empathetic concern and co-empowerment—and interprets relationships through the mindset of partnership, unconditional love, and equality. The abuser believes in control and domination, constantly seeking power over others. Evans described patterns of behavior that a verbal abuser uses: secrecy; unexpected angry outbursts; put downs when the victim is feeling happy, enthusiastic, or successful; familiar patterns of hostility; a disdain for the victim's interests alternating with attempts at reconciliation; a refusal to apologize for behavior; periods of functionality punctuated by times of dysfunction; isolation and loss of intimacy; defining the victim, the abuser, and incidents that do not make sense, often turning the victim's words around (Evans called this "crazy-making"); saying things the victim would never say, e.g., cursing, denigrating, or derogatory comments, etc.; and, deliberately creating an environment of intimidation and constant fear.

I felt that Evans was describing my marriage. Auguste's behavior toward me fit the description of a classic verbal abuser. I was shocked and embarrassed that I had spent twenty-eight years inside this marital relationship without realizing that it was not normal or acceptable.

I was ashamed of my victimhood. I was highly educated with a Master's degree; I was an acknowledged leader of national organizations, managing up to six associations at a time; I was a graduate of many personal development courses and a life coach for other people. I had difficulty reconciling this new information with the identity I had of myself and the way I viewed the world. From the personal development vantage point that we are responsible for our own perception of the world and from my own sense of responsibility for my behavior, I began to consider and examine how I might have been the cause of Auguste's behavior toward me. Had my personal feelings of lack of self-worth attracted his dominating behavior that then caused me to wrong him and keep the dynamic in place?

Evans wrote that the hardest path is to stay in the abusive relationship. My family had a history of long marriages—both sets of grandparents were married until their deaths—over fifty-five years together. My own parents had been married nearly that long. Both my brothers were still with the same woman. In two years' time, Auguste and I would be married for thirty years.

I decided to seek a therapist. I found one near my office that I could visit on my lunch hour and pay in cash. After five weeks of crying in his office and two more weeks telling him about coaching, we had not gotten anywhere to my satisfaction.

"You know what to do," the therapist eventually told me. I had no clue. I quit the therapy.

At the end of April, I received a notice at work about an association executives' gathering in Cleveland on May 15th. Although I would not normally attend a meeting of the Cleveland association executives, I thought, "Finally, a chance to fulfill my promise to visit Keir."

However, I had not received any response from Keir, or even Abigail, about the Honorary Member plaque. I wrote a short note to Keir that an opportunity had arisen for me to go to Cleveland on business and asked if he would like me to visit him. I enclosed a stamped, self-addressed postcard to make it easy to reply—he merely needed to check a box marked Yes or No. The day after I mailed it, I felt a punch of adrenaline in my stomach late that afternoon, so I imagined Keir had received my note. For two days, I could almost feel him thinking about what to respond and then make a decision. I waited a week for the postcard to come back. It never did. In hindsight, I realized I should have added a third check box: Not Now/Not Yet.

At this point, I was really in a quandary. None of my letters or the Honorary Membership plaque had garnered a response. (To be truthful, I had not written most of my letters, with exception of the last note, for a response but rather to keep Keir company in his lonelier moments.) Now I began to wonder if he and Abigail were being polite by ignoring my letters in the hope that I would eventually leave them alone.

I surmised that the Mervais family had installed caller identification on their home phone system. I certainly would have if my own husband was seriously ill. Who needed those marketing calls about lawn products, long-distance services, and carpet shampoo when you are enduring the side effects of chemotherapy? On the other hand, was *my* caller ID one of those being purposely ignored as well? With Abigail an attorney, I began to fear the possibility of her sending me a cease-and-desist letter. I decided to stop calling and writing.

But I did not stop praying, sending energy waves, or longing to see Keir again. It had been five years since he stood so forlorn in the doorway at Deerwood Lake Lodge to say goodbye. Did he have an intuition then that he would become so ill? That it would be the last time we would see each other?

I made an entry into my "hard times journal" on Father's Day addressed to Keir:

It's Father's Day. I hope it is happy for you. I remember how proud you were/are to be a father. It seems bittersweet—a beautiful June day but tinged with sadness.

At least this way I don't have to sanitize anything. I can just speak from my heart. So why didn't you return the postcard? Did it seem like the right thing to do at the time? Because No would have been as much of a lie as Yes? Because I need to move on? I still would like to say goodbye. Will I get the opportunity to say it in person?

A few days later, I recorded:

Okay, if goodbye is not forthcoming—or it's not time yet, may I just learn how you are doing? Am I merely being selfish and egotistical or am I being generous and loving? Does it matter?

No one in OAHIA talked about Keir, and I was afraid to bring him up. I did not know if he was dead or still alive. A month later, I protested in writing:

What do I have to give up in order to have the space for you to show up? Who do I need to BE???

In my work life, I was operating on all cylinders—transitioning new clients into AEMG while keeping my current clients happy and helping Jack Spencer market for new clients. (One staff member referred to me as "the company morale officer.") Additionally, I was working at the gallery on Saturdays and frequently on Wednesday afternoons during Mireille's Hebrew lessons, attending my weekly seminars, being coached, taking Coach University teleclasses and coaching others, working with Auguste to find a reliable roofer, and attempting to keep up with the housework and the homework from my classes as well as supervising Mireille's schoolwork. On a routine doctor visit, my physician remarked that I had the "adrenaline levels of a fighter pilot who had been out on too many missions."

One hot, sultry day in mid-summer, I was walking back from the apartment complex near my office at lunchtime. Along the sidewalk, a black metal gate separated the entrance to the complex from the portion of the neighborhood where our office was located. On the next block, between the gate and my office building, stood a vacant lot of wild grasses and young trees.

As I unlatched the gate to let myself through, I berated myself about Keir. "Why am I *still* so attached to this man? Obviously, he does not want to hear from me or have anything further to do with me! Why do I still *care so much*? Why can't I just let it go?"

By this time I had walked as far as the vacant lot. In the time it took me to walk two consecutive steps, I had a sudden, intuitive, *knowing* – a revelation. God, or at least a messenger directly from God, spoke to me.

"You CANNOT give up on him. You knew each other in a previous lifetime—specifically, the French-and-Indian War. He was a French soldier with a gunshot wound to his head. You were his caregiver, a British colonial woman. You fell in love with each other, but he died before you could tell each other. Your mission in this lifetime is to tell each other you love each other."

On the one hand, I was astounded. Up until this moment, I thought that, when one died, they dug a hole in the ground and buried you in dirt. I had interpreted "heaven" as humans remembering you fondly. God had never spoken to me before, and yet I had no question that this was a divine directive straight from The Almighty.

Suddenly, however, how Keir and I had previously interacted started to make perfect sense. This explanation was not something I would or could have thought up or imagined on my own. I knew next to nothing about the French-and-Indian War. Yet, it explained why, when Keir and I had spoken to each other years ago, we seemed to be holding two conversations at once: one coming out of our mouths and another, more important one—conveyed through body language—was unspoken with a deep understanding emanating from our hearts.

As I rapidly walked the rest of the way back to my office, I instantly had renewed hope and commitment. After all, the OAHIA convention the following month was to be held at the Cedar Palace Hotel in Sandusky where Keir had told me I was "the most beautiful woman in the room." My heart took wing as I thought, "Perhaps he and Abigail will be at their Lakeside vacation home and might even attend the convention so that he can be recognized as an Honorary Member in person!"

Over the next several weeks, however, I increasingly found the prospect of returning to the Cedar Palace emotionally daunting. At least the opening reception ballroom, although in the same room we used in 1995, was arranged differently. At one point during Thursday's opening reception, I overheard Greg Grisham mention Keir's name to a colleague. My ears perked up.

"You know, Keir Mervais was unfairly blamed for trying to block the establishment of the rating bureau," I heard Greg explain, "but it was really a case of shooting the messenger. Keir was generally in favor of the rating bureau, but after Alex McDowell retired, Cleveland Medical had no clear-cut leadership for about a year. Keir had been kept out of the rating bureau discussions and was just doing his due diligence to study the issues before committing his company's resources."

I was pleased that Greg, whom I respected and admired, was defending Keir's reputation in his absence. I had hoped to hear—or overhear—more current news about Keir's condition at the convention. The meeting rooms, the registration area in the foyer, and the refreshment break area all brought back memories of our last convention together there—but *he* was not there. I felt like I was living a double existence: carrying on as usual at the convention in the present, all the while sensing and missing Keir's presence from the past. I had hoped and expected that, after my extraordinary visit from God a month earlier, some breakthrough news or communication would be forthcoming.

By Friday afternoon, I had heard nothing further. An extremely hot, sweltering, humid weekend, I chose to walk slowly along Cleveland Road to Meigs Street and Battery Park, passing the restaurant where Sylvia and I had eaten six years earlier and had seen Keir hesitate then pass by.

Reaching the park, I rested on a bench in the shade of the oak trees, hoping to be cooled by the Lake Erie breeze. After sitting for about twenty minutes, I walked west on Washington Street and wandered around the historic district before turning east on Monroe Street to return to the Cedar Point Causeway, the road-bridge stretching to the entrance of the amusement park. To take advantage of air conditioning, I stopped in several art galleries along the route.

When I got back to the hotel, I went to the indoor pool for a swim. Several OAHIA families were already there. After speaking with Mark and

Marianne Thomas, Mike and Ruby Talbot, and a couple of attorney members, I noticed Eric Mitchell alone at the other side of the pool.

Eric worked in Cleveland and had served on the OAHIA Executive Committee along with Keir during my first year as executive director. His wife, Sandra, had just gone into the women's locker room to use the sauna. I swam over to where Eric was standing. After some initial, nonchalant chatting, I worked up my courage to ask what was foremost in my mind.

"Have you heard anything about how Keir Mervais is doing?" I tried to keep a casual tone in my voice.

"I ran into someone from his church a few weeks ago who said he was down to 120 pounds."

I quickly calculated in my mind: "One hundred twenty pounds— that's less than my ideal weight! Keir was at least five foot eight or nine inches and compactly built, perhaps weighing 165 or 175 pounds when he was healthy. That might explain why he might not have wanted me to visit him back in May…"

"Eric, if you hear anything else about him, would you please let me know?" Eric shook his head in agreement.

Contrary to my fervent wish, the Mervaises did not attend the Friday evening banquet. The evening's events proceeded as usual, with a lovely dinner followed by golf prizes for those who had braved the hot afternoon on the links. Since Kevin Raines had died twenty months earlier, no one had the heart to run a tennis tournament any more.

Having Saturday afternoon off, I decided to drive out to the Lakeside Daisy State Nature Preserve, across the Route 2 Bridge along East Bay Shore Road and County Road 135, to the Marblehead Peninsula. An old limestone quarry, the nineteen-acre preserve exists to protect the Lakeside daisy, a rare and threatened yellow wildflower. Other than a sea of yellow flowers against the grey limestone, the preserve did not hold much interest for me.

Getting back in my car, I continued my drive around the eastern tip of the peninsula on East Harbor Road into Marblehead but could not find a parking place in that vacation mecca on a Saturday afternoon in summer. As I continued driving, I found myself in Lakeside, speculating where the Mervaises' vacation home might be located.

The homes were large and impressive, representing a wealthy segment of the Ohio population, once again reminding me that Keir's socio-economic status greatly exceeded my own. I thought I would intuitively know the house but nothing specifically jumped out at me. As I neared the posh and gated community of Quarry Lake Resort and Golf Club, I relinquished my search and turned left onto South Bayshore Road, returning to Sandusky and the Cedar Palace Hotel, where I spent a wistful hour visiting a fine craft gallery near the hotel. Since retail sales were in a slump, sadly, at the end of July my partners had decided to close our Collectors Gallery in Columbus, selling everything down to the bare walls and equally dividing the rest.

At the closing reception that evening, I still had not heard anything more about Keir other than what Eric told me the previous day in the pool, so I approached Harry and Martha Whitfield. After all, if Keir and Abigail were in Lakeside this weekend, I reasoned, would not the Whitfields have gone to visit them?

"Did you have a pleasant afternoon?" I asked Harry and Martha.

"Yes, we went to the Marblehead Lighthouse and then to the East Harbor State Park," Martha replied. With no mention of Keir or Abigail, I tried a more direct approach.

"Have you seen Keir lately?" I asked Harry.

"Not recently," Harry admitted, "but I plan to call him soon." Martha shot him a sideways glance like only a wife can do.

"You'd better go *see* him," Martha insisted. I got the feeling Harry wished to avoid the reality and tragedy of the deteriorating health of his former colleague and long-time friend. I sought to lighten the mood a little while still fishing for more information about Keir.

"I remember, Harry, when you took us on that hike at Deerwood Lake Lodge on Friday afternoon —'The Plummet' I think they called it. We had stopped because that heavyset woman had hurt her knee. We were all sweaty, dirty, and tired when Keir and Abigail came along from the opposite direction, looking so fresh in contrast to us, but at least we knew we were near the end of the hike." Harry and Martha smiled at the memory. "Harry, when you hear how Keir is doing, will you let me know, please?" He shook his head in agreement.

Once the reception had ended and the sun had set, making for cooler air and a more pleasant evening, my co-worker Jennifer and I went to find a restaurant. Following the scorching heat of the day, the entire populace appeared to be out strolling along the Sandusky waterfront. After we ate, Jennifer and I ambled up toward the Cedar Point Causeway. We could hear the clack-and-whoosh of the roller coasters and the screams of delight of their riders in the distance. We walked out past the last dock to a point where there was some space to lean on the wooden railing.

The night was clear and star-studded and the breeze from the lake into Sandusky Bay was refreshing after the blistering heat of the day. Marine scents wafted our way while seagulls squawked above us. I turned toward what I thought was the direction of Lakeside and raised a silent prayer to the heavens:

"Oh, Lord, I have fretted and worried so much about Keir. But I can't do it anymore. You have to take care of him for me."

"Oh, look! A shooting star!" Jennifer excitedly pointed toward the sky over the Marblehead Peninsula. I knew in my heart that my prayer had been received, taken under advisement and, somehow, written into the Book of Prayers for God's consideration. After lingering a few moments longer, Jennifer and I then walked back to the hotel.

Driving back to Columbus on Sunday morning with Jennifer, I suddenly felt a sharp adrenaline slug in my stomach, and I knew my prayer had been delivered to God and been accepted. I looked at my watch: 10:45 a.m. I wondered if Keir was attending church at that moment.

One early September evening Keir stood in the large family room next to the built-in entertainment center staring out of the rear window of his house. He had just put on some soft music he had selected from the shelves containing an extensive collection of compact disks and videotapes, an expensive stereo system, and a large television set. The family room was sizeable, accommodating several overstuffed couches and four large tables on which were placed a scattering of coffee table books, novels, newspapers, and magazines. On the facing wall hung a larger-than-life-size oil painting of Sean, Keir's and Abigail's only son, playing with his wooden Brio train set. Underneath the painting were several shelves with a black telephone extension, paperbacks, a phone directory, and several knick-knacks.

The rear window stretched the entire width of the family room and was covered with mini-blinds. During the daytime, one could glimpse the professionally manicured back lawn and garden sloping down to a small creek. But tonight, even though the blinds were open, dusk was falling so it was almost too dark to see past the grove of trees that afforded protection from prying neighbors' eyes.

Abigail was stretched out on one couch reading. She and Keir had been married nineteen years, and a quiet comfort marked most of their time together. Since they were both attorneys involved in different sorts of practices, it was not uncommon for them to spend weekday evenings deep in thought or involved in paperwork without much conversation. They saved their playtime for the weekends, escaping to their second home in Lakeside, the peninsula jutting out into Lake Erie above Sandusky.

But this had been a long eighteen months for them—first the blackouts and sudden falling, the shock of the diagnosis, surgery, radiation, and finally the chemo treatments with their awful side effects, which, at least for the time being, were over. The tumor was stable. The doctors were cautiously optimistic.

Abigail had been a trooper; she had stood by him on this arduous and uncertain journey and had carried the burden of being the sole breadwinner, caring for both Keir and Sean, waiting helplessly through the hospital tests, surgery, MRIs, and chemotherapy. Occasionally, they had discussed what she would do if... He really owed her his life.

Keir thought about the letters Annie had sent him and the plaque. He had been very touched by the Honorary Membership. He did not think he deserved it. He was even surprised that Gordon had had anything to do with it, but he suspected Annie had been the driving force behind it.

Annie.

Several months had passed since Keir had gotten a letter from Annie. The last one in the spring told him she was coming to Cleveland and asked whether he would like her to visit him. She had even enclosed a postcard where he could mark Yes or No. But the real answer was Yes and No. Perhaps it was better to leave things as they were...

So much had changed since the last time they saw each other or even spoke on the phone. The treatments had taken their toll; he had lost a lot of weight as well as his hair, and he often felt tired and weak. Now the steroid treatments, although restoring him to a more normal weight, were causing other side effects, while the radiation and chemo were beginning to destroy the good cells as well. Besides, he had resolved, all those years earlier when Suzanne had married in the Amasa Stone Chapel, not to fall prey to that type of love again.

"What's wrong?" From the sofa on the other side of the room, Abigail's slightly apprehensive voice pierced Keir's stream of consciousness. So as to appear somewhat nonchalant, Abigail inquired of her husband without looking up from her reading.

Startled from his contemplation—caught in the act of daydreaming about Annie—Keir straightened up and looked over at his reclining wife in an attempt to ascertain how much she had divined. Reassured that her question was more general than specific, he picked up a nearby magazine and leafed through it absent-mindedly.

"Oh, nothing. I was just thinking," he said off-handedly. It was not *really* a lie. He had been thinking.

Of Annie...

He looked over at Abigail again. She seemed satisfied with his response. She had learned long ago not to probe uninvited into those moments when Keir was contemplating his illness, how much life he might have left, and how the family might cope without him.

The music had stopped. Keir walked over to the stereo, selected another CD, and placed it into the round slot to play. His mind returned to Annie and the way she had looked at him at the last OAHIA convention he had attended at Deerwood Lake Lodge.

On September 11th, the United States was devastated by terror attacks on the World Trade Center Towers in New York City, the Pentagon south of Washington, and on Flight 93 near Pittsburgh. At AEMG, two workers that

I supervised had caught the news after the first airplane hit the first Tower, and together we watched on our conference room television, frozen in horror-stricken astonishment, as the second plane hit.

Before I married Auguste, I had lived in New Jersey and worked in lower Manhattan, taking the PATH train daily into the bottom of the World Trade Center before ascending the escalators to the street to walk to my office. I had also interviewed for a job with Merrill Lynch in their office that had occupied an entire floor—a huge office stretching the length and width of one of the Towers. In addition, I had stood on the roof as a sightseer and eaten in the Windows on the World restaurant.

In the conference room, I was the first one among the gathering number of staff members to comprehend the extent of devastation that was about to occur as the top corner of the first Tower began to crumble, composting the people, desks, chairs, papers, file cabinets, girders, cement, electric wiring, plumbing, carpet, and dry wall, as explosions rocked the buildings causing black smoke and flames to burst forth from the double infernos. Tiny dots—people—leapt from the burning floors to their certain deaths on the stone plaza below. I began to sob uncontrollably. One female staff member pulled me onto her lap and rocked me until I could stop crying. Bystanders began to run from the crumbling Towers and the choking dust that rolled forth like a dustbowl storm to fill the surrounding streets. Newscasters described the scene in panic as reports of the Pentagon attack and later, Flight 93 came in. I could not watch any more.

We had five of our six executive managers and Jack Spencer out of the office that day. Two were in Chicago stuck on a plane grounded on the tarmac. One was in Bermuda at the end of a convention but stranded without any flights out. One was visiting his native Poland and was rounded up by the police for questioning but was later released. One had just arrived in Toronto to start a conference there, but half of the speakers and attendees had not arrived. Jack was in our Mansfield parent company headquarters. I was the senior staff member and had to pull myself together as the "morale officer."

I walked around the office to see how people were faring. The most serious chaos was in our travel agency. During the last round of layoffs we had reduced the travel staff to one agent. Now, she was trying to handle all the calls from travelers to the Toronto conference and figure out alternative travel plans or refunds. The accounting staff joined her to help field the calls and organize the paperwork. Invoices and tickets were strewn all over the floor amongst newly wired telephones as we recruited more staff to answer the phones. When it looked like that situation was under control, I went back to my office to try, unsuccessfully, to concentrate on work.

I received a phone call from a former co-worker and fellow New Jersey native. She lived alone, and having grown up across the Hudson River from the World Trade Towers, she needed to talk to someone. I realized that my coaching skills would be more useful that day than my association management skills.

Another co-worker showed up in my door way.

"Are you okay?" I asked.

"My brother works in Lower Manhattan," she said quietly. "No one in his family has heard from him."

"I'm sure he will be all right," I reassured her with a hug, lying hopefully.

I remembered that Keir might be home alone, too. I wondered if he had been watching the television and knew.

The next day, Jack Spencer came back to the office, and I encouraged him to hold a staff meeting to let everyone know the whereabouts of our staff members out of the office. We had been able to make contact with everyone by phone or email. One of the staff members in Chicago ended up in the hospital with an emergency appendectomy, but the other one had rented a car to drive home. While we were in the conference room for the staff meeting, President George W. Bush made his first post 9/11 speech. We all watched together on the same television that had revealed the horrible events the day before.

I do not know whether it was the preoccupation with the thousands of casualties on September 11th, but on September 30th I had a dream about Keir. Several months had passed since my last dream of him, all of which ended up with my waking and thinking, "That's *not* what he looks like anymore, but I don't *know* what he looks like now!"

In the dream, we were in the Bahamas. There was a long street lined with rainbow-colored buildings, at the end of which was a bank. In the bank were two rows of chairs back-to-back, like airport terminal seats. I sat in one chair with my back to the tellers. Keir was on the other side in a persimmon-colored, short-sleeved, cotton, sport shirt (not peach, not rose, not red, not orange, but persimmon; I later saw a shirt in that exact color at a J. Crew store). His shirt was uncharacteristically unbuttoned, revealing a white, sleeveless tee-shirt underneath. Keir took off the persimmon shirt, folded it in half lengthwise, left it on the back of one of the double-sided chairs, and then departed. For safekeeping, I took the shirt and draped it across my lap, folding my hands on top of it to await his return. I fell asleep in the chair, waking to feel Keir gently attempting to pull his shirt out from under my hands without disturbing my slumber. I was afraid to open my eyes—afraid to look up into his beautiful eyes and also afraid to look up in case he would vanish like the time in the Cedar Place Hotel foyer. Was this how he had come to say goodbye to me? Had he *died*?

I had a small card that I had bought for Keir and had held onto for a year because I had been afraid to send it to him. It consisted of three panels. On the front was written, *"Today you were in my thoughts"*; on the next panel it said, *"As you have been in days past"*; and on the inside, *"And you will be in days future"*. I felt I no longer had anything to lose. At first I was just going to send the card anonymously. But then I decided to type up and enclose the priestly benediction from synagogue services—a blessing I also knew from my childhood church services:

"May the Lord bless you and keep you. May the Lord make his face to shine upon you and be gracious unto you. May the Lord lift up his countenance upon you and give you peace."

At the last moment, I wrote across the top of the slip of paper with the benediction, "When there is nothing more you cpottean do for a friend, you can still pray." I did not sign it. The only identifying marks were my handwriting above the prayer and the Columbus postmark. I mailed it to Keir in mid-October. It had been over a year since I last talked to him. (After mailing it I realized, if he were already dead, the card would not be returned to me because I had not put a return address on the envelope.)

Due to Jack Spencer's contacts in the medical field and one of our already existing association clients, AEMG was awarded a major cardiology meeting hosted by the Cleveland Clinic on Mackinac Island, Michigan, for the following June. Since I did not have a national client to replace NIRS which had left at the end of 2000, Jack Spencer assigned me the task of organizing the scientific meeting that included major pharmaceutical sponsors, exhibits, a golf tournament, several food-and-beverage social functions, and five days of continuing education medical sessions. The meeting was scheduled immediately prior to another national convention for one of Jack's clients at The BroAdmoor for which I was also responsible. I would be away from home for ten days straight and finalizing aspects for the second convention while attending the one prior to it. To make my absence more palatable, I was encouraged to bring Auguste and Mireille along to the Mackinac meeting since we could make the drive in one day, but leave them home for The BroAdmoor trip that required air travel.

When I first began working at AEMG in 1985, we had a law student intern, Christine Morrow, who worked on government relations projects with David Fisher. With my therapist's words, "You know what to do," still ringing in my head, I looked up divorce attorneys in the phone book and found two familiar names: Christine Morrow and Allen Sayres, who had been a speaker at the 1994 OHIA convention. I consulted Christine first. She asked me a variety of questions, including, "How many friends does Auguste have?"

"Not many."

"How many friends do you have?"

"Lots!"

"If anyone needs a divorce, it's you." Chris explained how joint custody worked and even suggested that Auguste and I could alternate our own living arrangements rather than shuttling Mireille back and forth.

I was not sure. I did not know how a divorce would work logistically and financially, and I did not want to disrupt Mireille's life. By the time I sat in Allen Sayres' office the day before Thanksgiving, I realized that I did *not* want a divorce. Rather, I wanted an "extraordinary marriage." But how could Auguste and I get from where we were to that point? My solution was to register for another personal development course—this one focusing on love, generosity, and forgiveness, over a weekend in mid-

December in Mansfield. I would stay at the home of OAHIA President Alicia Tomlinson and her husband, Steven. Nicknamed "The Love Course," the program took place all day Saturday and Sunday with a completion evening on Thursday.

I made arrangements with my Cleveland Clinic contact, Adele Waters, to meet her at The Grand Hotel on Mackinac Island for a site visit on Wednesday following the weekend of my Love course, flying to Cleveland Hopkins Airport on Thursday. I asked Mark Thomas to pick me up at the Cleveland airport on Thursday afternoon and drive me back to Mansfield for the Love course finale, and my coach, Hillary, to drive me to the Columbus airport so that I could retrieve my car after the Thursday evening session was over.

At one point during 2000, I had explained to my potter friend and former AEMG co-worker, Marilyn Fields, my desire to see Keir again and the complete absence of communication. She suggested I drive to Cleveland, knock on his door, and tell him, "I'm not leaving until I speak to you!"

"I can't do that," I protested, "He's *ill!*"

One of the exercises in the Love course is to list all the people in our lives with whom we have "incompletions." In addition to most of my family members and some friends, Keir kept appearing on my list. On Sunday afternoon, we were assigned to do a paired-share role play with the person in the course sitting next to us. We were to play the role of someone for whom our Love course partner felt that love and/or relatedness was missing. Molly Abbott was my partner, so I asked her to assume the role of Keir should I show up at his door unexpectedly. Molly's responses demonstrated to me that my assumption that Keir did not wish to see me again was not necessarily true.

On Tuesday evening before I left for Mackinac Island, and under the influence of the love-generosity-and-forgiveness distinctions of the Love course weekend, I pulled my courage together and asked Auguste if we could talk.

"About what?" he asked, his eyebrows knitted together suspiciously.

"About us," I responded non-confrontationally. I could tell he was definitely curious.

"Last year when you said to me, 'Don't let the door hit you on your ass on the way out,' I fell out of love with you at that moment. In the past six months, I've been through therapy and have seen two divorce attorneys, but I realized I don't really want a divorce. I want an extraordinary marriage."

"I want that, too."

"Then, would you be willing to do the Level I Course?"

"No."

"Would you be willing to go to a therapist to address your anger and need to control people?"

306

"Yes."

Hopeful that we could work out our marital issues, I flew out on Wednesday to meet Adele Waters at The Grand Hotel on Mackinac Island to tour the conference space and begin planning for the June Cleveland Clinic scientific sessions. During our site visit, Adele suggested that I come to Cleveland in January and meet her boss, Dr. Schuster, the cardiologist who was responsible for the June scientific sessions.

When I arrived from Mackinac Island into Cleveland Hopkins airport several minutes early on Thursday, while waiting in baggage claim, I used a pay phone to call Keir's home. Perhaps, if he was avoiding my home and work caller IDs, the pay phone number would be different. There was no answer. I fetched my suitcase from the baggage carousel and went to meet Mark Thomas.

Ever since I had spoken to Mark about the Honorary Membership for Keir eleven months earlier, I felt I owed him a more substantial explanation for the times I had called him and cried on the phone to him, but on each occasion during the year when I had gone to Mansfield, Mark had been unable to meet with me in person. Finally, we had this drive alone together in his car. Mark was the only male I knew who was acquainted with Keir and the health insurance legal industry and with whom I could safely confide.

During the drive, after I requested attorney-client confidentiality, I related to Mark the message from God and summarized the significant events in my relationship with Keir: the "eye-drowning" instances at the Sandpiper Suites with Abigail nearby and at the Manor Grove Inn; Keir's breakdown around the news of his mother's cancer diagnosis and our walk to the Insurance Department together; his arm around my waist twice with the "You look GREAT!" and "You're the most beautiful woman in the room" comments; Sylvia's assessment of that interaction; and finally, our last two, "love-filled," phone conversations followed by over a year of silence.

"I don't know if Keir is alive or dead now, but I would be willing to give up the romantic part if I could just be his friend and in his life again," I vowed to Mark.

"If Keir were already dead, I suspect we would have heard about it by now. I think you need to develop a relationship with Keir outside of the health insurance legal field."

I was relieved and reassured that Mark, as a married man himself, did not scold me for infidelity, misbehaving, or breaking the Tenth Commandment but instead actually gave me permission to pursue some type of continued, supportive relationship with Keir. Neither did Mark lightly dismiss Keir's past behavior towards me as merely inconsequential flirtation; he saw something deeper at play. After dropping me off at the hotel where the final evening of the Love course was taking place, Mark went on to a holiday party with his attorney colleagues in the Richland Bar Association.

307

A few days later, Adele Waters emailed me to make arrangements for my visit to the Cleveland Cardiology Clinic to meet Dr. Schuster on Tuesday, January 22nd, at eleven o'clock. I looked up the directions on the internet mapping service and recognized the neighborhood and street names from my previous trips to University Circle. I typed Keir's home address into the direction box and found it was less than one-and-a-half miles away. I could scarcely believe it—this was the business trip to Cleveland that I had been hoping and waiting for—but how was I going to find out if Keir would let me, or even want me, to visit him? He had not returned the postcard last May, he had not answered any of my phone calls to his home, and I was not even sure he was still alive or even well enough to receive visitors.

I had waited over five years to see Keir again. There was only one person who would definitely know Keir's condition—Abigail. I would have to call her, but when? It was almost Christmas; the family might go away for the holidays if Keir was well enough. Abigail was a busy attorney—as Keir told me on several occasions—and now she had his illness and related disabilities to handle on top of all her other personal and professional obligations. And what would I say to her if she answered the phone? How would I explain who I was and my reason for calling? What if they really wanted me to stop pestering them? What if Keir had died several months ago, and my call would be an intrusion on her grief?

Maybe this was not such a good idea. Maybe Keir was in the hospital with tubes in him. Maybe I was the last person he wanted to see. Maybe it did not really matter. "But you promised him!" my conscience reminded me. "You told him in August 2000 that if you ever got up to Cleveland, you would visit him." How could I fulfill that promise if I did not attempt to contact Abigail? In the end, I knew I would regret it for the rest of my life if I did not at least try.

"What would I do if I was not afraid?" I would call Abigail.

Ohio, 2002

REDEMPTION

After all my rumination, I settled on January 2nd as the best evening to phone. If the Mervais family had been away for the holidays, they would have to return home for Sean to go back to school. The day after New Year's Day would likely be prior to any extracurricular evening activities gearing up again, and Abigail would likely be home from work. I would need to call after supper but before Sean's bedtime, between 7:00 and 7:30 in the evening.

What would I say if Abigail answered the phone? If Keir answered? If Sean answered? If no one answered and I got the answering machine again? For the last two weeks of December, I mentally rehearsed my opening sentences like variant scripts. I had one version if Abigail said, "I'm sorry, my husband died..." and another one for, "I'm sorry, Keir is in the hospital..." as well as one if Keir said, "I'm sorry, but I really don't want to see you."

As January second approached, a serious snowstorm was forecast. "Good!" I told myself. "Even more reason for Abigail to stay home." I had not spoken to her in fifteen years. I was not sure she even remembered who I was, and if she did, might it be because she wished me to stop harassing her husband with letters and phone calls?

At seven o'clock on January 2nd, Auguste went into our bathroom to take his shower, and Mireille watched a "Seinfeld" rerun on television. I finished tidying up the dinner dishes and put them into the dishwasher. I would have only a short period of time to make the call before Auguste came out of his shower. I began to panic with all the "what ifs" running through my head. I pulled the phone number out of my address book. This was it—now or never.

I picked up the receiver on the bedroom phone and sat on the edge of the bed. I dialed the Mervaises' phone number. It rang once. Twice. "Pick up the phone, Abigail," my mind pleaded. Third ring. "Pick up the PHONE!" Fourth ring. The little voice in my head realized, "It's going to the answer machine. Get *that* script ready."

"Hello?" a female voice answered.

My mind raced. ("Oh, *new* script...and say 'Abigail' with all the friendly warmth you can muster to let her know you are *not* a telemarketer!")

"Abigail...?" I managed to say out loud.

"Yes...?"

"I'm a former business associate of Keir's, and I haven't heard for a while how he is, so I called to see how he was doing." Whew! I had gotten it all out without stuttering or fumbling.

"He's okkaaaaayyyy..." she said in a monotone. (My mind rejoiced, "He's not *dead*! I'm not too late!") "...but he won't be going back to work anytime soon." ("Don't you get it, woman? He's still alive!") "Would you like to speak with him? He's right here." ("Speak to him?!?! You mean he can come to the phone? He's not in the hospital?")

"Sure," I said.

"Keir?" Abigail called him to the phone. In the pause, I started to panic about what Keir's reaction might be. Would he even remember who I was?

"Yes?" I heard his voice for the first time in a very long, year-and-a-half. A remarkable sense of relief washed over me, and I felt everything was going to be okay. I started to breathe again. "Hello?"

"Hello, Keir. This is Annie Weber..."

"How *are* you? How's Mireille? How's Auguste? How is your gallery?" Not only did he seem genuinely pleased to hear from me—and I had not made a complete fool out of myself with my letters—but he also remembered our last conversations and the content of those letters despite what had happened to his body and brain in the interim.

"We are all fine, but we closed the gallery last summer, prior to the events of 9/11. But, more importantly, how are *you*?"

"My tumor has been stable for some time now, but I've developed a necrosis that has created stroke-like symptoms on my left side, impairing my walking and some of my sight." His explanation seemed matter-of-fact, like it was no big deal.

"Keir, I will be coming to Cleveland to meet with a new client at the Cleveland Cardiology Clinic in a few weeks. I promised you before, if I had a trip to Cleveland I would come visit you. Would you like me to visit you...?"

"I *would* like that, but I need to check my calendar for doctor appointments and physical therapy sessions. Please hold on."

As I waited for him to retrieve his calendar, Auguste emerged from the bathroom and gave me a withering look as though to say, "Are you on the phone *again*?" I waved Auguste away in annoyance; every fiber of my being knew I was on the phone call *of my life*.

As the theme music from "Everybody Loves Raymond" filtered into our bedroom, I realized that "Seinfeld" had ended in the other room.

When Keir returned to the phone I attempted to eliminate the irritation I felt with Auguste from my voice.

"I don't do well with numbers, dates, and writing any more," Keir warned me in a light-hearted tone, "so please be patient with me." I waited while Keir struggled to get the January 22nd date right on his calendar. "I'm sorry you had to close the gallery—you enjoyed it so much."

"I now have another artistic outlet that I will tell you about when I see you on the 22nd." Keir seemed amused at my strategy to bait him in that flirtatious manner. ("A girl has got to have a hook," I rationalized.)

After we hung up, I joined Mireille in the living room in front of the television. I was relieved that we were watching a comedy because I was so giddy I laughed much harder than normal.

My prayers had been answered. Keir had been given a prognosis of two years to live and time was fast running out, but his tumor was stable. He wanted me to visit him. After over five years of waiting, I was finally going to see him again. This was indeed a miracle!

The next morning, we awoke to twenty-eight inches of snow and no school or work. Early the following week, Adele Waters sent me an email that Dr. Schuster had to postpone our January 22nd meeting until February 25th. I was dashed! "I will have to call Keir again to let him know of the change, but it was so difficult for him to make the appointment in the first place. Besides, I do not want to disappoint him, too." The new date was more than a month away, and Keir's biological clock was ticking; two years would soon be up.

After ruminating for a couple of days, I came up with the idea to offer Keir a compromise visit. Even if we could not visit in person yet, maybe we could at least visit by phone some more. I called Keir on January 11th and explained the change in plans, suggesting we hold a phone visit on January 21st, Martin Luther King Day. I would have the day off, and even though our respective children would be out of school, our spouses would be working. Keir explained that Sean had a nanny to supervise him. We agreed I would call Keir at nine o'clock on the morning of January 21st.

At the appointed time, Mireille was watching cartoons. With a combination of apprehension and excitement, I went upstairs to call the Mervais residence. I was surprised when Abigail answered because I thought she would already be on her way to work.

"Keir and I had set up an appointment for me to call him now," I explained.

"He's started yoga lessons. He probably forgot."

I did not know exactly what to do, but my brain suddenly prompted me to "get related," a concept from my professional development courses. Abigail was the "gatekeeper." For me to be able to continue to communicate with Keir, I would need to have Abigail on my side.

"My heart goes out to you," I said genuinely.

"What?"

"My heart goes out to you...for what your family has been through."

"Oh." Abigail seemed not quite sure how to take me.

"Do you remember who I am?" I wondered if she recalled meeting me either at the Sandpiper Suites in 1987 or at the Deerwood Lake Lodge in 1988.

"Something about a plaque...?" Abigail recalled vaguely. I figured she was referring to the Honorary Membership and surmised I no longer needed to be concerned about a cease-and-desist letter from her. "Do you realize your caller ID says 'Unknown' like a telemarketer?" she added hesitantly.

"No," I admitted. (The little voice in my head noted, "That would explain why my earlier calls had not been answered. I will have to fix that with the phone company.")

"Keir should be home by 10:30. You could try him then." I got the sense that she planned to leave for work before then.

"Would you please tell anyone who might answer the phone that I will call again at 10:30 and my caller ID says 'Unknown'?" She agreed.

Since Keir's speech pattern had slowed, I noticed that when I had spoken with him on previous occasions, I had a tendency to interrupt. I decided to create this call more like a coaching call. I chose my potentiality and "place to come from" as Gently Being With and Listening Fully. I made a short agenda of items I definitely wanted to discuss as well as a few more topics that were optional.

At 10:30 I called again—more nervous now because of my earlier failed attempt. A woman answered—the nanny, I assumed—who put Keir on.

"I'm sorry I missed your call earlier, Annie. I started a yoga class this morning. I am also doing water exercises at the Y."

"Abigail told me about the yoga class." Remembering her shy reluctance with me on the phone in contrast to Keir's own out-going personality, I probed lightly, "Is she the introvert in the family?"

Keir hesitated. I imagined him looking around to see if anyone was in earshot, even though no one else could have possibly heard my question.

"Yes," he replied quietly.

I thought it must be hard for him--naturally outgoing and friendly—to be so restricted now in his social activities while his more timid wife needed to be forthright in dealing with the medical community and the necessary legions of helpers.

"You were going to tell me what you are doing since closing the gallery," Keir changed the focus of our conversation.

"One of my half-cousins has been doing a considerable amount of genealogical research on the internet and found out that my great-great uncle on my mother's side of the family was a British Impressionist painter and my parents own two of his works. My mother and I are seeking an art conservator and researching auction prices to determine the value of the paintings. We took the pieces to the Columbus Museum of Art, and the curators who saw them were quite excited, suggesting we work with the art librarian there to find auction records. Since 1972, when the online auction records started, sixty-eight of his paintings have been sold. My half-cousin also found a website about him maintained by his grandson."

"That sounds like a great project. Can you email me a copy of the pictures? I'd like to see them."

"What's your email address?"

"It's kfootball@yahoo.com. I grew up in Canton where the Football Hall of Fame is. I never learned to type, so I can't reply by email, but someone can print out my messages. How's Auguste?" Keir and I always seemed to conduct this litany when we spoke with each other—sort of a boundary-setting reminder: "How's Abigail?" "How's Auguste? How's Mireille?" "How's Sean?"

"Last November, after Auguste said something mean to me, I told him, 'If you don't stop treating me this way, I'm going to leave,' and he replied, 'Don't let the door hit your ass on the way out!'"

"Uh-oh!"

"In the spring I went to a therapist and then to two divorce attorneys in the fall. Do you remember Allen Somers who spoke at the 1994 OAHIA convention at the Manor Grove Inn?"

"Yes, he was *very* funny."

"He was one of the divorce attorneys I visited. I was sitting in his office on the day before Thanksgiving when I realized, 'I don't want a divorce; I want an *extraordinary marriage!*'"

My purpose in confessing all this to Keir was so he would be reassured that, in my coming back into his life, rather than being in pursuit of him, I was still committed to working out my own marital issues.

"You don't want to settle..." Keir's tone of voice struck me like he was someone familiar with the experience of settling. (Meanwhile, the voice in my head protested: "If I can't have you, then I have *already* settled.")

"In mid-December Auguste and I talked about it, and he agreed to see a therapist." I switched the conversational focus. "What have you learned about life in the past two years since you've been ill?" Keir had always had a wonderful intelligence, so I expected some Buddha-like, enlightened, pronouncement from him.

"How caring and compassionate people can be...Like you sent me *all* those letters." He hesitated, gathering his thoughts. "I couldn't respond..." I could understand there was a physiological reason for his lack of response, his difficulty with writing and sequencing, but now I also sensed an emotional one, too. "I've had to learn to put the past behind me," he finished.

"I'm sure it is hard to stay positive..."

"My Cajun-Scottish background helps. We're a high-spirited sort."

"Does Sean have the Disney video, *The Lion King*?"

"Of course!" (I would later learn Keir had traveled to Africa.)

"Do you remember the part where Pumba, the warthog, says to Simba, 'You have to put your behind in your past'?" Keir chuckled softly. My heart gladdened to know I had made him laugh.

"I had forgotten about that!"

I suddenly heard some commotion in the background of the phone. "Hold on a second," Keir requested. Then I heard him say, "Why don't you boys go downstairs?" I imagined Sean and his friends were the disturbance. Keir returned his attention to the phone.

313

"I've been trying to walk regularly around the block in my neighborhood several days a week," I told him, shifting the conversation again while remembering Harry Whitfield telling me that Keir walked, too. "There is a large hill where I sometimes chant a Buddhist mantra in order to get up it."

"What's the mantra? I might know it. I've been to Nepal. That's a Buddhist country."

"When did you go to Nepal?" To me, Nepal was a very long way off and an exotic destination for a vacation. Was not Mt. Everest in Nepal?

There was a long silence on the other end of the phone as Keir struggled to answer my question. I immediately chided myself for asking him a question dealing with numbers.

"I don't remember. It was when I had a career crisis…sometime in the 1990s." Thinking back to his succession of jobs, I calculated it must have been between 1996 and 1999. Maybe when his father had died, he left an inheritance that Keir used for the trip?

"Am-Ni-Yah Ren-Gai-Kee-Yoh." Keir did not recognize my Buddhist mantra. "It's from that movie about Ike and Tina Turner, *What's Love Got To Do With It*? Tina became a Buddhist which eventually gave her the courage to split up with Ike."

We continued chatting for about fifteen more minutes, enjoying the sense of togetherness after a long separation. Similar to our two phone calls in August 2000 before Keir began chemotherapy, the sense of love and compatibility was palpable.

"My treatments have caused necrosis—the death of tissue surrounding the tumor—that is affecting the left side of my body. I will be going down to The Ohio State University Cancer Center for another opinion at the end of next week to see if I am a candidate for a clinical trial that Case Western does not currently offer."

"May I call you after that trip to see how things went?" I hoped to get his permission to continue our contact.

"Yes." A moment later he deliberately added, "I can feel the love." The voice in my head said "You had better, buster!" Nevertheless, I could tell he was fatigued.

"Good luck next week," I ended the call. We had talked for forty-eight minutes and had covered the items I had most wanted to discuss but not the optional ones. I called the phone company and straightened out my caller ID problem.

The weather during the two days when Keir and Abigail were scheduled to drive down to the OSU cancer center was cold and gray with a bleak, teeming, January rain.

"Lord, isn't it hard enough to make that two-and-a-half hour drive from Cleveland to Columbus without adding insult to injury by making it rain so hard?" my mind complained. I knew I should be grateful it was not snowy or icy. I prayed for their safe journey and wondered what a husband and wife talk about on such a journey when one of them is virtually under a death sentence. Do they keep it light and insignificant? Do they discuss burial and disposition of personal effects? Continued care and education of their child? Would Keir sleep most of the journey?

True to my promise, I called Keir on February 1st. A man answered.

"Keir?"

"No. I'll get him. He's right here." Keir picked up the phone.

"That was Tom, my personal secretary," Keir explained. I always figured Keir was relatively well off, but a nanny, a personal secretary, and a trip to Nepal gave me a greater sense of the socio-economic gap between us.

"How did your visit to OSU go?" My voice had a hopeful lilt.

"I don't match their criteria for the clinical trial. They had no new answers for me. They are keeping me on the steroids." Keir sounded a little discouraged. I hoped I could lift his spirits.

"My trip to the Cleveland Clinic has been rescheduled for Tuesday, February 25th. Would it be okay to visit you then?"

Keir must have covered the phone receiver because his voice was muffled.

"Tom, what do I have on the schedule for February 25th?" I could not make out the words of Tom's reply.

"That will be fine," Keir told me.

"Great! I'll call you a few days before when my schedule is firmer." We ended the call. I hoped Keir told Tom to write my visit on his calendar.

A fortnight later, I called again, but there was no answer, and I chose not to leave a message. That was a good choice because, a few days later, Adele Waters emailed me again that Dr. Schuster was postponing our meeting in Cleveland until March 6th. I called Keir a few days later and left a message on his answering machine that my trip had again been postponed. I wondered if I would ever get to Cleveland to see Keir. His two years had elapsed; he was now living on borrowed time.

In 2001 I had begun a co-coaching relationship with Carolyn Bigelow, a close friend I had met through the personal development seminars. She and her husband, Gary, often carpooled with me to the Monday evening seminars in Dublin. Carolyn had coached me on my 50th birthday trip to Disney World that year while I coached her about leaving a transportation coordinator job that she could no longer stomach to start a business as The Hobby Lady, a consultant to help people develop hobbies for stress relief.

In autumn 2001, Carolyn had been diagnosed with stomach cancer and began treatments. Surrounded by various teams from the personal development courses, Carolyn was supported with prayers, exercise, spiritual practice, food, transportation, flowers, and visits. We even had a "celebrate life" party during the snow and ice storm on January 6th that was also a send-off for her daughter to the Peace Corps in Guatemala. Carolyn entered a clinical trial in February and was making substantial progress. She

315

was also coaching me around the preparations for Mireille's *bat mitzvah*, making certain I was staying on top of invitations, catering, clothing, gifts, Hebrew practice, and writing my own speech. In turn, I served on her exercise and spiritual practice teams.

Since the tragic events of September 11, 2001, the travel and association businesses had experienced economic difficulties. While AEMG CEO Jack Spencer had made financial and client progress for our company, he had not yet been able to pull the management firm into the black. Jack was planning more layoffs, but this time, the choices were harder because, on the first round of layoffs he had kept only the best employees. Although I had been given a number of temporary assignments, a decent replacement for my former national client NIRS had not been found. Jack informed me that he would have to reduce my work hours from thirty per week down to twenty and eliminate paying for my health insurance through the company, effective March 1st. He encouraged me to pursue my coaching and art interests in my additional free time as potential sources of supplemental income.

Starting in mid-January, I began to experience a constant pain running from the base of my skull down to the middle of my back on the right side. I did not know if it was related to clenching my teeth from anxiety, the TMJ in my jaw, or any number of other stresses in my life. The doctor gave me a series of exercises and some muscle relaxants, but the pain did not subside.

On February 25th, I called Keir from my office, and Tom answered, but I was cut off while he was handing the phone to Keir. I called back immediately and got a busy signal twice. On the fourth attempt, I got the answer machine. On the fifth try, I got through.

"My meeting at the Cleveland Clinic is now scheduled for Wednesday, March 6th, if they don't postpone it again," I reminded Keir. I likely sounded a little flustered and annoyed by the phone trouble and postponements to my trip.

"We'll get there." His reassuring voice calmed me.

"I'll drive up in the morning for my eleven o'clock meeting and probably be done around 12:30 or 1:00."

"Okay. We could have some lunch or coffee."

Keir had not worked for over a year, and I was about to have my hours and paycheck cut, so I was not sure about having lunch; what was our protocol? Who was supposed to pick up the check?

In preparing my nine-year old Saturn for the trip to Cleveland, I went to a discount tire installer for new tires on Sunday, March 3rd. The manager told me my wheel drum ball bearing was dangerously loose on the car and needed immediate repair. Trying not to panic that my Cleveland trip would be postponed yet again, I was able to make an appointment at the Saturn dealership on Monday. The Saturn service manager reassured me that there was nothing wrong with the ball bearing, and my car was fine for the trip. I vacuumed out the interior and placed a new tissue box inside.

After checking with Adele Waters to re-confirm my meeting with Dr. Schuster the next day, I phoned Keir early Tuesday afternoon to confirm that he was still expecting me then as well.

"What time will you be coming? I have water exercise in the morning." He seemed nonchalant while I was apprehensive about our encounter and how he might act and look. I suspected the walk up his driveway would be the longest walk I might ever take.

"Around oneish. I'll call you when my meeting at the Cleveland Clinic is finished."

"That will be good."

The next morning dawned sunny and unseasonably mild for my drive to Cleveland. For several days, I had tried to figure out what to wear for meeting a new client at the Cleveland Clinic and visiting a male friend I had known professionally and whom I had not seen in nearly five-and-a-half years. I selected a business casual outfit of a navy blazer and navy Dockers with a new, lavender-striped, medium-blue, silk shirt and white pull-over sweater, adorned with a gold necklace and my special dichroic glass, blue-and-gold clip earrings that brought out the brown in my eyes. I carefully put on my makeup, some Jessica McClintock cologne (my favorite fragrance), a "healing" aromatherapy hand lotion, and was grateful that it was a good hair day.

"I will likely have supper on my return trip from Cleveland," I told Auguste. "Please remember to pick Mireille up after school." I headed out the door.

In the car, I switched on the radio and tried not to feel anxious, distracting myself with singing along with the popular tunes and going over the details of the Cleveland Clinic meeting later that summer. As I passed Mansfield, I thought about Mark Thomas and how he had encouraged me to forge a non-professional relationship with Keir.

I reached the Cleveland Clinic in good travel time and was pleased to find Adele Waters was dressed in a navy blazer and khakis, so my outfit was a slight cut nicer than, but in keeping with, hers. My meeting with Dr. Schuster only lasted thirty minutes, after which Adele and I went over a few more details for the June conference. When I was ready to leave her office at 12:45 p.m., I asked Adele if I could use the phone to make a local call. I dialed Keir's home, but he did not answer. I was not sure if it was the unfamiliar caller ID or if he had not yet come back home from his morning treatment. I left a message that I would call again a little later as perhaps he was running a bit late.

The sunny day held forth that bittersweet sense of the promise of almost, but not quite, spring. At 56 degrees, it was warm enough for me to shed the raincoat I had donned against the morning chill, but still just cold enough for me to be glad I had my pullover and suit jacket on. The bareness of the trees and beige dryness of the grass reminded me that winter was not over yet, but we could begin to hope for warmer days soon.

317

Returning to my car in the Cleveland Clinic parking deck, I quickly ate an apple and a package of Lanz crackers, washed down by some bottled water. I repaired my makeup and applied more hand lotion. Pulling out the driving directions I had printed from the internet, I headed out of the parking deck and made a right onto Euclid Avenue, hoping to find a pay phone in the next mile to Keir's house. I did not own a car phone (or cell phone, a device which was just beginning to become more widespread). Bearing right on Stearns and left onto Carnegie just before heading onto Cedar Glen Parkway, I realized that the area was largely academic and wooded, with no likelihood of a pay phone.

"God," I prayed, "you did not have me come *all* this way, within a mile of Keir's house, only for me not to see him. There has *got* to be a pay phone some place!" Just then, I noticed a vaguely familiar Sunoco station up ahead on Cedar Road as I entered Cleveland Heights. I pulled into the service station and an attendant approached as I got out of my car. I noticed there seemed to be an abundance of Mercedes-Benz, BMW, and Lexus cars parked on the street.

"Do you need some help?" the attendant asked.

"Do you have a pay phone I could use?" A little desperation rose in my voice.

"We don't have a *pay* phone, but we do have a phone you can use." I followed him inside the service booth where he pointed to a black phone hanging on the wall. I pulled Keir's phone number from my purse. I dialed 3-3-4-4-5-7-2. I heard a recording.

"You must use 10-digit dialing in this area. Please hang up and try your call again."

I looked at my watch. It was already 1:18, and I had not been able to reach Keir. I dialed again, including the area code this time: 2-1-6-3-3-4-4-5-7-2. The phone rang through this time. It rang again. Then again.

"Hello?" I heard Keir's familiar voice at the other end.

"Hi, Keir. It's Annie. I'm at the Sunoco Station on Cedar Road."

"Have you eaten?"

"I've had an apple." I refrained from mentioning the crackers.

"I've had an apple, too. We can get coffee, then."

"I should be there shortly."

"I'm waiting."

Turning right onto Cedar Road from the Sunoco station, I passed what appeared to be the commercial gateway to Cleveland Heights: a series of buildings in the stucco-and-half-timbered style of Tudor Revival, and then bore right onto Fairmount Boulevard. I was immediately awed by the stately and expensive manor homes on either side of the Boulevard. I knew I needed to backtrack to get to Keir's house but was not able to consult my written directions until I reached the stoplight at Fairmount Boulevard and Coventry Road. At the traffic light, I noticed a large, stone, Gothic Revival church, the Covenant-Coventry United Methodist Church. Its landmark, square bell tower rose majestically above the tree line.

"I wonder if that's Keir's church?" I thought. I consulted my map, noting the best way to get back to Keir's house, and turned right to drive south onto Coventry Road for two blocks, turned right onto Colchester Road, and headed back to North Park Boulevard.

Driving along the gently curving boulevard, I observed a park on the left that was beginning to show signs of budding and, on the right, a majestic assembly of custom-built homes in varied historic styles: Colonial Revival, Romanesque Revival, Georgian Revival, French Country Villa, and Tudor Revival. My art history education was immediately put to the test. I remembered having had a dream about Keir's house a week earlier and wondered if his home would be the white brick Georgian Revival with black shutters from my dream.

As I turned up Glencourt Drive, I saw a small historic marker noting the entrance to the National Trust Scottish Hills neighborhood. I made a left onto Findon and right onto Hawkins to number 2226. Rather than the traditional straight driveway I had imagined, the drive curved in a semicircle to the white stone porch of a red brick Colonial Revival with black shutters. As I pulled around to the front, I noticed a gold Lexus parked on the side of the house facing forward. I surmised that was Keir's car since he was no longer permitted to drive. I was embarrassed to park my nine-year-old Saturn in the front drive, thinking it should have more appropriately been left in the back at a servant's entrance.

Not as imposing as some of its neighbors on Fairmount, Keir's house was certainly far more elegant than those in my own neighborhood. Noting the size of his home, I expected it might take a few minutes for someone to answer the door, so after ringing the door bell, I waited on the porch and glanced around at the rest of the neighborhood.

The door was opened almost instantaneously. Keir threw his arms around me in an exuberant hug.

"You look *GREAT!*" he pronounced, pulling back as quickly as he had embraced me. I guessed he must have been waiting at a nearby window in order to see me before I saw him.

I quickly surveyed the middle-aged man standing before me. He was dapperly dressed in a black ball cap over his bald head, a charcoal grey cashmere turtleneck, and grey flannel slacks with a black belt. I had worried how his appearance might shock me. This was the man who, when he was healthy, could walk into the room and cause my heart to do a somersault in my chest and whose photo or printed name made my heart skip a beat. I knew he would be bald, but I had worried that he might look like a Holocaust victim after the radiation and chemotherapy treatments. Now, I was relieved that his body pretty much resembled how I remembered it— close to his former weight and with his broad shoulders and chest filling out his sweater—although perhaps slightly more puffy. After all, we were both middle-aged, I rationalized, and I was heavier than when he last saw me, too.

His face was slightly broader than I remembered, perhaps due to aging, to what was going on inside his skull, or to the steroids. To my surprise, he had a grown a thin moustache encircling his mouth that connected with a small beard. In all the phone calls we had had since January, he had never mentioned growing facial hair. If I had suddenly encountered him on the street, I would not have recognized him. It gave him a Bohemian flair.

"What is *THIS*?!?!" My forefinger reached up to touch the goatee on Keir's chin. I think he was even a bit amused that he had surprised me.

Keir stepped back to let me into the house, but almost as soon as I stepped over the threshold, he appeared nervous. From his demeanor, I surmised we were alone in his house. Somehow he had gotten rid of everyone—his personal secretary, Tom, the nanny, Abigail—and the old feelings of emotional chemistry began to resurface. I had come determined to visit as a friend, but I sensed that Keir was not sure he could trust himself alone with me. We needed to go somewhere public. I looked at him quizzically, trying to ascertain what he wanted me to do. Perhaps he was worried my perfume scent would linger in the air.

"Are you ready to go?" he asked. I turned to exit. "No. Wait. I want to show you something."

Turning, Keir led me across the hard wood floor of the foyer toward the back of the house. As I passed the dining room to my right, I noticed a large, honey oak table with seating for a dozen piled with several neat stacks of papers. ("I hope those are legal papers from Abigail's practice and not Keir's medical bills," I thought.) We passed the wooden staircase leading to the second floor and entered a sunlit family room. Five overstuffed sofas in an orange-and-beige striped pattern, interspersed with almost as many square, wooden, coffee tables covered in books and magazines, occupied much of the floor space. On the left wall was an entertainment center plus full shelving holding a television, a large collection of CDs, books, and videos. The right and back walls were lined with half-height shelves of books. Along the entire width of the room along the back wall, large windows illuminated the room; although covered in mini-blinds, the sun pouring into the room almost blinded me such that I could scarcely see outside.

"This is my favorite room. There is a small creek down there." Keir indicated the back garden.

I again looked at him to ascertain his meaning. I intuited that he wanted me to picture him in this room when I thought about him. At the same time my own thought process was studying Keir and asking, "Who is this man? Is this the same person I used to know?" I walked toward him, and he turned toward the front of the house, signaling it was time for us to leave.

Returning through the foyer, we exited the house. He locked the house door as I unlocked the passenger side door to my car. Keir slipped into the passenger seat. I indicated the shoulder seat belt.

"Is this thing going to decapitate me?" he joked. I was not sure whether I should tell him about the separate lap belt, and I certainly was not going to stretch it across his hips to fasten it for him like I did for my elderly mother-in-law. As I walked around to the driver's side, I promised myself to drive carefully so Keir would have no need for the lap belt.

"I saw Evonda recently." I wanted a safe topic to start our conversation as I slipped into my seat.

"She's a lovely woman. Please remember me to her. How is work?"

"Funny you should ask. I was cut back to twenty hours per week starting this week." At four hours a day, I had already used up this day's work hours and was now on my personal time.

I started the ignition and slowly began to drive out of Keir's driveway, stopping at the curb cut to the street. I had a moment of panic; would he know which way to go?

"Left or right?" I hoped my voice did not reflect my concern that the direction part of his brain might not be working.

"Oh, left. It's not far. Actually it's walking distance, but I can no longer walk that far." He was matter-of-fact. I did not wish to make him feel badly.

"I don't have my walking shoes on anyway." I had chosen a pair of shoes with two-inch heels to wear since I remembered Keir was a few inches taller than I. (Auguste was a few inches shorter, so I normally wore flats in his presence.) The truth was, however, I had thrown a pair of sneakers into my trunk in case Keir had wanted to walk.

At the next corner, Keir directed me to take a right onto Scottish Hills Lane and a left onto the northern end of Glencourt Drive.

"I drove in from the other direction," I remarked after seeing the Sunoco Station and realizing that Keir probably thought I was familiar with this entrance to his neighborhood. Across from the Sunoco was a Starbucks in one of the Germanic-looking Tudor Revival buildings I had seen earlier. Keir directed me into the parking lot behind it.

As we got out of my car, I locked both doors manually, and we started to walk toward the Starbucks entrance. I proceeded at my normal gait when I noticed Keir was not beside me. I stopped, turned, and returned to where he was slowly progressing forward. He limped slightly and accidently bumped into my right side.

"I'm sorry. I have a little trouble walking straight." I really did not mind him touching me. I wondered if I should offer him my arm but remembered this was his neighborhood Starbucks—they probably knew him and Abigail—it would be best not to enter arm-in-arm.

We passed some tables with patrons sitting outside in the sun enjoying their beverages. As we approached the entrance door, I wondered if he had the strength to open it. I stepped back slightly and lightly touched the small of his back with my finger tips to encourage him to go in first. Keir stepped back swiftly—whether to signal that he was a gentleman and

321

would open the door for me or as a reaction to the sensuality of my fingers touching him stealthily on a sensitive portion of his body.

Keir opened the door and stood back to let me enter first. The pungent smell of roasted coffee hit my nostrils while it took a moment for my eyes to get accustomed to the dark interior after the bright sunlight outdoors. We approached the counter to order.

"I'll have a tall Sumatra bold," Keir instructed the barista who then turned expectantly to me. I knew if Keir held the door for me, I had better let him buy my drink. I scanned the menu board behind and above the counter. Since I am not much of a coffee drinker, the Starbucks experience was not routine to me. I really did not want coffee. It felt like an eternity before I settled on a Tazoberry iced raspberry tea. From the corner of my eye, I saw Keir pull a twenty-dollar bill from his wallet. I mentally counted the $15.31 in change the girl returned to him to be sure she had not taken advantage of his illness and associated disabilities.

"Would you like to sit outside?" Keir motioned to the tables where customers were enjoying the mild weather at the café tables along the sidewalk. Peering out through the door, we noticed all the tables were already taken, so we turned back and surveyed the interior. We found a solitary table for two in an alcove beyond a glass-enclosed fireplace near the window.

I was still feeling a little disoriented by Keir's new look, especially the facial hair. I was determined to keep the tone as one of a professional friend but already there had been moments when something else was apparent beneath the surface of our demeanor. I wanted him to take the lead in selecting topics of conversation and to establish the tone of our meeting. I teased him a little about the potential health detriments of drinking strong, black coffee, but then relented after reminding myself that I should let him enjoy his small pleasures.

"Guess who I saw today?" Keir's eyes twinkled mischievously. I shook my head that I had no idea. "Peter Pascal!" I remembered that Peter was the founder of OAHIA and the only other Honorary Member living in Cleveland. I had heard that Peter had knee surgery recently. "I was doing my water exercise inside my roped off lane in the pool at the Y, and he was in the lane next to me. Every time we passed each other, he called me 'Byron.' Byron Watson is a British attorney we know who has a moustache and beard." I could tell Keir was trying to make light of the subject, but he knew I understood Peter's personality could be grating and that Peter's little joke about Byron got tiresome after the first or second time. I thought it ironic that OAHIA's only two Honorary Members (out of a total of four) in the Cleveland area were both doing water exercise in the same pool at the same time. Did Keir also feel badly that he could no longer work while Peter was still consulting in his retirement?

"What would you like to do next to make a contribution?" I led with a good coaching question to change the focus of our conversation.

"Abigail and I are on the advisory board of the Cleveland Clinic's Cancer Clinic. So many people have been helpful to us during this time that we wanted to give back." I remembered Keir's leadership skills and his sense of charity. "I think I'd like to work with seniors. Having spent time with my father in a nursing home, I would like to work someplace like that."

"I thought you would more likely be drawn to help young people."

"Children are too fast for me now." While not denying his disabilities, he touched ever so lightly on them. "I've been very lucky. I've had the best brain surgeon available. I've met some people whose surgery was badly done, and my surgeon was called in to try to repair the damage."

My own brain screamed: *"Surgery?!?!* Oh, NO! You mean someone cut inside that head—that mind that I loved so much to watch at work?" I noticed that Keir had not taken off his ball cap while inside, and now I surmised that it must cover the surgical scar. Had he not grown back his hair because he wore his baldness as a badge of honor and courage for other brain cancer survivors or because the new hair would not grow right over the scar? I noticed the embroidery on his cap for the first time, "The Merv Show," a play of words on his last name.

One of the coffee clerks came over to our table. I had forgotten anyone else was in the room.

"Pardon me, but may I close the blinds a little? The sun is in our eyes and blinding us." I wondered what the employees must think of us in our own little world in this corner. We shifted our chairs a little to allow the clerk to close the blinds.

After the clerk had walked out of earshot, Keir resumed.

"I'm sorry I could not respond to your letters."

"I assumed you were busy with your treatments and their side effects."

"Thank you for the plaque. It came at a good time." I could not ascertain whether he meant it arrived at a time when he was down and needed a psychological boost or when he was in a good place with his treatments and was able to appreciate it.

"I had wondered…" I replied simply. A bit of awkwardness set in again. "My friend Carolyn has been accepted for a clinical trial for her gastrointestinal cancer."

"I hope it works out for her. Those soft-tissue cancers can be tough." I thought Keir might be recalling his mother's own cancer battle. He shifted a little in his seat. "My family and I are planning a trip to the Grand Canyon this summer to go whitewater rafting. I've done that before, but Sean is now old enough to go along with us."

"Oh? That sounds like fun." I wondered how Keir would negotiate such a trip considering his current physical limitations. "When Greg Grisham was re-negotiating his contract with Buckeye Healthcare, Greg had told me in confidence that he might be leaving Buckeye. Since I am a close friend of Mark Thomas's—he did several personal development courses

323

with me—I tried to figure out how to warn Mark without betraying Greg's confidence since that change would affect Mark."

"I won't tell anyone," Keir wanted to reassure me he still abided by attorney-client confidentiality.

"That doesn't matter any more. Greg successfully re-negotiated the contract, so the subject is moot now. My point is that I had decided to warn Mark using a parable about rafting the Colorado River through the Grand Canyon that I got from a PBS show with Linda Ellerbee. I'll send you a copy of the parable."

"I'd like that." Keir smiled at me. "I'm glad Mark Thomas is your friend." I had not previously been sure they knew each other, but I was glad that Keir approved of Mark.

"Did you know that Kevin Raines died?" I was venturing into a more dangerous subject area since Kevin had died of brain cancer only a couple of months before Keir's own diagnosis with the disease. Keir nodded affirmatively. "He left behind three children under the age of five and a wife who did not work. They started a trust fund for his children's college education."

"I had heard Kevin passed away, but I did not know about his family." I could see tears forming in Keir's eyes. "Oh, these steroids make me prone to emotion."

I wondered if thinking of the likelihood of leaving Sean behind, not being there to watch him grow up, and being concerned for Sean's college education was mixed with sympathy for what Kevin had experienced in leaving three babies behind. Keir's attempt to dismiss his tears as steroid-induced failed with me because I knew how important his son was to him. He took a moment to re-compose himself.

"Please email me the address to contribute to the Raines' children's trust fund. It won't be much, but I'd like to make a donation." I was touched both by Keir's fatherly love and his generosity in spite of his own circumstances.

"I will." While still on the subject of children, I chose to change the focus to lighten the mood. "Did I tell you Mireille will make her *bat mitzvah* next month?" I could not remember if I had ever explained to Keir about my promise to Auguste to raise any children we had in the Jewish faith even though I had never converted to Judaism from my Christian-Methodist upbringing.

"Abigail and I recently attended the *bat mitzvah* of the daughter of one of her law partners. It was quite an event!" (I weighed in my mind whether I should invite Keir to Mireille's ceremony, but remembering it was a long drive for Abigail to make when she scarcely knew me, I dismissed the idea.) "In fact, that's how we hired Tom as my personal secretary. One night, Abigail and I went out for date night at a pizza restaurant—our friends insist that we go out at least once a week together while they take care of Sean—and we ran into her partner and his family. Their son, Tom, is going to enter law school next October. He helps me with my paperwork."

Keir glanced out of the window as though to collect his thoughts or find another topic for us to discuss, while I tried to imagine their date night conversation with Keir's health situation hanging over their marriage.

For the first time since I had arrived at his doorstep, I looked deeply into Keir's averted eyes. This time they were a light, transparent, sky blue with a small brown dot in his left iris—a freckle? A broken blood vessel?

I suddenly sensed Keir was disappointed that our conversation, and how we were being together, was not going along quite as he had hoped. But there was also something else unspoken. "This man has a *very deep* affection for me," my internal voice said, "but where it comes from, I don't know. However, if I don't change how I am acting right now, I am going to lose him. I have to get intimate and vulnerable somehow." The way to get intimate and vulnerable, I knew from my personal development training, was to reveal something deeply personal about one's self.

To regain Keir's attention, I reached out across the table and, with my pointer finger, touched his forearm which was lying across the table in front of his chest. I looked down to maintain the propriety of emotional distance.

"I have a story about myself that I am not good enough." I looked up again to gauge his reaction. "I want to thank you for not believing I was not good enough." I was specifically recalling his compliment seven years earlier that I was "the most beautiful woman in the room."

"I *never* thought you were not good enough." Keir glanced back at me then looked away again. "But I may have taken you...for granted..." He appeared to be searching for a more precise word which eluded him. Meanwhile, I was not sure what he had "taken for granted." Did he mean the compliment, the special services clause—my "lifetime contract," his forward behavior, or his lack of response to my letters?

I observed that Keir's hands were clasped together on top of the round table. His fingers were longer than I had remembered them to be. I noticed his gold watch and remembered the Native American bracelet he wore years ago. I had a sudden desire to put my hand on top of his in a reassuring and loving gesture, but I kept them respectfully in my lap.

"That's why I was thanking you for *not* thinking I wasn't good enough."

I looked at Keir, trying to reconcile this face that looked both familiar and different with the hair on his chin rather than on his head. I saw that one of his front teeth overlapped the other—a small defect in his formerly, orthodontic-perfect, smile. His voice sounded the same, the soft cadence like liquid velvet, only slower. His hand gestures were familiar. His thought pattern, the way he jumped through a maze of thoughts to his next articulation, leading me on a breathless mental chase, seemed almost the same. His eyes were still gorgeous, even though during our conversation he admitted to wearing contact lenses, now supplemented with the reading glasses hung around his neck because his vision was degenerating. All those pieces still fit, but I was still having a difficult time reconciling this image with the man I had known before. Did he sense this from me and was this also what he was regretting about how we were here together?

Keir suddenly stood up. "We have to go now. I've got someone picking me up soon for physical therapy." I did not see him consult his watch or a nearby clock. I glanced at my own watch. It was three o'clock. We had been talking in Starbucks for nearly an hour-and-a-half. We had never spent that much time alone together, and yet it had passed by too quickly.

At Keir's slower pace, we walked back to my parked car. When we neared it, I moved ahead to the passenger side to unlock and open the door for Keir. As I turned toward him, he stopped in the middle of the cement floor of the parking lot, confused as though he thought I expected him to be the driver before understanding that I was merely unlocking his door manually (a downside of an older, less expensive car without power locks). When Keir was again seated in the passenger seat (I still had not mentioned the lap belt) and I in the driver seat, we exited the parking lot.

"You cannot make a left back onto Glencourt from Cedar," Keir advised me, "so turn right onto Cedar, get in the right lane, and we'll go down Fairmount to the first right." I followed his directions and eased into the traffic.

"When things aren't going my way," I said. "I try to think of what's perfect about it. Like all the times this trip was postponed—it gave us an opportunity to get reacquainted by phone. I might have to come back to the Cleveland Clinic for another meeting in May or June. Do you want me to visit you again?"

"Sure." Keir seemed to be considering what I had said. "Turn left onto North Park Boulevard." As I shifted gears, I thought about how he could no longer drive himself and had the urge to grab his left hand and place it on top of the gear shift between us with my hand on top of his, just to allow him some sensation of driving. Up ahead we could see children exiting from the Park Elementary School. The streets were lined with school buses. I remembered it was a little after three o'clock. I slowed the car.

"Is that Sean's school?"

"No, he goes to school a few miles away." From the way Keir said it, I suspected that Sean attended a private academy. "We'll go another way. Turn right at the next corner." Halfway up the street we encountered a garbage truck blocking our forward progress. I stopped the car in idle.

I had a sudden, momentary, impulse to kidnap Keir and run away with him. I wanted to ask "How far is the Canadian border? Or maybe even the Mexican border?" I calculated that we probably had less than forty dollars in cash between us. We would have to use credit cards, and I suddenly remembered that story Keir had told at the Executive Committee meeting years ago about the attorney who faked his own death by drowning but gave himself away when he began to use his credit cards. What else could we discuss?

326

"OAHIA is having its 25th anniversary this year. I will soon be sending out letters to each of the past presidents requesting that they send me a remembrance from their term as president." I doubted Keir would be able to submit something in writing, so I figured he could tell me something verbally now that I could include for him. "Is there a highlight from your presidency that you'd like me to include?"

"I remember that crisis we had with the Insurance Department, but that was really during Liam's term..." Keir was visibly trying to recall some worthy event or legacy.

"How about writing the licensing exam for agents?" I prompted. Keir brightened at my suggestion.

"That's right! I liked developing the agent's exam for the Department of Insurance. As I recall, it took a lot of time and work, but I enjoyed it." His statement was straightforward and simple—and he seemed satisfied with its choice to mark his presidency. I noticed that he did not waste a lot time any more being wordy. I forced myself to memorize what he had said as I would need to write it down later.

Keir used his hand to brush the front of his grey turtleneck.

"After I got your message from the gas station, I decided to trim my beard before you came," he explained. I had not noticed the beard trimmings on his sweater, but I was touched by that gesture that he took the time to neaten up his appearance...that he wanted to look his best for me.

The garbage truck moved down the street. Keir indicated I should turn left onto Llewellyn Street. Mentally, I noted that had been my maternal grandfather's Welsh middle name. After a right turn onto Glencourt, a left onto Scottish Hills, and another left, we were back in Keir's driveway on Hawkins.

"My next door neighbor manages the Home Shows...." Keir reversed his thought. "But that's not what *you* want to do." I was touched that he was attempting to provide some employment assistance when his own career had finished somewhat ignominiously. And I was pleased that he had some sense of the type of work that might gratify me.

Keir turned his face toward me and leaned forward, as though expecting a goodbye kiss. I imagined nosy neighbors watching out of their windows—Abigail's spies, perhaps—keeping an eye on Keir, his comings and goings. In the past, he had kissed me on the cheek, so I knew that was acceptable. I leaned my head around to press my lips to his right cheek. His skin felt slightly puffy and looser than I expected, another side effect of the steroids, I surmised.

As Keir turned back in his seat to open the car door, I remembered something and grabbed his left forearm, feeling the soft cashmere of his sweater, bone, and muscle under my grip.

"I've never met Sean!"

"He won't be home for a while, but I can show you some pictures of him inside."

"I understand." I smiled. "We have a photo shrine to Mireille at our house."

"You don't have a shrine like we have a shrine!" Keir displayed a mischievous twinkle in his eye and pride in his voice. "I also want to get you some hats and bumper stickers."

After exiting my car, I followed Keir back up the curved steps. Opening the front door, he shouted out, "Maria?" I guessed that was the name of the nanny or housekeeper. There was no response. We were again alone in his house. I followed him back to the sunny family room, noticing as I passed the dining room again, a stunningly decorated, tall, ceramic, turquoise vase.

Keir stopped in front of the right side wall where an original oil painting hung of Sean playing with a set of wooden trains. At about three feet high by five feet wide, it was almost larger than life size.

Before I could comment, the phone on the shelf beneath the painting rang. Keir picked it up. I could tell from the first part of the conversation that this was his ride to physical therapy.

In order to give him a sense of privacy, I walked back through the foyer. On both sides of the hallway were two tables of family photographs. One picture of Abigail had a smaller school photo of Sean tucked in the bottom right corner of the frame. I could see Sean's resemblance to his mother, although he was blond and his parents were both brunettes. I speculated whether Keir might have been blonde as a young boy. My father had been, so it was possible.

Another photo dominating the display on the other side of the hallway was a black-and-white close up of Keir and Abigail, cheek-to-cheek. "So *that's* the 'great' photo by Liam to which Keir had referred back in 1988 and not the one that I keep in my briefcase!" I thought to myself. "It really is a wonderful shot of them as a couple."

Since Keir would soon be picked up to go to his physical therapy session, I suspected he wanted me to leave before his ride came.

How would we say goodbye? I knew earlier in the car that he wanted me to kiss him, and we were inside now, away from prying eyes. But seeing the photo of Keir and Abigail, I knew in my heart I could not compromise him or his marriage inside his house where he would remember and perhaps feel guilty. After all, Abigail was paying the bills.

I reached the front foyer of the house and, turning around, I noticed an original painting over the living room sofa. I heard Keir hang up the phone.

"Next time I come back," I raised and directed my voice in Keir's direction," I want the art tour." I did not think he heard me, so I walked back toward the family room. Just as I reached the arch of the entrance, Keir came back to hand me four of The Merv Show ball caps like the one he was wearing and four bumper stickers with "Kick Tumor Butt!" on them.

328

"Give these to your family," he said. Instead, I decided I would give them to people who actually knew Keir: Evonda, Sylvia, and Mark Thomas.

Thanking him, I took the hats and bumper stickers in my right hand, encircled my arms around both his shoulders, gave him a swift squeeze, spun around, and headed for the front door. Unlatching the door, I swiftly let myself out and headed toward my car, going around the front to the driver's side door. I figured Keir would stay inside. However, as I turned round to open my car door, I looked over the car roof to see Keir had followed me outside and was leaning his arms on the railing, smiling radiantly.

"I love you," my eyes said over the car roof just before I ducked into the driver's seat. I drove out of the driveway and headed to the end of Hawkins Drive. At the stop sign, I realized for the first time my clip-on earrings were painfully pinching my ear lobes. Before removing them, I glanced in my rearview mirror. Keir was still standing on his porch, smiling brilliantly, watching my car leave.

Still enveloped in the aura of our time together, I did not turn my car radio on until I approached the ramp entrance to the Interstate. I immediately heard the lyrics from "When Will I See You Again" by Three Degrees: "When will I see you again? When will we share precious moments? Are we in love or are we just friends?"

"Just *PERFECT!*" I said out loud to the radio.

On the drive home, two images alternated in my head in rapid succession, like two slides flipping back-and-forth: the way Keir had looked when he was well and the way he looked today. My visual mind could not marry the two together into the same person. As I drove, I went over our conversation in my head—what Keir had said as well as what had been in the space between us in the form of unsaid feelings, thoughts, and expressions.

Somewhere south of Mansfield I stopped to use the restroom and to eat some supper. As I pulled into the parking lot of the fast food restaurant, the dam of tears broke and washed over me. For the past couple of hours of driving, I had been buoyed up by the miracle of seeing Keir again, reassured that he appeared in better physical shape than I had feared and that my feelings for him were not only returned but still there. Most importantly, we had been able to convey wordlessly a sense of those feelings to each other without compromising our respective marriages.

But now I was in the letdown of anticlimax. The closer I drove to Columbus and Auguste, the more reluctant I became. As I entered the city limits of Columbus and turned off I-71 to drive along Morse Road, I heard the radio play Sarah MacLaughlin's lyrics, "I will remember you. Will you remember me? Don't let your life pass you by. Weep not for the memories"—another song that perfectly reflected my thoughts and wrung some more tears from me.

329

The next day, a surprisingly strong wave of grief overtook me. I recorded it in my "hard times journal." I felt like I had lost my rudder and my compass. Parts of the former Keir were there and some were gone. I had put so much stock into seeing him again. In some ways, the visit went much better than I had expected, but I was also aware that something deeper had gone unfulfilled. I was mourning the loss of who Keir had been—for him and for me—as well as the future that would not, could not, be.

I was also worried that my visit may have overtired Keir. He had water exercise in the morning, my visit midday, and physical therapy in the later afternoon. I waited a week and then telephoned him. With no answer, I left a voice message: "Hello, Keir. I just wanted you to know I got home safely and hope you are doing well."

A couple of weeks later, on March 25th, I called again but this time I did not leave a message.

Plans for Mireille's *bat mitzvah* intensified. We expected fifty people to attend the service and following luncheon on April 13th, mostly family members from out of state and local friends of mine and Mireille's. I was also planning her 13th birthday party sleepover at a nearby hotel for the following weekend, as well as a quick trip the weekend after that to southwestern Cleveland to visit Mireille's oldest friend from daycare and her mother; the trip also included a day trip to the Cleveland Metroparks Zoo in Brookside Park.

I felt guilty about going back to Cleveland and not calling or visiting Keir while we were there as I had promised him, but we were staying in the suburbs on the other side of the city and were only in town for twenty-four hours. I did not wish to appear rude to our overnight hostess by attempting to contact Keir while we were visiting, nor did I want to go into any lengthy explanations.

Instead, I wrote Keir a letter on April 22nd, Auguste's birthday, reporting on the *bat mitzvah*, enclosing an article on cancer patients in remission, letting him know that my friend Carolyn's tumors had shrunk by 50 percent in her clinical trial, mentioning our whirlwind trip to the Cleveland Zoo, and finally, sharing with him my decision take a watercolor class in the summer since my part-time work schedule now allowed me the liberty to schedule a daytime art class. Remembering his comment that his eyesight was deteriorating (whether due to the natural aging process, the cancer and necrosis, or other factors), this time I typed the letter using a twelve-point font. Finally, I enclosed the copy of the black-and-white photo of Keir and Abigail I had carried in my briefcase for six years.

In the beginning of the year, Keir and I had spoken on the phone about every two weeks just trying to make arrangements for my trip to visit him. Now, it had been nearly six weeks since we had spoken. I missed our communication; I missed him. I wondered whether, having had the actual visit, he was having second thoughts, feeling guilty, or regretting the in-person encounter. Was I supposed to continue to call? Did he expect me to continue to write?

330

On the afternoon of May 2nd, I called Keir again. His private secretary, Tom, answered and turned the phone over to Keir.

"How are you, Keir?"

"Well, I'm not doing any better." His usual upbeat attitude was tinged with discouragement.

"But you're not doing any worse…?"

"Actually, I am. I'm using a walker now." (I knew it took courage for him to admit that.) "But I am still the same person inside." (I wondered if he was sensing my ambivalence between who I knew him to be before he became ill and now, or if he was attempting to hold on to the remaining vestiges of who he knew himself to be.) "I look forward to your calls." (I thought, *But you don't know when I am going to call you!*) "I might not be in a good mood when you call, and I might not answer." (Was Keir letting me know why he had not answered my calls recently? In any case, I understood he was giving me clear permission to continue phoning him.)

"We've formed a number of support committees around my friend Carolyn. Would you like me to ask her prayer committee to pray for you as well?"

"I would appreciate that. I need all the help I can get!" A glint of his sense of humor had come back.

"When I collect the prayers, how do you want me to get them to you?" I was checking on his continued capacity to read and who might actually be privy to his correspondence.

"You can email them to me at kfootball@aol.com." He had already told me that other people would have to print off his email for him, so I figured either Tom or Abigail would be the one to retrieve the prayers from cyberspace.

I was pleased that, by the end of our call, I had been able to cheer Keir up a little, although whether by giving him hope through the prayer circle or by the simply act of calling, I was not sure. Although his health news was disappointing and worrisome, his granting me continued calling privileges buoyed me up.

I noticed Keir's communication style, always succinct and expectant that his listener was erudite and adept enough to follow his quicksilver thought process was becoming ever more concise and efficient. Maybe he felt he had precious little time left for long-winded chatter. He was not rude or impatient with his listener; he simply cut to the heart of the matter and left his listener to comprehend all the nuances he left in the spaces between his words.

Even though AEMG was paying me for only twenty hours of work each week, by mid-May, I was actually working twice that because I was in the midst of the last month of intensive meeting planning for the Cleveland Clinic's Scientific Seminar at Mackinac Island, to be followed immediately by my national client convention at The BroAdmoor, and two months later, by OAHIA's 25th anniversary convention. Adele Waters continued to mention that she might want me to drive up to Cleveland for a day prior to the Mackinac seminar. I was hoping that would give me another opportunity to visit Keir, but Adele and I were rapidly running out of spare time. I was reluctant to promise Keir that I was definitely going to Cleveland because of what had happened in the early part of the year when my previous trip had been postponed twice.

I sent out an email to Carolyn's prayer group asking them to pray for Keir as well. I accidently changed a letter in one person's email address, and the stranger who received the email in error—someone named Joanne— replied that she was so touched by my message that she offered to pray for Keir, too. Ten people agreed to pray for Keir, including Mark Thomas, Sylvia, and seven people from the professional development courses who were also Carolyn's friends.

The day following Mireille's *bat mitzvah*, Carolyn entered the hospital with dehydration. Even though her tumors had shrunk by 50 percent in mid-April, she experienced no further progress in the clinical trial. I tried to encourage her when she was facing five more months of chemotherapy.

"My friend Keir underwent nine months of chemo, surely you can do five!" I wasn't sure if Keir had done the full nine months, but I thought the white lie was justified because Carolyn cheered up.

Carolyn's husband, Gary, who had been out of work for nearly a year, landed a plum job with the premier corporate employer in Columbus, so we devised a care-giving schedule for Carolyn in morning and afternoon blocks of time when Gary was at work. Gary came home for his lunch hour and oversaw the changing of the guard.

One mild and sunny May afternoon when I was Carolyn's sitter, she requested that we take a walk. Since her front door led down a brick staircase, we exited through the rear door where there was only one low step. She held my arm to descend her steep front driveway to the sidewalk. I could feel her frailness. She wore a ball cap to cover her balding scalp, and her teeth now had a yellow pallor. In sharp contrast, a photographic portrait of her hung in their dining room depicting a strikingly beautiful and vital woman. When we arrived at the bottom of the driveway where it met the public sidewalk, Carolyn asked me to stop.

"I'm not sure I can go on."

Not wanting her to falter, I held Carolyn in my arms. At first, I was a little subconscious due to the homophobic nature of our society but almost immediately dismissed the thought, chiding myself. "This is my friend, and she needs my support." A few moments later, Carolyn pulled away, signaling her readiness to try to walk some more. We slowly walked past my car parked at the curb. As we neared the edge of her property line, she stopped and waivered.

"I can't do it," Carolyn whispered. I had a moment of panic since I was not strong enough to carry her back up the hill to her house. I spied my car sitting at the curb.

"Can you walk back to my car? You can sit and rest in it." Carolyn turned and, leaning heavily on my arm, we headed toward the oasis of relief several feet away. Luckily, I had my car keys in my pocket. Leaning Carolyn against the side of my car, I unlocked the passenger door, moved the seat back a bit, and helped her drop into it. I silently thanked whatever providence had persuaded me to park at the curb rather than in the driveway.

After closing the passenger side door and walking around to the other side, I climbed into the driver's seat. At least, this way, I could drive her halfway back up the hilly driveway. However, Carolyn would need sufficient strength to make it the rest of the way up the drive, around the back of the house, and through the house to either the living room or bedroom. We were going to have to sit in my car for a while. I remembered Carolyn's dehydration spell in the hospital.

"Do you want some water to drink?"

"No...just...rest." Carolyn leaned back against the seat and closed her eyes. We fell silent. I looked out the windshield at each of her neighbors' yards, observing their landscaping, birds in flight, and the occasional squirrel darting about. I took a swig from my water bottle in the cup holder next to the gear shift. Nothing to do; nothing to say; just sit, wait, and BE.

"Okay, I think I can make it now." Carolyn had opened her eyes again.

"I'll drive up the driveway." I turned my key in the ignition. I performed a U-turn in the street and parked my car as far as possible up the driveway behind Carolyn's own car already parked there. Going around to the passenger side of my car, I held the door against the downhill gravitational pull while easing Carolyn out of the passenger seat and around the door that slammed closed once I stepped away from it. Leaning heavily on me again, Carolyn and I walked slowly past her car and through the gate to her backyard.

"Let's sit outside." Carolyn pointed to the white resin chairs on the brick patio. I steered her to the closest one. She fell into it heavily.

Gary had bought Carolyn a Jack Russell terrier, Maggie, to keep her company at home. Maggie, and their two cats, Lerner and Lowe, came out through the doggie door to join us and frolic in the yard.

As I surveyed the backyard, I suspected Carolyn had been the gardener because the landscape was beginning to show the signs of lack of attention. Maggie brought me a tennis ball, green with mold and wet from dog saliva, which I took in my fingertips and threw across the yard; the cats high-stepped through the ivy in search of small prey. Maggie retrieved the ball in her jaws and bounded back to drop it at my feet. Mentally noting that I would need to wash my hands when we got inside, I gingerly picked up the ball again and threw it as far as my shoulder would allow. Maggie tore down the yard in its direction.

"Um, the sun feels nice," Carolyn observed quietly.

"Yes, it does." I thought about how much I take for granted—the sunshine, my ability to walk unaided...I could not fathom what must go through Carolyn's and Keir's minds faced with deteriorating abilities, treatments that caused nausea and diarrhea, and the greatly diminished prospects of living to see their grandchildren. Oh, I so wanted them to live to see their grandchildren!

"I'd like to go inside now." Carolyn's voice interrupted my reflection. I wondered if she, as someone who had coached me, had sensed my own shift to sadder thoughts. I approached her chair and helped Carolyn rise and go into the house.

"The bedroom," Carolyn replied to my unasked question. "I want to lie down." I steered her toward the hallway too narrow to walk along side of her. She used the wall as support as I followed behind. She sat down on the edge of her bed, fell over sideways, and pulled her feet up under her in a fetal position. I removed her ball cap, found a blanket and covered her, and quietly left the room to sit and read in the living room until my care-giver shift was over when Gary came home.

On Friday morning, May 17th, I phoned Keir's home but got no answer. At 1:40 p.m. I tried again. It was in the middle of a work day, so I was surprised when Abigail answered.

"Oh! Hello, Annie!" She answered too warmly as though I was now her new best friend. "I'll get Keir." I mused to myself that we had come a long way since January when she scarcely remembered who I was, and I had been concerned about her sending me a cease-and-desist letter. I assumed that Keir had told her about my visit, letters, and phone calls at their mealtime during the "How was your day?" conversations between a husband and wife. Maybe she brought in the mail and had seen my return address.

"We're leaving for our lake house in five minutes!" Keir was excited. We would only have a short time to talk. I heard a male voice in the background. "In twenty minutes," Keir corrected himself. "The suitcases are coming down now. How was the *bat mitzvah*?" His voice sounded over-excited, almost out-of-breath.

I imagined him in the family room on the phone beneath Sean's portrait with the train set. I remembered how much Keir loved their lake house and Harry's comment the previous year that the family was dependent on Abigail's work schedule to be able to go there. I now understood Abigail's eagerness to put Keir on the phone with me. I would be a convenient distraction to get him out from under foot while the rest of the adults packed the car.

"It was lovely." I repeated what I had written in my letter the previous month, not sure whether he had forgotten what I wrote or wanted a more in-depth description. I was concerned our call might over-tire him even before beginning the two-hour drive to Lakeside. He had shifted the conversation to me so that his own voice would not tire, but I wanted to know how *he* was faring. I attempted to get him to talk some more. "How are *you* doing?"

"I'm running out of gas," Keir's voice sounded worn out. I could tell he was having difficulty concentrating on our conversation amidst the excitement of his imminent sojourn.

"Enjoy your trip to Lakeside." I hoped the family was driving a vehicle in which Keir could lie down and rest.

When I had seen Keir in early March, I thought I would be back to Cleveland in late May or early June. (For the sake of appearances, I felt it was more prudent to visit Keir in conjunction with a *bona fide* business trip rather than make the trip solely as a personal junket.) Concerned now with his deteriorating health, I felt it was becoming more urgent to visit him again. During the next week, I emailed Adele Waters to ask when she wished me to return to the Cleveland Clinic to review the remaining details of the scientific seminar the next month.

"I was thinking it would make more sense for me to go to your office in Columbus," Adele replied.

Now I strongly suspected it was not likely I would return to Cleveland soon to visit Keir. Perhaps I could convince Adele that I should go up in July after the scientific sessions to reconcile the books and conduct a post-meeting evaluation. Keir had already passed the two-year mark for his prognosis. His biological clock was ticking loudly in my head. I continued to pray for him and Carolyn each night before bed, each morning as I woke up, and on my midday walks. My phone conversations with both were getting shorter as I sensed them both tiring sooner.

With a day off on Wednesday, May 29th, I called Keir around 11:30 a.m. Unexpectedly, a man with a British accent answered.

"Keir is out for lunch with a friend," the man said. "I expect him back around 1:30." I was encouraged that Keir was still able to go out to lunch with a friend.

"Please let him know Annie will call him back this afternoon. Thank you."

The neck and shoulder pain I had been experiencing on and off since January was increasing in intensity. My family physician had given me two new prescriptions to try. After downing my own lunch, I drove to the pharmacy to fill my prescriptions. In the car, I wondered if the British man was Abigail's father, perhaps come to visit the family over the past Memorial Day weekend and staying to help care for Keir for a bit.

The pharmacy was crowded with others who were on their lunch hour, so it was nearly two o'clock before I arrived back home. After storing my purchases and locating Keir's phone number, I sat down to calm myself before dialing.

This time Keir answered the phone himself but accidentally disconnected me. I dialed again.

"Keir, it's Annie."

"Sorry to cut you off. I'm lying down for a rest." The lunch out must have over-tired him.

"I'm sorry. I don't want to disturb your rest."

335

"No, it's fine. I'm glad to hear from you." He seemed very relaxed and peaceful—almost serenely so. I imagined him lying upstairs on his bed.

"How are you?"

"I'm using a wheelchair now, but a wheelchair could be fun!" I thought about the fortitude required to go out to lunch in a wheelchair, but I could also imagine him racing the wheelchair around the wooden floors of his hallway and family room. He was in an open, relaxed mood—perhaps because no one was within earshot. I was surprised a little that he was not discouraged by the physical deterioration that necessitated the move to a wheelchair. I attempted to make light of it.

"Be careful doing wheelies in your foyer!"

"I have a physical problem that has a spiritual solution," he said simply.

I knew instantly he was telling me he was dying. I did not want him to give up hope.

"There are always miracles."

"I'm all out of miracles." Despite Keir's profound observations, his spirit seemed open, warm, and exceedingly loving. I swore to myself that he would have miracles, even if I had to give them to him myself.

"How was your trip to Lakeside?"

"I enjoyed it."

"You are tiring. I'll let you go."

"Thank you for understanding."

In the sweetly tender and affectionate space that hung between us, there was only one more thing for me to say, but first my mind warned me: "Don't scare him; say it as a friend…and don't expect any response!"

"I love you."

"I love you, too." Without a split-second's hesitation, Keir's reply was too quick, like he had been waiting his whole life to say that, and he was relieved to let the truth out finally.

We hung up. I sat at my desk for a moment. I was stunned and giddy, in shock, and happy yet serene. I went downstairs and outside to take my walk.

The May sky was a perfect azure, the sun's warmth felt impeccable, and the air smelled fresh. The birds chirped their delight. Yet, by the time I reached the bottom of our hill, I felt dizzy and light-headed. Rather than risk tripping or fainting, I turned around and went back home to lie down on the sofa in our front living room.

Once safely back inside my cool living room and lying down, I reviewed our conversation in my mind. Had I waited countless years to hear Keir's declaration? Had he said it merely has a friend, too?

Resurfacing from my forgotten memory came the previous year's revelation from God: *"You knew each other in a previous lifetime, specifically, the French-and-Indian War. You fell in love with each other, but he died before you could tell each other. Your mission in this lifetime is to tell each other that you love each other."*

Had I just sealed Keir's fate? Had I been afraid to express my love to him earlier because, deep down, I knew it would mean his end? Keir seemed so accepting of his situation when he had said, "I have a physical problem that has a spiritual solution." Death was the only way he could be relieved of his body's deterioration. I was still mulling these thoughts over when Auguste and Mireille arrived home.

"I was feeling a little dizzy, so I lay down."

"Are you going to make dinner?" August asked bluntly. "I have some work outside I need to do."

"Yes." I sighed reluctantly and rose slowly, steadying myself on the coffee table. "Mireille, do you have homework to do?" My daughter nodded and headed upstairs to her room, sensitive to, and desirous of, getting away from the tension mounting between her parents.

I awoke that Saturday, my 51st birthday, and realized I needed to have sex with *someone*. Auguste was lying next to me. As my husband, legally and morally, he was the obvious choice. I started off patiently, although I felt a little detached. About halfway through the act of intercourse, however, I realized I was having sex with the wrong man. I could not wait until Auguste had finished. I felt emotionally flattened.

Later that afternoon, we drove to my parents' home for my birthday party. After dinner and cake, I noticed an issue of *Readers' Digest* on their coffee table with a cover story about Michael J. Fox having Parkinson's disease. I remembered that Keir's father had died of PD. I suddenly realized that Michael J. Fox reminded me physically of Keir when he was healthy: the boyish charm, quick wit, wide face, and thick, dark hair in the same style. Since I learned of Keir's illness, I had avoided watching television episodes of "Spin City" in which Fox had starred. Now I sat down and devoured the magazine article. My father was watching the news—even the Pope had Parkinson's. "If Keir was diagnosed with PD on top of his brain tumor," I reasoned, "he could not survive *both* genetic inheritances from his parents."

Adele Waters decided she did not have enough time to come to Columbus nor for me to drive to Cleveland. We would have to plan the rest of the scientific sessions by email and phone. At the same time, Colorado was experiencing a series of summer wild fires. Now, added to my daily action list of working fulltime to plan the three upcoming conventions, I had to keep tabs on the fires' proximity to Colorado Springs and The BroAdmoor, as well as the direction of the wind. Worrying about Keir and Carolyn, trying to plan three meetings, working fulltime hours with halftime pay and stress at home heightened the pain in my neck and right shoulder.

For two weeks that love declaration between Keir and me hung in the air like the wildfire smoke. Sharing the air was my speculation that he might also have an onset of PD. I needed to talk with him again. I picked up the phone at my office on Wednesday, June 11th, to call him, but I chickened out. My anxiety level was too high to be upbeat with him on the phone.

I was scheduled to leave for Mackinac Island on Sunday, June 16, Father's Day, along with Auguste and Mireille. For them, the week would be a vacation while I worked every morning, three afternoons, and two evenings for the Cleveland Clinic Scientific meeting. I wanted to speak with Keir before I left, because, along with The BroAdmoor convention immediately following the week of the scientific sessions, I would be away from home nearly two weeks and predictably exhausted upon my return. I might not get to talk to him for at least two or three weeks. I also wanted to assure him that I would visit him in July but did not know when his family was going to the Grand Canyon; although, now that he was using a wheelchair, I wondered whether they would still be able to go.

I resolved again to phone Keir on Thursday, June 12th. At 11:45 a.m., my hand hovered over my office phone as I talked myself into the courage to call Keir. To my surprise, he answered on the first ring.

"Hello!" he said harshly. He sounded rushed and frustrated. Had I phoned at an inconvenient time?

"Keir, it's Annie. Are you going out?"

"Yes." He sounded unusually abrupt and annoyed. "I can't talk to you today." His words came across the phone line like a slap in my face. I heard it like he had said, "I can't talk to you ever again!" This was the antithesis of our last, loving call. Keir must have felt me recoil because he added in a tired monotone, as though he had said it a million times before, "Thank you for caring."

I hesitated for a second, but sensed it would not be wise to prolong the call to inform him of my travel plans. I had other methods of communicating with him at my disposal, whereas he did not.

"You take care," I said with a mixture of sadness and hope then hung up.

"Fine! Don't ever expect me to call *you* again!" my angry, upset mind roared at the phone receiver now back in its cradle. Then my personal development and coaching training came to the forefront of my mind.

Underneath Keir's annoyance, I sensed a deeper fear. To his fears, I added my own—especially of his potential rejection of me. A couple of weeks ago he was serenely accepting the inevitable proximity of his premature death. Now, he was scared, and that made him angry. Had he received more medical bad news? Was he frustrated because he was trying to go out and his body was not cooperating? Did our saying "I love you" frighten him? Did he expect bad news from a doctor's appointment to which he was headed? Was Abigail standing right there, and he did not feel he could converse with me freely?

I needed to separate his fear, anger, and upset from my own. First, I had expected a warm, love-filled reception from him and had received the contrary. Second, my intention was to let him know of my travel plans, and that communication had been thwarted. Once I was able to get clear about my emotions, I forgave his behavior and resolved to let him know of both my forgiveness and my travel plans by writing him a letter.

Within the next twelve hours, first at night in my journal, then the next morning on our home computer, I wrote and rewrote a letter to Keir until it distilled everything I wanted to communicate into one double-spaced page in a large, readable, font:

Dear Keir,

I am so sorry you are having a difficult time now. You have been through so much.

What I wanted to let you know is that I will be traveling on business during the next few weeks. However, I didn't want another month to go by without an opportunity to say "hello." I will try you again upon my return in July, and maybe then we will both have more time and energy to talk.

Meanwhile, I have e-mailed you the prayers from the Central Ohio chapter of "The Merv Show" in the hope that they will help uplift your spirits during your more difficult moments.

I hope you have a Happy Father's Day.

Fondly,

Annie

I ended the letter that way, because if nothing else, I was certain of his love of Sean. I mailed the letter directly from the post office so that it had a chance to be delivered on Friday or Saturday before Father's Day. I did not wish to go to Mackinac Island with this awful feeling hanging between us.

Although I could have telephoned Keir again on Thursday, Friday, or Saturday, I was afraid he might refuse to answer my phone call if he was reacting to our saying "I love you."

Early Sunday morning, my family departed for the drive to Mackinac Island's Grand Hotel Resort. After the wearying, eight-hour, drive plus a thirty-minute ferry ride, we were all glad to arrive. The Scientific Sessions opened with an outdoor welcome reception that evening, marred by running out of *hors d'oeuvres* and a rain shower that closed the event early.

A young male co-worker from AEMG, Tyrrell, also arrived to assist Adele Waters and me with registration, exhibits, and the golf program. Tyrrell, a cheerful, patient, upbeat person, seemed to get along with everyone, which was important for the several hundred doctors and their families who were registered to attend, as well as with Adele and her boss, Dr. Schuster, who had the egotistical expectations of a famous medical specialist at the top of his field; or at least Adele worshipped the ground he walked on and expected the rest of us to do the same.

On Monday, Adele, Tyrrell, and I worked the entire day, with the evening off. Mireille and Auguste occasionally stopped by our registration desk when they became bored or got on each other's nerves. On Tuesday afternoon, June 18th, we had the afternoon off, so I joined Mireille and Auguste poolside. I had brought along one of The Merv Show ball caps Keir had given me since the colors matched my bathing suit. I wore it to keep the sun off my face at the pool. Auguste eyed my cap suspiciously.

339

"Where did you get the hat?"

"A friend of mine gave it to me." I hoped my tone of voice warned him not to question me any further on the subject. After I warmed up in the sun, I went into the pool to swim with Mireille. Following our afternoon swim, my family retired to our room for a room service dinner and to watch television.

On Wednesday afternoon while Tyrell joined the golfers and Adele and her husband went shopping, the resort conference service manager told me that the high humidity and the potential for rain had reached 30 percent; therefore, he wanted our permission to move the evening dinner event indoors. I could reach neither Adele nor Dr. Schuster, who was on the golf course, so I made the executive decision alone to hold the dinner indoors.

I retired to the business center to await the potential fallout regarding my decision from Adele and Dr. Schuster as well as to read emails from my office as part of the last planning stages for The BroAdmoor convention scheduled to begin the following Sunday. I was relieved to learn that the wind direction for the Colorado wild fires had turned away from Colorado Springs, temporarily, at least.

Initially, for Wednesday evening's dinner, I had planned to wear a new, matching, Hawaiian shirt and shorts set. However, I remembered that I would also need to wear the dress and jacket I had originally planned to wear for Friday's luau two days afterwards in Colorado Springs. Therefore, I decided to switch and wear the dress and jacket on Wednesday instead so that I could wash them and have them ready to repack on Saturday, saving the Hawaiian outfit for Friday's luau.

Returning from his hot and humid golf outing, Dr. Schuster told Adele that he approved of my decision to move Wednesday's dinner indoors. We all breathed a sigh of relief and enjoyed the evening.

A light rain began on Thursday. Having the afternoon off again, Mireille and I used the indoor pool, alternately running outside to the heated jacuzzi with raindrops falling on our heads. We had never before swum in the rain, and this experience, minus Auguste's disapproving presence at the pool, gave my daughter and me a sense of childish freedom. Our flip-flops squeaked on the flagstones as we slip-slided our way back to the room to change. For dinner, Auguste, Mireille, and I ventured into town for a Japanese dinner.

My neck pain was increasingly uncomfortable. I was very happy that the resort provided each room with neck pillows—long, narrow, pillows that slide between your shoulder and the regular pillow. Nevertheless, I still had difficulty sleeping and took some pain killers. I assumed the double stress of two back-to-back national conventions was wearing on me. My TMJ jaw pain was also throbbing.

Since the weather report for Friday, June 21st indicated heavy showers later in the day, we also moved that evening's luau inside to the large ballroom. Around 6:00 p.m., I donned my Hawaiian shirt-and-shorts outfit and headed downstairs to survey the last of the banquet set-up, including the video deejay and Margaritaville props and games. The rain turned from heavy to pouring.

Auguste and Mireille participated in the early part of the evening, eating their fill of seafood and other thematic buffet items. Adele and her husband decided to drive home to Cleveland that night, so they left at 8:30 in the pouring rain to catch the last ferry for their seven -hour trip, leaving me to sign the last banquet checks and pay the deejay. Toward nine o'clock, Auguste took Mireille up to bed since we were scheduled to depart Mackinac Island on the 6:00 ferry the next morning before the drive back to Columbus so that I would be in time to catch my four o'clock flight out to Colorado Springs.

Once they were upstairs, I asked Tyrell if he wanted to fast-dance with me. Since we were staff members—the hired help—it was not likely that anyone else would dance with us, so we decided we might as well enjoy each other's company until the end of the event. The banquet staff removed the food, we gave a last call at 10:15, and most of the guests left the ballroom by 10:30. After signing the banquet checks, I rode the elevator up to our room around eleven o'clock.

The thunder and rain were so loud through the night that I had trouble sleeping. The wine, heavy food, and strenuous dancing late in the evening did not help, and I dreaded the long drive home. Even the neck pillow offered little relief as I tossed and turned.

Rising before daybreak, our family packed the car, checked out, and stopped for a quick breakfast before boarding the ferry. Thirty minutes later, we were on I-75 heading south for most of the length of Michigan. For the first five hours that I drove, the rain fell heavily, but it started to ease up near Toledo when Auguste took the wheel.

I tried to rest in the passenger seat with my eyes closed, knowing I had a very long flight to Colorado Springs. I began to daydream about taking Keir to his Lakeside house. "If only we could spend a week together, we could say everything we wanted to tell each other," I wished, although I knew that it would take a pretty clever explanation to get Auguste's and Abigail's permission. "Perhaps we could take Mireille and Sean along as chaperones? After all this traveling and full-time hours, AEMG owes me some serious time off," I mused. As I had promised in my letter to Keir, I resolved to call him when I returned from Colorado Springs and make plans to visit him again.

Finally arriving back home in Columbus at 2:00, I only had an hour to empty my suitcase and repack it for Colorado Springs, check my phone messages, of which there were several calls to return, and drive to the airport in time for my 4:00 p.m. flight. I tried to rest on the airplane, but I have always had difficulty sleeping on moving vehicles of any kind. When I arrived at The BroAdmoor at 12:30 a.m. Mountain Time (2:30 a.m. Eastern Time, for my body), I had been traveling for most of the past twenty-one hours.

The cheerful front desk clerk at the West Building, where most of our meetings would be held, greeted me enthusiastically.

"Ms. Weber, we are pleased to give you an upgrade to one of our lovely cottage suites in the lakeside villas across the lake."

"I appreciate the offer, but I've been traveling since 6:00 yesterday morning Eastern Time," I began in a terse, don't-you-dare-argue-with-me voice. "I am the meeting planner, and I want to stay in *THIS* building!"

"Of course, Ms. Weber."

By the time I crawled into bed, it was 3:30 a.m. Eastern Time. Luckily, the time difference was in my favor for sleeping late.

Since Jack Spencer and Jennifer Erwin had flown into Colorado Springs on Saturday from Columbus, we caught up with each other at Sunday brunch, followed by the pre-conference meeting with the hotel staff. I supervised the exhibitor room set-up, while Jennifer handled registration, and Jack attended the Executive Committee meeting. The keynote speaker kicked the convention off with a five o'clock presentation.

Our opening social event, the Welcome Reception, was scheduled for poolside at 6:30 p.m. I ducked out of the keynote talk early to check on the reception set-up.

As I walked over to the new, vanishing edge pool, memories of Kevin Raines and the last time I walked here flooded back to me. In constructing the new poolscape, they had removed the man-made island that I had dedicated to Kevin three years earlier on my walk around Cheyenne Lake. I had asked our convention services manager earlier what had happened to the island.

"The trees and rocks from the island have been added to the west side lake edge as a rock garden near the water slide tower." I passed by the tower on my way over to the pool gate.

The reception set-up was well in hand, and soon our convention delegates joined us for the reception with heavy hors d'oeuvres set on buffet-stations and an open bar and musical trio. Even after the sun set the members were still conversing and enjoying themselves. I walked over to Jack Spencer.

"As you know, Jack, It's been a long week for me already. Do you mind if I leave now to return to my room? I'll be up early tomorrow for the exhibit hall breakfast."

"That's fine, Annie. You've done a good job here. Everyone seems happy. We'll see you tomorrow morning. Have a good night."

As I walked back past the rock garden-island remnants, I looked up at the starlit sky. Two stars shone particularly brightly—almost like Kevin Raine's eyes glinting with humor.

"Kevin," I prayed, "would you please help Keir? He is having a hard time right now."

I returned to my room bone weary, ready to take a shower and fall asleep. As I began to doze in bed, I saw a halo-glow vision with Kevin's face, his spirit manifesting strongly to me, followed by Keir's face and spirit, and then by that of Mark Thomas. During the night, I dreamt I spoke with Keir on the phone.

Even while dressing the next morning, the images and feelings from the night before stayed with me. I suddenly thought, "These prayers are NOT working! What else do I need to do or be to help Keir?"

Down in the exhibit hall, I ate breakfast with Jack Spencer and a few other convention delegates then went out to the registration desk to relieve Jennifer so she could eat her breakfast as well. While I was sitting at the registration table, I noticed a pay phone on a nearby wall and decided to check my voicemail messages at the office since it was around 10:15 Monday morning back East.

I only had one message. It was from former OAHIA President Marcia Tuttle.

"I hate to leave this on your voicemail," Marcia's voice said, "but Keir Mervais died on Friday evening at six o'clock. His funeral service is tomorrow at 11:00 in Cleveland at the Covenant-Coventry United Methodist Church."

Putting the phone receiver back into its silver cradle, I turned away and moaned under my breath, "Oh! Keir!" I walked into the exhibit hall where Jennifer was sitting and told her calmly, trying to hold down my mounting emotion, "Keir Mervais just died on Friday night. I am going to our staff office room down the hall because I am about to lose my composure." Jennifer, who also worked on OAHIA with me, was aware that Keir had been ill with cancer.

I turned and began to walk, and then run down the hall. I fumbled with the door key, eventually opened the door, closed it behind me, and sat down. I hyperventilated for ten minutes while staring out the window at the Rocky Mountains with Pike's Peak in the distance.

It was *déjà vu*. The BroAdmoor was where I had learned that Kevin Raine's brain cancer had worsened, and now I learned of Keir's death here. I had missed Kevin's funeral because I had learned about it too late to attend. Now, I was stuck in Colorado Springs at a convention and would miss Keir's service, too, even though I was so much closer to him than I ever was to Kevin. My heart was breaking.

"So that's why Kevin's spirit came to me last night, bringing Keir and Mark!" I thought. "Kevin *knew* I was at The BroAdmoor because I had prayed to him on the walk back to my room, but Keir only knew from my letter that I was out of town. Was this their way of telling me Keir had died but I didn't understand? That Kevin could not help Keir in the way I had asked because Keir had already died? Was this Keir's way of saying goodbye? And why had they included Mark?"

"Mark! I have to call Mark. It's about 10:30 or 11:00 a.m. back home. It's Mark's first day back from vacation." I pulled my OAHIA directory out of my briefcase and dialed the phone number for Buckeye Healthcare's Mansfield office. "Please, Mark, be there!" my mind implored.

He was. He had not yet heard about Keir. I cried again with fresh grief. He spoke comforting words. I calmed down a little.

Next, I called my personal coach, Hillary. She also comprehended the depth of my loss, having coached me through the months of Keir's illness, the unanswered letters and phone calls, and the triumphs of reconnecting with him over the last six months.

I called Marcia Tuttle.

"Marcia, I called to let you know I received your message. I am out of state, but I appreciated your willingness to leave me the message."

"I thought you would want to know. I can send you the facsimile of the *Cleveland Plain-Dealer* obituary." I gave her the fax number at The BroAdmoor.

Jennifer, now concerned about me, came to the staff office to check on me.

"Do you need anything?" she asked. I made a quick scan of my emotional state.

"Probably tranquilizers," I admitted. Jennifer left, and a little while later, the convention services manager came into the room.

"Jennifer told me you've had a death. Is there anything we can do? Do you need a car to the airport?"

"I don't think I can go to the funeral," I said plaintively. "I might need some tranquilizers…"

"I'll see what we can do." He left and returned with the concierge.

"Do you want us to locate a doctor?" she asked. I was not thinking very clearly. Everything seemed to be moving in slow motion. But I had stopped hyperventilating and was now just crying softly.

"I'm not sure…"

"Well, if you do, please let us know if we can help in any way." She politely retreated.

A few minutes later, Jack Spencer came into the room. Jennifer had told him what had occurred. He took one look at me and sized up the situation.

"When's the funeral?"

"Tomorrow at eleven in Cleveland."

"You need to go to this memorial service. It's very important to you. You've planned the convention well. Jennifer and I can take it from here. Go to Cleveland. Go. Get out of here."

A wave of relief washed over me as if the Red Sea had suddenly parted before me. I grabbed the nearest piece of blank paper and quickly wrote a list as if I had been given a jolt of electricity:

1. Change airline tickets – Cleveland or Columbus?
2. Pack suitcase
3. Go to airport
4. Call Mark
5. Call Auguste

In my grief-stricken state, I was not thinking very reliably, so I would have to focus on one thing at a time. First, I called our travel agent who told me I would need to call the airline directly to change my flight. The convention service manager returned with Keir's faxed obituary. I read it quickly and realized, "I will need a place to stay in Cleveland Heights." I called Eric Mitchell who assured me he was planning to attend the funeral and I could stay with him and Sandra. I thought the Covenant-Coventry UMC was the one I had passed when I had visited Keir in March. I called Jim Frasier in Cleveland who had originally faxed the obituary to Marcia and asked him the street address of the church. He confirmed it was at the corner of Coventry and Fairmount.

I went upstairs to my room to call the airline and pack. I was told I could not change my flight to fly directly to Cleveland but would have to return to Columbus, my original return ticket's destination. I was put on hold while the agent checked flights. I held the phone in one hand while I pulled out my suitcase and walked back-and-forth to the closet, pulling out garments and laying them inside the suitcase with the other hand. I had planned to wear a black skirt and top with colored flowers the next day at the convention, but realizing it would now be my funeral attire, I lay it on top. When the airline agent came back on the line to apologize for the delay, I reassured her. "I just *know* you will be able to get me on the next flight."

A few minutes later, she came back on the phone and announced in her crisp, professional voice, "I've confirmed you on the 3:15 flight out of Colorado Springs, due to arrive in Columbus at 11:00 p.m." I thanked her and called The BroAdmoor spa to cancel my 3:15 massage appointment. I called the convention services manager and asked him to arrange for a car to the airport for my new flight. Then I called Mark back.

"Mark, my boss has given me permission to fly back today to Columbus so that I can drive to Cleveland for Keir's funeral tomorrow. Do you want to go with me? I can pick you up in Mansfield at 9:00 a.m."

"When I thought you could not attend, I had decided to go as your surrogate, but I'll be happy to carpool with you. I'll meet you out in my office parking lot at 9:00 because parking spaces are assigned and you'll have trouble locating a spot."

Then I called Sylvia to tell her the sad news. I read Keir's obituary to her out loud. New details of his life became apparent to me. His birthday was June 18th; he had just turned 54 years old (I had thought he was a little younger, 51 or 52) just three days before he died on the eve of summer solstice, his favorite season. He had been a community leader, serving as the head of several organizations besides OAHIA and the Health Law Section, as well as active in his church and the YMCA's program for children, including being the dragon mascot for them. The obituary listed his deceased parents, his brother and sister-in-law, their children, Abigail's siblings, and, of course, Abigail and Sean. Thinking, "Poor Sean! He must be only ten years old!" I was overcome with another moment of emotion.

Like me, Keir had been a Gemini, a Methodist (preferable to a guilt-ridden Catholic or bible-thumping Baptist). Sylvia, who had been raised in Cleveland Heights, confirmed to me that Keir's church was the one I had seen on March 6th. He and Abigail had been married for 20 years and both had graduated from Case Western Reserve. Keir had been a teacher for three years before entering law school at the University of Akron. The photo used for the obituary was a cropped headshot from the black-and-white photo of Keir and Abigail that I had sent to Keir only back in April.

Upon hanging up with Sylvia, I called Eric back and told him I would have to return to Columbus and would not need accommodations at his home. I then called Auguste at his office and informed him that I would be home around midnight but would need to leave for a funeral at 7:00 the next morning, so his care giving duties for Mireille would not change.

I noted that I still had an hour-and-a-half before I needed to leave for the airport. Following the first shock and my torrent of tears, I now entered a numbed phase and was more under control. I decided to take a last walk around Cheyenne Lake.

The clear, sunny day seemed to mock my inner darkness. When I arrived at the southern tip of the Lake, bells at a nearby church rang the noon hour: "For whom the bell tolls." The weight of the shock of recognition was too heavy for me to bear; I collapsed down onto the nearest bench.

After resting for several minutes, I gathered my strength and returned to our registration desk where box lunches had just been put out. I briefly informed Jennifer of the plans I had made, and we went over some of the convention details for which she and Jack would now be responsible in my absence. As the members filed out of the morning's general session, I explained to a few of the officers the reason for my hasty departure. I said goodbye and thank you to Jack.

The BroAdmoor limousine driver attempted to engage me in conversation on our way to the airport. I was not in a talkative mood, staring glumly out of the car window, barely aware of the passing scenery. I had hoped to call, maybe even see Keir again, on my return from Colorado Springs. Now, I was returning early for his funeral. The finality of it hung over me like an ominous storm cloud over the Rockies. When I reached the airport and checked my bags like an automaton, I learned that one of the x-ray machines—heightened airport security measures introduced in response to the 9/11 terrorist attacks the year before—was broken and the security process was expected to take longer than normal. I was so numb, I did not care.

When I finally arrived at my gate for the 3:15 p.m. flight home, I pulled out a notebook and wrote two letters to Keir: one listing all my regrets and the other one listing my gratitude. The flight home through Dallas-Ft. Worth was less than memorable, just something I had to endure, and I arrived home at midnight.

346

I lay in bed next to Auguste, weeping silently until 5:00 a.m., when I realized sleep was not forthcoming. I rose and went into the bathroom. Sitting there in the dark, I observed, "This is the first day of the rest of my life without Keir." His positive attention toward me had been the antidote to Auguste's mean, unsupportive, comments. I felt desolate. However, I also noticed that there was one thing I did *not* feel any more: the searing pain from my neck to my upper right back. I remembered the onset of the pain had been in January after my first call to Keir. I understood now it was my "please don't die" pain. And, now, Keir *was* dead.

After drying my fresh set of tears, I made my way upstairs to the computer to read nine days of personal email messages. To my astonishment, among the most recent was an email from kfootball@aol.com which I recognized immediately as Keir's email address. Had he sent me a response to my last letter? But then I noticed the date: Sunday, June 23, at 10:30 a.m., 36 hours after his death. How was that possible?

The email message was actually from Abigail:

"Oh, Annie. Keir died on Friday evening. There is so much to do, I cannot reply adequately. His obituary will appear in the Cleveland paper tomorrow after some corrections. Due to his various and growing disabilities, Keir could not maintain contact with his friends, and most seemed to forget about him. There were many lonely times for him these past couple of years. You were among a small cadre of special friends who reached out to him. This was so kind, so precious—the simplest yet very best support—for which Keir and I felt extremely grateful. Thank you and your friends for your prayers.

This confirmed to me that Abigail knew of my last letter and had found the prayer support group email that I had sent to Keir a couple weeks earlier. My letter had not detailed where I was or when exactly I would return, so she did not know when I might read her email message. And I had already received a copy of the obituary.

I was deeply honored that Keir's widow, in the fresh hours of her own grief, had taken the time and energy to attempt to communicate with me, someone she scarcely knew. I had wrongly assumed that many of Keir's friends and colleagues from OAHIA *had* stayed in contact with him but had just not communicated that to me. (Keir, of course, would never have let on to me about his loneliness.) Perhaps my letters and phone calls had been more important to him than I had ever imagined. I had been afraid for so many months that no one would tell me when Keir died, and here I was on Abigail's short list. And, thanks to Marcia Tuttle's voicemail and Jack Spencer's magnanimity, I was able to arrive home in time for the funeral.

Ten days ago, prior to leaving for Mackinac Island, while at the drugstore looking for encouragement cards for Keir, on impulse I had purchased a sympathy card. On its cover was a Native American prayer:

"I give you this one thought to keep—
I am with you still – I do not sleep.
I am a thousand winds that blow;

I am the diamond glints on snow;
I am the sunlight on ripened grain;
I am the gentle autumn rain.
When you awaken in the morning's hush,
I am the swift, uplifting rush
Of quiet birds in circled flight.
I am the soft stars that shine at night.
Do not think of me as gone—
I am with you still—in each new dawn."

I shut down the computer, tiptoed back downstairs, and located the card. At 6:00 a.m., I sat down, and without a single error I wrote Abigail a note inside the card.

"Words cannot express how infinitely sorry I am over your loss. I, too, shall miss Keir's warm voice and gentle laughter, his engaging smile, his beautiful eyes, easy manner, and gentlemanly charm.

"May you hold him close forever in your hearts.

"Although I cannot do any more for Keir, if you ever need to talk, please feel free to call me. I can be a good listener."

My last letter to Keir had gone through twelve rewrites. My sympathy note to Abigail was perfectly expressed the first time. I enclosed the card inside the accompanying envelope and placed it inside my purse, then proceeded to dress in my funeral outfit, adding a gold heart pin to the lapel of my black jacket.

Auguste and Mireille awoke—the latter delighted for her mother's early return, albeit, short-lived. After arranging that Auguste would fetch Mireille home from school in the afternoon, she and I left at 7:00 a.m. for her middle school where I dropped her off before driving to Mansfield to meet Mark Thomas.

Tuesday, June 25th, had dawned as a clear, sunny, perfect, summer day—except for the heaviness in my heart. I turned on the car radio for company only to hear Enriqué Iglesias' song "(You Can Be My) Hero": If you witnessed me crying, would you cry also? If I were to kiss you, would you tremble from my touch? Luckily, I was driving out of the city, against most of the heaviest traffic, because I could hardly see the road through my tears. Grabbing for the box of tissues on the floor behind my driver's seat, I realized it was the box I had stowed in the car for my visit to Keir on March 6th. I would definitely need them today.

About an hour later, I pulled off of Exit 169 for a quick pit stop and to alert Mark Thomas by phone that I would be arriving shortly at his office. He was waiting in the already-full parking lot.

"Hello, Mark. I have not slept all night. Would it be possible for you to drive?"

"We will have to take your car because there is no space for you to park your car here, and I have an assigned space."

"Can you drive stick?"

"Yes."

348

The day was already promising to be a warm one. I put the car in neutral and got out of the driver's seat, adjusting it for Mark's longer legs, and placed my suit jacket on the hook behind it above the back seat. Mark placed his suit jacket on the opposite hook, behind the passenger seat, and came around to the driver's side. After Mark adjusted the seat and mirrors, we headed out of the parking lot toward Route 30 to get back on I-71 North.

After our initial pleasantries, I recalled for Mark in detail the events of the past six months: my phone calls, Keir's increasing physical reliance on walkers and wheel chair, our mutual declaration of love foretold by the visit from God to me the previous summer, our awful last phone call when Keir "pushed me away," my subsequent letter with the prayer emails, the spiritual communications at The BroAdmoor with Kevin Raines that suggested I needed Mark, the Sunday email from Abigail I had read earlier, and the sympathy card I had written to her in response that was now resting inside my pocketbook.

"Mark, Keir told me he was glad you were my friend."

"I didn't know him very well, but we did serve on a couple of Health Law Section committees together."

Mark listened to my saga with heartfelt attention. Instead of being a health insurance lawyer, I think Mark should have been a pastor. As mutual graduates of all three Levels of the same personal development courses, we had been trained to have the capacity to suspend judgment of others. Mark accepted my account of the events with kindness and sympathy, occasionally asking questions for clarification or adding in his own observations, but completely without disapproval or condemnation. Not only did Mark not judge my behavior over the last six months, he seemed to endorse my efforts to stay connected with Keir.

Mark's attitude relieved me of some of the duplicitous guilt I was feeling toward Abigail, and even for unintentionally precipitating Keir's death by telling him I loved him. True, we had not had a physically intimate relationship—I was not even sure now if I had overplayed Keir's feelings for me or taken advantage of the situation of his illness—but something had occurred between us, time and time again, something that Sylvia had witnessed in those few moments of Keir's greeting me during the opening reception at the Cedar Palace Hotel back in 1995.

I needed Mark to reflect my story from the viewpoint of a male, a spouse, a member of OAHIA, a lawyer, and a former colleague of Keir's in order to provide me with the more balanced opinion of a neutral bystander. At this point, only Mark, Sylvia, and Hillary were privy to what had occurred between me and Keir, and I knew I could not trust my own interpretation of the events, skewed and fueled as they were with feelings of self-doubt, culpability, denial, and self-reproach.

During the course of our drive, Mark revealed to me facts about him that I had not known or had forgotten. He and Kevin Raines had known each other as teenagers when Mark was a counselor at church camp and Kevin was a camper. Then they had been sworn in at the Ohio Bar in the same ceremony, eventually ended up in the same legal specialty field, and even served on the OAHIA Executive Committee together for a short while.

In addition, Mark's mother, a smoker, had died of breast cancer. I started to understand Mark's own aversion to, and fear about, cancer—why he had not told me that Keir had been diagnosed with brain cancer when he learned about it two years earlier from Greg Grissom, because it brought back those other painful memories.

We talked about other subjects: our respective daughters, who were close in age and Mark's marriage to Marianne, a "preacher's kid."

Approaching the Covenant-Coventry UMC in Cleveland Heights, we noticed that a church expansion construction project required some church attendees to park in an overflow lot across the street. The lot was almost full, but Mark managed to steer my Saturn into the last remaining open spot.

Mark and I stepped out of my car and walked around to the opposite sides to retrieve our respective suit jackets from the back seat hooks.

"I usually wear my heart on my sleeve," I quipped to Mark, pointing to the gold heart pin on my jacket, "but today I am wearing it on my lapel."

"You are still wearing your heart on your sleeve," Mark observed gently.

A Golden Retriever trotted up to greet us, his blue eyes turning first to look at me and then to look at Mark, first a bit puzzled, but then, appearing satisfied, trotted off towards the parking lot exit. The incident was a bit curious, but I dismissed it as typical dog behavior.

After locking my car, Mark and I walked through the parking lot toward Coventry Road to cross over toward the sanctuary's main entrance.

"Do you believe that animals can take on human spirits?" Mark asked.

"I don't know..." I did not follow Mark's meaning.

Suddenly, I felt weak in my knees at the prospect of entering the church which would require me, at some level, to acknowledge what I did not wish to admit—that Keir was now dead. The emotional weight of what was about to happen and my anticipation bore down on me.

"I'm not sure I am going to be able to walk across the street." My voice trembled with my body. "May I have your arm?"

"I'd be honored." Mark allowed me to slip my arm through his right elbow and then patted my hand with his left. I could feel his solidness and strength buoying me up as we waited for the traffic to clear and then walked across the avenue to join the streams of people mounting the steps of the Indiana limestone, Gothic Revival church to enter under its square bell tower.

Inside, the sanctuary was the largest capacity Methodist Church I had ever entered, and the pews, from front to back, were filled with hundreds of fellow mourners. Mark steered me to the left side aisle.

350

Walking about half way toward the front, we spotted Harry and Martha Whitfield in one of the pews, so Mark and I slid into the pew behind them which was still relatively empty. Harry and Martha stood up and turned to greet us. Harry and Mark, both attorneys from Mansfield although working at different companies, shook hands as colleagues, murmuring their condolences.

Martha and I just looked at each other, burst out in fresh tears, and hugged each other wordlessly. We mutually recognized that neither of us knew what we could possibly say to the other to provide comfort or adequately express the depth of our sadness for the loss of a man who had been so dear and special. That alone spoke volumes.

Harry and Martha turned around and re-seated themselves, while Mark and I took our seats. I fumbled to pull more tissues out of my purse to wipe my eyes and blow my nose. I suddenly was aware the processional music being played was an instrumental version of Elvis Presley's "Can't Help Falling in Love with You." I was not sure how I was going to be able to make it through this funeral in one piece.

Mark was reading the small pamphlet that we were each given that listed Keir's birth and death dates, his surviving relatives, and his biography. Mark leaned over toward me, his finger pointing to the words, "...member of the Golden Retriever Book Club..." I recalled the dog with blue eyes in the parking lot and Mark's question to me about animal spirits. Had Keir, in the guise of the dog, come to check that Mark and I had made it to the funeral after Keir and Kevin had visited me at The BroAdmoor? Was that why they had included Mark in the vision, too?

The next song in the processional medley of Keir's favorites had a Zydeco beat. "To acknowledge Keir's Cajun heritage," I thought. Following it was a piece with bagpipes for his Scottish side. I took a moment to look around to see whom else I recognized from OAHIA.

Allen Farmer sat on the other side of Mark but further down our pew closer to the center aisle. Allen had been one of Keir's former Cleveland Medical colleagues and one of the "gang of four" along with Keir, Harry, and Diane Dudley managing Cleveland Medical back in 1995-97 before Kenneth Sven had been hired and then let Keir go. I had not liked Allen because he had been an impediment to Keir's promotion, but now I was touched that he, too, had driven up from Columbus for the funeral. Across the aisle from Allen but in the same pew row sat Brent Tillett, Jr., Keir's friend and Abigail's law partner, curiously dressed in a brightly-colored, luau shirt rather than the somber black of the standard funeral attire.

A few pews in front of Harry and Martha, I spied Jim Frazier and Peter Pascal, founding past president of OAHIA, sitting together. As my eyes scanned the assemblage of mourners, I did notice, dotted here and there, others sporting vibrant Hawaiian shirts. I tried to make out the family members in the front pew—to identify Abigail, Keir's brother, and especially Sean, but it was difficult from the backs of heads. Adding to the difficulty, Abigail's siblings and their spouses were seated with the other family members.

At eleven o'clock the minister rose to the pulpit and recited the same blessing prayer that I had written in a card and sent to Keir the previous October. Then the congregants rose to sing Cat Stevens' "Morning Has Broken," one of my favorite songs from the seventies. This was definitely not going to be your typical funeral, although some of the later songs were more religious in tone.

Following a scripture reading, the minister began his eulogy, explaining that, during the previous evening's visitation at the funeral home, Keir's friends remembered his extensive wardrobe of, and fondness for, colorful Hawaiian shirts and decided to wear them today to honor his vibrant personality, love of life, and casual, humorous nature. (I already knew I would be writing Keir's obituary for the OAHIA newsletter. I had in the back of my mind been wondering which photograph of him to select, and now I was certain which one I would use.)

The minister talked about Keir's love of storytelling, cooking, swimming, and Elvis music; his travels abroad to exotic locales and how he was a great traveling companion; his leadership contributions to various professional organizations, cultural institutions, and social service agencies; and, his involvement in church activities such as Sojourners and the Disciples course. (I remembered that my mother and Sylvia had both taken the Disciples course.) The minister mentioned Keir's love of music, his extensive music library (I remembered the entertainment center wall in his family room opposite the painting of Sean), and his intellectual curiosity that made him an avid and wide-ranging reader. (I admonished myself for how little I had actually known about Keir. How could I have felt so close to someone about whom I had known so little?)

Continuing on, the minister told of Keir's valiant battle against cancer, undergoing any treatment that offered hope of a cure. He had been dunked twelve times in a deep water tank, marking each dive on the pool wall so he would not lose track of the count, and had done water aerobics and yoga to keep his balance and maintain strength while the disease took away so many of his physical and mental abilities. (I remembered Keir telling me about encountering Peter Pascal in the YMCA pool as well as the morning call back on January 21st when Abigail told me he was starting a yoga class.)

"On his birthday last Tuesday," the pastor concluded, "Keir had a good day. He told his son, Sean, 'I think I want to take a cruise, but I'd like to go casual.' Keir fell into a coma on Thursday and passed away at six o'clock on Friday evening, surrounded by his family and listening to music." Looking heavenward, he added, "Father, into Thy hands I commend the spirit of our dear friend, Keir Mervais, loving husband of Abigail, loving father to Sean, and loving brother."

After another hymn and blessing, the minister and family proceeded out of the sanctuary to the campy tune of "Ease on Down the

352

Road." The rest of the assembly of mourners followed slowly. I caught sight of Abigail in a blue-and-beige flowered dress heading up the aisle. Instead of the curly brown hair I had remembered from our first two meetings, her hair had turned grey and was dyed blonde. (Vainly, I noted my own hair was still a natural brunette with only a few grey strands.)

Harry and Martha Whitfield stood and turned around. Once again, Martha and I looked at each other wordlessly, broke into tears again, and hugged each other. Mark and Harry shook hands again.

As we filed out of our pew, up the side aisle, and made our way to the vestibule, Mark and I nodded or murmured greetings to the other OAHIA members we saw. Since many of the church members had formed a line to greet the minister and the family, we exited by a side door into the bright noonday sun. Together, we approached Brent Tillett standing on the lawn in his luau shirt and exchanged greetings.

"I went to visit Keir on Friday morning," Brent explained with regret in his voice, "but because he was in a coma by then, I was not allowed to see him. Back in 1986, when I first spoke at the OAHIA conference at the Beaver Ridge Inn, my first son had just been born prematurely, and I was very worried. Keir sat with me on the porch..." Brent stopped to control the catch in his voice, "...and told me everything would be all right. And it was." I could tell this was an unforgettable bonding experience in Brent's and Keir's friendship.

Looking around, I noticed Abigail had come outside and was surrounded by a knot of people who took turns hugging her. I pulled the sympathy card I had written six hours earlier out of my purse and stood, waiting at a respectful distance until Abigail was momentarily alone, then stepped forward.

"I'm Annie."

"*You're* Annie!" We embraced.

"I liked you the first time I met you." We stepped apart. "I got your email message this morning at five o'clock."

"And you *came!*"

"I came all the way from Colorado Springs" I did not mention I had received news of Keir's death from Marcia Tuttle.

"You were *so* very special to Keir."

"And he was *very special* to me, too." I handed Abigail my card and then moved back so that others could approach her. What a difference from January, I thought, when she only remembered me from a plaque. Keir had not let on—or at least I had not realized—to what extent I had been unique in my support of him during his illness over the last couple of years, or what it may have meant to him. For so long I had been afraid that I was intruding, being an unwanted nuisance, or worse. And he had only told me he couldn't respond to my letters.

Beyond Abigail, I saw three, black, stretch limousines lined up at the curb. I did not know where they would take the family next. I walked back to Mark. Brent had gone off, and there was no one else around we knew.

"What do you want to do?" Mark asked. I looked at my watch: it was 12:15 p.m.

"Would you like to go to the Fine Art Garden in Wade Park?" Mark nodded as though a quiet period of meditation in a natural setting was just what he needed, too. We crossed the street back to my car. This time I took the driver's seat.

"Would you like to see where Keir lived? I can swing through his neighborhood on the way to the Garden," I asked before starting the engine. Mark again nodded in acquiescence.

From Fairmount Boulevard, I turned left onto Parkside Drive, quickly entering the Scottish Hills neighborhood. I turned right onto Glencourt and took a quick left onto Findon and right onto Hawkins.

"It's over there on the left, number 2226." Although I was sure Mark was in a substantially higher income bracket than Auguste and I, from Mark's silent reaction, he was impressed that the property values in this part of Cleveland Heights exceeded his own.

Turning right onto Scottish Hills Lane and left onto the upper end of Glencourt, we merged our way out of the quiet seclusion of Keir's neighborhood and back in to the noisy traffic of Cedar Glen Parkway, heading toward University Circle and Wade Lagoon. We finally found a parking spot on the street and walked over to the Garden in front of the art museum.

Selecting a bench in the shade, I explained to Mark how I had mentally dedicated the Garden to Keir two summers earlier when I had visited the Cleveland Museum of Art during the OAHIA convention. A gentle breeze slightly ruffled our hair as we smelled the scent of newly mowed grass and the new growth of flowers and leaves. For a while, we sat in companionable silence, each lost in our own thoughts about the memorial service, life, and loss. On the other side of the park, across the lagoon, we watched as two Golden Retrievers frolicked with a black dog near a large oak tree. Were the Retrievers Kevin Raines and Keir, I wondered? If so, who was the black dog? I was afraid it might be an omen about Mark.

"Are you ready to go?" Mark asked after about 30 minutes. We both stood up and walked back to my car. "Thank you for sharing the Garden and your dedication with me."

"Thank you for going with me," I smiled back at Mark.

"If we head back to Mansfield now, we can get some lunch near my office. I might be able to get some work done this afternoon." I remembered Mark had just returned from vacation the previous day and would likely have been behind in his paperwork even if he had not taken the day off for Keir's funeral.

"Okay, but we'll need to get some gas for the car. I know there is a Sunoco station on Cedar Road."

"I know how to get back to the highway from Cedar Road." We knew our choices were to drive through downtown Cleveland on Carnegie to I-90 or to head west through the fashionable neighborhoods of Cleveland Heights, University Heights, and Lyndhurst to Route 271 and skirt the city to the south, linking up with I-71 near Medina—a much more pleasant route. Mark paid for the tank of gas, and we switched drivers again so that he could take the wheel.

Although I was still profoundly sad, and probably still in some shock about Keir's death, I was also relieved that, rather than a blubbering fool through the ceremony, I had been able to keep a quiet dignity. I was now buoyed by what Abigail had told me, hopeful that Keir had received and been able to decipher my message of forgiveness and comprehend the prayers mentioned in my last letter.

On the return drive to Mansfield, Mark shared with me more about dealing with his mother's breast cancer and his frustration in trying to get her to stop smoking. I was touched by the measure of courage it took for him to accompany me to this funeral.

"Promise me something, Mark, if you ever hear of any news about OAHIA members, that you will let me know, and I will do the same for you." He agreed.

We spoke more of our families, Keir and Kevin, and other subjects for the remaining drive until we arrived near Mark's office building.

"There is a submarine sandwich shop here." He parked my car at the curb. "Come on, I'll buy you some lunch."

Now, close to two o'clock I was starting to notice my hunger as I had not eaten since before 7:00 a.m. when I had left home. Past the normal lunch hour, Mark and I were the only customers in the lunch room. The place smelled of a mix of freshly baked bread, tuna, mayonnaise, and pickles. We ordered our sandwiches and sat at a black-and-white metal and linoleum table in the center of the dining area.

"Thank you for going with me today, for driving, for buying the gas and my lunch. It has meant a lot to me."

"Thank you for trusting me to confide in me about your relationship with Keir and honoring me with the privilege of accompanying you."

After consuming our sandwiches and tossing the wrappings in the waste receptacle, we exited into the bright sunlight. We exchanged hugs at the curb.

"Are you okay to drive back to Columbus?" Mark was understandably concerned about my emotional state and possible fatigue.

"I'm okay now. It helped a lot that you drove half the trip."

Mark watched me get in the driver's seat. We both waved as I checked the traffic and pulled out into the driving lane. Glancing into my rearview mirror, I saw that Mark had begun walking down the street in the opposite direction toward his office.

In life, we are taught how to accumulate things, but losing them is a totally different experience. We continue to conduct ourselves in a normal routine—eating, dressing, walking, bathing, driving, etc. and, we do not look much different with broken hearts—no casts or surgical scars—but the experience is akin to being two-headed. One head goes on normally, and the other head might as well have had a frontal lobotomy. One minute you are fine, maybe even laughing at a joke, and the next minute you are curled up in a fetal position awash in tears that seem like they will never stop.

Even though I had previously experienced the deaths of all four of my grandparents, two teachers in junior high school, a junior high classmate, the former treasurer of another association, and Kevin Raines, I was more profoundly affected by Keir's death than by any of the others. Waking up on the morning after his funeral, my first thought was: "Without Keir, who will salve my wounds when Auguste says something hurtful?"

The entire time I knew Keir was ill, I had avoided watching the television comedy "Spin City" with Michael J. Fox. That Thursday evening, I watched the episode as if I was glued to the television, again noting Fox's striking resemblance to Keir.

One of Keir's friends from the Golden Retriever reading group was a columnist for the *Cleveland Plain-Dealer* and wrote a personal obituary describing Keir's upbeat approach to life, symbolized by the Hawaiian shirts, how the club members learned he was ill, his love of Elvis, the funeral music, and Keir's last trip to Lakeside. Jim Frazer faxed me a copy of the article, which again used the same black-and-white photo by Liam that I had mailed to Keir after my visit with him in March. The information in the article augmented my limited knowledge of Keir's life.

While I had been traveling in June, the deadline for the summer issue of the OAHIA newsletter had passed. We were also planning to hold OAHIA's 25th anniversary convention in August. I called Alicia Tomlinson to formulate the timeline and content for the newsletter. (I remembered that, ironically, Alicia had gotten her job at Cleveland Medical when Keir had lost his.)

"I want to write a column on the latest legislation the Ohio General Assembly is considering," Alicia told me. "Why don't you write a little something about Keir Mervais? You knew him better than I did."

"A *little* something?!" my mind protested. "Why I scarcely knew him at all! There were so many things I did not know about him, so many questions I still wanted to ask him." Besides, I was not sure I wanted to reveal to the OAHIA members or Keir's family the content of our relationship as it had unfolded predominantly in private conversations. I just was not too sure I was up to the task, but I certainly did not want to leave it to anyone else. Alicia and I agreed on a deadline of July 15th for the newsletter copy. I would need some time to think about what I wanted to write.

Finally back in Columbus after my travels, I made arrangements to visit Carolyn on Monday, July 1st, in the morning. The U.S. Postal Service was raising the price of stamps that day, so I decided to swing by the post office to get some stamps before going to Carolyn's house. On my drive out of my neighborhood, the car radio played a new song by a teen-aged, classically trained, songwriter; the lyrics and music went straight to my heart. When I arrived at the post office, the parking lot was so full I could not find a spot, and the line to purchase new stamps filled the lobby.

I calculated that I did not have enough time to wait in line and still get to Carolyn's house by ten o'clock when Gary had to leave for work. I circled through the parking lot and headed out of the drive toward the stop light at the entrance. I changed the radio station, still a little perturbed that my stamp-buying plan had been thwarted. "There must be a perfect reason for this," I rationalized.

The same song was playing on the radio as before. I listened more closely. "(Fly Me Up) To Where You Are" was pleading to the composer's deceased loved one to fly him up to heaven so he can be with her for a few moments to see her smile again; she is still only a heartbeat away, and he can still feel her spiritual presence in the darkness.

The traffic light turned green, and I pulled out and turned left onto the main street as the radio announcer was talking about the song. "Josh Groban was trained at Julliard. His first album, 'Josh Groban,' is great. That's Groban—G-R-O-B-A-N."

I wondered if this was a sign from the universe. Rarely any more do radio disk jockeys even tell the names of the songs or the artists, much less spell their names. Maybe this was why my post office visit had turned out the way it had? I resolved to buy Josh Groban's album.

I knew I would need to tell Carolyn that Keir had died, but I knew I could not share the sad news with her over the phone. I had used his cancer treatment progress to motivate her, and I had even given her one of Keir's The Merv Show baseball caps. After Carolyn greeted me at the door and invited me inside the living room, we exchanged the normal courtesies.

"Please sit down," Carolyn indicated the gold suede sofa to her right. She was definitely showing the fatigue and physical signs of the chemo treatments. Her teeth had taken on a brownish-yellow tinge and most of her fine blonde hair was gone, leaving only a few strands and tufts. We seated ourselves on the sofa. Sunlight was coming in through the window curtains on both sides of the entertainment center on the other wall.

"How was your trip?" she asked, referring to my two convention jaunts to Mackinac Island and Colorado Springs.

"I had to come back from Colorado Springs early." I took both of Carolyn's hands in mine and raised my eyes to hers. I took a deep breath so that I could speak in a quiet and measured tone. "Keir died Friday evening while I was on Mackinac, but I didn't know until Monday morning when I was at The BroAdmoor. My boss, Jack, permitted me to fly back early to Columbus so that I could drive to the funeral in Cleveland on Tuesday. Mark Thomas drove me from Mansfield and back." I thought Carolyn might remember Mark from our professional development seminars together.

Carolyn looked like someone had punched her in the stomach. She glanced away to take in the information. I described the funeral's upbeat character but was afraid she was becoming disheartened, so I changed the subject.

"Would you like to try a walk today?" My voice was an octave higher than normal.

"No. I think I'd like to eat something. There is some pudding in the refrigerator." I stood up and headed through the dining room to the kitchen. Although the house had been cleaned by a friend on Carolyn's support team, the refrigerator had the telltale signs of neglect dictated by her disease and someone on a soft food diet. Inside there were also remains of a pizza that I assumed belonged to Gary. I found a container of chocolate pudding, opened it, and found a clean spoon, returning to the living room to hand it to Carolyn.

"Did you want something?" I knew she was trying to be hospitable.

"No, thanks. I had breakfast before I came." I waited while she slowly took a few spoonsful of pudding. She put the cup down on the coffee table with the spoon inside.

"That's all." I wondered if her taste buds were affected by the chemo treatments as well as her appetite. "I'd like to take a nap now." I helped Carolyn down the hallway to the master bedroom. Carolyn crawled into the unmade bed, slipping her shoes off as she curled her feet under the coverlet and closed her eyes.

"Do you need anything else?"

"No," she whispered.

I left the bedroom and walked back down the hall to the living room. I took the pudding from the coffee table, went to the kitchen, found some aluminum foil to cover it, returned it to the refrigerator, and placed the spoon in the dishwasher. I checked around the house a bit, locked the front door, and let myself out the back door to sit outside for a while. Gary came home around noon to relieve me of my care giving responsibilities.

I recalled that when I had written Keir before I left for Mackinac Island, I had promised myself that I would call him on July 2nd. Instead, I wrote Abigail a letter of encouragement and sympathy. I had a desire to support Keir's family—after all, he had loved them—but maybe I also had a need to assuage some of my guilt. (I had tried to keep my relationship with Keir one of friendship, not crossing that unspoken line in the sand, but our toes had come right up to that line on a few occasions.)

Some of the OAHIA past presidents had sent me their recollections of their terms for inclusion in the 25th anniversary booklet that included history and photos. I already had memorized Keir's statement. Now I would need to prepare his obituary for the OAHIA newsletter, something I had been resisting all week. That Saturday evening, while Auguste was on the sofa watching television, I went upstairs to our office/computer room to begin. What could I write about him? Between the church eulogy and the *Plain-Dealer* obituary, I realized I scarcely knew the man.

Since my coaching training urged me to "start where you are," I began to type what I did not know about Keir, and then I wrote what I did know about him. I knew about his family and I knew I wanted to share my article with Abigail when I was done. I knew he respected and admired her, but if I had been his widow and had struggled through two-and-a-half years of cancer, I would have wanted more, so I wrote that he had adored her. In my professional development courses, we learned to acknowledge people for "who they are for us" and seek to "touch, move, and inspire" others. Inside that context, I wrote about what I had learned about Keir from our conversations over the previous half year and what I had gleaned about him from our earlier interactions since 1986. The words seemed to flow out of me, almost as if composed by someone outside of me.

As I typed, I would remember something about Keir and decide how to word it, cry, and then type. Then I would remember something else, cry, and then type. Many times the tears would arise from a combination of sadness, joy, regret, and being touched. In the process of writing, for the first time I experienced my own creative expression. I had always written journalistically before, but creative writing was a new format for me.

When I reached a point in the obituary where I wished to describe how Keir had affected other people, I stopped. I needed and wanted input from his friends and colleagues. The following Monday, I composed an email to the OAHIA members requesting a short memorial paragraph from those who wished to submit one.

Through this process, I learned even more aspects of Keir's life and the depth and breadth of his relationships. The first contribution to my obituary was from Rick Northfield, the attorney from Newark who had helped to extricate me from the Arts Council position back in 1985. Rick wrote about Keir's travels, including trips to Africa, India, and the Himalayas. In reading Rick's email message, I was suddenly struck with the profound blessing that, by losing the Newark arts council job, I had been given the opportunity to join AEMG, OAHIA, and, especially, to meet Keir.

Larry Hammersmith wrote about attending Case Western Law School together with Keir and their thirty-year friendship, Keir's unique sense of humor, and his distinct way of viewing the world. Charlie Lincoln wrote about Keir's leadership and devotion to the health insurance industry. Charlie Parker shared thoughts about Keir's warmth and how he made everyone feel special.

As the week wore on, I was still hoping for a contribution from Brent, Liam, or Harry—three people with whom I knew Keir had been friends. I was fully aware that I was asking for emotional writing during a period when many people were on vacation, and I had only given them a week to produce it. In addition, I recalled my difficult experiences in the past with trying to extract president's columns from these men for the newsletter.

On the following Monday, Liam sent me an email explaining he had been on vacation but hoped his memorial writing was not too late. He wrote how Keir had changed the OAHIA convention dress code to Hawaiian shirts back in 1987—a perfect accompaniment to the photo I had selected to include in the obituary. I was now ready to finish writing the piece, but I was still stuck without an ending that succinctly wrapped up who Keir embodied for me. I still had a few more days to finish the article before our deadline.

Back in April, I had registered for a watercolor class on Monday afternoons at the local arts center. Keir had been disappointed for me that my partners and I had closed the art gallery the year before, and now that I was only working half-time, Jack Spencer—my boss and a former ceramic artist himself—gave me permission and encouragement to take the afternoon painting class. In addition, before she became ill, I had coached Carolyn on being The Hobby Lady, a person who encouraged people to engage in hobbies for fun and relaxation. Two weeks after Keir's funeral, I started the six-week watercolor class.

Painting requires focus, planning, and visual study, using the right and left sides of our brains. Neuroscientists describe the neural process of art creation as being akin to being in a meditative state. For me, it provided a sense of quiet joy and bliss, a period when I was elevated out of my sadness to express my admiration for the beauty of form and nature. It allowed me an outlet for my grief in a way I did not expect. I invited Keir's spirit along to the classes with me. I felt a shift in the atmosphere, like he was delighted to come along, and sometimes I could feel him watching over my shoulder as I painted.

In our Monday evening personal development seminars, we had finished Being Exceptional: Living Beyond the Ordinary, which had coincided with Keir's last three months of life, and now we were beginning the Profoundly Related seminar. My relationships, however, did not feel full of potential. Carolyn was becoming more ill, Keir was dead, Mireille was acting out as a thirteen-year-old, Auguste was criticizing me for not acting like a wife, and I was crying daily in the shower or in my walk-in closet so that I could hold it all together at work and in front of my family. The only time I felt I could just be myself was on my thirty-minute weekly coaching calls with Hillary and while painting.

The 25th OAHIA anniversary convention was only one month away. I needed to finish Keir's obituary for the newsletter and prepare the anniversary booklet with the OAHIA presidential memories. Despite a few reminders, I had only collected about a third of the presidential quotes I needed. I began reading the Association's minutes from 1977 to create the memorial portions for the OAHIA past presidents whose entries were missing.

Our memories are interesting critters. They hide and morph and disappear and reappear in different shapes altogether. For example, I had forgotten that I had actually met Keir at my *second* OAHIA Executive Committee meeting at his office in Cleveland (he missed the first meeting I attended in Mansfield). That was the meeting on the day following the

ACOO board meeting when the latter voted to leave AEMG, and it was the time when I told Liam (within Keir's earshot) that Auguste was moving to Pittsburgh. The minutes also reminded me that it was also the meeting when, at my urging, the officers agreed to take action to turn OAHIA around financially, even though Keir, as Treasurer, had warned them all the previous year of their impending financial difficulties.

As I read more in the minutes, I remembered that those early months of knowing Keir had coincided with Auguste living away in Pittsburgh. (Perhaps I had been more carefree, independent, and open when Auguste was not living with me on a daily basis?) The revelations from reading the minutes posed a different interpretation for me of the "special services clause" that Keir had fashioned—the one that he had termed in 2000 as my "lifetime contract."

After a week of mulling over potential endings for Keir's obituary, I found a greeting card I had bought for him but had not sent. On the front of the card was a photograph of two hands on a potter's wheel molding a clay pot:

"As the Potter's adept hands molds our CLAY, we feel BENT, STRETCHED and PULLED in many directions as we implore, 'Are You not done with me yet?' But the Potter answers, 'You must be PATIENT and cede to My touch, as I am making you into a BEAUTIFUL thing.'

"...we are the clay, and thou our potter, and we all are the work of thy hand."– Isaiah 64:8

"When the Lord sends us moments of trial, we don't always understand why, but we are His ever-evolving work in progress. May God's love grant you continued strength as He casts you into one of His own precious works of art."

I inserted the quote into the obituary and, as a last thought, added a small box at the end with instructions on making donations in Keir's memory. Once our graphic designer had created the newsletter proof, I mailed a photocopy of the obituary to Abigail. On the next day, Thursday, July 18th, a month after Keir's 54th birthday, I emailed the newsletter to the OAHIA membership. After pushing the send button, I sat at my computer terminal to cry from the weighty sense of finality. After several minutes, I dried my eyes, donned my sneakers, and went out for a walk.

I had no idea how the OAHIA members and Keir's family would react to my presumption in authoring the obituary myself, to my portrayal of Keir, or to my audacity in dedicating two full pages of the newsletter to extol him. Although I had begun the article mentioning his interests and his family, buried deep on the second page was the statement that was the most nakedly revealing: *"I was blessed to play a role in his last inning, and during that short time, I learned something of his capacity for love, strength, and courage...and my own."*

At 9:38 p.m. that evening, I received the first reaction to the obituary by email, from Keir's brother, Mark, whom, ironically, I had forgotten to mention in the obituary. I concluded he must have received a copy of my tribute from either Abigail or one of the OAHIA members. He admitted to *"typing through a few tears"* (something he did not have to confess to me but which endeared me to him immediately). He thanked me for my *"kind words and obvious warm friendship"* with his brother and for writing the memorial.

I replied that I could not possibly fathom what his family had been through. I went on to relate to him the incident in the summer of 1987 when Keir had cried in front of me upon learning about their mother's cancer diagnosis and that, having two brothers of my own, I knew I would miss them painfully if they had died. I took the opportunity of this email exchange to ask where the family had decided to bury Keir.

Mark replied that Keir had been cremated and his remains stored at the funeral home awaiting construction to be completed for a columbarium at the church. I regretted that Keir's eyes, hands, mind, body, and voice, not only were dust in a box but shelved in a dark room rather than free and scattered at the lake he had loved so much.

Abigail took the weekend to compose her response. She wrote she had been very touched by what I had written and wanted to include my obituary in a collection of items about Keir she was saving for Sean and perhaps for any children he might have. She pointed out that, *"It had been difficult during Keir's illness and increasingly debilitating disabilities for him to stay in touch with people."* (I now wondered whether he could have even dialed the phone himself unless a family member's number was already on speed dial.) She noted that Keir had experienced loneliness, except for *"a small number of special people"* who *"took the extra time to reach out to him."* She also praised my generosity.

All this time I had assumed Keir's many friends and OAHIA colleagues had stayed in touch with him; after all, there were hundreds in attendance at his funeral. I knew it was uncharacteristic of Keir to have admitted to being lonely, or that I was one of the few who had remained supportive through his illness. Now, I wished I had known he was lonely—I would have called him every day and written him every week. However, I reminded myself, my affection for him would have been more obvious and a cease-and-desist letter from Abigail more likely. At least now she thought I was a hero.

It was exactly that affection that I had been trying to hide from Abigail, from Auguste, from the OAHIA members, from my co-workers, and even from Keir and myself. There were only a few people I trusted enough with the secret of my broken heart: Mark Thomas; Hillary; my coach, Carolyn; a few other friends in my professional development community; and, Sylvia, who witnessed Keir calling me "the most beautiful woman in the room" and had sent me a sympathy card. Abigail could mourn her loss openly, but my grief was kept in the closet.

Whenever someone I know dies, I have felt their personality lingering with me very strongly for a few days following their death. The same experience now occurred with Keir, only it did not subside as it had

362

with the others. I bought the Josh Groban album and found an even more poignant song on it: "You're Still You." Clearly, Groban had experienced the lingering spirit of his deceased grandmother in much the same way that I was still feeling Keir's presence. Despite my jam-packed schedule and especially while I was pre-occupied with more mundane tasks like driving or doing the dishes, I felt Keir's personality, his soul-spirit, for a fleeting second. I would try to grab onto it to hold it, but it dissipated as quickly as it came.

As I drove home from work one afternoon that summer, I felt Keir's hand reach from the back seat of my car and touch my right shoulder as though to say, "This one is for you." The car radio then played Elvis Presley's "Can't Help Falling in Love with You", the song from Keir's funeral. Hot tears coursed down my cheeks. No sooner had Presley stopped crooning when Celine Dion's lyrics from *The Titanic* movie, "My Heart Will Go On," began, its lyrics penetrating my heart like a fundamental truth.

Towards the end of July, I was scheduled to take care of Carolyn one afternoon. I brought along Groban's CD and played the songs for her. When I dissolved into tears at the crescendo of "You're Still You," she gently asked me to stop playing the music. Then I read my tribute to Keir out loud to her.

"I've been thinking," she said quietly. "I want to have a celebrate life memorial service like your friend Keir did, perhaps in the morning before people have to rush off to work." I realized Carolyn was dictating her end-of-life-directives and quickly grabbed a sheet of paper out of my seminar notebook and a pen from my purse. "I'd like an outdoor service with my priest, but not a formal Catholic service. Then maybe everyone can go out for breakfast together."

I remembered Carolyn had enjoyed walking around the lake at Sharon Woods Metropark and had been a member of a breakfast group before she had gotten cancer. Many of those group members were now her core cancer support team. I wrote it all down.

"Now, I'm tired, and I'd like to rest." Carolyn leaned back on her pillow and closed her eyes. I gathered my own belongings and went out to the living room. In the foyer, a collection of the family's books stood in a bookcase. Among the Gary Zukar spiritual books and real estate investment guides, one narrow volume caught my attention, *I Hope You Dance*. The song had always reminded me of Keir when sung by Lee Ann Womack, but this book was authored by the lyricists, Mark D. Sanders and Tia Sillers. One particular passage resonated with me, (paraphrased):

> *"Hope is an amazing thing…*
> *With it, you bare your soul…*
> *You wear your heart on your sleeve…*
> *You wait with bated breath,*
> *To hear*
> *'I love you, too…'*
> *Having faith*

That you will be given a second chance
That you can make a difference
That tomorrow may be better than today...
That what you do will matter."

When Gary, Carolyn's husband, arrived home from work to relieve me of caretaker duty, I told him Carolyn had given me her funeral instructions.

"I don't know why she gave them to me...?" I thought Greg might be offended that she had given a non-family member this crucial information.

"That's because you're her coach."

"Do you want them?" I handed him the piece of notebook paper which he grabbed from my hand, crumpled into a ball, and tossed behind him. He headed for the kitchen. I picked up the paper from the floor, smoothed it out, and laid it on the bookshelf in the foyer before letting myself out the front door.

Mireille and I rented the movie *Moulin Rouge* with Nicole Kidman and Ewan MacGregor over the weekend. The film opens with MacGregor typing that the most important lesson in life is to love and allow yourself to be loved in return.The film includes many popular songs, including Elton John's "This is your song", which includes lyrics about not remembering the color of someone's eyes—whether they were blue or green. But I had *not* forgotten the color of Keir's eyes depending on his contact lenses—at one time, light green, and another, light blue.

Some days later, I went with a girlfriend to see the movie *Unfaithful* with Dianne Lane and Richard Gere. In a horrifying scene when Gere discovers his wife, Lane, had had an extramarital affair, Gere smashes her snow globe over her lover's head and kills him. Since Lane and Gere are married in the film and therefore protected by spousal immunity, she lies to investigators about the incident, and they continue to live together sharing their tragic secret. As I watched in dismay and, remembering Auguste's temper, I was relieved Keir and I had not ever had an affair.

The summer Disney movie, *Lilo and Stitch*, used Elvis songs in its soundtrack. Mireille had already seen it with her friends, so I went alone on a Saturday afternoon. The film is cute in typical Disney fashion, but when the credits began to roll, the music of "Can't Help Falling in Love with You" nailed me to my seat.

"Are you alright, ma'am?" One of the ushers sweeping the floor had noticed me. Peeling my eyes away from the screen, I looked around. I was the only patron still seated in the theater.

"Uh, yes..." I quickly stood up, gathered my purse and sweater, and exited the theater.

I knew grief is a series of emotional states: shock, anger, denial, sadness, relief, disbelief, guilt, panic, depression, resignation, acceptance, and moving on. What I did not know is that it is not linear but more of a vortex. Just when you think you have safely completed one phase, it comes

364

around again, springing upon you like a tiger from behind. I had hours of productivity followed by an overwhelming desire to sleep in the mid-afternoon, slipping into oblivion, unable to go on. I felt like I was sleep-walking or had a split personality, living two concurrent lives.

On July 28th, I again pulled out my "hard times journal,' the one where I had recorded letters to Keir I had never sent, and wrote to him of my pain, loneliness, and feeling that I was going insane, drop by drop. The previous day, I mentally attempted to make our whole reunion a mistake, but I felt him not allowing me that train of thought. I listed a series of unanswered questions.

I suspected Abigail might be the only one who could answer some of my lingering questions. I phoned her on July 31st to see how she was doing. A woman, perhaps Sean's nanny, answered the phone.

"Abigail is out having dinner with some friends, but I will tell her you called." She took my name and number.

"Dinner with friends is good," I thought to myself, recalling my own attempts at normalcy.

One of the women in my Profoundly Related seminar group had worked for a hospice. I knew Keir had been under hospice care at the end, but I knew very little about what it entailed. I called to speak with her but left a message when there was no answer.

On the morning of August 1st, I was scheduled to visit Carolyn again. Since she had wanted to be The Hobby Lady, I wanted to show her the watercolors I had produced from my class. Carolyn was seated in a wheelchair when I arrived. Nearly completely bald, she had lost a lot of weight and looked like someone with the collapsed shoulders of osteoporosis. We chatted for a while, and then I pulled out my paintings.

"Beautiful," she said wanely as I showed her each one. "Lovely." As I finished, I watched something happen to Carolyn: a clouding of the eyes, a withdrawal of the mind, and a shift in consciousness. "I'm tired now," she whispered. I wheeled her into the bedroom and helped her into bed. I waited until Gary came home for lunch to leave.

After I arrived home, the woman knowledgeable about hospice returned my call.

"How long does someone grieve the death of a good friend?" I asked.

"Family members usually grieve for twelve to eighteen months."

"What about for *two* friends?"

"It depends on whether you grieve them separately or together."

I related to her what had happened to Carolyn during my visit. The woman was already familiar with the circumstances since Gary and Carolyn had been in the seminar with us.

"It's time for Gary to call in hospice," she advised.

That evening Abigail also returned my call. We exchanged a few pleasantries before I introduced my main reason for calling.

"I realize you probably aren't ready to deal with cleaning Keir's effects out yet, but when you do, only if you don't want to keep them, I would appreciate your returning the letters and vase that I sent him." I felt a little awkward broaching the subject but wanted to get my request in before it was too late.

"What was the vase like...?"

"About six or eight inches high, with a burgundy shino glaze and about six faceted sides."

"Oh, those items must be in Keir's room."

My mind reacted. "*Keir's room*? You mean you two had *separate* bedrooms?" All along, I had assumed they shared a master bedroom like Gary and Carolyn. Had they converted Keir's home office into a sick room when he became ill so as not to disturb either's rest, especially during periods of cancer treatment side effects?

Out loud, I related Carolyn's situation to Abigail.

"Your friends should call hospice. There is a website that was very helpful to Keir and me in describing the end of life process. It is called 'passingover.com.' It was written by a hospice worker."

"Thank you." After our goodbyes, I went upstairs to our computer and spent the next hour-and-a-half reading the website:

> "*...about the process of dying from someone who had witnessed it firsthand numerous times. The dying person usually withdraws into a type of 'coma' but instead of being totally unconscious, it is more like a speeded up transformational process of readiness to 'pass-over.' Herein derive the accounts of an accelerated reviewing of one's lifetime near the point of death. At times the person dying may see a deceased loved one coming for them or talk about going on a journey* (as Keir had mentioned a cruise). *Hospice workers may administer morphine or other drugs to ease any physical pain to allow the people under their care to focus completely on their spiritual transition.*"

When I finished reading, I emailed the URL to Gary.

While at work the next morning, Hillary phoned me.

"Gary called in hospice for Carolyn last night. They have sent word to their daughter, Pamela, in the Peace Corps in Central America to come home and are urging anyone who wants to say goodbye to Carolyn to visit her today."

I related to Hillary what had transpired the previous morning at Carolyn's house and what I had read on the website.

"I'll go by their house again tomorrow," I promised.

I had only planned to stop by for a few moments on Saturday for moral support, but Gary invited me into the bedroom where Pamela (only just arrived home from Central America), her brother Isaac, and the hospice worker were seated on or adjacent to Carolyn and Gary's bed. Carolyn was lying on her back, semi-conscious, with her eyes half-closed. After murmuring greetings and exchanging hugs, Gary suggested I sit down on the side of the bed near Carolyn's legs. I picked up her right hand and held it in my own.

When Carolyn had become ill, I had promised her that if she died our professional development community would support and take care of her family emotionally.

"It's okay," I said to her simply. An important part of coaching is "giving permission," and I had just given Carolyn permission to die. I knew she understood me, because she closed her eyes. In that moment, I understood to my core what it meant to be a "life coach." I was coaching Carolyn to let go of her life, and she was silently coaching me how to die with dignity.

The hospice worker administered a dose of morphine. There was no concern about addiction; Carolyn was not expected to live long enough to become addicted. Pamela pulled out the wrinkled paper whereon, only a week ago, I had written Carolyn's end-of-life directives. Together with her immediate family, we planned Carolyn's memorial service in accordance with her wishes. I left an hour later.

With the OAHIA 25th anniversary convention only four days hence, I spent Sunday morning compiling an album of photographs from past OAHIA conventions. I had just finished organizing and laying down Liam's black-and-white shots of Keir's convention and presidential term in 1987-88 (choosing to leave out the photos of Keir and Abigail), when the phone rang.

"This is Adrienne Rush. Carolyn passed away at 8:00 this morning." Adrienne had been one of the organizers of Carolyn's support team. I thanked her for calling me, then sat on the bed while I let the news sink in for a few moments, noting the ironic timing of placing Keir's photos in the album with Carolyn's news. They were both fifty-four years old. I reached for the phone again and dialed Hillary's number. We cried together on the phone. After composing myself, I called Carolyn's family to offer my condolences. Carolyn's daughter, Pamela, answered.

"Visitation is scheduled for 6:30 tomorrow evening at the Granville Funeral Home. The memorial service will be Tuesday morning at Sharon Woods. The priest will read something, we'll sing, and then we'll walk around the lake together since Mom loved walking there. We've made arrangements for breakfast at the Embassy Suites."

"Is there anything I can do?"

"Having your notes about what Mom wanted was a godsend. Thank you for all that you did to help her. I think we've got most of it under control."

"I'll see you tomorrow night then."

The next afternoon I had my watercolor class. I painted a beach scene, but it was missing something. I added in two figures—a man and a woman walking hand-in-hand. I knew they represented Gary and Carolyn.

I arrived a little early at the funeral home for the visitation. Gary took both my hands in his and looked me straight in the eyes.

"I'm so glad *you* were the first to arrive!" I handed him my beach painting, and he hugged me. "I'll put it with Carolyn's photo montage and an angel picture painted by her cousin." Gary led me over to the casket where we stood together silently for a few moments. I noticed the unnaturally waxy cast to Carolyn's embalmed body. I had not seen an open casket since my grandmother's funeral nearly thirty years ago. (Silently, I wondered if Keir's visitation had been open casket and whether I would have been able to withstand peering at his body in this same manner.)

Other friends began to arrive. I was glad to focus on other thoughts. Gary introduced me to his mother and brother, explaining that Carolyn's mother could not make the journey. I learned that Carolyn would be cremated following the visitation. I remembered my Buddhist neighbor's memorial service a couple of years earlier when his widow, ten-year-old daughter, Auguste, Mireille, Mireille's twelve-year old female neighbor friend, and I had watched the father's casket enter one side of an oven on a conveyor belt and come out the other in an urn. I walked over to Gary.

"Do you need me to stay with you?"

"No. I'm okay. I've got Pamela and Isaac with me and the rest of the family. Are you coming tomorrow morning?"

"Yes, of course." We hugged goodbye.

As I lay in bed that night awaiting sleep, I felt Carolyn's presence strong and clear. My mind addressed her.

"Hey, sweetie! How are you? What's it like?"

"I miss my friends and family, but I can go wherever I want in an instant: to Philadelphia where my mom is, to Columbus to be with Gary and Isaac, and even to Central America where Pamela is teaching." Then she was gone. Just like the brief visits I had had from Keir and Kevin on June 23rd and from Keir over the previous six weeks, this experience was natural, peaceful, reassuring, and joyous to me.

Arriving in the parking lot at Sharon Woods Metro Park on Tuesday at 6:45 a.m., I saw a woman from our seminar unloading a large quantity of white helium balloons out of her SUV. There were 54 balloons—one for each year of Carolyn's life. Each person attending the service held one, and at the end of the formal service led by the priest, we let our balloons fly heavenward from the bridge over the lake before walking the 3.8 mile trail circuit. Gary carried Carolyn's urn in his left arm and walked her Jack Russell terrier with his right hand. I recognized many of the mourners from our seminars, including a few seminar leaders, but Carolyn's neighbors, family, and friends were also there. We must have been a curious sight to the regular joggers on their normally quiet path: a loose parade of nearly sixty people. Afterwards, we all adjourned to the Embassy Suites hotel for a buffet breakfast before going to work—just as Carolyn had wished.

On Wednesday, Jennifer Erwin and I finished convention preparations for OAHIA's 25th anniversary convention and packed our respective cars with the educational and registration materials, the photo album I had finished only the day before, and the bound copies of the anniversary history I had prepared since Keir's death. I had written an especially touching introduction for the history and, at the last moment, decided to dedicate the volume to Kevin Raines and Keir Mervais. Ironically, the same day that Carolyn had died, so had one of OAHIA's founding private practicing attorney members, so the association had yet another death to grieve.

However, one convention item was curiously missing. I could not find the green-and-gold OAHIA banner. I recalled bringing it back from the Cedar Palace convention the year before and placing it in the office storeroom, but it was no where to be found in our offices. (I began to wonder if Keir had some how "spirited" it away so that I would never stretch up to take it down again.)

As Auguste, Mireille, and I drove northwest to the Sheraton Swiss Inn in Mentor-on-the-Lake for the OAHIA convention, I thought about Keir's, Kevin's, and Carolyn's love of Lake Erie; two had owned lakeside vacation homes and Kevin had lived in Toledo, on the lake's shore. Even though Keir had not attended the 1998 convention at the Swiss Inn, it had been the last one Kevin had attended while he was still in good health, and traveling up I-71 and 271, bypassing Cleveland, was a strong reminder of my last trip—to Keir's funeral. Luckily, Auguste had elected to drive because I was staring out the window watching the Ohio countryside as the tears coursed down my cheeks. This would be my first OAHIA convention since writing and publishing Keir's obituary in the newsletter, about as public I had ever been about my feelings for him. I knew it was going to be an emotionally difficult experience—everything about the Association reminded me of him. Drawing on my professional development training, I resolved to have the potentiality of Courage and Honor present for the convention weekend.

During the Thursday afternoon OAHIA Executive Committee meeting in President Alicia Tomlinson's suite, I proposed that the Association honor the memories of Keir and the attorney who had passed away the previous Sunday with a donation to the Education Trust Fund for Kevin Raine's children, keeping the money within the industry's family. My proposal was approved unanimously.

Unbeknownst to me, however, thirteen members of OAHIA— current and former officers—had collected monies privately to honor my seventeen years as Executive Director. Greg Grisham and Gordon Geddes had spearheaded the collection to give to the Brain Cancer Center at The Ohio State University Hospital. As I stepped to the podium during Friday evening's banquet to make my impromptu Thank You speech, my brain was screaming, "NO! Not to the Brain Cancer Center! They didn't do what they were supposed to do! They were supposed to keep Keir *alive!*"

Both mornings while at the lake, I woke up early, donned sneakers, and took a lakeside stroll, thinking about my three friends who had died of cancer. Carolyn's ashes would be scattered at the lake by her family. With the cool lake air touching my face and the sun starting to ascend in the sky, I stopped walking, faced the water, and cried.

Upon my return to the office on Monday, I mailed extra copies of the 25th anniversary booklets to the OAHIA past presidents who were unable to attend the convention as well as to widows Rebecca Raines and Abigail Mervais.

Soldiering my way through three conventions and three deaths in three months had taken its toll. I was exhausted. I still had so many questions lingering in my mind about Keir, and I missed him *so* much. I dreamt I held his hand while he was dying as I had held Carolyn's hand. One evening in mid-August, I began to cry at the dinner table.

"What's *your* problem?" Auguste eyed me suspiciously.

"My friend Carolyn just died a couple of weeks ago…"

"I knew her. She was a nice lady. But now she's dead. Get over it."

I pushed the plate with my half-eaten supper away from me, stood up, and went into the bedroom, closing the door behind me. I crawled under the covers of the bed and cried harder. I heard the crash of dishes in the sink and then the back door slamming as Auguste went outside, followed by the sound of Mireille climbing the stairs to her room.

It hurt too much to look at Keir's photograph yet I longed to paint him—to get to know that face intimately, every curve and nuance. I peppered my "hard times journal" with lamentations and questions: *"After 15 years you finally tell me you love me, and then you die three weeks later. That really sucks!!! Did you have anything more you wanted to say to me? Were you afraid, too?"*

Due to the conventions, I had put in many extra hours at work. Jack Spencer approved my taking a week off before the Labor Day weekend. I planned to catch up on laundry and some neglected housekeeping plus take some time to rest.

On Monday morning the late summer sun was coming through my bedroom window. I walked across our bedroom floor in the direction of our clothes hamper to fetch the next load of laundry.

"I didn't know you would be so sad." Keir's melodic cadence was instantly recognizable to me.

"Of course, I am sad!" my brain replied, a little indignantly. "First you tell me you love me then you push me away!"

"I was crazy with grief…" I immediately understood that, although we were losing *him*, during his last weeks, he was losing *everyone* he loved and everything he knew—*life itself*. He *had been* scared. I could now reconcile and forgive him for that last phone call between us. The communication had occurred so naturally, like we were speaking to each other on the phone or in person, yet I had heard it inside my head. I would never have thought of that particular phrase of explanation, "crazy with

370

grief," on my own. Besides, Keir was replying to what I had written in my journal. Could he actually *hear* my thoughts and *feel* my emotions?

Still having difficulty reconciling how Keir looked when he had been healthy (in all the OAHIA photographs) and how he looked on my March 6th visit, I unsuccessfully attempted to sketch his portrait freehand. I resorted to enlarging and tracing the photo that I had included in the OAHIA newsletter obituary of Keir. The photo of Keir and Mike Johnson in Hawaiian shirts was taken fifteen years earlier by Liam in the lobby of the Sandpiper Suites only a few hours before I first found myself "drowning" in Keir's eyes as Evonda and Abigail were conversing a mere dozen feet behind me. I transferred the image onto two pieces of watercolor paper.

Under the effects of the steroids, and possibly aging, Keir's face on March 6th was slightly puffier than when he was thirty-eight years old in the photo and in good health. Using a soccer ball with one of his The Merv Show ball caps atop (similar to "Wilson," the volleyball who kept Tom Hanks company in the movie, *Castaway),* I altered the second image to resemble the bald man with thin moustache and beard that I recalled from my visit nearly six months earlier.

Playing the Josh Groban compact disk in our stereo, I sat down to mix my paints. The transparency of the watercolors translated the crystal clear green and blue of Keir's eyes. I used the same green in his luau shirt while trying to remember how it had looked fifteen years earlier. I watered down the black pigment from his hair in the healthy picture to render his gray turtleneck for the more recent depiction.

Since I had only begun my painting lessons six weeks earlier, the resulting dual portraits were nothing akin to a Rembrandt, but they did accomplish my primary purposes: to reconcile for me the two strikingly different views I had of Keir into one and to create a likeness to aid my memory of our last visit in the absence of a photograph. Once dry, I placed the portraits with my growing collection of works inside an artist portfolio.

Auguste and I spent our 29th wedding anniversary over Labor Day weekend with my parents, his mother, and Mireille. On the following Friday, exactly six months after my visit with Keir, I went to Sylvia's house for lunch.

After having her second child, Sylvia had quit working at AEMG, but her house was only a five-minute drive from the AEMG offices, so it was relatively easy for me to visit her for lunch. I showed her my watercolors, including my portraits of Keir. As Sylvia held them in her lap, her daughter innocently exclaimed,

"Oh! Two boys!"

"No." Her mother quietly corrected while gazing at the images before her. "They are pictures of the same man."

"Thank you for letting me spend part of this anniversary day with you," I said when I got ready to leave. "You are one of the few people who understand the situation and the depth of feelings I am processing. I've decided to go to a local Starbucks in remembrance."

As I drove into the parking lot of the strip mall containing the coffee shop, the radio played Joe Cocker's song, "You Are So Beautiful to Me." Once inside, I ordered a Tazoberry iced tea—the same drink I had selected the afternoon I was with Keir—and found a seat in the corner where I read the copy of Proust's *Swann in Love* I had recently borrowed from the library. Keir's Golden Retrievers Book Club had read Proust at his insistence, and I wanted to understand why.

The following Monday morning I received an email at work from Abigail announcing that the Cuyahoga County Bar Association would be holding a Memorial Service for Keir on Thursday, September 26th, in the Cleveland Courthouse Building. After asking Abigail's permission and ascertaining the dress code (luau versus black suit), I forwarded the announcement to the OAHIA membership list. I also obtained Jack Spencer's permission to attend the service as part of my OAHIA executive director duties. After all, Keir had been an Honorary Member of the Association.

The next night I dreamt Keir held my hand.

"What do I *do?*" I asked him.

"Just miss me."

As I woke the next morning, reflecting on the dream, I felt Keir's presence and heard him speak.

"One of the things I am going to miss the most is being able to witness my son's achievements as he grows up—in school, his first date, learning to drive, graduation…"

My heart constricted tightly in my chest with that knowledge.

I wrestled with the decision whether or not to send Abigail copies of Keir's dual portrait. What if Keir, in his normal human vanity, had not wanted his picture taken after he had become ill? Would not she and Sean want to have a way to remember him both well and ill? I went to the copy center and made five sets of color copies: one for Abigail, one for Mark Thomas, one for the Whitfields, and a couple of extra sets. I was concerned that, with Abigail's fine taste in art as evidenced in her home décor, she might scoff at my amateurish depiction and destroy the originals if I sent them to her. If, on the other hand, she received the copies with enthusiasm, I could send her the originals later. I also made her copies of Keir's president's columns from the archived OAHIA newsletters.

I was not sure whether I should drive to Cleveland for the Cuyahoga County Bar Memorial Service alone or carpool with someone. Mark Thomas declined to attend. I made a few additional discreet inquiries among the OAHIA membership; only Eric Mitchell was planning to attend, and he lived in Cleveland. I steeled myself for the return drive to Cleveland. However, I got the sense that Keir wanted me to attend to support his brother, Mark, and son, Sean.

Although the Bar Memorial Service was not scheduled to begin until 1:30 p.m., once I dropped Mireille off at middle school at 7:15 a.m., I drove north out of Columbus. It was teeming rain. I recalled that Abigail and

Keir had driven to The Ohio State University Brain Cancer facility in the pouring rain back in January. I again empathized with making such an emotionally-fraught, roller-coaster of a journey in wretched weather. I wondered again what a married couple would discuss on such a trip. The car radio played Enrique Iglesias' "(You Can Be My) Hero" and Whitney Houston's "I Will Always Love You," and I knew this would be a difficult journey for me, too.

With several hours to spare, I took a detour fueled by curiosity. Instead of proceeding directly north to Cleveland, when I reached Mansfield on I-71, I exited and turned eastward on Route 30 toward Canton, Keir's home town. The road led through farm country and was more relaxing than the truck-laden interstate. After a little more than an hour of driving on Route 30, I reached Canton and merged onto I-77 north until reaching the Tuscarawas Street exit. I was in search of Keir's childhood; where would a doctor have raised his two sons in the 1950s?

After driving around a few neighborhoods, I headed for the Stark County Historical Center in the McKinley Monument and the relief of a restroom. My curiosity pilgrimage had answered some questions but also had provoked some new ones.

At eleven o'clock after my tour of Canton, I left to continue onto Cleveland. I wanted to be there before noon to find a parking place near the Courthouse and eat some lunch. As I got back on I-77 north, it started raining again, hard. My mind, once again, went over—for perhaps the hundred-thousandth time—what had transpired between Keir and me over the past sixteen years.

An eighteen-wheeler, coming down the entrance ramp too fast, cut me off and splashed my windshield, startling me back to the present. I removed my foot from the accelerator and let the weight of my car slow me down a little. "Wow! That was close!" I thought. "No need for me to get killed on the way to a memorial service!"

As I entered the Cleveland metropolitan area the traffic became heavier. I especially wanted to be alert for my exit where I-90 and I-77 intersected. The rain and passing traffic made it difficult to see the green highway signs ahead. I needed to take the Ninth Street exit.

Just as I entered the curve of the exit ramp, I was startled to hear the radio play the lyrics of "I know you are shining down on me from heaven," and I nearly lost control of my car. Pulling the car back from the direction of the guard rail of the exit ramp, I guided it onto Ninth Street.

The towering skyscrapers of downtown lined the sidewalks on both sides. There was a No Left Turn sign above the traffic signal at Superior, but the next block, Rockwell, had a left turn signal, which I took. I drove west three blocks to Public Square and made a right onto Ontario Street. Straight ahead of me, I saw the five-story Beaux-Arts-style, Cuyahoga County Court House Building. I scanned the sides of Ninth Street for the universal public parking sign, "P." I located the Court House garage and pulled in, grabbing the ticket spit at me from the machine.

The rain, now steady, was no longer teeming. I found a parking space and changed from my sneakers to high heels, pulling out my latest reading material (a book called *Finding Your Own North Star*) and my umbrella, and headed out of the garage in search of a place to eat lunch.

I navigated the puddles in the sidewalk as I headed toward a neon beacon announcing "Open" in a delicatessen near the Courthouse. Since it was only 11:30 a.m., the lunch crowd was still relatively thin. Reading the large board above the row of cash registers, I was reminded of the lunch I shared with Keir when he was first OAHIA president so long ago in Columbus before we went to the Insurance Department to write the licensing exam. Remembering I had a chicken salad sandwich then, I ordered one on pita bread and took my platter over to an empty booth near the window. I chose not to eat the dill pickle (even though it smelled delicious) because I had no way to brush my teeth or disguise my breath after lunch. Opening my *North Star* book, I ate my lunch slowly while reading.

When I finished my sandwich, I looked up to see that the restaurant was filling up with the lunch crowd. I gathered my belongings and headed across Lakeside Avenue to the imposing Courthouse. Climbing the two sets of granite steps, I passed between the two bronze statues of Thomas Jefferson and Alexander Hamilton and walked through the center arch under the six-columned colonnade. I entered the gleaming white marble rotunda whose elegance was now marred by the metal detectors, conveyor belts, plastic buckets, and guards installed after the terrorist attacks of the previous year. My purse was searched. I surrendered to the guard the small Swiss army knife Auguste had given me that was attached to my key ring so that I could pass into the Courthouse lobby.

I still had an hour to kill before the memorial service. I located the ladies room to use the toilet and apply fresh lipstick. Back in the lobby, I sat on a marble bench next to the mural of *The Magna Carta* to continue reading. Under the lofty arches upholding a second floor balcony, I felt alone, small, and conspicuous in alien territory like a misguided, stealth invader of this intimidating world of lawyers, justices, and the court system. I tried to concentrate on my book.

At one o'clock, I gathered my things. My stomach was tight from anxiety. I walked over to the building directory. The courtroom reserved for the memorial service was on the third floor. Stepping inside the small elevator, I rode to that floor and found Courtroom 301. I tried the door, but it was locked. Turning around, I noticed a small, flat bench next to the window overlooking Lakeside Avenue. Again I sat down and took out my book to read, grateful that I had the foresight to bring it.

About five minutes later, a middle-aged man in a black suit entered the foyer and headed toward the courtroom door, attempted to turn the handle, and discovered it locked. He turned around.

"Are you here for the memorial service?" I asked tentatively.

"Yes." He approached me with his hand proffered. "I am Steve Garber. I chair the Cuyahoga County Bar's Memorial Committee." I rose to shake his hand, remembering his name from the printed announcement Abigail had emailed me.

"I'm Annie Weber." I also had another insight: Abigail's law firm was Garber, Gay, Jones, and Siegel. This man was Abigail's law partner. I would need to be careful about what I said. "I'm the executive director of the Ohio Association of Health Insurance Attorneys."

I stood as Mr. Garber explained to me how the service would proceed. A few more people arrived and also tried the door unsuccessfully. Mr. Garber greeted them in a familiar fashion. Feeling awkward, I was relieved to see the familiar figure of Brent Tillett enter the foyer. I recalled that he, too, was Abigail's law partner, and remembered what he had told me and Mark Thomas at Keir's funeral.

"Hi, Brent," I walked over to him. "I'm glad to see someone I know."

"Hey, Annie. Did you drive up from Columbus?"

"Yes, it was quite a rainy ride."

Brent tilted the handle of his closed golf umbrella outward from his hip, the metal point of which was resting on the floor.

"Yeah, I walked the six blocks from my office."

"Eric Mitchell told me he was coming today, but I didn't hear from anyone else."

Brent recognized some co-workers and excused himself to greet them. I began a conversation with the man next to me, another attorney. While we were talking, I saw Abigail enter holding Sean's hand, with another woman following—the nanny, I assumed.

Several people rushed to greet Abigail, including a woman in a leopard print dress who hugged Abigail dramatically. Keir's widow was wearing a black suit with a colorful floral blouse—a mixture of mourning and Keir's penchant for Hawaiian shirts. I was relieved I had chosen a conservative navy suit, pearl necklace, and the sweater and blouse I wore the last day I saw Keir. I waited my turn to greet her.

"Thank you for sending me copies of Keir's newsletter columns," Abigail said. "Reading them, I could hear his voice again." I recalled having the same reaction.

"That's why I sent them to you."

A couple of others joined us, so I backed away and resumed small talk with the attorney I had been conversing with earlier while still gazing about for people I recognized. I noticed Sean, adorably dressed in a beige sports jacket with a luau shirt underneath. He was seated Indian style on the bench that I had occupied earlier, reading a history book out loud to himself in an attempt to drown out the adults around him. I suspected, at only about ten years old, he was likely feeling out-of-place himself.

Across the foyer in the direction of the elevators, I observed a very handsome man with dark hair graying at the temples and a blonde woman of the Junior League type joining the gathering crowd in the foyer.

"Oh, my God!" my brain automatically responded, "There is a *gorgeous* man here!" I surprised myself since it had been a very long time since I had had that reaction to anyone. I had not felt that way since...well, since I had seen Keir enter the reception room at Deerwood. "That's got to be Keir's brother, Mark, and his wife, Leah. That's how Keir would have looked if he had not become ill."

I noticed that Mark Mervais was wearing a navy sports jacket, white shirt, grey pants, and a red tie—all similar to what Keir had worn to the OAHIA Executive Committee meeting in February 1989 when I had noticed he was wearing the Native American bracelet.

To exercise some self-control, I turned back to my fellow conversationalist.

"I've been taking some watercolor classes."

"We've got some artwork in our office. My law partner is a better judge of artwork than I am, however."

I noticed Mark cross the foyer to join Sean on the bench and speak softly to his nephew. The tender, caring scene between uncle and nephew caused me to feel as though my heart had fallen straight out of my chest and gone splat on the floor. My internal voice observed, "I never saw Keir with Sean. If Keir had been here, he, too, would have noticed the people on the periphery and spoken with them to make them feel included. Oh, good," I admonished myself. "Now you are starting to fall for Keir's brother—that's just *transference*! Don't do that!"

The woman in the leopard-print dress approached me, blocking my view of Mark and Sean. I sensed something threatening and territorial in her manner and was immediately on high-alert and defensive.

"Are you the one who painted the watercolors of Keir?" She must have overheard my painting conversation with the attorney. I surmised Abigail had shown her or told her about the portraits I had done of Keir. I immediately sensed that this woman had had a "thing" for Keir, too. I felt my fingernails figuratively grow six inches. I was aware we might have to take this cat fight outside the courthouse. At the same time, I knew somehow that Keir had never cared for her, so I stood my ground as though to say "And what's it to *you*?" Out loud, I replied firmly.

"Yes."

"What's this about watercolors?" a male voice to my right asked. Either sensing trouble or just being inclusive with the outliers, Mark Mervais had somehow come to my aid. The woman in the leopard-print dress backed away into the crowd. Relieved that the confrontation had been averted, I turned to reply to Mark's question.

"I painted two watercolor portraits of Keir."

I noted with interest that Abigail had told the woman about the paintings but not her brother-in-law. Mark was taller than I remembered

Keir, especially since I was wearing the same high heels as when I had been with Keir at Starbucks, and Mark was more classically handsome, with an oval face versus Keir's more square one. I also noticed Mark's eyes were brown, as were Abigail's, but Sean had inherited his father's sky blue eyes and squarer face.

"I'm sorry. I did not catch your name. I'm Mark Mervais."

Standing next to Mark, I suddenly felt like a thirteen-year-old standing next to the cutest boy in school and thoroughly tongue-tied. We were at his brother's memorial service, but in true Mervais fashion, he had come to my rescue, sparing me further interaction with the woman in the leopard-print dress and seeking to include me in the social milieu in which, he, himself, was likely feeling a little foreign as well.

"I'm Annie Weber." I did not know how much or what he knew about me or OAHIA, so I did not elaborate. I was also afraid that, if I told him I was the one who wrote the obituary in the newsletter that had made him cry, and if I was to witness any emotion float across this man's face as I had seen cross Keir's, I would not be able to keep my own emotions under control. "I'm sorry about your brother."

I recalled that only a few hours earlier I had driven through this man's home town of Canton trying to guess where he and Keir might have lived as boys. I felt embarrassed for what seemed like an invasion of this gracious and noble man's privacy.

An awkward silence ensued. I scolded myself for not knowing what else to say: "You're a coach, for goodness sake! Talk about his career. Ask him a question."

"Are you an attorney, too?" I ventured out loud.

"Oh, NO!" Mark took two steps backwards as if I had accused him of being a vampire. I could almost imagine him pulling out a cross and a cluster of garlic to ward off the evil.

I watched him a moment wondering if he was going to divulge his career to me when the courtroom clerk unlocked and opened the door. I looked at my watch. It was exactly 1:30 p.m. The crowd in the foyer filed into the courtroom for the proceeding and found seats among the solid oak benches facing the judge's stand. Keir's family sat in the front row on the right side; Steve Garber sat alone in the front row on the left. I sat in the third row along the aisle; Brent Tillett sat directly behind me.

Once everyone was seated, the bailiff called the court to order, asking us to rise in honor of the Chief Superior Court Judge, an African-American woman, who was to preside. The court reporter typed furiously.

Steve Garber asked the Judge's permission first, to approach her bench and, then, asked her indulgence to turn his back to her in order to address the assembly. Her Honor granted him permission. Garber pulled out a sheaf of prepared remarks. I crossed my arms across my stomach to steel myself against the rising emotions I was experiencing.

I learned more things I had not known about Keir. He *had* graduated from Canton High School. He had visited Africa in addition to

India and Nepal. (Had he gone on a safari? This was another indication of his wealth and adventurous, risk-taking, personality.) He had majored in history at Case Western Reserve (explaining why he taught social studies before going to law school). As an Elvis admirer, he had visited Graceland in a pink Cadillac (more evidence of his *joie-de-vivre* and sense of humor). His music collection had a reputation for being extensive, and the last CD playing when he died was African music.

When Garber finished, another one of Abigail's and Garber's law partners asked the Judge's permission to present some extemporaneous remarks. (I was beginning to wonder if I was one of the few people in attendance *not* employed by that law firm.)

"We considered Keir a silent partner at Garber, Gay, Jones, and Siegel and respected his fine legal mind. Of course, we were very grateful when he introduced us to Abigail who has added so much to her specialized legal field. Keir was a *very* attractive man—both outwardly physical and on the inside."

My mind involuntarily observed, "No shit, Sherlock!" and considered that now it was official—the court reporter had recorded it in the permanent records of Cuyahoga County—and this "very attractive" assessment was issued from a male.

Yet another law partner rose and asked the Judge for permission to speak. (All this protocol made me wonder if this was what law students practiced in Moot Court.)

"Keir was a great father and proud as punch of his son, Sean."

Hearing his name, Sean shot both arms above his head in a Rocky-like victory sign, and shouted, "YES!!!" Even the Judge had to chuckle and then gaveled the laughing courtroom back to order.

Behind me, Brent stood and requested permission to speak. He told the same story that he had shared with Mark Thomas and me at Keir's funeral: How his first son had been born prematurely just before Brent was scheduled to speak at the Beaver Ridge Inn during the 1986 OAHIA convention. Keir had spent time on the Inn's porch reassuring Brent that his son would be okay. This bond had turned into a close friendship over the years, and Brent had stopped by the Mervais home to see Keir on the morning the latter passed away but was not admitted because Keir had entered his death coma the evening before.

With all the courtroom formalities that each attorney had to go through, I determined that I was definitely *not* going to make any public comments. I had already had my say in the obituary I had written for the OAHIA newsletter.

Since no one else offered to speak, the Judge adjourned the memorial session and left the courtroom while all of us stood again. I turned to Brent to say goodbye.

I noticed Sean had moved up the center of the aisle and was standing by himself in the sea of adults. I realized I would have only thirty seconds to make a difference in this boy's life—a boy that I might never see

378

again. If his father had ever felt that he did not matter, perhaps Sean felt the same way, especially during the two years when Keir's health had been the family's chief concern. The young boy may have not been the center of attention that most young children expect. I wanted to assure Sean that the one thing I was absolutely certain about his father was that Sean had been the light of his life. I walked over to him and bent down a little to face him. Politely, Sean extended his hand to me.

"I'm Annie. I've wanted to meet you your entire life." I hesitated, allowing my intent to sink in. "The last words I said to your dad were 'Happy Father's Day,' because I know how *very important* you were to him."

Sean's head shot back a little, and his blue eyes grew wide and round, as though he had seen the ghost of his father over my shoulder reassuring him that what I was telling him was true. He turned around and headed for the main exit. I guessed that he felt the room had suddenly shrunk in on him with the momentousness of this news, and he needed to escape. Unfortunately, his way was blocked by a crowd of talking adults, and Sean stopped. I could tell from the set of his back that it now dawned on him that his mother was not with him. He turned around again and walked past me, seeking his mother in the front of the courtroom. He hugged her leg in a gesture of childhood vulnerability and need for comfort. Absent-mindedly, her arm encircled his shoulders.

I approached Abigail myself and gave her a hug.

"Thank you for inviting me. I'm glad I came." I then headed toward the front door, shaking in turn Mark and Leah Mervais's hands, before walking out the double doors to the foyer. I stopped in the ladies room before descending the elevator to the main lobby.

As I reached my Saturn in the parking deck, I spotted the woman in the leopard-print dress pulling out of her parking spot in her Mercedes-Benz. She nodded through the window on the driver's side in recognition of me. I nodded back with the instantaneous thought, "There goes trouble!" I changed from my heels back to my sneakers for the drive home.

Making my way back to the interstate, it started raining hard again. As I drove toward the juncture of I-77 and I-90 and saw the sign for I-77 Akron/Canton, all the emotion I had been holding back broke forth. I was crying so hard, and it was raining so hard, I could not see the road. "Keir," I prayed, "you are going to have to drive, because I cannot see. I promise I'll keep my hands on the wheel and my foot on the gas pedal, but you'll have to steer."

"YES!" I heard his spirit answer me. "This will be great. It's been so long since I've driven."

I do not recall how, about an hour later, I arrived at the rest stop at I-71 and Route 30, the point at which I had cut off earlier that morning and headed to Canton. I noticed my water bottle was empty and the rain had eased almost to the point of stopping.

"I have to leave you now to return to comfort my family members in Cleveland," Keir's spirit told me then he slipped away, disengaging me to continue the rest of my journey home.

The next morning I emailed Brent a thank you for being at the memorial service and helping me feel a little less like an interloper. A couple of weeks later, I sent an email to Abigail: *"I've been meaning to let you know that I was impressed with how well Sean handled himself during the Cuyahoga Bar memorial service (not surprised, but impressed). He certainly has Keir's irrepressible* joie de vivre*...I think I even saw the Judge crack a smile! My heart literally constricted when Keir told me that one of the things he was going to miss the most was being there to witness Sean's achievements—in school, his first date, learning to drive, graduation, etc. I hope as Sean grows, he will find special ways to still continue to be connected to his father."* I did not tell Abigail that Keir had told me that *after* he had died.

A few days later I received a thank you note from Abigail—in the shape of a Hawaiian shirt—she must have special-ordered them from a stationery store. In it, she wrote me a personal note thanking me for my memorial donations, my presence at Keir's services, and my written tribute to him in the newsletter. There was no mention of the paintings.

I was trying to find my way through the sorrow of grieving and the nagging feeling of guilt. The following Saturday, in mid-October, I picked my mother up to spend the afternoon visiting artist studios in Westerville, a suburb northeast of Columbus. We had enjoyed our stops at several studios on the outskirts of Westerville and were making our last stop at two downtown craft galleries. As I stood on the outdoor porch of the second gallery looking at the glass, pottery, metalwork, and cards displayed there, the too familiar strains of the first bars of the first song on Josh Groban's album, *All Luce del Sole* (literally, "Under the sunlight" but with the overall theme of "Where are you?") drifted through the loudspeaker to penetrate my ears and psyche.

"Not *THAT* album!" my mind protested. I was overcome with tears. My mother hugged me, not sure what to do or say to comfort her suddenly and inexplicably distraught daughter.

"I'm going back up to the car," I said after gaining a little composure. "When you are done looking around here, you can come to the car." I walked down the front steps and up the short street to my Saturn. Probably more worried about me than interested in the gallery art, my mother returned to my car about five minutes later and sat inside. I knew it was about five o'clock, and time to head to our respective homes.

"I've fallen in love with another man, but he's dead," I blurted out. For the first time out loud I admitted both to myself and mother my feelings for Keir that I had denied and suppressed for so long. I cried some more.

"I'm sorry." My mother was aware of the tensions that existed in my marriage.

380

"Do you remember at the Deerwood Lake Lodge after the OAHIA banquet when a handsome man came over to speak to me and you offered to get Mireille from the children's program for me so that I could talk to him?" I could see she was trying to recall the incident. Keir had the ability to act a bit invisible at times. "He was the man who died of brain cancer back in June. I flew back early from my conference at The BroAdmoor to attend his funeral...We did not have an affair or anything...We told each other we loved each other just three weeks before he died."

I let my mother absorb the news. She did not say much; she let me confess bits and pieces of my past with Keir: the "eye drowning" incidents, the "most beautiful woman in the room" comment, the kisses on the cheek, his arm around my waist, the visit from God informing me of our past lifetime together, and my last visit with him.

About an hour later, my emotional storm was spent after sharing my truth with my mother. I drove her home and proceeded to return to my house and supper.

That night, I had a long, luxurious dream about Keir. He was buying me coffee (similar to our Starbucks "date"). I sat on a sofa next to Sean's nanny, but Keir came over and, using his knee, indicated to the nanny that he wanted her to move so that he could sit next to me.

"I'm sorry I could not make you happy," he said. I used the fingernail of my thumb to slide down his bicep to let him know that he had made me happy. When I woke, I tried to hold onto the feeling of the presence of his spirit as long as I could but it soon dissipated in the light of day.

To soothe my guilt, I mailed Abigail a copy of Anne Morrow Lindbergh's book, *A Gift from the Sea,* which I had recently read. The book's theme addresses women's periodic need to replenish their souls. I offered it to her as a way to find a measure of tranquility. For myself, I had also read Nicholas Sparks' new novel, *Nights in Rodanthe,* about a married woman who has an affair with a handsome stranger during a stormy week on the Outer Banks of North Carolina, but he dies suddenly some months later from a mudslide in South America while reconnecting with his son.

I continued searching for a book or movie that would confirm or explain my relationship with Keir. I commenced a charcoal portrait of Keir. One day, while painting a fairy for Mireille, I tried to paint a fierce dragon as well, but the harder I worked, the sillier the dragon looked.

"Are you messing with my dragon?" I asked Keir's spirit. I could feel him smile mischievously. I then remembered his role as a dragon mascot for Sean's YMCA group.

I still had dozens of questions about Keir. I wrote them in my "hard times journal." Almost every song on the radio reminded me of something about Keir (including "There is always something there to remind me"). I thought about him before I fell asleep at night and when I awoke each morning. I could feel his spirit three or four times a day, but just for a fleeting moment.

I was frequently worried about thirteen-year-old Mireille. If I did not know where she was (and often she would not think to tell me), I would ask Keir to find her for me. Often, within ten minutes of my prayer to him, she would call me or arrive home, except one night.

Mireille had called in the afternoon, likely prompted by her friend's mother, to tell me she was going to the movies with some girlfriends. When she failed to return home by 7:30 p.m. that late autumn evening, I asked Keir's spirit where she was.

"I can't have her contact you right now, but she is okay," was his response.

Thirty minutes later, Auguste came home demanding to know "Where's Mireille? It's eight o'clock on a school night!" Trusting Keir's guidance, I was able to reply calmly.

"She's at the movies with some of her girlfriends."

At nine o'clock, Mireille called to say she was on her way home in the car of the mother of her friend. Instead of attending the five o'clock matinee, as I had assumed they would, they had gone to the seven o'clock showing. Just as Keir had reassured me, she was unable to contact me during the movie.

Back in January, I had registered for a Leadership Team (LT) program through my personal development education. My first weekend of this year-long course, consisting of five weekends away, was held in mid-November in Washington, DC. The other two Columbus-area participants, a man and a woman, drove with me to Washington. On the return trip, I shared with them my story about Keir. The woman confessed that she herself was having an extramarital affair. The man described us both as "honorable women." I was not quite sure how the description fit us both since her situation differed from mine, but I was touched by his understanding and the woman's own marital struggle. (She eventually divorced her husband.)

With so few of us in the LT course living in Columbus, and the requirements of the course to be in communication with the rest of the Midwest Team–participants, to conduct registration phone calls several nights a week, and to attend local classrooms every other Friday, I found myself spending five nights a week doing LT phone work. Auguste was visibly perturbed and verbally resentful.

During a routine doctor's visit before Thanksgiving, Mireille confessed to having tried cutting herself (a popular, teenaged girl's way of "cutting her pain" ironically, by slitting her arms multiple times). The amount of blood had frightened Mireille, so she had used up our household supply of Band-Aids. Then, in an effort to get to sleep, Mireille took five of my over-the-counter sleeping pills. Since she was under eighteen, Mireille's physician was required to tell me of her near-suicide attempts and advised us to seek psychological assistance for her apparent depression.

When I had originally registered for LT, life was good—I had reconnected with Keir and was scheduled to see him again, and Carolyn's tumors had shrunk. Now, eleven months later, both Keir and Carolyn were dead, Mireille was trying to kill herself, and Auguste blamed me and my not being emotionally available to him and our daughter. I am not generally a quitter, but I called the course development office in Cincinnati and quit the LT program. We started family psychotherapy with Mireille a week later in early December.

That same week I asked Keir in my journal, "I know you loved me, but were you *in love* with me?" That night, while lying in bed waiting to fall asleep, I felt Keir's spirit—his personality—very strongly followed by a vision, similar to a movie trailer running inside my mind. In it, I was dressed in a long, brown skirt and white apron with a shawl over my light blue blouse. In snow almost up to my hips, I was trying to run after two, nearly nude, Native Americans wearing snowshoes who were dragging Keir, dressed as a French soldier in a dirty white uniform, backwards by his upper arms. Blood was seeping through a bandaged wound on his left forehead. Hampered by the depth of the snow, I fell forward, crying in frustration as the Native Americans and Keir disappeared over a ridge and into the woods.

Immediately, I knew this scene was from the French-and-Indian War. When God had visited me nearly eighteen months earlier and told me "the French soldier had died before you could tell each other you loved each other," I had assumed that the soldier had died in my care. But this vision revealed to me that he had been abducted away from my care; I was not the one responsible for his death.

Our analytical minds will often overrule our hearts. I did not trust the truth of this vision. I needed proof that this was not a dream my subconscious mind had fabricated. A few days later, I researched the French-and-Indian War on the internet. Very little about this war is taught in U.S. schools other than it was when George Washington began his military career at some frontier forts in Ohio and Pennsylvania and that it was related to the Seven-Year War raging in Europe. Certainly, I did not know a lot about it.

In my research, I learned the war had been romanticized by Washington Irving in *The Last of the Mohicans* and made into a movie starring Daniel Day-Lewis as the heroic frontiersman who tries to maintain the idyllic frontier life in the face of the bitter British-French fight over the North American colonies.

I also learned from the internet that most of the French-and-Indian War took place along Lake George, New York, where I had vacationed multiple times during my teen years with my family. At the time, I had been bored by our visit to Fort Ticonderoga (formerly called Fort Carillon when it was held by the French). Now I read with investigator-like fascination the web pages detailing the events of the war.

From various web pages, I discovered that, on March 21, 1757, as the French made their way south from Fort Carillon at the north end of Lake George (formerly Lake Horican) to attack the British garrison holding Fort William Henry at the south end of the lake, a freak, three-foot, snowstorm hindered their progress. After a few skirmishes, the French were forced to retreat back to Fort Carillon. The French were called "white coats" after the design of their uniforms. A photograph I found of a colonial woman's costume dated to the period 1750-1760 showed a long, dark, homespun skirt, covered with a light, homespun apron. A flannel shawl was placed over the mannequin's shoulders, partially covering a plain blouse. A drawing of some Oneida braves—the only tribe to support the French— depicted Native Americans very similar to the ones from my vision. By this time, I had goose bumps on my arms and the little hairs on the back of my neck were on end as the details of my vision were confirmed by the historical facts I was reading.

Some days later, I felt Keir's spirit presence again. In a second vision, he, the French soldier, was in a battle with General Montcalm. Running forward on a battlefield, he was mortally wounded by a cannon ball in the chest. Returning to my internet research the next day, I learned that Montcalm had joined the French forces in July 1757 at Fort Carillon to plan a second offensive on Fort William Henry early the next month. This time the French reached Fort William Henry, encamping nearby, building trenches and moving them ever nearer to the fort, and engaging in several close battles before the British, still awaiting reinforcements from Fort Edward to the south, eventually surrendered to the French. Although the French assured the British women and children safe passage to Fort Edward, the Oneida, not happy with the deal struck between the French and British, attacked and massacred the women and children enroute to Fort Edward.

Was the French soldier (Keir) coming back to the British colonial woman (me) who had nursed his wound and with whom he had fallen in love only to be shot in the chest during combat? Had she died in the Oneida massacre, neither one having been able to tell each other of their love? Was this the mission God wanted Keir and me to rectify in this lifetime? Was this Keir's answer to my question, "Were you in love with me?"

I borrowed Irving's book *Last of the Mohicans* from the library to read and rented the video from Blockbuster. While at the Blockbuster store, I saw in the section of used videos for sale an award-winning foreign film *Himalaya* about a ten-year old boy following in his deceased father's footsteps as a leader trekking through the Nepalese mountains. I was curious why Keir had chosen to visit Nepal and what he had seen there. I bought the video. After watching it, I sent a note to Abigail offering her the video for Sean.

We had an ice storm in Columbus on December 6th, the nine-month anniversary of my visit with Keir. As I sat on the foot of my bed, putting on my shoes that morning, I felt my bed depress a little as Carolyn's spirit sat down next to me.

"Your heart will heal," she said reassuringly.

"But WHEN?" I protested. Carolyn's spirit slipped away as quickly as she had arrived.

A few days before Christmas, while sitting in the waiting room of Mireille's psychotherapist, the Muzak on the loud speaker played, "Sleep my child and peace attend thee, all through the night," I felt as though an electric bolt went through the center of my body, and I knew Keir was there with me.

Anonymously, I purchased a white, memorial poinsettia for Christmas display at Covenant-Coventry Methodist Church so that Keir would be represented at his church during the holidays. On Christmas Eve, I went to the florist from whom we had bought flowers for Carolyn when she was sick, and I purchased three roses with white exterior petals and red, velvet-like, interior petals. Placing them in a tall vase on our mantle with the accompanying fern and baby's breath, I rendered them in charcoal. Each flower represented one of my deceased friends: Kevin, Keir, and Carolyn. I drew the roses first on Christmas Evening, but was not sure how to depict the fern and baby's breath. I finished the charcoal on December 26th, very pleased with how I had drawn everything but the vase.

WHEREVER YOU WILL GO

So lately, been wondering
Who will be there to take my place?
When I'm gone, you'll need love
To light the shadows on your face.
If a great wave shall fall,
It would fall upon us all.
And between the sand and stone,
Could you make it on your own?

If I could, then I would
I'll go wherever you will go;
Way up high or down low
I'll go wherever you will go.

And maybe, I'll find out
A way to make it back someday--
To watch you, to guide you
Through the darkest of your days.
If a great wave shall fall,
It would fall upon us all.
Well, I hope there's someone out there
Who can bring me back to you.

Run away with my heart
Run away with my hope
Run away with my love

I know now, just quite how
My life and love might still go on
In your heart and your mind--
I'll stay with you for all of time.

If I could turn back time,
I'll go wherever you will go.
If I could make you mine,
I'll go wherever you will go.

Ohio, 2003

FOREVER

I did not want to start a New Year without Keir! His comments had been the salve to the wounds inflicted by Auguste's words. Three or four times a day—while working, driving, cleaning, painting, or even napping—I thought of Keir, sensed him, remembered him, missed him, mourned him. Was it his spirit visiting or just my grieving mind acting up? Was it just a coincidence that immediately following a thought about Keir I would feel a sensation of his spirit or hear a befitting song on the radio?

Over New Year's weekend, Auguste and I headed out to Sharon Woods Metropark for a walk. Trudging along in silence, Auguste on my right, and lost in our own thoughts as joggers and bicyclists passed us by, I suddenly felt a jogger catch up with us from behind me on my left side. I turned my head quizzically to face the jogger and found myself looking at Kevin Raines!

"Thank you for helping to take care of my kids," I heard his spirit say. I knew he was referring to the donations I had made in the past couple of years to his children's education trust fund. Then, as quickly as he had appeared, Kevin jogged off into thin air.

I turned to Auguste to see his reaction to this apparition. Auguste, gazing straight ahead, was oblivious to what had just occurred. I decided not to tell him about my vision lest he inform me that I was losing my grip on reality—something I was already questioning myself.

I felt like I was living in two separate worlds—one of every day existence, interacting with live people at home, work, and in various social venues (like the Art Center and my seminars), and a second, more nebulous and unfamiliar, in which I did not know where the boundaries lay.

"You are having too many of these instances to call them coincidences," my coach, Hillary, observed after I told her of Kevin's appearance. Reassuring as her words were, however, I still was having doubts about my sanity.

While conducting some internet research one January afternoon, I ran across the Cleveland Clinic's web page with a short test for depression. Out of nine classical symptoms, I had six. If a person has five or more, they are advised to seek professional help. I made an appointment with our family physician. He confirmed a diagnosis of situational depression and prescribed an anti-depressant for me, the same medicine that Mireille was using for her ADHD symptoms.

Since I was heading out of town for a few days to a medical society conference at the Quail Hollow Golf Resort in Painesville, and since I knew from Mireille's experience with the ADHD drugs that nausea and dizziness were likely side effects in the beginning as one's body gets accustomed to the medicine, I postponed starting on the anti-depressants until the weekend following my return. I hid the bag of starter kit drug samples my doctor gave me in the back of my closet inside a box; I did not want Auguste to know I was officially depressed. I did not trust him not to use it to berate me further and make me feel even worse.

I left home Wednesday evening, January 15th, to drive to Quail Hollow for the medical society conference. Driving up I-71 and I-271 in the dark alone in my car and listening to the car radio, I could feel Keir riding alongside me in the passenger seat. I suspected, when he was alive, that he had been to Quail Hollow for the Health Law Section conferences held there on a rotating basis. I had never been to the resort.

After I arrived, checked in, and went to my room, I wrote a short note to Keir in my journal thanking him for "accompanying me" and then, before drifting off to sleep, I had a reverie of what it would be like to have him there with me in person.

In the morning I was scheduled to tend a booth at the medical society meeting in the foyer outside the conference room. During the long stretches of time when the doctors were attending their scientific sessions, I did some charcoal sketches of flowers and a horse from an oil painting that I could see from my booth.

After lunch, I took a walk around the quaint downtown area. A snowstorm was predicted. I sat on a park bench to watch the gray clouds boiling and rolling their way across the sky—one of those times when you can smell that it is going to snow.

Sitting on the bench, I reflected that Abigail had not responded to my gift to her of the Anne Morrow Lindbergh book, to my Thanksgiving note, nor to my offer to Sean of the *Himalaya* video. Again, I felt Keir's presence palpably nearby.

"I haven't heard from Abigail recently," my thoughts reached out to Keir. "Should I call her?"

"NO!" I was taken aback by the vehemence and immediacy of Keir's response. "Wait for her to contact you." The wind blew stronger, as though to underscore Keir's instructions. Feeling cool, I returned to the hotel and went to my room to dress for dinner.

As an exhibitor, I was not included in the medical society's banquet held that evening in one of the resort ballrooms, so it was unlikely I would run into anyone I knew while eating dinner. I was shown to a table for two near a window. The votive candle on my table was reflected in the glass panes through which I could just see the dark outlines of bushes and trees swaying in the wind. I was seated facing the piano and a wooden dance floor where an older couple was slow dancing to a romantic song from the 1940s. The waiter, noticing I was alone, offered me a newspaper which I declined. Instead, I imagined Keir sitting across from me.

When I was a young child, I had an imaginary friend named Bee-ghos. Whenever I spilled milk or did something wrong, I blamed it on Bee-ghos. Sitting at the dining table, it occurred to me that Bee-ghos was my childish pronunciation of "Big Ghost," a spirit entity whom as an innocent child I could see and sense but dismissed by my parents as mere childhood imaginings. As a child, I was aware of ghosts from the television cartoon, "Casper, The Friendly Ghost," who had three, larger, protective ghosts who frequently created mischief but were not frightening.

If Keir had really been there, I would have been nervous, shy, modest. He, in contrast, would have been reassuring and casual. I experienced a flash of guilt from my moral conscience admonishing me about an extra-marital affair, but Keir was no longer married, I rationalized, and I was only indulging in harmless fantasy. To ease the jaw pain of my TMJ, I imagined dancing with Keir to the slow melodies of the pianist like the other couples on the dance floor.

Before retiring, I wrote a note to Keir in my journal thanking him for dinner and the two dances. I admitted that my self-concept had been another barrier stopping me from ever seriously considering Keir's advances when he was well, but when his physical changes and limitations from his illness evened the score between us, I was afraid he could not, physically— and should not, morally—be disloyal and unfaithful to Abigail.

An overnight snow deposited a light dusting of white crystals covering the ground. Again, I spent the morning at my booth station but packed up at noon and then drove back to Columbus. The warm sun melted the snow, and by the time I had reached Mansfield, there was no evidence that the storm had affected the middle of the state.

Since Mireille was still in school and Auguste at work when I arrived home, I called a sick friend to chat for a while. Then, at 3:45 p.m., I headed upstairs to the computer to respond to email messages.

The very first message I saw, sent at 3:41 p.m., was from Abigail: *"As I have written before, I do appreciate your kindnesses toward Keir and the article for the OAHIA newsletter. However, although this is difficult to explain, as a widow I am sorting my grief out with my close friends. Your continued contact with me hurts, and unless I give you permission, I do not want you to contact me further."*

Here was the cease-and-desist letter I had been expecting for a few years. In addition, I remembered Keir had forewarned me the day before to let Abigail contact me. I knew immediately what I wanted to write in response, but spent the next twenty minutes reading and responding to other emails so as not to appear to be lurking on the email. When I finished with the rest of my messages, I replied to Abigail: *"The last thing I want to do is to cause you or your family any further pain. I apologize if I have and will certainly respect your wishes."* I turned off the computer.

I realized that the possibility of obtaining any further knowledge or questions answered from Abigail was now ended. I walked downstairs, beseeching out loud, "Give me drugs!" I walked to my closet and pulled out my prescription samples of anti-depressants. Pouring myself a glass of water, I took the first dose.

I spent the weekend dizzy and ill on the sofa suffering side-effects from the medication.

"I must have caught something when I was in Painesville," I explained to Auguste. "It's flu season."

One of the benefits of Abigail cutting off communication with me was that I could now experience my own grief without associated guilt. In fact, I wondered if she sensed my feelings of guilt which may have tainted my sympathy toward her. (For years I had been committed to not hurting her, and yet had done so in spite of my intentions.) I was now doubtful that she would ever return the vase and letters I had sent to Keir.

I reflected that Abigail had scarcely known who I was on January 21, 2002; she was very friendly when I called Keir on May 17; she was close enough to email me thirty-six hours after Keir's death in June; she told me she had "learned volumes about generosity" from me in July; she invited me to the Cuyahoga Bar memorial service in September; and on January 17, 2003, I was *persona non grata* to her. Throughout it all, I had attempted to act with kindness, compassion, gentleness, generosity, and restraint. Some readers may think I was two-faced. But if what God had told me about the French-and-Indian War was true, then Abigail was extraneous to my and Keir's soul mission.

I dreamt Keir lived two houses down the street from me, but we had not realized it. In the dream, we signed into a Level seminar together, and I baked cookies in his kitchen, but the best part was that I was able to be in his presence, sweetly.

A few nights later, I dreamt of him again; this time we were at a New York art museum, and we were working on preparing exam questions to administer. Abigail was there, too, and Keir had recovered, growing back his head of hair.

Some days I could sense Keir's presence briefly checking in with me. At times, he was sad, at other times there was an angelic sweetness. I did not know when to expect any of these "visits."

On February 12th, I flew to Tucson, Arizona, for a site visit to a luxury resort and had the opportunity to meet a fellow coach, Diane, with whom I had been communicating by telephone for about a year. Remembering the Native American bracelet that Keir had worn once when he was OAHIA president fifteen years earlier, I resolved to find one like it while I was in Tucson.

Although Diane and I visited seven art and jewelry stores on February 13th, none of the bracelets looked anything like how I remembered Keir's, and they all cost several hundred dollars.

"Tomorrow is Valentine's Day," my mind spoke to the universe . "If I am meant to have a bracelet like Keir's, then tomorrow would be an appropriate day to find one."

I was too busy the next morning even to visit the hotel gift shop. When I arrived at the airport, I went over to the Paradies Store, the only shop there likely to have jewelry for sale. In the glass case by the entrance I spotted a bracelet that was vaguely similar to Keir's but was priced at $200.

"May I help you?" I looked up at the woman standing behind the counter.

"I am looking for a bracelet..."

The saleswoman indicated a glass display case to the left side of the register and pulled out a grey, velvet stand from which hung about twenty bracelets. "These are on sale."

Among the array, I saw one with a simple design of black onyx, alabaster, turquoise, and red coral stone embedded in a silver band with its encircling prongs narrowing with two alabaster stones near their tips. Although not exactly identical to Keir's, it was very similar but more feminine.

"How much is this one?"

"Forty dollars. Forty-one sixty-seven with tax."

I looked in my wallet. I had two 20-dollar bills, a single, and 82 cents in change. If I paid in cash, I reasoned, I would not have to explain my purchase to Auguste. I handed the woman all my bills and all the change minus a dime and a nickel. She put the bracelet in a small, white box and rang up my purchase. I silently thanked Keir for my Valentine's present.

Sitting in my seat on the airplane, I took the bracelet out of its box and examined it more closely. Inside, stamped onto the silver curve was the word, "ZUNI." I slipped the silver band over my left wrist and tightened it to the underside of my wrist.

After I arrived home, I learned from the internet that the Zuni are the present-day descendants of the Anasazi, a people who had lived in the Grand Canyon area of Arizona. I wondered if Keir had purchased his bracelet during a trip to the Grand Canyon.

On March 6th, I took the day off from work and drove back to Cleveland to commemorate the anniversary of my last visit with Keir. I told Auguste that there was an exhibition at the Cleveland Museum of Art I wanted to see, so that was my first stop. Inside the museum, a woman in a wheelchair was trying to access the ladies room when I was exiting it, and I offered to assist her. "After all," I reminded myself, "Keir had been in a wheelchair, too."

I finished visiting the exhibit at 11:15—too early for lunch. I wondered if Keir had been able to walk to the museum from his home, so I decided to see how long it would take to walk. As it had rained earlier in the day, the weather was cloudy, cool, and damp. I strode down East Boulevard past Wade Lagoon and the Fine Arts Garden, turned left around Severance Hall onto Euclid Avenue and crossed over it at the Amasa Stone Chapel. I continued down Adelbert Road, bearing right at Ambleside. At Cedar Glen Parkway, I turned left and strolled along the tree-lined avenue until I reached the Scottish Hills Historic District. I turned right onto Glencourt, another right onto Scottish Hills Lane, and, two blocks later, arrived at Hawkins Drive, Keir's street.

As I walked past his house, I noticed a basketball hoop, obviously for Sean, and a very sturdy looking Volvo parked in the front drive. I was not sure whether the Volvo belonged to Abigail—who might be home—or to the hired help. To escape possible recognition, I walked quickly down the street until I reached Findon, turned left and left again onto Celadon, then looked at my watch. It had been a fifteen-minute walk and, it was getting close to lunch time. I turned right onto Scottish Hills, returned to Glencourt Drive, and retraced my steps back to the museum.

Having reached my car again, and having accomplished my daily thirty-minute walk, my next destination was the Starbucks where Keir and I had lingered a year earlier. Driving down the same streets where I had just walked, this time I passed Glencourt and headed onto Cedar Road to drive the three extra blocks to the Starbucks.

"Our table" was still in the same location and empty, but the staff had rearranged the retail display near it. I did not recall the interior having being quite so loud before; the jazz music felt a bit intrusive. I felt like a fish out of water; it was obviously a university student hangout, but Keir's spirit seemed at ease. I was a bit concerned if Abigail might drop in for a coffee and recognize me, even consider me a stalker. I purchased a Tazoberry tea, some pound cake, and a yogurt, not much of a lunch but what was available, and seated myself at "our table," then recorded my thoughts and observations in my journal which I had brought along.

I had expected to feel sadder, but maybe the residual happiness and joy we had shared the year before in each other's company lingered with me.

About an hour later, having eaten my lunch, accomplished my memorial pilgrimage, and finished my journal writing, I returned to my car for the drive home. Getting on Route 90 towards I-71, the radio played Lionel Ritchie's "Once, Twice, Three Times a Lady," and I sensed Keir was thanking me for making the trip in his memory.

A couple of weeks later, I dreamt that Keir wanted to walk around our house, but Auguste's garden tools were scattered on the ground like an obstacle course, and Keir had trouble walking, so he sat in the wheelbarrow. When I touched his shoulder, I awoke.

On March 23rd, Mireille and I watched her video of *The Lion King*. I noticed that the lyrics to Elton John's song, "The Circle of Life," are different in the movie than on the radio. I was touched remembering how Keir had chuckled over Timon and Pumba discussing "put your behind in your past." When Simba and Nala, the male and female lions who had not seen each other for years, frolicked and played to the song, "Can You Feel the Love Tonight?", I was struck to my heart when I suddenly discerned the connection between the movie's song and Keir's ending statement on the phone to me fourteen months earlier: "I can feel the love…"

A few weeks later, I was dialing a Cleveland phone number from work, and I heard Keir's voice say, "Hello?" I was so startled that I forgot whom I was calling. I had to hang up to restore my emotions.

I learned that the Covenant-Coventry United Methodist Church was holding a mass inurnment to dedicate its new columbarium on Easter

Sunday, the Day of Resurrection. I wondered if Keir's ashes, that had been stored for months at the funeral home, would be part of the inurnment.

On the unseasonably warm and sunny Good Friday afternoon in April when I had the day off, I sat outside on our deck to watercolor while listening to a transistor radio. Taking my Zuni bracelet and a thicker bracelet as a dummy model, plus my dream-catcher necklace, I painted Keir's and my bracelets intertwined together. I named the painting, "The Covenant," representing a solemn promise made between two people. Ironically, Auguste deemed it the best painting I had done.

I had also pulled out the double portrait of Keir that I had painted the previous August to touch up a few spots. I had planned to name the portraits, "How Can I Live Without You?" but when I heard the radio play Josh Groban's song, "You're Still You"—the song to which I had originally painted the portraits; I selected that title instead.

My extended family, visiting for the Easter holiday, went to see *Everest* at the IMAX Theater. As the large screen image of the helicopter flew over Katmandu, I saw the white water in the river below and wondered if Keir had rafted on his trip to Nepal, or even if that was the impetus for him traveling there.

One overcast and cloudy morning while taking my walk around the neighborhood, I asked "Will your eyes come out?" referring to the sky blue of Keir's eyes. The clouds parted just enough to reveal an eye-shaped, almond patch of light blue sky. Later that night, I dreamt that Keir was in the library reading. When I called his name, he looked over at me and smiled beguilingly.

One warm, Monday afternoon toward the end of April, as I was walking around our neighborhood in shorts, I was stung in the right ankle by a yellow jacket. By the evening, while sitting in my professional development seminar, my ankle had swollen painfully and turned red. I promised the person sitting next to me that I would see a doctor in the morning.

When I awoke the next day, I bent over to clean out the cats' litter box, and then stood up too quickly to return the litter scoop to our laundry room and passed out. As I slumped to the floor, my front teeth hit the metal edge of the washing machine. As I came back to consciousness, I was sitting in the dark laundry room with my back leaning against the door connecting to our bathroom. I felt the sharp, jagged edge of my front tooth with my tongue. "Oooh! That's going to be expensive— about a thousand dollars for a new crown."

"Auguste!" I shouted out loud. He must have heard the thump of my body hit the washer, door, and floor.

"Where *are* you?"

"In the laundry room," I said a little weaker. Auguste opened the connector door from the kitchen. "I fainted and broke my tooth." A disparaging look crossed his face but he helped me to my feet so we could both inspect the dental damage. A few spots of blood had dripped onto my bathrobe. I got dressed and made arrangements to go to the dentist and get off from work while Auguste drove Mireille to school.

"How come you did not stop my fall?" I mentally asked Keir.

"You fell too fast to catch you," he replied. I sensed he did attempt to mitigate my fall, since it could have been worse; the tooth only needed to be capped, since the root was still intact, and I did not hit my head or get a concussion.

In the midst of all this, I completed all my courses through Coach University and received my diploma plaque.

Leading up to May 2nd and May 17th, I experienced some volatile emotions. I did not immediately associate my feelings with the dates of two phone calls with Keir the previous year—one when he told me he was using a walker but let me know that he wanted me to continue to call him, and the other when his family was packing to take him for what was to be his last trip to Lakeside.

I dreamt about Keir and Abigail again. This time, Keir sported unruly hair and a scraggly beard similar to Gary Sinese playing "Captain Dan" in the movie, *Forrest Gump*. I must have made the symbolic association with the wheelchair.

The night of May 29th, the anniversary of the day when Keir and I had told each other we loved each other—essentially fulfilling our "mission" left over from the French-and-Indian War—Auguste was already in bed, either asleep or feigning so, when I finally lay down myself around eleven o'clock. I started with some deep breathing exercises while on my back, but eventually, at some point in that place between sleep and awake, rolled over onto my stomach.

Keir appeared to me, standing beneath a shower of other-wordly golden light.. Clasping both of my hands together, Keir pulled me gently toward him (for now I was standing up somewhere above my prone body), kissed my entwined hands, then threw his arms around my shoulders in a hug. I knew telepathically that he wanted me to know he still loved me.

Taking my left hand in his right, Keir and I lifted off the ground and were suddenly flying, like Peter Pan and Wendy. Skimming over the trees below us toward Cleveland, we landed at the corner of Scottish Hills Lane and Hawkins Drive in his former neighborhood and stood looking at his (former) house. He conveyed to me that he knew I had been back—once after his funeral and again a few months ago on the anniversary of our afternoon at Starbucks.

We flew again a short distance and hung, suspended in the kitchen ceiling, watching Keir's brother, Mark, and sister-in-law Leah chop vegetables together standing at a kitchen island in their home. Keir wanted me to understand that he knew I had met them at his Cuyahoga County Bar memorial service.

Next we flew to Canton, his hometown. He knew I had been there, too. Keir conveyed to me that he had to leave to go back up toward the Light to rejoin his deceased parents. I floated back down into my body lying face down on my bed with Auguste beside me.

"THAT was an out-of-body experience!" I knew instantly and without question, although I had never had one before. I had not even read about them, but I was certain it had not been a dream because I had not yet fallen asleep. I felt peaceful, loved, and happy. I fell into a deep slumber until morning.

I needed to understand these messages I had been receiving—was my depression-drugged mind playing tricks on me or was there something legitimately occurring to me? I ordered some books about spiritual and psychic experiences: *Lilydale* and *Astral Dynamics* (induced out-of-body travel).

For my birthday and Memorial Day Weekend, Auguste, Mireille, and I drove to the vacation home of my widower friend, Gary. We arrived in the dark before he did and while another visiting couple was out, so we did not have a key to enter the house. We all needed to use the restroom.

"Mom, why don't you contact your friend Carolyn?" Mireille suggested referring to Gary's deceased wife. I stood under the stars looking up and prayed for Carolyn's help. A few minutes later, we saw the visiting couple strolling down the street toward the house. Using their key, they let us inside. Gary arrived about thirty minutes later. After spending the weekend together with my family, Gary privately told me, "Your husband is a jerk not to understand how special you are."

Since Abigail had never returned the letters I had written to Keir, I felt the need to create some memento of him for myself. I laid out and considered all the remnants I had gathered in the past year: a couple of photos, his funeral and memorial service documents, color photocopies of his double portrait, and some scraps of paper with his phone number, my notes from one of our calls, Abigail's and Mark's emails about my obituary in the OAHIA newsletter and a few other emails from Abigail, my maps to Keir's house and around Canton, the thank you note from Abigail, the words from my sympathy card to her, and the lyrics to Josh Groban's songs. I knew I could retrieve other documents from the OAHIA records: Keir's president's columns, the 25th anniversary brochure, my obituary in the newsletter, and more photographs. In the end, it was a sufficient collection for a scrapbook. Together, the items helped remind me of who Keir had been for OAHIA, for his friends, for his family, and for me.

On June 12th, the anniversary of my last phone call with Keir (the one in which he pushed me away), I watched a public television broadcast about Pueblo spiritual buildings The spiritual buildings were aligned to the moon's eighteen-year cycle. In my journal, I worked Keir's life backward in nine-year segments and hit major points in his life. I asked his spirit, "Were you a Native American in a former lifetime?"

I was inspired to paint a watercolor of the Grand Canyon from the river level since Keir had planned to raft there. I was very pleased that it turned out so well, almost as if I had some spiritual assistance. (I still consider it one of my best works.) Six days later, on what would have been Keir's 55th birthday, I sent a memorial donation to the Grand Canyon National Park Foundation, explaining what type of man he had been and why I had chosen the Grand Canyon Foundation as the recipient of this first, annual donation from me. The Foundation staff was so touched by my description, they called and wrote me how moved they were reading my letter.

Knowing I would likely be emotional on June 21st, the anniversary of Keir's death, and would also be in Washington, DC at the commencement of a client's national convention, I made arrangements with my boss, Jack Spencer, to take off that evening to visit the National Cathedral. After a call to the Cathedral office, I learned that, although the main part of the Cathedral would be closed at 4:00 p.m. for a wedding, there was a small meditative chapel, the Good Shepherd Chapel, at the rear of the Gothic-style edifice that was always open to the public.

On the morning of June 21st, before leaving our house for my flight to DC, I noticed that a gardenia had bloomed in our garden overnight. Since I was wearing a white dress with red and blue flowers and a white jacket, I clipped the gardenia and placed it on my jacket lapel. While on the airplane, the flight attendant remarked on how fragrant my flower was.

Having arrived in the Capital and checked in at our hotel, I hailed a taxi to drive me from the Foggy Bottom area through Embassy Row to the National Cathedral. Armed with a diagram of the 59-acre Cathedral Close, I walked up the South Road drive, where the taxi driver had deposited me, to the front of the Western, or main, façade.

Perched atop Mount St. Alban, at 676 feet above sea level and the highest point in Washington, DC, I paused for some moments in front of the Cathedral to take in the impressive and spiritually uplifting sight. On this façade, the Cathedral's three massive, Indiana lime-stone portals depict the creation of day, mankind, and night in the tympana arches above the bronze doors portraying scenes from the lives of Abraham and Moses in the center and Saints Peter and Paul on either side. The pointed arches of the awe-inspiring building pulled my gaze upward to the two, parallel towers and their pointed finials reaching heavenward into the cerulean blue sky. As a former art history major, I would have loved to have reveled in the architectural beauty before me, but I was on a mission of a different kind.

I continued around the façade to the left, walking to the North Road, and turned right alongside the north bays with their flying buttresses and gargoyles to just beyond the north transept where an archway connected the Cathedral to the Administrative Building. Passing beneath the arch, I entered a small, enclosed garden, the Garth, with a stone fountain at its center. A well-worn, stone staircase to my right descended into a cool and slightly musty corridor. A small opening in the wall led to the secluded Good Shepherd Chapel. Three wooden pews to the right sat empty facing a small altar upon which lay a small wreath of ivy and a red rose bud. Above the altar was a granite reredos, holding a half-body sculpture of a hooded

Christ looking down affectionately and reassuringly at a lamb held in His arms.

I slid quietly into the second pew and sat for a moment, taking in the sacred, intimate, and private stillness of this place in contrast to the mammoth, imposing, public building of which it was a part.

With a sigh, I pulled out the manila envelope in which I had placed the documents that would form my personal *Yahrzeit* (Hebrew death anniversary service) or *Yizkor*: the Reformed Mourner's *Kaddish* (prayer for the deceased), the obituary I had written, and a copy of some quotations I had typed from Marcel Proust's *Swann's Way: Remembrance of Things Past*, the tome Keir's book club had read at his insistence. In the hymnal holder on the back of the pew before me were a *Book of Common Prayer*, a bible, and a hymnal. When I finished reading my own documents, I reverently read the funeral services from the *Book of Common Prayer* and those located at the back of the hymnal.

When I had completed my readings, I looked at my watch; it was a few minutes before six o'clock. After returning the books to their resting places in the rack before me and rising from the pew, I walked purposely toward the altar. I removed the gardenia from my jacket lapel and placed the flower gently on the stone surface next to the red rose. I turned around and, grabbing my envelope, exited the chapel, retracing my steps through the cool corridor, up the steps, and back out into the Garth.

Once outside again, I noticed the waning early summer evening light and heat. I continued walking around the exterior of the Cathedral toward the eastern, semi-circular nave end which enclosed the high altar, and around to the south side transept. Passing a series of steps to my left, The Pilgrim Steps, and through the Norman archway, I entered the Bishop's Garden, a medieval-style, walled garden, comprised of a more formal rose garden and less formal, stone-paved walkways amongst other flowers—day lilies, irises, and gladioli.

In the middle of this verdant urban preserve stood an octagonal stone gazebo, the Shadow House, built with stones from President Cleveland's summer home. Passing through a fragrant, boxwood-lined herb garden surrounding a medieval baptismal font, I stepped onto the crunching pebble path leading toward the quiet shade of the Shadow House with its eight cut-out windows. Mounting the few steps, I seated myself on the wooden bench encircling the edges of the gazebo. I opened my journal and wrote to Keir, detailing my day.

Just as I concluded my writing, the quiet was broken by a couple approaching the gazebo. I picked up my belongings and headed for the rose garden. As I stopped to smell the fragrant blooms in many shades of red, pink, yellow, peach, and white, I thought, "It would be nice to have a red rose for my jacket lapel now that my gardenia is gone. I don't want to cut a rose for myself, but it would be nice simply to find one that has recently fallen."

Nearing the eastern end of the rose garden, I stopped to admire the granite sculpture of the Father embracing his Prodigal Son, noting the similarity in style to that of the Good Shepherd in the chapel. I looked down at the plaque at the foot of its pedestal to confirm that it, too, was sculpted by Heinz Warneke. In the right corner of the pedestal base, partially hidden by the boxwood hedge in front of it, lay an almost perfect red rose that had been cut from its stem. I bent over, picked up the flower, and fastened it onto my lapel with the safety pin that I had used for my gardenia.

Leaving the rose garden, I ascended the Pilgrim Steps back up to the South Road. It was 6:45 p.m., so I thought it time to head back to my hotel. As I walked up the drive to my left I noticed another small stone building, the Herb Cottage Gift Shop, closed at this hour. In front of the Herb Cottage sat a bronze statue of a small boy with his legs drawn up under him and resting his arms on top of his legs. I suspected the sculpture was meant to depict the boy Jesus but I thought about Sean, Keir's son, as I walked past it. I did a double-take when I noticed resting in the crook of his right arm was a single, long-stemmed, red rose.

"Is that one for me, too?" my mind asked. "Or was it placed there on purpose by the sales staff of the gift shop or by a gardener?" I hesitated a moment debating whether or not to take it but erred on the side of caution and left it. Having noticed it was sufficient. I continued on my way down the South Road and out onto Wisconsin Avenue.

Looking about me, I thought I would have better luck catching a cab if I crossed over and walked down Wisconsin Avenue to the corner island at the intersection with Massachusetts Avenue.

Traffic was relatively light at this dinner hour and most of the buildings outside the Cathedral Close appeared to be brick apartments. Two taxis sailed past me, already occupied. A few minutes passed before I spied another yellow taxi headed in my direction. When it was close enough for me to see the "on duty" light, I lifted my arm to signal the driver's attention. He swerved to drive over to where I was standing and unlocked the curbside door so that I could climb into the back seat.

"Ritz-Carlton Hotel on M Street," I directed. The driver peered at me through his rearview mirror, nodded, and pulled away from the curb.

"Do you have any idea how hard it is to get a cab at this time on a Saturday night around here?" the driver asked me. "I had just dropped off a fare when I saw the red rose on your white jacket!" I silently thanked Keir for the rose as we drove down Embassy Row, the part of Massachusetts Avenue lined with international embassies.

Upon returning home from the convention in Washington, DC, my family and I flew out to California for my older brother's wedding reception followed by a camping trip to Yosemite. Auguste had taken our cats to the veterinarian for boarding. Unfortunately, they acquired a nasty case of fleas and infected our house within a week. Not knowing what the pest control's spray might do to my watercolors, I took them out, two at a time, and stacked them in the trunk of my car between large bath and beach towels to protect the glass and frames. Later that evening, I was on the phone in the midst of my weekly coaching call with Hillary.

"Oh, my God!" My voice was fraught with consternation.

"What's wrong?"

"I just noticed there are three stones missing from my Zuni bracelet—the one from Keir!" I frantically searched all around the floor beneath my chair. "I don't have any idea where I could have lost them."

For the next three days I looked everywhere around the house and work, but the stones were so small they could be anywhere.

The flea treatment had worked, so I retrieved my framed paintings from my car trunk, grateful I had not been accidentally rear-ended in the interim. Lifting the last painting from my trunk, the double-portrait of Keir, I found the three stones from my bracelet had stayed securely under the frame despite three days of driving. I understood intuitively that Keir had not liked having his portraits thrust in my car trunk and had gotten my attention by temporarily pinching the stones. I glued them back in place and resolved to be more respectful of his picture, stacking it under its towel again back in our bedroom, along with the other paintings.

One mid-July afternoon, exhausted from my recent travels and work plus the extra emotional burden of hiding my lingering grief, I lay down on the bed to nap. As I began to drift off to sleep, I felt Keir's spirit strongly present.

"I keep these things in my heart," his voiced whispered to my brain. I knew instantly that he was referring to the vase and letters I had sent him. He was letting me know I could no longer expect Abigail to return them—whether because Keir had destroyed them before he died or because she had put them in Sean's keepsake box or even destroyed them herself. (I also realized his statement was a paraphrase of the Biblical reference to Mary, Jesus' mother, who "kept these things [the Wise Men's gifts] in her heart.")

The OAHIA annual convention returned to Louisville, KY, for its 26th anniversary. I do not know whether it was the out-of-state location, the educational program, or the convention chair, but the membership stayed away in droves. We only had twenty-five delegates in their seats on Friday morning, half the normal contingent. The convention chair had attempted to add some creativity to the program by introducing some music and theater bits to the normal lecture delivery. One of the national speakers, a health insurance executive from Colorado, played an amusing song on his banjo. Marcia Tuttle, who had been sitting next to me, got up ostensibly to visit the restroom, and I felt Keir's presence slip into her seat and heard his soft chuckle in tune with the general amusement in the audience. Behind me, I also heard Kevin Raines' louder laugh, and I turned around to see an "empty" chair between Charles Lincoln—who had first hired Kevin into the industry—and Henry Spaulding—who had shared an office with Kevin. I knew then that the industry's "guardian angels" would be with us whenever we gathered.

At the end of July, an acquaintance of mine put me in contact with a local frame shop owner who exhibited works of emerging artists. I assumed when I showed the owner my first year's labors he would dismiss them out of hand and suggest I come back in five years.

"Can you hang your show next month?" he asked instead. In the course of our conversation, I learned he taught a five-week matting-and-framing course at the local arts center, so I immediately registered and spent the rest of August readying my work for display in September.

One of my former gallery partners helped me mount the show. When I stepped back from hanging the last picture, I had the uncanny experience—similar to severing an umbilical cord—of separating myself from my creations. "Who did these?" my mind queried from a paradoxical sense both of reverence and of no longer having the ability to recognize my relationship to my work. My gallery partner affirmed that he had felt similarly upon hanging the first exhibit of his paintings. My mother helped me set up the wine and cheese appetizers and a bevy of friends showed up for the opening.

I had already painted portraits of Keir and Carolyn and had made a charcoal portrait of Mireille, so I made another one of Kevin Raines, adding that the purchase price of the piece would be donated to his children's education fund. Although no one bought the drawing, several people made a donation, and at the end of the show, I mailed the charcoal to his widow along with the collected donations.

"When are you going to quit association work and be the artist you truly are?" Mark Thomas had come to my opening and purchased my first painting, a still life done in art class. "I like to have art work by my friends at my house."

Out of twenty-five paintings, I sold seven and a series of greeting cards. Gary, Carolyn's widower, purchased a winter scene.

"This is part of Carolyn's Hobby Lady legacy." We both smiled as I handed him the painting. After the exhibit closed, I gave him her portrait as well.

In the next year, I held two more solo exhibits, one in the conference room at work where I sold a couple more paintings and one at the arts center where I had taken classes, plus I entered some group shows. In a short time, I sold fifteen paintings.

"This is too easy," I told myself. "They probably only bought the paintings because they are my friends After all, Van Gogh only sold *one* painting in his entire lifetime, and *his* brother was an art dealer."

Inspired by the trip Keir had taken to Nepal and the IMAX movie, *Everest*, I painted the mountain and added a small, male hiker in the forefront, dwarfed by the snow-covered peak behind him.

"That's the ugliest painting I have ever seen," Auguste pronounced. I pulled out every mountain picture I had done and evaluated them side-by-side in the living room.

"No, it's not. It's the best one I've done." Silently, I remembered that Keir had encouraged my artistic interests while Auguste tended to resent them, even after he had taken up pottery at my behest, and I encouraged even his small successes.

In mid-October, I learned that Jim Frazier, former OAHIA president, had a heart condition that landed him in the Cleveland Clinic. Although Jim and I had not gotten along very well, I knew he had been friends with Kevin and Keir, so that afternoon, while I walked from my laundry room to my bathroom, I prayed to Keir for help with Jim's health.

"Kevin and I are already on the case," Keir reassured me immediately. Jim was soon out of the hospital and on the mend.

Although I was experiencing some success with my art, coaching private clients, and participating as a coach in a leadership program, I was still racked with doubts and fears that these post-death communications were hallucinations. One night I wrote in what had now become my Dear Keir journal, "What am I *supposed* to do???"

"Just love me."

A few days later, while driving to pick Mireille up at her friend's house, I mentally asked Keir, "Can you *really* hear my thoughts?" The car radio played Elvis' "Can't Help Falling in Love with You"—the song from Keir's funeral.

"Okay, that *could* have been a coincidence," I thought. "Now, *REALLY* prove you can hear me." The next song on the radio was "Annie" by John Denver.

While I was at the library looking for something compelling to read, my attention was drawn to a non-fiction book, *In the Shadow of Everest.* Keir had not told me anything about his trip to Nepal, and despite watching the movie *Himalaya,* I was still curious what drew him to that part of the world.

One night, as I was lying in bed, I felt Keir's spiritual presence very strongly. I felt and saw us running together in the mesa of the southwest of what is now the United States. I knew it was 900 A.D. (now called C.E.), and my parents had forbidden our relationship. I did not understand what to make of this vision.

Another evening, I again felt Keir's presence and watched a scene play out before my closed eyelids. This time I was a young woman in Africa with many beads around my neck. Two young tribal warriors were fighting over me for my affections—one, I knew, was Keir, who was beaten and died. I knew they weren't dreams because they were not illogical or surreal as my dreams could be. Besides, I could accurately recall them several days later without writing them down.

Were these scenes, these sleep-onset (hypnagogic) hallucinations, perhaps a new side effect of my anti-depressants? But I was seeing things I had never thought about and places I had never visited while receiving knowledge of aspects of the visions about which I would have no previous conscious memory.

A newly mandated lobby report from OAHIA to the Secretary of State's office did not arrive, as I had neglected to mail it Certified, and OAHIA was assessed a $500 fine. Eric Mitchell, who had returned to the Executive Committee to serve as OAHIA's general counsel, wrote an appeal letter while I prayed fervently to Keir and Kevin. The next day—even before Eric's letter could have been received—a representative from the Secretary of State's office called to inform me the fine had been rescinded since they had not taken appropriate steps to create their administrative rules after the statute had passed mandating the lobbying report. I thanked Keir in my journal that evening.

By Thanksgiving, Keir had now been deceased for nearly a year-and-a-half, and I had not yet visited the columbarium where his ashes were inurned in Cleveland at his former church. Knowing that every time I saw Keir's name printed, I felt as though an arrow pierced my heart, I suspected it would be even more emotionally painful for me to see his name and the dates of his lifetime engraved on a bronze plaque or carved into cement. However, I knew I needed to experience that phase of completion around his death.

When I was required for the Level III leadership program to meet my course coach, Melissa, who lived in Cleveland, to discuss my future plans for professional development, I suggested that I drive to Cleveland rather than meet her in Mansfield where the course classrooms had been held. We made an appointment for four o'clock on December 1st to meet at That Place on Bellflower, a French country restaurant located adjacent to University Circle and only a mile from Keir's former neighborhood.

I planned to arrive in Cleveland in sufficient time to visit the columbarium. Rather than head into downtown and drive through the urban streets, I took Route 480 to skirt the southern side of the city and then Route 271 to the more prosperous suburbs, exiting onto Cedar Road for the drive westward toward Cleveland Heights. However, I turned left too soon onto Lee Road and admitted telepathically to Keir that I was lost.

"Turn right here," Keir instructed at Corydon Road. I made my way through tree-lined streets into the affluent neighborhood. Just before the street intersected with Coventry, Keir spoke again.

"Turn left." There ahead, on the right side was the parking lot for the church. I silently thanked Keir for his directional assistance.

As I parked my car in one of the empty spaces and got out of the driver's seat, I looked around for something indicating where I would find the columbarium. I spotted a small wooden sign at the far end of the parking lot that said, "Church Office," so I walked over and entered the stone building.

"May I help you?" a middle-aged woman in glasses looked up from her desk-top terminal.

"Where is the columbarium?" I asked, feigning nonchalance to hide my inner, anticipatory nervousness.

"Around the front of the church," the woman made a half-circle with her right arm, "and up the hill through the gate."

I thanked her and exited the building, walked down an alley way and then emerged onto the sidewalk on the next street. Turning right, I saw a path leading up a hill through a wrought-iron gate into a small, park-like area on top of the hill. I stopped for a moment in the warm sun of the early December day. I had left my raincoat in the car and was comfortable in my red suit. I took a deep breath to summon my courage and ascended the hill. Unlatching the bar that held the gate closed, I swung it open wide enough for me to pass and then closed it with a slight clang.

I mounted the cement path to the two, three-foot high, curved, brick walls facing each other. Along the top of the walls were small brass plaques, aligned vertically in fives, and horizontally numbering about twenty or thirty. The plaques did not appear to be in alphabetical order but rather in some chronological order, although not completely. I concluded they were in the order that the resting places of the deceased had been purchased. My eyes skimmed the names while I steeled myself for the one that would be recognizable to my heart and mind.

I slowed down when I got near the date of Keir's death but did not find his plaque. At the end of the wall, I started over, working backwards. I walked over to the other wall and repeated my scanning process.

Keir's plaque was not there!

What could have happened? Maybe his family had decided against inurnment here after all, since the building of the columbarium had taken nine months? Maybe they scattered his ashes at the Lakeside house or in Lake Erie? Or perhaps Abigail kept them on her mantelpiece? But why would Keir clearly direct me to his church only for me to be dismayed and frustrated? Why did he not simply say, "I'm not there"?

Confused and bewildered, wondering if my emotions had blinded me from seeing his plaque, I slowly turned away and returned through the gate and alley way to my car. I turned right out of the parking lot and made another right onto Fairmont Boulevard from Coventry Road. Immediately after passing the front of the Covenant-Coventry United Methodist Church, I passed St. James Episcopal Church on the next block. Continuing on Fairmont, I soon saw the now familiar, half-timbered buildings of the Cedar Road shopping area. After turning left onto Cedar Road, I passed the Starbucks where Keir and I had spent our halcyon afternoon visit and then the entrance to his Scottish Hills neighborhood. The memories just added to my bewilderment. By the time I reached my meeting place with Melissa, the only conclusion I could draw was that Keir was protecting me from an experience for which he knew I was not yet emotionally ready. My journal entry that night was filled with questions.

A few nights later, I composed a confessional letter to Abigail. I did not intend to send it, but I was tired of pretending. In the course of writing the letter, I realized that she actually *knew*, maybe not while Keir was still alive, but the scales must have fallen from her eyes at some point;

maybe when she received the copies of Keir's portraits, or her friend in the leopard-skin dress from the Cuyahoga County Bar memorial service had said something. Or perhaps Keir spoke to her after he had passed on, or maybe she had always known that they had never been soul mates but just an intellectual match.

I had been carrying all my memories of Keir around in my head since meeting him in 1986. In my continuing effort to "get complete," I began writing them in a notebook every night before I went to bed while Auguste was watching television. Sometimes I would remember other incidents and have to squeeze them into the margins or insert additional pages. As I recalled the visit from God during the summer of 2001 wherein He told me that Keir and I had fallen in love during the French-and-Indian War and had a karmic mission to fulfill in this lifetime, I also wrote that story, incorporating the two visions Keir had brought me the previous year. I do not know what Auguste thought I was writing so intensely, but he never asked and I never volunteered to tell him.

On December 21st, 18 months after Keir's death, I sent a Christmas donation in his memory to the Amasa Stone Chapel at Case Western University to support the music program there. It was the chapel for Keir's undergraduate college, and he had loved music; I thought it would be sufficiently removed from Abigail's interests to escape her notice.

The next evening, the blockbuster movie *The Titanic* was re-broadcast on television. The story of one night of passion with a tragic ending for Jack while Rose lives the rest of her life without forgetting him, topped off with Celine Dion's hit, "My Heart Will Go On," easily elicited my tears.

404

Ohio, 2004

CHERISH

Once in a while, a book comes along that alters your life. In the case of *Journey of Souls* by Michael Newton, Ph.D., it also saved my sanity. When inducing his past life regression patients to a state of deep hypnosis— super consciousness—Dr. Newton discovered that they were remembering and revealing what occurred between the moment of their human death to the time of their re-incarnated rebirth—the entire state of being discarnate. Between the 29 case studies in *Journey of Souls* and 75 more in his subsequent book, *Destiny of Souls*, Dr. Newton made a compelling and convincing argument for the evolution of souls through multiple lifetimes.

More important for me, however, was his portrayal of soul mates encountering each other on Earth and recognizing each other through the eyes—a description that reverberated through me. I instantly recognized the uncanny experience of "eye drowning" I first experienced with Keir in the lobby of the Sandpiper Suites in 1987, again in 1994 at the Manor Grove Inn, and finally at Starbucks. Coupled with remembering God's message of our French-and-Indian War lifetime together (plus the ongoing, after-death communications from Keir's spirit), Dr. Newton's depiction pointed to the possibility that Keir was my soul mate. And, yet, all the time Keir was alive, I had talked myself out of falling for him because of my fidelity promise to Auguste, my determination not to pursue other women's men, and my low self-esteem, especially around my looks and weight.

Instead of continuing to fight, resist, and deny my love for Keir— and his for me—I began to allow it to wash over me. Books like *Visits from the After Life* and *The Five People You Meet in Heaven* further helped me to understand our connection. What if Keir was as incomplete about our relationship when he died as I had been? What if, although we had told each other we loved one another, we had stopped short of admitting that we were *in love* with each other?

As I began sharing, cautiously at first, with a few more of my friends (beyond Hillary, Sylvia, and Mark Thomas) these incidents, my story of Keir, and these unusual—at least to me—communications I had received, they suggested books to me containing similar experiences written by other authors, including Betty Eadie and, most notably, Shirley MacLaine.

In mid-January, I finished writing my own memories of Keir in my notebook.

In another attempt to save my marriage, I registered to repeat the Level I course since it had been newly redesigned. While I was away from home on the first night on the course in early February, Auguste called my room and left me a blistering voice message that Mireille had run away from home and her father's care. Even though she had returned home by the time

I had the opportunity to return his call, Auguste was still furious with us both. He blamed me for "abandoning" him with Mireille and was unwilling to discuss the situation with me.

Mireille, however, was willing to speak with me on the phone. I tried unsuccessfully to find out what had occurred and where she had gone.

"Mom, you are my *best* friend, but you are *still* my Mom." From this, I concluded our relationship was still intact and she was safe, but I allowed Mireille her privacy and did not probe any further.

On Sunday of the Level I, the course leader asked us how many of us had ever had a "peak experience?" I easily remembered Mireille's birth and several episodes with Keir. Half the course participants in the room, including me, raised our hands in response to the question.

"How about two peak experiences?" About one-third of the room kept their hands up.

"Three?" Only a quarter of the participants still had their hands raised.

"Four?" The number dropped down to about eight.

"Five or more?" Only one other person and I kept our hands raised. For someone who had a view of life that things are never good enough, I suddenly realized that, to the contrary, I had been blessed to experience far more than the normal number of life-enhancing incidents.

A few nights later, I dreamt Abigail had hired me to be Sean's and Keir's caregiver, responsible for getting them both out the door every morning after breakfast and driving them to their respective daycare locations and back. The dream also included a scene where Keir and I made love.

I asked Keir in my journal: *"What exactly did you mean by 'I may have taken you for granted'?"* I telepathically understood him to reply that, hitherto, he had had an unquestioning expectation of my unceasing devotion to him until my letters to him stopped arriving, at which point he had realized his presumption.

Another time, I asked him, *"Where in Africa did you go?"*

In late winter, I became involved in a network marketing business with an older friend, Lorraine, formerly a neighbor of my parents and also a fellow Level I graduate. Together, we decided to attend a half-day, women's networking event in Cleveland on Tuesday, March 13th. The prior Monday evening, we left our seminar in Dublin at 10:30 p.m. and headed north to Cleveland, stopping on the southern outskirts to stay at a less expensive motel before attending the downtown event the next morning. That afternoon, we planned to visit the "Dead Sea Scrolls" exhibition at the Great Lakes Science Museum. However, I had one caveat. I told Lorraine that I wanted to visit the Covenant-Coventry UMC columbarium again to see if Keir's plaque—and ashes—had finally been placed there.

While checking into the ticket desk at the museum for the exhibit, the clerk urged us to view the IMAX film there, *The Mystery of the Nile*. The film was a documentary of a white-water rafting expedition from the headwater origins of the Blue Nile in Ethiopia to the Nile Delta in Alexandria. Since Keir had enjoyed white-water rafting and, Auguste had lived in Alexandria as a boy, I was curious to know where Keir had traveled in Africa as well as where the vision he had presented to me the previous year may have taken place. I thought to myself, "This seems like an answer to one of my journal questions."

"Let's do it," I told Lorraine, so we bought our IMAX tickets.

After the first vertiginous moments of the movie filmed from a small airplane banking that had Lorraine and me grabbing each other's hands in an effort to ward off our dizziness, the film was a lush and exciting travelogue that approximated the sensation of rafting while exploring the exotic and dangerous journey from the Ethiopian highlands, through Saharan Sudan, the ancient lands of the Egyptian pyramids, modern-day Cairo, and finally to the bustling port of Alexandria. We were very grateful that the ticket clerk had suggested we view the film.

After exiting the theater, Lorraine and I returned to her car. From the Great Lakes Science Center, we drove down Ninth Street, past the Cuyahoga County Courthouse--site of Keir's Bar memorial service, and straight along Carnegie Avenue toward University Circle and Cleveland Heights.

A crisp and sunny March day, the weather and lighting were very reminiscent of my last visit with Keir. When we passed the Starbucks on Cedar Road, I could feel my emotional tension rising, my stomach tightening, and my blood pumping faster. Once on Fairmont Boulevard, I directed Lorraine into the church parking lot where I had come four months earlier. I suggested Lorraine park near the alleyway so I did not have as far to walk.

"Do you want to come with me?" I asked politely, not even sure I wanted the company.

"No, I'll stay in the car." Lorraine knew it was a journey I needed to take on my own.

I got out of the car and again walked up the hill toward the brick columbarium. As I strode toward the wrought iron gate, my eye caught sight of a low sign on the ground to my left: St. James Episcopal Church. I slowed my previously determined gait then stopped. I looked up at the church before me, its Gothic stone tower rising into the cerulean sky. Turning my gaze toward my left, looking beyond the alleyway where Lorraine's car was, I saw another, almost identical, Gothic tower.

Turning on my heels, I strode purposefully back down the hill, past Lorraine's car, and along Fairmont Boulevard around to the front of the Covenant-Coventry United Methodist Church. As I neared the double wooden front doors, a young woman in her thirties was also approaching the entrance from the main parking lot in the opposite direction. I slowed my pace.

"May I help you?" she asked.

"Where is the columbarium?" The woman began to direct me then thought better of it.

"I'll show you." She appeared sympathetic. "I'm the assistant pastor here. Is it a recent bereavement? Can I help you?"

"No." I did not wish to explain my visit lest it reach Abigail through the parson. Respecting my wishes for privacy, the assistant minister led me into the dark foyer of the entrance, through the narthex, and out the back into an enclosed, sunken garden, area.

"Are you sure I can't help?"

"No. I'm fine. Thank you." She retreated indoors while I descended the cement stairway onto the parterre.

In the center of this grassy lawn, surrounded by the stone wall enclosing the garden, rose a high cement wall with drawers engraved in cement or fronted by brass plaques with names and dates. Reverently, I walked to the wall, reading up and down the rows and columns as I made my way slowly down its length, rounded the end, and continued reading.

Midway down the second side of the wall, halfway between top and bottom, my eyes, body, and soul, locked onto a single, engraved, rectangle:

KEIR MERVAIS

June 18, 1948 – June 21, 2002

For about ninety seconds I stood transfixed in front of his name permanently embedded in cement while this undeniable finality sunk into my psyche.

I remembered I had wanted to bring a red-and-white rose but had not had an opportunity to visit a florist. I had wanted to bring newsprint and charcoal to do a rubbing but had not brought my supplies. I had nothing to leave or take as a reminder of my visit other than this hard, dull, feeling in my chest as stone cold as the cement before me. I reached my right hand out and gently touched the intaglio letters of Keir's name for a split second, then turned and ran toward another stone staircase ascending to the alleyway.

As quickly as possible, I made it to Lorraine's car and sat down heavily inside before bursting into hysterical tears. I cried for nearly fifteen minutes before I could actually speak. Lorraine silently handed me tissues.

"Thank...you," I finally managed. "It was just...seeing his name...in cement like that...The finality of it...The weather is...just like that day...when I last saw him...This neighborhood..." I took a deep, shuddering breath. "The last time I came...I must have gone to the wrong church. There are *two* churches on this corner! I realized when I saw that sign over there—it had the wrong church name!" I took another deep breath. "We can go now." Lorraine started her car, and we drove back out onto Fairmont Boulevard for the drive back to Columbus.

The OAHIA Executive Committee was considering the location of its 2006 annual convention. The officers wanted some place where the Association had not previously been before in the Sandusky area. Somewhat selfishly, I suggested the Lakeside Inn in Lakeside since I had secretly wanted to visit Keir's vacation home there that he had loved so much. To camouflage my desire and to provide a fair, more cost-effective, comparison, I suggested and the officers agreed that I would visit four resort properties in the vicinity--Lakeside Inn, Lakeside; South Beach Resort, Marblehead; Catawba Bay Peninsular Resort, Catawba Island; and, the Island House in Port Clinton--to compare them and report back to the Executive Committee with my recommendations.

Mireille had a spring break from middle school for a week in April, so I made arrangements for her to accompany me while her father stayed home with our cats. On the way to Lakeside, I planned to stop at a Jesuit monastery, Serenity Abbey in Castalia, where Keir had visited during his last trip to Lakeside—the trip his family took moments after I had spoken him.

Mireille slept in the backseat for most of our drive through the central Ohio countryside northward toward Lake Erie. It allowed me the time to be alone with my thoughts about visiting these key places from Keir's last weeks. When we arrived at the Abbey, Mireille still wanted to sleep in the car, so I obtained a map of the grounds from the gift shop and plotted my course through the monastery's complex.

I could easily understand why it was called Serenity; the quietude seemed sacred. Pink, white, fuchsia, and purple azaleas were in their peak of bloom under ancient, spreading oak trees. A small pond lay in a hollow beyond the gravel parking lot. Birds called sweetly to each other while a slight breeze lifted my hair.

According to the map, there was a library, a cloister, and a small chapel on the other side of the pond. The monks were required to maintain silence, so guests were asked to refrain from speaking to them. I could now comprehend why Keir thought this a special place to visit. I headed down the gravel path that circumvented the pond and led to the other buildings.

My artist's gaze absorbed the spring colors of new growth while my other senses took in the fresh smells and soothing sounds of the private enclave. I captured several photographs as potential painting scenes.

The monastic buildings were constructed of cream-colored stucco. An arcade with a row of arches led between the library and the square bell tower. Passing beyond that, I came to a stone staircase surrounded by azaleas and dogwood trees with soft white and pink blossoms. A small wooden sign posted on the ground said, Chapel, with an arrow pointing to the left along a flagstone pathway. Ahead on the right, stood a low stone-and-wooden structure in an austere, yet welcoming, Danish-modern style. In front were two raised beds of colorful spring flowers and three, wide, stone steps leading to glass doors with wooden handles in the shape of crosses.

Inside, the sun streamed through a window, making the sparkling dust particles appear like fairy dust slanting down toward the flagstone floor. The holy presence of God was palpable. Turning to my right, I entered the sanctuary. Wooden stalls lined both walls where I imagined the monks would sit. In addition, about a dozen wooden pews faced the altar. I stood still, taking in the divine tranquility, my soul absorbing its healing nature.

I wondered what thoughts may have crossed Keir's mind while at this abbey. Did he just enjoy the natural surroundings or did he seek a more spiritual experience?

Remembering Mireille was alone and asleep in the car, I exited the chapel to retrace my steps. Once back on the path, I saw an old monk, dressed in a hooded tunic fastened with a rope belt, walking toward me. In greeting, he smiled a huge, toothless grin, his eyes twinkling in limitless joy. I returned his smile with a nod, passed him, and continued back to my car.

Mireille, who was just beginning to stir, sat up and now joined me in the front seat. As we drove out of the Abbey gates and onto the main road, we both spotted a rainbow up in the sky.

About thirty minutes later, we turned into the gated community of Quarry Lakes Resort and Golf Club, part of the Lakeside Chautauqua. (I realized now that I had not driven far enough in 2001 to find Keir's house because I had stopped short of the Resort gate.)

"We have a reservation at the Lakeside Inn," I told the gatekeeper. After checking his list for our last name, he raised the bar and waved us through to the tree-lined main road of the prestigious development. We were definitely in the presence of some pricey real estate! Huge vacation and permanent homes with expansive porches lined with rockers and hammocks graced both sides of the street, each one more impressive than the last. Mireille and I silently acknowledged that we had entered a much classier neighborhood than to which our own socio-economic background had accustomed us.

After driving several blocks, we turned into the entrance to the Lakeside Inn, located where Lakefront Street intersects with Plum Avenue. I knew Keir's home—more accurately, his former vacation home—was located two blocks west on Laurel Avenue.

Pulling up under the Inn's portico, I gave the valet my car keys while the bellman retrieved our suitcases from the trunk. Mireille and I mounted the sweeping, columned front porch, lined with a multitude of rockers, and stepped through the door opened by the doorman onto the lobby's expansive, hardwood floor polished to sheen to check in at the front desk.

Beyond the open doors at the far end, we could see the sunlit lake sparkling in the distance, feel the cooling breeze, and smell the aquatic aroma. I tried not to appear as nervous as I felt. Once we were checked in, the bellman accompanied us to our room. Since we were on a site visit, the hotel salesperson had provided us with a complimentary lakefront suite with a king-sized bed and separate parlor.

Mireille, my independent and impulsive fourteen-year old, wanted to go out and explore the beach on her own. I calculated the risk, assured myself that we were in a relatively safe neighborhood, and permitted her freedom.

Once she left and I was alone in the room, I knew I had an exploration of my own. Donning my walking shoes and slipping the room key and an ID card into my pocket, I nonchalantly exited the hotel lobby, cutting through the parking lot at Kenton Row, and headed east onto Second Street. I tried to appear like a calm tourist although my heart was beating strongly inside my chest.

From the internet maps I had printed off at home, I knew Keir's vacation house was on Laurel Avenue, but as I passed Jasmine Avenue, I noticed a tree-lined, public-access walkway to the lake. I continued on a little further. Turning left onto Laurel, four lots down toward the lake, I saw #103 on the mailbox. I slowed my walk enough to turn my head to view the house while trying not to appear as though I was gawking.

The house was huge; not necessarily any larger than its neighbors, but certainly more than a cut above my own home. The two-story, blue-grey cottage with white trim, was surrounded by stately oaks. I could see the house had a glass-enclosed porch with an open balconied deck on top. A newer home, likely built around 1995 when Keir and Abigail bought it, it had the typical Victorian Revival hipped roof and board-and-batten architecture necessary for withstanding lake-effect snow. I noticed the steep wooden steps leading to the front door and wondered how, on his last visit, Keir had been able to mount them relying on his walker. Had he needed help from his friends and family?

As I reached the end of Laurel Avenue, I noticed a dirt path to my right between the row of lakefront homes before me and the last home on the side of the avenue where Keir's house stood. This dirt path connected with the public-access pathway, so I quickly stepped onto the path and made my way towards the lake. Recalling that on his last trip here nearly two years earlier, Keir had reportedly walked a half mile on the moist, sandy beach with his walker, I had a greater respect for how difficult it must have been for him physically and how determined he must have been to attempt it. I imagined and empathized with the personal anguish Abigail must have felt if she had been an eye-witness to her husband's struggle. I also wondered whether Keir had headed east or west along the lakefront.

Turning my back to the lake, I walked across Lakefront Street again and returned to the access path. The overhanging tree branches and leaves created a feeling of intimate privacy in contrast to the open, exposed, sunshine of the lakefront. Approaching Keir's home from the back side, I saw a large, ground-level, deck surrounded by wooden benches as well as a black, gas grill. I could imagine him grilling steaks for a party of his neighbors during the all too few summers when he was still well, and it saddened me to realize Keir experienced only four such summers. I suspected the multi-windowed first floor contained a great room with a view of the lake and a dining space, while the bedrooms were housed on the second floor with their own balconies.

Almost completely past the house now, I turned quickly for one last look. I was not sure if Abigail had sold the house yet or not. She may

411

have needed the additional funds to pay off Keir's medical bills, felt the house had too many memories, or decided it was simply too large for her to maintain on her own. Both doors to the two-car garage were closed, so I could not tell if anyone was home. In any case, I disliked the idea of trespassing on what felt like sacred territory.

I finished walking the rest of the path and emerged back into the full sunshine of Second Street and retraced my steps back to the Inn, juggling my thoughts and emotions. Evidently, Keir had been even more well-to-do than I had imagined. Had he merely toyed with me or had he felt sorry for me? And yet, he had been through so much—surely having such a magnificent second home was fair compensation for his suffering. And how poignant must have been Keir's last visit here: his last walk on the beach, his physical effort to ascend and descend the house steps, both inside and outside, as well as the lake access path, his visit to Serenity Abbey, and his no longer being able to carry out the duties of being a gracious party host for his guests—something that he must have loved.

Bittersweet anger and sadness rose to sting my throat, and I could feel the white-hot tears starting to mount as I unlocked the hotel room door. I knew I needed some distraction, so I grabbed my recently purchased copy of Nicholas Sparks' latest book, *The Guardian*, and began reading.

The first chapter contained an episode on Christmas Eve when a young widow, living in a North Carolina beach town, receives a posthumous gift—a Great Dane puppy— from her husband who had recently died of brain cancer. Accompanying the puppy was a touching note he had written to her explaining the reason for the gift (companionship) and urging her to find someone else and be happy again. In trying to distract myself, I had reinforced my own sadness. I cried for twenty minutes before I heard Mirielle's key in the door and quickly wiped my eyes.

"How was your walk?" I attempted to be cheerful.

"Okay. I met some teenagers. I might hang out with them later. I'm going to take a shower before dinner." I watched as she rummaged through her suitcase, pulled out some clean clothes, and headed into the bathroom. When I heard the water flowing from the shower, I telephoned my office to check my voicemail then changed into a clean skirt and top for supper in the hotel dining room.

After a quiet dinner, Mireille joined her new acquaintances for a while, as I returned to our room and attempted to continue reading my book. Once past the initial, emotion-triggering, similarity to my own life, I was able to sink into Sparks' bestselling prose with my usual level of admiration and enjoyment. I was still reading in bed when Mireille returned to the room around ten o'clock.

"Did you have fun with your friends?"

"It was okay. I think they are rich. They acted a little stuck up. One guy asked me how long I was going to be here. I told him we're leaving tomorrow." She headed into the bathroom.

"Do you want to sleep in tomorrow or join me downstairs for breakfast and a hotel tour with the sales manager?" I asked when Mireille came back out.

"Sleep in."

"Okay. What do you want to order for room service?" I handed her the door hanger menu from the nightstand. Once she had marked her selections and placed it outside the door, we settled into the king-sized bed and turned off the lights.

"You'll need to be up, packed, and ready to check out at eleven tomorrow," I spoke to the petite, dark figure beside me.

"Umhuh," was the muffled response from the other pillow.

After my breakfast and property tour with the sales manager, Mireille and I checked out and got packed back into my car.

"Do you remember me telling you about my rich friend in Cleveland and his house with the wall of windows in the den with five sofas?" I asked Mireille.

"Yeah. I always wanted to see that house."

"Well, he's dead now...but his former lake house is two blocks away. Would you like to drive by to see that?"

"Yeah." Mireille was a bit noncommittal but trusted her mother's judgment. Besides, there was probably not much she could do to stop me since I was the driver. We proceeded up Kenton Row to head east on Second Street and turned left onto Laurel Avenue. Three houses later, I proceeded slowly.

"That one," I pointed right toward the house I had studied the previous day.

"Wow!"

Satisfied that my unimpressionable teenager had now been impressed, I made a U-turn at the end of Laurel Avenue and headed back south. Both of us took another quick look over our left shoulders before making our way back to Second Street. However, this time, I continued eastward on Second Street, passing Plum Avenue to drive along the lake. We were headed to our next stop, the South Beach Resort in Marblehead.

"Mireille...I've fallen in love with another man—the one who owned that house. We did not have an affair, and he's dead now..." I started to cry hard. Not only was this news a startling confession to my daughter, although she may have suspected something, she was also worried I could not see the road sufficiently through my tears. Sensing her fear of a potential accident, I collected myself, grabbing a tissue to dry each eye in succession. Mireille's silence was acknowledgement that she was mulling over my revelation and relief that we were not about to crash.

"I'm glad you did not cheat on Dad," she finally said. "What was his name?"

"Keir."

"Oh."

We drove the rest of the way around the tip of the peninsula through Marblehead in silence, both deep in our own thoughts. We crossed the short causeway to Johnson's Island and checked into the resort where we were directed to a two-bedroom, cottage suite, complete with screened in porch, living room, and kitchen. Mireille elected to read while I met the salesperson for a tour of the property and meeting space. When I got back to the cottage, Mireille was napping, so I opened the windows to take advantage of the cool breeze and lay down on the sofa, soon drifting off to sleep myself and allowing the emotional roller-coaster from the Abbey, Lakeside, and my confession to Mireille to dissolve in slumber.

I knew the OAHIA members preferred a resort where everyone was lodged in the same hotel rather than housed in scattered villas, so I silently ranked the Lakeside Inn above the South Beach Resort on Johnson Island but reserved final judgment until I could visit the other two properties.

After breakfast the next morning, Mireille and I repacked my car and headed toward Catawba Island Peninsula Resort back on the north side of the peninsula between Sandusky Bay and Lake Erie. Due to hotel schedule conflicts, we were not able to drive a logical, counter-clockwise, itinerary from Johnson Island, to Lakeside, to Catawba Island but had to take a crisscross route instead.

The Catawba Island resort was even more spread out than the one on Johnson Island with lodging in townhouses and condominiums dispersed throughout the complex, not even within walking distance of either the meeting space or the beach.

Our final stop was the huge Island House Hotel in Port Clinton. Although a beachfront facility with guest rooms all in the same building, OAHIA's convention would be a small fish in a big pond, lacking the personalized attention of a more boutique property like the Lakeside Inn. I could imagine Keir's satisfaction with having his former association colleagues savoring a location he had loved so much. The one potential stumbling block was that the room rate at the Lakeside Inn was substantially higher than at the three other locations because it was ranked as a higher-end, four-diamond property. I decided to present the OAHIA Executive Committee with an objective comparison of all four resorts, only giving them my opinion and recommendation if asked.

After returning to Columbus, I experienced a bout of anger, resentment, and jealousy that Keir had been rich enough to own two beautiful homes. I felt inadequate and out-classed. One night as I lay in bed, hot tears of anger coursing from the outside edges of my eyes, I heard his voice.

"That's *not* what it was about!" He wanted me to understand that he was endowed with these riches as a compensation for the illness and suffering he had endured. My anger faded.

Since January 2003 I had feared that Abigail had dismissed me after my trip to the Quail Hollow Golf Resort because she had discovered my hidden love for Keir by sensing my guilt and figuring out my unusual attentiveness to her husband was deeper than friendship. Still, it continued to bother my ego. One April day while walking around my neighborhood, I asked, "Why did Abigail blow me off?"

"Because she felt inadequate to you and your big heart," was Keir's immediate response. Ironically, I had always felt deficient to Abigail's intellect, petite attractiveness, and marital situation. Now, the tables were turned.

During one of our family counseling sessions for Mireille who had been diagnosed with Attention Deficit Hyperactivity Disorder, high-level impulsivity, and a propensity to addiction, Auguste was blaming her for some teenage infraction.

"Anger is normal, but you are abusively angry!" the therapist remarked to Auguste. I held my breath, not knowing how Auguste would react. However, he did not seem to notice the therapist's comment.

"May I speak to you privately at the end of our session?" I asked the therapist.

"Certainly."

Once our session was over, Mireille and Auguste retired to the waiting room while I stayed.

"Have you ever read the book, *The Verbally-Abusive Relationship*?" I asked.

"No," he said, "but if you are in one, you need to get out. It's not helping you or your daughter." Now I had a third-party, professional, opinion of Auguste's behavior toward me.

Pulling into the parking lot at work one April morning, I heard the radio announce a joint Cleveland Clinic-OSU Hospital fundraising walk for brain cancer research called "Angels Amidst Us" to be held on the OSU campus in Columbus a few days later. I knew that this event had my name on it, as it had come time for me to let go of being irked at the brain cancer center medical staff for not being able to cure Keir's tumor. I immediately went into my office and registered for the event online.

Arriving at the populous fundraiser walk registration area near the football stadium, I felt small and out-of-place since I did not recognize anyone and I was not specifically representing a team supporting a current patient or recently deceased one. Once I retrieved my "Angels Amidst Us" T-shirt, I turned around to find a place to sit and wait for the walk to begin.

The day was warm and sunny after a shower the night before. All around me, teams with brightly-colored shirts gathered in groups to hug and encourage each other. I found an empty spot along a cement parapet upon which to sit and wait. I donned my T-shirt, pleased that the primary colors of the design complimented The Merv Show ball cap I had elected to wear. Looking out on the crowd, I noticed a familiar couple from my personal development seminar and waved them over. They told me they were walking to support a child in their daughter's grade school class and invited me to walk with them. My own "angels" had appeared to keep me company.

One early morning in mid-May, Keir woke me up insisting that I send his son, Sean, tickets to the IMAX movie, *The Mystery of the Nile* for Father's Day. "But Abigail will have a royal conniption fit if I do that!" my mind protested. Keir was adamant. I retrieved my calendar: Father's Day fell on the same day as would have been Keir's 56th birthday. I pulled on my bathrobe and made my way upstairs to the computer room.

While waiting to log on and open Google, I tried to figure out how to comply with Keir's request. How would I pay for Sean's ticket? How would I send it? Which date would I purchase the ticket for? How would I explain what I was doing and why? I had promised Abigail not to trouble her, and now I was about to bother her precious son, perhaps bringing up unwanted emotions; and the only explanation I had was a telepathic message from her deceased husband.

Navigating my internet search to the IMAX page for ticket sales in Cleveland, I learned that the movie was scheduled to end its run at the IMAX two weeks before Father's Day, which explained Keir's urgency but complicated selecting the movie date. Instead of purchasing the tickets online—my original intention—I chose instead to send a $20 bill and a note detailing what had transpired. I remembered having painted that silly dragon the previous year, understood now that Keir had meant it for Sean, located the JPEG scan among my digital pictures, and printed out a greeting card with the dragon on its face.

Dear Sean,

This may seem very unusual, but your father wants very much for you to see the IMAX movie, The Mystery of the Nile, *for Father's Day and his birthday. Take your cousin, your mother, your uncle, your best friend, or your best girl, but you must go soon because the film is ending its run in two weeks, on June 5th. I was worried your mother would have a royal conniption fit about this, but your Dad said it would be okay.*

P.S. Save a seat next to you in case your Dad shows up.

I signed my name, enclosed the twenty dollars, and mailed it with a prayer to Keir, "Please tell Abigail not to have a 'royal conniption fit' and use those exact words so she knows that this is not a hoax."

When it came time for me to present the results of my Sandusky area site visit to the OAHIA Executive Committee at their May meeting, the officers asked for, received, and endorsed my recommendation to select the Lakeside Inn for their 2006 annual convention. Some weeks later, while researching activities in Lakeside, I learned that the Chautauqua of Lakeside was planning a downtown revitalization project and selling memorial bricks for the plaza it was erecting. Through the internet, I had already learned that Abigail had sold their lake house. I purchased a brick in Keir's memory so that he would continue to own a small piece of real estate in the lakeside community he had so loved.

On May 29th, to honor the second anniversary of my phone conversation with Keir when we said we loved each other, I took the day off to drive to Cleveland again and spend the day at the Art Museum and in the

Fine Arts Garden around Wade Lagoon. Taking a sketchbook and watercolor pencils with me, I found I was more drawn to the peace and beauty of the natural setting than to the manmade artifacts inside the museum. The clear blue sky above reminded me of Keir's own eyes, and I wondered if he had found solace visiting this garden when he was ill.

"I wonder if there are any irises?" I mused half out loud as I wandered through the pathways.

"Turn here," Keir's voice instructed. I turned down a walkway narrowed by overhanging tree limbs, emerging out on the other side to see a breathtaking array of yellow and lavender irises clustered around a small stone pagoda at the edge of the lagoon. Seating myself on a rock facing the classic Japanese scene, I sketched the idyllic landscape before me, followed by writing in my journal, grateful to have been led to this secluded area. When I gathered my belongings and continued walking around the lagoon, I noticed a plaque embedded in a stone near the pagoda: Garden of Peace.

While reflecting on my day during my drive home, I also thought about the coming week with my birthday. I sent Keir a silent prayer request to give me a birthday gift. "Surprise me," I asked.

Nothing unusual occurred on my birthday beyond the expected family celebrations and greetings from friends. Ten days later, midway between my birth date and Keir's, I was lingering in bed that Saturday morning halfway between sleeping and awake. Auguste had already gone outside to work in our yard. Suddenly I found myself standing in my art studio directly above my bed on the second floor. Keir was standing in the hallway at the top of the stairs, sporting a black-and-purple Hawaiian luau shirt and holding a white gift box under his left arm. He was pointing beyond me directly at a group of towel-covered, framed paintings, including a charcoal portrait I had drawn of him. However, the towel from that picture had fallen to the floor to reveal the drawing. I knew that he was both acknowledging the portrait and warning me it was exposed. I was so surprised to see him that I "fell" back down onto my bed, fully awake now to this second out-of-body experience.

Immediately, I rose from bed and headed upstairs to re-cover the portrait and to see if my sleeping daughter had any sense of this encounter. Peeking into the door of her room, just two feet from where Keir had appeared just moments before, Mireille was still slumbering undisturbed. However, on the shelf inside her room was an empty white gift box, a remainder from her opened birthday present exactly two months earlier. Then I remembered that the night Keir and I had first drowned in each other's eyes at the Sandpiper Suites, I was wearing a black-and-purple dress similar to the shirt he wore in this vision. He had indeed delivered on my birthday surprise. I firmly replaced the towel over his picture and went back down stairs. To honor his birthday, a week later I mailed a second memorial donation to the Grand Canyon National Park Foundation.

The following Saturday, as I drove to a nearby restaurant to celebrate my mother's 80th birthday, I heard Elton John singing "Can You

Feel the Love Tonight?" on the radio. The lyrics were so perfect! I prayed that Sean could feel his father's presence of love surrounding, protecting, and warming him on Father's Day and wondered if Sean had been to the movie.

Monday evening, around six o'clock while I was driving to my seminar, I had a sensation of what it was like when Keir's soul left his body as he died and rose above his bedroom where his body still lay. When I arrived at the seminar and entered the restroom, my friend Becky looked shell-shocked.

"What's *wrong*?" I asked urgently. She fell into my arms crying and sobbing, unable to speak for what seemed like five minutes.

"John Waters...died yesterday," she finally choked out, then cried some more. John, a charming and gracious older man, had coached the Level III leadership program with Becky, Gary, Melissa, and me the previous autumn. Like me, he had been an Association executive and a good friend of our deceased friend and Gary's wife, Carolyn. "John had gone to Florida to care for his father-in-law who has cancer. Instead, John had a heart attack," Becky explained.

Immediately, I recalled my last few encounters with John. He was the first person with whom I had dared visit a Starbucks for coffee after Keir had died. Another time, he, my current coach Hillary, Gary, and I had met for dinner to discuss creating a scholarship program in Carolyn's memory that, sadly, never came to fruition. And there had been the Level III leadership coaches' reunion party when John had enthralled us with a story of how he, as a young man, had once had the opportunity to dance with the former Grace Kelly before she became a famous actress and the Princess of Monaco. John would be sorely missed.

As I lay down to sleep that night, Keir's spirit sent me a vision of myself on the deck of a black schooner in the English Channel in 1810. I was dressed in a long silver dress. The ship captain had my back pinned against the railing making unwelcome, amorous advances to me as I struggled to free myself. I knew my husband—Keir—had been tossed overboard by this captain, and I no longer was under my husband's protection.

Later, when I did some internet research about schooners, clothing, and the period 1810, I learned that schooners were a popular form of naval transportation in the nineteenth century. A break in the Napoleonic Wars around 1810 allowed for trade on the English Channel to resume, although piracy was rampant. The style of my dress was the height of fashion in Paris 1806, but it was likely there was a few years' delay before that fashion reached England.

On June 21st, the second anniversary of Keir's death, I had purposely scheduled myself for an hour massage, redeeming a gift certificate given to me by a friend for my birthday. About two-thirds into the massage, I heard Abigail's voice in my mind.

"Sean enjoyed the film." I was glad she had allowed him to go, but there was something else I wanted to know.

"Of course he did," my mind replied, "but I want to know—*did his father show up?*"

"Of course I did," Keir's amused voice broke in to my consciousness. "Why would I have asked you to send Sean, if I wasn't planning to be there?"

Two days later, I departed for a national conference I was coordinating in the Napa Valley. I had wanted to take a hot-air balloon ride for a long time and once had priced a Columbus-area balloon ride company for my mother's birthday, but at $250 per person, that was more money than I could justify to Auguste. However, I now had an independent source of coaching income with my own checking account and credit card, so I was able to funnel some expenses through that without having to explain them to Auguste.

Due to the competition among hot-air balloon companies in the Napa Valley, the cost of a dawn ride was less expensive than in Columbus. In addition, my body would still be operating on East Coast time, so the 4:30 a.m. wake up call would not be such a hardship for me. Since our conference staff would have to fly out on Friday to be in California on Saturday to prepare for the conference, I made a reservation for an early Saturday morning balloon ride.

The wind that morning in the Napa Valley was so strong that our balloonists, rather than cancel the trip as several competitors chose to do, took the chance that heading further inland toward the vegetable-growing valleys east of Napa would be safer. Four valleys over, toward Sacramento and Davis, they located a field cleared of crops with short, hay-like stubble, and began to inflate the colorful balloon cavities above the square, straw baskets divided into six sections each. Once fully inflated by the propane gas burners, we passengers were invited to climb inside—two passengers per section.

I was nervous, excited, and sleepy. Stepping onto the low, plastic stool in front of the basket, placing my right foot into the small "foot hole" in the basket wall and then my left foot into the hole a little higher in the basket wall, I lifted my right leg over the basket wall and dropped my foot onto the basket floor, quickly following with my left foot, landing with a thud. Once inside, the basket wall reached to my mid-chest. We were warned not to lean too far out as there were no seat belts or safety straps. Too much weight on one side would tip the basket.

After some souvenir photos were taken, I looked at my watch: 7:30 a.m. California time and 10:30 a.m. back home where John Water's funeral was about to commence in Dublin. Suddenly, I felt John's presence with me as though in a quandary: "Hot-air balloon ride with Annie? Or a party with my friends in Dublin?"

"John," my mind spoke to him. "I am sorry I cannot be at your memorial service today, but I know you would wholeheartedly support me

419

taking this hot-air balloon ride. However, you need to be with the rest of your friends in Dublin." John's spirit disappeared as with a loud whoosh of hot air my basket lifted off the ground.

We soared over mustard fields, tomato fields, and my favorite, sunflower fields, descending so close to the ground, you could almost lean over (forbidden!) and pick a sunflower, then ascended aloft again to the same elevation as the single-engine, crop-dusting airplanes. Ahead of us, like colorful lollipops dotting the sky, we could see the five other balloons that had lifted off before us. Other than the whoosh-whoosh of the occasional bursts of propane-heated air into the balloon's cavity, the conversation amongst my fellow passengers, and the distant hum of the crop-dusters, there was only quiet as we drifted over the farmlands, our progress measured by the shadow cast by the balloon and basket against the crops beneath us.

"Normally, a hot-air balloon travels at five or six miles per hour," our pilot told us, "but today, with the winds, we are doing fifteen!" I savored the trip even more, realizing how close we had come to having it cancelled, even while I wondered if we would blow as far south as San Jose. I checked the position of the tiny, white, chase-vehicle below us. About forty-five minutes into the flight, the pilots signaled each other to begin looking for a safe place to land and instructed us in safe landing procedures.

"We're looking for a large, clear-cut field where we can avoid touching utility wires," the pilot said. "Usually a farmer will be fine with us landing, as long as we leave fairly quickly. Although, one time, the landowner came out with a shotgun; so we've learned to land, deflate the balloon, pack everything on the van, and get out of there in ten minutes. Sometimes the basket tips over, or it skips along a bit, so you need to be prepared for that. Otherwise, as soon as we land, you all need to climb out of the basket quickly before the balloon drops to the ground. Then head for the van, and we'll do the rest."

Our basket cleared the electrical wires, hit the ground with a slight thud, then skipped a few times, and landed upright. We scrambled out of the basket as quickly as possible and over the stubbly ground to the waiting chase vehicle, which drove us back to the balloon company's headquarters in Napa for our champagne brunch.

I was continuing to struggle with my marriage to Auguste. Arguments were plentiful, and we were constantly in a state of mutual resentment. Mireille was invited for a sleepover at the home of one of her friends for the July Fourth holiday weekend. Auguste and I were eating breakfast alone on that Independence Day morning. While chewing my bagel, I had the thought: "I can continue on in this marriage for the rest of my life, or I can strike a blow for freedom." I turned to Auguste.

"This marriage isn't working for me," I stated simply. "Do you want to move out or should I?"

"I think you should stay here with Mireille, and I'll move out." He was equally as calm. That was it. No arguments, threats, fireworks,

420

protestations, or criticism. Three days later, Auguste found an apartment a mile away, within walking distance of Mireille's high school. I helped him locate and purchase some basic furniture and provided him with other household items from our house: a television and a VCR, some pots and pans, sheets and towels, and dishes. Meanwhile, my divorce attorney drafted a settlement agreement for Auguste's and my review. He accepted all the provisions without any rebuttal.

The day following our separation talk, I felt Keir's spirit very strongly throughout the day. Sometimes it was so powerful, I had to rest from the sense of him. Other times, I just allowed myself to be present to it.

The following weekend, Becky and her husband invited me, Gary, and several other mutual seminar friends, including a couple from Mansfield, Adrianne and Rusty Rush, over for a cookout. In the process of chatting, I learned that Adrianne was a hypnotist, helping people with their smoking and weight issues as well as assisting the Mansfield police department with criminal investigations.

"Have you ever heard of a past-life regression?" I asked her.

"Oh, I do those, too," the cheerful blonde replied. "I've done about a hundred of them."

"I've been having these visions…snippets, like movie trailers, of earlier historic periods…preceded by a very strong spiritual presence of a close friend who died. When I research the details of the dress and events on the internet, the information corresponds accurately with the visions."

"Oh, that definitely sounds like past lives! You should set up an appointment with me the next time you are planning to be in Mansfield." For a couple of weeks, I worried how much the hypnosis session would cost, imagining something akin to a hot-air balloon ride, but I finally called Adrianne and learned her fee was closer to that of a psychotherapy session.

"I'm coming to Mansfield on July 25th for the evening session of the Love course that I am repeating. Do you think you could give me a regression that afternoon?"

"Sure, how about 3:30?" Adrianne gave me directions to her office.

In contrast to the questionable psychic types advertising in the New Age tabloids, Adrianne was a friend of mutual friends and had done the same personal development programs I had done. She came across as a no-nonsense, practical woman who reassured me that her type of hypnosis did not have her patients "do silly things they do not remember like depicted on TV magic shows." I was about to undergo a procedure I did not completely understand, so I needed to trust Adrianne's experience, professionalism, and integrity.

Before entering her office, I had resolved not to tell Adrianne much of the details of my visions so as not to prejudice the process, but Adrianne explained that she needed to know what to listen for, so I gave her a brief summary of my relationship with Keir, before and after his death. Before starting our session, we first reviewed hypnosis protocols and patient agreements and releases.

"Now, lie down with that blanket over you and get comfortable," Adrianne indicated the navy futon in her therapy room. "I'm going to put you into something of a meditative state, and then I'll ask you some guided questions." I lay down and closed my eyes.

Beginning with deep breathing, Adrianne guided me through a relaxation process then mentally took me "down an elevator" which opened onto a space of – nothingness.

"What do you see?" she asked.

"Nothing. It's black. Are you sure I am hypnotized?"

"Yes, you are hypnotized. What do you feel?"

"I feel...nauseous...and shackled."

"Hmmm. Okay, let's move ahead some. Now, what do you see?"

"It's all white." I was starting to feel a little frustrated. After all, I was paying for this.

"Are you still nauseous?"

"No."

"Move ahead a little more. What do you see now?"

In my mind, I could see the whiteness lift a little, like fog or mist, and my surroundings become clearer. Below in the distance, I began to perceive a curving shoreline.

"I think it is a fishing village on the coast."

"Look down at your feet, what are you wearing?"

"My feet are bare."

"Ask someone if they recognize you." In my mind, I moved down the grassy, sloped path to the beach below where fishermen were repairing their nets and asked one of them if he recognized me. The crinkled eyes in the wizened and unshaven face peered up at me.

"No'um, Miss," he replied in an accented voice, very puzzled and concerned, almost to the point of thinking I was crazed. He turned away.

"No, he didn't recognize me," I told Adrianne.

"Go find a mirror and look at yourself," she instructed. Picking my way barefoot over the stones and shells of the beach, I mentally made my way up the stone steps to the esplanade where the seafront taverns and stores lined a cobblestone street. My long, silver gown felt stiff, heavy, and stained with dried salt brine.

"I doubt they will have a mirror here," I warned Adrianne. But I did find a large, lobster pot hanging with its round, copper bottom facing outward. Peering at it, I saw the vague reflection of a young, upper middleclass, woman with disheveled blonde curls looking gaunt and half-drowned. "No wonder the fisherman was wary of me," I thought to myself.

"Let's move on," Adrianne prompted. In my mind I strode uphill walking on a cobblestoned street towards a square, stone church in the distance. Something about the church was familiar and welcoming to me.

"I see a church," I told Adrianne. A friendly pastor was in the garden, so I told him my plight. He made arrangements for me to stay with a widow nearby. "I think I have amnesia," I said out loud to Adrianne.

"Move ahead a year," Adrianne encouraged. "What do you see now?" I was meeting in a tavern with an older man and interviewing to be a governess for his children. I am feeling resigned to my fate.

"I'm going to be a governess," I explained to Adrianne.

"Okay. Let's try something else." I sensed that Adrianne, too, was feeling frustrated by the lack of clarity of the information being revealed to us. "Imagine you are entering a temple, what do you see?" First, I saw the Taj Mahal and then a smaller temple in a different architectural style.

"It's gold and red with black doors." It appeared to me like an elaborate Buddhist temple from the Far East somewhere.

"Open the doors and go inside. What do you see?"

"A small man sitting on a black cushion. He wants me to sit on a cushion facing him."

"Okay. Imagine he hands you something. What is it?"

"It's a scroll." Actually, it was a glass-tube encased in gold filigree containing a parchment scroll.

"What does the scroll say?"

"I cannot read it. The letters are foreign to me. But I think they mean something like '*Hakuna Mata—No Worries!*' Are you sure I am hypnotized?"

"Yes, I am sure. Now I am going to bring you out of it slowly. When you are fully conscious again, you will remember everything you saw, felt, heard, and understood." Adrianne rode me back up the mental elevator, back to my body and breathing, and to the futon and her therapy room.

"Wow! You were under for an hour-and-a-quarter!" Adrianne said when I was fully awake. "I felt like we were being prevented from getting any place, though, because I sensed a powerful, male presence in the room the whole time."

We debriefed further, and Adrianne gave me her notes about what I had reported to her. The images felt jumbled in my head. "Let me know if anything else comes to you in the days ahead. Sometimes the process can open up a floodgate of spiritual experiences." Adrianne then bid me goodbye and good luck with my Love course evening session.

Now five o'clock, I found a Subway restaurant for dinner. Collecting my sandwich, chips, and drink, I found a lone table towards the rear of the store. Suddenly, Keir's presence was palpable.

"Why did you prevent Adrianne's attempt to regress me?" I protested telepathically to him. Just then, the loudspeaker in the restaurant played "Once, Twice, Three Times a Lady," and I understood immediately that the scenes from the dark, the nausea, the white fog, and the fishing village were related to the vision about the ship captain on the schooner. I also understood that Keir wanted to be the one "scripting" these revelations of our past lifetimes to me.

The next day, I sent Adrianne an email, telling her what occurred at the Subway and including a link to the OAHIA newsletter with the obituary

I had written about Keir. She agreed he had been very handsome and felt he had complimented me highly by continuing to communicate to me his love and interest.

Just as Adrianne predicted, Keir's spirit hung around me for several days as though attempting to soothe me: "Are you okay? Are you okay? Are you okay?" while the pieces of the revelations fell into some understandable pattern for me.

A week later, I had another vision after feeling Keir's presence just before falling asleep; in it, I was a Native American on the American Plains. A medicine man, my grandfather, is leaning over me to ascertain whether I am okay. I am tightly swaddled in and lying on a stretcher made of tree limbs and deer hide attached behind a horse. As my grandfather pulls back from the front of my face, I see an unpleasant warrior-chief standing at the foot of the travois, glaring down at me, his arms akimbo. The stretcher begins to move, and I catch a glimpse of my love—an earlier reincarnation of Keir—dead on the ground, his face and head bloodied from having fought for me and been beaten. I sense I am being taken back to my village to marry the warrior-chief to whom I am betrothed, even while I am in love with the dead brave.

August 25, Journal Entry: *Often I have feelings that I cannot seem to put into words. It's an ache, a longing, a slide, and a tremor of sadness—adrenaline, a reaching for—I do not know what, only that it is out of my reach. It's a yearning, an almost recognition, and then a loss; an almost remembering and an empty handedness.*

That Sunday, a couple who regularly conducted past-life regressions visited the Columbus Unity Church. I invited Adrianne and her husband to attend the session with me. Once inside the sanctuary, I telepathically requested to Keir "no more death scenes; only happy, joyful times." The leader of the regression session requested three volunteers up front for a group regression. In my pew, I closed my eyes.

After taking a few deep breaths, I was in India, walking through the hallway of a Muslim palace, wearing a yellow sari and holding my young son's hand. I looked back over my shoulder at a handsome, dark guard—a former version of Keir. Our eyes met, and I smiled at him.

Then, another lifetime came. I was running over a stone bridge into the arms of my beloved fiancé waiting for me in front of his carriage, handsomely dressed in a nineteenth century, green velvet, tailcoat. The regressionist told us to skip ahead, and in my mind's eye, I was exiting a stone church with my just-wed husband—Keir again. As we mounted our open carriage, I turned to wave to the well-wishing villagers standing in the churchyard and saw—to my astonishment—my OAHIA and seminar friend, Mark Thomas, who appeared in an ill-fitting suit—probably his best clothes for the occasion, standing with his hat in hand, simultaneously joyous and sad to see his best friend married. But I did not have long to ponder the fact that I had known both Mark and Keir in that previous lifetime.

"Now, move ahead to the end of that lifetime," the regressionist instructed. I saw myself lying on my deathbed, my white curls under a mob cap. A very nice, young man in a green velvet jacket with a high collar—a Dickensian style—is visiting me; he was once one of my governess "charges." I am eagerly awaiting the final reunion with the spirit of my deceased husband.

When the regression session was over, impatient to impart these new pieces to my past-life puzzle, I asked Adrianne what she had learned.

"I fell asleep," she said, a bit annoyed.

"I didn't get anything either," Rusty admitted. I felt badly they had driven to Columbus for nothing.

"I got four visions from two different lifetimes," I had to confess. "And they were all happy visions, too!"

"You were lucky. We're not always ready to receive what spirit can tell us." We hugged, and then Adrianne and Rusty left to drive back to Mansfield.

Now separated from Auguste, for the first time in my life, I was going to take a vacation by myself. I asked Auguste to care for Mireille for a week while I attended a week-long watercolor workshop at the Hideaway Country Inn, the rustic resort in Bucyrus where Evonda and her husband had encountered Keir, Abigail, and Sean in April 1996. Mark Thomas had once told me he had practiced law in the town of Bucyrus when he was a young attorney.

In addition to the enjoyable watercolor lessons with a vibrant teacher and fun students, we shared our meals—groaning board buffets—in the picturesque wooden dining hall. However, my favorite times were the quiet moments when I took solitary walks in the woods, despite a painful knee, or along the golf trails in the early mornings when the dew and mist clung to the grass. My room had a small deck with two rockers affording me some moments of serenity as well. The smell of the wood paneling permeated my nostrils—so different from most hotel rooms in which I had slept.

"Abigail is no longer part of the equation," I heard Keir say to me as I drifted off to sleep one evening. I was puzzled by his pronouncement. Did that mean she had moved on? Did that mean that she no longer mattered in the relationship?

One afternoon, as I left the watercolor class and passed through the bar lounge area, I heard Keir's voice again.

"This chair—*here!*" I passed my hand across the top of a high-backed, upholstered, wing chair, knowing that Keir had sat in it during his stay at the Inn eight years earlier. Another evening, as we gathered for supper, and I made my way through the lobby of the Main Inn towards the dining room, I felt Keir's spirit in one area near the glass cases of historic memorabilia, and I knew, with his interest in history, he had read these same display cases.

425

The night after I returned home from my trip to the Hideaway Country Inn, I had a long dream about Keir. Just before falling asleep, I wondered what he would have looked like if his hair had grown back after the surgery, radiation, and chemotherapy treatments. In the dream, I drove to Cleveland to visit him but ended up in a crowded, office building where I searched for a ladies room to change from my shorts into a business suit. I grabbed Keir's hand and held it tightly so as not to be separated from him in the crowd. Keir's hair was a bit unruly, similar to Michael J. Fox's in *Teen Wolf*. I wanted to hold onto his hand and spirit long after I awoke.

OAHIA returned to the Grove Manor Inn in Cincinnati for its 2004 annual convention. The meeting room where Keir and I had "drowned" in each other's eyes had been turned into a culinary shop. Ironically, one of the general session presentations was a panel on which all of the speakers had worked with and/or served on the OAHIA Executive Committee with Keir: Eric Mitchell, Harry Whitfield, Jonathan Patrick, and Phyllis Buckley. During the session, I had an "empty" seat next to me where I felt Keir's spirit. Just as the panel presentation was about to begin, I felt Keir suddenly "stand up" as Katherine Shipley entered and sat down in the seat. She turned and smiled at me, while I wondered if she had any clue that Keir, always the gentleman, had relinquished his seat to his former, female co-worker whom he had hired, with whom he had worked for thirteen years, and who now held the state manager's job Keir had so dearly wanted.

I had wanted to honor Keir's memory in some way at the convention, so I planned an optional, white-water rafting excursion on the Whitewater River west of Cincinnati. It would be my first time rafting. In the end, only about a dozen people registered, but my raft contained some of Keir's closest friends and colleagues: Harry and Martha Whitfield, Phyllis Buckley, and a younger couple, the husband of which was a fairly new employee of Cleveland Medical, where Keir had worked.

On the rickety bus ride back from where our rafting excursion had ended to return our starting point, I shared a seat with Phyllis. I recalled that she was the woman who originally told me that Keir had brain cancer and wondered if she remembered.

"Where is the convention next year?" she asked me.

"At the Lakeside Inn," I replied tautly, aware that she would likely make the association with Keir's vacation home.

"Did you know that Keir Mervais had a home there?" I nodded in response. "He had many happy moments at that house," she remarked wistfully. We sat together in silence until we returned to the raft launching site where we changed our clothes before driving back to the Grove Manor Inn.

Once back at the Grove Manor Inn, I showered and changed into dinner clothes. We had a small group—mostly rafting trip participants—who were staying an additional night to go out to dinner together at a restaurant in downtown Cincinnati. Although we had ordered a van, the transportation provider opted to send us a stretch limousine for the ride into

426

town. Delighted by this unexpected surprise, we climbed into the black interior and settled ourselves onto the leather seats. Sitting across from me, Harry Whitfield leaned forward.

"How come OAHIA doesn't get to meet at The BroAdmoor?" His question caught me by surprise.

"I don't think I *ever* want to go back to The BroAdmoor. That's where I was when Kevin Raines told me he had to quit the OAHIA presidency because his cancer had spread and where I was when I learned Keir Mervais had died." My throat was tight from emotion. "Besides, we're a state association. You'll probably need to attend a national convention at The BroAdmoor." I don't think Harry expected to receive the intense seriousness of my response.

Our dinner reservations were in a private upstairs dining room at the restaurant. When we had all ordered, Harry's wife, Martha spoke to Patty Tippett, a manager of one of Cleveland Medical's satellite offices.

"Did you ever know Keir Mervais?" At the mention of his name, I turned to listen to Martha.

"No," Patty replied.

"He was *wonderful!*" Martha gushed while I silently agreed. "One of our mutual friends, an Appellate Court Justice, had cancer a year before Keir came down with it." I mentally calculated that to be 1999 while I hung on Martha's every word. "He drove her *every*where—doctor's appointments, radiation treatments, whatever she needed…" I hoped Martha would say more about Keir, but the waiter came with our salads and the conversation drifted onto other topics.

I considered the unfair irony of Keir's attentiveness to the judge only to be followed by his own, similar illness. I wondered who—besides Abigail and Keir's brother, Mark—had driven Keir to his appointments. I wanted to get Martha alone and beg her to tell me everything she knew about Keir, but I could not bring myself to disclose the true reasons behind my deep interest.

I had absolutely no desire to hurt Abigail, Sean, Mark, or any of Keir's family. I doubted most of the OAHIA members would believe my story about God's pronouncements to me of "our mission" and our previous French-and-Indian War life together, much less stories about other past lifetimes. And I did not trust that anything I said on the subject would not eventually get back to Abigail in some fashion. So, besides confessing to Mark Thomas—who had assured me of attorney-client confidentiality, my former co-workers Sylvia and Evonda, and a few, close seminar friends, I did not reveal what I had experienced to anyone else in OAHIA.

Upon my return to Columbus following the OAHIA convention, I was writing in my "Dear Keir" journal, telling him about the rafting trip, when I came up with and recorded the idea that I should raft through the Grand Canyon myself since Keir had not been able to take his own family trip in the summer of 2002. I had no idea what that would entail or how I would do that, but the goal was inspiring, exciting, and scary at the same time.

Later that evening, while almost falling asleep, I had a vision of Keir standing in the back of the Amasa Stone Chapel on Case Western Reserve University's campus. The Chapel was almost full, and a wedding was about to begin. Keir was anxiously standing behind the last pew while I was standing in the third pew from the rear looking backwards toward the sunlit entrance as the wedding march music began. The bride and her father came down the aisle together. As they made their way toward the altar, Keir bolted outside, jumped into his convertible, gunned the motor, and sped out of the parking lot, swearing to himself that he would never fall that "out-of-control in love" with any woman ever again.

Was this vision Keir's way of explaining to me why he had (what had seemed to me) an "arranged" marriage with Abigail—an intellectual and socio-economic match but without the emotional intimacy and intensity I would have expected from someone with such a joy of life? Did this also explain his sometimes reluctance to pursue me beyond the moral factor of infidelity? Had he actually been *afraid to love me*?

A week later, I lay on my back on my living room sofa listening to a meditation CD, breathing in and out, calming my mind. Suddenly, I was back at Keir's funeral outside on the church lawn standing between Mark Thomas and Brent Tillett while Brent was relating the story of the Beaver Ridge Inn in 1986 when Keir had reassured Brent about his premature son, the story that was now permanently recorded in the Cuyahoga County court records. But instead of being *inside* my body, Keir and I were standing *behind* my body and Mark.

"Look—all my friends are here!" Keir was very excited but then disappointed. "They can't seem to hear me..." I was experiencing Keir's feelings *with* him. We watched together as I walked over to speak with Abigail. Keir was nervous about this encounter, but I already knew that it had gone well. We watched me hug Abigail, give her the sympathy card, and exchange our few words.

Then, Keir and I were floating aloft and looking down on the mourners in the churchyard. The scene below changed a little and we both saw my lone figure in my red suit looking for Keir's name on the wrong church's columbarium wall.

We pulled upward, and we were above Cleveland and Lake Erie, then we were above Ohio, and the United States. We floated higher, looking back at the Earth like astronauts, only we had no spaceship around us. We passed through the stars and planets of our solar system, through the Milky Way, and further into deep space.

Then, I was back down on my living room sofa, meditating, breathing in and out, having experienced my third out-of-body experience in two years. In this manner, Keir had confirmed to me that he had been present at his funeral, that he was admittedly nervous about Abigail's and my interaction, that he knew I had been to the wrong columbarium at first—

428

and maybe he had even misdirected me—and that deceased souls can float through space at will.

Since then, not a starry night goes by that I do not pause and look up into the heavens and recall that spiritual flight with awe, love, and gratitude.

"Did you ever think of me?" I wrote in my journal. The response came one night through a vision of Keir in his family room one evening. Abigail was stretched out on a sofa reading while Keir was unsettled. He put some music on the entertainment center and stared out the back window. He seemed to morph from being well and having hair to after he had his cancer treatments and was bald. Without looking up from her reading, Abigail sensed Keir's mood.

"What's wrong?" Retrieved from his reverie by his wife's inquiry, Keir shifted a little and shrugged.

"Oh, I was just thinking..." I knew he had averted her question because he had been thinking about me...and, that he thought about me both before and after he was ill.

I was presenting a four-week workshop, Finding the Artist Within, to a small group of would-be artist friends at one of the women's homes. In our third session of the course, the participants worked with me to develop their twelve-month creativity plans.

"And what would *you* like to accomplish creatively a year from now?" one asked me after the participants had finished their respective plans.

"I've always wanted to write a book..." I admitted, perhaps for the first time out loud.

"What about?"

"Well, I've been having these visions about past lifetimes. One in Africa, one in India, the French-and-Indian War..." The woman who was hosting the workshop stood up and went to her bookshelf. She retrieved a National Geographic book on the Maasai tribe of Africa and a novel about multiple lifetimes. Although it has taken me many years rather than one year to write, that evening was the genesis of this book.

Within a month after Auguste had left our household, Mireille and I weaned ourselves from our anti-depressant medications. The sessions with the family therapist ended with Mireille and the therapist agreeing that the best thing to come out of them was that her parents had separated and were getting along much better now that they were no longer living together under the same roof.

From time to time, I would get more visions, each preceded by a strong sense of Keir's spirit. The following three appeared to be specifically related:

I am a young girl, about nine or ten years old, in tattered clothing, almost like a gunny sack. I am being led across a rock-strewn, icy river on a wooden bridge and into the streets of a bustling marketplace in the center of the capital city of a snowy, mountainous country. As a young child would be, I am delighted with all the new sights, sounds, and smells, but I am also nagged by a question, *"Where is he?"* until we round the corner and stretching upward before me is a large, white building with a very tall and steep, stone staircase leading up to the main entrance. Instinctively, I know *he* is inside that building. I am left with a single word: "Shangri- La."

He and I are merrily strolling on a dirt path through a large stretch of open field. He is wearing a black robe, belted at the waist, similar to that of a black-belt in karate. His smile is warm and content. My mind gladly notes, "It's been a long time since I saw him *this* happy!"

I am climbing the stone steps from the marketplace with my purchases in a cloth sack. Oddly, there is a crowd of people on the staircase leading up to the front of the building. At first I am curious, but as I make my way further up the stairs, I sense a growing feeling of dread. About two-thirds of the way up the steps, I am pulled to the side by some bystanders as the main, wooden doors to the monastery open to reveal a group of monks carrying a stretcher. Since this is a new experience for me, I share the anticipation of the crowd as the monks and the stretcher descend the stairs, until I recognize the face of the monk on the stretcher.

"NO!!!" I scream out and lunge at the stretcher bearing *his* body, but someone stronger pulls me back and restrains me in my struggle to get free. My purchases of fruits and vegetables roll out of my dropped bag and down the steps.

As the crowd follows the stretcher down to the river's edge, I sit on the steps and cry inconsolably. No one pays attention to me. Later, after the ceremony is over and the crowd has disbursed, I make my way down to the cremation bier at the river's edge. Curious to see where they have taken my beloved monk, I walk along the wet rocks toward the bridge over which I first entered the city. I slip on the rocks, hit my head, and am carried away with the current.

Searching the word "Shangri-La" on the internet, I found the Himalayan country of Bhutan whose governmental and religious authority rests with the monasteries housed in tall, white buildings called *dzongs*. I even found a photograph of one of these fortresses alongside a wooden bridge spanning a river. The men wear jackets (often black) called *gho*, tied with cloth belts, similar to those worn by karate instructors. I even located a photograph of a red and gold Buddhist temple similar to the one from my past-life regression with Adrianne.

I started a series of file folders with the countries and time periods of all the visions and used the library to supplement my internet research. The number of similarities between the events and clothing in my visions and those found in my research readings was too uncanny to ignore. When I sat down to write the Anasazi Indian chapter, it only took me two, ninety-minute, sessions because the words flowed out of my pen so easily, I must have been tapping into some deep recollection.

My life was not completely consumed with my research. Auguste willingly sold me his half of our house. We went through the divorce and house closing legal transactions. After thirty years of a contentious marriage, he put up very little resistance to its dissolution.

Now that the house was mine, Mireille and I went shopping for colorful wall paint. As an artist, living for thirty years with white walls virtually without pictures had stifled me. I was ready for an explosion of color to offset my growing number of paintings, especially those that reminded me of Keir: his double portrait, the Grand Canyon, Mt. Everest, Lake Erie, the fine arts garden at the Cleveland Museum of Art, the Hideaway Country Inn, and Serenity Abbey, but especially the painting of our two, entwined Zuni bracelets.

I chose to paint two walls of my bedroom the sky blue of Keir's eyes and the other two the pale green of his eyes when he wore yellow tinted contact lenses. After three days painting the ceiling, walls, and trim, I suddenly felt so tired that I lay down on a patch of drop cloth-covered floor since the bed was still covered with a chair, two night tables, and a bookshelf under more drop cloths. My throat was very sore, like I was swallowing razor blades, and I could feel the dizzying sensation of a fever mounting.

Fading in and out of consciousness, I was not surprised to sense Keir's presence, but when I felt Kevin Raine's spirit pass into my bedroom as though to say to Keir, "Nope, she doesn't look too good," I knew that they were both trying to save my life by rousing me to go to the doctor. I was diagnosed with a particularly virulent form of strep throat, likely aggravated by the paint fumes. I needed two penicillin shots and a steroid-booster shot to affect a cure.

By Christmas time, I was recovered. A friend of mine who lived in Cleveland, Cindy, invited me to visit her for the holidays since Mireille was with Auguste for Hanukkah. Cindy suggested we attend the midnight Christmas Eve service at Amasa Stone Chapel. Remembering Keir's vision of the wedding from that Chapel, I agreed to Cindy's suggestion.

Although we arrived an hour before the service was scheduled to begin, the Chapel was already pretty full, and we ended up sitting behind a column with our view of the altar partially obstructed. We could see the pulpit where the local and state dignitaries spoke, but the area where the choir was seated was hidden.

During the first choral hymn, I closed my eyes to hear the music better rather than stare at the stone column before me. Soon, I sensed Keir's presence bringing me a new vision. Dressed in a long, black, velvet dress with a bustle of Victorian vintage, I was standing up inside an open, horse-drawn carriage. I was wearing a small hat tilted forward on my forehead as I had a mass of curls piled high on the back crown of my head. I reached out to grasp the hand of a bespectacled man dressed in a more middle-class style suit standing outside the carriage. I felt emotionally numb as well as out-of-place since I was the only woman in attendance. We were attending my husband's funeral.

431

Once the hymn was finished, I opened my eyes again to listen to the service. When the Chapel choir sang a second hymn, I again closed my eyes and was transported back to the Victorian age. This time, I wore a brown, orange, and white plaid taffeta skirt and white lace blouse with puffed sleeves. Our infant son was sleeping in his bassinet with a white gauze cover. I regretted my husband would never see his boy grow up. When I opened my eyes in the Amasa Chapel, I was saddened to remember Keir would not see Sean grow up either.

EPILOGUE

As the intervening years have passed and my grief over Keir's death has subsided, his visits have also diminished in intensity and frequency. There have been no more out-of-body experiences, and the past life visions now only occur when I do meditations specifically geared to past lifetimes—and then only when the revelation is one that will not affect my karma or life plan in a detrimental manner.

I have also discovered other persons with whom I have led previous lifetimes: my mother (in France during the reign of Louis XIV), a neighbor (my Comanche grandfather), co-workers and former OAHIA officers during the English time periods, and even Keir's brother in this lifetime, Mark, was a fellow monk brother with us in Bhutan. I also discovered that during the MiddleAges, I was a young boy and Keir was a knight. I have previously known two current friends during the Florentine reign of Lorenzo de Medici.

Occasionally, I can still feel Keir drop in on me for a second or two, or he will send along a song or answer a request. And sometimes, he'll make a request of me.

Thankfully, Keir has answered many of my questions that lingered after his death, frequently reassured me of his eternal love, and explained why our relationship was so incomplete in this lifetime. He has also shown me that we will be together again in a future life.

On the Friday preceding Mother's Day weekend in 2012, while heading to visit and spend a recreational weekend with a male friend in Chautauqua, New York, I detoured to stop at the Coventry-Covenant Methodist Church columbarium where Keir's ashes are entombed. Sitting on a bench in the shade of a tree facing Keir's memorial stone, I realized that my visits here had become a form of penitence.

"I am so sorry I did not come back to Cleveland to visit you when I had promised," I prayed.

Keir's voice immediately replied to my consciousness: *"I forgave you a long time ago, but you haven't forgiven yourself."*

Instantaneously lightened from the burden of long-carried guilt, I stood up and left the memorial garden behind to continue my trip to Chautauqua. That weekend became my first romantic tryst since my divorce...and Keir's death. Later, I learned, in a karmic twist, that male friend had been Frederick, the valet of my Victorian husband, Ralph.

POSTSCRIPT

As I was putting the final touches on this book, readying it for print, ironically, Auguste moved back to Columbus after living for several years in Canada with his second wife from whom he is separated.

I realized I may have portrayed Auguste in a more singularly negative light than is completely true. Overall, he is not a bad man. He entered our marriage with his set of issues as did I. These issues collided from time to time and resulted in unhealthy, co-dependent, behaviors. (I suspect that we, too, may have lived together in a previous life time; perhaps he was the Comanche Chief Red Cloud or my husband from colonial New York near Lake Horican.)

"The Lord giveth, and the Lord taketh away." In any case, Auguste's return has provided us both—now older and wiser with the added perspective of time and distance—with an opportunity to grant ourselves some measure of mutual forgiveness and understanding.

Resources Consulted

Anasazi/SW US/Cohonino
http://www.desertusa.com/ind1/du_peo_ana.html
http://www.mnsu.edu/emuseum/cultural/northamerica/anasazi.html
http://sipapu.gsu.edu/timeline/index.html
http://www.fs.fed.us/r3/kai/recreation/historic/tusayan.shtml
http://www.passportintime.com/summaries/2006/kaibab.html
http://jan.ucc.nau.edu/d-antlab/Southwestern%20Arch/Anasazi/pueblo1.htm
http://www.clayhound.us/images/anaz-hoho-mogo%20Map.jpg

O'Reilly, Sean, ed., O'Reilly, James and Habegger, Larry. *Grand Canyon: True Stories of Life Below the Rim.* San Francisco, CA, Traveler's Tales, Inc., 1999.

Petersen, David. *The Anasazi.* Danbury, CT, Children's Press Inc., 1991.

Africa
Nubian culture
http://oi.uchicago.edu/OI/PROJ/NUB/NUBX/NUBX_brochure.html
http://www.thenubian.net/
Samburu morans (warriors)
http://www.on-the-matrix.com/africa/samburu_people.asp

Maasai/Masaai/Masai
http://www.on-the-matrix.com/africa/masai_people.asp
http://website.lineone.net/~yamaguchi/culture/kencult.html
http://www.watchtower.org/library/g/2002/2/22/article_01.htm
http://www.bing.com/images/search?q=masai+tribe&qs=AS&sk=IM2AS4&FORM=QBIR&pq=masaa&sc=8-5&sp=7&qs=AS&sk=IM2AS4
http://www.maasai-association.org/maasai.html
http://www.quenchthirst.org/massai_facts.html

Saitoti, Tepilit Ole. *Maasai,* 1993 ed. New York, Harry N. Abrams, Inc., 1980.

Himba
http://www.on-the-matrix.com/africa/himba.asp
Ngorongoro Crater -Tanzania
http://www.watchtower.org/library/g/2005/1/8/article_01.htm
http://www.bing.com/images/search?q=Ngorongoro+Crater+-Tanzania&qpvt=Ngorongoro+Crater+-Tanzania&FORM=IGRE
Mt. Kilimanjaro - Tanzania
http://www.tusker.com/kilimanjaro_goog_us_fortis.cfm
http://www.bing.com/images/search?q=mount+kilamanjaro&qs=IM&form=QBIR&pq=mount+kila&sc=8-10&sp=3&sk=IM2

India/Fatehpur Sikri/Emperor Akbar
http://www.mapsofindia.com/maps/uttarpradesh/agra.htm
http://www.indianvisit.com/ivnew/destinationguides/culture/agra.htm
http://www.indianvisit.com/taj-mahal/travel-packages/maharajas-retreat.html
http://edweb.cnidr.org/india/akbar.html
http://www.indiaprofile.com/heritage/fatehpursikri.htm

http://www.libasdesigns.com/Indian_Fashion_Glossary.html
http://en.wikipedia.org/wiki/Uttar_Pradesh
http://en.wikipedia.org/wiki/Delhi_Sultanate
http://en.wikipedia.org/wiki/Agra
http://en.wikipedia.org/wiki/Akbar
http://en.wikipedia.org/wiki/Jodhabai
http://en.wikipedia.org/wiki/Mariam-uz-Zamani
http://en.wikipedia.org/wiki/Fatehpur_Sikri
http://encyclopedia.jrank.org/PYR_RAY/RAJPUT.html
http://www.skidmore.edu/academics/arthistory/ah369/Intropg2.htm
http://www.homeindia.com/catalogue/fashion/sharara33777.shtml

Dalal, Anita. *Nations of the World: India.* Oxford, England, Raintree Publishers, 2002.

Dersin, Denise, ed. *What Life Was Like in the Jewel in the Crown: British India AD 1600-1905.* Alexandria, VA, Time-Life Books, 1999.

Goodwin, William. *India: Modern Nations of the World.* San Diego, CA, Lucent Books, Inc. 2000.

Moorcroft, *The Taj Mahal: How and Why It Was Built.* Austin, TX. Steck-Vaughn Co., 1998.

Bhutan/Himalayas
Bhutan map, Department of Tourism, Bhutan, Wangchuk.
http://www.kingdomofbhutan.com/kingdom/kingdom_.html
http://www.kingdomofbhutan.com/regions/regions_.html
http://www.pbs.org/edens/bhutan/Bhu_resource.htm
http://www.indianvisit.com/india/himalayas/bhutan/index.html
http://www.bhutanmajestictravel.com/images/detailed_tourism_bhutan_map.jpg
http://www.bing.com/images/search?q=dzong&qpvt=dzong&FORM=IGRE

Balf, Todd. *The Last River: The Tragic Race for Shangri-La.* New York, Crown Publishers, 2000.

Choedon, Yeshi, and Norbu, Dawa. *Tibet.* London, Tiger Books International, 1997.

Cooper, Robert, and Lin, Youg Jui. *Cultures of the World: Bhutan.* Tarrytown, NY, Marshall Cavendish Corp., 2001.

Kincaid, Jamaica, *Among Flowers: A Walk in the Himalaya*, Washington, DC: National Geographic Directions, 2005.

Salak, Kira. "Trekking Bhutan's Higher Planes," *National Geographic*, vol. 10, no. 3, April 2008, 62-99.
Zeppa, Jamie. *Beyond the Sky and the Earth: A Journey into Bhutan.* New York: Riverhead Books, 1999.

Central Plains Indians/US
http://www.legendsofamerica.com/NA-Commanche.html - Comanche

436

http://www.crystalinks.com/comanche.html
http://www.archaeolink.com/northern_plains_indians_page_2.htm
http://en.wikipedia.org/wiki/Great_Plains
http://en.wikipedia.org/wiki/Comanche
http://www.encyclopedia.com/html/t1/travois.asp
http://en.wikipedia.org/wiki/Travois
http://en.wikipedia.org/wiki/Arapaho
http://en.wikipedia.org/wiki/Sioux
http://en.wikipedia.org/wiki/Kiowa
http://en.wikipedia.org/wiki/Apache
http://en.wikipedia.org/wiki/Cheyenne
http://www.tolatsga.org/ComancheOne.html
http://www.dickshovel.com/ComancheTwo.html
http://www.accessgenealogy.com/native/tribes/kiowa/index.htm
http://www.accessgenealogy.com/native/tribes/kiowa/chief.htm
http://www.accessgenealogy.com/navtive/tribes/kiowa/kiowaapachehist.htm
http://www.nativeamericans.com/Kiowa.htm
http://www.accessgenealogy.com/native/tribes/kiowa/kiowahist.htm
http://www.comanchenation.com/Education/history.html
http://www.venomousrepitles.org/librafies/showfilepage/407?offset=41
http://www.sdsnake.com/Rat.htm#Find
http://www.venomousreptiles.cor/articles/345

Bial, Raymond. *Lifeways: The Comanche*. New York, Benchmark Books, 2000.

Gwynne, S. C. *Empire of the Summer Moon: Quanah Parker and the Rise and Fall of the Comanches, the Most Powerful Indian Tribe in American History.* New York. Scribner, 2010.

Josephy, Alvin M., Jr. *500 Nations: An Illustrated History of North American Indians*. New York, Alfred A. Knopf, 1994.

Mails, Thomas E. *The Mystic Warrior of the Plains*. Garden City, NY, Doubleday and Co., Inc., 1972.

Taylor, Colin F., ed. cons. *The Native Americans: The Indigenous People of North America*. New York, Smithmark Publishers, 1991.

French & Indian War -- March 19-22, 1757 and August 3-9,1757
http://www.militaryheritage.com/wm_henry.htm: "An Account of Two Attacks on Fort William Henry, 1757"
http://en.wikipedia.org/wiki/Battle_of_Fort_William_Henry
http://www.historiclakes.org/wm_henry_battle.html
http://www.historiclakes.org/Timelines/timeline1d.html
http://www.historiclakes.org/Timelines/timeline1c.html
http://www.philaprintshop.com/frchintx.html
http://web.syr.edu/~laroux/lists/alpha.html
http://www.fortwilliamhenry.com/History/index.cfm
http://www.fwhmuseum.com/archaeology.html
http://www.accessgenealogy.com/native/tribes/algonquian/mahicanhist.htm
http://www.accessgenealogy.com/native/tribes/oneida/oneidahist.htm

http://www.accessgenealogy.com/native/tribes/seneca/senecahist.htm
http://www.u-s-history.com/pages/h1175.html
http://www.nativeamericans.com/Natives.htm
http://fttoulousejackson.org/Toulouse/GUIDEBOOK.HTM
http://www.shpect.org/index.php/early-american/clothing-in-the-colonies-1700-to-1770/290-costume-1750s-1760s
http://histoiresdancetres.com/vaillancourt/henri-ardouin-a-defendu-la-nouvelle-france-contre-les-anglais/attachment/8-the_victory_of_montcalms_troops_at_carillon_by_henry_alexander_ogden-2/
http://media.oneidanation.net/images/120*90/LACROSSE+DRAWING+7.jpg
http://www.essortment.com/all/huronindians_rjru.htm
http://www.tolatsga.org/hur.html
http://www.mohicanpress.com/from_the_ramparts1.htm
http://www.mohicanpress.com/mo08009.html

Cooper, James Fenimore. *The Last of the Mohicans.* New York. Bantam Dell, 2005.

"The Last of the Mohicans," directed by Michael Mann, executive producer James G. Robinson. Twentieth Century Fox, 1992.

Regency England/1810
    Costumes of Ladies 1810-1823 England
http://digitalgallery.nypl.org/nypldigital/dgkeysearchresult.cfm?parent_id=355551&word
http://www.museumofcostume.co.uk/collections/collection_search.aspx
    Schooners/sailing ships:
http://www.bruzelius.info/nautica/Ships/Schooners/Schooners.html
http://www.schoonerman.com/home.htm
http://www.vallejogallery.com/item.php?id=1481&cat=&title=Brig_and_Cutter_Off_the_English_Coast
http://www.pepsiamericassail.com/intrototallships.html
    Coast of English Channel
http://www.williamtrostrichards.org/the-complete-works-3-96-3-0.html
http://www.chycor.co.uk/gorran-haven-holiday-cottages-hillside/images/gorranhaven.jpg
http://cyper-heritage.co.uk/maps/cook.jpg
http://www.cyber-heritage.co.uk/maps/nile.jpg
http://www.cornwall365.co.uk/cornwall_image/3.Gorran-Haven-Beach.PICT2635_260806.JPG
http://www.cornwall-calling.co.uk/gazetter-cornwall/gorran-haven.htm
    Stone Bridges, England
http://www.geograph.org.uk/list.php?square=SX
http://www.bing.com/images/search?q=stone+bridges+Dorset+England&id=64651CDD74A4183B2BF8A440898E565756ADC78A&FORM=IQFRBA
    Weymouth/Georgian Architecture
http://www.users.globalnet.co.uk/~wykedh/webgeorge/Title%20Content%20Page.htm

Feden, Robin and Rosemary Joekes, ed. *The National Trust Guide to England, Wales, and Northern Ireland.* New York. Alfred A. Knopf, 1974.

Hughes, Kristine. *The Writer's Guide to Everyday Life in Regency and Victorian England from 1811-1901* Cincinnati, OH. Writer's Digest Books, 1998.

Cunnington, C. Willett. *English Women's Clothing in the Nineteenth Century: A Comprehensive Guide with 1,117 Illustrations.* Mineola, NY. Dover Publications, 1990.

Austen, Jane. *Emma.* Ware, England. Wordsworth Editions, Ltd., 1994.

Austen, Jane. *Pride and Prejudice.* New York. Tor Doherty Associates, Inc., 1994.

Erickson, Carolly. *Our Tempetuous Day.* London. Robson Books, 1996.

Feather, Jane. *Almost a Lady.* New York. Bantam Dell, 2005.

Murray, Venetia. *An Elegant Madness: High Society in Regency England.* New York. Viking Penguin, 1999.

Ross, Josephine. *Jane Austen: A Companion.* New Brunswick, NJ. Rutgers University Press, 2003.

Victorian England
http://www.musicwithease.com/flying-dutchman-synopsis.html
http://www.1911encyclopedia.org/Influenza
     Barristers/Inns of Court
http://en.wikipedia.org/wiki/Barrister
http://enwikipedia.org/wiki/Inns_of_Court
http://www.fathom.com/feature/122359/index.html
http://www.victorianweb.org/authors/dickens/ge/courtroom.html
     London Cemeteries
http://homepage.ntlworld.com/lhitch/gendocs/cem.html
http://www.timetravel-britain.com/articles/london/cemetaries.shtml
     Women's Clothing/1870s
http://www.villagehatshop.com/glossary_e.html
http://www.gogmsite.net/_Media/sissi_and_gisela_detail_fro.jpg
http://demodecouture.com/images/1880_afternoon.jpg
http://imgc.artprintimages.com/images/art-print/women-s-hats-by-le-follet-paris-1870s_i-G-37-3725-J6SAF00Z.jpg
http://farm4.static.flickr.com/3058/2900552224_f2be2a60ef.jpg
http://img2.photographersdirect.com/img/16398/wm/pd776470.jpg
http://www.costumegallery.com/
     Derby
http://en.wikipedia.org/wiki/Derby
http://www.localhistories.org/derby.html
http://www.visitderbyshire.co.uk/about_history.ihtml

Flanders, Judith. *Inside the Victorian Home: A Portrait of Domestic Life in Victorian England.* New York. W.W. Norton & Co., 2003.

Gernsheim, Alison. *Victorian and Edwardian Fashion: A Photographic Survey.* New York. Dower Publications, 1981.

Hibbert, Christopher. *The English: A Social History, 1066-1945.* New York. W.W. Norton & Co., 1987.

Hughes, Kristine. *The Writer's Guide to Everyday Life in Regency and Victorian England from 1811-1901* Cincinnati, OH. Writer's Digest Books, 1998.

Mitchell, Sally. *Daily Life in Victorian England.* Westport, CT. Greenwood Press, 1996.

Picard, Liza. *Victorian England: The Tale of A City, 1840-1870.* New York. St. Martin Press, 2005.

Ziegler, Philip. *Britain: Then and Now.* London. Weidenfield & Nicolson, 1999.

Ohio
  Canton
http://en.wikipedia.org/wiki/Canton,_Ohio
http://www.cityofcanton.com/gallery12.html
  Sandusky/Lakeside
Lake Erie Islands Area: A Great Lake Adventure 1999, Ottawa County (Ohio) Visitors Bureau, Port Clinton, OH, 1999.
  Cleveland
http://music.case.edu/weddings/amasahist.php
http://cleveland.about.com/od/eastsidesuburbs/p/clevelandhts.htm
http://clevelandheights.com/historyarch_landmarks.asp
http://www.clevelandskyscapers.com/
  Brain Cancer
Http://cancer.about.com/od/braintumors/a/brain_cancer.htm?p=1
  Law Schools
http://stu.findlaw.com/schools/usaschools/ohio.html

Google Maps

"Ohio/West Virginia" map, Heathrow, FL, AAA, 2008.

"Cleveland" map, Heathrow, FL, AAA, 2007-2008.

Illinois, Indiana & Ohio Tour Book, 2008 ed. Heathrow, FL, AAA, 2008.

Gaede, Robert C., *et.al. Guide to Cleveland Architecture,* 2nd ed., Cleveland, OH, Cleveland Chapter of the American Institute of Architects, 1997.

Johannesen, Eric. *Cleveland Architecture, 1876-1976.,* Cleveland, OH, The Western Reserve Historical Society, 1979.

Encyclopedia of Home Designs. Tucson, AZ, Home Planners, 1997.
Murray, James C., and Maxwell, Shirley. *House Styles in America.* Kalamazoo, MI, Dovetail Publishers, 1996.

440

Reincarnation/Soulmates/Past Lifetimes/Death and Dying

Albom, Mitch. *The Five People You Meet in Heaven.* New York, Hyperion, 2003.

Baker, Elsa. *Letters from the Afterlife: A Guide to the Other Side.* Hillsboro, OR. Beyond Words Publishing, Inc., 2004.

Botkin, Allan L., with R. Craig Hogan. *Induced After Death Communication: A New Therapy for Healing Grief and Trauma.* Charlottesville, VA. Hampton Roads Publishing Co., Inc. 2005.

Browne, Sylvia. *Visits from the Afterlife: The Truth about Hauntings, Spirits, and Reunions with Lost Loved Ones.* New York, Dutton/Penguin Group, Inc., 2003.

Bruce, Robert. *Astral Dynamics: A New Approach to Out-of-Body Experience.* Charlottesville, VA. Hampton Roads Publishing Co., Inc., 1999.

Cohen, Doris Eliana. *Repetition: Past Lives, Life, and Rebirth.* Carlsbad, CA. Hay House, Inc., 2008.

Dale, Cyndi. "Healing Across Time: Guided Journeys to Your Past and Future" Compact Disk. Sounds True, Inc., Boulder, CO, n.d.

Dale, Cyndi. *"Illuminating the Afterlife: Your Soul's Journey through the Worlds Beyond.* Boulder, CO, Sounds True, Inc., 2008.

Gootman, Marilyn E. *When a Friend Dies.* Minneapolis, MN. Free Spirit Publishing, Inc. 1994.

Guggenheim, Bill, and Judy Guggenheim. *Hello from Heaven!* New York. Bantam Books, 1996.

Hanh, Thich Nhat. *No Death, No Fear: Comforting Wisdom for Life.* New York. Riverhead Books, 2002.

Holland, John. *Psychic Navigator: Harnessing Your Inner Guidance.* Carlsbad, CA. Hay House, Inc. 2004.

Holland, John. *The Spirit Whisperer: Chronicles of a Medium.* Carlsbad, CA. Hay House, Inc. 2010.

Horn, Stacy. *Unbelievable: Investigations into Ghosts, Poltergeists, Telepathy, and Other Unseen Phenomena, from the Duke Parapsychology Laboratory.* New York. HarperCollins Publishers, 2009.

Howe, Linda. *How to Read the Akashic Records: Accessing the Archive of the Soul and Its Journey.* Boulder, CO, Sounds True, Inc., 2009.

Kessler, David. *Visions, Trips, and Crowded Rooms: Who and What You See Before You Die.* Carlsbad, CA. Hay House, Inc. 2010.

Lucas, Sabine. *Past Life Dreamwork: Healing the Soul through Understanding Karmic Patterns*. Rochester, VT. Bear & Company, 2008.

MacLaine, Shirley. *It's All in the Playing*. New York, Bantam Books, 1987.

MacLeod, Ainslie. *The Transformation: Healing Your Past Lives to Realize Your Soul's Potential*. Boulder, CO, Sounds True, Inc., 2010.

Newton, Michael. *Destiny of Souls: New Case Studies of Life Between Lives.* Saint Paul, MN. Llewellyn Publications, 2003.

Newton, Michael. *Journey of Souls: Case Studies of Life Between Lives.* Saint Paul, MN. Llewellyn Publications, 2003.

Roland, Paul. *Explore Your Past Lives.* London. Godsfield Press, 2005.

Rosen, Rebecca. *Spirited: Connect to the Guides All Around You.* New York, HarperCollins Publishers, 2010.

Van Praagh, James. *Unfinished Business: What the Dead Can Teach Us about Life.* New York. Harper One, 2009.

Weiss, Brian L., MD, *Only Love is Real: A Story of Soulmates Reunited.* New York, NY, Warner Books, 1996.

Wicker, Christine. *Lily Dale: The True Story of the Town that Talks to the Dead.* New York. HarperSanFrancisco, 2003.

Verbally Abusive Relationships
Evans, Patricia. *The Verbally Abusive Relationship: How to Recognize It and How to Respond.* Holbrook, MA. Adams Media Corp., 1996.

Quotations in the Public Domain
http://silveropossum.homestead.com/Prayers/NativeAmericanPrayer.html

The Holy Bible, King James Version. New York: Oxford Education 1769; King James Bible Online, 2008 http://www.kingjamesbibleonline.org/

Made in the USA
Charleston, SC
31 October 2013